Lecture Notes in Artificial Intelligence   9868

Subseries of Lecture Notes in Computer Science

T0236225

More information about this series at http://www.springer.com/series/1244

Oscar Luaces · José A. Gámez
Edurne Barrenechea · Alicia Troncoso
Mikel Galar · Héctor Quintián
Emilio Corchado (Eds.)

Advances in Artificial Intelligence

17th Conference of the Spanish Association
for Artificial Intelligence, CAEPIA 2016
Salamanca, Spain, September 14–16, 2016
Proceedings

 Springer

Editors

Oscar Luaces
Artificial Intelligence Center
University of Oviedo
Gijón
Spain

José A. Gámez
University of Castilla-La Mancha
Albacete
Spain

Edurne Barrenechea
Public University of Navarre
Pamplona
Spain

Alicia Troncoso
Universidad Pablo de Olavide
Sevilla
Spain

Mikel Galar
Public University of Navarre
Pamplona, Navarra
Spain

Héctor Quintián
University of Salamanca
Salamanca
Spain

Emilio Corchado
University of Salamanca
Salamanca
Spain

ISSN 0302-9743   ISSN 1611-3349   (electronic)
Lecture Notes in Artificial Intelligence
ISBN 978-3-319-44635-6   ISBN 978-3-319-44636-3   (eBook)
DOI 10.1007/978-3-319-44636-3

Library of Congress Control Number: 2016938377

LNCS Sublibrary: SL7 – Artificial Intelligence

Printed on acid-free paper

This Springer imprint is published by Springer Nature
The registered company is Springer International Publishing AG Switzerland

Preface

This volume contains a selection of the papers accepted for oral presentation at the 17th Conference of the Spanish Association for Artificial Intelligence (CAEPIA 2016), held in Salamanca (Spain), during September 14–16, 2016. This was the 17th biennial conference in the CAEPIA series, which was started in 1985. Previous events took place in Madrid, Alicante, Málaga, Murcia, Gijón, Donostia, Santiago de Compostela, Salamanca, Seville, La Laguna, Madrid, and Albacete.

This time, CAEPIA was coordinated with various symposia, each one corresponding to a main track in Artificial Intelligence (AI) research: 11th Symposium on Metaheuristics, Evolutive and Bioinspired Algorithms (MAEB); 6th Symposium of Fuzzy Logic and Soft Computing (LODISCO); 8th Symposium of Theory and Applications of Data Mining (TAMIDA); and the 3rd Symposium on Information Fusion and Ensembles (FINO).

CAEPIA is a forum open to researchers worldwide, to present and discuss the latest scientific and technological advances in AI. Its main aims are to facilitate the dissemination of new ideas and experiences, to strengthen the links among the different research groups, and to help spread new developments to society. All perspectives — theory, methodology, and applications — are welcome. Apart from the presentation of technical full papers, the scientific program of CAEPIA 2016 included an App contest, a Doctoral Consortium and, as a follow-up to the success achieved at previous CAEPIA conferences, a special session on outstanding recent papers (Key Works) already published in renowned journals or forums.

With the aim of maintaining CAEPIA as a high-quality conference, and following the model of current demanding AI conferences, the CAEPIA review process runs under the double-blind model. The number of submissions received by CAEPIA and associated tracks was 166; however, only 47 submissions were selected to be published in the LNAI Springer volume. These 47 papers were carefully peer-reviewed by three members of the CAEPIA Program Committee with the help of additional reviewers from each of the associated symposia. The reviewers judged the overall quality of the submitted papers, together with their originality and novelty, technical correctness, awareness of related work, and quality of presentation. The reviewers stated their confidence in the subject area in addition to detailed written comments. On the basis of the reviews, the program chairs made the final decisions.

The six distinguished invited speakers at CAEPIA 2016 were Serafín Moral (University of Granada, Spain), Xin Yao (University of Birmingham, UK), Enrique Alba Torres (University of Málaga, Spain), Sancho Salcedo Sanz (University of Alcalá de Henares, Spain), Richard Benjamins (BI & DATA, Telefonica, Spain), and Alberto Bugarín Diz (University of Santiago de Compostela, Spain). They presented six very interesting topics on current AI research: "Algoritmos de Inferencia Aproximados para Modelos Gráficos Probabilísticos" (Moral), "Ensemble Approaches to Class Imbalance Learning" (Yao), "Sistemas Inteligentes para Ciudades Inteligentes" (Alba Torres),

"Nuevos Algoritmos para Optimización y Búsqueda Basados en Simulación de Arrecifes de Coral" (Salcedo), "Creating Value from Big Data" (Benjamins), and "A Bunch of Words Worth More than a Million Data: A Soft Computing View of Data-to-Text" (Bugarín).

The Doctoral Consortium (DC) was specially designed for the interaction between PhD students and senior researchers. AEPIA and the organization of CAEPIA recognized the best PhD work submitted to the DC with a prize, as well as the best student and conference paper presented at CAEPIA 2016. Furthermore, and with the aim of promoting the presence of women in AI research, as in previous editions, a prize was set at CAEPIA 2016: the Frances Allen award, which is devoted to the two best AI PhD Thesis presented by a woman during the last two years.

The editors would like to thank everyone who contributed to CAEPIA 2016 and associated events: authors, members of the Scientific Committees, additional reviewers, invited speakers, etc. Final thanks go to the Organizing Committee, our local sponsors (BISITE and the University of Salamanca), the Springer team, and AEPIA for their support.

September 2016

Oscar Luaces
José A. Gámez
Edurne Barrenechea
Alicia Troncoso
Mikel Galar
Héctor Quintián
Emilio Corchado

Organization

General Chairs

Oscar Luaces   University of Oviedo at Gijón, Spain
Emilio Corchado   Univesity of Salamanca, Spain

Program Chairs

Co-chair of MAEB

Francisco Herrera   University of Granada, Spain
José A. Gámez   University of Castilla-La Mancha, Spain

Co-chair of LODISCO

Luis Martínez   University of Jaen, Spain
Edurne Barrenechea   Public University of Navarre, Spain

Co-chair of TAMIDA

José Riquelme   University of Seville, Spain
Alicia Troncoso   Universidad Pablo de Olivine, Spain

Co-chair of FINO

Emilio Corchado   University of Salamanca, Spain
Mikel Galar   Public University of Navarre, Spain
Bruno Baruque   University of Burgos, Spain

Program Committee

Jesús S. Aguilar-Ruiz   University Pablo de Olavide, Spain
Pedro Aguilera Aguilera   University of Almería, Spain
Enrique Alba   University of Málaga, Spain
Rafael Alcala   University of Granada, Spain
Jesus Alcala-Fdez   University of Granada, Spain
Francisco Almeida   University of La Laguna, Spain
Amparo Alonso-Betanzos   University of A Coruña, Spain
Ada Álvarez   Universidad Autónoma de Nuevo León, Spain
Ramón Álvarez-Valdés   University of Valencia, Spain
Alessandro Antonucci   IDSIA, Switzerland

Lourdes Araujo	UNED, Spain
Olatz Arbelaitz	University of País Vasco, Spain
Marta Arias	Polytechnic University of Cataluña, Spain
Ángel Arroyo	University of Burgos, Spain
Gualberto Asencio	University Pablo de Olavide, Spain
Jaume Bacardit	Newcastle University, UK
Emili Balaguer-Ballester	Bournemouth University, UK
Edurne Barrenechea	Public University of Navarra, Spain
Senén Barro	University of Santiago de Compostela, Spain
Bruno Baruque	University of Burgos, Spain
Iluminada Baturone	Instituto de Microelectrónica de Sevilla-CSIC, Spain
Joaquín Bautista	Polytechnic University of Cataluña, Spain
José Manuel Benítez	University of Granada, Spain
Pablo Bermejo	University of Castilla-La Mancha, Spain
Concha Bielza Lozoya	Polytechnic University of Madrid, Spain
Christian Blum	IKERBASQUE, Spain
Fernando Bobillo	University of Zaragoza, Spain
Daniel Borrajo	University Carlos III de Madrid, Spain
Julio Brito	University of la Laguna, Spain
Alberto Bugarín	University of Santiago de Compostela, Spain
Humberto Bustince	Public University of Navarra, Spain
Pedro Cabalar	University of A Coruña, Spain
Rafael Caballero	University of Málaga, Spain
José M. Cadenas	University of Murcia, Spain
Tomasa Calvo	University of Alcalá, Spain
Jose Luis Calvo-Rolle	University of A Coruña, Spain
David Camacho	Universidad Autónoma de Madrid, Spain
Vicente Campos	University of Valencia, Spain
Andrés Cano	University of Granada, Spain
Cristóbal Carmona	University of Burgos, Spain
Pablo Carmona	University of Extremadura, Spain
Andre Carvalho	University of Saõ Paulo, Brazil
Jorge Casillas	University of Granada, Spain
José Luis Casteleiro Roca	University of Coruña, Spain
Pedro A. Castillo	University of Granada, Spain
Francisco Chávez	University of Extremadura, Spain
Francisco Chicano	University of Málaga, Spain
Carlos A. Coello	CINVESTAV – IPN, Spain
José Manuel Colmenar	Universidad Rey Juan Carlos, Spain
Ángel Corberán	University of Valencia, Spain
Emilio Corchado	University of Salamanca, Spain
Juan Manuel Corchado	University of Salamanca, Spain
Oscar Cordón	University of Granada, Spain
Carlos Cotta	University of Málaga, Spain
Inés Couso	University of Oviedo, Spain
Javier Cózar	University of Castilla-La Mancha, Spain

Leticia Curiel	University of Burgos, Spain
Sergio Damas	European Centre for Soft Computing, Spain
Rocío de Andrés Calle	University of Salamanca, Spain
Luis M. de Campos	University of Granada, Spain
Cassio De Campos	Queen's University Belfast, UK
Luis de la Ossa	University of Castilla-La Mancha, Spain
José del Campo	University of Málaga, Spain
Juan J. del Coz	University of Oviedo, Spain
María José del Jesús	University of Jaén, Spain
Irene Díaz	University of Oviedo, Spain
Julián Dorado	Universidad da Coruña, Spain
Bernabé Dorronsoro	University of Cádiz, Spain
Abraham Duarte	Universidad Rey Juan Carlos, Spain
Richard Duro	University of A Coruña, Spain
Thomas Dyhre Nielsen	Aalborg University, Denmark
José Egea	Polytechnic University of Cartagena, Spain
Francisco Javier Elorza	Polytechnic University of Madrid, Spain
Sergio Escalera	University of Barcelona, Spain
Anna Esparcia	ITI – UPV, Spain
Francesc Esteva	Instituto de Investigación en Inteligencia Artificial-CSIC, Spain
Javier Faulín	Public University of Navarra, Spain
Francisco Fernández	University of Extremadura, Spain
Alberto Fernández	University of Granada, Spain
Antonio J. Fernández	University of Málaga, Spain
Elena Fernández	Polytechnic University of Cataluña, Spain
Javier Fernandez	Public University of Navarra, Spain
Alberto Fernández Hilario	University of Jaén, Spain
Antonio Fernández-Caballero	University of Castilla-La Mancha, Spain
Juan M. Fernández-Luna	University of Granada, Spain
Francesc J. Ferri	University of Valencia, Spain
Aníbal Ramón Figueiras-Vidal	Universidad Carlos III de Madrid, Spain
Maribel G. Arenas	University of Granada, Spain
Mikel Galar	Public University of Navarra, Spain
José Gámez	University of Castilla-La Mancha, Spain
Mario Garcia	Instituto Politécnico de Tijuana, Spain
Nicolás García	University of Córdoba, Spain
Salvador García	University of Granada, Spain
Carlos García Martínez	University of Córdoba, Spain
Nicolás García Pedrajas	University of Córdoba, Spain
José Luis García-Lapresta	University of Valladolid, Spain
Josep M. Garrell	Universitat Ramon Llull, Spain
Karina Gibert	Polytechnic University of Cataluña, Spain

Gabriel J. Luque	University of Málaga, Spain
Rafael M. Luque-Baena	University of Extremadura, Spain
Andrew Macfarlane	City University London, UK
Nicolas Madrid	University of Málaga, Spain
Luís Magdalena	European Centre for Soft Computing, Spain
Lawrence Mandow	University of Málaga, Spain
Felip Manya	IIIA-CSIC, Spain
Rafael Martí	University of Valencia, Spain
Luis Martínez	University of Jaén, Spain
Francisco Martínez Álvarez	Universidad Pablo de Olavide, Spain
María Martínez Ballesteros	University of Sevilla, Spain
Carlos David Martinez Hinarejos	Polytechnic University of Valencia, Spain
Ester Martinez-Martín	University Jaume I, Spain
Sebastià Massanet	University of les Illes Balears, Spain
Vicente Matellán	University of Leon, Spain
Gaspar Mayor	University of les Illes Balears, Spain
Belén Melián	University of La Laguna, Spain
Alexander Mendiburu	University of País Vasco, Spain
Juan Julián Merelo	University of Granada, Spain
Pedro Meseguer	IIIA - CSIC, Spain
José M. Molina	University Carlos III de Madrid, Spain
Daniel Molina	University of Cádiz, Spain
Julián Molina	University of Málaga, Spain
Javier Montero	Universidad Complutense de Madrid, Spain
Susana Montes	University of Oviedo, Spain
Eduard Montseny	Polytechnic University of Cataluña, Spain
Antonio Mora García	University of Granada, Spain
Serafín Moral	University of Granada, Spain
J. Marcos Moreno	University of La Laguna, Spain
José Andrés Moreno Pérez	University of La Laguna, Spain
Pablo Moscato	The University of Newcastle, Spain
Manuel Mucientes	University of Santiago de Compostela, Spain
Antonio J. Nebro	University of Málaga, Spain
Juan Nepomuceno	University of Sevilla, Spain
Manuel Ojeda-Aciego	University of Málaga, Spain
Jose Ángel Olivas	University of Castilla-La Mancha, Spain
Eugénio Oliveira	Universidade do Porto, Portugal
Eva Onaindia	Polytechnic University of Valencia, Spain
Julio Ortega	University of Granada, Spain
Sascha Ossowski	University Rey Juan Carlos, Spain
José Otero	University of Oviedo, Spain
Joaquín Pacheco	University of Burgos, Spain
Miguel Pagola	Public University of Navarra, Spain
Juan J. Pantrigo	Universidad Rey Juan Carlos, Spain
Eduardo G. Pardo	Universidad Rey Juan Carlos, Spain

Francisco Parreño	University of Castilla La Mancha, Spain
Daniel Paternain	Public University of Navarra, Spain
Juan Pavón	University Complutense de Madrid, Spain
María del Carmen Pegalajar	University of Granada, Spain
David A. Pelta	University of Granada, Spain
José M. Peña	Linköping University, Sweden
Rafael Peñaloza	Free University of Bozen-Bolzano, Italy
Antonio Peregrin	University of Huelva, Spain
M. Elena Pérez	University of Valladolid, Spain
Jesús Mª Pérez	University of País Vasco, Spain
Raul Perez	University of Granada, Spain
María Pérez Ortíz	University of Córdoba, Spain
Filiberto Pla	University Jaume I, Spain
Héctor Pomares	University of Granada, Spain
Ana Pradera	Universidad Rey Juan Carlos, Spain
José Miguel Puerta	University of Castilla La Mancha, Spain
Oriol Pujol	University of Barcelona, Spain
Héctor Quintián	University of Salamanca, Spain
José Carlos R. Alcantud	University of Salamanca, Spain
Julio R. Banga	CSIC, Spain
Juan R. Rabuñal	Universidad da Coruña, Spain
Helena Ramalhinho Lourenco	Universidad Pompeu Fabra, Spain
Mª José Ramírez	Polytechnic University of Valencia, Spain
Jordi Recasens	Polytechnic University of Cataluña, Spain
Raquel Redondo	University of Burgos, Spain
Roger Ríos	Universidad Autónoma de Nuevo León, Spain
José C. Riquelme	University of Seville, Spain
José Luis Risco-Martín	Universidad Complutense de Madrid, Spain
Víctor Rivas	University of Jaén, Spain
Ramón Rizo	University of Alicante, Spain
José Carlos Rodríguez	University of Salamanca, Spain
Rosa Mª Rodríguez	University of Granada, Spain
Juan J. Rodríguez	University of Burgos, Spain
Tinguaro Rodríguez	Universidad Complutense de Madrid, Spain
Ignacio Rojas	University of Granada, Spain
Emma Rollon	Technical University of Catalonia, Spain
Jesús Ángel Román Gallego	University of Salamanca, Spain
Carlos Andrés Romano	Polytechnic University of Valencia, Spain
Alejandro Rosete Suárez	CUJAE, Cuba
Rubén Ruiz	Polytechnic University of Valencia, Spain
Daniel Ruiz-Aguilera	University of les Illes Balears, Spain
Rafael Rumi	University of Almería, Spain
Yago Sáez	Universidad Carlos III de Madrid, Spain
Sancho Salcedo	University of Alcalá, Spain
Jorge Sales	Universitat Jaume I, Spain

Antonio Salmerón	University of Almería, Spain
Luciano Sánchez	University of Oviedo, Spain
Daniel Sánchez	University of Granada, Spain
Miquel Sànchez i Marrè	Polytechnic University of Cataluña, Spain
Javier Sánchez Monedero	University of Córdoba, Spain
Santiago Sánchez Solano	Instituto de Microelectrónica de Sevilla-CSIC, Spain
Araceli Sanchís	Universidad Carlos III de Madrid, Spain
Roberto Santana	University of País Vasco, Spain
José Antonio Sanz Delgado	Public University of Navarra, Spain
Ángel Sappa	Computer Vision Center, Spain
Javier Sedano	Instituto Tecnológico de Castilla y León, Spain
Miguel-Angel Sicilia	University of Alcalá, Spain
Alejandro Sobrino Cerdeiriña	University of Santiago de Compostela, Spain
Emilio Soria	University of Valencia, Spain
Thomas Stützle	Université Libre de Bruxelles, Spain
Luis Enrique Sucar	INAOE, Spain
J. Tinguaro Rodríguez	Universidad Complutense de Madrid, Spain
Vicenc Torra	University of Skövde, Sweden
Joan Torrens	University of les Illes Balears, Spain
M. Inés Torres	University of País Vasco, Spain
Isaac Triguero	Gent University, Spain
Enric Trillas	Public University of Navarra, Spain
Alicia Troncoso Lora	Universidad Pablo de Olavide, Spain
Leonardo Trujillo	Instituto Tecnológico de Tijuana, Spain
Ángel Udías	Universidad Rey Juan Carlos, Spain
Belén Vaquerizo García	University of Burgos, Spain
Pablo Varona	Universidad Autónoma de Madrid, Spain
Miguel Ángel Vega	University of Extremadura, Spain
Sebastián Ventura	University of Córdoba, Spain
José Luis Verdegay	University of Granada, Spain
Joan Vila	University of Valencia, Spain
Gabriel Villa	University of Sevilla, Spain
José Ramón Villar	University of Oviedo, Spain
Pedro Villar	University of Granada, Spain
Mateu Villaret	University of Girona, Spain
Juan Villegas	Universidad Autónoma Metropolitana, Spain
Jordi Vitria	University of Barcelona, Spain
Gabriel Winter	University of las Palmas de Gran Canaria, Spain
Amelia Zafra	University of Córdoba, Spain
Marta Zorrilla	University of Cantabria, Spain

Contents

Clustering

Multiagent Systems

Machine Learning

Applications

Evolutionary and Genetic Algorithms

Metaheuristics

Optimization

Fuzzy Logic: Foundations and Applications

Image and Video

Frame Size Reduction for Foreground Detection in Video Sequences

Miguel A. Molina-Cabello[1(✉)], Ezequiel López-Rubio[1],
Rafael Marcos Luque-Baena[2], Esteban J. Palomo[1,3], and Enrique Domínguez[1]

[1] Department of Computer Languages and Computer Science,
University of Málaga, Bulevar Louis Pasteur, 35, 29071 Málaga, Spain
{miguelangel,ezeqlr,ejpalomo,enriqued}@lcc.uma.es
[2] Department of Computer Systems and Telematics Engineering,
University of Extremadura, University Centre of Mérida, 06800 Mérida, Spain
rmluque@unex.es
[3] School of Mathematical Science and Information Technology,
University of Yachay Tech, Hacienda San José s/n, San Miguel de Urcuquí, Ecuador
epalomo@yachaytech.edu.ec

Abstract. A frame resolution reduction framework to reduce the computational load and improve the foreground detection in video sequences is presented in this work. The proposed framework consists of three different stages. Firstly, the original video frame is downsampled using a specific interpolation function. Secondly, a foreground detection of the reduced video frame is performed by a probabilistic background model called MFBM. Finally, the class probabilities for the reduced video frame are upsampled using a bicubic interpolation to estimate the class probabilities of the original frame. Experimental results applied to standard benchmark video sequences demonstrate the goodness of our proposal.

Keywords: Foreground detection · Video size reduction · Interpolation techniques

1 Introduction

Within the field of artificial vision, the research on video surveillance systems mainly focuses on detecting, recognizing and tracking the movement of the foreground objects in a sequence of images. Any video surveillance system begins its activity by detecting moving objects in the scene. However, this process is more complex than subtracting the current frame and the background image previously calculated, which is considered a naive approach, but there are several problems to be solved which increase its complexity. Unfavorable factors such as illumination changes both abrupt as continuous, casting shadows of objects on the background or repetitive motions of stationary objects such as tree branches, should be taken into account by the developed methods.

There are several proposals which try to manage the problem. In [2] a temporal average of the sequence is used to obtain a background image. The Kalman

© Springer International Publishing Switzerland 2016
O. Luaces et al. (Eds.): CAEPIA 2016, LNAI 9868, pp. 3–12, 2016.
DOI: 10.1007/978-3-319-44636-3_1

filter is applied for each pixel [7] to cope with the variability of the illumination in a scene. Additionally, in [9] a Gaussian distribution is considered to model the background color of each pixel, while in [3], the previous model is extended by a mixture of Gaussian distributions. Unlike the two previous parametric methods, in [1] the background is modeled by using a nonparametric method, which is more robust and invariant especially in outdoor scenes with a lot of variability in the stationary background objects. Haritaoglu et al. [4] presents a statistical model called W4 to represent each pixel with three values: its minimum and maximum values, and the maximum difference intensity between consecutive frames observed during the training period.

However, one of the main issues of the pixel-level foreground detection techniques is that the model approach for data analysis must be applied to each of the pixels which belongs to the scene, which involves a considerably high computational load. This kind of proposals restrains the development of more complex models if we want to maintain the same ratios of efficiency and real time. Thus, other techniques based on the consensus paradigm [8] achieve very good results combining the masks of several object detection methods, with the drawback of not fulfilling the temporal requirements needed for real-time processing.

Unlike other approaches which cluster the data by their color similitude [6], the objective of this paper is to present a frame resolution framework which groups the data of the neighborhood of each pixel and estimates a prototype for each region. Thus, several interpolation methods are studied in order to downsample the sequence. Since the sequences of frames are usually compressed with a video codec to reduce the size and improve the transmission rate, the use of interpolation techniques could alleviate the artifacts generated by the compression, and slightly overcome the output of the pixel-level methods. In order to analyze the frame resolution reduction approach, a probabilistic foreground detection technique [5], which is a pixel-level method, is considered and incorporated in the proposal for studying the quality of the foreground mask and the reduction of the computational load obtained by our methodology.

The rest of the paper is structured as follows: Sect. 2 states the methodology of the proposal, specifying the downsampling and upsampling process. Section 3 shows the experimental results obtained by the model, while Sect. 4 presents some conclusions about the work.

2   Methodology

In this section we present a frame resolution reduction framework for the foreground detection problem. The base probabilistic background model is that of [5]. This approach models the distribution of pixel feature values $\mathbf{t}(\mathbf{x}) \in \mathbb{R}^D$ at frame coordinates $\mathbf{x} \in \mathbb{Z}^2$ by employing a Gaussian mixture component $K(\mathbf{t}(\mathbf{x})|\boldsymbol{\mu}, \boldsymbol{\Sigma})$ for the background, and a uniform mixture component $U(\mathbf{t}(\mathbf{x}))$ for the foreground, where D is the number of pixel features of interest. The use of a uniform mixture component has the advantage that all incoming foreground objects are modelled equally well by the mixture, no matter their features. On the other hand, the set of features to be used can be tuned to suit the application at hand.

Our goal is to reduce the computational load of the base algorithm, while at the same time the resilience against noise is sometimes improved. The proposed procedure is composed of three stages: first the original video frame is downsampled (Subsect. 2.1), then the base background model is applied to the reduced video frame, and finally the class probabilities for the reduced video frame are upsampled (Subsect. 2.2).

2.1 Downsampling

Let us consider a video sequence with frame size $M \times N$ pixels, so that each pixel has D distinctive features such as color or texture. Here our aim is to reduce the size of the frame to be processed by the basic background model to $m \times n$ pixels, where $m < M$ and $n < N$, while at the same time the final foreground detection mask is size $M \times N$ pixels. For each pixel of the reduced size frame with frame coordinates $\mathbf{x}$, $\mathbf{x} \in \{1, \ldots, m\} \times \{1, \ldots, n\}$, its features $\mathbf{t}(\mathbf{x}) \in \mathbb{R}^D$ are computed from the features $\mathbf{t}(\mathbf{y})$ of the original video sequence:

$$\mathbf{t}(\mathbf{x}) = \varphi(\{\mathbf{t}(\mathbf{y}) \mid \mathbf{y} \in \mathcal{N}(\mathbf{x})\}) \tag{1}$$

$$\mathcal{N}(\mathbf{x}) \subset \{1, \ldots, M\} \times \{1, \ldots, N\} \tag{2}$$

where $\mathcal{N}(\mathbf{x})$ is a suitable neighborhood of the point $\mathbf{x}' = \left(\frac{Mx_1}{m}, \frac{Nx_1}{n}\right)$ in the original video frame and φ is a suitable interpolation function which takes a set of feature vectors from the original frame and outputs an interpolated feature vector for the reduced frame pixel. For example, one can choose φ to return the feature vector of the nearest neighbor of $\mathbf{x}'$:

$$\mathbf{t}_{NN}(\mathbf{x}) = \mathbf{t}(\mathbf{y}_{NN}) \tag{3}$$

$$\mathbf{y}_{NN} = \arg \min_{\mathbf{y} \in \{1, \ldots, M\} \times \{1, \ldots, N\}} \|\mathbf{y} - \mathbf{x}'\| \tag{4}$$

Another possibility is to divide the original image into non overlapping square blocks of size $B \times B$ pixels, and then compute the average of the feature vectors over each block:

$$\mathbf{t}_{AVG}(\mathbf{x}) = \frac{1}{B^2} \sum_{\mathbf{y} \in \mathcal{N}_{AVG}(\mathbf{x})} \mathbf{t}(\mathbf{y}) \tag{5}$$

$$\mathcal{N}_{AVG}(\mathbf{x}) = \{1 + B(x_1 - 1), \ldots, Bx_1\} \times \{1 + B(x_2 - 1), \ldots, Bx_2\} \tag{6}$$

We also consider bilinear and bicubic interpolations computed from the original frame data at the point $\mathbf{x}'$.

2.2 Upsampling

The reduced feature data $\mathbf{t}(\mathbf{x})$ are processed by a probabilistic background model such as [5]. The model yields the class probabilities $P(i|\mathbf{t}(\mathbf{x})) \in [0,1]$ of the observed values $\mathbf{t}(\mathbf{x})$ of the reduced frame pixels, for classes $i \in \{Back, Fore\}$. After that, it is necessary to estimate the class probabilities for the original frame pixels:

$$P(i|\mathbf{t}(\mathbf{y})) = \varphi'(\{P(i|\mathbf{t}(\mathbf{x})) \mid \mathbf{x} \in \mathcal{N}'(\mathbf{y})\}) \tag{7}$$

where $\mathcal{N}'(\mathbf{y})$ is a suitable neighborhood of the point $\mathbf{y}' = \left(\frac{my_1}{M}, \frac{ny_1}{N}\right)$ in the reduced video frame and φ' is a suitable interpolation function which takes a set class probabilities from the reduced frame and outputs an interpolated class probability for the original frame pixel. In our experiments we have always taken φ' to be a bicubic interpolation, since it produces smooth class probability estimations.

3 Experimental Results

In this section the foreground detection performance and the run time of different compression methods and compression factors is analyzed. First of all, the software and hardware used in the experiments are detailed in Subsect. 3.1. The tested sequences are presented in Subsect. 3.2 and the set of parameters by each compression method are specified in Subsect. 3.3. Finally the results are reported in Subsect. 3.4.

3.1 Methods

The underlying object detection method is the MFBM algorithm [5], which was previously published by our research group and it is based on the stochastic approximation theory.

Several compression methods are tested, namely: Blockwise average (AVG), Nearest neighbor (NN), Bilinear interpolation (LIN), and Bicubic interpolation (CUB). We note as the original size method (ORIG) if no compression method is applied and each pixel is individually processed. The key features that characterize each method are shown in Table 1.

Table 1. Summary of the model key features used by each proposal.

Name	Model key features
ORIG	Original size
AVG	Blockwise average
NN	Nearest neighbor
LIN	Bilinear interpolation
CUB	Bicubic interpolation

We do not use any additional post processing in any of the methods studied in order to make the comparisons as fair as possible. All the experiments have been carried out on a 64-bit Personal Computer with an eight-core Intel i7 3.60 GHz CPU, 32 GB RAM and standard hardware.

3.2 Sequences

The set of the videos we have tested have been chosen from the 2014 dataset of the ChangeDetection.net web site[1]. The sequences selected are the videos from the Baseline category, which is composed by videos with no special difficulties. There are two outdoor videos: *Highway* presents a highway with cars moving from top to bottom (320×240 pixels and 1700 frames), and *Pedestrians* shows people walking from left to right and vice versa (360×240 pixels and 1099 frames). Also, there are two indoor sequences: *Office*, whose peculiarity is a person remains static in a room during a time interval and then continues its movement (360×240 pixels and 2050 frames); and PETS2006, with people moving on in a train station (720×576 pixels and 1200 frames).

3.3 Parameter Selection

We have chosen a range of values for the Compression Factor parameter, which is the test parameter and can take different values. For the MFBM parameters we have run the method with the parameter values recommended by their authors, so these parameters are fixed. The combination of the parameter values forms the set of all configurations we have tuned for each benchmark sequence. These values are shown in Table 2.

Table 2. Considered parameter values for the competing methods. The combinations of them form the set of all experimental configurations.

Method	Parameters
MFBM	Step size, $\alpha = 0.01$
	Features, $F = [1, 2, 3]$
	$Compression Method = \{ORIG, AVG, NN, LIN, CUB\}$
	Compression Factor, $\rho = \{1, 0.875, 0.75, 0.625, 0.5, 0.375, 0.25, 0.125\}$

3.4 Results

Our aim is to determine the influence of the analyzed compression methods on the foreground mask produced by the object detection method and its execution time.

From a qualitative perspective, our experiments show how the compression methods affect the result, as we can see in Fig. 1. As the Compression Factor

---

[1] http://changedetection.net/.

Frame	GT	MFBM

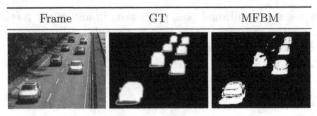

(a) A raw frame, the Ground Truth (GT) mask and the output of the MFBM method, respectively.

	0.875	0.75	0.625	0.5	0.375	0.25	0.125
AVG							
NN							
LIN							
CUB							

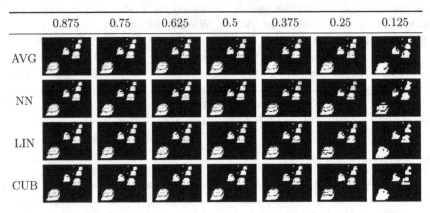

(b) Output masks after applying the MFBM with combinations of the Compression Methods (first column) and Compression Factors (first row).

Fig. 1. Results of this approach for the *Highway* sequence.

decreases, the result loses details, so that the objects appear highly pixellated and they look like squares. On the other hand, the downsampling process also has favorable consequences: in most of cases the result has a lower noise level, and the interior of the objects is better defined than in the original result.

From a quantitative point of view, three performance measures have been considered, namely the accuracy, the execution time and the used memory. The best performing configuration for each sequence is shown in Fig. 2. In the same way, Fig. 3 shows the results of each method for the tuned configurations.

As it can be observed in Fig. 2, as the Compression Factor decreases, the time and memory requirements are smaller. Furthermore, all tuned configurations need less memory than ORIG, except the AVG compression that uses more memory for Compression Factor values higher or equal than 0.75. This is not the case for the CPU time, since there are many tuned configurations with a higher execution time than ORIG.

In addition to this, applying downsampling to the images does not always lead to a smaller accuracy. There is a large amount of downsampled configurations which exhibit a similar or higher accuracy value than the original configuration.

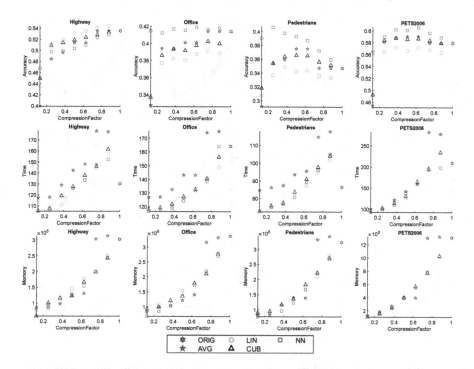

Fig. 2. Quantitative results: accuracy (first row), execution time (second row), and used memory (third row), all of them versus the compression factor. Each tested video corresponds to a column.

The most interesting benchmark is the PETS2006 sequence because this video has the biggest frame size among the tested sequences. As seen in Fig. 3 the differences in the used memory and the execution time are higher than for the other sequences.

The memory used by our algorithm is very similar with each Compression Method and the same Compression Factor (except the AVG compression, which uses more memory for Compression Factor values higher or equal than 0.75), while the execution time and the accuracy values vary significantly depending on the Compression Factor. In Fig. 4 the obtained accuracy and the required execution time are listed for each method and sequence.

The Office, Pedestrians and PETS2006 videos yield similar results. The NN method yields the best compromise between the accuracy and the execution time. CUB and AVG present a similar accuracy but AVG spends more time. LIN is fast but its accuracy is worst than the others. On the other hand, the comparison with the Highway sequence yields the LIN method as the best one.

According to this results, the NN method applied to a foreground detection system it will decrease the usage of the memory and it could reduce the execution time without affecting the accuracy significantly. In some cases, the accuracy could even be improved.

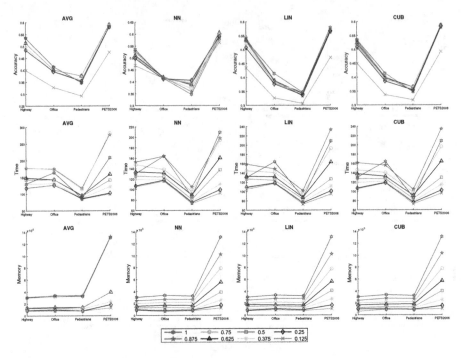

Fig. 3. First, second and third rows show the accuracy, the execution time (in seconds) and the used memory (in bytes) for all sequences tested for each method, respectively. Please note that the values of each method are connected between them with lines to better compare the methods in each video, but this does not mean that the videos are related.

4   Discussion and Conclusions

In this work, a frame size reduction method for foreground detection in video sequences is presented. This method is divided into three different stages, namely downsampling of the original video frame using a specific interpolation function, foreground detection of the reduced video frame by a probabilistic background model, and upsampling of the class probabilities for the reduced video frame to estimate the class probabilities of the original frame. For the downsampling process the blockwise average (AVG), nearest neighbor (NNN), bilinear interpolation (LIN), and bicubic interpolation (CUB) were used, whereas the MFBM [5] probabilistic background model was chosen to perform the foreground detection.

Four different well-known video sequences were selected for our experiments, where the accuracy and execution time were analyzed for several compression configurations. These results yielded similar or better results than those obtained by the same method without any compression method applied (ORIG), with the advantage of decreasing significantly the computational load of the algorithm.

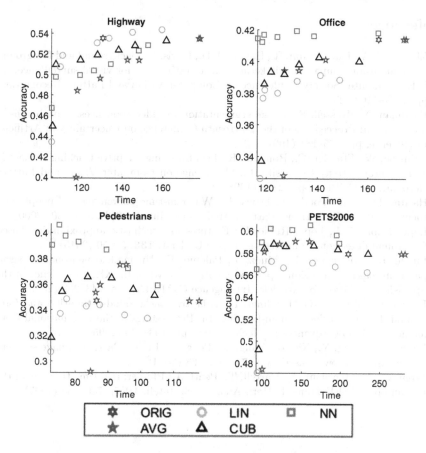

Fig. 4. Accuracy and execution time (in seconds) for all tested configurations and videos.

Acknowledgments. This work is partially supported by the Ministry of Economy and Competitiveness of Spain under grant TIN2014-53465-R, project name Video surveillance by active search of anomalous events. It is also partially supported by the Autonomous Government of Andalusia (Spain) under projects TIC-6213, project name Development of Self-Organizing Neural Networks for Information Technologies; and TIC-657, project name Self-organizing systems and robust estimators for video surveillance. Finally, it is partially supported by the Autonomous Government of Extremadura (Spain) under the project IB13113. All of them include funds from the European Regional Development Fund (ERDF). The authors thankfully acknowledge the computer resources, technical expertise and assistance provided by the SCBI (Supercomputing and Bioinformatics) center of the University of Málaga.

References

1. Elgammal, A., Duraiswami, R., Harwood, D., Davis, L.: Background and foreground modeling using nonparametric kernel density estimation for visual surveillance. In: IEEE Computer Society Conference on Computer Vision and Pattern Recognition, pp. 1151–1163 (2002)
2. Friedman, N., Russell, S.: Image segmentation in video sequences: a probabilistic approach. In: Proceedings of the Thirteenth Conference on Uncertainty in Artificial Intelligence, pp. 175–181 (1997)
3. Grimson, W., Stauffer, C., Romano, R., Lee, L.: Using adaptive tracking to classify and monitor activities in a site. In: Conference on Computer Vision and Pattern Recognition (CVPR), pp. 22–29 (1998)
4. Haritaoglu, I., Harwood, D., Davis, L.: W4: real-time surveillance of people and their activities. IEEE Trans. Pattern Anal. Mach. Intell. 22(8), 809–830 (2000)
5. López-Rubio, F.J., López-Rubio, E.: Features for stochastic approximation based foreground detection. Comput. Vis. Image Underst. 133, 30–50 (2015)
6. Luque, R., Dominguez, E., Muoz, J., Palomo, E.: Un modelo neuronal de agrupamiento basado en regiones para segmentacin de vdeo. In: XIII Conference of the Spanish Association for Artificial Intelligence (CAEPIA), pp. 243–252 (2009)
7. Ridder, C., Munkelt, O., Kirchner, H.: Adaptive background estimation and foreground detection using kalman-filtering. In: Proceedings of the International Conference on Recent Advances in Mechatronics, pp. 193–199 (1995)
8. Wang, H., Zhang, Y., Nie, R., Yang, Y., Peng, B., Li, T.: Bayesian image segmentation fusion. Knowl.-Based Syst. 71, 162–168 (2014)
9. Wren, C., Azarbayejani, A., Darrell, T., Pentl, A.: Pfinder: real-time tracking of the human body. IEEE Trans. Pattern Anal. Mach. Intell. 19(7), 780–785 (1997)

Visual Navigation for UAV with Map References Using ConvNets

Fidel Aznar[✉], Mar Pujol, and Ramón Rizo

Departamento de Ciencia de la Computación e Inteligencia Artificial,
Universidad de Alicante, San Vicente del Raspeig/Sant Vicent del Raspeig, Spain
{fidel,mar,rizo}@dccia.ua.es

Abstract. In this paper, a visual system for helping unmanned aerial vehicles navigation, designed with a convolutional neural network, is presented. This network is trained to match on-board captured images with several previously obtained global maps, generating actions given a known global control policy. This system can be used directly for navigation or filtered, combining it with other aircraft systems. Our model will be compared with a classical map registration application, using a Scale-Invariant Feature Transform (SIFT) key point extractor. The system will be trained and evaluated with real aerial images. The results obtained show the viability of the proposed system and demonstrate its performance.

1 Introduction

Unmanned aerial vehicle (UAV) navigation is an active research area. There are some situations, places and even devices, where visual perception is the best option for navigation. To develop visual navigation systems is complex because there are many factors that affect perception. However, given various assumptions this complexity can be reduced. In this paper we will assume that we have a prior record of recent images of the area to be overflown. Moreover, the path to be developed by the UAV is known given the UAV position and a global control policy. Thus, we firstly need the UAV to be able to locate itself on a previously obtained global map.

Most state of the art approaches rely on global localization based on visual matching between current view and available georeferenced satellite/ aerial images [1–4] using feature detection. For example, in [2] geo-referenced is aided by Google Maps. Feature detectors and descriptors, that exploit the self-similarity of the images, are paired to establish the correspondence between the on-board image and the map. Subsequently, template matching using a sliding window approach is confined in the search region predicted by inter-frame motion obtained from optical flow. In [4] the matching is based on scale-invariant feature transform (SIFT) features and the system estimates the position of the UAV and its altitude on the base of the reference image.

This work has been supported by the Spanish Ministerio de Economia y Competitividad, project TIN2013-40982-R. Project co-financed with FEDER funds.

O. Luaces et al. (Eds.): CAEPIA 2016, LNAI 9868, pp. 13–22, 2016.
DOI: 10.1007/978-3-319-44636-3_2

After the incredible success of deep learning in the computer vision domain, there has been much interest in applying Convolutional Network (ConvNet) features in robotic fields such as visual navigation. There are several papers related to visual matching using convNets. For example, [5] shows how to learn directly from image data a general similarity function for comparing image patches. In [6] the effectiveness of convNets activation features for tasks requiring correspondence is studied. This paper claims that convNet features localize at a much finer scale than their receptive field sizes. They can be used to perform intra-class alignment as well as conventional hand-engineered features, and that they outperform conventional features in keypoint prediction.

This article describes a navigational aid system for UAVs based on the registration of perceptions on a previous map using convNets. A Convolutional Network will be trained to generate actions for every visual perception given a global motion plan. Our intention is to provide a useful navigation system for drones that can be combined or filtered with other aircraft systems.

The organization of the paper is as follows. Firstly, a global navigation policy for a specific map will be defined. Secondly, we will describe the system and the tests to be performed with real aerial maps. Next, we will introduce a convolutional network to develop visual navigation. Finally, we will validate our system with real aerial images and will compare it with a classical visual matching strategy related to [4].

2 Global Navigation Map

Our motion model is based on building a global motion plan, defined specifically for the task to be developed. For this purpose we have defined a potential function $U(x)$ so that the global navigation plan will be defined by its gradient. There are many studies and different alternatives to define potential functions that behave desirably as feedback motion plan. We use a potential function U quadratic with distance. This function allows us to calculate the potential field for a given space point x. The system presented here does not depend on a specific potential function and will not be deeply discussed here.

$$U(x) = \alpha \sum_{i=1}^{N} q_i \frac{x - x_i}{\|x - x_i\|}, \ A(x) = \cos^{-1}\left(\frac{-\nabla U(x) \cdot a}{\|\nabla U(x)\| \|a\|}\right)$$

We are interested in developing an interface where the user could touch different areas adding repulsion or attraction forces. Therefore, we will use N particles. For each particle i we will define its intensity q_i (that can be attractive or repulsive) and position x_i, where α is a normalization term. More specifically, we will focus on the angle of the gradient of this potential function, $A(x)$, as we are only interested in the direction of the aircraft. This direction is obtained through a reference vector a.

In Fig. 1(a), an aerial image of the University of Alicante campus is presented. All the introduced particles for generating the potential field are shown, where

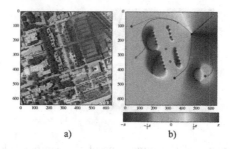

Fig. 1. (a) Aerial image of the University of Alicante campus with the attractive parti-cles (circles) and repulsors (stars) (b) $A(x)$ function of the previous map, where colour represents the navigation angle in radians. Seven different routes developed with this map for different starting positions are also shown

circles are attractive forces and stars repulsive ones. The radius of the particle represents its intensity. In Fig. 1(b) the $A(x)$ function, calculated for the previous particles is presented. A simulation of movement using this map is also presented, for seven different starting positions, where a circle represents the initial position and a star the final one. For this simulation, we have iterated 500 times, adjusting the vehicle angle using $A(x)$ function with a translational velocity equal to one meter per iteration.

3   Test Design

For the development of our task we require the UAVs to be equipped with a compass and a barometer (both are very common sensors for even low cost drones). The usefulness of the barometer is to ensure a uniform altitude for capturing the images. This is a key advantage of this type of vehicle, because we can reduce and even eliminate the need to extract multi-scale features (they can fly at the same altitude as the map was obtained). Moreover, a compass is needed for registering the images in an independent point of view.

As was discussed above, the presented system allows us to have several points of attraction and repulsion placed on a global visual map. The perceptions of a UAV will be used to determine the action to be proposed by the system given a registration process (carried out internally by the network). Therefore, we could use the system in several ways: to create reactive sensors to avoid or direct the drone to different areas, such as the work presented in [7] or to provide support for visual navigation, as will be used in this paper.

To accomplish this task we need a visual global map. We will use five orthophotos of the same area of the campus, taken at different time of the day of different years. These photos are sufficiently different (different shadow areas, camera types, changes in vegetation...) to test the robustness of the system. The first four images (Fig. 2(a) will be used as global map for network training. One last image (Fig. 2(b) will be used as validation.

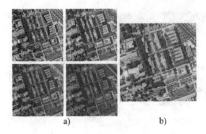

Fig. 2. (a) Different images of the same zone of the campus taken in several flights used for training. Capture years are (from left to right) 2002, 2005, 2007 and 2009. Different shadow orientations indicate different day times captures. (b) Image used for test taken in 2012. A perceptual window of size $w = 32$ is represented

These images will be reduced by 80 % to decrease the amount of computation and memory needed by the system. Once reduced, the perceptual window represented in Fig. 2(b) will correspond to 32×32 pixels. Although there is a noticeable data reduction we have determined that there is sufficient information to make a smooth visual navigation, as we will see shortly. With the same philosophy we have discretized the global navigation map with 20 possible angles (the allowed turns that can develop the aircraft for each input image).

4   ConvNet Navigation

Recent progress in the computer vision and machine learning community has shown that the features generated by Convolutional Networks (convNets) outperform other methods in a broad variety of visual recognition, classification and detection tasks. ConvNets have been demonstrated to be versatile and transferable, i.e. even although they were trained on a very specific target task, they can be successfully deployed for solving different problems and often even outperform traditional hand engineered features [8].

In this section we will provide a convNet network model for developing our navigation task. We will also discuss the training strategy followed for network convergence. Is worth highlighting that we have used Theano Library (http://deeplearning.net/software/theano/) for the implementation of our models.

4.1   Proposed Model

As previously discussed, convolutional networks have several features that make them particularly suitable for working with real images. We propose to use the network model presented in Fig. 3 for this task. The first four layers are responsible to extract visual features while the last one, the softmax layer, is responsible to select from desired action for the input. All the internal layers utilize Parametric Rectified Linear Units (PReLU) [9], because they have shown greater results in network convergence and generalization.

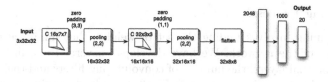

Fig. 3. Proposed convNet model. The first four layers are responsible to extract visual features while the last one, the softmax layer, is responsible to select from desired action for the input.

Layers responsible for the visual scene analysis will serve mainly for two purposes: the convolution step, where a fixed-size window runs over the image defining a region of interest, and the processing step, that uses the pixels inside each window as input for the neurons that, finally, perform the feature extraction from the region. This iterative process results in a new image (feature map), generally smaller than the original one. However, in our case this filter will be extended with zeros (zero padding) to generate more uniform filters for subsequent phases. After each convolutional layer, there are pooling layers that were created in order to reduce the variance of features by computing the max operation of a particular feature over a region of the image. This process ensures that the same result can be obtained, even when image features have small translations or rotations, being very important for object classification and detection.

Finally, the network processing units lose their spatial notion, lining up in a fully connected layer. All these 2048 neurons will be connected to another full connected layer of 1000 neurons, ending with the final classification layer of 20 neurons (the 20 allowed turns that can develop the aircraft for each input image). More specifically, we must learn 1061164 parameters including weights, bias and the PReLU coefficients for this network.

The most common classifier layer is the softmax function, also called normalized exponential. It is a generalization of the multinomial logistic function that generates a K-dimensional vector of real values, which represents a categorical probability distribution:

$$P(y_i|\boldsymbol{Z};\boldsymbol{W}) = \frac{e^{\boldsymbol{Z}^T\boldsymbol{W}_i}}{\sum_j e^{\boldsymbol{Z}^T\boldsymbol{W}_j}}$$

That can be interpreted as the (normalized) probability assigned to all the network outputs given the image z_i of the sample vector $\boldsymbol{Z}$ and parameterized by $\boldsymbol{W}$. One of the reasons for discretizing the action map is to be able to use a classification cost function, because regression problems require different cost functions (such as Mean Squared Error, MSE) much more difficult to converge. Intuitively, regression cost functions require very fragile and specific properties from the network to output exactly one correct value for each input.

4.2   Training Process

Network training involves finding the set of weights that minimize the classification error of the network. We have developed several tests, increasing the number of internal layers, the number of convolutional filters and their size. The more balanced network is presented in Fig. 3. In order to avoid overfitting several techniques have been tested, such as batch normalization layers, dropout or L2/L1 weight decay penalty. Our final network architecture uses a L2 penalty of 0.006 and a dropout factor of 0.5 for fully connected layers. Batch normalization layers achieved without L2 or dropout, better training accuracy values but do not generalize well on our test set. Therefore, the final cost C of the network to be minimized is presented, where N is the number of samples, λ is the intensity of the L2 penalty and k, l are weight iterators:

$$\underset{W}{\text{argmin }} C(W) \text{ where } C(W) = \frac{1}{N} \sum_i -\log P(y_i|Z;W) + \frac{1}{2}\lambda \sum_k \sum_l W_{k,l}^2$$

It should be noted that the process of generating training data for the four global image maps has big memory requirements. We have to extract patches from the images presented in Fig. 2 with a window size of $3 \times 32 \times 32$. For each global image 47045 patches must be extracted. Therefore, we calculate, for each phase of training, the patch extraction in an online way. More specifically, we extract random patches (24000 per epoch) for each of the training maps (6000 for each map) in order to train the network.

This training process involve to calculate the global navigation map of Sect. 2 and extract, for each random patch, the action that the UAV must develop. Because both maps have the same size and represent the same space, is trivial to obtain which action must be taken given a specific position. In this case, to train the network, we have taken the action found in the global motion map at the central position of the patch. In this way, the network has been trained to generate the required output (the turn angle extracted from our global navigation map) for every presented patch.

5   Results

As can be seen in Fig. 4, this network is able to learn the actions to be emitted depending on the perception of the drone (developing internally a global matching process with the four training maps). We have observed that the network has emitted the correct action for the 88 % of the presented images and the 75 % for the test set. It is important to underline that all the test images are extracted for a map not previously seen, captured three years later that the last training image set (even taken in a different time of the day). For this work, the training dataset extracted from Fig. 1(a) is not extended artificially (which could further increase the generalization ability of the network).

Previously, we have stated that for this application to work, recent global maps must be taken. But as we have seen, the network is able to generalize even without these conditions.

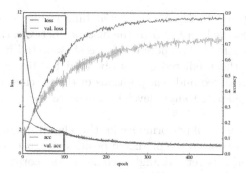

Fig. 4. Evolution of network error and accuracy for the training and validation data for each epoch. At every epoch 24000 random patches are presented to the network (6000 for each training map)

Is worth highlighting that once the network is trained we have calculated a mean runtime for prediction of 1.36 ms for an Intel core i7. This is the time required to calculate, given a patch input, the turn to be developed by the aircraft.

5.1 Comparing with a SIFT Registration Application

As has been discussed above, most global localization applications based on visual matching use feature detectors such as SIFT, Features from accelerated segment test (FAST) or Oriented FAST and Rotated BRIEF (ORB). In order to compare our system with this approximation we have implemented a global registration application based on [4].

As presented in Fig. 5 we use a SIFT extractor to obtain both, the robot perception (patch) features and the global map features. More specifically, we have used the SIFT key extractor provided by the openCV library (http://opencv.org). Once these features are extracted we perform a matching process using FANN algorithm [10] to determine which patch features correspond to

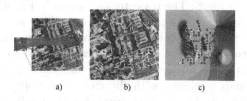

Fig. 5. (a) Matching of a drone perception (patch) through the map using SIFT. (b) Distance between real position and estimated position for 100 random patches of size 32×32 where a dot represents the real position and a cross the estimated one. (c) Same test with a window size of 64×64 and represented over the discretized global action map

the global map features. In Fig. 5(a), the matching results for one patch of size 32×32 pixels is presented. In Fig. 5(b) the distance between the actual position and the estimated one for 100 random patches is showed. In Fig. 5(c) the distance of real position an the predicted one is observed for 100 random patches of size 64×64. The predicted and real positions of the patches are plotted on the discretized motion map (20 angle levels) to observe the error on the emitted action.

To calculate a measure of performance for this algorithm, in order to compare it with our system, we obtain the predicted position of a patch and calculate the corresponding action (discretized angle), counting the correct predicted angles regards our global policy angle. We perform this test for several global maps sizes, increasing the perception size in a proportional way.

The following table shows the percentage of correct predicted actions by applying this algorithm to 10,000 randomly selected perceptions of size w in a previously presented global map. We also include the accuracy rate obtained by our convNet. It must be underlined that the train accuracy of SIFT algorithm is calculated based on patch extraction and matching from the 2009 map presented in Fig. 2(a). The test accuracy for this approximation is obtained calculating the matching process from the previous map over the 2012 test map presented in Fig. 2(b).

Base algorithm	Perception size (w in pixels)	Map size	Training accuracy (as decimal)	Test accuracy (as decimal)
Sift	32	128	0.35	0.15
Sift	64	256	0.61	0.13
Sift	160	640	0.80	0.11
ConvNet	32	128	0.88	0.75

5.2   Using the System for Reactive Visual Navigation

Finally, several trajectory predicted by the network for various selected start positions are shown in Fig. 6. The trajectories showed in Fig. 6(a) are developed using the four training maps. As can be seen, most of the predicted movements make the vehicle to reach the zones of attraction. However, there are some circumstances where this is not the case: there are zones where the combination of repulsion and attraction forces could nullify the potential field. In addition, some zones of the map combined with the movement policy could suffer from visual ambiguity. These problems could cause that the predicted trajectory may not match the global movement policy.

As it was presented before, the network is able to generalize and emit correct actions from not previously seen images. We have used our network to predict reactive trajectories using a not previously seen map, obtaining good results as can be seen in Fig. 6(b).

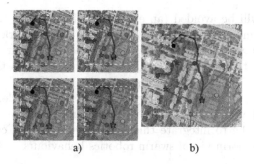

Fig. 6. Movement of ten aircraft navigating through the training and test maps. The initial positions (circles) and final (starts) are shown. The simulation is carried out for 120 iterations, with a velocity vector size of 1 m per iteration

Is worth highlighting that the results presented here are obtained without any filtering (it is a reactive navigation) using only the most likely angle defined by $P(y_i|\boldsymbol{Z};\boldsymbol{W})$, discarding the rest of information of this distribution. Obviously, including these two factors could substantially improve the robustness of the aircraft navigation.

6   Discussion

This paper presents an aid system for UAV navigation using the registration of perceptions through a global map. A convolutional neural network, to extract the essential features of the global visual maps given a global movement policy is used. The resulting model is able to generalize and work with no previously seen images, captured with different sensors and with changes in light conditions. Although this application does not require multi-scale matching (the UAV will fly at the same altitude of the global map), it easy to extend it, extracting multi scale patches for the network training process.

The accuracy of the network for training maps is higher than the obtained by matching features using SIFT key point extractors (even with larger maps and window perception size). Only using a much bigger global map (80 % larger) we could achieve a similar accuracy for training global maps. One of the reasons for the convNet proper functioning is that the network is able to extract the essential features of the map with respect to the global navigation policy. Thus, the more complex areas force the network to devote more resources to find visual indicators that characterize it. This explains its better performance in this task compared with specialized key point extractors. Moreover, the generalization of this network is far better that the key point matching approach, although we have discarded so much visual information to reduce the amount of resources required for network training.

In this approximation we have tested our system using real aerial maps. A coherent set of global maps (or previous perceptions) with a global control policy must be provided so that the production of two distinct actions for the same perception will be avoided (an expansion of the perception window or a filtering step can smooth this problem). Although this network has been shown generic enough for working with new images we must ensure that the set of images that define the global map will be generic enough so that the network will be able to draw general characteristics.

As future plans we will test this system in a UAV vehicle, combining this sensor with the other aircraft modules to develop navigation and security tasks. Our next step will be to integrate this system within a low cost module that could be used to perform visual swarm robotics behaviours with low cost UAV.

References

1. Nogueira, K., Miranda, W.O., Dos Santos, J.A.: Improving spatial feature representation from aerial scenes by using convolutional networks. In: 2015 28th SIBGRAPI Conference on Graphics, Patterns and Images (SIBGRAPI), pp. 289–296. IEEE (2015)
2. Shan, M., Charan, A.: Google map referenced UAV navigation via simultaneous feature detection and description. In: IEEE/RSJ International Conference on Intelligent Robots and Systems (IROS) (2015)
3. Cesetti, A., Frontoni, E., Mancini, A., Zingaretti, P., Longhi, S.: A vision-based guidance system for UAV navigation and safe landing using natural landmarks. In: Valavanis, K.P., Beard, R., Oh, P., Ollero, A., Piegl, L.A., Shim, H. (eds.) Selected Papers from the 2nd International Symposium on UAVs, pp. 233–257. Springer, Heidelberg (2009)
4. Cesetti, A., Frontoni, E., Mancini, A., Ascani, A., Zingaretti, P., Longhi, S.: A visual global positioning system for unmanned aerial vehicles used in photogrammetric applications. J. Intell. Robot. Syst. **61**, 157–168 (2011)
5. Long, J.L., Zhang, N., Darrell, T.: Do convnets learn correspondence? In: Advances in Neural Information Processing Systems, pp. 1601–1609 (2014)
6. Zagoruyko, S., Komodakis, N.: Learning to compare image patches via convolutional neural networks. In: Proceedings of the IEEE Conference on Computer Vision and Pattern Recognition, pp. 4353–4361 (2015)
7. Mejias, L., Fitzgerald, D.L., Eng, P.C., Xi, L.: Forced Landing Technologies for Unmanned Aerial Vehicles: Towards Safer Operations. In-Tech, Rijeka (2009)
8. Sunderhauf, N., Shirazi, S., Dayoub, F., Upcroft, B., Milford, M.: On the performance of convnet features for place recognition. In: 2015 IEEE/RSJ International Conference on Intelligent Robots and Systems (IROS), pp. 4297–4304. IEEE (2015)
9. He, K., Zhang, X., Ren, S., Sun, J.: Delving deep into rectifiers: surpassing human-level performance on imagenet classification. In: Proceedings of the IEEE International Conference on Computer Vision, pp. 1026–1034 (2015)
10. Muja, M., Lowe, D.G.: Fast approximate nearest neighbors with automatic algorithm configuration. VISAPP (1) **2**, 331–340 (2009)

Vessel Tree Extraction and Depth Estimation with OCT Images

Joaquim de Moura, Jorge Novo, Marcos Ortega$^{(\boxtimes)}$, Noelia Barreira,
and Manuel G. Penedo

Departamento de Computación, Universidade da Coruña, A Coruña, Spain
{joaquim.demoura,jnovo,mortega,nbarreira,mgpenedo}@udc.es

Abstract. The identification of the retinal arterio-venular tree is a relevant issue for its analysis in a large variability of procedures. Classical methodologies employ 2D acquisition strategies that obtain a limited representation of the vascular structure. This paper proposes a new methodology for 2D vessel tree extraction and the corresponding depth estimation using Optical Coherence Tomography (OCT) images. This way, the proposal defines a more complete scenario for an adequate posterior vasculature analysis. The methodology employs different image analysis techniques to initially extract the 2D vessel tree. Then, the method maps these 2D positions in the corresponding histological sections of the OCT images and estimates the corresponding depths along all the vessel tree. To test and validate this proposal, this work employed 196 OCT histological images with the corresponding near infrared reflectance retinographies. The methodology provided promising results, indicating an acceptable accuracy in a complex domain as is the vessel tree identification. It provides a coherent 2D vessel tree extraction with the corresponding depth estimations that constitute a scenario with high potentially useful information for posterior medical analysis and diagnostic processes of many diseases as, for example, hypertension or diabetes.

Keywords: Computer-aided diagnosis · Retinal imaging · OCT · Vessel tree

1 Introduction and Previous Work

Eye fundus is, nowadays, a frequently used way of analyzing and diagnosing many different diseases. The study of retinal images provides the doctors useful information that can be of a great utility to obtain accurate diagnosis in a large variability of pathologies. In these diagnostic procedures, Computer-Aided Diagnostic (CAD) systems have demonstrated its utility as many different approaches. These computational approaches help the doctors to increase their productivity, minimize the risks of possible mistakes and help to establish preventive and therapeutic strategies.

CAD systems for the identification and analysis of the eye fundus main structures were appearing over the years. The vessel tree extraction is one of the most relevant issues, as its analysis is fundamental for the microcirculation analysis

© Springer International Publishing Switzerland 2016
O. Luaces et al. (Eds.): CAEPIA 2016, LNAI 9868, pp. 23–33, 2016.
DOI: 10.1007/978-3-319-44636-3_3

due to the fact that the retinal microcirculation is the easiest and less invasive way to access to the circulatory system in human body. Different studies arised over the years stating this relevance. For example, the vessel caliber was demonstrated to be a parameter of high relevance in the analysis of diabetic patients [1]. Others indicated that the microcirculation constitute a relevant biomarker for cerebrovascular diseases [2] or cardiovascular illnesses [3].

The task of vessel tree extraction was faced by different authors over the years, and interesting methodologies were appearing. Despite that, most of them proposed segmentation methodologies for 2D vessel tree segmentation using angiographies or retinographies, image modalities that provide 2D projections of the real 3D layout of the vasculature. We include a representative set of proposed methodologies as illustration.

Thresholding approaches were employed in this issue. Hence, Zhang *et al.* [4] or Yong *et al.* [5] designed adaptive thresholding processes to extract the vessel tree in retinographies. Tracking approaches also demonstrated its utility as the work of Wink *et al.* [6], who implemented a methodology that begins from a set of user-defined image coordinates and provides the central axis of tubular structures, as is the case of the retinal vasculature. Edge detectors were also used, as the work of Dhar *et al.* [7] testing Canny and Laplacian of gaussian detectors. The authors stated that Canny is more robust in these particular image conditions. Region growing approaches were also proposed, as the work of Mendonça and Campilho [8] that proposed a method that firstly extracts the vessel centerline and then uses a region growing process to fill the extracted vessels. Wavelet transform was also included in different proposals as the one of Fathi *et al.* [9] where information over multiple classification scales was integrated to obtain the vessels.

Regarding Optical Coherence Tomography (OCT) images, few works appeared for vessel extraction. Wu *et al.* [10] proposed a methodology that uses Point Drift to obtain the retinal vessel point sets. Then, this set is used as landmarks for image registration. Niemeijer *et al.* [11] proposed a method that segments the retina in multiple layers performing a posterior classification in the projected image to extract the vessels. In the work of Xu *et al.* [12] a 3D boosting learning approach is employed for vessels detection. Then, a post-processing step is done to remove false positive detections.

Given the high potential of a 3D analysis of the vessel tree, we present in this work a new methodology to identify the vessel tree in OCT images. The method firstly extracts the 2D vessel tree that is posteriorly mapped with the corresponding histological sections. Finally, the corresponding depth coordinates are estimated for each detected vessel point. This way, this proposal offers a methodology that provides a more complete information set of the retinal arterio-venular tree that could facilitate further and more precise retinal microcirculation analysis than simple 2D extractions.

2   Methodology

The proposed methodology makes use of, as input, the OCT image. The OCT imaging technique let us obtain tomographic images of the biological tissue with high resolution, performing consecutive measurements, the histological sections, that provide the depth at the progressive bands over the eye fundus. Hence, these consecutive histological sections compose the 3D representation of the eye fundus of the patient. This 3D visualization is complemented with the corresponding near infrared reflectance retinography, automatically registered with the histological sections, that offer a classical 2D visualization of the corresponding eye fundus region where the histological section were obtained. Figure 1 includes a illustrative example of an OCT image. The input images include the representation of the region of interest (ROI), region that indicates the part of the retinography that is mapped with the histological sections. Both are the parts where we can search and analyze the retinal vessel tree of a patient.

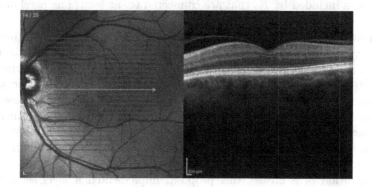

Fig. 1. Near infrared reflectance retinography and histological section example.

The new approach is mainly composed of three consecutive stages: a first one, where the vessel tree is extracted in the near infrared reflectance retinography, providing a 2D vasculature extraction; a second one, where this initial 2D identifications are mapped in the corresponding histological sections; and a third one, where the approach searches for the vessel location in the histological sections and derives the corresponding depth positions at the mapped points. This process is performed over the entire vessel tree obtaining, finally, a complete set of (x, y, z) coordinates over all the vasculature. Next subsections detail the process.

2.1   2D Vessel Tree Extraction

As said, we firstly segment the vessels in the 2D near infrared retinography for its simplicity and given that there is well-established techniques to achieve that. In particular, a segmentation process based in morphological operators [13] is used to enhance the vessels and identify an initial vessel representation.

The vessel enhancement stage employs a multi-scalar approach where the eigenvalues, λ_1 and λ_2, of the Hessian matrix [14] are combined to filter geometric tubular structures with variable size, that is, the vessels. Thus, a function $B(p)$ is defined as:

$$B(p) = \begin{cases} 0 & \lambda_2 > 0 \\ exp(\frac{-R_B^2}{2_\beta^2})(1 - exp(-\frac{S^2}{2c^2})) & otherwise \end{cases} \quad (1)$$

where $R_b = \lambda_1/\lambda_2$, c is the half of the max Hessian norm, S represents a measure to "second order structures". Pixels that belongs to vessels are normally represented by small λ_1 values and higher positive λ_2 values. After this enhancement, the vascular segmentation is achieved in two steps: an early segmentation and a posterior removal of isolated structures. The early segmentation is done by a hysteresis based thresholding. A hard threshold (T_h) obtain pixels with a high confidence of being vessels while a weak threshold (T_w) keeps all the pixels of the tree, including also spurious ones. The final vessel segmentation is formed by all the pixels included by T_w that are connected to, at least, one pixel obtained by T_h.

Segmentation approaches in 2D can not be directly used for reconstruction as they typically present cumulative errors due to misrepresentation of the edges. This way, a centerline-based approach is normally used to correct deviation in the detected structure. The main purpose of this stage is the identification of the approximate central line of the vessels in order to obtain a set of consecutive coordinates that represents all the vasculature. This process is performed with an approach that exploits the concept that vessels can be thought of as creases (ridges or valleys) when images are seen as landscapes. Hence, curvature level curves are used to calculate the creases (crest and valley lines).

As definition of a crease, this proposal implemented a level set extrinsic curvature or LSEC, Eq. 2, given its invariant properties. This approach segment the vessel tree that is going to be 2D structure of the identified vessel tree. Given a function $L : \mathbb{R}^d \rightarrow \mathbb{R}$, the level set for a constant l consists of the set of points $x|L(x) = l$. For 2D images, L can be considered as a topographic relief or landscape and the level sets as its level curves. Negative minima of the level curve curvature k, level by level, form valley curves, and positive maxima form ridge curves.

$$k = (2L_xL_yL_{xy} - L_y^2L_{xx} - L_x^2L_{yy})(L_x^2 + L_y^2)^{-\frac{3}{2}} \quad (2)$$

where

$$L_\alpha = \frac{\partial L}{\partial \alpha}, \ L_{\alpha\beta} = \frac{\partial^2 L}{\partial \alpha \ \partial \beta}, \ \alpha, \beta \in x, y \quad (3)$$

However, the usual discretization of LSEC is ill-defined in a number of cases, giving rise to unexpected discontinuities at the centre of elongated objects. Due to this, the Multilocal Level Set Extrinsic Curvature with Structure Tensor, MLSEC-ST operator, originally defined [15] for 3D landmark extraction of CT and MRI volumes, is used:

$$k = -div(\bar{w}) = -\sum_{i=1}^{d}(\frac{\partial \bar{w}^i}{\partial x^i}), \ d = 2; \quad (4)$$

where $\bar{w}^i$ is the component at the position i of $\bar{w}$, the normalized vector field of $L : \mathbb{R}^d \to \mathbb{R}$. This last is defined by Eq. 5, where O_d is the d-dimensional zero vector.

$$\bar{w} = \begin{cases} \frac{w}{\|w\|}, \; if \; \|w\| > 0 \\ O_d, \; if \; \|w\| = 0 \end{cases} \tag{5}$$

This work does not face the extraction of the caliber of the vessel tree, just a 3D coordinate representation of the entire points of the vasculature. The employed crease method does not return a 1-pixel width segment as there are degrees of creaseness along the vessel. For that reason, all the pixels are labeled with a tracking process that checks all the crease image and guarantees that all the detected pixels are grouped belonging to a particular vessel. The aim of this process is the obtaining of a skeleton vessel tree structure with all the vessels represented by one-pixel width segments. Moreover, small detected vessels are removed considering that belong to detections of different structures than vessels as noisy artifacts in the image. This way, this process offers the detection of the (x, y) coordinates for the entire vessel tree. Examples of this process can be seen in Fig. 2 where the original image, 2D vessel tree extraction and skeletonization are included in Figs. 2(a), (b) and (c), respectively.

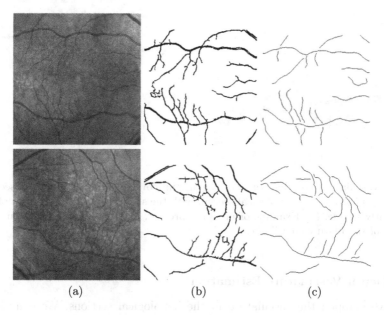

(a)   (b)   (c)

Fig. 2. 2D vessel tree extraction and skeletonization. (a) Input retinography. (b) 2D Vessel tree extraction. (c) Skeletonized vessel tree.

2.2   Vessel Coordinates Mapping in the Histological Sections

Once the (x, y) coordinates of the vasculature is detected, we need to calculate the corresponding depth, or z, at all these detected points. The depth can be obtained with the OCT scans, as the histological sections provide the depth information over the entire eye fundus analyzed region. In the histological sections, the vessels are visualized as structures that blocks the transmission of light, leaving a shadow and revealing, therefore, its location. This can be seen in Fig. 3(a), where a histological section with the presence of several vessels is presented. As we know, each histological section corresponds to a band in the 2D retinography. We can identify in the intersection of the band and the 2D vessel tree the vessel positions that appear in this particular band visualized in the histological section.

Therefore, we analyze all the bands that correspond with the histological sections and identify all the vessel points that intersect with the band. This way we can map all the 2D coordinates of the vasculature that are present in the histological sections, identifying their projection zones, that is, the region that corresponds with each vessel shadow. This process is illustrated in Fig. 3(b), where this mapping process can be clearly seen. In these projection zones, we can posteriorly identify the depth at which each vasculature points is located.

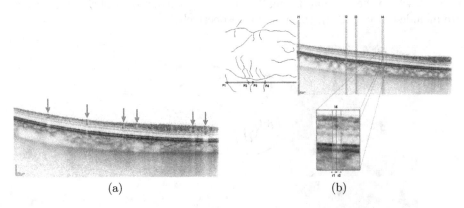

(a)   (b)

Fig. 3. Vasculature coordinates mapping in the corresponding histological sections process. (a) Example of histological section with the shadow projection of a set of vessels clearly visible. (b) Example of mapping process, identifying the projection zones of a set of vasculature coordinates.

2.3   Depth Vasculature Estimation

Once we mapped the vasculature in the histological sections, We can obtain the corresponding depth coordinates z for each vasculature position. Hence, we can search in the mapped region a dark structure that produce a shadow, as commented before. This process is performed in two consecutive steps.

ILM and RPE Layers Identification. In the histological sections, the vessels can only appear between the retinal layers Inner Limitant Membrane (ILM), the first intraretinal layer, and the Retinal Pigment Epithelium (RPE), formed by pigmented cells at the external part of the retina. Taking advantage of this, we can reduce the search space to the region between those layers, minimizing the risk of possible miscalculations.

We employed the Canny edge detector to find where these layers are placed considering that both ILM and RPE layers contain the edges with the highest contrast of intensities among all the layers. Firstly, we apply the gradient to the image in the horizontal direction to gain information, producing strongest detections and guaranteeing that both layers are correctly obtained. In this resultant image, the upper and lower connected lines of these edges identify the limits of the ILM and RPE layers, respectively. An example of this process is shown in Fig. 4(a).

Vessel Point Depth Detection. In this reduced search space, each vessel coordinates can be clearly searched, appearing as a small dark elliptic region, due to its particular reflectance properties compared to retinal layers. Firstly, a mean filter with a window of 3×3 is applied to smooth the ROI and avoid noisy detections. Then, the darkest spot inside the region of interest is identified as the vessel location. This is illustrated in Fig. 4(b). Finally the depth value is derived by taking RPE layer lower limit as baseline and computing the height of the vessel center related to the baseline:

$$z = |C_v - P_i| \tag{6}$$

where z is the distance that measure the depth value, C_v indicates the y coordinate of the center of the detected vessel in the histological image, and P_i indicates the y coordinate of the lower limit of the RPE layer.

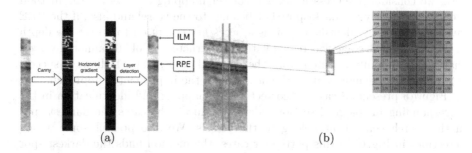

(a) (b)

Fig. 4. Vessel depth identification process. (a) Detection of ILM and RPE layers. (b) Detection of the vessel in the search region.

3   Results

The implemented methodology was tested with a dataset of 196 OCT histological images that were taken with a confocal scanning laser ophtalmoscope, a CIRRUS^{TM}HD-OCT–Carl Zeiss Meditec. This OCT images also provided the corresponding near infrared reflectance retinographies. All the scans are centered in the macula and were obtained from both left and right eyes. The images have a resolution of 1520 × 496 pixels. For all the tests, the groundtruths were constructed in the collaboration with an expert of the field.

Vessel Coordinates Mapping in the Histological Sections. After the 2D vessel tree detection, we tested the accuracy of the vasculature mapping in the corresponding histological sections. From the entire dataset, we randomly selected a set of vessel points, calculate their corresponding mappings and measure if this process was correctly performed. In particular a set of 607 points were analyzed obtaining a success rate of 86,49 %, as shown in Table 1.

Table 1. Results obtained at the different stages of the methodology.

	Vessel mapping in OCT	Depth calculation
Correctly processed	525	641
Test set size	607	704
Success rate	86,49 %	91,05 %

Depth Vasculature Estimation. We also tested the method to identify the location of the vessel inside the histological sections and the adequate estimation of the depth position with respect to the RPE layer lower limit. In this particular case, we consider a success if, after a correct mapping of a vessel, the method identifies correctly the dark spot that belongs to the vessel and also, if the RPE layer was correctly identified, as it is a necessary condition to derive the depth of the vessel. This stage was tested with a constructed set of 704 annotated vessels that were randomly selected from the entire dataset. Table 1 shows a success rate of 91,95 %, demonstrating the accuracy of the implemented approach.

Figure 5 presents 8 cases of correct vessel mapping and identification in the corresponding histological sections, detecting in all the cases the darkest spot in the search space that belong to the vessels. We also present some wrong detections in Fig. 6. In this particular cases, the method finds the darkest spot between the ILM and RPE layers but belong to noisy artifacts or overlapped vessels instead of the desired one. Normally incorrect detections are mainly due to: (1) noisy artifacts or vessels that are too close and appear in the same region of the histological section as the objective vessel position; (2) alterations of a particular layer that can produce dark regions that can be confused with a vessel; (3) impossibility of detecting the dark spot of a vessel, as sometimes vessels can be parallel to the histological section, without producing the typical dark spot of a vessel intersection.

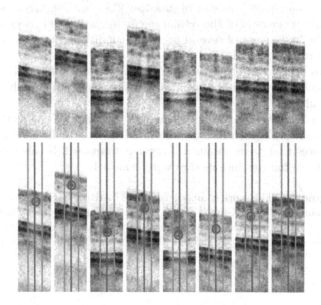

Fig. 5. Examples of correct vessel depth identifications. 1st row, vessels to locate. 2nd row, obtained detections.

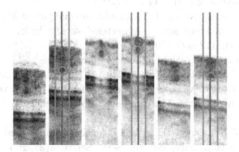

Fig. 6. Examples of wrong vessel depth identifications. 1st row, vessels to locate. 2nd row, results: red circle, the obtained vessel location: green circle, real vessel location. (Color figure online)

4   Conclusions

This paper presented a new methodology for arterio-venular tree extraction and depth estimation using OCT images. The method provides the combination of the 2D vasculature structure extraction, done in the infrared reflectance retinographies, with their corresponding depth estimation over the positions of the entire vessel tree, thanks to the depth information that the histological sections provide. This way, we finally obtain the entire set of (x, y, z) coordinates over the entire arterio-venous tree. Thanks to that, doctors are provided with a more complete information set, instead of classical 2D vessel segmentations, to be able to do further analysis of the retinal microcirculation that constitute a key analysis for the assessment of several prevalent conditions such as hypertension, diabetes or cardiovascular risk.

Key stages of the approach were tested with a set of 196 OCT histological sections and the corresponding near infrared reflectance retinographies, showing promising results.

In future works, we plan to improve each of the stages of the method, trying to overcome some of the identified drawbacks of the issue and, therefore, increase the success rates that were obtained. Larger datasets will be also analyzed, in order to reinforce the conclusions that were achieved.

Acknowledgments. This work is supported by the Instituto de Salud Carlos III, Government of Spain and FEDER funds of the European Union through the PI14/02161 and the DTS15/00153 research projects and by the Ministerio de Economía y Competitividad, Government of Spain through the DPI2015-69948-R research project.

References

1. Nguyen, T.T., Wang, J.J., Sharrett, A.R., et al.: Relationship of retinal vascular caliber with diabetes and retinopathy: the multi-ethnic study of atherosclerosis (MESA). Diab. Care J. **31**(3), 544–549 (2007)
2. Smith, W., Wang, J.J., Wong, T.Y., et al.: Retinal arteriolar narrowing is associated with 5-year incident severe hypertension: the blue mountains eye study. Hypertens. J. **44**(4), 442–447 (2004)
3. Wong, T.Y.: Quantitative retinal venular caliber and risk of cardiovascular disease in older persons. Arch. Intern. Med. J. **166**(21), 2388–2394 (2006)
4. Zhang, Y., Hsu, W., Lee, M.L.: Segmentation of retinal blood vessels by combining the detection of centerlines and morphological reconstruction. J. Sig. Process. Syst. **55**(1), 103–112 (2008)
5. Yong, Y., Yuan, Z., Shuying, H., et al.: Effective combined algorithms for retinal blood vessels extraction. Adv. Inf. Sci. Serv. Sci. J. **4**(3), 263–269 (2012)
6. Wink, O., Niessen, W.J., Viergever, M.A.: Adaptive local thresholding by verification-based multithreshold probing with application to vessel detection in retinal images. IEEE Trans. Med. Imaging **23**(1), 130–133 (2004)
7. Dhar, R., Gupta, R., Baishnab, K.L.: An analysis of Canny, Laplacian of gaussian image filters in regard to evaluating retinal image. Int. Conf. Green Comput. Commun. Electr. Eng. **31**(8), 1–6 (2014)
8. Mendonça, A.M., Campilho, A.: Segmentation of retinal blood vessels by combining the detection of centerlines and morphological reconstruction. IEEE Trans. Med. Imaging **25**(9), 1200–1213 (2006)
9. Fathi, A., Naghsh, N., Reza, A.: Blood vessels segmentation in retina: preliminary assessment of the mathematical morphology and of the wavelet transform techniques. Biomed. Sig. Process. Control J. **8**(1), 71–80 (2013)
10. Wu, J., Gerendas, B., Waldstein, S., et al. Stable registration of pathological 3D-OCT scans using retinal vessels. In: Proceedings of Ophtalmic Medical Image Analysis (2014)

11. Niemeijer, M., Garvin, M.K., van Ginneken, B., Sonka, M., Abrámoff, M.D.: Vessel segmentation in 3D spectral OCT scans of the retina. In: SPIE Proceedings (2008)
12. Xu, J., Tolliver, D.A., Ishikawa, H., Wollstein, G., Schuman, J.S.: 3D OCT retinal vessel segmentation based on boosting learning. Med. Image Anal. **25**(11), 179–182 (2009)
13. Calvo, D., Ortega, M., Penedo, M.G., Rouco, J.: Automatic detection and characterisation of retinal vessel tree bifurcations and crossovers in eye fundus images. Comput. Methods Programs Biomed. **103**, 28–38 (2011)
14. Frangi, A.F., Niessen, W.J., Vincken, K.L., Viergever, M.A.: Improvement of retinal blood vessel detection using morphological component analysis. In: Proceedings of MICCAI, pp. 130–137 (1998)
15. López, A., Lloret, D., Serrat, J., Villanueva, J.J.: Multilocal creaseness based on the level set extrinsic curvature. Comput. Vis. Image Underst. **77**, 111–144 (2000)

Classification

How to Correctly Evaluate an Automatic Bioacoustics Classification Method

Juan Gabriel Colonna[1]([⊠]), João Gama[2], and Eduardo F. Nakamura[1]

[1] Institute of Computing (Icomp), Federal University of Amazonas (UFAM),
Avenida General Rodrigo Octávio 6200, Manaus, Amazonas 69077-000, Brazil
{juancolonna,nakamura}@icomp.ufam.edu.br
[2] Laboratory of Artificial Intelligence and Decision Support (LIAAD),
INESC Tec, Campus da FEUP, Rua Dr. Roberto Frias, 4200-465 Porto, Portugal
jgama@fep.up.pt

Abstract. In this work, we introduce a more appropriate (or alternative) approach to evaluate the performance and the generalization capabilities of a framework for automatic anuran call recognition. We show that, by using the common k-folds Cross-Validation (k-CV) procedure to evaluate the expected error in a syllable-based recognition system the recognition accuracy is overestimated. To overcome this problem, and to provide a fair evaluation, we propose a new CV procedure in which the specimen information is considered during the split step of the k-CV. Therefore, we performed a k-CV by specimens (or individuals) showing that the accuracy of the system decrease considerably. By introducing the specimen information, we are able to answer a more fundamental question: Given a set of syllables that belongs to a specific group of individuals, can we recognize new specimens of the same species? In this article, we go deeper into the reviews and the experimental evaluations to answer this question.

Keywords: Automatic anuran call recognition · Cross-validation · Bioacoustics · One-against-all · One-against-one

1 Introduction

Nowadays Wireless Acoustic Sensor Networks (WASNs) are used in several environmental applications including bioacoustic monitoring programs [1]. These networks are composed by small sensor nodes that can: collect, process and transmit the audio data and correlated environment variables. In this context, the problem of automatic bioacoustic monitoring can be addressed by embedding a Machine Learning (ML) classification technique into the sensor nodes [2,3]. Thus, by combining ML and WASNs, we can identify different animal calls without human intervention. However, the low cost of the sensor nodes imposes restrictions on the hardware and software, and consequently, affects the classification techniques.

Among all the species commonly used in bioacoustic monitoring programs anuran (frogs and toads) are natural indicators of the environmental health [4].

© Springer International Publishing Switzerland 2016
O. Luaces et al. (Eds.): CAEPIA 2016, LNAI 9868, pp. 37–47, 2016.
DOI: 10.1007/978-3-319-44636-3_4

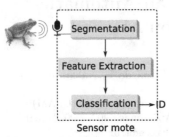

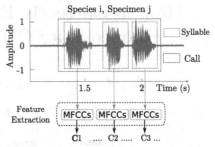

(a) Automatic Call Recognition System (ACR).

(b) An audio record of the species **Adenomera hylaedactyla**.

Fig. 1. A framework for automatic frog's calls recognition.

Thus, tracking the variations of frog populations can help to identify ecological problems in early stages [5]. Moreover, with WASNs, we can develop an autonomous system to support researchers in long-term ecological studies.

The general framework for recognizing frog species, based on their calls, is shown in Fig. 1(a). This system consists of three main blocks. The first block performs an acoustics signal segmentation that recognize the start and end time where a minor vocalization unit occur, named **syllable** (see Fig. 1(b)) [6,7]. The second block maps each syllable into a set of Low Level acoustic Descriptors (LLDs or feature vector). The last block, is a ML algorithm that makes a pattern matching between the unknown input feature vector and a feature set representing all the species included into the dataset (see Table 3).

In the related literature, presented in Sect. 3, we found works concerned with the segmentation and pre-processing steps [7], also works mainly concerned with feature analysis and selection [6,8–10] and, finally, works comparing different ML algorithms for classification [11,12]. These are examples on how this framework can be flexible. However, most of these systems are based on syllable recognition approaches that use Cross-Validation (k-CV) to evaluate the classification performance and the generalization capabilities of the system. In these cases, the k-CV procedure splits the dataset in two subsets: one for training and another for testing, ignoring if all the samples chosen (or syllables in this case) belong to the same individual (or specimen). This becomes a problem when syllables of one particular specimen are at the same time in these two subsets. When it happens, we noticed that the accuracy of the classifier increases being over estimated. Our new evaluation and validation proposal incorporates the specimen information as additional label and considers this new information during the k-CV split procedure to avoid mixing syllables from the same individual in the training and testing sets at the same time.

To the best of our knowledge, this is the first work proposing a CV strategy dividing the testing and training sets by specimens. We believe that specimen-based cross validation is the best way to test the generalization capabilities of recognition models, without falling in a bias problem and overestimate the final accuracy.

2   Fundamentals

Bioacoustics classification systems are traditionally composed of three main steps with different purposes (see Fig. 1(a)). Formally, the input bioacoustic signal $X = \{x_1, x_2, \cdots, x_N\}$ is a time series of length N, in which its values represent the acoustics pressure levels (or amplitude). A syllable $\mathbf{x}_k = \{x_t, x_{t+1}, \cdots, x_{t+n}\}$ is a subset of n consecutively signal values. Thus, the pre-processing step segments the signal X by identifying the beginning and the endpoints of $\mathbf{x}_k$.

After the syllable extraction we need to represent each $\mathbf{x}_k$ by a set features, commonly called Low Level Descriptors (LLDs). The most frequent LLDs are the Mel-Frequency Spectral Coefficients (MFCCs). The MFCCs perform a spectral analysis based on a triangular filter-bank logarithmically spaced in the frequency domain [2,3,12]. The feature extraction using the MFCCs allows to represent any syllable by a set of coefficients (MFCC($\mathbf{x}_k$) → $\mathbf{c}_k$), i.e.: $X \rightarrow \{(\mathbf{c}_1, y_i), (\mathbf{c}_2, y_i), \ldots, (\mathbf{c}_k, y_i)\}$, where each $\mathbf{c}_k = [c_1, c_2, \ldots, c_l]$ is a feature vector with l coefficients (Fig. 1(b)), and y_i is the species name (or label). The representation of $\mathbf{x}_k$ through $\mathbf{c}_k$ is more robust, compact, and simpler for recognizing, compared to raw data.

Finally, the challenge is how to assign the species name to a new syllable by using the MFCC values. This is a supervised classification task and is performed by the last step of the system. For this purpose several ML algorithms could be applied to create and train a model $f(\cdot)$ with capabilities to predict new incoming samples, i.e., given an unknown $\mathbf{c}$ estimates the most probable label by evaluating $f(\mathbf{c}) \rightarrow y_i$, where $S = \{s_1, s_2, \ldots, s_i\}$ is the set of species names. To test how well the model performs and, estimate the expected error, a common choice is the use of stratified k-CV. However, there is a main problem related to the classical k-CV in this type of application (see Sect. 4). This is the main concern of this work and, therefore, we propose a different Cross-Validation procedure, especially adapted for this task. We present our proposal in the Sect. 5.

3   Related Work

Amphibians are directly affected by environmental changes [4,5]. This observation has motivated many researchers to develop Automatic Calls Recognition (ACR) systems to monitor anuran populations. Thus, the general idea consists of treating the problem of species recognition as an audio classification task. In this context, there are three possible approaches: (1) classify the entire audio recorded without segmentation; (2) use a fixed size segmentation by frames; or (3) classify by syllables [6,7,12,13]. However, the last approach is widely adopted among related works, because signal segments between syllables do not carry useful information about the acoustic frequencies of the species. Therefore, the syllable-based approach achieves better results.

Several comparative studies about ACR can be found in the literature. Table 1 summarizes the related works. Note that commonly these methods achieves high accuracy rates, even with very different features and ML methods.

Table 1. Summary of few related works. The # stands for the number of different frog species, **ML** for Machine Learning Algorithm, **Acc** for the accuracy, and GMM for Gaussian Mixture Models.

Author	#	ML	Acc	Author	#	ML	Acc
Colonna et al. [12]	9	kNN, SVM	97 %	Dayou et al. [14]	9	kNN	90 %
Huang et al. [6]	5	kNN, SVM	100 %	Han et al. [8]	9	kNN	100 %
Jaafar et al. [15]	28	kNN, SVM	98 %	Vaca-Castaño et al. [16]	20	kNN	91 %
Xie et al. [17]	4	GMM	90 %*	Yuan et al. [18]	8	kNN	98 %

* identify the F-score measure.

In this paper, we investigate why this happens. One insight about this is the way in which k-CV is applied to this task. However, in the majority of the related works the description of the CV procedure adopted is not always explicit, this fact makes the reproduction of the results, and the critical analysis, difficult.

Briggs et al. [19] had used 5-CV to evaluate their method although they express concern about this, pointing that it may be a problem: *"(. . .) We expect that prediction accuracy would decrease in an experiment where the classifier is applied to individuals that do not appear in the training set (. . .)"*. Other example can be found in Dong et al. [20]: *"(. . .) The selection of recordings was made so as to ensure that no two queries within one call class came from the same site on the same day. This was to minimize the probability that calls of the same individual appeared in more than one recording (. . .)"*. Therefore, the community is concerned about the problem caused when syllables of the same specimen are present in the testing and training sets at the same time. However, there is no consensus on how to evaluate the gains over the recognition rate and which is better suited to this context.

4   Problem Description

This section describes the major problem related with the performance validation of the bioacoustic classification approaches used to recognize anuran calls. We called this "the generalization problem", exemplifying the problem as follow. The Fig. 1(b) represents an audio signal (or a call) with three syllables of one specimen from the species Adenomera hylaedactyla. Visually these syllables appear slightly different, but in the frequency domain their differences are not very noticeable. Table 2 shows 10-MFCC values extracted from these three syllables. The last row summarize the mean and the standard deviation (Std) of each column. The low Std indicates that these syllables are very similar. For instance, assuming that we choose a kNN classifier with the Euclidean distance separating the first syllable for testing and the two remaining syllables for training. After running the classifier the dissimilarity score is 0.0545 between the first and second syllables, and 0.0546 between the first and third syllables. This situation is likely to result in a high recognition rate. Technically, this situation may not be considered as overfitting, but as bias. This illustrative example helps understand why some related works achieve almost 100 % of accuracy.

Table 2. MFCCs example.

	MFCCs									
syllable$_1$	0.00	0.14	0.42	0.69	0.81	0.90	0.93	0.97	1.00	0.91
syllable$_2$	0.00	0.13	0.42	0.72	0.84	0.93	0.94	0.96	1.00	0.92
syllable$_3$	0.00	0.14	0.44	0.72	0.83	0.91	0.92	0.95	1.00	0.92
Mean	0.00	0.14	0.42	0.71	0.83	0.91	0.93	0.96	1.00	0.92
±Std	±0.000	±0.005	±0.010	±0.018	±0.017	±0.014	±0.012	±0.008	±0.000	±0.003

Learning the parameters of the classification function and testing it on syllables arising from the same specimen is a methodological misconception. The model would have a perfect score repeating the labels of the samples, but could fail to predict syllables from new specimens. To avoid it, and to increase the generalization capabilities of the system, a common practice when performing a ML experiment is to adopt Cross-Validation. Thus, part of the available examples are separated for testing and other part for training, but in this context, we must avoid generating a random split containing syllables of the same specimen into two subsets. So the classical k-CV procedure is not suitable to this application context. Now we can define our research question as: Given a classification's model $f(\cdot)$, trained on a subset of j specimens from the ith species, is possible to recognize a new specimen of the same species? Thereby, we want to know how well the trained model generalizes the concept learned for unknown specimens.

5   Proposed Methodology

Cross-Validation (CV) is used to estimate the expected error in a real situation. With k-CV the original dataset is split into k disjoint folds, and for each one the conditional error (e_k) is estimated training the model $f(\cdot)$ with k-1 folds. Thus, this procedure is repeated k times and the expected generalized error can be obtained as the mean of e_k. As mentioned earlier, we might hope that k-CV estimates the real error, but when the information of the specimen is omitted we fall in a situation in which the split could leave syllables from one specimen in the testing and training sets.

To address this problem, we propose to consider the specimen information during the k-CV splitting, leaving all the syllables that belongs to the same specimen (or individual) together, avoiding mixing them in the testing and training sets. Then, we propose a Leave-one-Out CV (LOOCV) by individuals (or records) for measuring the performance of the classification algorithms, i.e., being k equal to number of different specimens. Because we are dealing with a supervised problem, and we want to consider this new information during the LOOCV evaluation, now each syllable must be associated with two labels: one for the specimen (s_j) and one for the species (y_i), e.g., $\mathbf{c}_k = [c_1, c_2, \ldots, c_l, s_j, y_i]$. Therefore, the individuals are separated into two groups, one for testing and the others for training. These steps are repeated until every individual (or record) has been used as test set. In each k step, the predictions for every syllable are saved.

This way of splitting shows two main particularities. First, at least two specimens of each species are needed. Second, the number of examples in each fold could be not balanced. On the other hand, we assume that the generalization error will be more realistic, because we are training with one specimen to predict a different one. However, apply this procedure to solve a multiclass problem could be more complex when increasing the number of specimens, but these can be simplified by creating and combining a pool of binary problems. For this purpose there are two well know strategies: One-against-All (1AA) and One-against-One (1A1 or Round Robin) [21]. These approaches are also useful to adapt a binary classifier to a multiclass task.

The 1AA procedure begins by separating all the syllables of the first specimen in testing set and grouping the remaining syllables of the same species in training set for the target class ("+1"). The syllables of all remaining species, that not belongs to the target species, are grouped in the negative class ("−1"). Then, the model $f(\cdot)$ is trained and applied to estimate the labels of the testing group. In the second round, this procedure is repeated but separating all the syllables of the second specimen for testing. The validation is repeated until all specimens in the dataset are evaluated. It is analogous to perform a Leave-one-Out CV using specimens instead off syllables. With the 1AA and the classical k-CV setting the number of rounds are equal to $r = i \times k$, but after incorporating the specimen information the amount of rounds become $r = i \times j$. However, with this decomposition the complexity of trained model $f(\cdot)$ is smaller than in the multiclass configuration.

The second procedure we propose, called 1A1, breaks the original problem in smaller problems than 1AA. The label estimation proceeds similar to the Leave-one-Out by specimen, but with the main difference that the negative class is breaking down into several small groups, considering one group for each species. After that, the result of each sub-problem is combined by using the majority voting rule. Typically, with 1A1 and k-CV the number of rounds increases with the rule $\frac{i \cdot (i-1)}{2} \times k$, but, in our case, this rule becomes $\frac{i \cdot (i-1)}{2} \times j$. This decomposition reduces the complexity of each sub-problems, compared to the multiclass approach.

6   Experiment Setting and Results

The dataset used in our experiments is summarized in Table 3. It has 10 different species, 55 specimens and 5799 syllables. These samples were collected *in situ* under real noise conditions. Some species are from the Federal University of Amazonas, Brazil*, other from Mata Atlântica, Brazil**, and the last from Córdoba, Argentina[+]. These recordings were stored in *wav* format with 44.1 kHz of sampling frequency and 32 bit, which allows us to analyze signals up to 22.05 kHz. From each extracted syllable, 24 MFCCs were calculated by using 44 triangular filters. For the segmentation task we based our approach on the work of Colonna *et al.* [7], but using only the energy of the signal. The segmentation code is available at http://goo.gl/kaWCrc. Finally, the frame size was 0.0464 s with 66 % of overlap to obtain a good energy-time resolution.

Table 3. Species dataset. The *s* and the *k* stands for the amount of specimens and syllables respectively.

Species	it s	k	Species	s	k
Adenomera hylaedactyla**	11	3039	Adenomera andreae*	8	471
Leptodactylus fuscus*	4	222	Ameerega trivittata**	5	493
Hyla minuta**	11	227	Hypsiboas cinerascens*	2	361
Hypsiboas cordobae+	4	703	Osteocephalus oophagus*	3	96
Scinax ruber**	4	77	Rhinella granulosa*	3	110

Table 4. Comparison result using 1AA decomposition.

Species	kNN k = 1	kNN k = 3	kNN k = 5	Tree	QDA	SVM RBF	SVM p = 1	SVM p = 2	SVM p = 3
Adenomera andreae	33.46	32.66	34.67	30.64	86.69	72.58	59.27	74.79	72.98
Ameerega trivittata	89.88	89.33	88.23	42.83	88.60	67.46	57.90	64.52	70.77
Adenomera hylaedactyla	98.68	99.37	99.50	94.29	98.29	99.77	99.77	99.73	99.60
Hyla minuta	61.57	53.71	53.27	34.49	52.40	55.02	25.32	55.02	65.06
Hypsiboas cinerascens	96.39	98.06	96.95	71.74	90.02	93.35	90.02	96.67	97.50
Hypsiboas cordobae	100.00	100.00	100.00	98.29	95.86	98.29	96.43	97.86	98.57
Leptodactylus fuscus	63.96	59.90	49.09	9.00	0.45	9.45	0.45	70.27	57.20
Osteocephalus oophagus	42.70	34.37	32.29	17.70	11.45	0.00	0.00	0.00	9.37
Rhinella granulosa	39.84	32.81	30.46	9.37	0.78	28.12	12.50	37.50	45.31
Scinax ruber	0.00	0.00	0.00	3.94	0.00	0.00	0.00	3.94	1.31
Micro-accuracy	86.21	85.80	85.36	73.52	85.38	84.34	80.09	86.93	**87.61**
Average-accuracy	**62.65**	**60.02**	**58.45**	41.23	**52.45**	**52.40**	44.16	**60.03**	**61.77**
Precision	0.62	0.60	0.59	0.53	0.65	0.66	0.63	0.72	0.70
Recall	0.63	0.60	0.58	0.41	0.52	0.52	0.44	0.60	0.62

We compared the results showed in the Tables 4 and 5 by using four classifiers: kNN; Quadratic Discriminant Analysis (QDA); Decision Tree; and Support Vector Machine (SVM) using RBF and polynomial kernels with degrees $p = \{1, 2, 3\}$. For each configuration we calculated the micro-accuracy and average accuracy per species. The baselines results for comparison are: 52.40 % in the case of micro-accuracy and 10 % in the case of average-accuracy, i.e. the baseline value for a classifier, which always chooses the most numerous species is the micro and for a classifier, which randomly chooses one species is the average. In the Average-accuracy rows we applied the t-Test to compare the means obtained against the best value in the row. Therefore, the boldface values could be considered a tie with confidence level $p = 0.05$. In the last row of each table, we have the standard deviation values of each column.

Table 5. Comparison result using 1A1 decomposition.

Species	kNN k = 1	kNN k = 3	kNN k = 5	Tree	QDA	SVM RBF	SVM p = 1	SVM p = 2	SVM p = 3
Adenomera andreae	33.46	32.05	31.45	26.00	26.61	31.85	28.42	28.62	30.24
Ameerega trivittata	89.88	89.70	88.97	70.40	99.26	92.83	91.36	78.86	63.78
Adenomera hylaedactyla	98.68	99.37	99.50	98.19	98.49	99.86	99.96	99.77	99.34
Hyla minuta	61.57	53.71	53.27	58.07	84.27	61.57	62.44	66.81	68.99
Hypsiboas cinerascens	96.39	98.06	97.22	88.36	88.64	97.22	96.95	96.12	94.18
Hypsiboas cordobae	100.00	100.00	100.00	95.58	95.72	99.85	99.00	99.71	100.00
Leptodactylus fuscus	63.96	59.90	50.90	45.49	1.351	59.00	36.93	67.56	62.16
Osteocephalus oophagus	42.70	36.45	34.37	20.83	15.62	6.25	1.04	14.58	36.45
Rhinella granulosa	39.84	33.59	33.59	17.96	1.56	31.25	28.12	32.81	46.87
Scinax ruber	0.00	0.00	0.00	0.00	0.00	9.21	18.42	23.68	32.89
Micro-accuracy	**86.21**	85.83	85.34	80.85	82.66	86.14	84.82	85.32	84.43
Average-accuracy	**62.65**	**60.28**	**58.93**	52.09	**51.15**	**58.89**	**56.26**	**60.85**	**63.49**
Precision	0.62	0.61	0.60	0.57	0.53	0.67	0.63	0.68	0.70
Recall	0.63	0.60	0.59	0.52	0.51	0.59	0.56	0.60	0.63

Table 6. Gains of 1A1 over 1AA.

	kNN k = 1	kNN k = 3	kNN k = 5	Tree	QDA	SVM RBF	SVM p = 1	SVM p = 2	SVM p = 3
Gains	0.00	**+0.26**	**+0.48**	**+10.86**	−1.30	**+6.49**	**+12.10**	**+0.82**	**+1.72**

Among these results, we note that Scinax ruber was the most difficult species. However, Adenomera hylaedactyla and Hypsiboas cordobae appear to be easier to classify. The configuration using polynomial SVM with $p = 3$ and 1A1 is the better option. In general, comparing the standard deviation of the methods we can conclude that 1A1 decrease the variance showing a more uniform accuracy among all the species tested. In the last table of results 6 we compare the average-accuracy gains of 1A1 against 1AA. This values are presented in percentage. The gains obtained by the Tree classifier and by the linear SVM show that these methods take advantages from the 1A1 decomposition.

For comparison purpose we have tested two additional configuration applying the traditional k-CV with ten folds and LOOCV by syllables, i.e., without taking care about individuals information, with kNN ($k = 3$ and $k = 1$). In the first case, the Micro- and Average-accuracy were 99.45 % and 99.14 %, and in the second case, were 99.66 % and 99.53 % respectively. These results are equivalent to the approaches described by several authors [6,8,12,14–16,18], but using our own dataset. Comparing these against the results obtained using our k-CV by individuals, showed in last lines of the Tables 4 and 5, we realize that when the specimen information is not considered, the accuracy is overestimated due the problem described in Sect. 4.

7 Discussion and Conclusion

In this work we introduced a different k-CV procedure to evaluate a bioacoustic recognition framework. The main contribution is the incorporation of the specimens information (or individuals) as an additional label and consider it when performs the k-CV. This extra label helps to split the dataset without mixing up syllables from the same specimen into the testing and training groups avoiding an overestimate of the accuracy. Thus, the results are more representative of a real situation, in which different specimens would be found in the rainforest. In addition, we showed a problem simplification using 1A1 and 1AA approaches.

Comparing the related works against our results we notice a considerably difference from similar configurations, showing that not separate the testing by specimens causes a high bias of the accuracy, and consequently, the model has less generalization capabilities. Moreover, the difference between the avearge- and micro-accuracy exposes the problem of working with unbalanced datasets as commonly happens in these type works. Inspecting several confusion matrix of our experiments we also note that the information about others individuals was not enough to recognize new ones in some cases, as the Scinax ruber. This may be caused by: (1) the features were insufficient to extract the shared information between specimens of the same species; or (2) the discriminatory power of the MFCCs was very detailed capturing fine-grained differences of the frequencies. Anyway, others LLDs should be investigated and evaluated with our methodology. Finally, we recommend to the authors of future works give more details about the adopted evaluation procedures and the generalization capabilities of the proposed approaches.

Acknowledgements. This work was partly supported by the European Commission through MAESTRA (ICT-2013-612944) and the Project TEC4Growth - Pervasive Intelligence, Enhancers and Proofs of Concept with Industrial Impact/NORTE-01-0145-FEDER-000020 is financed by the North Portugal Regional Operational Program (NORTE 2020), under the PORTUGAL 2020 Partnership Agreement, and through the European Regional Development Fund (ERDF). Juan G. Colonna gratefully acknowledge to National Council of Technological and Scientific Development (CNPq, Brazil) by the PhD fellowship. Eduardo F. Nakamura acknowledge to FAPEAM by the support granted through the Anura Project (FAPEAM/CNPq PRONEX 023/2009).

References

1. Bertrand, A.: Applications and trends in wireless acoustic sensor networks: a signal processing perspective. In: 2011 18th IEEE Symposium on Communications and Vehicular Technology in the Benelux (SCVT), pp. 1–6, November 2011
2. Ribas, A.D., Colonna, J.G., Figueiredo, C.M.S., Nakamura, E.F.: Similarity clustering for data fusion in wireless sensor networks using k-means. In: IEEE International Joint Conference on Neural Networks (IJCNN), pp. 1–7, June 2012

3. Colonna, J.G., Cristo, M.A.P., Nakamura, E.F.: A distribute approach for classifying anuran species based on their calls. In: 22nd International Conference on Pattern Recognition (2014)
4. Cole, E.M., Bustamante, M.R., Reinoso, D.A., Funk, W.C.: Spatial and temporal variation in population dynamics of andean frogs: effects of forest disturbance and evidence for declines. Glob. Ecol. Conserv. 1, 60–70 (2014)
5. Carey, C., Alexander, M.A.: Climate change and amphibian declines: is there a link? Divers. Distrib. 9(2), 111–121 (2003)
6. Huang, C.J., Yang, Y.J., Yang, D.X., Chen, Y.J.: Frog classification using machine learning techniques. Expert Syst. Appl. 36(2), 3737–3743 (2009)
7. Colonna, J.G., Cristo, M.A.P., Salvatierra, M., Nakamura, E.F.: An incremental technique for real-time bioacoustic signal segmentation. Expert Syst. Appl. 42(21), 7367–7374 (2015)
8. Han, N.C., Muniandy, S.V., Dayou, J.: Acoustic classification of Australian anurans based on hybrid spectral-entropy approach. Appl. Acoust. 72(9), 639–645 (2011)
9. Jaafar, H., Ramli, D., Shahrudin, S.: MFCC based frog identification system in noisy environment. In: IEEE International Conference on Signal and Image Processing Applications (ICSIPA), pp. 123–127, October 2013
10. Xie, J., Zhang, J., Roe, P.: Acoustic features for hierarchical classification of Australian frog calls. In: In 10th International Conference on Information, Communications and Signal Processing (2015)
11. Yen, G., Fu, Q.: Automatic frog call monitoring system: a machine learning approach. In: Proceedings of SPIE, vol. 4739, pp. 188–199. SPIE (2002)
12. Colonna, J.G., Ribas, A.D., dos Santos, E.M., N., E.F.: Feature subset selection for automatically classifying anuran calls using sensor networks. In: IEEE International Joint Conference on Neural Networks (IJCNN), pp. 1–8, June 2012
13. Xie, J., Towsey, M., Truskinger, A., Eichinski, P., Zhang, J., Roe, P.: Acoustic classification of Australian anurans using syllable features. In: IEEE Tenth International Conference on Intelligent Sensors, Sensor Networks and Information Processing (ISSNIP 2015). IEEE (2015)
14. Dayou, J., Han, N.C., Mun, H.C., Ahmad, A.H., Muniandy, S.V., Dalimin, M.N.: Classification and identification of frog sound based on entropy approach. In: International Conference on Life Science and Technology, vol. 3, pp. 184–187 (2011)
15. Jaafar, H., Ramli, D.A., Rosdi, B.A.: Comparative study on different classifiers for frog identification system based on bioacoustic signal analysis. In: Proceedings of the 2014 International Conference on Communications, Signal Processing and Computers (2014)
16. Vaca-Castaño, G., Rodriguez, D.: Using syllabic mel cepstrum features and k-nearest neighbors to identify anurans and birds species. In: 2010 IEEE Workshop on Signal Processing Systems (SIPS), pp. 466–471 (2010)
17. Xie, J., Towsey, M., Yasumiba, K., Zhang, J., Roe, P.: Detection of anuran calling activity in long field recordings for bio-acoustic monitoring. In: IEEE Tenth International Conference on Intelligent Sensors, Sensor Networks and Information Processing (ISSNIP 2015). IEEE (2015)
18. Ting Yuan, C.L., Athiar Ramli, D.: Frog sound identification system for frog species recognition. In: Vinh, P.C., Hung, N.M., Tung, N.T., Suzuki, J. (eds.) ICCASA 2012. LNICST, vol. 109, pp. 41–50. Springer, Heidelberg (2013)
19. Briggs, F., Lakshminarayanan, B., Neal, L., Fern, X.Z., Raich, R., Hadley, S.J.K., Hadley, A.S., Betts, M.G.: Acoustic classification of multiple simultaneous bird species: a multi-instance multi-label approach. J. Acoust. Soc. Am. 131(6), 4640–4650 (2012)

20. Dong, X., Towsey, M., Truskinger, A., Cottman-Fields, M., Zhang, J., Roe, P.: Similarity-based birdcall retrieval from environmental audio. Ecol. Inform. **29**(Part 1), 66–76 (2015)
21. Fürnkranz, J.: Round robin rule learning. In: Proceedings of the Eighteenth International Conference on Machine Learning, ICML 2001, pp. 146–153 (2001)

Shot Classification and Keyframe Detection for Vision Based Speakers Diarization in Parliamentary Debates

Pedro A. Marín-Reyes[1(✉)], Javier Lorenzo-Navarro[1],
Modesto Castrillón-Santana[1], and Elena Sánchez-Nielsen[2]

[1] Instituto Universitario SIANI, Universidad de Las Palmas de Gran Canaria,
35017 Las Palmas, Spain
`pedro.marin102@alu.ulpgc.es`
[2] Departamento de Ingeniería Informática y de Sistemas,
Universidad de la Laguna, 38271 Santa Cruz de Tenerife, Spain

Abstract. Automatic labelling of speakers is an essential task for speakers diarization in parliamentary debates given the huge amount of video data to annotate. In this paper, we address the speaker diarization problem as a visual speaker re-identification issue with a special emphasis on the analysis of different shot types. We propose two approaches that makes use of convolutional neural networks (CNN) and biometric traits for keyframe extraction. Experimental results have been evaluated with challenging real-world datasets from the Canary Islands Parliament, and contrasted with a similar approach that does not analyze the shot type. Results show that the use of CNN for shot classification and biometric traits help to improve the performance of the re-identification outcomes in an average rate of 9.8 %.

Keywords: Visual diarization · Re-identification · CNN classification · Biometric traits

1 Introduction

Speaker diarization is a common topic for the speech research community. The aim is to identify the number of participants and creation of the list of time intervals of each participant speech, e.g. "who spoke when" [1,15]. Although this problem has received the interest of the speech processing community, just recently the use of visual features has been considered to strength the performance of audio-only diarization systems [5,6,9,12,16].

In [5] the scenario is restricted to a meeting. The diarization is done using an agglomerative clustering method using Mel Frequency Cepstral Coefficients (MFCCs), head pose and motion intensity. Vallet et al. [16] also employ an

This work has been partially supported by the Spanish Government under the projects TIN2011-24598 and TIN2015-64395-R.

agglomerative clustering in a talk-show scenario. They use as visual features HSV color components cumulative histograms of the clothes for shots presenting lip movement. In a recent work, Sarafianos et al. [12] implement a semi-supervised variant of the Fisher Linear Discriminant Analysis named FLsD. Gabor based features are extracted after a face detection and normalization stage. Feature reduction is applied in FLsD followed by a C-means clustering process. In another recent work [6], also a fusion of audio and visual features is employed. In this case, the visual features are based on Local Binary Patterns (LBP) and two variants Center-Symmetric LBP (CS-LBP) and Thresholded CS-LBP (tCS-LBP).

Unlike previous works that rely on the combination of audio and video features to perform the diarization process, in this work we focus only on the use of visual information. Debates in the Canary Islands Parliament is the chosen scenario, that although is a well defined scenario, it poses some challenging situations that the system must cope with. The contribution of the paper is twofold. First, the identification of different shot types with the use of a Convolutional Neural Network that allows to implement the proper strategy to identify the speaker without the sound cue. Second, the proposal of a measure based on anthropometric relations of facial elements to discard non frontal faces that introduce noise in the diarization process. To validate the proposals, they have been tested on 31 videos that add up more than 100 h.

1.1 Parliamentary Sessions Scenario

The parliamentary sessions scenario is challenging given that the recording does not provide a single field of vision focused on each speakers intervention. Instead of it, several and different views of the Parliament are captured by a camera network including different individuals and changes in pan, tilt and zoom. This scenario is also characterized by clothing similarities among speakers, changing lighting conditions and automatic color adjustment during speakers speeches, viewpoint variations across camera views when a speaker is giving the speech, cluttered background and occlusions. Given our aim is to roughly label in each time interval speaker apparence, the developed system must know the different types of shots in order to process only valid shots and avoid redundant computation.

Recent computer vision literature is rich in people detection approaches [14]. There are different visual patterns that have been taken into account for that purpose: the face/head, the upper body, the entire body, or just the legs. For our scenario, even if the speaker will be looking at the audience instead of the camera, his/her pose will be typically frontal. Hence, the speaker could be standing surrounded by the audience while they are sitting near him/her. Therefore, face and upper body detectors fit the problem restrictions depending upon the shot type (Fig. 1).

Fig. 1. Different camera views during a parliamentary session.

2   Methodology

The proposed system is composed by six modules, see Fig. 2. Input frames feed a shot detector which determinates if the frame is a new shot. Shots are classified into four types (Fig. 3), considering only the two leftmost of interest. The image is processed by a upper body detector if the shot satisfies some conditions, returning a new cropped image. After that, a face detector is used to identify the area of the speaker and the position of eyes and mouth. These metrics are computed in order to verify that the area of the frame corresponds to a real face. This area is modelled by visual features and then the label of the most similar speaker is given if it is similar enough, or a new label is created.

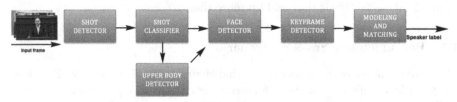

Fig. 2. System pipeline overview.

2.1   Shot Boundary Detector

Shot boundary detection is a required task for automatic video indexing. Their detection provides semantics about the video stream processed. Different techniques have been described in the literature mainly based on statistics computation and the definition of a threshold between frames. In this work, the shot boundary detection method presented in [11] is used. The method is based on the comparison of consecutive frames using the Kullback-Leibler (KL) divergence [4] between the HSV histograms of the frames.

Fig. 3. Shot types. (a) Medium close up. (b) Mid shot. (c) Long shot. (d) Others.

2.2   Shot Classification

In a parliamentary debate, deputies can participate from their own seat or from the platform. We call *medium close up* a shot where only the speaker appears and the face pose is mainly frontal. The second type is called *mid shot*, where a speaker is the main subject of the frame but it can be surrounded by other deputies. The other two types corresponds to *long shot* that are general views of the parliament and *others* which are ratings and titles.

In order to differentiate among the four types of shots under consideration a convolutional neural network (CNN) [8] has been trained. The architecture of the CNN is as follows. The input to the network is a 227×227 RGB image. Then, three convolutional layers each one with a ReLU activation function, followed by a maximum pooling and a local response normalization stage. The sizes are 96, 256 and 384 respectively. The two next layers correspond to fully connected both with size of 512, each of these levels has ReLU activation function and a dropout phase. The last layer is a fully connected layer with 4 outputs.

2.3   Speaker Detection

As mentioned above, the scenario configuration allows the system to introduce some restrictions in the kind of shots that belong to the speaker exposition. Long shots are excluded from the detection process because normally they correspond to a general view. Face detector is used for medium close up shots due this kind of shots are close and only the speaker appears. Mid shots introduce a limitation to face detecton based systems, e.g. [10] because face detectors localize all the faces of the image and the biggest detected one could not correspond to the speaker due to the angle of the camera. Some samples of this problem are shown in Fig. 4. As commented before, in this kind of shots the speaker is standing. This fact can be detected with an upper body detector obtained as region of interest only the standing person area. Figure 4 shows some frames where the introduction of the standing person detection (in blue) has removed the false speaker detection obtained with only a face detector. After upper body detection, a face detector is used on this region. See Algorithm 1 for a brief description of the method.

Fig. 4. Face detection samples using face and upper body detectors. (Color figure online)

Algorithm 1. Speaker face detector algorithm

1: $shotType \leftarrow$ **classifyShot**($frame$)
2: $faceRect \leftarrow []$
3: **if** $shotType =$ **MediumCloseUp then**
4:     $faceRect \leftarrow$ **faceDetector**($frame$)
5: **if** $shotType =$ **MidShot then**
6:     $upperBodyRect \leftarrow$ **detectorUpperBody**($frame$)
7:     $frameRegion \leftarrow$ **crop**($frame, upperBodyRect$)
8:     $faceRect \leftarrow$ **faceDetector**($frameRegion$)
        return $faceRect$

The upper body detector [2] is used to detect standing speakers in *mid shots*. On the other hand, to detect faces we have made use of Viola-Jones face detector [17]. The areas of the images detected as faces are validated by means of the detection of both eyes and mouth. Additionally, it is checked that distance between eyes and distance between the middle point of eyes and mouth correspond to a real face.

2.4   Biometric Keyframe Extraction

In [10] all faces detected in a shot are considered to label the speaker because a majority voting approach was used. However, some non-frontal faces can be detected and this introduces noise in the process. To alleviate this fact, the detection of keyframes is considered in this work.

Keyframe is the frame that represents the relevant content of the shot. It reduces the amount of images that the system has to process and it deletes possible noise errors. There are diferent methods to extract the keyframe [13] such as visual frame descriptors, motion attention model or camera motion and object motion. We propose a biometric keyframe based on the facial element interdistances, distance of eyes and distance between the middle point of eyes and mouth. Statistically we analyzed the influence of these metrics to define a coefficient, Eq. (1), that represent a non-dimensional measure.

$$c = \frac{D_{eyes}}{D_{eyes/mouth}} \qquad (1)$$

where c represent dimensionless relational coefficient between eyes distance (D_{eyes}) and the distance from the middle point of the eyes respect with the mouth ($D_{eyes/mouth}$). The following decision rule is implemented according to Eq. (2)

$$frame_i \text{ is keyframe} \begin{cases} \text{true} & \text{if } shotType \text{ is MediumCloseUp and } 0.76 \leq c \leq 0.82 \\ \text{true} & \text{if } shotType \text{ is MidShot and } 0.83 \leq c \leq 0.89 \\ \text{false} & \text{otherwise} \end{cases}$$

$$(2)$$

where $frame_i$ corresponds to each video frame and $shotType$ is the type of shot of the frame.

2.5   Speaker Modeling

Once the face of the speaker is detected, three areas of interest are considered to model her/him. One of those areas is the face where Histograms of Oriented Gradients (HOG) are computed using a 3×3 grid to obtain nine HOG cell histograms. Another area of interest is the one surrounding the head that carries out information about hair styles and can introduce a discriminant element between speakers with similar faces. In this area, also a HOG is computed but as the information is coarser than in the face a 2×2 grid is defined. Finally, the color of the clothes is also used to model the speaker given the fact that during a debate session the deputies wear the same outfits. This is done with the YCbCr color components histogram of the region just under the face because it is always visible both in medium close up and mid shots.

The matching process between speakers is done using the previous described visual features. As the nature of the visual features extracted from the individual are different, two similarity measures are used in the matching. The comparison of the HOG features is done with the cosine distance and the comparison between color histogram is calculated with the KL divergence.

The approach proposed by Sánchez et al. [10] for parliamentary debate scenarios is not based on clustering the different detected speakers after recording. Instead they realize an on-the-fly assignment to previously seen speakers, or create a new label for different enough individuals. This is done by combining the three above mentioned matching measures into a decision rule to create a new label or assigning to an existing one. Re-identification techniques are considered based exclusively on visual features extracted from the upper body. Most computer vision identity modeling approaches are based on the face pattern, working with identity models that are previously pre-computed based on the image [18] or facial descriptors [7].

3   Experiments

This section presents the experimental evaluation of the approaches proposed in this paper. The video dataset consists of 31 videos extracted from http://www.parcan.es/video/canales.py. Table 1 summarizes the main details for each specific video. In our experimental evaluation, we compared three approaches for speaker detection. The first one, taken as baseline, is the method described in Sánchez et al. [10] where only a single face detector is used to localize speakers. The second one, is Diarization Shot Classification (DSC) method that combines a CNN shot classifier and a people standing person detector previous to detecting the face in mid shots. The third, is our complete method, called Diarization Shot Classification Keyframe (DSCK) that uses DSC method and biometric verification of the face.

Four videos have been used for training the CNN shot classifier. Shots were manually labelled into four classes: general shot (4,740 samples), mid shot (1,395 samples), medium close up (4,309 samples) and others contains 143 items that represent title and rating shots.

Table 1. Features and re-identification measures results in percentage of the whole set of evaluated videos.

Video features				Measures results per method					
				Baseline		DSC		DSCK	
Id	Frames	Shots	Speakers	TRR	TDR	TRR	TDR	TRR	TDR
2770	314050	660	8	100.0	100.0	100.0	100.0	93.8	100.0
2785	242850	325	32	40.0	99.6	50.0	99.4	100.0	100.0
2786	265500	396	17	75.0	100.0	76.9	100.0	80.0	100.0
2787	464000	738	24	80.8	99.2	88.5	99.2	79.4	97.8
2789	232350	334	26	92.3	99.8	100.0	100.0	50.0	100.0
2790	243450	451	13	94.1	96.9	93.3	96.7	100.0	100.0
2791	442625	636	25	82.8	99.6	80.7	98.8	83.8	97.3
2792	162000	318	11	100.0	100.0	100.0	100.0	83.3	96.2
2799	241925	269	33	0.0	99.9	0.0	100.0	100.0	100.0
2800	273300	255	19	66.7	98.8	70.6	99.3	57.1	97.2
2817	299450	281	18	73.9	98.7	72.0	98.7	85.7	97.9
2818	540350	713	14	73.3	100.0	92.3	99.4	47.1	98.9
2904	247725	389	30	100.0	100.0	100.0	100.0	100.0	100.0
2905	293400	325	20	73.9	97.8	66.7	97.8	62.5	95.1
2907	210500	257	15	87.5	97.4	87.5	97.4	100.0	100.0
2908	350025	503	24	90.5	99.1	95.0	99.1	89.3	97.6
2918	122075	143	7	90.0	94.7	90.0	94.7	83.3	90.5
2940	297250	402	17	71.4	97.9	71.4	97.9	66.7	96.4
2959	217925	265	24	28.6	99.4	100.0	100.0	60.0	98.4
2960	317850	340	22	66.7	99.3	60.0	99.1	66.7	97.8
2977	247575	447	32	0.0	99.8	0.0	100.0	100.0	100.0
2978	323175	371	20	80.0	99.8	80.0	99.8	69.0	95.5
2992	192900	149	2	100.0	100.0	100.0	100.0	100.0	100.0
2995	265475	580	9	76.5	99.0	76.5	99.0	52.2	98.1
3011	182550	315	25	0.0	98.7	0.0	98.3	100.0	100.0
3012	325750	365	24	71.4	98.7	63.2	98.1	75.0	98.4
3013	382900	501	19	66.7	97.8	72.2	98.5	84.2	98.5
3014	251050	270	20	33.3	98.5	50.0	99.1	62.5	96.7
3015	274100	252	13	80.0	97.3	83.3	97.3	80.0	99.3
3017	278400	291	18	100.0	100.0	100.0	100.0	92.9	98.2
3020	332950	390	14	72.2	98.0	91.7	99.5	66.7	97.6
Mean	**277672**	**376**	**19**	**69.9**	**98.9**	**74.6**	**98.9**	**79.7**	**98.2**
Median	**273300**	**340**	**19**	**75.0**	**99.2**	**80.7**	**99.2**	**83.3**	**98.4**

The assignment of the thresholds for the coefficient of Eq. 2 has been calculated using four videos. Biometric measures are calculated for each frame and shot type to obtain the corresponding coefficients. The median value of these coeficients is used as the center value of the thresholds, with an interval of ±3.

For each video a coarse-grained annonation is provided by the Canary Islands Parliament Media Service. As our approach is not based on a clustering technique but in a matching process similarly to a re-identification task, to evaluate the performance of the proposal, the measures described in [3] are used:

– True Re-identification Rate (TRR): the system declares two speakers as the same speaker and they are the same person.
– False Re-identification Rate (FRR): the system declares two speakers as the same speaker but they are different person.
– True Distinction Rate (TDR): the system declares two speakers as different speaker and they are different.
– False Distinction Rate (FDR): the system declares two speakers as different speaker and they are the same person.

4   Results

This section presents the speakers labelling results in the parliamentary sessions scenario. In Fig. 5, "Baseline" is the baseline strategy [10], "DSC" is our initial proposed strategy and "DSCK" is our completed proposed strategy. The summarized rates are presented in Table 1.

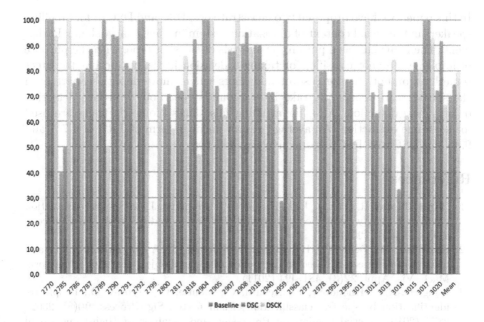

Fig. 5. Comparison methods per video using TRRs (y axis) achieved per video (x axis).

In general, the proposed methods give better results than the baseline. This fact can be explained because the baseline method fails in the detection of the speaker in mid shots since deputies that are next to the speaker act as distractor for the face detector. A clear example appears in video 2959, the most part of the video are mid shots with a few medium close up shots. The TRR improvement in this video is 71.4 %. On the other hand, the use of biometric traits reduce the error rate of the face detector. We obtain in three videos an improvement of 100 %.

On the contrary, in videos 2905 and 2960, the most of the shots are medium close up, the shot classification errors affect negatively to the performance. When there is a shot misclassification, the shot is not processed, or the system tries to find an upper body where there is not, resulting an unpreprocessed shot. Also, at the time to identify a keyframe, the misclassification can introduce an error in the evaluation of the threshold.

Summarizing, the mean TRR with our proposals are better than the baseline, and only just a reduced number of videos reported slightly worse results. Thus, observing Table 1, we can remark that in 80.6 % and 61.3 % of the videos the DSC and DSCK approaches increases or equals the performance. DSC obtains an average of 4.7 % improvement of all processed videos for the TRR, while keeping a similar TDR. Compared to DSC, DSCK obtains a mean of 5.1 % TRR improvement. Finally, the TRR increment of DSCK with respect to the baseline is 9.8 %.

5   Conclusions

In this paper, we have proposed two new strategies, DSC and DSCK, for labelling speakers in the visual context of diarization system in the Canary Islands Parliament. The focus has been put on the analysis of the shot type, with the purpose of implement a shot classifier for taking a decision if the system has to detect something or not. In the case of mid shots where more deputies apart from the speaker can appear, we take into account upper body and face detection or only face detection. Also, for avoiding false faces biometric traits are used for keyframe extraction. An average improvement in term of TRR of 4.7 % and 9.8 % for DSC and DSCK respectively is achieved.

References

1. Barra-Chicote, R., Pardo, J.M., Ferreiros, J., Montero, J.M.: Speaker diarization based on intensity channel contribution. IEEE Trans. Audio Speech Lang. Process. **19**(4), 754–761 (2011)
2. Castrillón, M., Déniz, O., Hernández, D., Lorenzo, J.: A comparison of face and facial feature detectors based on the violajones general object detection framework. Mach. Vis. Appl. **22**(3), 481–494 (2011)
3. Cong, D.-N.T., Khoudour, L., Achard, C., Meurie, C., Lezoray, O.: People re-identification by spectral classification of silhouettes. Sig. Process. **90**(8), 2362–2374 (2010). Special Section on Processing and Analysis of High-Dimensional Masses of Image and Signal Data

4. Cover, T.M., Thomas, J.A.: Elements of Information Theory. Wiley, London (2006)
5. Garau, G., Bourlard, H.: Using audio and visual cues for speaker diarisation initialisation. In: IEEE International Conference on Acoustics Speech and Signal Processing (ICASSP), pp. 4942–4945 (2010)
6. Kapsouras, I., Tefas, A., Nikolaidis, N., Peeters, G., Benaroya, L., Pitas. I.: Multimodal speaker clustering in full length movies. Multimed. Tools Appl. 1–20 (2016). doi:10.1007/s11042-015-3181-5
7. Kumar, N., Berg, A.C., Belhumeur, P.N., Nayar, S.K.: Describable visual attributes for face verification and image search. IEEE Trans. Pattern Anal. Mach. Intell. **33**, 1962–1977 (2011)
8. Lecun, Y., Bottou, L., Bengio, Y., Haffner, P.: Gradient-based learning applied to document recognition. Proc. IEEE **86**, 2278–2324 (1998)
9. Noulas, A., Englebienne, G., Krose, B.J.A.: Multimodal speaker diarization. IEEE Trans. Pattern Anal. Mach. Intell. **34**(1), 79–93 (2012)
10. Sánchez-Nielsen, E., Chávez-Gutiérrez, F., Lorenzo-Navarro, J., Castrillón-Santana, M.: A multimedia system to produce and deliver video fragments on demand on parliamentary websites. Multimed. Tools Appl. 1–27 (2016). doi:10.1007/s11042-016-3306-5
11. Sao, N., Mishra, R.: A survey based on video shot boundary detection techniques. Int. J. Adv. Res. Comput. Commun. Eng. (IJARCCE) **3**(4) (2014)
12. Sarafianos, N., Giannakopoulos, T., Petridis, S.: Audio-visual speaker diarization using fisher linear semi-discriminant analysis. Multimed. Tools Appl. **75**(1), 115–130 (2016)
13. Sujatha, C., Mudenagudi, U.: A study on keyframe extraction methods for video summary. In: 2011 International Conference on Computational Intelligence and Communication Networks (CICN), pp. 73–77 (2011)
14. Teixeira, T., Dublon, G., Savvides, A.: A survey of human-sensing: methods for detecting presence, count, location, track, and identity. ACM Comput. Surv. **5**, 1–77 (2010)
15. Tranter, S.E., Reynolds, D.A.: An overview of automatic speaker diarization systems. IEEE Trans. Audio Speech Lang. Process. **14**(5), 1557–1565 (2006)
16. Vallet, F., Essid, S., Carrive, J.: A multimodal approach to speaker diarization on TV talk-shows. IEEE Trans. Multimed. **15**(3), 509–520 (2013)
17. Viola, P., Jones, M.J.: Robust real-time face detection. Int. J. Comput. Vis. **57**(2), 151–173 (2004)
18. Zhao, W., Chellappa, R., Phillips, P.J., Rosenfeld, A.: Face recognition: a literature survey. Assoc. Comput. Mach. **35**(4), 399–458 (2003). http://doi.acm.org/10.1145/954339.954342

Online Multi-label Classification with Adaptive Model Rules

Ricardo Sousa[1]([✉]) and João Gama[1,2]([✉])

[1] LIAAD/INESC TEC, Universidade do Porto, Porto, Portugal
rtsousa@inesctec.pt, jgama@fep.up.pt
[2] Faculdade de Economia, Universidade do Porto, Porto, Portugal

Abstract. The interest on online classification has been increasing due to data streams systems growth and the need for Multi-label Classification applications have followed the same trend. However, most of classification methods are not performed on-line. Moreover, data streams produce huge amounts of data and the available processing resources may not be sufficient. This work-in-progress paper proposes an algorithm for Multi-label Classification applications in data streams scenarios. The proposed method is derived from multi-target structured regressor AMRules that produces models using subsets of output attributes (output specialization strategy). Performance tests were conducted where the operation modes global, local and subset approaches of the proposed method were compared to each other and to others online multi-label classifiers described in the literature. Three datasets of real scenarios were used for evaluation. The results indicate that the subset specialization mode is competitive in comparison to local and global approaches and to other online multi-label classifiers.

Keywords: Multi-label · Classification · AMRules · Data streams

1 Introduction

Nowadays, data streams systems are very common (sensors systems, network monitoring logs, video streams, ...) [1]. These systems produce data unlimitedly in real time at high rates. Collected data can not be all stored and processed in just one procedure but one example at a time. Moreover, the data may present changes over time [2]. Therefore, systems such as regressors and classifiers need to perform training and prediction operations dynamically through online systems [3]. Some classification problems require that more than one class label should be assigned to an example. Two different examples may have a different number of class labels assigned [4]. The process that tries to solve this problem is called Multi-label Classification (MLC) [2]. Formally, representing $\mathcal{D} = \{..., (\mathbf{x}_1, \mathbf{y}_1), (\mathbf{x}_2, \mathbf{y}_2), ..., (\mathbf{x}_i, \mathbf{y}_i), ...\}$ as an unbounded data stream, where $\mathbf{x}_i = [x_{i,1} \cdots x_{i,j} \cdots x_{i,M}]$ is a M-dimensional vector containing the data descriptive variables $x_{i,j}$ (input attributes) of the ith example (considering an example

© Springer International Publishing Switzerland 2016
O. Luaces et al. (Eds.): CAEPIA 2016, LNAI 9868, pp. 58–67, 2016.
DOI: 10.1007/978-3-319-44636-3_6

as a reference) and $\mathbf{y}_i$ corresponds to the response (output attributes) that consists of subset of nominal labels λ_k such that $\mathbf{y}_i \subseteq \{\lambda_1, ..., \lambda_k, ..., \lambda_L\}$, where L is the number of possible labels. The objective of MLC is to learn a function $f(\mathbf{x}_i) \rightarrow \mathbf{y}_i$ that maps the input values of $\mathbf{x}_i$ into the output values of $\mathbf{y}_i$. Online MLC is used in several domains such as Biology (gene and protein function classification) [5], Engineering (Network Monitoring and sensor applications) [6], Economics (online stock market data) [7], Social Sciences (social networks evolution) [8], Library and Information Science (text categorization) [7] and Multimedia (image, video and music categorization and annotation) [4]. Among classification techniques, structured classifiers present the advantage of selecting the most discriminative features implicitly, without requiring variables scaling. Moreover, these classifiers are resilient to outliers and the produced models are easily interpreted [8]. From structured classifiers, Rules Learning algorithms presents high modularity due to the fact that each rule can be interpreted individually [9]. The rule learning is independent which is an advantage when compared to tree-based algorithms. Modularity of rule sets can be explored to overcome the global and local methods thought rule specialization on a subset of output variables [10]. This work suggests a solution for MLC on data streams based on the algorithm AMRules and inspired on a regression approach [10]. This method was evaluated through a comparison of performance measures against other methods found in the literature. In addiction, the local and global operation mode were also compared to the subset approach. This paper presents the following structure. Section 2 summarizes related work (small presentation of online multi-label classifiers found in literature) and Sect. 3 describes the proposed rule-based algorithm for online MLC. The performance tests are described in Sect. 4. The results are discussed on Sect. 5 and the conclusions are remarked in Sect. 6.

2   Related Work

In this section, some existing online MLC approaches are briefly described. Typically, most approaches are based on problem transformation [8]. The output set of labels $\mathbf{y}_i$ are transformed into a vector of outputs variables $[y_{i,1} \cdots y_{i,k} \cdots y_{i,L}]$, where $y_{i,k} \in \{0,1\}$ are binary. If label λ_k is assigned to the ith example then $y_{i,k} = 1$, otherwise $y_{i,k} = 0$. Here, the outputs variables are redefined as $\mathbf{y}_i = [y_{i,1} \cdots y_{i,k} \cdots y_{i,L}]$. The Binary Relevance (BR) is a simple multi-label classifier that uses directly the problem transformation. An online binary classifier trains and predicts for the kth output variable only. The prediction procedure is represented by $\hat{\mathbf{y}}_i = [f_1(\mathbf{x}_i), ..., f_k(\mathbf{x}_i), ..., f_L(\mathbf{x}_i)]$, where f_k represent the classifier of the kth output variable. This classifier is used as a baseline in the performance tests. Classifier Chains (CC) also uses the problem transformation like the BR method [11]. The L outputs variables indexes are shuffled in a sequence. Then, a classifier k is used to model the inputs and the first $(k-1)$ outputs variables. The prediction can be expressed as $\hat{\mathbf{y}}_i = [f_1(\mathbf{x}_i), ..., f_k(\mathbf{x}_i, \hat{y}_{i,1}, ..., \hat{y}_{i,k-1}), ..., f_L(\mathbf{x}_i, \hat{y}_{i,1}, ..., \hat{y}_{i,L-1})]$ (posteriorly reordered as before shuffling). Multi-label

Hoeffding Trees (MHT) is an online structured classifier based on a decision tree that uses the Hoeffding bound criterion in the induction. The algorithm uses the information gain in the split decision and multi-label classifiers at the tree leaves [2]. The process can be modelled as $\hat{\mathbf{y}}_i = f_n(\mathbf{x}_i)$, where f_n is a basic online multi-label classifier of n leaf.

3 Multi-label AMRules for Classification

In this section, Multi-label AMRules (ML-AMRules) algorithm and its underlying principles are presented. As main principle, this algorithm is based on the adaptation of the multi-target AMRules regressor to the MLC problem through problem transformation [10]. This section also presents the underlying Rule Learning theory, the description of ML-AMRules training and prediction (multi-target adaptation to the MLC problem) and the description of the local and global modes.

3.1 Rule Learning

Rule R is defined as $\mathcal{A} \Rightarrow \mathcal{C}$ implication where the antecedent $\mathcal{A}$ is a conjunction of conditions (called literals) of the input variables $\mathbf{x}_i$, and the consequent $\mathcal{C}$ is a predicting function (in this context, it is a basic online multi-label classifier). For numerical data, literals may present the forms $(X_j \leq v)$ and $(X_j > v)$, where X_j represents the jth input variable, meaning that $x_{i,j}$ must be less or equal to v, and $x_{i,j}$ must be greater than v, respectively. Regarding nominal data, literals may present forms $(X_j = v)$ expressing that $x_{i,j}$ must be equal to v or $(X_j \neq v)$ indicating that $x_{i,j}$ must be different than v. R is said to cover $\mathbf{x}_i$ if, and only if, $\mathbf{x}_i$ satisfies all the literals in $\mathcal{A}$. The support of the input variables of an example, $S(\mathbf{x}_i)$, corresponds to a set of rules that cover $\mathbf{x}_i$. Function (the basic classifier) in $\mathcal{C}$ returns a prediction $\hat{\mathbf{y}}_i$ if a rule R_r covers the example input variables $\mathbf{x}_i$. Data structure $\mathcal{L}_r$ containing the necessary statistics (about the rule and the examples) to the algorithm training and prediction (expand the rule, detect changes and identify anomalies, ...) is associated to each rule R_r. A particular rule D, called default rule, exists for initial conditions and for the case of none of the current rules covers the example ($S(\mathbf{x}_i) = \emptyset$). The antecedent of D and its statistics $\mathcal{L}_D$ start as an empty set. Rule set is formed by a set of U learned rules defined as $\mathcal{R} = \{R_1, \cdots, R_r, \cdots, R_U\}$ and a default rule D as depicted in Fig. 1. In summary, Rule Learning allows to create partitions on the input variables space and build a model on each partition. Consequently, the linear model can fit more easily to data.

3.2 ML-AMRules Training (Rule Induction)

Algorithm 1 illustrates the pseudo-code for the ML-AMRules training. The algorithm initializes the statistics $\mathcal{L}_D$ of the default rule and starts the rule set $\mathcal{R}$ out empty. When an example $(\mathbf{x}_i, \mathbf{y}_i)$ is received, the algorithm searches for rules

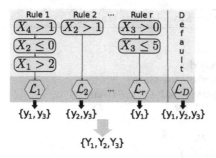

Fig. 1. Multi-label AMRules based on subsets specialization.

that covers the example input variables $\mathbf{x}_i$. Considering one rule $R_r \in S(\mathbf{x}_i)$, the example input variables $\mathbf{x}_i$ are submitted to anomaly ($\texttt{isAnomaly}(\mathcal{L}_r, \mathbf{x}_i)$) and change ($\texttt{changeDetected}(\mathcal{L}_r, \mathbf{x}_i)$) detection in order to prune the examples. For change detection, the Page-Hinkley (PH) is used [12]. For anomaly detection, a method based on probability of example occurrence was used [10]. In case of anomaly, the example is simply rejected and in case of change detection, R_r is removed from the rule set (the rule is outdated). Otherwise, the statistics $\mathcal{L}_r$ are updated ($\texttt{update}(\mathcal{L}_r)$).

Rule expansion (addition of new literal) is attempted and in an affirmative case ($\texttt{expand}(R_r)$), specialization of the rule on the output subset and rule addiction to $\mathcal{R}$ are performed (Sect. 3.4). This specialization leads to more accurate predictions and it increases the speed of processing. The example input variables $\mathbf{x}_i$ may not be covered by any rule. Consequently, the statistics of the default rule $\mathcal{L}_D$ are updated and the expansion is attempted. If an expansion occur, the default rule D is added to the rule set $\mathcal{R}$ and a new default rule is initialized. The training process also involves the computation of a weight parameter for the case of more than one rule covers the example, in the prediction operations. The parameter is the mean error with a fading factor, for the rule r and output variable k, $e_{r,k} = \frac{T_{r,k}}{W_r}$. $T_{r,k}$ is the accumulated error and W_r is the number of examples observed since the last expansion, both affected by a fading factor $0 < \alpha < 1$. These parameters are computed as

$$T_{r,k} \leftarrow \alpha T_{r,k} + |\hat{y}_{i,k} - y_{i,k}|, \; W_r \leftarrow \alpha W_r + 1, \tag{1}$$

where and $y_{i,k}$ is the true value and $\hat{y}_{i,k}$ is post-training prediction. Each output variable under the rule R_r is associated to a linear and to an output mean predictors. The output-mean predictor is simply defined as $\hat{y}_{i,k}^r = \frac{1}{n} \sum_{u=1}^{n} y_{u,k}$, where n is the number of examples seen since last expansion. The purpose is to allow fast training convergence of the linear predictor. The error $e_{r,k}$ is computed for each predictor.

3.3   Rule Expansion

Rule R_r expansion consists of adding a new literal to the antecedent A_r. The new literal is determined by finding the input variables and by computing the

Algorithm 1. Adaptive Model Rules training

1: $\mathcal{R} \leftarrow \emptyset,\ D \leftarrow 0$
2: **for all** $(\mathbf{x}_i, \mathbf{y}_i) \in \mathcal{D}$ **do**
3:     **for all** $R_r \in S(\mathbf{x}_i)$ **do**
4:         **if** ¬isAnomaly($\mathcal{L}_r, \mathbf{x}_i$) **then**
5:             **if** changeDetected($\mathcal{L}_r, \mathbf{x}_i$) **then**
6:                 $\mathcal{R} \leftarrow \mathcal{R} \setminus \{R_r\}$
7:             **else**
8:                 $R_c \leftarrow R_r$
9:                 update($\mathcal{L}_r$)
10:                 $expanded \leftarrow$ expand(R_r)
11:                 **if** $expanded = $ TRUE **then**
12:                     Compute $\mathcal{O}'_c$
13:                     $\mathcal{O}_c \leftarrow \mathcal{O}'_c$
14:                     $\mathcal{R} \leftarrow \mathcal{R} \cup \{R_c\}$
15:     **if** $S(\mathbf{x}_i) = \emptyset$ **then**
16:         update($\mathcal{L}_D$)
17:         $expanded \leftarrow$ expand(D)
18:         **if** $expanded = $ TRUE **then**
19:             $\mathcal{R} \leftarrow \mathcal{R} \cup \{D\}$
20:             $D \leftarrow 0$

---

split-points that maximize the uniformity of two groups of values, divided by v. This procedure uses an Extended Binary Search Tree (E-BST) with limited depth that keeps data statistics [13]. Mean Information Gain (MIG) is the maximizing function for splitting an input X_j given the split-point v with respect to the output variables. MIG is defined as

$$MIG(X_j, v) = \frac{1}{|\mathcal{O}_r|} \sum_{u \in \mathcal{O}_r} IG_u(X_j, v), \qquad (2)$$

where $IG_u(X_j, v)$ is the Information Gain of splitting X_j given v considering the output variable Y_u, and $\mathcal{O}_r$ is the set of output variables indexes currently being considered by the rule R_r. The Information Gain (IG) is defined as

$$IG_u(X_j, v) = H_u(E) - \frac{|E_L|}{|E|} \frac{H_u(E_L)}{H_u(E)} - \frac{|E_R|}{|E|} \frac{H_u(E_R)}{H_u(E)}, \qquad (3)$$

where,

$$H_u(E) = -[p \log(p) + (1 - p) \log(1 - p)],$$

is the entropy, p is the probability of $Y_u = 1$ and E denotes the set of examples processed since the last expansion. If the input variables are numerical, $E_L = \{\mathbf{x}_i \in E : x_{i,j} \leq v\}$ and $E_R = \{\mathbf{x}_i \in E : x_{i,j} > v\}$. Considering nominal input variables, $E_L = \{\mathbf{x}_i \in E : x_{i,j} = v\}$ and $E_R = \{\mathbf{x}_i \in E : x_{i,j} \neq v\}$. The rule expansion procedure uses the Hoeffding bound [14] to determine the minimum number of examples n required to expand, which states that the true mean of a random variable β, with range P, will not differ from the sample mean more than ϵ with probability $1 - \delta$. The Hoeffding bound is defined as $\epsilon = \sqrt{\frac{P^2 \ln (1/\delta)}{2n}}$. This procedure suggests several candidates for splitting $[MIG(X_j, v_1)...MIG(X_j, v_c)]$ that are organized in decreasing order. A comparison between the two best splits is performed using the difference: $\beta = MIG(X_j, v_1) - MIG(X_j, v_2)$. The range of β is $[0, 1]$, therefore $P = 1$. In case of $\beta > \epsilon$, $MIG(X_j, v_1)$ is the best split with the probability of $1 - \delta$. Threshold τ is defined to limit ϵ for numerical instabilities. If $\epsilon < \tau$ is met, the split with higher $MIG(X_j, v_1)$ is selected and the expansion takes place. The relation sign is determine by finding the set of example(E_L or E_R) with the lowest $H(E)$. This incremental algorithm presents $\mathcal{O}(n)$ complexity which makes it suitable for online scenarios.

3.4   Specializing on Subsets of the Output Variables

Let $\mathcal{O}_r$, E_{best} be the set of the current learning outputs indexes for rule R_r and the set of examples with the lowest $H(E)$ in the splitting, respectively. $\mathcal{O}'_r$ denotes the new learning outputs that consists of set of output variables indexes that reduce in entropy after the split:

$$\mathcal{O}'_r = \left\{ u : u \in \mathcal{O}_r \wedge \frac{H_u(E_{best})}{H_u(E)} < 1 \right\}. \tag{4}$$

A complementary rule R_c which contains the set of the pruned output variables is also added to the rule set in order to keep their information. The antecedents of R_c and R_r are equal before the expansion. R_c learns only from the output attributes $Y_u \in \mathcal{O}'_c$ in order to satisfy $\mathcal{O}'_c = \mathcal{O}_r \setminus \mathcal{O}'_r$.

3.5   ML-AMRules Prediction

In the prediction, the rules R_r that covers the example are considered $\Lambda = \{r : R_r \in \mathcal{S}(\mathbf{x}_i)\}$. The next step consists of choosing the predictor that presents lower error (the output-mean or linear predictor) to retrieve an estimation $\hat{y}^r_{i,k}$ for the output k. The final prediction is defined as

$$\hat{y}_{i,k} = \begin{cases} 1 & \text{if } m_{i,k} > 0.5 \\ 0 & \text{if } m_{i,k} \leq 0.5 \end{cases} \tag{5}$$

$$m_{i,k} = \sum_{u \in \Lambda} \theta_{u,k} \hat{y}^u_{i,k}, \quad \theta_{u,k} = \frac{(e_{u,k} + \varepsilon)^{-1}}{\sum_{t \in \Lambda} (e_{t,k} + \varepsilon)^{-1}}, \tag{6}$$

where ε is a small positive number used to prevent numerical instabilities. If the output attribute Y_u can not be predicted by any rule, the prediction is given by the default rule D.

3.6 Local and Global Approaches

Two ML-AMRules operation modes are presented in this subsection according to local and global methods. The local approach is based on an instantiation of the ML-AMRules for each output variable. This operation mode resembles the BR approach. Each output variable has an independent rule set that models it. The final prediction is produced by combining the individual predictions. Considering the global approach, the rules are learned and predicted for all output attributes using one instantiation. For implementing the global algorithm the rule specialization is not performed (steps 11 and 12 in Algorithm 1).

4 Experimental Setup

This section presents the evaluation tests of the proposed algorithm described in Sect. 3. The proposed algorithm is compared to three online multi-label algorithms described in Sect. 2 in terms of their performance. The same comparison was performed for local and global operations mode described in Subsect. 3.6. The algorithm CC is incorporated in the open source MEKA platform that includes both batch and online multi-label algorithms. The algorithms were implemented in JAVA programming language and are based on WEKA [2]. BR, MHT and the proposed methods ML-AMRules were implemented in the Massive Online Analysis (MOA) platform. Its an open source platform of Machine Learning and Data Mining algorithms applied to data streams. This platform was also implemented in JAVA programming language. Real scenarios datasets 20NG, mediamill and OHSUMED were used to simulate data streams. These datasets are described on literature [8] and some features are presented in Table 1.

Table 1. Dataset description

Dataset	#Examples	#Outputs	#Inputs
20NG-F	19300	20	1006
mediamill	43907	101	120
OHSUMED-F	13929	23	1002

The examples of the datasets were replicated four times and shuffled due to the need of a significant number of examples by these algorithms. Performance example-based measures, Exact Match, Accuracy, Precision, Recall and F-measure were used [15]. This evaluation used the prequential mode where the algorithm starts by predicting the output values and the example-based measures. Posteriorly, it uses the example for training [16]. Datasets examples were divided into 100 windows and the above mentioned measures were computed for each window. Finally, the mean and the standard deviation of the measures of all windows were computed. Perceptron with a logistic activation function was used as linear predictor by all algorithms due to its models simplicity, low computational cost and low error rates [17].

5   Results

In this section, the evaluation results are presented. The results are organized by performance measures. Tables 2, 3, 4, 5 and 6 present the Accuracy, Exact Match, Precision, Recall and F-measure results of the online multi-label algorithms for each dataset. The ML-AMR(S), ML-AMR(G) and ML-AMR(L) correspond to the subset, global and local ML-AMRules operation modes, respectively.

Table 2. Accuracy. Mean and standard deviation values.

Dataset	ML-AMR(S)	ML-AMR(G)	ML-AMR(L)	BR	MHT	CC
20NG	0.65 ± 0.07	**0.67 ± 0.07**	0.63 ± 0.06	0.65 ± 0.07	0.66 ± 0.07	0.64 ± 0.05
mediamill	**0.37 ± 0.01**	0.35 ± 0.01	0.35 ± 0.01	0.34 ± 0.01	0.35 ± 0.01	0.34 ± 0.01
OSHUMED	0.46 ± 0.06	0.46 ± 0.06	0.44 ± 0.05	**0.47 ± 0.06**	**0.47 ± 0.06**	0.44 ± 0.05

Table 2 shows that the ML-AMRules approaches present values that have competitive accuracy. Among ML-AMRules approaches, the subset and global approaches seem to stand out.

Table 3. Exact match. Mean and standard deviation values.

Dataset	ML-AMR(S)	ML-AMR(G)	ML-AMR(L)	BR	MHT	CC
20NG	0.62 ± 0.06	**0.65 ± 0.07**	0.61 ± 0.06	0.64 ± 0.07	0.64 ± 0.07	0.62 ± 0.06
mediamill	0.04 ± 0.01	0.04 ± 0.01	0.04 ± 0.00	0.04 ± 0.01	**0.04 ± 0.01**	0.04 ± 0.01
OSHUMED	0.30 ± 0.04	0.30 ± 0.05	0.29 ± 0.04	**0.31 ± 0.04**	0.31 ± 0.05	0.30 ± 0.05

Table 3 presents low values for mediamill dataset due to high number of possibles labels for all algorithms. In this aspect, the ML-AMRules approaches present lower values in comparison to other algorithm.

Table 4. Precision. Mean and standard deviation values.

Dataset	ML-AMR(S)	ML-AMR(G)	ML-AMR(L)	BR	MHT	CC
20NG	0.68 ± 0.07	**0.69 ± 0.07**	0.65 ± 0.06	0.69 ± 0.07	0.68 ± 0.07	0.65 ± 0.06
mediamill	0.40 ± 0.02	0.41 ± 0.02	**0.41 ± 0.01**	0.41 ± 0.01	0.41 ± 0.01	0.40 ± 0.01
OSHUMED	0.50 ± 0.06	0.50 ± 0.06	0.48 ± 0.05	0.51 ± 0.06	**0.51 ± 0.06**	0.50 ± 0.05

Table 4 displays favourable precision values for ML-AMRules approaches. Among ML-AMRules modes, global and local present better values.

Table 5. Recall. Mean and standard deviation values.

Dataset	ML-AMR(S)	ML-AMR(G)	ML-AMR(L)	BR	MHT	CC
20NG	0.66 ± 0.07	$\mathbf{0.68 \pm 0.07}$	0.64 ± 0.06	0.67 ± 0.07	0.67 ± 0.07	0.65 ± 0.07
mediamill	$\mathbf{0.68 \pm 0.02}$	0.67 ± 0.01	0.66 ± 0.01	0.67 ± 0.01	0.67 ± 0.01	0.66 ± 0.01
OSHUMED	0.59 ± 0.06	0.59 ± 0.06	0.57 ± 0.05	0.59 ± 0.06	$\mathbf{0.60 \pm 0.06}$	0.58 ± 0.05

Table 5 exhibits predominance of the ML-AMRules approaches. The global and subset approaches present better performance.

Table 6. F-Measure. Mean and standard deviation values.

Dataset	ML-AMR(S)	ML-AMR(G)	ML-AMR(L)	BR	MHT	CC
20NG	0.66 ± 0.07	$\mathbf{0.68 \pm 0.07}$	0.64 ± 0.06	0.67 ± 0.07	0.67 ± 0.07	0.64 ± 0.06
mediamill	0.46 ± 0.01	0.47 ± 0.01	0.47 ± 0.01	$\mathbf{0.47 \pm 0.01}$	0.47 ± 0.01	0.46 ± 0.01
OSHUMED	0.51 ± 0.06	$\mathbf{0.52 \pm 0.06}$	0.50 ± 0.05	0.50 ± 0.06	0.51 ± 0.06	0.50 ± 0.05

Table 6 reveals the preponderance of the ML-AMRules approaches. The global and subset approaches present better performance. In general, the mean values present very close values due to the fact that all algorithms use the same linear predictor and due to datasets complexity.

6   Conclusions

This paper is the result of a preliminary work suggests a multi-target algorithm adaptation to the multi-label problems using Rule Learning methods. It can be concluded that the proposed approach is competitive when compared to online multi-label algorithms from the literature. The subset approach has shown to be competitive against local and global approaches. The experiments have shown that the datasets implicit models should be characterized in order to understand the data distribution.

Acknowledgments. This work was partly supported by the European Commission through MAESTRA (ICT-2013-612944) and the Project TEC4Growth - Pervasive Intelligence, Enhancers and Proofs of Concept with Industrial Impact/NORTE -01-0145- FEDER-000020 is financed by the North Portugal Regional Operational Programme (NORTE 2020), under the PORTUGAL 2020 Partnership Agreement, and through the European Regional Development Fund (ERDF).

References

1. Bifet, A., Holmes, G., Pfahringer, B., Kirkby, R., Gavaldà, R.: New ensemble methods for evolving data streams. In: Proceedings of the 15th ACM SIGKDD International Conference on Knowledge Discovery and Data Mining, KDD 2009, pp. 139–148. ACM, New York (2009)

2. Read, J., Bifet, A., Holmes, G., Pfahringer, B.: Scalable and efficient multi-label classification for evolving data streams. Mach. Learn. **88**(1–2), 243–272 (2012)
3. Gama, J.: Knowledge Discovery from Data Streams. Chapman and Hall/CRC Data Mining and Knowledge Discovery Series. CRC Press, Boca Raton (2010)
4. Madjarov, G., Kocev, D., Gjorgjevikj, D., Deroski, S.O.: An extensive experimental comparison of methods for multi-label learning. Pattern Recogn. **45**(9), 3084–3104 (2012)
5. Clare, A.J., King, R.D.: Knowledge discovery in multi-label phenotype data. In: Siebes, A., De Raedt, L. (eds.) PKDD 2001. LNCS (LNAI), vol. 2168, pp. 42–53. Springer, Heidelberg (2001)
6. Aggarwal, C.C.: Data Streams: Models and Algorithms. Advances in Database Systems. Springer, New York (2006)
7. Kong, X., Yu, P.S.: An ensemble-based approach to fast classification of multi-label data streams, pp. 95–104, December 2011
8. Osojnik, A., Panov, P., Dzeroski, S.: Multi-label classiffcation viamulti-target regression on data streams. In: Proceedings of the Discovery Science - 18th International Conference, DS 2015, Banff, AB, Canada, 4–6 October 2015, pp. 170–185 (2015)
9. Fürnkranz, J., Gamberger, D., Lavra, N.: Foundations of Rule Learning. Springer, Heidelberg (2012)
10. Duarte, J., Gama, J.: Multi-target regression from high-speed data streams with adaptive model rules. In: IEEE Conference on Data Science and Advanced Analytics (2015)
11. Read, J., Pfahringer, B., Holmes, G., Frank, E.: Classifier chains for multi-label classification. In: Buntine, W., Grobelnik, M., Mladenić, D., Shawe-Taylor, J. (eds.) ECML PKDD 2009, Part II. LNCS, vol. 5782, pp. 254–269. Springer, Heidelberg (2009)
12. Page, E.S.: Continuous inspection schemes. Biometrika **41**(1/2), 100–115 (1954)
13. Ikonomovska, E., Gama, J., Dzeroski, S.: Learning model trees from evolving data streams. Data Min. Knowl. Discov. **23**(1), 128–168 (2011)
14. Hoeffding, W.: Probability inequalities for sums of bounded random variables. J. Am. Stat. Assoc. **58**(301), 13–30 (1963)
15. Sorower, M.S.: A Literature Survey on Algorithms for Multi-label Learning. Oregon State University, Corvallis (2010)
16. Gama, J., Sebastião, R., Rodrigues, P.P.: On evaluating stream learning algorithms. Mach. Learn. **90**(3), 317–346 (2013)
17. Mencía, E.L., Fürnkranz, J.: Pairwise learning of multilabel classifications with perceptrons. In: Proceedings of the International Joint Conference on Neural Networks, IJCNN 2008, Part of the IEEE World Congress on Computational Intelligence, WCCI 2008, Hong Kong, China, 1–6 June 2008, pp. 2899–2906 (2008)

Predicting Hardness of Travelling Salesman Problem Instances

Miguel Cárdenas-Montes[(✉)]

Department of Fundamental Research,
Centro de Investigaciones Energéticas Medioambientales y Tecnológicas,
Madrid, Spain
`miguel.cardenas@ciemat.es`

Abstract. Travelling Salesman Problem is a classical combinatorial problem which is used to check the performance of heuristics and meta-heuristics. However, for fairly comparing the performance of these algorithms, it is necessary an in-depth understanding of the hardness of the Travelling Salesman Problem instances. This requires to recognize which attributes allow a correct prediction of the hardness of the instances of Travelling Salesman Problem. In this work, the hardness of the instances was predicted based on the statistical distribution of the distance between the cities, the areas arisen from the Dirichlet tessellation, and the areas from the Delaunay triangulation. As a consequence of this work, the attributes which separate the ease and difficult instances of the Travelling Salesman Problem are stated.

Keywords: Travelling Salesman Problem · Instance difficulty · Random forests · Dirichlet tessellation · Delaunay triangulation

1 Introduction

Travelling Salesman Problem (TSP) is intensively used for checking the performance of combinatorial algorithms [1,2]. However, not always the proposed algorithms are confronted to TSP instances with the adequate hardness intensity; even if TPS is declared as NP-hard problem [3].

In the past, some efforts for finding hardness evaluators have been done [4,5]. Not only these are necessary, but also which features allow an accurate classification of instances as ease or difficult to solve. By understanding these features, and specifically the ranges of values for these features which separate high-difficult instances from others, they can be used as criteria for creating hard-to-solve instances. This will allow confront the new algorithms to a set well-recognized hard TSP instances. In this work, some spatial features were evaluated as attributes to classify, by using Random Forests, TSP instances as hard or ease. To the author' knowledge, no similar works in this line have been proposed.

The rest of the paper is organized as follows: Sect. 2 summarizes the Related Work and previous efforts done. Relevant aspects of the methodology are introduced in Sect. 3. The Results and the Analysis are shown in Sect. 4. And finally, the Conclusions and Future Work are presented in Sect. 5.

© Springer International Publishing Switzerland 2016
O. Luaces et al. (Eds.): CAEPIA 2016, LNAI 9868, pp. 68–78, 2016.
DOI: 10.1007/978-3-319-44636-3_7

2   Related Work

Regarding the previous efforts done in this area, in [6] two algorithms for solving TSP are presented. This work uses as benchmark two TSP instances with 13 cities and 9 cities respectively. Comparing with the current problem sizes, these tiny problem sizes are revealing how the capacity to produce high-quality solutions has evolved, and how to rely on high-difficult instances is currently more necessary. For a more complete review of the problem, the reader is referred to [1,7] for more information.

The existence of a transition phase in TSP is cited in [4]. This issue arises from the transformation of the TSP into a binary decision problem under the question, *can an algorithm find a solution with a tour length less that l?*. The transition phase ease-hard-ease in relation to the difficulty to find a new solution to a TSP instance with a shorter tour length is analysed. Authors place this transition phase at $\frac{l}{\sqrt{N \cdot A}} \approx 0.75$, where N is the number of particles, A the area covered by the cities and l the tour length.

In [8], a prediction of the relationships between the performance of the algorithms and the critical feature of TSP instances is investigated. The paper provides a methodology to determine if the metadata is sufficient for predicting the instances hardness. In this work, the experimental set-up is composed of instances of 100 cities randomly generated in a squared area of 400 units. The TSP instances are evolved using a evolutionary algorithm, particularly a genetic algorithm: new instances are created by using uniform crossover and mutation. The criterion for classify as easy or as hard the instances is based on the effort done by two Lin-Kernighan heuristic methods [9] to solve the TSP instance: chained Lin-Kernighan [10] and Lin-Kernighan with cluster compensation [11]. In [12] a major revision and extension of [8] is done by extending the methodology to the most popular combinational problems.

3   Methodology

In this work, Random Forests is used for classifying TSP instances in hard- or ease-to solve through spatial features. They included the distribution of area emerging from the Dirichlet tessellation and from the Delaunay triangulation. The minimum and maximum sizes, the mean, variance, skewness and kurtosis of the distribution of the normalized areas were used as attributes. The same information from the Euclidean distance between the cities was also checked as attributes for the hardness classification of the instances.

The process was as follows: initially the instances were classified as ease or difficult by their closeness to the phase transition ease-hard-ease [4]. This phase transition takes place in the nearby of $\frac{l}{\sqrt{N \cdot A}} \approx 0.75$, where N is the number of particles, A the area covered by the cities and l the tour length (see Sect. 3.2). Two outputs were considered in this work. On the one hand, the value of the numerical parameter $|\frac{l}{\sqrt{N \cdot A}} - 0.75|$; and on the other hand, the categorical labels: ease "E" and difficult "D". These label were assigned to the instances depending on the following expression for the difficult instances $|\frac{l}{\sqrt{N \cdot A}} - 0.75| < 0.10$; and ease label otherwise. Later, by using Random Forests (see Sect. 3.3) based on the previous mentioned spatial features, both outputs were predicted.

3.1 Travelling Salesman Problem

The TSP can be expressed as shown in Eqs. 1 and 2.

$$x_{ij} = \begin{cases} 1 & \text{the path goes from city } i \text{ to city } j \\ 0 & \text{otherwise} \end{cases} \tag{1}$$

where $x_{ij} = 1$ if city i is connected with city j, and $x_{ij} = 0$ otherwise.

For $i = 0, ..., n$, let u_i be an artificial variable, and finally take c_{ij} to be the distance from city i to city j. Then TSP can be written as shown in Eq. 2.

$$\begin{aligned} \min \sum_{i=0}^{n} \sum_{j \neq i, j=0}^{n} c_{ij} x_{ij} & \\ 0 \leq x_{ij} \leq 1 \qquad & i, j = 0, \cdots, n \\ u_i \in \mathbf{Z} \qquad & i = 0, \cdots, n \\ \sum_{i=0, i \neq j}^{n} x_{ij} = 1 \qquad & j = 0, \cdots, n \\ \sum_{j=0, j \neq i}^{n} x_{ij} = 1 \qquad & i = 0, \cdots, n \\ u_i - u_j + n x_{ij} \leq n - 1 \qquad & 1 \leq i \neq j \leq n \end{aligned} \tag{2}$$

The purpose of TSP is to find the shortest tour between a set of cities. In the symmetric version of TSP —variant used in this work—, the cost of joining two cities does not depend on the departure city, only on the pair of cities.

The TSP instances used as benchmarks in this work have been extracted from http://comopt.ifi.uni-heidelberg.de/software/TSPLIB95/. Among the instances published in this site, 20 instances with optimal solution have been selected. The figure in the names indicates the number of cities conforming the TSP instance.

3.2 Ease-Hard-Ease Phase Transition

In [4], for Euclidean TSP instances in the plane the existence of a phase transition – ease-hard-ease – for the TSP decision problem when seeking an answer to the question if a tour with length less than l exists for a certain instance is indicated. Given the parameters, A the area where the cities are spread out and N the number of cities, the decision problem becomes more difficult for instances with $\frac{l}{\sqrt{N \cdot A}} \approx 0.75$. Therefore, the closeness of $\frac{l}{\sqrt{N \cdot A}}$ to 0.75 can provide an auxiliary hardness rank for comparison purposes. In Table 1, this parameter is presented

Table 1. Values of the transition phase parameter $\frac{l}{\sqrt{N \cdot A}}$ in [4] for the TSP instances used in this work. Transition phase ease-hard-ease occurs at $\frac{l}{\sqrt{N \cdot A}} \approx 0.75$.

	Critical parameter: $\frac{l}{\sqrt{N \cdot A}}$	$\left\lvert \frac{l}{\sqrt{N \cdot A}} - 0.75 \right\rvert$
gr202	1.86	1.11
eil51	1.05	0.80
ulysses22	1.12	0.37
ulysses16	1.10	0.35
eil76	1.03	0.28
eil101	0.98	0.23
bays29	0.96	0.21
pa561	0.87	0.12
gr666	0.64	0.11
st70	0.86	0.11
gr120	0.81	0.06
rd100	0.81	0.06
gr96	0.70	0.05
ch130	0.78	0.03
ch150	0.78	0.03
kroD100	0.77	0.02
kroA100	0.77	0.02
berlin52	0.74	0.01
att48	0.76	0.01
kroC100	0.75	0.00

for the TSP instances of this work. Based on this criterion, the instances with $\left\lvert \frac{l}{\sqrt{N \cdot A}} - 0.75 \right\rvert < 0.10$ were classified as difficult, class "D", whereas the remaining ones were classified as ease, class "E". This limit is completely arbitrary but it allows a division of the data set in two balanced classes.

3.3 Random Forests

Random Forests [13] is a decision tree which incorporates ensemble learning. Random Forests is composed of many independent classification trees. Each tree is grown to the largest extent possible (no pruning). Random Forests incorporates Bagging [14] for creating each tree – each tree corresponds to a individual model in the ensemble. Each tree is trained with a slightly different training set, each one is a bootstrap set.

Additionally to the use of a different bootstrap sample for each tree (bagging), Random Forests proposes an extra layer of randomness. A random selection of features is executed to split each node, random subspace method [15].

In each node split, the best ones among a subset of predictors, randomly selected among the overall predictors, are employed. Thanks to this construction, Random Forests minimizes the overfitting risk and at the same time it is specially recommended when dealing with high-dimensional data sets.

In order to perform a classification or a regression action for an instance, it is predicted by each tree composing the Random Forests. In case of classification, the class of the instance is assigned by the majority of votes. If the case corresponds to a regression, the average value of each tree is calculated and assigned to the instance.

In detail the algorithm works as follows: for each tree a training set sampled with replacement is drawn from the original data set. This is the training or learning sample, LS. The LS is used to fit a tree without pruning. In each split only a randomly sub-set of predictors, approximately one tier, is used. Due to this sampling method, about one-third of the cases are left out of the training set. This is the *out of bag data*, OOB, and it is used for estimate of the classification error and the variable importance.

Due to the construction mechanism, Random Forests encompasses some relevant features, among others: high accuracy, estimation of the importance of variables, handling of unbalanced data set, or proximity measure. In this work the R package *randomForest* [16] is used with a configuration of a total of 500 trees and the vote not normalized, and deldir package [17] for the calculation of the areas emerging from the Dirichlet tessellation and from the Delaunay triangulation.

3.4   Matthews Correlation Coefficient

Matthews Correlation Coefficient (MCC) (Eq. 3) [18] is an elaborated index, applicable to binary classification, ranking from -1 to 1, where a value of 1 means a perfect prediction, -1 a fully incorrect prediction, and 0 a random prediction. MCC is an aggregate objective function aimed at resuming the information of the confusion matrix. In the analysis, it is employed to assess the quality of the prediction.

$$MCC = \frac{TP \cdot TN - FP \cdot FN}{\sqrt{(TP + FP)(TP + FN)(TN + FP)(TN + FN)}} \tag{3}$$

4   Analysis

In this section, diverse sets of spatial attributes of the TSP instances are used to predict ease and hard instances. They include the statistical distribution of the distance between the cities, the areas arisen from the Dirichlet tessellation, and the areas from the Delaunay triangulation. The hardness of the instances is predicted by using Random Forests.

4.1 Delaunay Triangulation Based Prediction

In order to asses the quality of the prediction when using the attributes arisen from the distribution of the normalized area[1] of Delaunay triangles, the confusion matrix was used (Table 2). From the distribution of these areas the following information was incorporated in the prediction model: minimum, maximum, mean, variance, skewness and kurtosis of the normalized areas. Random Forests with these attributes produced an error rate of 10 % for predicting the instances of class "D", whereas for the class "E" the algorithm exhibited a larger error rate, 30 %. The value of the MCC quality index for this prediction was 0.61.

Table 2. Confusion matrix from the classification of the TSP instances when predicting hardness variable with the attributes of the area of Delaunay triangulation. The OOB estimate of error rate for class "E" is 30 %, and for class "D" is 10 %, so that the mean error rate is 20.0 %.

	Classified D	Classified E
True D	9	1
True E	3	7

Random Forests algorithm permits interrogating about the percentage of votes of each class obtained by the instances (Table 3). This allows discovering which TSP instances are being misclassified. Concretely, for instances gr202, eil76, pa561 and att48 the majority vote for the class and the actual class did not coincide.

If the prediction is performed over the parameter $|\frac{l}{\sqrt{N \cdot A}} - 0.75|$, instead of over the categorical variable hardness (classes "D" and "E"), then the mean of squared error[2] was 0.11. The difference with the previous parameter for each TSP instance is presented in Table 3 (forth column).

4.2 Dirichlet Tessellation Based Prediction

When replacing the Delaunay triangles areas by the areas generated by the Dirichlet tessellation – both normalized to the total area of the TSP instance, then an improvement in the class prediction was produced (Table 4). As previously, the following information relative to the distribution of cells areas was incorporated in the prediction model: minimum, maximum, mean, variance, skewness and kurtosis. Regarding the comparison with the previous study, while maintaining an error rate of 10 % for the prediction of class "D", the prediction with the Dirichlet tessellation areas achieved an error rate of 10 % also for class "E" (for Delaunay triangulation the error rate for class "E" as 30 %).

---

[1] The area of the Delaunay triangles are normalized to the total area covered by the cities.

[2] The mean squared error (MSE) is the average of the squares of the differences between the predicted and actual values, $MSE = \frac{1}{N} \sum_N (\hat{y}_i - y_i)^2$, where N is the number of samples and $\hat{y}_i$ is the prediction of the value y_i.

Table 3. Percentages of votes for classes "E" and "D" for each TSP instances when predicting with the attributes of the area of Delaunay triangulation. The differences between the value $|\frac{l}{\sqrt{N \cdot A}} - 0.75|$ and the predicted one are also presented.

TSP instance	% Votes D	% Votes E	Hardness class	Difference with $|\frac{l}{\sqrt{N \cdot A}} - 0.75|$
gr202	54	46	E	0.53
eil51	18	82	E	0.34
ulysses22	27	73	E	−0.06
ulysses16	14	86	E	−0.10
eil76	52	48	E	0.07
eil101	45	55	E	0.00
bays29	20	80	E	−0.15
pa561	74	26	E	−0.01
st70	35	65	E	−0.09
gr666	42	58	E	−0.26
gr120	57	43	D	0.00
rd100	93	7	D	0.01
gr96	60	30	D	−0.01
ch150	63	37	D	−0.04
ch130	74	26	D	−0.06
kroA100	95	5	D	−0.01
kroD100	98	2	D	−0.01
berlin52	55	45	D	−0.10
att48	42	58	D	−0.15
kroC100	98	2	D	−0.02

Table 4. Confusion matrix from the classification of the TSP instances when predicting hardness variable with the attributes of the area of Dirichlet tessellation. The OOB estimate of error rate for class "D" is 10 %, and for class "E" is 10 %, so that the mean error rate is 10.0 %.

	Classified D	Classified E
True D	9	1
True E	1	9

As a consequence of the use of attributes of Dirichlet tessellation instead of Delaunay triangulation, the MCC index improved from 0.61 to 0.80.

When using the attributes from the distribution of the areas of the Dirichlet tessellation, two instances were misclassified – eil101 and att48, each one corresponding to one of the classes. The instance att48 was also misclassified with the attributes of the previous study.

Table 5. Percentages of votes for classes "E" and "D" for each TSP instances when predicting with the attributes of the area of Dirichlet tessellation. The differences between the value $|\frac{l}{\sqrt{N \cdot A}} - 0.75|$ and the predicted one are also presented.

TSP instance	% Votes D	% Votes E	Hardness class	Difference with $|\frac{l}{\sqrt{N \cdot A}} - 0.75|$
gr202	49	51	E	0.38
eil51	18	82	E	0.34
ulysses22	36	64	E	0.00
ulysses16	14	86	E	−0.07
eil76	28	72	E	0.03
eil101	92	8	E	0.10
bays29	40	60	E	−0.11
pa561	46	3	E	−0.03
st70	21	79	E	−0.06
gr666	30	70	E	−0.16
gr120	65	35	D	−0.02
rd100	81	19	D	−0.01
gr96	73	27	D	−0.02
ch150	74	26	D	−0.03
ch130	80	20	D	−0.01
kroA100	70	30	D	−0.03
kroD100	76	26	D	−0.04
berlin52	64	36	D	−0.08
att48	42	58	D	−0.13
kroC100	76	24	D	−0.03

When the prediction was performed over the parameter $|\frac{l}{\sqrt{N \cdot A}} - 0.75|$, the mean of squared error diminished until 0.09 (Table 5). This suggests that Dirichlet tessellation attributes better predicts the hardness – categorical and numerical outputs – of the TSP instances.

4.3 Distance Based Prediction

Additionally to the information extracted from the distribution of areas coming from the Dirichlet tessellation and the Delaunay triangulation, the distribution of distances between the cities can be used for constructing a predictor of the hardness of the TSP instances. Similarly to the previous studies, the minimum distance between the cites, the maximum, the mean, the variance, the skewness and the kurtosis of the distances were used as attributes. In Table 6, the confusion matrix for the classification is presented. As can be appreciated, for the attributes coming from the statistic of the distance between the cities, the lowest success

Table 6. Confusion matrix from the classification of the TSP instances when predicting hardness variable with the attributes of the statistic of distance. The OOB estimate of error rate for class "E" is 40 %, and for class "D" is 20 %, so that the mean error rate is 30 %.

	Classified D	Classified E
True D	8	2
True E	4	6

Table 7. Percentages of votes for classes "E" and "D" for each TSP instances when predicting with the attributes of the statistic of distance. The differences between the value $|\frac{l}{\sqrt{N \cdot A}} - 0.75|$ and the predicted one are also presented.

TSP instance	% Votes D	% Votes E	Hardness class	Difference with $|\frac{l}{\sqrt{N \cdot A}} - 0.75|$
gr202	07	93	E	0.39
eil51	28	72	E	0.23
ulysses22	4	96	E	−0.13
ulysses16	4	96	E	−0.14
eil76	28	72	E	−0.03
eil101	35	65	E	−0.03
bays29	83	17	E	0.08
pa561	98	2	E	0.04
st70	64	36	E	−0.01
gr666	76	24	E	−0.02
gr120	30	70	D	−0.02
rd100	61	39	D	−0.01
gr96	3	97	D	−0.14
ch150	51	49	D	−0.03
ch130	53	47	D	−0.03
kroA100	86	14	D	−0.00
kroD100	95	5	D	−0.00
berlin52	64	36	D	−0.03
att48	71	29	D	−0.02
kroC100	70	30	D	−0.02

ratios were achieved. The error rate for class "D" was 20 %, whereas for class "E" was 40 %. With this quality values, the MCC index diminished to 0.41.

By using the statistical distribution of distances for predicting the hardness class of the TSP instances, the largest number of misclassification cases was produced: bays29, pa561, st70, gr666, gr120 and gr96. It is appreciated a clear increment in the number of instances misclassified.

On the other hand, when predicting the parameter $|\frac{l}{\sqrt{N \cdot A}} - 0.75|$ (forth column in Table 7), then the mean squared error obtained was the lowest of the three studies performed, 0.06. Although the prediction based on the distribution of distances produced the largest number of misclassified cases, at the same time it was able to generate the best prediction on the parameter $|\frac{l}{\sqrt{N \cdot A}} - 0.75|$.

5 Conclusions and Future Work

In this paper, a study of the attributes which allow an efficient prediction of the hardness of instances of Travelling Salesman Problem – the class and the numerical value of hardness parameter – was performed. Three main groups of spatial attributes were used. They derive from the characterization of the distribution of distances between the cities, and the distribution of normalized areas coming from the tessellation of Dirichlet and the triangulation of Delaunay.

From the prediction of the hardness class point-of-view, the better prediction was obtained when using the information obtained from the Dirichlet tessellation, whereas the lowest mean squared error for the hardness-parameter prediction was achieved when using the attributes based on the distance between the cities. This divergence in the results suggests merging the information sources for a better prediction.

As future work, an in-depth follow-up of the research about the difficulty of the TSP instances, their attributes for allowing an efficient prediction of the instance hardness and, the mechanism to create hard-to-solve instances are proposed.

Acknowledgement. The research leading to these results has received funding by the Spanish Ministry of Economy and Competitiveness (MINECO) for funding support through the grant FPA2013-47804-C2-1-R, and "Unidad de Excelencia María de Maeztu": CIEMAT - FÍSICA DE PARTÍCULAS through the grant MDM-2015-0509.

References

1. Gutin, G., Punnen, A.P. (eds.): The Traveling Salesman Problem and Its Variations. Combinatorial Optimization. Kluwer Academic, Dordrecht (2002)
2. Blum, C.: Hybrid metaheuristics in combinatorial optimization: a tutorial. In: Dediu, A.-H., Martín-Vide, C., Truthe, B. (eds.) TPNC 2012. LNCS, vol. 7505, pp. 1–10. Springer, Heidelberg (2012)
3. Garey, M.R., Johnson, D.S.: Computers and Intractability: A Guide to the Theory of NP-Completeness. W. H. Freeman, New York (1979)
4. Gent, I.P., Walsh, T.: The TSP phase transition. Artif. Intell. **88**(1–2), 349–358 (1996)
5. Cárdenas-Montes, M.: Evaluating the difficulty of instances of the travelling salesman problem in the nearby of the optimal solution based on random walk exploration. In: Martínez-Álvarez, F., Troncoso, A., Quintián, H., Corchado, E. (eds.) HAIS 2016. LNCS, vol. 9648, pp. 299–310. Springer, Heidelberg (2016). doi:10.1007/978-3-319-32034-2_25

6. Lin, S.: Computer solutions of the traveling salesman problem. Bell Syst. Tech. J. **44**(10), 2245–2269 (1965)
7. Applegate, D.L., Bixby, R.E., Chvatal, V., Cook, W.J.: The Traveling Salesman Problem: A Computational Study. Princeton Series in Applied Mathematics. Princeton University Press, Princeton (2007)
8. Smith-Miles, K., van Hemert, J., Lim, X.Y.: Understanding TSP difficulty by learning from evolved instances. In: Blum, C., Battiti, R. (eds.) LION 4. LNCS, vol. 6073, pp. 266–280. Springer, Heidelberg (2010)
9. Lin, S., Kernighan, B.W.: An effective heuristic algorithm for the travelling-salesman problem. Oper. Res. **21**, 498–516 (1973)
10. Applegate, D., Cook, W.J., Rohe, A.: Chained Lin-Kernighan for large traveling salesman problems. INFORMS J. Comput. **15**(1), 82–92 (2003)
11. Johnson, D.S., McGeoch, L.A.: Experimental Analysis of Heuristics for the STSP. Wiley, London (2001)
12. Smith-Miles, K., Lopes, L.: Measuring instance difficulty for combinatorial optimization problems. Comput. OR **39**(5), 875–889 (2012)
13. Breiman, L.: Random forests. Mach. Learn. **45**(1), 5–32 (2001)
14. Breiman, L.: Bagging predictors. Mach. Learn. **24**(2), 123–140 (1996)
15. Ho, T.K.: The random subspace method for constructing decision forests. IEEE Trans. Pattern Anal. Mach. Intell. **20**(8), 832–844 (1998)
16. Liaw, A., Wiener, M.: Classification and regression by randomForest. R News **2**(3), 18–22 (2002)
17. Turner, R.: deldir: Delaunay Triangulation and Dirichlet (Voronoi) Tessellation. R package version 0.1-9 (2015)
18. Matthews, B.: Comparison of the predicted and observed secondary structure of T4 phage lysozyme. Biochim. Biophys. Acta (BBA) - Protein Struct. **405**(2), 442–451 (1975)

Learning from Label Proportions via an Iterative Weighting Scheme and Discriminant Analysis

M. Pérez-Ortiz[1]([✉]), P.A. Gutiérrez[2], M. Carbonero-Ruz[1],
and C. Hervás-Martínez[2]

[1] Department of Quantitative Methods,
Universidad Loyola Andalucía, Córdoba, Spain
mariaperez@uloyola.es

[2] Department of Computer Science and Numerical Analysis,
University of Córdoba, Córdoba, Spain

Abstract. Learning from label proportions is the term used for the learning paradigm where the training data is provided in groups (or "bags"), and only the label proportion for each bag is known. The objective is to learn a model to predict the class labels of individual instances. This paradigm presents very different applications, specially concerning anonymous data. Two different iterative strategies are proposed to deal with this type of problems, both based on optimising the class membership of the instances using the estimated pattern distribution per bag and the label proportions. Discriminant analysis is reformulated to deal with non-crisp class memberships. A thorough set of experiments is conducted to test: (1) the performance gap between these approaches and the fully supervised setting, (2) the potential advantages of optimising class memberships by our proposals, and (3) the influence of factors such as the bag size and the number of classes of the problem in the performance.

Keywords: Weakly supervised learning · Discriminant analysis · Label proportions · Classification

1 Introduction

With the advent of the big data era and the increased popularity of machine learning, the number of scientific data-driven applications is growing at an abrupt pace. The recently coined term weak supervision [3] refers to those classification learning problems where the labelling information is not as accessible as in the fully-supervised problem. An example is the semi-supervised setting, where one tries to learn a predictive function using both labelled and unlabelled data.

Recently, a new paradigm, known as learning from label proportions, has emerged and joined these learning settings, drawing significant attention from the machine learning community [2,4,6]. In this setting, training instances are provided as disjoint groups or "bags", and only the proportions of the labels are available for each bag. In the same vein than classical supervised classification,

© Springer International Publishing Switzerland 2016
O. Luaces et al. (Eds.): CAEPIA 2016, LNAI 9868, pp. 79–88, 2016.
DOI: 10.1007/978-3-319-44636-3_8

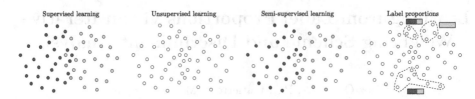

Fig. 1. Graphical representation of different learning paradigms, where each colour is a class (and non coloured instances are unsupervised).

the objective remains that of classifying new individual instances, as opposed to multiple-instance learning, where the objective is to classify new bags. This paradigm presents very different applications concerning problems of black-box nature, anonymous data and non-monitoring processes. For example, suppose that we aim to create a model for poll prediction, given a set of socioeconomic variables of the person. The commonly available data is the information obtained from the different polling stations, i.e. different sets or bags of people, where we do not know what each person has voted, but the final vote proportions.

Although learning from incomplete label information (e.g., semi-supervised learning) has been extensively studied, there are relatively few works on learning from label proportions (also known as aggregate outputs) [1,2,4–8]. Most works concerning learning from label proportions consider probabilistic classifiers [2, 4,7], since these are able to work with class-probabilities. But other algorithms have also been adapted, such as artificial neural networks [5] or support vector machines [5,8]. Recently, a complexity upper bound has been derived for binary classification [2], stating that the complexity scales exponentially with respect to the number of samples of each bag and that the performance of such algorithms decreases universally as the number of classes increases. Despite the novelty and promising results of related works, further research should be done in this topic.

In this paper, two simple new approaches are proposed to be used with discriminant analysis, although other classifiers can be used as well. The basic idea behind our proposal is to refine iteratively the initial class-probabilities (estimated through label proportions) based on two different sources of information (the location of the examples in the input space or, alternatively, the probabilities estimated by the classifier). Instead of approaching the problem using a transductive setting, we reformulate the linear discriminant analysis to deal with this uncertainty. We devise two differentiated approaches: a filter approach, which relies on a distance-based measure, and a wrapper one, which uses discriminant analysis internally. The experiments conducted comprise a total of 28 classification datasets: 14 binary and 14 multiclass, with up to 21 classes (note that the multiclass setting has been barely explored in this area [2,4,6,8]). In this sense, our experiments try to answer different questions with a thorough experimental setting: Firstly, whether is it possible to build a useful classifier given only data groups and the associated label proportions of each group. Secondly, how does our approach solves this problem when compared to the fully-supervised case. Finally, whether the data complexity (represented by different bag sizes and multiple classes) poses a serious hindrance for the learning.

The rest of the paper is organised as follows: Sect. 2 presents previous notions and the proposed methodologies; Sect. 3 analyses the experiments and results; and finally, Sect. 4 outlines some conclusions and future work.

2 Methodology

The goal in supervised classification is to assign an input vector $\mathbf{x} \in \mathbb{R}^m$ to one of K discrete classes c_k, where $k \in \{1, \ldots, K\}$. Let N be the number of instances in the sample and N_k the number of samples for the k-th class. The final objective is to find a prediction function $f : X \to Y$ by using an i.i.d. sample $D = \{\mathbf{x}^i, y^i\}_{i=1}^N \in X \times Y$. A more formal definition of the learning from label proportions setting is given now. Suppose, a dataset composed of N training data and divided in b bags $D = B_1 \cup B_2 \cup \ldots \cup B_b$, where $B_i \cap B_j = \emptyset$, $\forall i \neq j$. A bag $B_i = \{\mathbf{x}^{i1}, \mathbf{x}^{i2}, \ldots, \mathbf{x}^{iN_i}\}$ groups N_i instances and provides the only supervised information: the counts C_{ik} which indicate the number of instances in B_i that belong to class label c_k. Similarly, bag class information can be provided in terms of proportions, $p_{ik} = \frac{C_{ik}}{N_i} \in [0, 1]$ with $\sum_{c_k \in Y} p_{ik} = 1$.

Figure 1 shows a comparison between the considered paradigm and other learning settings. Note that in the case of label proportions only some of the instances have been grouped. As said, the only information known is the label proportions per bag The difficulty resides in associating each instance with its label, which can be thought as uncertainty associated to the label proportions. Given that each bag would have its own label proportion and involves different uncertainty, we could define two types of bags: full bags (composed of instances of the same class) and non-full bags (composed of data from different classes).

The approach proposed considers Linear Discriminant Analysis (LDA), although it can also be applied with its kernel version and other classifiers. Although the original LDA method does not consider probabilities or pattern-weights, its formulation can be easily transformed to take them into account.

2.1 Fully-Supervised LDA

This learning paradigm is one of the pioneer techniques in the machine learning area, given its wide use for supervised dimensionality reduction and classification. The main goal is to find the optimal linear projection for the data. To do so, the algorithm analyses two objectives: the maximisation of the between-class distance and the minimisation of the within-class distance, by using covariance matrices ($\mathbf{S}_b$ and $\mathbf{S}_w$ respectively) and the so-called Rayleigh coefficient ($J(\boldsymbol{\beta}) = \frac{\boldsymbol{\beta}^T \mathbf{S}_b \boldsymbol{\beta}}{\boldsymbol{\beta}^T \mathbf{S}_w \boldsymbol{\beta}}$, where $\boldsymbol{\beta}$ is the projection). To achieve these objectives, the K eigenvectors associated to the highest eigenvalues of $\mathbf{S}_w^{-1} \cdot \mathbf{S}_b$ are computed, which represent the projection, later used as a discriminant or visualisation technique.

2.2   Weakly-Supervised LDA

The LDA relies on a representation of the classes via covariance matrices. To use label proportions and assist this representation, the class means and within-class covariance matrix can be reformulated using a weighting scheme as follows:

$$\mu_k = \frac{\sum_{i=1}^{b} \sum_{j=1}^{N_i} p_{ik} \mathbf{x}^{ij}}{\sum_{i=1}^{b} p_{ik} \cdot N_i}, \; k = 1, \ldots, K, \tag{1}$$

$$\mathbf{S}_w = \frac{1}{p} \sum_{k=1}^{K} \sum_{i=1}^{b} \sum_{j=1}^{N_i} p_{ik} [\mathbf{x}^{ijk} - \mu_k][\mathbf{x}^{ijk} - \mu_k]^T, \tag{2}$$

where $\mathbf{p}_{ij} = \{p_{i1}, \ldots, p_{iK}\}$, $p = \sum_{k=1}^{K} \sum_{i=1}^{b} p_{ik} \cdot N_i$, and p_{ik} are the initial class probability for B_i and c_k (derived from the label proportions). By this approach, we consider that all instances in the bag have the same probability distribution, i.e. the one established for the bag in the dataset (p_{ik}). Moreover, these equations indicate that the data with a higher membership for class c_k (e.g. those within full bags) will contribute more to the mean and within-class covariance of this class, which are thereafter used for the projection computation step. This approach will be referred as Simple Weighting Scheme (SWS-LDA).

2.3   A Distance-Based Filter Approach to Weakly-Supervised LDA

As stated before, the given label proportions can be used as a preliminary estimation of the associated class probabilities per pattern. Instead of assuming the same probability distribution for all instances in the bag, our first proposal is to refine these class probabilities iteratively based on the location of each pattern in the input space (i.e. refine pattern-class membership using the distance to the different classes of the problem). To do so, our methodology relies on the previous definition of mean per class (Eq. 1) and makes use of a specific distance relation. One of the most important characteristics of our proposal is that when refining these class memberships, original label proportions are maintained, as this is the only true supervised information available.

For a visual analysis of the proposal see Fig. 2, where a hypothetical bag of three examples B_1 and the class distributions are represented in the input space. In this case, it can be seen that the main uncertainty is posed on $\mathbf{x}^{12}$, which lies in the intersection between c_1 and c_2. The original label proportions for this bag are $p_{11} = \frac{2}{3}$ and $p_{12} = \frac{1}{3}$ (i.e. two instances within B_1 belong to c_1 and one of them to c_2). In this case (and specially for $\mathbf{x}^{11}$ and $\mathbf{x}^{13}$), it is clear that these initial probabilities can be refined using the pattern distribution, since this distribution gives us additional information about their potential class membership. Note that without any prior information, because of the location of x^{12} (in an overlapping region between c_1 and c_2), it would have equal probability of belonging to both classes, however, in this case, as label proportions are used for the refinement step as well, $\mathbf{x}^{12}$ would be assigned to c_1.

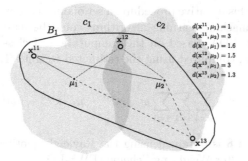

Fig. 2. Representation of the proposal where $p_{11} = \frac{2}{3}$ and $p_{12} = \frac{1}{3}$. These class probabilities can be refined using a distance relation to class centroids, resulting in $\mathbf{x}^{11}$ and $\mathbf{x}^{12}$ presenting a greater probability of belonging to c_1 and $\mathbf{x}^{13}$ to c_2.

The first step is the computation of the means per class using Eq. 1. In this sense, μ_k estimates the value of the mean for class c_k. Then, the relative distance of each pattern to each mean is computed using the approximated means:

$$P(y^{ij} = c_k|\mathbf{x}^{ij}) = p^*_{ijk} = 1 - \frac{d(\mathbf{x}^{ij}, \mu_k)}{\sum_{z=1}^{K} d(\mathbf{x}^{ij}, \mu_z)}, \tag{3}$$

where $j = \{1, \ldots, N_i\}$, $k = \{1, \ldots, K\}$, and d represents a distance relation (e.g. the Euclidean distance). The vector $\mathbf{p}^*_{ij} = \{p_{ij1}, \ldots, p_{ijK}\}$ provides information about the relative closeness of $\mathbf{x}^{ij}$ to all the classes, where $\sum_{k=1}^{K} p^*_{ijk} = 1$.

The next step is to refine the associated probabilities based on this distance relation. Note that it is crucial to maintain the original ratios p_{ik} (as this is the only true labelling information). To maintain these ratios while optimising the weights per pattern, the following formulation can be used:

$$w_{ijk} = \frac{p^*_{ijk}}{\sum_{z=1}^{N_i} p^*_{izk}} \cdot C_{ik}, \tag{4}$$

where the first term represents a ranking of relative distances of the instances inside bag B_i, and w_{ijk} represents the associated weight of pattern $\mathbf{x}^{ij}$ with respect to class c_k. Note this formulation ensures $\frac{p^*_{ijk}}{\sum_{z=1}^{N_i} p^*_{izk}} = 1$, $k = 1, \ldots, K$, and thus, when multiplying this by C_{ik}, the original label proportions are maintained.

By the described approach, the initial probability p_{ik} (for pattern $\mathbf{x}^{ij}$) is updated considering the location of the instances of the bag in the space, and a new estimated weight w_{ijk} is obtained. This process could be made iterative, refining again the class means using the new estimated weights as follows:

$$\hat{\mu}_k = \frac{\sum_{i=1}^{b} \sum_{j=1}^{N_i} w_{ijk} \mathbf{x}^{ij}}{\sum_{i=1}^{b} w_{ik} \cdot N_i}. \tag{5}$$

where $w = \sum_{i=1}^{b} \sum_{j=1}^{N_i} \sum_{k=1}^{K} w_{ijk}$. The process is repeated until convergence.

After applying this iterative procedure, a set of optimised weights is obtained. As said, different machine learning algorithms could be used. In this case, we use the well-known LDA, based on the computation of class means and class covariance matrices, computed using the estimated weights (Eq. (5)) and:

$$\hat{\mathbf{S}}_{\mathrm{w}} = \frac{1}{w} \sum_{k=1}^{K} \sum_{i=1}^{b} \sum_{j=1}^{N_i} w_{ijk} [\mathbf{x}^{ijk} - \mu_k][\mathbf{x}^{ijk} - \mu_k]^T. \tag{6}$$

The final projection $\boldsymbol{\beta}$ is obtained using the Rayleigh quotient. This approach will be referred as Filter Weighting Scheme (FWS-LDA).

2.4 A Wrapper Approach to Weakly-Supervised LDA

In this case, the class-membership is refined using the classifier output. Roughly speaking, the classifier (LDA) can be constructed in each iteration using the estimated weights $\mathbf{w}$ (defined previously). Class-probabilities are then estimated from the trained classifier (in the case of LDA, using the projections and the soft-max function). These probabilities are used to further refine $\mathbf{w}$ considering the number of instances in B_i that belong to class label c_k (i.e., C_{ik}).

In the same way than in Sects. 2.2 and 2.3, the methodology here proposed begins with the computation of a set of means per class using Eq. (1), where each pattern $\mathbf{x}^{ij}$ associated to bag B_i contributes with a weight of p_{ik} to the computation of μ_k. Apart from these means per class, the corresponding LDA model is trained: the associated covariance matrix is computed by Eq. (2), and the $\boldsymbol{\beta}$ data projection is obtained using the Rayleigh coefficient.

Once that the initial $\boldsymbol{\beta}$ have been obtained, the probability that pattern $\mathbf{x}^{ij}$ has of belonging to class c_k can be estimated from the projection using the soft-max function:

$$P(y^{ij} = c_k | \mathbf{x}^{ij}) = p^*_{ijk} = \frac{e^{((\mathbf{x}^{ij})^\mathsf{T} \boldsymbol{\beta}_k)}}{\sum_{z=1}^{K} e^{((\mathbf{x}^{ij})^\mathsf{T} \boldsymbol{\beta}_z)}}. \tag{7}$$

In the next step, these probabilities could be refined using the original proportions by applying Eq. (4). This refinement is captured in the associated weights $\mathbf{w}$, which are then used again for constructing the mean per class, the covariance matrix and a new LDA model, using Eqs. (5) and (6). This process is also repeated until convergence. This approach will be referred as Wrapper Weighting Scheme (WWS-LDA).

3 Experiments

The most common application of the studied paradigm involves private data, which reduces the public availability of datasets. Because of this, it is common to use synthetic or classical supervised datasets, and transform them into label proportions. We compare our two proposals for weakly supervised learning in a set of 28 originally supervised benchmark datasets (14 binary and 14 multiclass, with up to 21 classes). We test these proposals using different bag sizes (3, 5 and 10 instances per bag) to study its influence in the classifier performance. These bags are chosen randomly and the same bags are used for all the algorithms. Finally, we also compare the standard supervised learning setting versus learning from label proportions, to analyse the potential difficulties of this paradigm.

The methods considered in these experiments are the following:

- Linear Discriminant Analysis (LDA) using the standard supervised learning setting (i.e. using the labelling information).
- Simple Weighting Scheme (SWS-LDA). This method considers the approach in Sect. 2.2, where the class weights for each pattern are fixed to the initial label proportions. Three different results are obtained in this case depending on the bag size (SWS-LDA-3, SWS-LDA-5 and SWS-LDA-10).
- Filter Weighting Scheme (FWS-LDA). This method implements the approach in Sect. 2.3, where the class weights are iteratively optimised using a distance-based approach. Three different results are obtained in this case depending on the bag size (FWS-LDA-3, FWS-LDA-5 and FWS-LDA-10).
- Wrapper Weighting Scheme (WWS-LDA). This method implements the approach in Sect. 2.4, where the class weights are iteratively optimised using a classifier-based approach. Three different results are obtained in this case depending on the bag size (WWS-LDA-3, WWS-LDA-5 and WWS-LDA-10).

For FWS and WWS, the stop criterion is that new estimated weights change in total less than 10^{-5}.

The metric considered for measuring the performance is the Accuracy (*Acc*).

The experiments have been performed using a 10-fold partition. The characteristics of the datasets can be seen in Table 1 as well as the LDA mean results.

The results of the experiments performed can be seen in Table 2, where the best performing method for each bag size is highlighted in bold face and the second in italics. From these results, several conclusions can be drawn. Firstly, comparing the results of FWS-LDA-3 to the supervised approach (results of LDA in Table 1), it can be seen that generally, the fully supervised setting yields better or similar results when compared to the label proportions proposal. For the binary datasets, the performance is similar in six cases (within a range of 1 % accuracy), better in seven (within a range larger than 1 % of accuracy) and worst for one case (range also larger than 1 %). Using the same ranges, for the multiclass datasets, the fully supervised setting yields similar results to our proposal in four cases, better in nine cases and worst in one. Comparing also WWS-LDA-3 to the supervised approach the results are the following. For the binary setting, the supervised approach obtains similar performance in five datasets (range within 1 %), better in seven cases (within a range larger than 1 %), and worst in two cases. In the multiclass setting and using the same ranges, the supervised approach obtains similar results in seven cases, better in six and worst in one. Although the results could be considered as acceptable with respect to the fully supervised setting, there is still room for improvement, demonstrating the difficulty of this paradigm in the presence of multiple classes and the necessity of refining the proposed and existing

Table 1. Characteristics of the datasets used: number of instances (N), features (m), classes (K) and baseline *Acc* LDA fully supervised results.

Dataset	N	m	K	LDA *Acc*	Dataset	N	m	K	LDA *Acc*
Binary datasets					Multiclass datasets				
Appendicitis	106	7	2	86.73 ± 9.40	Cleveland	297	13	5	58.97 ± 7.60
Bands	365	19	2	66.31 ± 4.36	Dermatology	358	34	6	96.07 ± 3.58
Breast	286	15	2	70.28 ± 5.96	Ecoli	336	7	8	78.29 ± 4.62
Card	690	51	2	86.38 ± 4.17	Flare	1066	38	6	75.70 ± 3.24
Colic	368	60	2	82.23 ± 3.88	Glass	214	9	6	45.78 ± 7.66
Credit-a	690	43	2	85.77 ± 4.72	Hayes-roth	160	4	3	54.38 ± 14.15
Haberman	306	3	2	74.19 ± 4.94	Horse	364	58	3	65.16 ± 8.38
Heart	270	13	2	82.96 ± 5.00	Hypothyroid	3772	33	4	93.03 ± 0.28
Hepatitis	155	19	2	84.54 ± 6.28	Iris	150	4	3	98.00 ± 4.50
Housevotes	232	16	2	96.96 ± 3.58	Nursery	12960	26	5	91.13 ± 0.80
Mammographic	830	5	2	80.36 ± 4.65	Primary-tumor	339	23	21	25.68 ± 5.09
Pima	768	8	2	77.60 ± 4.29	Soybean	683	84	19	94.14 ± 2.94
Sick	3772	33	2	95.57 ± 0.90	Wine	178	13	3	98.86 ± 2.41
Wisconsin	683	9	2	96.04 ± 1.84	Zoo	101	21	7	95.00 ± 5.27

approaches. Moreover, it also shows that the proposed approaches capture the underlying supervised information for most problems.

Secondly, Table 2 shows the superiority of refining the class probabilities by our proposed approaches (FWS-LDA and WWS-LDA), as opposed to using the initial probabilities (SWS-LDA) for all bag sizes (compared to SWS-LDA, FWS-LDA wins in 58 cases out of 84 and WWS-LDA wins in 53 cases). To see this, analyse for example the drastic drop in performance for the iris and wine datasets. Furthermore, it can also be appreciated that WWS-LDA performs slightly better than FWS-LDA (WWS-LDA wins globally on 50 datasets out of 84 when compared to both SWS-LDA and FWS-LDA). Finally, as the difficulty of the problem increases (e.g. when using a larger bag size or number of classes), the FWS-LDA approach presents similar results to SWS-LDA, deviating to a larger extent from the results obtained by LDA and WWS-LDA (e.g. analyse the case of zoo). This shows the complexity of optimising the class probabilities in such domains (specially using only a filter approach) and in general of learning a classifier from only label proportions. However, the wrapper approach (WWS-LDA) maintains good performance even for larger bags and multiclass datasets (see zoo, wine, soy-bean, iris datasets for 5 and 10 instances per bag, where the performance improvement of WWS-LDA with respect to FSW-LDA and SSW-LDA is noticeable). Table 2 shows also the mean results and ranking for each method and situation tested (binary or multiclass datasets and different bag sizes). It can be seen that both methods yield similar results for binary datasets. However, the wrapper approach (WWS-LDA) is more indicated for more complicated scenarios (bigger bag sizes and multiclass datasets), with a

Table 2. Acc test experimental results obtained (in mean and standard deviation) for the different methods and bag sizes (3, 5 and 10).

Binary	SWS-LDA-3	FWS-LDA-3	WWS-LDA-3	SWS-LDA-5	FWS-LDA-5	WWS-LDA-5	SWS-LDA-10	FWS-LDA-10	WWS-LDA-10
appendicitis	79.27 ± 3.55	85.82 ± 8.96	89.55 ± 8.62	80.18 ± 2.77	83.91 ± 4.70	83.09 ± 10.46	80.18 ± 2.77	83.00 ± 5.88	83.91 ± 9.21
bands	65.47 ± 2.70	65.47 ± 2.99	62.74 ± 7.94	63.83 ± 1.27	63.83 ± 1.80	57.24 ± 6.37	63.30 ± 1.02	63.30 ± 1.02	58.09 ± 7.29
breast	70.30 ± 1.43	71.70 ± 2.82	68.17 ± 6.79	70.28 ± 1.69	70.28 ± 1.69	68.84 ± 7.30	70.64 ± 1.49	70.30 ± 1.43	67.44 ± 8.67
card	84.49 ± 6.07	84.20 ± 5.89	85.65 ± 3.58	75.51 ± 4.71	76.52 ± 5.15	84.93 ± 3.50	61.01 ± 3.51	62.61 ± 4.03	85.36 ± 3.45
colic	72.02 ± 6.20	73.91 ± 5.44	81.25 ± 4.52	66.88 ± 6.94	67.95 ± 6.13	75.03 ± 8.92	64.41 ± 2.89	65.50 ± 3.46	73.37 ± 11.80
credit-a	81.88 ± 3.07	82.32 ± 3.39	84.78 ± 4.39	76.67 ± 5.53	79.19 ± 4.98	84.64 ± 4.69	62.75 ± 4.21	64.93 ± 3.73	84.93 ± 5.03
haberman	73.20 ± 1.25	73.54 ± 2.25	76.15 ± 4.03	73.53 ± 1.00	73.86 ± 1.40	74.19 ± 4.91	73.53 ± 1.00	73.86 ± 1.40	73.85 ± 4.38
heart	77.78 ± 7.20	82.59 ± 4.95	77.41 ± 8.63	69.63 ± 7.57	76.67 ± 6.06	76.30 ± 8.41	61.85 ± 3.51	70.37 ± 8.00	73.33 ± 10.00
hepatitis	80.63 ± 4.36	81.29 ± 4.74	74.79 ± 7.69	80.00 ± 1.86	81.29 ± 4.74	75.38 ± 7.68	79.38 ± 2.38	79.38 ± 2.38	80.13 ± 11.35
housevotes	93.48 ± 6.87	95.22 ± 4.78	96.96 ± 3.58	90.07 ± 6.81	91.38 ± 4.59	96.96 ± 3.58	75.85 ± 9.34	89.22 ± 6.87	95.65 ± 5.80
mammographic	80.72 ± 4.29	80.60 ± 4.15	78.67 ± 4.44	80.72 ± 4.95	80.60 ± 4.11	77.71 ± 2.91	78.43 ± 6.26	80.24 ± 4.41	77.11 ± 3.01
pima	70.06 ± 2.88	74.22 ± 4.17	73.91 ± 3.06	65.50 ± 1.17	68.62 ± 1.68	70.19 ± 5.83	64.98 ± 0.59	65.97 ± 0.84	67.32 ± 4.10
sick	93.88 ± 0.08	93.88 ± 0.08	92.58 ± 2.06	93.88 ± 0.08	93.88 ± 0.08	90.27 ± 2.51	93.88 ± 0.08	93.88 ± 0.08	88.23 ± 2.70
wisconsin	85.79 ± 3.96	95.31 ± 2.06	95.46 ± 1.61	75.10 ± 4.37	95.16 ± 1.56	95.32 ± 1.80	65.01 ± 0.48	95.31 ± 1.67	95.02 ± 1.42
Mean	79.21	81.43	81.25	75.84	78.79	79.29	71.09	75.52	78.84
Ranking	2.36	1.71	1.93	2.46	1.68	1.86	2.54	1.75	1.71

Multiclass	SWS-LDA-3	FWS-LDA-3	WWS-LDA-3	SWS-LDA-5	FWS-LDA-5	WWS-LDA-5	SWS-LDA-10	FWS-LDA-10	WWS-LDA-10
cleveland	54.22 ± 1.22	54.56 ± 1.85	57.57 ± 6.11	53.89 ± 0.89	53.89 ± 0.89	50.86 ± 9.18	53.89 ± 0.89	53.89 ± 0.89	49.79 ± 7.54
dermatology	91.61 ± 3.76	93.29 ± 3.78	96.07 ± 3.58	85.74 ± 7.52	87.12 ± 8.10	96.36 ± 2.98	53.09 ± 4.52	56.15 ± 4.69	95.23 ± 4.04
ecoli	56.85 ± 4.95	58.32 ± 4.67	75.00 ± 4.00	48.52 ± 5.11	51.24 ± 5.83	71.69 ± 4.49	43.15 ± 2.24	43.15 ± 2.24	62.21 ± 5.33
flare	75.33 ± 3.33	75.51 ± 3.29	75.61 ± 3.28	71.67 ± 4.20	72.51 ± 3.74	75.23 ± 3.47	37.23 ± 2.98	38.26 ± 3.74	74.30 ± 3.29
glass	32.73 ± 0.78	32.73 ± 0.78	32.73 ± 0.78	32.73 ± 0.78	32.73 ± 0.78	32.73 ± 0.78	32.73 ± 0.78	32.73 ± 0.78	32.73 ± 0.78
hayes-roth	45.63 ± 12.52	47.50 ± 12.22	60.00 ± 9.41	44.38 ± 9.06	45.00 ± 10.54	51.25 ± 9.22	35.63 ± 8.36	38.18 ± 10.40	53.75 ± 12.22
horse	67.33 ± 6.31	67.33 ± 6.13	60.15 ± 9.41	63.48 ± 4.74	62.39 ± 5.15	54.69 ± 7.96	61.82 ± 1.69	61.82 ± 1.69	58.88 ± 10.55
hypothyroid	92.52 ± 0.63	92.55 ± 0.83	88.34 ± 2.30	92.50 ± 0.56	92.42 ± 0.59	89.98 ± 3.37	92.34 ± 0.34	92.34 ± 0.34	88.34 ± 2.62
iris	84.00 ± 10.04	85.33 ± 11.24	98.00 ± 4.50	82.67 ± 11.42	85.33 ± 10.80	98.00 ± 4.50	77.33 ± 7.17	84.00 ± 9.53	98.00 ± 4.50
nursery	90.24 ± 0.71	90.25 ± 0.75	89.97 ± 0.84	89.43 ± 0.72	89.48 ± 0.70	98.97 ± 1.13	86.39 ± 0.65	86.50 ± 0.60	87.99 ± 0.98
primary-tumor	24.79 ± 1.64	24.79 ± 1.64	24.79 ± 1.64	24.79 ± 1.64	24.79 ± 1.64	24.79 ± 1.64	24.79 ± 1.64	24.79 ± 1.64	24.79 ± 1.64
soybean	91.94 ± 2.45	92.08 ± 2.72	93.26 ± 2.54	89.15 ± 3.30	89.30 ± 3.36	93.41 ± 2.80	80.23 ± 3.23	80.08 ± 4.26	90.62 ± 2.24
wine	89.90 ± 6.82	92.71 ± 5.39	99.41 ± 1.86	86.54 ± 11.30	93.89 ± 6.65	98.86 ± 2.41	78.69 ± 9.32	87.68 ± 7.79	98.86 ± 2.41
zoo	79.09 ± 12.07	80.09 ± 12.56	94.00 ± 5.16	59.36 ± 8.88	62.36 ± 12.28	89.09 ± 11.98	46.55 ± 6.68	47.55 ± 6.33	83.09 ± 15.72
Mean	69.73	70.50	74.64	66.06	67.32	72.57	57.42	59.08	71.33
Ranking	2.61	1.82	1.57	2.39	1.89	1.71	2.43	2.00	1.57

12, 25 % of average *Acc* difference for multiclass datasets and bags of 10 instances. It is important to note that this method poses an additional computational load.

4   Conclusions

This paper presents two approaches for learning from label proportions used in conjunction with discriminant analysis. In this setting, the only supervised information is the label proportions for different bags of instances. The proposed methods are based on an iterative refinement of class probabilities or weights. These weights are later used to estimate the class distributions (mean per class and covariance matrices), in order to compute the optimal linear discriminant projection. The results show that this refinement is beneficial and leads to promising results, even when considering the multiclass setting. Moreover, our experiments demonstrate that the complexity grows when increasing the size of the bag and the number of classes.

As future work, the kernel version of this algorithm can be developed, comparing it to previous approaches in the literature. Furthermore, other classification paradigms could be explored such as monotonic classification or ordinal regression, since the problems here considered arise in those settings as well.

Acknowledgment. This work was financed by the TIN2014-54583-C2-1-R project of the Spanish MINECO, by FEDER Funds and by the P11-TIC-7508 project of the Junta de Andalucía, Spain.

References

1. Chen, S., Liu 0015, B., Qian, M., Zhang, C.: Kernel K-means based framework for aggregate outputs classification. In: ICDM Workshops, pp. 356–361. IEEE Computer Society (2009)
2. Fan, K., Zhang, H., Yan, S., Wang, L., Zhang, W., Feng, J.: Learning a generative classifier from label proportions. Neurocomputing **139**, 47–55 (2014)
3. Hernández-González, J., Inza, I., Lozano, J.A.: Weak supervision and other nonstandard classification problems: a taxonomy. Pattern Recognit. Lett. **69**, 49–55 (2016)
4. Hernández-González, J., Iñza, I., Lozano, J.A.: Learning Bayesian network classifiers from label proportions. Pattern Recognit. **46**(12), 3425–3440 (2013)
5. Musicant, D.R., Christensen, J.M., Olson, J.F.: Supervised learning by training on aggregate outputs. In: Proceedings of the 7th IEEE International Conference on Data Mining (ICDM), pp. 252–261
6. Quadrianto, N., Smola, A.J., Caetano, T.S., Le, Q.V.: Estimating labels from label proportions. J. Mach. Learn. Res. **10**, 2349–2374 (2009)
7. Stolpe, M., Morik, K.: Learning from label proportions by optimizing cluster model selection. In: Gunopulos, D., Hofmann, T., Malerba, D., Vazirgiannis, M. (eds.) ECML PKDD 2011, Part III. LNCS, vol. 6913, pp. 349–364. Springer, Heidelberg (2011)
8. Yu, F.X., Liu, D., Kumar, S., Jebara, T., Chang, S.F.: ∝SVM for learning with label proportions. In: Proceedings of the 30th International Conference on Machine Learning, ICML, pp. 504–512 (2013)

WekaBioSimilarity—Extending Weka with Resemblance Measures

César Domínguez, Jónathan Heras$^{(\boxtimes)}$, Eloy Mata, and Vico Pascual

Department of Mathematics and Computer Science,
University of La Rioja, Logroño, Spain
{cesar.dominguez,jonathan.heras,eloy.mata,vico.pascual}@unirioja.es

Abstract. The classification of organisms is a daily-basis task in biology as well as other contexts. This process is usually carried out by comparing a set of descriptors associated with each object. However, general-purpose statistical packages offer a limited number of methods to perform such a comparison, and specific tools are required for each concrete problem. Weka is a freely-available framework that supports both supervised and unsupervised machine-learning algorithms. Here, we present WekaBioSimilarity, an extension of Weka implementing several resemblance measures to compare different kinds of descriptors. Namely, WekaBioSimilarity works with binary, multi-value, string, numerical, and heterogeneous data. WekaBioSimilarity, together with Weka, offers the functionality to classify objects using different resemblance measures, and clustering and classification algorithms. The combination of these two systems can be used as a standalone application or can be incorporated in the workflow of other software systems that require a classification process. WekaBioSimilarity is available at http://wekabiosimilarity.sourceforge.net.

1 Introduction

The classification and resemblance-analysis of objects is one of the most important concerns in several areas such as biology [23], text comparison [14], chemistry [30], geology [15], biometrics [29], complex networks [22], and web data-mining [20] among others. The similarity among objects is obtained through the comparison of a set of descriptors (encoded by means of feature vectors); and such a similarity is the basis to classify the objects into groups. The descriptors depend on the concrete problem, and their possible types are binary, multi-value (also known as nominal), string or numerical.

The most common procedure to classify objects consists of two steps: the computation of a *distance matrix*, and the construction of *clusters*. In the former step, the resemblance information is gathered into a square matrix called the distance matrix: given a list of n objects L, the distance matrix of L is an $n \times n$ matrix where the element of row i and column j encodes the distance between the ith and jth object of L. In the latter step, the distance matrix is used to group objects using clustering algorithms [31]. In several contexts, it is common

© Springer International Publishing Switzerland 2016
O. Luaces et al. (Eds.): CAEPIA 2016, LNAI 9868, pp. 89–98, 2016.
DOI: 10.1007/978-3-319-44636-3_9

to use a special kind of clustering algorithms called hierarchical; the clusters produced by these methods can be visualised using a tree representation (e.g. dendrograms, cladograms and evolutionary trees). The classification process is summarised in Fig. 1.

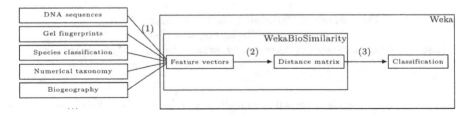

Fig. 1. *Workflow of the classification process proposed by the authors.* In our case, Step (1) is a preprocessing stage that depends on the concrete problem, Step (2) is provided by WekaBioSimilarity using several resemblance measures, and Step (3) is carried out using Weka algorithms.

Estimating the distance between objects is the crucial aspect of the classification process, and several *distance* and *similarity* measures (in general, *resemblance* measures) have been proposed in the literature [4]—similarity measures usually range from 0 to 1; and given a similarity measure S, its associated distance D can be computed as $D = 1 - S$, $D = \sqrt{1 - S}$, or $D = \sqrt{1 - S^2}$ [11].

General-purpose statistical packages (e.g. R, Matlab, Octave, Weka, or SPSS) provide the functionality to classify data using clustering algorithms, but they only support a few resemblance measures for either binary or numerical feature vectors—a summary of the resemblance measures included in these systems is provided in Table 1. This means that problems like the comparison of DNA sequences [16] (uses multi-value/string vectors), DNA fingerprints [7] (uses numerical vectors), or, in general, phylogenetics [17] or data-mining [1] (might work with heterogeneous descriptors) cannot be directly handled in these systems, and special-purpose packages are required.

Weka [5] is an open-source interface that serves to run a wide variety of machine-learning algorithms. It features several variants of clustering; however, it only supports 4 distance measures to compare objects (all of them related to numerical descriptors, see Table 1). In this paper, we present *WekaBioSimilarity*, a Weka extension implemented in Java that enhances this system with several resemblance measures and comparison modes for different types of descriptors. WekaBioSimilarity includes resemblance measures that have not been included in any other package; it is open, free, easily extensible and integrable in other systems.

The rest of this paper is organised as follows. In Sect. 2, we explain how WekaBioSimilarity computes the similarity among feature vectors of different type—for the sake of explanation, several simple examples are provided in this section. The integration of WekaBioSimilarity in Weka is presented in Sect. 3. Section 4 is devoted to present a case study where WekaBioSimilarity is applied

Table 1. Statistical packages and their resemblance measures.

System	Measures
Matlab	**Numerical measures:** Euclidean, Standarized Euclidean, CityBlock, Minkowski, Chebychev, Mahalanobis, Cosine, Correlation, Spearman, Hamming, Jaccard.
Octave	**Numerical measures:** Euclidean, Squared Euclidean, Chi-Squared, Cosine, Earth Mover's, L1.
R	**Numerical measures:** Euclidean, Maximum, Manhattan, Canberra, Binary, Minkowski. **Binary measures:** soerensen, jaccard, ochiai, mountford, whittaker, lande, wilsonshmida, cocogaston, magurran, harrison, cody, williams, williams2, harte, simpson, lennon, weiher, ruggiero, lennon2, rout1ledge, rout2ledge, rout3ledge, sokal1, dice, kulcz1insky, kulcz2insky, mcconnagh, manhattan, simplematching, margaleff, pearson, roger, baroni, dennis, fossum, gower, legendre, sokal2, sokal3, sokal4, stiles, yule, michael, hamann, forbes, chisquare, peirce, eyraud, simpson2, legendre2, fager, maarel, lamont, johnson, sorgenfrei, johnson2.
SPSS	**Numerical measures:** Euclidean, Squared Euclidean, Pearson correlation, Cosine, Chebychev, Block, Minkowski, Customized. **Binary measures:** Euclidean, Squared Euclidean, Size difference, Pattern difference, Variance, Dispersion, Shape, Simple Matching, Phi 4-point correlation, Lambda, Anderberg's D, Dice, Hamann, Jaccard, Kulczynski 1, Kulczynski 2, Lance and Williams, Ochiai, Rogers and Tanimoto, Sokal and Sneath 1, Sokal and Sneath 2, Sokal and Sneath 3, Sokal and Sneath 4, Sokal and Sneath 5, Yule's Y, Yule's Q
Weka	**Numerical measures:** Chebyshev, Euclidean, Manhattan, Minkowski
WekaBioSimilarity	**Numerical measures:** Chebyshev, Euclidean, Manhattan, Minkowski. **Numerical, binary, multi-value/string, and heterogeneous measures:** Jaccard, Dice, Czekanowski, Jaccard3W, NeiLi, SokalSneathI, SokalMichener, SokalSneathII, RogerTanimoto, Faith, GowerLegendre, Intersection, InnerProduct, GilbertWells, OchiaiI, Forbesi, Fossum, SorgenFrei, Mountford, Otsuka, McConnaughey, Tarwid, KulczynskiII, DriverKroeber, Johnson, Dennis, Simpson, BraunBanquet, Ample, Tarantula, Eyraud, Peirce, BaroniUrbaniBuserII, BaroniUrbaniBuserI, GoodManKruskal, Anderberg, Michael, Hamann, Disperson, Tanimoto, KulczynskiI, Yulew, Yuleq, OchiaiII, Stiles, Cole, SokalSneathIII, PearsonHeronII, PearsonHeronI, PearsonIII, PearsonI, PearsonII, Gower, SokalSneathIV, ForbesII, FagerMcGowan, Hamming, Euclidean, SquareEuclidean, Manhattan, MeanManhattan, Vari, SizeDifference, ShapeDifference, PatternDifference, LanceWilliams, BrayCurtis, Hellinger, Chord

to compare DNA fingerprints, and Sect. 5 introduces how resemblance measures can be compared using supervised-learning algorithms in Weka. The paper ends with the Conclusions and the Bibliography. WekaBioSimilarity is available at http://wekabiosimilarity.sourceforge.net—installation instructions, examples and videos can also be downloaded from this webpage.

2 Resemblance Measures in WekaBioSimilarity

WekaBioSimilarity works with data of different type: binary, multi-value, string, numerical and heterogeneous. Each type of data has its particularities, and, therefore, the comparison of feature vectors is different in each case. The comparison of binary data is tackled by SPSS and the Simba [8] package of R, but Weka together with WekaBioSimilarity is the only general-purpose tool that works with the other kind of data (see Table 1).

In this section, we explain how WekaBioSimilarity carries out the comparison of feature vectors of different types. We will illustrate the functionality for each case considering real-world examples obtained from the UC Irvine Machine Learning Repository [12]—for the sake of explanation, we will use fragments of those datasets.

2.1 Binary Data

In the simplest case, objects are represented by means of binary feature vectors that encode the presence/absence of a set of attributes (or properties). Given two objects, A and B, represented by means of binary vectors, four values are computed: M_{11} (the number of attributes present both in A and B), M_{10} (the number

Patient	F1	F2	F3	F4	F5	F6	F7	F8	F9	F10
P1	Yes	Yes	No	No	Yes	Yes	No	No	No	Yes
P2	Yes	Yes	No	No	Yes	Yes	No	No	No	No
P3	Yes	No	No	No	Yes	No	Yes	No	No	Yes
P4	Yes	No	Yes	Yes	Yes	No	No	Yes	No	Yes
P5	Yes	No	No	Yes	No	No	No	Yes	No	No

$$\begin{array}{c|ccccc} & P1 & P2 & P3 & P4 & P5 \\ \hline P1 & 1 & 0.9 & 0.7 & 0.5 & 0.4 \\ P2 & 0.9 & 1 & 0.6 & 0.4 & 0.5 \\ P3 & 0.7 & 0.6 & 1 & 0.6 & 0.5 \\ P4 & 0.5 & 0.4 & 0.6 & 1 & 0.5 \\ P5 & 0.4 & 0.5 & 0.5 & 0.5 & 1 \end{array}$$

Fig. 2. *Fragment of SPECT heart dataset.* **Left.** Table wit the first 10 binary features of the first 5 patients in the dataset. **Right.** Similarity matrix obtained using the simple-matching measure.

of attributes present in A but not in B), M_{01} (the number of attributes present in B but not in A), and M_{00} (the number of attributes present neither in A nor in B). From these values, several resemblance measures can be defined; for instance, $S(A, B) = \frac{M_{11}+M_{00}}{M_{11}+M_{10}+M_{01}+M_{00}}$ is the simple-matching similarity measure.

The WekaBioSimilarity package features the 76 binary resemblance measures surveyed in [4] including widely employed measures like Dice or Jaccard (see Table 1 for the complete list of measures included in WekaBioSimilarity).

Example 1. The SPECT heart dataset [9] is a database that describes diagnosing of cardiac Single Proton Emission Computed Tomography (SPECT) images. This dataset contains 267 instances that are described by means of 23 binary features indicating partial diagnosis at different stages. A fragment of this database is shown in Fig. 2. Using such information and the simple-matching measure, the similarity matrix obtained by WekaBioSimilarity is given in Fig. 2.

2.2 Multi-value/String Data

In the binary case, the resemblance of two objects is computed through a pairwise comparison of the feature vectors associated with the objects. Therefore, the length of the vectors must be the same and the position of the elements is relevant. This approach can also be applied to multi-value and string feature vectors (e.g. in the comparison of DNA sequences, each descriptor is one of the four nucleobases [16]). To compare multi-value/string vectors, we must consider *agreements* and *disagreements* (descriptors for which the two objects have, respectively, the same and different values), and extend, when possible, the binary measures. For instance, the generalisation of the simple-matching measure is $S(A, B) = \frac{agreements}{agreements+disagreements}$.

Example 2. The HIV-1 protease cleavage dataset [21] contains lists of octamers (8 amino acids)—each one of the 8 attributes is a letter denoting an amino acid (e.g. G is Glycine and P is Proline)—and a flag (-1 or 1) depending on whether HIV-1 protease will cleave in the central position (between amino acids 4 and 5). If we compare the three first instances of this dataset (I1: AAAKFERQ,-1, I2: AAAMKRHG,-1, and I3: AAAMSSAI,-1) using the simple-matching measure,

WekaBioSimilarity can compute the similarity between them obtaining the following results: $S(\mathtt{I1},\mathtt{I2}) = 0.44$, $S(\mathtt{I1},\mathtt{I3}) = 0.44$, and $S(\mathtt{I2},\mathtt{I3}) = 0.55$.

A different situation occurs when a string feature vector represents the set of components of an object (e.g. in the study of the distribution of species [13], or for tracking the different areas of a web site that are visited by users [3]). Hence, the size of the vectors associated with two objects might be different, and the position of the attributes in those vectors is no longer relevant. In this situation, the similarity of two objects A and B (which associated sets are S_A and S_B, respectively) is obtained using three values: $|S_A \cap S_B|$, $|S_A \setminus S_B|$ and $|S_B \setminus S_A|$; and generalising the binary measures. For instance, the simple-matching measure is given by $S(A,B) = \frac{|S_A \cap S_B|}{|S_A \cap S_B| + |S_A \setminus S_B| + |S_B \setminus S_A|}$.

Example 3. The USDA plants database [25] contains the plants of the USA and the states where they occur (the original dataset consists of almost 35000 instances, and each plant inhabits from 1 to 69 regions). Some instances of such a database are: *abelia*: fl, nc; *abelia x grandiflora*: fl, nc; *abel.*: ct, dc, fl, hi, il, ky, la, md, mi, ms; and, *abel. esc.*: ct, dc, fl, il, ky, la, md, mi, ms. Using the simple-matching measure, the similarity between the species abelmoschus (abel.) and abelmoschus esculentus (abel. esc.) is given by

$$S(abel., abel.\ esc.) = \frac{|\{ct, dc, fl, il, ky, la, md, mi, ms\}|}{|\{ct, dc, fl, hi, il, ky, la, md, mi, ms\}| + |\{hi\}| + |\emptyset|} = \frac{9}{10}.$$

When working with multi-value/string feature vectors, the user of WekaBioSimilarity must select the kind of comparison that is performed: pairwise (former scenario) or set-occurrence (latter scenario)—see Fig. 3. In the pairwise case, the 25 binary measures that can be generalised are supported; and, in the set-occurrence case, all the measures supported for binary data are available.

2.3 Numerical Data

The comparison of numerical data is usually performed using measures like the Euclidean distance or the Pearson correlation coefficient [11]—4 of these measures were already implemented in Weka (see Table 1). In addition, the two situations presented in the previous subsection also make sense when working with numerical feature vectors (e.g. to compare regions based on age demographics, or to classify DNA fingerprints [7]). Hence, the pairwise-comparison and set-occurrence modes have been implemented for numerical feature vectors in WekaBioSimilarity.

Working with numerical descriptors has a particularity: there exists a notion of "closeness": values that, in spite of not being equal, are close enough to be considered the same. To deal with this issue, WekaBioSimilarity provides a configurable parameter called *tolerance*—see Fig. 3. This parameter allows the user to fix the "closeness" depending on the concrete problem, and it is essential, for instance, when precision errors must be taken into account. A detailed example will be introduced in Sect. 4.

2.4 Heterogeneous Data

In general, the attributes that describe an object may have different types—e.g. when comparing animals, descriptors like the presence of hair (binary), habitat (multi-value), or number of limbs (numerical) might be considered. In this context, only a pairwise comparison can be applied, and WekaBioSimilarity implements 25 measures for heterogeneous data (analogously to the multi-value/string and numerical situations). In the case of numerical descriptors included in heterogeneous data, the user can also fix a tolerance value as explained in the previous subsection. We will introduce an example of heterogeneous data in Sect. 5.

3   Integration of WekaBioSimilarity in Weka

In this section, we explain how Weka integrates WekaBioSimilarity. Weka implements several supervised and unsupervised algorithms that require the selection of a distance measure; for instance, k-means or hierarchical clustering in the former case, and k-nearest neighbour or locally-weighted learning in the latter. Once WekaBioSimilarity is installed in Weka, the resemblance measures implemented in this plugin become available for those algorithms, see Fig. 3.

WekaBioSimilarity automatically recognises the kind of data that the user is processing and acts accordingly as explained in the previous section; additionally, there are some parameters that might be configured by the user using the interface presented in Fig. 3: *resemblance measure* (the user can select among the different resemblance measures available for each kind of data), *distance computation* (if the user selects a similarity measure S, she must fix how the distance measure D is computed from S using one of the following formulas $D = 1 - S$, $D = \sqrt{1 - S}$, or $D = \sqrt{1 - S^2}$), *matching* (if this option, only available for string

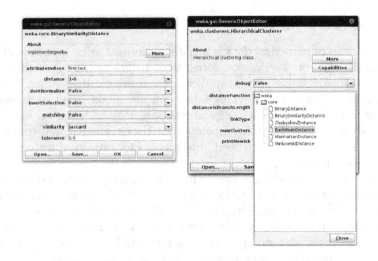

Fig. 3. Left: WekaBioSimilarity interface. **Right:** Distances available in Weka.

and numerical data, is fixed as true, the set-occurrence mode is used; otherwise, the pairwise mode is applied), and *tolerance* (this parameter, only available for numerical data, and heterogeneous data that contain numerical attributes, allows the user to fix the closeness value).

4   Case Study: DNA Fingerprinting

In this section, we present an application that illustrates some of the features supported by WekaBioSimilarity. The problem presented here cannot be handled using general-purpose software packages, and specific tools are required.

DNA fingerprinting [7] is a genetic typing technique that allows the analysis of the genomic relatedness between samples, and the comparison of DNA patterns. This technique has multiple applications in different fields (medical diagnosis, forensic science, parentage testing, food industry, agriculture and many others) [19]. The comparison of DNA fingerprints follows the workflow presented in Fig. 1: (1) construction of feature vectors, (2) computation of similarity matrix, and (3) classification (using hierarchical clustering).

In the first stage, a feature vector for each DNA pattern is constructed. Each DNA pattern consists of a set of bands (see Fig. 4), and in turn, each band has associated a numerical value called "molecular weight" (see Fig. 4 for the molecular weights of the bands of Fig. 4); the molecular weights of a DNA pattern correspond to its feature vector. In the second step, DNA patterns are compared considering the matchings of the molecular weights of their bands (i.e. a set-occurrence comparison is necessary). In this task, two bands are matched even if their molecular weights are not exactly the same, but they are close enough; hence, a tolerance value is required—in our concrete example, we take a tolerance value of 3. Finally, the DNA patterns are grouped together using hierarchical clustering, and the result is visualised using a dendrogram.

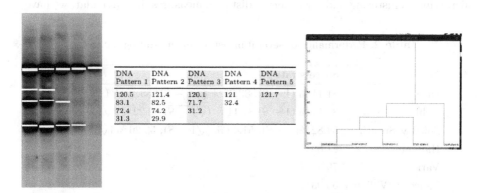

Fig. 4. Left: Image of DNA fingerprints. The image contains 5 DNA patterns (the 5 vertical lanes). In white, the bands of each pattern. **Centre:** Molecular weights of the bands of the image. **Right:** Dendrogram associated with the DNA patterns.

Given a file containing the feature vectors of several DNA patterns, Weka combined with WekaBioSimilarity can generate the dendrogram of such patterns (see Fig. 4) using the most common resemblance measures (Dice, Jaccard, and simple-matching [26]) and hierarchical clustering algorithms (UPGMA, single linkage, neighbour joining [26]) applied in this context.

Several software systems have been developed for DNA fingerprint analysis. Some of them internally implement the whole classification process generating a dendrogram as a final result. However, several systems (e.g. GelAnalyzer [10] or Dolphin 1D [28]) only generate the molecular weights of bands (i.e. Step (1)). In the latter packages, their output might be fed as input to WekaBioSimilarity to compare DNA patterns using the most common measures applied in this subject—as in the former packages, the final result will be a dendrogram.

5   Comparing Resemblance Measures

In the previous section, we have presented the application of WekaBioSimilarity in a context where some resemblance measures are considered as standards (works related to DNA fingerprinting mainly employ Dice, Jaccard, and simple-matching measures). In other situations, it is useful to explore different alternatives as shown in [2,6,24,27]; WekaBioSimilarity can also be used to this aim as we will illustrate in this section.

The statlog dataset [18] is a heart disease database that consists of 270 instances having 13 attributes (7 numeric, 3 binary, and 3 multi-value)—i.e. it is a heterogeneous dataset. From such a dataset, several classifiers can be trained in Weka to make predictions using supervised machine-learning algorithms. Some of those algorithms (e.g. k-nearest neighbour or locally-weighted learning) can work with the resemblance measures implemented in WekaBioSimilarity.

We consider the *ClassificationViaClustering* algorithm of Weka—a meta-classifier that uses clustering for classification. For this classifier, we can pick hierarchical clustering and try different distance measures. In particular, we have

Table 2. Performance of several measures in the statlog dataset.

Measure	Success rate
Dice	81.11 % $(1 - S)$, 83.33 % $(\sqrt{1 - S})$, 55.19 % $(\sqrt{1 - S^2})$
Ochiai	81.11 % $(1 - S)$, 81.11 % $(\sqrt{1 - S})$, 82.22 % $(\sqrt{1 - S^2})$
Sokal & Sneath	54.82 % $(1 - S)$, 51.49 % $(\sqrt{1 - S})$, 59.26 % $(\sqrt{1 - S^2})$
Hamming	81.85 %
Vari	79.63 %
Lance & Williams	55.93 %
Chebyshev	55.93 %
Euclidean	80.37 %
Manhattan	81.11 %

selected 3 similarity measures (Dice, Ochiai, and Sokal & Sneath, using the 3 different formulas available to compute the distance value) and 3 distance measures (Hamming, Vari, and Lance & Williams) of WekaBioSimilarity, and 3 measures (Chebyshev, Euclidean, and Manhattan) included by default in Weka. As can be seen in Table 2, different success rates are obtained when the resemblance measure is changed.

In this example, we have not pretended to be exhaustive in the analysis of the different measures for predicting heart diseases, but just show that several alternatives can be easily explored thanks to WekaBioSimilarity.

6 Conclusions

The classification of objects is a common problem in several contexts, and it is highly dependent on computing the resemblance among the feature vectors of the objects. Usually, this task is carried out by special-purpose packages developed for each concrete problem. Weka is a general-purpose tool that offers several supervised and unsupervised machine-learning algorithms, but it only supported a few methods to obtain the similarity between numerical feature vectors. This drawback has been overcome with the WekaBioSimilarity package: a Weka extension that enhances this system with several resemblance measures and comparison modes. Namely, WekaBioSimilarity features: (1) the same (and even more) binary measures than other general-purpose statistical packages; (2) a generalisation of the binary measures to multi-value, string, numerical, and heterogeneous data; (3) a configurable tolerance parameter for numerical data; and, (4) two comparison modes: pairwise and set-occurrence. As far as we are aware, functionalities (2)–(4) have not been previously implemented in other general-purpose systems. As a result, we have a tool that can be applied in a wide variety of contexts either used as a standalone application, or integrated into other software packages.

References

1. Arif, M., Basalama, S.: Similarity-dissimilarity plot for high dimensional data of different attribute types in biomedical datasets. Int. J. Innovative Comput. Inf. Control **8**(2), 1173–1181 (2012)
2. Boriah, S., Chandola, V., Kumar, V.: Similarity measures for categorical data: a comparative evaluation. In: Proceedings of the 8th SIAM International Conference on Data Mining, pp. 243–254 (2008)
3. Breese, J., Heckerman, D., Kadie, D.: Empirical analysis of predictive algorithms for collaborative filtering. In: Proceedings of the 14th Conference on Uncertainty in Artificial Intelligence (1998)
4. Choi, S.S., et al.: A survey of binary similarity and distance measures. J. Syst. Cybern. Inform. **8**(1), 43–48 (2010)
5. Hall, M., et al.: The weka data mining software: an update. SIGKDD Explor. **11**(1), 10–18 (2009)

6. Hubálek, Z.: Coefficients of association and similarity, based on binary (presence-absence) data: an evaluation. Biol. Rev. **57**(4), 669–689 (2008)
7. Jeffreys, A.J., Wilson, V., Thein, S.L.: Hypervariable 'minisatellite' regions in human DNA. Nature **314**, 67–73 (1985)
8. Jurasinski, G., Retzer, V.: simba: a collection of functions for similarity analysis of vegetation data (2012)
9. Kurgan, L.A., et al.: Knowledge discovery approach to automated cardiac SPECT diagnosis. Artif. Intell. Med. **23**(2), 149–169 (2001)
10. Lazar, I.: Gelanalyzer 2010a (2010). http://www.gelanalyzer.com/
11. Legendre, P., Legendre, L.: Numerical Ecology. Elsevier, Amsterdam (1999)
12. Lichman, M.: UCI machine learning repository (2013). http://archive.ics.uci.edu/ml
13. MacArthur, R.: Geographical Ecology: Patterns in the Distribution of Species. Princeton University Press, New Jersey (1984)
14. Manning, C., Schütze, H.: Foundations of Statistical Natural Language Processing. The MIT Press, Cambridge (2001)
15. Michael, H.: Binary coefficients: a theoretical and empirical study. Math. Geol. **8**(2), 137–150 (1976)
16. Miyamoto, M., Cacraft, J.: Phylogenetic Analysis of DNA Sequences. Oxford University Press, Oxford (1991)
17. Nei, M., Kumar, S.: Molecular Evolution and Phylogenetics. Oxford University Press, Oxford (2000)
18. Nutt, C.L., et al.: Gene expression-based classification of malignant gliomas correlates better with survival than histological classification. Cancer Res. **63**(7), 1602–1607 (2003)
19. Read, M.M. (ed.): Trends in DNA Fingerprint Research. Nova Science Publishers Inc., New York (2005)
20. Rettinger, A., et al.: Mining the semantic web. Data Min. Knowl. Disc. **24**, 613–662 (2012)
21. Rögnvaldsson, T., You, L., Garwicz, D.: State of the art prediction of HIV-1 protease cleavage sites. BioInformatics **31**(8), 1204–1210 (2015)
22. Silva, T.C., Zhao, L.: Machine Learning in Complex Networks. Springer, Heidelberg (2016)
23. Sneath, P., Sokal, R.: Numerical Taxonomy: The Principles and Practice of Numerical Classification. W.H. Freeman & Co., San Francisco (1973)
24. Spertus, E., Sahami, M., Buyukkokten, O.: Evaluating similarity measures: a large-scale study in the orkut social network. In: Proceedings of the 11th ACM SIGKDD Conference on Knowledge Discovery in Data Mining, pp. 678–684 (2005)
25. USDA, NRCS: The plants database (2008). http://plants.usda.gov
26. Vauterin, L., Vauterin, P.: Integrated databasing and analysis. In: Stackebrandt, E. (ed.) Molecular Identification, Systematics, and Population Structure of Prokaryotes. Springer, Heidelberg (2006)
27. Wang, X., et al.: Experimental comparison of representation methods and distance measures for time series data. Data Min. Knowl. Disc. **26**, 275–309 (2013)
28. Wealtec: Dolphin-1D software version 2.4 (2006). http://www.wealtec.com/products/imaging/software/dolphin-1d-software.htm
29. Willett, P.: Similarity-based approaches to virtual screening. Biochem. Soc. Trans. **31**, 603–606 (2003)
30. Willett, P., Barnard, J.M., Downs, G.M.: Chemical Similarity Searching. J. Chem. Inf. Comput. Sci. **38**, 983–996 (1998)
31. Xu, R., Wunsch, D.C.: Clustering. IEEE Computer Society Press, Washington, DC (2008)

Age Classification Through the Evaluation of Circadian Rhythms of Wrist Temperature

M. Campos[1]([⊠]), A. Gomariz[1], M. Balsa[1], M.A. Rol[2], J.A. Madrid[2], and F.J. Garcia[3]

[1] Computer Science Faculty, University of Murcia, Murcia, Spain
manuelcampos@um.es
[2] Chronobiology Laboratory, Department of Physiology,
University of Murcia, Murcia, Spain
[3] Geriatrics Section, Hospital Virgen del Valle, Toledo, Spain

Abstract. Chronobiology is the scientific discipline that deals with the study of the biological rhythms and their underlying mechanisms. The alteration of biological rhythms, such as blood pressure or temperature begins to be considered as a good marker of certain diseases and senescence. Among the variables, the wrist skin temperature has proven to be a good marker of the circadian rhythms of the subject. In this paper we evaluate the wrist temperature of four groups of subjects with different age in order to gain some knowledge on the evolution of the circadian rhythms and its application to age classification.

Keywords: Circadian rhythms · Data mining · Wrist temperature

1 Introduction

Chronobiology is the scientific discipline that deals with the study of the biological rhythms and their underlying mechanisms. Much of the biological variable suffer variations over different time intervals. Some biological variables vary over the life of individuals and others vary annually, seasonally, monthly, daily or even every few hours. The rhythms included in a near-daily frequency, with periods between 20 and 28 h are called circadian rhythms. This group includes many of the rhythms studied in chronobiology, and among them are the sleep-wake variations in body temperature, alertness and some neuroendocrine functions, such as cortisol and melatonin secretion.

The alteration of blood pressure or temperature rhythms begins to be considered as a good marker of certain diseases and senescence. Thus the temperature rhythm is an excellent biomarker of aging degree in laboratory animals [15] and

---

M. Campos—The authors wish to thank the Instituto de Salud Carlos III, the Ministry of Science and Innovation and the Ministry of Economy and Competitiveness for their financial support through the Ageing and Frailty Cooperative Research Network, RD12/0043/0011, RD12/0043/0020, SAF2013-49132-C2-1-R, the latter including FEDER cofunding, granted to Juan Antonio Madrid.

© Springer International Publishing Switzerland 2016
O. Luaces et al. (Eds.): CAEPIA 2016, LNAI 9868, pp. 99–109, 2016.
DOI: 10.1007/978-3-319-44636-3_10

it shows age-related changes in human [10]. Circadian rhythmicity has shown to be a predictor of effective weight-loss [2].

Little is known about how circadian system evolves over time [9]. The existence of a circadian regulation is considered beneficial to the body and an abnormal pattern lifestyle habits can be considered an additional risk factor that contributes to the development of many diseases of aging such as cardiovascular disease, diabetes and cancer, although the underlying molecular mechanisms are unclear. The rest-activity circadian rhythm appears to be an objective indicator of physical welfare. Numerous publications have shown in recent years that aging causes a series of changes in biological rhythms, which are summarized as follows [4]: decreased amplitude, advancement of phase, instability of phase.

However, sometimes it is not so clear which is the circadian response to aging. For example, there is still no certain answer as to whether the shortening of nocturnal sleep and increased napping during the day is a characterization of the aging process of the human circadian system. The wrist skin temperature has proven to be a good marker of the circadian rhythms of the subject [12], being the acrophase and mesor the most robust parameters for its characterization [7]. It also has the advantage of being easily measured for a sufficient number of days and at an appropriate frequency as opposed to other markers such as core body temperature or melatonin. In the analysis of biological rhythms, the aim should be the characterization of rhythmic patterns, and its great variability is a major problem. In this paper we try to characterize these series for different age groups in which the wrist skin temperature has been registered.

These series have some basic characteristics: firstly, they are sampled at low frequency; secondly, they have different lengths; and thirdly, by nature the series are non-stationary. Because of all these, we opted for an approach based on feature extraction for classification. Feature extraction technique is a well established method for time series comparison because from it serves three purposes: it removes both noise and redundancy and offers a higher semantic interpretation of results [8]. The advantages of this approach are known [1], and arose mainly because of the difficulty of comparing raw complete time series.

The structure of the paper is as follows. In Sect. 2 describes the data, the technique of data acquisition, the feature extraction methods and the classification techniques. In Sect. 3 we show the results of the classification techniques. Finally, we offer some conclusions about these results.

2   Materials and Methods

2.1   Data and Data Acquisition

The Murcia University Chronobiology Laboratory has validated a method for the evaluation of the circadian system [6]. The method consists on recording the wrist skin temperature, which shows a wide amplitude and its daily pattern is the reverse of body core temperature with an advance in the phase. The data are recorded by a data logger iButtom (Thermochron, Dallas) placed on the wrist of the nondominant hand with the help of a wristband that neither bothers the subject nor requires his active cooperation. This is a miniaturized data logger ($16 \times 6\,mm^2$) capable of recording up to 2048 values with the frequency and scheduled set up. Its low cost, reliability and robustness make it an ideal tool for an ambulatory assessment of the temperature rhythm in individuals who carry out their normal life.

In the population of the study, the temperature is logged every 10 min (sampling period) for a number of days (ranging from 2 to 7) for subjects of four different groups of ages, from infants at primary school to elderly (over 65 years old). Table 1 shows the main characteristics of the population.

Table 1. Study population and main characteristics by age group.

GROUP	Number of series	Average age ($\pm$std)
G1: At primary school	15	9,46 (0,52)
G2: Students at university	46	20,14 (3,77)
G3: Adults	29	45,75 (10,57)
G4: Elderly people	39	70,12 (3,48)

Since in some registers there exist missing data, we have established a procedure in which we are removing and/or replacing non-reliable data. These data appear when a subject has removed the wristband with the sensor or when it is bad positioned for some time, for example, during the shower. This preprocessing is too extensive to describe in this article, and therefore it is left out. For simplicity, suffice to say that missing data in some concrete part of the day, that is extreme values below the minimum temperature defined, have been replaced with the average values within that time range.

2.2 Feature Extraction and Classification

There are different approaches to the problem of time series classification such as direct comparison of time series, symbolic transformations [5], morphological characterization [13] or feature extraction [8,16]. There are two reasons why we initially have used an approximation based on feature extraction. First, the need for high legibility on the model obtained. The model should provide some insights for the biologist to understand which features are more relevant for classification. Second, by the characteristics of their own series of temperature: The different series cover a varying number of cycles for each subject, therefore, direct comparison is not possible. Moreover, the global morphology of the series is different for each group of subjects.

Among existing tools for the study of circadian rhythms, we find methods from statistics and signal processing. On the one hand we will find basic features of rhythm, such as frequency, phase, amplitude, trend, etc. On the other hand we will use the knowledge of domain experts to generate some variables that may be significant in the problem.

From the statistical point of view, we have extracted the values that characterize the data distribution in subjects (max, min, mean, kurtosis, standard deviation, and skewness). Other techniques of the time series analysis are the method ARIMA or Box-Jenkins. The basic objective of time series analysis is the prediction of future values or control values of the series, and his primary interest lies in areas such as the economy where there are long series, and therefore they are not suitable in this domain.

Among classical techniques of chronobiology, we have used the chi-square periodogram and the cosinor analysis. More detail of basic techniques of study of circadian rhythms can be seen in [11]. Cosinor method allows us to determine the parameters of a cosine fit the data. This cosine would represent a normal life cycle of the subjects. The parameters are amplitude, phase, and mesor (mean estimated statistic over rhythm). We also get values that establish the goodness of the fit such as the Rayleigh test and the Percentage Rhythm. Despite being widely accepted, this technique has several problems since it does not properly characterize subjects with cycles of different duration or cycles or that show more than one predominant cycle in their behavior (such as bimodal subjects).

To overcome this limitation the Fourier analysis is used. The methods of analysis in the frequency domain have proven relevant to the study of biological signals such as ECG and FCG. The use of a limited number of harmonics allows the characterization of the appearance of other regular periods in the subjects in the same way as the cosinor does. The basic limitation of Fourier analysis is the resolution that it can obtain, as only fractions of the initial set (24-h circadian rhythms) are obtained.

The periodogram is an exploratory technique that is appropriate for measuring short period cycles (or fewer cycles), and it allows us to get any resolution. Thus, it is possible to characterize the shortening of the periods if we find periods of 23 h. Some periodograms used in the literature are the chi-square-Bushel Solokov, the regressive and Lomb-Scargle. We used the chi-square periodogram [11] to obtain the number of statistically significant periods, the length of the periods, and the maximum value of the chi-square statistic.

Due to the non-seasonal nature of the signals, we also opted to use a nonparametric indexes for the characterization: Intradaily stability, Interdaily variability, Relative Amplitude, and dichotomy index ($I < O$). Interdaily stability serves as a measure of the degree of resemblance across activity patterns of individual days. Higher values indicate a more stable rhythm across days. Intradaily variability represents fragmentation of periods of rest and activity. Lower values indicate normal cycles. The relative amplitude is the non-parametric version of the cosinor amplitude. The dichotomy index is a ratio between the amount of activity while in and out of bed.

Finally, based on knowledge of the specific domain we will obtain other parameters that initially could help to characterize the groups. First, the significant moments L and M. L and M are as a parameter a number of hours (e.g. L2, M5) are the minimum and maximum points in a moving average of the behavior of the subject. L and M can characterize the minimum and maximum moments in the rhythm of the subject, which is a nonparametric version of the bathyphase and acrophase respectively. Another circadian characteristics of aging is the progressive differentiation between dominant and other sub-rhythms. Therefore, we will establish as characteristics the differences in phase, amplitude and mesor between the first harmonic and other harmonics of Fourier. Also, as stated in the introduction, we expect to find a decrease in the complexity of the subject's behavior in older subjects and very young subjects. Therefore we have calculated two measures of complexity, Approximate Entropy and Detrended Fluctuation Analysis, previously used in some studies [14].

As classification methods we will use some of the most representative shown in [17]: C4.5, SVM, Naive Bayes, kNN. We will use the weka implementation of these algorithms with their default configuration except when otherwise mentioned. Since our objective is also to know the relationship of the most relevant features for classification, we will pay special attention to the decision trees as it is a method that produces a readable model. The C4.5 (J48 in weka) algorithm has been configured with a different values of the minimum number of objects at the leaves (parameter M). The kNN (IBk in weka) has been also tested with different number of neighbors (parameter k).

The stratified 10-fold cross validation was chosen to train the classifiers. As comparison measure for the classifiers we have used accuracy and the ROC curve. In order to summarize the information contained in the ROC curve, the AUC of a ROC curve is recommended as a single number evaluation method.

3   Results and Discussion

The total number of features extracted is 142, being all of them real numbers. As a first experiment, we have considered only the classic cosinor approach. Results can be seen in Table 2.

Table 2. Accuracy of classification using only the cosinor data.

	JRIP (N2)	J48 (M5)	SMO	NB	IBk-5
Accuracy	56, 67	63, 59	51, 92	57, 24	62, 05
AUC	0, 59	0, 70	0, 62	0, 81	0, 69
Accuracy (discretized)	61, 15	67, 37	63, 59	65, 13	62, 76
AUC (discretized)	0, 69	0, 74	0, 75	0, 80	0, 73

We see that classification with the cosinor is not very accurate. Although from the biology perspective it provides a simple and useful model for explaining the temperature rhythm of an individual, it is difficult to assume that the cosinor features are similar for the subjects in the same group.

We show in Fig. 1 the accuracy of the classifiers for subsets of different sizes when we consider all the numeric features. As a second step, we have proceed

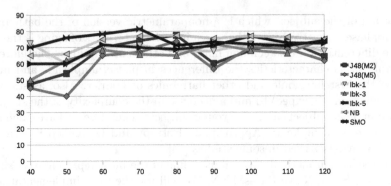

Fig. 1. Classifier accuracy for different sizes of the datasets with non discretized attributes.

to discretize all the attributes in order to get a more simplified interpretation of the results. The same results for this second experiments are shown in Fig. 2. In this figures we see that all the classifiers perform quite similar, about 70 %, when more than sixty individuals are considered. The paired t-test showed no difference at 0,05 level.

For the end user, it is important to see if there are some attributes more relevant than other. To that end, we have performed an attribute selection procedure with several methods. As a first approach to reducing the number of features, features we have perform an ANOVA analysis to rule out those attributes whose mean is not different among the groups. A correlation based attribute selection method [3], the gain ratio and chi square were also used (see Table 3). We have performed the attribute selection before and after discretization but we did not observe any significant difference. In that table, the dash means that the attribute did not appear in the first twenty positions of the corresponding method while the asterisk means that it did.

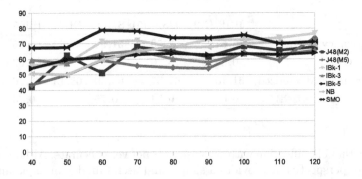

Fig. 2. Classifier accuracy for different sizes of the datasets with discretized attributes.

Table 3. Attribute selection

Order	CFS	IG	Chi
1	Kurtosis	-	-
2	rayleigh	-	-
3	maxchi	*	-
4	LV-2-2	-	-
5	LH-2-5	*	*
6	LH-2-10	*	-
7	LH-5-5	*	*
8	MLH-5-10	*	*
9	MH-10-2	*	*
10	ApEnMax	-	-
11	DFAOrdinate	-	-
12	F2-phase	*	*
13	F3-amp	-	-
14	F1-F2-phase	*	*
15	F1-F3-amp	-	-

From the results of the attribute selection algorithms, we see what the features represent. In the first place, we see that several of them (attributes 4, 5,6,7) represent the lowest hour (LH) and lowest value (LV) of the moving average during the day considering 2 or 5 h as windows. This attributes are very related to the acrophase of the cosinor. We see that the non-parametric version of the cosinor seems to be preferred by the attribute selections methods. It is also relevant to see that the phase of the second series (F2-phase) and the difference between the phases of the two first harmonics (F1-F2 phase) is also included by all the attribute selection methods. These attributes and all other relevant moments (MLH-5-10, MH-10-2) should be very related.

In the second place the result of the Rayleigh test and the maximum value of the chi-square periodogram give us an idea of the strength of the rhythm. The higher the values, the stronger the rhythm.

In the third place, the kurtosis attribute tell us the how the values are distributed around the mean value. Finally, two of the attributes that characterize the complexity of the signals (maximum value of the approximate entropy and the ordinate of the straight line found in the DFA) and the has been selected.

The accuracy in all the classifiers shown in Table 4 is higher than in the case of using all the features as input for the algorithms. It is clear that algorithms such as NaiveBayes obtain more benefit than others when the attributes are not correlated. Again, the accuracy is increased when the discretized version of the attributes is used. The values of accuracy and AUC showed not difference at level 0.05 with the paired t-test.

Table 4. Accuracy of classification with attribute selection.

		J48(M2)	J48(M5)	SMO	NB	IBk-1	IBk-3	IBk-5
Numeric	ACC	78, 33	78, 97	73, 59	82, 18	79, 04	82, 18	78, 21
	AUC	0, 90	0, 90	0, 90	0, 99	0, 77	0, 89	0, 94
	CE	0, 33	0, 34	0, 39	0, 32	0, 37	0, 33	0, 38
Discrete	ACC	85, 96	82, 12	83, 72	87, 56	85, 19	86, 79	87, 50
	AUC	0, 88	0, 88	0, 95	0, 98	0, 89	0, 96	0, 95
	CE	0, 26	0, 31	0, 31	0, 24	0, 28	0, 25	0, 23

For our problem we have also considered an entropy based measure calculated on the confusion matrix (see last line of Table 4). This measure can give us an approximation to the expected classifier since not all the errors are equal. It can be notice in the confusion matrix that it is coherent to think that subjects of each group are probably misclassified as subjects of a neighbor group. Thus, errors are usually found around the diagonal of the confusion matrix. That is, subjects belonging to the elder group are more probably misclassified as adults than as students (Table 5).

Table 5. Confusion matrix of the classifiers

(a) NB

Real \ Classified	G1	G2	G3	G4
G1	13	0	1	1
G2	2	39	4	1
G3	0	3	26	0
G4	1	1	2	35

(b) J48(M5)

Real \ Classified	G1	G2	G3	G4
G1	11	2	0	2
G2	3	38	4	1
G3	0	5	21	3
G4	0	1	2	36

Finally, in Fig. 3 we provide the J48 classification tree build with all the data. In that tree we see that the time of the L2 moment (which is the non-parametric acrophase) seems to clearly differentiate between elderly people (G4), and infants (G1). On the bottom of the tree, we can see that, without considering G4, values of kurtosis and the time of the M10 moment seem to differentiate between groups G1 and G3. On the upper part of the tree, it is interesting to see that the second decision in the tree is done based on the complexity of the signal. The low complexity values seems to be associated to elderly people.

```
LH_2_5 = '(-inf-14.0835]'
|   ApEnMax = '(-inf-0.9955]'
|   |   F1_F3_amp = '(-inf-0.5875]': G4 (14.0/2.0)
|   |   F1_F3_amp = '(0.5875-1.106]': G4 (24.0)
|   |   F1_F3_amp = '(1.106-inf)'
|   |   |   F2_fase = '(-inf-7.4215]': G2 (0.0)
|   |   |   F2_fase = '(7.4215-17.6385]': G3 (2.0)
|   |   |   F2_fase = '(17.6385-inf)': G2 (2.0)
|   ApEnMax = '(0.9955-inf)'
|   |   F2_fase = '(-inf-7.4215]': G2 (3.0/1.0)
|   |   F2_fase = '(7.4215-17.6385]': G3 (12.0)
|   |   F2_fase = '(17.6385-inf)': G3 (3.0)
LH_2_5 = '(14.0835-inf)'
|   Kurtosis = '(-inf--0.7085]': G1 (2.0/1.0)
|   Kurtosis = '(-0.7085--0.521]': G3 (6.0/1.0)
|   Kurtosis = '(-0.521-inf)'
|   |   MH_10_2 = '(-inf-4.5835]'
|   |   |   F3_fase = '(-inf-8.5445]': G1 (15.0/2.0)
|   |   |   F3_fase = '(8.5445-inf)': G2 (5.0)
|   |   MH_10_2 = '(4.5835-inf)'
|   |   |   F2_fase = '(-inf-7.4215]': G2 (14.0)
|   |   |   F2_fase = '(7.4215-17.6385]': G3 (6.0/1.0)
|   |   |   F2_fase = '(17.6385-inf)': G2 (21.0/1.0)
```

Fig. 3. Decision tree trained with all the data.

4   Conclusions

The aim of this article was the characterization of circadian rhythms of wrist skin temperature of subjects of different ages. Given the characteristics of the series, we decided to use an approach based on feature extraction and a number of the most representative classifiers that used those features for the classification of the individuals in one of four age group: infants, students at university, adults, and elderly people.

In order to get more insight on the data, we have also used some attribute selection techniques. It is interesting to note that these methods did pointed out some attributes of the different approaches considered: descriptive statistical values, non-parametric values, rhythm characterization, complexity, and frequency domain. So, it seems that all of them contributes to the correct classification of the individuals in their groups. The experts confirm that attributes selected are coherent with the current knowledge about the evolution of the circadian rhythms in aging such as progressive differentiation between the dominant and other sub-rhythms. Among them, kurtosis was not previously pointed out by the biologist as a feature to be studied.

Regarding the results of the classifiers, some conclusions can be drawn. On the one hand it can be said that the classical method of cosinor is not sufficient to characterize the evolution of the wrist temperature rhythm. On the other hand, some groups are clearly distinguishable from the rest, such as the elderly through the L2 feature. A factor that influences the classification errors is the dispersion of the subjects of the same group. For example, the group of adults contains individuals that are from 30 years old, that are near the university group, up to 60 years old, that are close to the group of elderly people. We think the results in accuracy and AUC of the classifiers are very good considering also that most errors are close to the diagonal in the confusion matrix.

Recently the study of biological rhythms from the perspective of more complex mathematical models, such as chaos theory, has recently arose. Given the results we have obtained, there seems to be a trend that corroborates the expected behavior in a subgroup of subjects. Nevertheless, we can not get any conclusion about the importance of these characteristics on the population studied since initially these measures can be influenced by the short length of data series, which normally include a few days and are not always significant for the subject.

For future work, first we propose the use of DWT to extract new features on the series. In addition, we plan an approach based on some abstraction of the time series that represent an average behavior pattern of each subject.

Finally, it is worth to mention that this process of knowledge discovery can be applied to the study of other populations such as the shift workers.

References

1. Alcock, R.J., Manolopoulos, Y.: Time-series similarity queries employing a feature-based approach. In: 7th Hellenic Conference on Informatics, Ioannina, pp. 27–29 (1999)
2. Bandn, C., Martinez-Nicolas, A., Ordovs, J.M., Madrid, J.A., Garaulet, M.: Circadian rhythmicity as a predictor of weight-loss effectiveness. Int. J. Obes. **38**(8), 1083–1088 (2014)
3. Hall, M.A., Smith, L.A.: Feature subset selection: a correlation based filter approach. In: Kasabov, N. et al. (ed.) Proceedings of Fourth International Conference on Neural Information Processing and Intelligent Information Systems, Dunedin, New Zealand, pp. 855–858 (1997)
4. Hofman, M.A., Swaab, D.F.: Living by the clock: the circadian pacemaker in older people. Ageing Res. Rev. **5**(1), 33–51 (2006)
5. Lin, J., Keogh, E., Lonardi, S., Chiu, B.: A symbolic representation of time series, with implications for streaming algorithms. In DMKD 2003: Proceedings of the 8th ACM SIGMOD Workshop on Research Issues in Data Mining and Knowledge Discovery, pp. 2–11. ACM, New York (2003)
6. Madrid, J.A., Sarabia, J.A., Rol de Lama, M.A.: Circadian rhythm of wrist temperature in normal-living subjects: a candidate of new index of the circadian system. Physiol. Behav. **5**(1), 570–580 (2008)
7. Martinez-Nicolas, A., Ortiz-Tudela, E., Rol, M.A., Madrid, J.A.: Uncovering different masking factors on wrist skin temperature rhythm in free-living subjects. PLoS ONE **8**(4), e61142 (2013)
8. Mörchen, F.: Time series feature extraction for data mining using DWT and DFT. Technical report, Department of Mathematics and Computer Science Philipps-University Marbur, TechReport n 33 (2003)
9. Mrosovsky, N.: Rheostasis: The Physiology of Change. Oxford University, New York (1990)

10. Raymann, R.J.E.M., Swaab, D.F., Van Someren, E.J.W.: Skin temperature and sleep-onset latency: changes with age and insomnia. Physiol. Behav. **90**(2–3), 257–266 (2007)
11. Refinetti, R., Cornélissen, G., Halberg, F.: Procedures for numerical analysis of circadian rhythms. Biol. Rhythm Res. **38**(4), 275–325 (2007)
12. Sarabia, J.A., Rol, M.A., Mendiola, P., Madrid, J.A.: Circadian rhythm of wrist temperature in normal-living subjects: a candidate of new index of the circadian system. Physiol. Behav. **95**(4), 570–580 (2008)
13. Toshniwal, D.: Feature extraction from time series data. J. Comput. Methods Sci. Eng. **9**, 99–110 (2009)
14. Varela, M., Jimenez, L., Fariña, R.: Complexity analysis of the temperature curve: new information from body temperature. Eur. J. Appl. Physiol. **89**, 230–237 (2003)
15. Vivanco, P., Ortiz, V., Rol de Lama, M.A., Madrid, J.A.: Looking for the keys to diurnality downstream from the circadian clock: role of melatonin in a dual-phasing rodent, octodon degus. J. Pineal Res. **42**(3), 280–290 (2007)
16. Wang, X., Smith, K., Hyndman, R.: Characteristic-based clustering for time series data. Data Min. Knowl. Disc. **13**, 335–364 (2006). doi:10.1007/s10618-005-0039-x
17. Wu, X., Kumar, V., Quinlan, J.R., Ghosh, J., Yang, Q., Motoda, H., McLachlan, G., Ng, A., Liu, B., Yu, P., Zhou, Z.H., Steinbach, M., Hand, D., Steinberg, D.: Top 10 algorithms in data mining. Knowl. Inf. Syst. **14**(1), 1–37 (2008)

Selection of the Best Base Classifier in One-Versus-One Using Data Complexity Measures

Laura Morán-Fernández[✉], Verónica Bolón-Canedo,
and Amparo Alonso-Betanzos

Laboratory for Research and Development in Artificial Intelligence (LIDIA),
Computer Science Department, University of A Coruña, 15071 A Coruña, Spain
laura.moranf@udc.es

Abstract. When dealing with multiclass problems, the most used approach is the one based on multiple binary classifiers. This approach consists of employing class binarization techniques which transforms the
multiclass problem into a series of binary problems which are solved
individually. Then, the resultant predictions are combined to obtain a
final solution. A question arises: should the same classification algorithm
be used on all binary subproblems? Or should each subproblem be tuned
independently? This paper proposes a method to select a different classifier in each binary subproblem—following the one-versus-one strategy—
based on the analysis of the theoretical complexity of each subproblem.
The experimental results on 12 real world datasets corroborate the adequacy of the proposal when the subproblems have different structure.

1 Introduction

Classification problems with multiple classes are common in real life applications.
The simplest way to classify a dataset with more than two classes is to use
classification algorithms that can directly deal with multiple classes. However,
it is not a very extended choice because not all the machine learning algorithms
have this ability, as Support Vector Machines, for instance. Furthermore, this
approach runs the risk of focusing on the majority classes, so good results cannot
be expected [5]. The alternative is to reduce the original multiclass problem to
a series of binary problems that are solved individually. Usually, it is easier
to build a classifier to distinguish only between two classes than to consider
multiple classes in a problem, since the decision boundaries in the former case
can be simpler. This is why binarization techniques have come up to deal with
multiclass problems by dividing the original problem into easier to solve binary
problems that are faced by binary classifiers. These classifiers are usually referred
to as *base classifiers* [6].

Different decomposition strategies can be found in the literature [7]. The
most common strategies are called *one-versus-one* (OVO) and *one-versus-rest*
(OVR).

- OVO consists of learning one classifier for each pair of classes. This technique
  transforms a c-class problem into $c(c-1)/2$ two-class problems, one for each

© Springer International Publishing Switzerland 2016
O. Luaces et al. (Eds.): CAEPIA 2016, LNAI 9868, pp. 110–120, 2016.
DOI: 10.1007/978-3-319-44636-3_11

set of classes $\{i, j\}$. The binary classifier is trained with examples of its corresponding classes i, j whereas examples of the rest of classes are ignored for this problem.

- OVR strategy learns a classifier for each class, where one takes each class in turn and learns binary concepts that discriminate that class from all other classes. These two-class problems are constructed by using the examples of class i as the positive examples and the examples of the rest of the classes as the negative problems.

In a multiclass problem, the standard procedure is to select the optimal base classifier and to manage all binary subproblems. As in binarization strategies there are too many subproblems, it is possible that this base classifier could have difficulties to deal with all the subproblems appeared, returning non satisfactory results in some of them. This raises the question of how to perform model selection: should the same model and parameters be used on all subproblems, or should subproblems be tuned independently?

There exist in the literature several works that propose the selection of different base classifiers in each subproblem. Szepannek et al. [16] investigated the possibility of combining classifiers in multiclass problems, where an optimal classifier is determined using cross-validation and class pairwise models are trained. The results gave an interesting indication of the robustness of *Naive Bayes* and *Linear Discriminant Analysis* as well as they produced a "map" that shows whether using one of the single classifiers or a combination. Mendialdua et al. [13] proposed a method to select the best base classifier in OVO dynamically for each test pattern, which showed its usefulness due to the competitive results obtained. In [11] a new method (ODOAO) is presented. ODOAO is based on meta-learning where the base classifiers are trained according to the one-versus-one approach using various candidate classification algorithms and a meta-classifier is trained to optimally combine the outputs of the base classifiers. In other works, the aim is not to select the best base classifier for each subproblem but the parameters of a particular classification algorithm, as for example, the kernel function of a SVM. Lorena et al. [12] developed an automatic system, using genetic algorithms, for the selection of the parameter values of the binary SVMs contained in multiclass divisions.

In this study we focus our attention on OVO strategy, which gives the option to consider each subproblem independently and thus to select a different base classifier for each. In [14], the author deals with this problem and concludes that independent optimization is more productive than shared-hyperparameter optimization when the different subproblems in multiclass classification have different structure with respect to model selection. Otherwise, it is better to use the same base classifier. Based on this work, we propose a method to select a different base classifier in each subproblem making use of several data complexity measures. Data complexity analysis, a relatively recent proposal by Ho et al. [9], identifies data particularities which imply some difficulty for the classification task, such as overlaps between classes, class separability or decision boundary linearity. The novel procedure was tested over 12 real world datasets and has proved to be useful when the different subproblems do not have the same shape, showing competitive results in terms of classification accuracy.

The remainder of this paper is organized as follows. Section 2 describes the OVO strategy and the three decoding techniques to obtain the proper output of the model. Section 3 presents the data complexity measures. Section 4 describes the proposed method to deal with multiclass problems. Section 5 provides a brief description of the specific datasets that will be dealt with, as the classification algorithms. Moreover, the experimental study of our method over several datasets is described in this section. Finally, Sect. 6 contains our concluding remarks and proposals for future research.

2   Classification in Datasets with Multiple Classes

Class binarization approaches can be summarized using a coding matrix $M_{b \times c}$, being b the number of classifiers and c the number of classes. Once each classifier is individually trained, the global performance must be checked using a test dataset. Then, a test sample x is fed to each learning algorithm that finds an hypothesis for it. The vector predictions of these classifiers on an instance x is denoted as $h(x) = (h_1(x), \ldots, h_b(x))$ and the yth column of the matrix $M_{b \times x}$ is denoted by M_y.

Several class binarization techniques are proposed in the literature. However, this research is focused on the *One-versus-one*. To obtain the proper output there exist different techniques [3], detailed below, the first two use a measure distance between the vector $h(x)$ and the columns of matrix $M_{b \times c}$, M_y and they are described in the following paragraphs. Finally, the third measure was designed based on probability.

– *Hamming decoding.* This technique counts up the number of positions in which the sign of the vector of predictions $h(x)$ differs from the matrix column M_y. The distance measure is:

$$d_H(M_y, h(x)) = \sum_{s=1}^{b} \left(\frac{1 - sign(M_y(s)h_s(x))}{2} \right)$$

where $sign(z)$ is $+1$ if $z > 0$, -1 if $z < 0$ and 0 if $z = 0$. For an instance x and a matrix M, the predicted label $y \in \{1, \ldots, c\}$ is therefore:

$$\hat{y} = arg \min_c d_H(M_y, h(x))$$

– *Loss-based decoding.* This method takes into account the magnitude of the predictions which can often be an indication of a level of *confidence* as well as the relevant *loss function L*. The idea is to choose the label y that is most consistent with the predictions $h_s(x)$ in the sense that, if instance x were labeled y, the total *loss* on instance (x, y) would be minimized over choices of $y \in \{1, \ldots, c\}$. This means that the distance measure is the total loss on a proposed instance (x, y).

$$d_L(M_y, h(x)) = \sum_{s=1}^{l} L(M_y(s)h_s(x))$$

where $L(z)$ is the corresponding *loss function*. The loss function L adapts to each learning algorithm. In this research, where kNN and SVM are used, the more suitable for the first one is the loss function employed in logistic regression, $L(z) = log(1 + e^{-2z})$ whilst for SVM we will use the function $L(z) = (1 - z)_+$.

- *Weighted voting.* The binary classifier, for each sample, obtains a probability p for the winning class (positive or negative) while the probability for the remaining class is $1 - p$. Therefore, the accumulative probability sum of each class is computed. Then, the desired output is the one with the highest value.

3   Data Complexity Measures

Data complexity measures are a recent proposal aimed at analyzing the nature of the input dataset and at helping us to decide which classifier could be the most promising one. To analyze the theoretical complexity of the problems, we used some of the measures proposed in [9].

- *F*1: Maximum Fisher's discriminant ratio. This measure, which computes the maximum discriminative power of each feature, is defined as $f = (\mu_1 - \mu_2)^2/(\sigma_1^2 + \sigma_2^2)$, where μ_1, μ_2 are the means and σ_1^2 and σ_2^2 are the variances of the two classes, in that feature dimension. We compute f for each feature and take the maximum as the F1 measure. The range of this measure is $[0, +\infty]$. Small values represent strong overlapping.
- *F*3: Maximum (individual) feature efficiency. In a procedure that progressively removes unambiguous points falling outside the overlapping region in each chosen dimension, the efficiency of each feature is defined as the fraction of all remaining points separable by that feature. To represent the contribution of the most useful feature, we use *maximum feature efficiency* as measure *F*3. In this case, the range is $[0, 1]$. Small values of this measure indicate high overlap.
- *L*1: Minimized sum of the error distance by linear programming. This measure evaluates to what extent the training data is linearly separable. It returns the sum of the differences between a linear classifier predicted value and the actual class value. Unlike Ho et al. [9], we use SVM with a linear kernel. Small values of *L*1 indicates that the dataset is linearly separable. The measure has its domain in the range $[0, +\infty]$.
- *N*1: Fraction of points on class boundary. This measure constructs a class-blind minimum spanning tree over the entire dataset, counting the number of points incident to an edge going across the two classes. The index thus reflects the fraction of such points over all points in the dataset. The N1 measure domain is $[0, 1]$. Large values of this index indicate that the majority of points lay closely to the class boundary which could affect to the classifier to define the class boundary accurately.

– N2: Ratio of average intra/inter class NN distance. This measure starts by computing the Euclidean distance from each data point to its nearest neighbor from the same class and its nearest neighbor from the other class. It then calculates the ratio between the average (over all points) of all distances to intraclass nearest neighbors and the average of all the distances to interclass nearest neighbors. The range of this measure is $[0, +\infty]$. High values suggest that samples from the same class are disperse.

4 Proposed Method: Classifier Selection in OVO Making Use of Data Complexity Measures (CSC)

The binary subproblems in which the original multiclass dataset is divided can have very different structure, hence the use of the different base classifiers can be appropriate. Because of that, we proposed a new method, called CSC (Classifier Selection based on Complexity), that tries to select the best base classifier in each binary subproblem making use of several data complexity measures. The pseudo-code for the proposed method is shown in Algorithm 1.

Two of the measures described in Sect. 3, F1 and F3, refer to the overlaps in feature values from different classes whilst the other three (L1, N1 and N2) relate to the separability of the classes. As it is concluded in [4], F1 presents the most marked and robust effect on all the classifiers' accuracy. In the case of F3, its variation affects to all classifiers, but their accuracy rates are robust just when the metric reaches its maximal values. The behavior of each separability measure is different. L1 variation affects significantly to all the classifiers, being SVM the most robust one. N1, due to its nearest neighbor base definition, shows a remarkable effect on kNN classifier. N2 presents a behavior similar to N1 (useful for kNN classifier), but it is not as robust. The information supported by these measurements will restrict us to select either kNN or SVM as classifiers.

Algorithm 1. Pseudo-code for Classifier Selection based on Complexity

---
　　Divide the dataset in $c(c-1)/2$ binary subproblems
　　for each binary subproblem **do**
　　　　N1 ← value of the data complexity measure N1 computed on subproblem data
　　　　N2 ← value of the data complexity measure N2 computed on subproblem data
　　　　if (N1<0.1 **and** N2<0.4) **then**
　　　　　　apply kNN classifier
　　　　else
　　　　　　apply SVM classifier
　　　　end if
　　end for
　　Combine the resultant predictions to obtain a final solution

---

The domain of competence of the kNN classifier is located in problems with compact classes and little interleaving. Particularly for problems with less than

10 % of points in the boundary and intra-interclass nearest neighbor distances less than 0.4, the kNN has good applicability [10]. For problems outside this region, the kNN classifier is hardly recommended. Because of that, we will apply kNN when the subproblem matches the rule ($N1 < 0.1\ and\ N2 < 0.4$). In other case, SVM will be applied.

5   Experiments

In this section we present and discuss the experimental results of our proposed method over 12 datasets with multiple classes. A comparative study will be carried out between our proposed method CSC and the approaches which use the same classifier for all the binary subproblems. Then, we will analyze in depth the theoretical complexity of the datasets chosen in order to study if our method obtains better results than the other approaches when the different classes have different structure.

5.1   Experimental Setup

The proposed method is applied to nine real world problems from the UCI Machine Learning Repository and three microarray datasets (braintumor-2, cll-sub111 and leukemia-1), which are described in Table 1 in terms of the number of features, the number of samples and the number of classes. In the case of missing values we removed those samples from the datasets. The datasets are available with only training set, then we have opted for computing a 5-fold cross-validation to estimate the error rate.

Table 1. Characteristics of the 12 datasets.

Dataset	#Features	#Samples	#Classes	Download
braintumor-2	10367	50	4	[15]
cllsub111	11349	111	3	[17]
dermatology	33	366	6	[2]
glass	9	214	6	[2]
iris	5	150	3	[2]
leukemia-1	5327	72	3	[15]
optdigits	64	5620	10	[2]
page-blocks	10	5473	5	[2]
pendigits	16	10992	10	[2]
satimage	36	6435	6	[2]
waveform	21	5000	3	[2]
wine	13	178	3	[2]

Two different classifiers, each belonging to a different family, were chosen to evaluate complexity: non-linear (kNN) and linear (SVM using a linear kernel). Both classifiers were executed using the Weka [8] tool, using default values for the parameters.

- **kNN** [1] is a classification strategy that is an example of a "lazy learner". An object is classified by majority vote of its neighbors and is assigned to the class most common among its k nearest neighbors. If $k = 1$ (as is the case in this study), then the object is simply assigned to the class of the single nearest neighbor.
- A **Support Vector Machine** (SVM) is a learning algorithm, used for classification, regression and other tasks, which constructs a hyperplane or set of hyperplanes in a high—or infinite—dimensional space [18].

5.2   Results

In this section we compare our proposal with the methods using the same classifier for all the subproblems. OVO will be applied in all the approaches with the three decoding techniques: Weighted voting (WV), Hamming (H-dec) and Loss-based (LB-dec).

- OVO-kNN: the method applies the kNN classifier in all the binary subproblems.
- OVO-SVM: the method applies the SVM classifier in all the binary subproblems.
- OVO-CSC: our proposed method, which selects the best base classifier (kNN or SVM) in each binary subproblem making use of several data complexity measures.

Table 2 shows the classification accuracy obtained by the three approaches for the 12 datasets chosen (highest accuracy rates highlighted in bold). As can be seen, our proposed method achieved the best results in 5 of the 12 datasets. For the leukemia-1 and waveform datasets our proposal matches with the method OVO-SVM, which means that OVO-CSC has selected SVM as classifier for all the subproblems. These results show that our proposal obtains good results, but not the best for all situations. However, the aim of this work is to analyze if our method obtains better results than those which use the same classifier for all the subproblems when the different classes had not the same structure, not to achieve the highest classification performance for all the problems. Because of that, we analyze the theoretical complexity of these datasets using the measures mentioned above. Figure 1 illustrates the behavior of the data complexity measures F1, F3, L1, N1 and N2, where the values of the metric is the average of the binary subproblems into which each multiclass dataset was decomposed. Standard deviations are also shown, where the larger the value, the greater the difference in structure between the subproblems.

As can be seen, datasets as iris or cllsub111 show high standard deviation values in most of the data complexity measures. To make it clearer, we calculate

Table 2. Classification accuracy of different methods for the 12 datasets.

	OVO-kNN			OVO-SVM			OVO-CSC		
	WV	H-dec	LB-dec	WV	H-dec	LB-dec	WV	H-dec	LB-dec
braintumor-2	54.00	54.00	54.00	**74.00**	**74.00**	**74.00**	64.00	64.00	64.00
cllsub111	60.30	60.30	60.30	**75.70**	**75.70**	**75.70**	74.62	74.62	74.62
dermatology	96.37	96.37	96.37	96.65	96.65	96.65	97.48	**97.84**	**97.84**
glass	64.53	64.53	64.53	53.34	53.34	53.34	**65.87**	65.39	**65.87**
iris	95.33	95.33	95.33	94.00	94.00	94.00	**97.33**	**97.33**	**97.33**
leukemia-1	77.60	77.60	77.60	**97.10**	**97.10**	**97.10**	**97.10**	**97.10**	**97.10**
optdigits	98.56	98.56	**98.57**	98.27	98.27	98.31	98.42	98.42	98.43
page-blocks	**96.13**	**96.13**	**96.13**	93.90	93.90	93.90	93.90	93.90	93.90
pendigits	99.34	99.34	99.34	97.88	97.88	97.87	**99.35**	**99.35**	99.34
satimage	86.40	86.40	86.39	87.44	87.44	87.44	**90.10**	**90.10**	**90.10**
waveform	76.24	76.24	76.24	**87.92**	**87.92**	**87.92**	**87.92**	**87.92**	**87.92**
wine	94.36	94.36	94.36	**97.75**	**97.75**	**97.75**	96.65	96.65	96.65
Mean	83.26	83.26	83.26	87.83	87.83	87.83	**88.56**	88.55	**88.59**
	(83.26)			(87.83)			**(88.57)**		

the average of the deviations of the data complexity measures—normalizing F1 because it is not in the range $[0, 1]$—for each dataset (see Table 3). With the average of all the measures, a significant difference arises between the obtained values, with a clear cut under 0.13 value, corresponding to the wine dataset (see Table 3). In order to find out the appropriate threshold, we should also take into account the average of the measures used in our proposal, N1 and N2. In this case, the biggest gap takes place in the value 0.101 that corresponds to the iris dataset. Among these five datasets with mean values higher than 0.101, glass is the dataset with the lowest average of the deviations for all the measures. Thus, the threshold is established at that value. As the final result of the procedure, the datasets are separated into two clusters; one containing iris, cllsub111, braintumor-2, satimage, pendigits, dermatology and glass and other containing optdigits, page-blocks, wine, waveform and leukemia-1.

Five of the seven datasets with the highest mean values are those obtaining the best classification performance through our proposed method. The other two datasets are cllsub111 and braintumor-2, both microarray datasets, for which best performance was not achieved by our proposed method. This might be happening because SVMs were specifically designed to handle high dimensional data, such as these microarray datasets (also leukemia-1). In fact, OVO-CSC obtain the best results for leukemia-1, trying with OVO-SVM, and thus selecting SVM as base classifier for all binary subproblems.

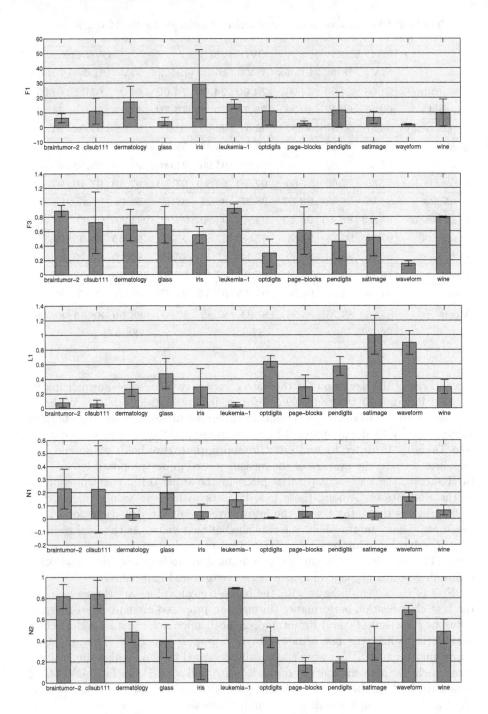

Fig. 1. Theoretical complexity of the 12 datasets based on the measures F1, F3, L1, N1 and N2.

The results for these datasets indicate that when binary subproblems have significantly different shape—high deviation standard values—it is advisable to allow each binary subproblem to select its own classifier.

Table 3. Average of the standard deviations of the data complexity measures for each dataset. Thresholds are indicated with an asterisk (*) whilst values higher than the respective thresholds (All measures or N1 & N2) are highlighted in bold.

	iris	cllsub111	braintumor-2	satimage	pendigits	dermatology	glass	optdigits	page-blocks	wine	waveform	leukemia-1
All measures	**0.313**	**0.264**	**0.196**	**0.188**	**0.187**	**0.181**	**0.172**	**0.158**	**0.133**	**0.130***	0.059	0.057
N1 & N2	**0.101***	**0.234**	**0.133**	**0.105**	0.030	0.072	**0.138**	0.051	0.056	0.077	0.038	0.031

6   Conclusions

There are two main approaches for dealing with classification problems that involve more than two classes. One tries to transform the multiclass problem in several binary subproblems, while the other deals directly with the multiclass problem. Several class binarization techniques are proposed in the literature, and in this work we have applied the widely used OVO strategy in combination with three decoding techniques. In this approach, should the same base classifier be used on all binary subproblem? Or should these subproblems be tuned independently? Trying to answer this question, in this paper we propose a method to select a different base classifier in each subproblem making use of several data complexity measures. The novel procedure tested in 12 datasets has proved to be useful when the different subproblems in multiclass classification have different structure with respect to model selection, showing competitive results in terms of classification accuracy.

For future work, it would be interesting to make use of other classification algorithms, not only kNN and SVM. Another future research lines are studying if the combination model selected affects the performance of the method and also apply feature selection, specially when dealing with microarray data.

Acknowledgments. This research has been financially supported in part by the Spanish Ministerio de Economía y Competitividad (research project TIN2015-65069-C2-1-R), by European Union FEDER funds and by the Consellería de Industria of the Xunta de Galicia (research project GRC2014/035).

References

1. Aha, D.W., Kibler, D., Albert, M.K.: Instance-based learning algorithms. Mach. Learn. **6**(1), 37–66 (1991)
2. Bache, K., Linchman, M.: UCI machine learning repository. Univerity of California, Irvine, School of Information and Computer Sciences. http://archive.ics.uci.edu/ml/

3. Bolón-Canedo, V., Sánchez-Maroño, N., Alonso-Betanzos, A.: Feature selection and classification in multiple class datasets: an application to KDD cup 99 dataset. Expert Syst. Appl. **38**(5), 5947–5957 (2011)
4. Cano, J.-R.: Analysis of data complexity measures for classification. Expert Syst. Appl. **40**(12), 4820–4831 (2013)
5. Forman, G.: An extensive empirical study of feature selection metrics for text classification. J. Mach. Learn. Res. **3**, 1289–1305 (2003)
6. Fürnkranz, J.: Round robin classification. J. Mach. Learn. Res. **2**, 721–747 (2002)
7. Galar, M., Fernández, A., Barrenechea, E., Bustince, H., Herrera, F.: An overview of ensemble methods for binary classifiers in multi-class problems: experimental study on one-vs-one and one-vs-all schemes. Pattern Recogn. **44**(8), 1761–1776 (2011)
8. Hall, M., Frank, E., Holmes, G., Pfahringer, B., Reutemann, P., Witten, I.H.: The weka data mining software: an update. ACM SIGKDD Explor. Newsl. **11**(1), 10–18 (2009)
9. Ho, T.K., Basu, M., Law, M.H.C.: Measures of geometrical complexity in classification problems. In: Basu, M., Ho, T.K. (eds.) Data Complexity in Pattern Recognition, pp. 1–23. Springer, London (2006)
10. Ho, T.K., Bernadó-Mansilla, E.: Classifier domains of competence in data complexity space. In: Basu, M., Ho, T.K. (eds.) Data Complexity in Pattern Recognition, pp. 135–152. Springer, London (2006)
11. Kang, S., Cho, S.: Optimal construction of one-against-one classifier based on metalearning. Neurocomputing **167**, 459–466 (2015)
12. Lorena, A.C., De Carvalho, A.C.: Evolutionary tuning of svm parameter values in multiclass problems. Neurocomputing **71**(16), 3326–3334 (2008)
13. Mendialdua, I., Martínez-Otzeta, J.M., Rodríguez-Rodríguez, I., Ruiz-Vázquez, T., Sierra, B.: Dynamic selection of the best base classifier in one versus one. Knowl.-Based Syst. **85**, 298–306 (2015)
14. Reid, S.R.: Model combination in multiclass classification. University of Colorado at Boulder (2010)
15. Statnikov, A., Aliferis, C., Tsardinos, I.: Gems: gene expression model selector. http://www.gems-system.org/
16. Szepannek, G., Bischl, B., Weihs, C.: On the combination of locally optimal pairwise classifiers. Eng. Appl. Artif. Intell. **22**(1), 79–85 (2009)
17. Arizona State University. Feature selection datasets. http://featureselection.asu.edu/datasets.php
18. Vapnik, V.N., Vapnik, V.: Statistical Learning Theory, vol. 1. Wiley, New York (1998)

Using Data Complexity Measures
for Thresholding in Feature Selection Rankers

Borja Seijo-Pardo[✉], Verónica Bolón-Canedo, and Amparo Alonso-Betanzos

Department of Computer Science, University of A Coruña,
Campus de Elviña s/n, 15071 A Coruña, Spain
borja.Seijo@udc.es

Abstract. In the last few years, feature selection has become essential to confront the dimensionality problem, removing irrelevant and redundant information. For this purpose, ranker methods have become an approximation commonly used since they do not compromise the computational efficiency. Ranker methods return an ordered ranking of all the features, and thus it is necessary to establish a threshold to reduce the number of features to deal with. In this work, a practical subset of features is selected according to three different data complexity measures, releasing the user from the task of choosing a fixed threshold in advance. The proposed approach was tested on six different DNA microarray datasets which have brought a difficult challenge for researchers due to the high number of gene expression and the low number of patients. The adequacy of the proposed approach in terms of classification error was checked by the use of an ensemble of ranker methods with a Support Vector Machine as classifier. This study shows that our approach was able to achieve competitive results compared with those obtained by fixed threshold approach, which is the standard in most research works.

1 Introduction

Over the last years, the real-world scenarios have incremented considerably their size, both in number of instances, known as *sample size*, and number of features, known as *dimensionality*. Feature selection (*FS*) has become one of the essential steps in preprocessing for many data mining applications, since it allows to eliminate irrelevant and redundant information, and thus reducing storage needs and improving computational time needed by the machine learning algorithms. Several studies have demonstrated that *FS* can greatly contribute to improve performance of posterior classification methods [4,6,18].

Feature selection algorithms can be classified in three different categories, according to their structure [8]: *filters*, *wrappers* and *embedded* algorithms. *Filter methods* [3] use an evaluation function which is fast to compute and is independent of the classifier used. *Wrappers* [3] work hand in hand with a classification algorithm, in such a way that the error committed in each iteration by the latter gives the scoring for the evaluation function of the former. Wrappers require greater computational resources than filters. Lastly, *embedded methods* [3] are in

O. Luaces et al. (Eds.): CAEPIA 2016, LNAI 9868, pp. 121–131, 2016.
DOI: 10.1007/978-3-319-44636-3_12

the middle of the other two. In the first place, they work with a classification algorithm, but they do not use the error, like wrappers do, but some intermediate result. In the second place, they are more computationally intensive than filters, but lesser than wrappers. Thus, in this paper, and after a preliminary study involving the three approaches, filters and embedded methods were chosen because they allow to reduce the dimensionality of the data without compromising the time and memory requirements of machine learning algorithms.

In feature selection, there are two different approaches when conducting the evaluation of the features of a dataset: (i) *individual evaluation* and (ii) *subset evaluation* [21]. In the first case, an ordered ranking of all features is returned by assigning a level of relevance to each of these features. In the second case, successive subsets of features are generated and evaluated iteratively, according to an optimality criterion, until reaching the final subset of selected features. Since subset evaluation methods can suffer from a problem of computational efficiency, most of the feature selection methods follow the individual evaluation approach, also known as ranker methods, and so this paper will be focused on them. As mentioned above, ranker methods return an ordered ranking of all the features, and eventually it is necessary to establish a threshold to reduce the number of features to deal with. However, how to establish this threshold is not an easy to solve question, and will be the focus of this work.

In particular, we will try different approaches for the automatic selection of a threshold when using an ensemble of ranker methods which we have successfully presented in a previous work [19]. Ensemble learning builds on the assumption that combining the output of multiple experts is better than the output of any single expert [10]. Typically, ensemble learning has been applied to classification, although it can be also thought as a means of improving other machine learning disciplines such as *FS*.

Therefore, the idea of this paper is the use of different complexity measures to automatically establish the threshold and obtain a practical subset of features, since it is a recent proposal to represent characteristics of the data which are considered difficult in classification tasks beyond estimates of error rates [2]. We assume that good candidate features would contribute to decrease the complexity and thus should be maintained. This approach is tested on an ensemble of ranker methods (four filters and two embedded methods), combining the different individual rankings by the *Minimum union method (Min)* and using a Support Vector Machine (SVM) with a Radial Basis Function (*RBF*) kernel as a classifier. The results obtained by four different fixed thresholds (which is the regularly established procedure) are taken as baseline to compare the results of the proposed approach.

In this study, an extensive experimentation on different DNA microarray datasets is carried out. DNA microarray experiments generate a high number of gene expressions (*dimension*) for a low number of patients (*samples*). This kind of datasets pose an enormous challenge for feature selection researchers due to the high dimensionality and the small sample size. The experimentation shows the adequacy of our proposed method for automatically determining the threshold.

The remainder of this paper is organized as follows: In Sect. 2 the proposed data complexity measures are introduced, and their functions are presented. Next, Sect. 3 shows the methodology and the specific configuration of each step. Section 4 describes the datasets and provides the experimental results. Finally, Sect. 5 details some concluding remarks.

2 Data Complexity Measures

Ranker methods return an ordered ranking of all the features and, in order to obtain a practical subset of these features, a threshold is necessary. In this work, instead of choosing an arbitrary threshold, we propose herein the use of data complexity measures to establish the threshold value both automatically and tailored for the dataset. Data complexity measures were originally developed with the aim of identifying and solving possible problems in the classification process. When popular classifiers do not achieve the required or anticipated accuracy in a practical application, possible causes can be deficiencies in the algorithms, intrinsic difficulties in the data, and a mismatch between methods and problems. Complexity measures provide a basis for analyzing classifier behavior beyond estimates of error rates. The complexity measures can be divided into several categories [2]:

1. *Measures of overlaps in feature values from different classes:* These measures consider the effectiveness of a single feature dimension separating the classes, or the composite effects of a number of dimensions.
2. *Measures of separability of classes:* These measures evaluate to the extent to which two classes are separable by examining the existence and shape of the class boundary.
3. *Measures of geometry, topology, and density of manifolds:* These measures assume that a class is made up of a single or multiple manifolds that form the support of the probability distribution of the given class. They give indirect characterizations of a class separability.

In this work, complexity measures of category 1 are used since they can estimate the relevance of each feature individually and, therefore, can help to establish a cutoff threshold for the ordered ranking of features. In this category three different complexity measures exist, which are briefly described below:

1. *Maximum Fisher's Discriminant Ratio (F1).* This measure is defined for a multidimensional problem as:

$$F1 = \frac{\sum_{i=1,j=1,i\neq j}^{c} p_i p_j (\mu_i - \mu_j)^2}{\sum_{i=1}^{c} p_i \sigma_i^2}, \tag{1}$$

where μ_i, σ_i^2, and p_i are the mean, variance, and proportion of the ith class c, respectively. The Fisher discriminant ratio values are calculated for each feature of the dataset individually. In practice the inverse of the Fisher ratio $(1/F1)$ is preferred, such that a small complexity value represents an easy problem.

2. *Volume of Overlap Region (F2).* Let the maximum and minimum values of each feature f_i in class c_j be $max(f_i, c_j)$ and $min(f_i, c_j)$, then the overlap measure *F2* is defined to be:

$$F2 = \prod_i \frac{MINMAX_i - MAXMIN_i}{MAXMAX_i - MINMIN_i}, \tag{2}$$

where $i = 1, \ldots, d$ for a d-dimensional problem, and

$$MINMAX_i = MIN(max(f_i, c_1), max(f_i, c_2))$$
$$MAXMIN_i = MAX(min(f_i, c_1), min(f_i, c_2))$$
$$MAXMAX_i = MAX(max(f_i, c_1), max(f_i, c_2))$$
$$MINMIN_i = MIN(min(f_i, c_1), min(f_i, c_2))$$

In the original definition of this measure, the authors compute the product (volume of the overlap) instead of a sum (length of the overlap). The side effect of employing the product is that the value of this measure decreases drastically as dimensionality increases and, therefore, it is easy to obtain a value of 0 for this measure, which would not give any information. Thus, as this can be a problem when dealing with high input dimensionality datasets, such as microarrays, it has been opted for using the sum (length of the overlap region). For multiclass problems, *F2* is computed for each pair of classes, then the absolute value is obtained for all of them, and finally the sum of all these values is returned as output. A low value of this measure means that the features can discriminate between the instances of different classes.

3. *Maximum (Individual) Feature Efficiency (F3).* In a procedure that progressively removes unambiguous points falling outside the overlapping region in each chosen dimension [1], the efficiency of each feature is defined as the fraction of all remaining points separable by that feature. To represent the contribution of the most useful feature in this sense, the maximum feature efficiency (largest fraction of points distinguishable with only one feature) is used as a measure. The maximum feature efficiency *F3* is defined for a d-dimensional problem as:

$$F3 = \sum_{i=1}^{d} \frac{|\{f_i \in [MINMAX_i, MAXMIN_i]\}|}{d}, \tag{3}$$

where

$$MINMAX_i = MIN(max(f_i, c_1), max(f_i, c_2))$$
$$MAXMIN_i = MAX(min(f_i, c_1), min(f_i, c_2))$$

For multiclass problems, *F3* is computed for each pair of classes, then the absolute value for all of them is obtained, and finally the maximum of all these values is returned. The *F3* values are calculated for each feature of the dataset individually. In practice the inverse of this measure $(1/F3)$ is preferred, such that a small complexity value represents an easy problem.

3   Proposed Methodology

The experimental study consists of a comparison between the proposed approach, for automatically determining a threshold, and the fixed threshold approach, which is the standard in most research works. The experiments performed can be divided into four main steps according to Fig. 1.

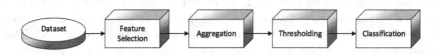

Fig. 1. Diagram of the experimental methodology applied in this study.

First, a feature selection process is carried out in order to eliminate the redundant and irrelevant features, and maintain the relevant ones. An ensemble approach was chosen to perform this process (aiming at obtaining a better result than using individual methods), where all the feature selection methods are rankers, i.e. they do not select a subset of features, but sort all the features. Then, as an ensemble is chosen, it is necessary to perform an aggregation step, combining the different feature rankings achieved above to obtain a final single ranking. Subsequently, since the feature selection methods employed are rankers, a cutoff threshold is required, allowing to obtain an optimal subset of features. Finally, a classification step is performed to check the adequacy of the proposed approach in terms of classification error. The sections below detail the particular settings of each step of the proposed methodology.

3.1   Feature Selection Methods

The feature selection methods used to conform the ensemble are rankers. Among the broad suite of ranker methods available in the literature, four filters (*Chi-Square* [11], *Information Gain* [16], *mRMR* [15] and *ReliefF* [9]) and two embedded methods (*SVM-RFE* [7] and *FS-P* [12]) were chosen. This set of ranker methods was selected because (i) they are based on different metrics so they ensure a great diversity in the final ensemble; and (ii) they are widely used by researchers in feature selection.

3.2   Aggregation Method

The outputs of the components of the ensemble, i.e. the different feature selection methods aforementioned, have to be combined in order to produce a unique final output. The combination methods, also known as 'aggregators', are responsible for conducting the fusion of several rankings using some reduction function. A single final ranking is derived as output of the union method that combine all the input rankings. In this paper, the *Minimum union method (Min)* was chosen to perform the combination of the different input rankings. The reduction function of this 'aggregator' is based on simple arithmetic operations, selecting the minimum of the relevance values granted by the rankings [20]. Despite its simplicity, it proved to achieve the best results on DNA microarray datasets in a previous work [19]. The behavior of this method will be illustrated with a simple example. Imagine that we apply an ensemble of 3 different feature selection methods on a dataset with 4 different features to be ranked $\{a, b, c, d\}$. Therefore, as can be seen in Table 1, we obtain 3 different rankings of features $\{R_1, R_2, R_3\}$, one for each feature selection method in the ensemble. The last column of the table illustrates the calculations made by the *Min* method. This method computes the best value achieved by each ranking along the different rankings, where best means the highest position. Notice that using this method can cause ties between features. In this case, the elements which are tied will be returned in their original position. Thus, in this example, the *Min* method will return the ranking $\{a, b, c, d\}$.

Table 1. Example of how the *Min* 'aggregator' works with multiple rankings.

Element	R_1	R_2	R_3	R_{Min}
a	1	2	3	1
b	2	1	1	1
c	3	3	2	2
d	4	4	4	4

3.3   Cutoff Thresholds

Finally, to calculate the cutoff threshold for the ordered ranking and to obtain the final subset of features, Algorithm 1 is applied. This algorithm obtains the optimal number of features that should be selected in the final ranking. The main part of Algorithm 1 is the function that calculates the complexity value of each feature, taken from [13]:

$$e = \alpha \times C + (1 - \alpha) \times \rho \tag{4}$$

where α is a parameter with value in the interval $[0, 1]$ to control the relative emphasis on both the number of features to retain and the weight given to the complexity measure ($\alpha = 0.75$ empirically established for this work), C is one of the aforementioned complexity measures in Sect. 2 (note that C takes the value of the inverse in the case of *F1* and *F3* measures), and ρ is the percentage of features retained (ranging from one to the total number of features of the dataset). A small complexity value e represents an easier problem. If the cumulative complexity measure of the partial subset is less than that obtained by total subset, the features of the partial subset become part of the total subset and added their complexity values. The process ends when the cumulative complexity measure of the partial subset is greater than that obtained by total subset, and the selected features are those that form this total subset.

Algorithm 1. Pseudo-code to limit the final ordered ranking

Input: $F = (f_1, \ldots, f_{nF})$ ▷ Ordered feature vector obtained from the aggregation step
Input: C ▷ Complexity measure to be used

Output: S ▷ Final subset of features

1: $E = \infty$ ▷ Cumulative complexity measure of the total subset
2: $Ep = 0$ ▷ Cumulative complexity measure of the partial subset
3: $I = \text{Calculate } \lfloor log_2(nF) \rfloor$ ▷ Dimension of comparable subsets
4: **for** each feature $f(pos)$ in F **do**   ▷ pos takes values from 1 to nF
5:      Calculate $\rho = pos/nF$ ▷ Percentage of selected features
6:      Calculate $e(f) = \alpha \times C(f) + (1 - \alpha) \times \rho$ ▷ Complexity value of feature f
7:      Obtain $Ep = Ep + e(f)$ ▷ Cumulative complexity value
8:      **if** $f \bmod I = 0$ **then**   ▷ Compares the complexity between the subsets
9:          **if** $Ep < E$ **then**
10:              **if** $f == I$ **then**   ▷ Checks if the current iteration is the first
11:                  $E = 0$ ▷ Sets the E value to 0 to perform the next step
12:              **end if**
13:              $E = E + Ep$
14:          **else**
15:              **break**   ▷ Obtains the number of features pos that form the final subset
16:          **end if**
17:      **end if**
18: **end for**
19: $S = F(1, \ldots, pos)$ ▷ Obtains a final subset of features S (first pos features in the vector F)

3.4 Classification Method

A Support Vector Machine (SVM) with a Radial Basis Function (RBF) kernel has been chosen to check the adequacy of the proposed approach in terms of classification error. This classifier has been selected as it tends to obtain better results than other classifiers over microarray datasets [14].

4 Experimental Study

The proposed methodology has been tested over microarray datasets. Specifically, DNA microarray experiments generate a high number of gene expressions (dimension) for a low number of patients (samples). An important application of DNA microarray data is to separate healthy patients from cancer patients based on their gene expression "profile". Thus, due to their high dimensionality, classifiers tend to overfit, and it is necessary to eliminate irrelevant and redundant information as can be seen in the review of feature selection methods applied to microarray datasets [5].

Six different DNA binary microarray datasets, which are listed in Table 2, were chosen to perform the experiments. The datasets originally divided into training and test sets were maintained, whilst, those with only training set were randomly divided using the common rule 2/3 for training and 1/3 for testing for the sake of comparison. This division introduces a more challenging scenario since, in some datasets, the distribution of the classes in the training set differs from the one in the test set. Table 2 shows the number of attributes and samples and also the distribution of the binary classes, indicating unbalances.

Table 2. Binary microarray datasets employed in the experimental study.

Dataset	Features	Samples		Train distribution (%)	Test distribution (%)	Download
		Train	Test			
Colon	2 000	42	20	67–33	60–40	[17]
DLBCL	4 026	32	15	50–50	53–47	[17]
CNS	7 129	40	20	65–35	65–35	[17]
Leukemia	7 129	38	34	71–29	59–41	[17]
Lung	12 533	32	149	50–50	90–10	[17]
Ovarian	15 154	169	84	35–65	38–62	[17]

The results obtained by the different configurations are displayed in Table 3. This table shows the test classification error of different methods and the number of relevant features selected by each threshold is shown in parenthesis. Table 3 is divided in two parts: (i) the first three rows represent the classification error obtained by using measures of complexity to define the cutoff threshold (*F1*, *F2* and *F3* respectively), and (ii) the last four rows refer to baseline results, which correspond to the application of three different fixed thresholds over the final ensemble ranking. These values are:

- *10 %*: selects the 10 % most relevant features of the final ordered ranking.
- *25 %*: selects the 25 % most relevant features of the final ordered ranking.
- *50 %*: selects the 50 % most relevant features of the final ordered ranking.

In addition, the classification error without performing the feature selection preprocessing has been added as the last row of the Table 3.

The experimental results demonstrate the suitability of performing the feature selection preprocess on DNA microarray datasets. In addition, it is demonstrated the adequacy of using complexity measures to establish the threshold value in feature selection ensembles composed by ranker methods since they match or improve upon the results obtained by fixed thresholds. In fact, it can be seen that the complexity measures *F2* and *F3* always achieve the best error results on the different datasets. Also, the complexity measure *F1* achieves the best error results in 5 out of 6 datasets. In addition to this, the proposed thresholds have the added benefit of reducing significantly the dataset dimensionality, using a very small subset of features for the classification process.

Table 3. Test classification error for DNA microarray datasets. The value shown in parenthesis represents the number of relevant features selected by each method. The best error for each dataset is highlighted in bold face.

Threshold	Colon	DLBCL	CNS	Leukemia	Lung	Ovarian
F1	40.00 (231)	**6.67** (12)	**35.00** (13)	**14.71** (13)	**0.67** (14)	**0.00** (14)
F2	**20.00** (11)	**6.67** (12)	**35.00** (13)	**14.71** (13)	**0.67** (14)	**0.00** (14)
F3	**20.00** (11)	**6.67** (12)	**35.00** (13)	**14.71** (13)	**0.67** (14)	**0.00** (14)
10 %	40.00 (200)	13.33 (403)	**35.00** (713)	41.18 (713)	**0.67** (1253)	4.76 (1515)
25 %	40.00 (500)	13.33 (1007)	**35.00** (1782)	41.18 (1782)	**0.67** (3133)	7.14 (3789)
50 %	40.00 (1000)	13.33 (2013)	**35.00** (3565)	41.18 (3565)	1.34 (6267)	9.52 (7577)
Without FS	40.00 (2000)	20.00 (4026)	**35.00** (7129)	41.18 (7129)	4.70 (12533)	38.10 (15154)

5   Conclusions and Discussion

Over recent years, the volume of the massive data is constantly growing, both in size and dimensionality, and therefore, it is important to identify which information does not contribute to machine learning models. For this purpose, and as it has been demonstrated in this study, a feature selection preprocess is essential to confront the high dimensionality problem, choosing the best features and remove irrelevant and redundant attributes from data. Ranker methods are the best approach due to they do not compromise the computational efficiency and can determine an order of significance of the features, also known as ranking. These rankings perform an ordering of all the features, and therefore, a threshold is necessary in order to obtain a practical subset of features.

In this paper, we have opted for the use of data complexity measures to establish the threshold value, releasing the user from the task of choosing a fixed threshold in advance. Three different complexity measures were selected to obtain the final practical subset of features. The results achieved by three fixed thresholds, which is the regularly established procedure, are taken as baseline to compare the accuracy of our approach. In addition, the results obtained by not performing the feature selection process are included in the study.

An ensemble of ranker methods for feature selection was used to test the proposed approach. Six well-known feature selection algorithms were chosen to form part of the ensemble and the individual rankings were combined with the *Minimum union method (Min)*. The experiments on six DNA microarray datasets, which have brought a difficult challenge for researchers, using a *SVM-RBF* classifier to check the adequacy in terms of error test, showed that our proposal was able to obtain competitive results compared with the baseline. In addition, it has the added benefit of significantly reducing the dataset dimension and selecting automatically the threshold to establish the final number of features to consider in the classification stage.

Acknowledgments. This research has been financially supported in part by the Spanish Ministerio de Economía y Competitividad (research project TIN2015-65069-

C2-1-R), by European Union FEDER funds and by the Consellería de Industria of the Xunta de Galicia (research project GRC2014/035).

References

1. Ball, G.H., Hall, D.J.: Some implications of interactive graphic computer systems for data analysis and statistics. Technometrics **12**(1), 17–31 (1970)
2. Basu, M., Ho, T.K.: Data Complexity in Pattern Recognition. Springer Science & Business Media, Berlin (2006)
3. Boln-Canedo, V., Snchez-Maroo, N., Alonso-Betanzos, A.: Feature Selection for High-Dimensional Data. Springer, Heidelberg (2016)
4. Bolón-Canedo, V., Sánchez-Maroño, N., Alonso-Betanzos, A.: A review of feature selection methods on synthetic data. Knowl. Inf. Syst. **34**(3), 483–519 (2013)
5. Bolón-Canedo, V., Sánchez-Maroño, N., Alonso-Betanzos, A., Benítez, J.M., Herrera, F.: A review of microarray datasets and applied feature selection methods. Inf. Sci. **282**, 111–135 (2014)
6. Gao, K., Khoshgoftaar, T.M., Wang, H.: An empirical investigation of filter attribute selection techniques for software quality classification. In: IEEE International Conference on Information Reuse and Integration, IRI 2009, pp. 272–277. IEEE (2009)
7. Guyon, I., Weston, J., Barnhill, S., Vapnik, V.: Gene selection for cancer classification using support vector machines. Mach. Learn. **46**(1–3), 389–422 (2002)
8. Guyon, I.: Feature Extraction: Foundations and Applications, vol. 207. Springer Science & Business Media, Berlin (2006)
9. Kononenko, I.: Estimating attributes: analysis and extensions of RELIEF. In: Bergadano, F., De Raedt, L. (eds.) Machine Learning: ECML-94. LNCS, vol. 784, pp. 171–182. Springer, Heidelberg (1994)
10. Kuncheva, L.: Combining Pattern Classifiers: Methods and Algorithms. Wiley-Interscience, Hoboken (2004)
11. Liu, H., Setiono, R.: Chi2: feature selection and discretization of numeric attributes. In: 2012 IEEE 24th International Conference on Tools with Artificial Intelligence, pp. 388–388. IEEE Computer Society (1995)
12. Mejía-Lavalle, M., Sucar, E., Arroyo, G.: Feature selection with a perceptron neural net. In: Proceedings of the International Workshop on Feature Selection for Data Mining, pp. 131–135 (2006)
13. Morán-Fernández, L., Bolón-Canedo, V., Alonso-Betanzos, A.: A time efficient approach for distributed feature selection partitioning by features. In: Puerta, J.M., et al. (eds.) CAEPIA 2015. LNCS, vol. 9422, pp. 245–254. Springer, Heidelberg (2015). doi:10.1007/978-3-319-24598-0_22
14. Navarro, F.F.G.: Feature selection in cancer research: microarray gene expression and in vivo 1H-MRS domains. Ph.D. thesis, Universitat Politècnica de Catalunya (2011)
15. Peng, H., Long, F., Ding, C.: Feature selection based on mutual information criteria of max-dependency, max-relevance, and min-redundancy. IEEE Trans. Pattern Anal. Mach. Intell. **27**(8), 1226–1238 (2005)
16. Quinlan, J.: Induction of decision trees. Mach. Learn. **1**(1), 81–106 (1986)
17. Ridge, K.: Bio-medical dataset. http://datam.i2r.a-star.edu.sg/datasets/krbd. Accessed May 2016

18. Rodríguez, D., Ruiz, R., Cuadrado-Gallego, J., Aguilar-Ruiz, J.: Detecting fault modules applying feature selection to classifiers. In: IEEE International Conference on Information Reuse and Integration, IRI 2007, pp. 667–672. IEEE (2007)
19. Seijo-Pardo, B., Bolón-Canedo, V., Alonso-Betanzos, A.: Using a feature selection ensemble on DNA microarray datasets. In: Proceeding of 24th European Symposium on Artificial Neural Networks, pp. 277–282 (2016)
20. Willett, P.: Combination of similarity rankings using data fusion. J. Chem. Inf. Model. **53**(1), 1–10 (2013)
21. Yu, L., Liu, H.: Efficient feature selection via analysis of relevance and redundancy. J. Mach. Learn. Res. **5**, 1205–1224 (2004)

Clustering

Using CVI for Understanding Class Topology in Unsupervised Scenarios

Beatriz Sevilla-Villanueva[1,2(✉)], Karina Gibert[1,3],
and Miquel Sànchez-Marrè[1,2]

[1] Knowledge Engineering and Machine Learning Group (KEMLG),
Universitat Politècnica de Catalunya-BarcelonaTech, Barcelona, Spain
bea.sevilla@gmail.com
[2] Department of Computer Science,
Universitat Politècnica de Catalunya-BarcelonaTech, Barcelona, Spain
[3] Department of Statistics and Operations Research,
Universitat Politècnica de Catalunya-BarcelonaTech, Barcelona, Spain

Abstract. Cluster validation in Clustering is an open problem. The most exploited possibility is the validation through cluster validity indexes (CVIs). However, there are many indexes available, and they perform inconsistently scoring different partitions over a given dataset. The aim of the study carried out is the analysis of seventeen CVIs to get a common understanding of its nature, and proposing an efficient strategy for validating a given clustering. A deep understanding of what CVIs are measuring has been achieved by rewriting all of them under a common notation. This exercise revealed that indexes measure different structural properties of the clusters. A Principal Component Analysis (PCA) confirmed this conceptual classification. Our methodology proposes to perform a multivariate joint analysis of the indexes to learn about the cluster topology instead of using them for simple ranking in a competitive way.

1 Introduction

Clustering is an approach of unsupervised learning that finds some hidden structure in unlabeled data. The aim of clustering is to group a set of objects into distinguishable classes, groups, or clusters of similar subjects [1]. These groups can characterize a set of different profiles which is one of the main applications of clustering in order to understand the data.

The different clustering approaches, the different configurations and the selection of the number of clusters (when required) lead to different solutions for the same dataset [1]. Therefore, the evaluation of which partition is correct or better than others becomes a crucial task.

Usually, the real partition of the data is unknown and, therefore, the results from a clustering process cannot be compared with a reference partition by computing misclassification indexes, as in the case of supervised learning.

In the literature, most of used techniques for evaluating the clustering results are based on numerical indexes which evaluate the validity of the resulting partition from different points of view, known as Cluster Validity Indexes (CVI).

© Springer International Publishing Switzerland 2016
O. Luaces et al. (Eds.): CAEPIA 2016, LNAI 9868, pp. 135–149, 2016.
DOI: 10.1007/978-3-319-44636-3_13

A wide number of CVIs can be found in literature and also, some reviews of those indexes which compare them [2–10]. However, there are currently no clear guidelines for deciding which is the most suitable index for a given dataset [3–6]. In fact, there is not an agreement among those indexes, but it seems clear that each one can give some information about a different property of the partition like homogeneity, compactness of clusters, variability, etc. All these CVIs refer to structural properties of the partition, which are context-independent, and the evaluation based on them is mainly made in terms of the cluster' topology.

In this work, some of these indexes are analyzed with some additional indicators of the structure of the partitions provided by statistical packages. A new methodology is proposed based on the joint multivariate interpretation of all these indexes that provides valuable information about the topology of the clusters and constitutes a richer method of evaluation.

This work differs from those found in literature because it does not perform a simple comparison among several indexes to see which is the best index. Instead, a multivariate analysis of indexes is performed to better understand the nature of those indexes and which of them have similar behavior. Since, in most of clustering real applications, one has no idea about the structure of the best partition which fits the data, we think that, at least, the proposed approach brings a valuable information about the properties of the clustering recognized.

Concretely, a principal component analysis (PCA) is performed in order to analyze the relationships among different indexes and in this way, to establish the methodology for further analysis of a real dataset.

The structure of this paper is the following: first, Sect. 2 contains the background of CVIs. In the methodology (Sect. 3), the PCA is explained and a definition of the indexes with a common notation is provided. Then, a classification and analysis of these indexes is presented in Sect. 4. Section 5 proposes how to use the indexes. Finally, the discussion, conclusions and future work of this study are presented.

2   Background

Cluster validity methods aim at the quantitative evaluation of the results of the clustering algorithms. These methods try to cope questions such as "how many clusters are in the dataset?" or "is there a better partitioning for our dataset?" [8].

Most of the works done in cluster validation on unsupervised context are centered in the internal validation of the clusters [2,4–11] using what is known as a *cluster validity index (CVI)*. Previous works have shown that there is no single CVI outperforming the rest [3–6] and there are few works that compare several CVIs in order to draw some general conclusions [2–4,6] and no general guidelines exists to help the analyst to choose the best CVI in front of a real case.

A reference in this area is [6] which compares 30 CVIs using artificial datasets and Monte Carlo simulation. Other popular study is [7] which compares Davies-Bouldin Index and a modification of Hubert Γ Statistic using Monte Carlo method.

In [11], they evaluate two clustering methods (hard c-means and simple linkage) and the results are compared using Davies-Bouldin, Hubert's statistics, Dunn and variants of Dunn indexes. They suggest in this study that there is not an index which provides consistent results across different clustering algorithms and data structures.

The performance of 15 indexes for determining the number of clusters in 162 synthetic binary datasets is analyzed in [4]. Based on the ability to recommend the correct number of clusters, they proposed to use Ratkowsky-Lance and Davies-Bouldin followed by Calinski-Harabasz and Xun indexes regarding to point the correct number of classes.

A comparison of a proposed CVI against others is performed in [5]. In this work, they conclude that there is not a unique index which it is good enough to determine the number of clusters.

In [3], they compare different cluster indexes of different types, some evaluating the properties of the partition itself (internal criteria), some comparing with a reference partition (external criteria that usually corresponds to accuracy error measurement) and some comparing several partitions among them (relative criteria). Authors claim that the external criteria are better when a reference partition for comparing is available. In other cases, they conclude that Silhouettes index outperforms in their experiments.

A comparison of the most popular CVIs are performed in [2]. In this work, CVIs are compared using 720 synthetic datasets and 20 datasets from the UCI. The synthetic datasets are all possible combinations of the following 5 factors: number of clusters (2,4,8), dimensionality (200,400,800), cluster overlap (yes, no), cluster density (equal, asymmetry) and noise level (without, with). For each dataset 3 clustering methods (k-means, Ward and Average-linkage) are run using a k from 2 to n, being n the size of the dataset. This work concludes that indexes with better performance seem to be Silhouettes, David-Bouldin and Calinski-Harabasz.

All these works run a sort of competition among indexes to search for a winner. However, our belief is that most of these indexes are measuring different properties of the clusters, and that all of them are related with structural characteristics of the classes. It is very probable that for certain structures some indexes perform better than others. In most of clustering real applications, the main limitation is that one has no idea about the sphericity of classes or whether they are tangent nor other features that could help to select the best index. Instead, we think that an interesting reverse reading of this scenario is suitable, by using all those indexes to get knowledge about classes' structure based on their joint performance, and this is the contributions of this work: the idea of making a joint interpretation of all indexes to get structural knowledge from the partition.

3   Methodology

In this work, the 17 most commonly used CVIs and indicators found in the literature are evaluated over 17 UCI datasets which contain their real classification. The multivariate relationships among indexes are analyzed by means of a

PCA. The first 2D and 3D factorial subspaces are analyzed to identify groups of indexes behaving similarly over several datasets and conclusions are extracted about how to use those indexes to get information about classes' topology.

3.1 Principal Component Analysis

Although Principal component analysis (PCA) [12] appears at the beginning of the XXth century, it becomes popular in the late 50's when computer had sufficient capacity. PCA is a multivariate statistical method that finds a reduced set of factors keeping as much information as possible from the original dataset. The factors are orthogonal and they are linear combinations of original attributes. The quantity of information from the original dataset conserved in each factor coincides with the eigenvalues of the covariance matrix of the original dataset. The factors are defined by the eigenvectors. From an algebraic point of view, vectorial base changing operations are found by means of diagonalization of the covariance matrix build over X, to get the most informative projection of the original dataset. From a geometrical point of view, the most informative orthonormal rotation of the original attributes is found.

Given the matrix $X = \{X_1, \ldots, X_K\}$ of K attributes and n objects and being W a diagonal matrix of individual weights, the matrix $Cov(X) = X^T W X$ is diagonalized

$$X^T W X \overline{u} = \lambda \overline{u}$$

The solutions provide the eigenvectors $u_\alpha, \alpha = \{1, .., K\}$ and corresponding eigenvalues $\lambda_\alpha, \alpha = \{1, .., K\}$. The Principal Components are linear combinations of original attributes and $P_\alpha = \sum\limits_{\alpha=1}^{K} u_\alpha X_\alpha$. Sorting both u_α, λ_α according to decreasing λ_α the first r Principal Components such that $\sum\limits_{\alpha=1}^{r} \lambda_\alpha \geq 0.80$ are conserved.

However, in most of real applications the first factorial plane is analyzed, the one determined by $\langle \overline{u}_1, \overline{u}_2 \rangle$, as it is the one conserving as much information as possible from the original dataset [13]. In this work PCA has been used to analyze synergies and oppositions of CVIs.

3.2 Cluster Validity Indexes

The evaluation of a resulting clustering is commonly assessed with internal CVIs and indicators because they do not need additional information other than data and clusters themselves. The internal validation evaluates the resulting clusters in base to its topography or structure. This evaluation is mostly based on the compactness (cohesion) of the clusters and the separation between clusters. Literature on CVIs is abundant (see Sect. 2). Most of the indexes estimate cluster cohesion (within or intra-variance), cluster separation (between or inter-variance) or combine both to compute a quality measure [14].

The formulation of the 17 indexes is provided under a common notation. Given,

- Datasest $\mathcal{X}$ composed by n individuals $I = \{i_1, \ldots, i_n\}$ and K attributes $X = \{X_1, \ldots, X_K\}$.
- Partition $P = \{C_1, \ldots, C_\xi\}$ contains ξ clusters where $n_c = card(C)$, $C \in P$ and $C \cap C' = \varnothing$, $C, C' \in P$.
- Being $d(i, i') = \sqrt{\sum_{k=1}^{K}(x_{i_k} - x_{i'_k})^2}$ the distance between two individuals i, $i' \in I$.

Entropy index measures the entropy associated with partition P [15]. Entropy is always non-negative and it takes value 0 only when there is no uncertainty (when only one cluster). So, it measures chaos, values ranges from $[0, 1]$ and it is better to minimize. Note that the uncertainty does not depend on the number of objects in I but on the relative proportions of the clusters.

$$Entropy = -\sum_{C \in P} \frac{n_c}{n} log\left(\frac{n_c}{n}\right) \tag{1}$$

Maximum Cluster Diameter (Δ) is the maximum distance between any two points that belongs to the same cluster [16]. In other words, it is defined by the higher diameter among all the clusters belonging to P (see Fig. 1). Therefore, it measures *compactness*, values range from $[0,)$ and it is better to minimize.

Fig. 1. Maximum cluster diameter

$$\Delta = \max_{C \in P} \Delta_c, \quad \Delta_c = \max_{i, i' \in C} d(i, i') \tag{2}$$

Widest Gap (wg) is the maximum within-cluster gap for all clusters. The widest within-cluster gap (wg_c) is defined as the largest link in within-cluster minimum spanning tree [17] (see Fig. 2). Thus, it measures *compactness*, values range from $[0,)$ and it is better to minimize.

$$wg = \max_{C \in P} wg_c, \tag{3}$$

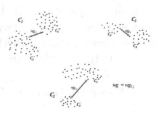

Fig. 2. Widest gap

$$wg_c = \max_{\substack{C', C'' \\ C' \cap C'' = \varnothing \\ C' \cup C'' = C}} g(C', C''), \quad g(C', C'') = \min_{\substack{i' \in C', \ i'' \in C'' \\ C' \cap C'' = \varnothing \\ C' \cup C'' = C}} d(i', i'')$$

Average Within-Cluster Distance ($\overline{W}$) is the average of the distances between all pairs of objects within the same cluster. This measures *compactness* (better to minimize) and values range in $[0,)$.

$$\overline{W} = \frac{\sum_{C \in P} W_c}{\sum_{C \in P} n_c(n_c - 1)}, \quad W_c = \sum_{i, i' \in C} d(i, i') \tag{4}$$

Within Cluster Sum of Squares **(*WSS*)** is the sum of squared distances between all pairs of objects within a cluster [10]. This measures compactness (better to minimize) and values range in $[0,)$. Let i_c be the barycenter of cluster C,

$$WSS = \sum_{C \in P} WSS_c, \quad WSS_c = \sum_{i \in C} d(i, i_c)^2 \tag{5}$$

Average Between-Cluster Distance **($\overline{B}$)** is the average of all distances between pairs of objects which do not belong to the same cluster. It measures *separation* (better to maximize) and values range in $[0,)$. Given a pair of classes $C, C' \in P$,

$$\overline{B} = \frac{\sum_{\substack{C,C' \in P, \\ C \neq C'}} dist(C,C')}{\sum_{\substack{C,C' \in P, \\ C \neq C'}} n_c n_{c'}}, \quad dist(C,C') = \sum_{i \in C} \sum_{i' \in C'} d(i,i') \tag{6}$$

Minimum Cluster Separation **(δ)** is the minimum distance between any two objects that do not belong to the same cluster. In other words, it is defined by the lower separation among all the clusters (See Fig. 3). It measures *separation* (better to maximize) and values range in $[0,)$. $\delta_{c,c'}$ is highly related with wg_c measure. $\delta_{c,c'}$ finds gaps between clusters whereas wg_c finds gaps inside each cluster.

Fig. 3. Minimum cluster separation

$$\delta = \min_{C,C' \in P} \delta_{c,c'}, \quad \delta_{c,c'} = \min_{i \in C, i' \in C'} d(i,i') \tag{7}$$

Separation Index **(*Sindex*)** is based on the distances for every point to the closest point not in the same cluster. The separation index is the mean of the S smallest separations [16,17] being S a certain proportion of the dataset. This allows formalizing separation less sensitive to a single or a few ambiguous points. It measures separation (better to maximize) and values range in $[0,)$.

$s \in [0,1], S = E[ns]$ an object $i \in I, c(i)$ is the class of object i

$\forall i \in I, sep(i) = \min_{i' \notin c(i)} d(i,i')$

Let $\{sep(i)_m\}_{m=1:n}$ be the sorted sequence where $sep(i)_m \leq sep(i)_{m+1}$

$$Sindex = \frac{\sum_{m=1}^{S} \{sep(i)_m\}}{S} \tag{8}$$

Dunn Index **(*D*)** is a cluster validity index for crisp clustering proposed in Dunn (1974) [18]. It attempts to identify "compact and well separated clusters" [19]. If a data set contains well-separated clusters, the distances among the clusters are usually larger than the diameters of the clusters. We present a formulation from [4]: (see Sect. 3.2 for $\delta_{c,c'}$ and 3.2 for Δ_c). It measures separation vs compactness, then its better to maximize and values range from $[0,)$.

$$D = \frac{\min_{C,C' \in P} \delta_{c,c'}}{\max_{C \in P} \Delta_c} \tag{9}$$

Dunn-like index is one of the generalizations of Dunn index [18] proposed by Bezdek and Pal [11]. It attempts to identify compact and well separated clusters. From all generalizations proposed in [11,20], the one available in FPC-R package [21] is the one substituting point to point distance of the original Dunn index by average inter-class distance in numerator and average point to point intra-class distance in the denominator. This version is more robust than the original Dunn Index [8,11]. Also, it measures *separation vs compactness*, it is better to maximize and values range in $[0,)$.

$$D = \frac{\min_{C,C' \in P} \overline{\delta_{c,c'}}}{\max_{C \in P} \overline{\Delta_c}}, \quad \overline{\delta_{c,c'}} = \frac{\sum_{i \in C, i' \in C'} d(i, i')}{n_c n_{c'}} \quad \overline{\Delta_c} = \frac{\sum_{i,i' \in C} d(i, i')}{n_c(n_c - 1)}$$

$$(10)$$

Calinksi-Harabasz Index (CH) [22] is based on getting a compromise between both the between-cluster distances (*separation*) and the within-cluster distances (*compactness*). Thus, it is better to maximize and values range in $[0,)$. CH is defined as following:

$$CH = \frac{BSS/(\xi - 1)}{WSS/(n - \xi)}, \quad BSS = \sum_{C \in P} n_c d(i_c, \bar{i})^2$$

$$(11)$$

i_c is the barycenter of the cluster C $\bar{i}$ is the barycenter of I, WSS is already defined. This index is interpreted as higher values as better clustering partition.

Normalized Hubert Gamma Coefficient $(\hat{\Gamma})$. This index is a Pearson version of Hubert's gamma coefficient [8]. It gives information on how good the clustering is as an approximation of the dissimilarity matrix. It is especially useful when clustering is used for dimensionality reduction. This index takes values between -1 and 1, it is a compromise between *separation and compactness* and it is better to maximize. It introduces an auxiliary indicator Y such that evaluates to 1 for pairs of objects in the same cluster and to 0 otherwise. Being D the matrix with distances between subjects; the $\hat{\Gamma}$ index is defined as the correlation between D and Y:

$$y(i, i') = \begin{cases} 1 & c(i) = c(i') \\ 0 & c(i) \neq c(i') \end{cases}, \quad \hat{\Gamma} = \frac{\sum_{i,i' \in I} (d(i,i') - \bar{d})(y(i,i') - \bar{y})}{\sum_{i,i' \in I} (d(i,i') - \bar{d})^2 \sum_{i,i' \in I} (y(i,i') - \bar{y})^2}$$

$$(12)$$

Being $c(i)$ the class of i, $\bar{d}$ the barycenter of all distances and $\bar{y}$ the barycenter of Y.

Silhouettes Index [23] provides a succinct graphical representation of how well each object lies within its cluster. It measures the separation vs compactness to the nearest cluster. In principle, this index is assessed for each object, but in order to be used is reduced to the average of all dataset or the average for each cluster.

For each object $i \in I$, let

$$s(i) = \frac{b(i) - a(i)}{max(a(i), b(i))} \tag{13}$$

$a(i)$: average dissimilarity of i with all other data within the same cluster. $a(i)$ shows us how well clustered i is to the cluster assigned (smaller value means better matching).

$$a(i) = \frac{\sum_{i,i' \in C} d(i, i')}{n_c - 1}$$

$b(i)$: the lowest average dissimilarity of i with the data of another single cluster. The cluster with this lowest average dissimilarity is said to be the "neighbouring cluster" of i as it is, aside from the cluster i is assigned, the cluster in which i fits best.

$$b(i) = \min_{C' \neq C} \frac{\sum_{i \in C, i' \in C'} d(i, i')}{n_c - 1}$$

Then, the value of $s(i)$ belongs to $[-1, 1]$ and a higher value indicates that i is better clustered.

The Silhouettes index of a cluster C is

$$S_C = \frac{\sum_{i \in C} s(i)}{n_c}$$

The overall Silhouettes index for a given dataset with a partition is

$$Silhouettes = \frac{\sum_{i \in I} s(i)}{n} = \frac{\sum_{C \in P} n_c S_C}{\sum_{C \in P} n_c} \tag{14}$$

Baker and Hubert Index (BH) [24] is a variant of Goodman and Kruskal's Gamma [25]. Comparisons are made between all within-cluster distances (*compactness*) and all between-cluster distances (*separation*). A comparison is considered to be *concordant* if a within-cluster distance is strictly less than a between-cluster distance. Values are in $[-1, 1]$ and it is better to maximize.

$$BH = \frac{S^+ - S^-}{S^+ + S^-} \tag{15}$$

S^+: number of concordant quadruples,
S^- : number of discordant quadruples.

For this index, all possible quadruples (q, r, s, t) of input parameters are considered.

A quadruple (q, r, s, t) is called *concordant* if one of the following two conditions is true:

- $d(q, r) < d(s, t)$, q and r are in the same cluster, and s and t are in different clusters.

- $d(q,r) > d(s,t)$, q and r are in different clusters, and s and t are in the same cluster.

By contrast, a quadruple is called *discordant* if one of following two conditions is true:

- $d(q,r) < d(s,t)$, q and r are in different clusters, and s and t are in the same cluster.
- $d(q,r) > d(s,t)$, q and r are in the same cluster, and s and t are in different clusters.

Within Between Ratio (WBR) index is the ratio between the average within-cluster distance (compactness) and the average between-cluster distance (separation). Then, as lower is the value means that the partition P is more *compact* and more *separated*. Values range in $[0,)$. See the previous definitions of $\overline{W}$ and $\overline{B}$

$$WBR = \frac{\overline{W}}{\overline{B}} \tag{16}$$

C-Index [26,27] is computed using the within-cluster distances.

$$C = \frac{W - W_{min}}{W_{max} + W_{min}} \tag{17}$$

Where, W is Sum of distances over all pairs of objects from the same cluster.

$$W = \sum_{C \in P} \sum_{i,i' \in C} d(i,i')$$

Let $\{d_m\}_{m=1:n^2}, d_m \leq d_{m+1}$ be the ordered list of distances between all possible pairs of objects.

$$W_{min} = \sum_{m=1}^{n_W} d_m, \quad W_{max} = \sum_{m=n^2-n_W+1}^{n^2} d_m, \quad n_W = \sum_{C \in P} n_c^2$$

Let n_W be the number of those pairs. Then W_{min} is the sum of the n_W smallest distances if all pairs of objects are considered (the objects can belong or not to the same cluster). Similarly, W_{max} is the sum of the n_W largest distances out of all pairs. This index measures compactness and separation, it is better to minimize and values range in $[0,)$

Davies-Bouldin Index (DB) [28] is a cluster separation measure. The overall index is defined as the average of indexes computed from each individual cluster. An individual cluster index is taken as the maximum pairwise comparison involving the cluster and the other clusters in the solution. Values range in $[0,)$ and it is better lower values.

$$DB = \frac{1}{\xi} \sum_{C \in P} max_{C' \in P, C' \neq C} \left(\frac{S_{p_c} + S_{p_{c'}}}{d_p(C, C')} \right),$$ (18)

$$d_p(C, C') = \sqrt[p]{\sum_{k=1}^{K} |\overline{X_{c_k}} - \overline{X_{c'_k}}|^p}, \qquad S_{p_c} = \sqrt[p]{\frac{\sum_{i \in C} d_p(i, i_c)^p}{n_c}}$$

Where, i_c is the barycenter of the cluster C defined as $i_c = (\overline{x_{c_1}}, \ldots, \overline{x_{c_k}}), \overline{x_{c_k}} = \frac{\sum_{i \in C} x_i}{n_c}$;

p is the Minkowski factor ($p = 1$ Manhattan distance, $p = 2$ Euclidean distance)

S_{p_c} is the dispersion measure of a cluster C (for $p = 1$ the average distance of objects in cluster C to the barycenter of cluster C; for $p = 2$ the standard deviation of the distance of objects in cluster C to the barycenter of cluster C).

4   Results

The first contribution of this paper is that, after rewriting all the indexes under a common notation, we can observe that these indexes evaluate a reduced set of characteristics of a partition and, according their definition, all indexes can be grouped around 4 basic concepts:

(A) Indexes measuring compactness of clusters: Δ, WG, $\overline{W}$ and WSS.
(B) Indexes measuring separation between clusters: $\overline{B}$, δ, Sindex.
(C) Indexes measuring relationships between compactness and separation: Dunn, Dunn-like, CH, $\hat{\Gamma}$, Silhouettes, BH, WBR, C-Index and DB.
(D) Indexes measuring chaos in the clusters: Entropy

In this work, the same 17 datasets from the UCI Machine Learning Repository in [2] are considered. Table 1 shows the main characteristics of each dataset, each one contains an attribute with the real partition, and this will be used as a class-variable to our purpose. The mentioned 17 CVIs and indicators have been computed for every dataset using the real partition of each one and the behavior of the indexes is analyzed with multivariate techniques to understand both relationships among indexes and how they perform in front of certain class topologies.

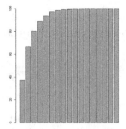

Fig. 4. Histogram of the inertia of the principal components

A Principal Component Analysis (PCA) has been performed over Table 2 in order to understand the relationships among different indexes. The eigenvalues recommend to keep 3 factors with a total conserved inertia of 80.2 % (see Fig. 4).

Table 1. 17 dataset from the UCI repository and the main characteristics

Dataset	Num. clusters	Data type	Num. attributes	Num. instances
breast_w	2	Numerical	30	569
Ionosphere	2	Numerical	34	351
Parkinsons	2	Numerical	22	195
sonar_all	2	Numerical	60	208
Transfusion	2	Numerical	4	748
Haberman	2	Numerical	3	306
Musk	2	Numerical	166	476
Spectf	2	Numerical	44	267
Iris	3	Numerical	4	150
Wine	3	Numerical	13	178
vertebral_column	3	Numerical	6	310
Vehicle	4	Numerical	18	846
breast_tissue	6	Numerical	9	106
Glass	6	Numerical	9	214
Ecoli	8	Numerical	7	336
vowel_context	11	Numerical	10	990
movement_libras	15	Numerical	90	360

Table 2. The 17 indexes computed for the 17 UCI datasets

Dataset	Num Clusters	Chaos Entropy	Compactness Δ	wg	W	WSS	Separation B	δ	Sindex
breast_w	2	0,66	4350,55	1145,67	382,43	$1,2110^8$	1030,1	10,922	18,52
ionosphere	2	0,65	9,75	5,29	3,58	3086,17	4,47	0,467	0,79
parkinsons	2	0,56	487,14	202,93	108,82	$2,1810^6$	140,68	3,269	4,66
sonar_all	2	0,69	3,53	1,53	1,77	351,59	1,83	0,507	0,59
transfusion	2	0,55	12250,48	3500,13	1188,38	$1,5110^9$	1558,94	0,000	0,00
Haberman	2	0,58	64,03	23,69	15,93	$5,3110^4$	17,18	0,000	0,60
Musk	2	0,68	2604,64	1437,21	1429,7	$5,2110^8$	1433,84	288,376	403,54
Spectf	2	0,51	230,33	142,11	87,24	$1,110^6$	76,46	22,956	26,41
Iris	3	1,10	3,82	0,91	0,96	89,3	3,32	0,224	0,35
Wine	3	1,09	1000,03	133,22	192,22	$5,2310^6$	434,53	4,785	6,87
vertebral_column	3	1,03	427,19	298,80	46,62	$4,7410^5$	64,54	3,020	5,90
Vehicle	4	1,39	747,47	97,01	186,52	$2,4410^7$	228,83	7,071	12,43
breast_tissue	6	1,78	173088,92	134397,35	8694,6	$2,7210^{10}$	11426	12,630	27,56
Glass	6	1,51	10,15	5,94	2,05	911,2	3,2	0,157	0,21
Ecoli	8	1,52	1,07	0,84	0,32	21,31	0,63	0,052	0,07
vowel_context	11	2,40	7113,94	2214,04	2412,79	$3,3410^9$	3165,12	427,639	651,67
movement_libras	15	2,71	4,26	2,63	1,72	627,23	2,33	0,169	0,49
Target		Min	min	min	min	min	max	max	max

Dataset	Num Clusters	Relational Dunn	Dunn-like	CH	Γ	Silhouette	BH	WBR	C-Index	DB
breast_w	2	0,003	1,32	633,63	0,49	0,51	0,64	0,37	0,17	0,91
ionosphere	2	0,048	0,89	17,75	0,27	0,15	0,29	0,80	0,33	4,42
parkinsons	2	0,007	0,97	13,05	0,16	0,19	0,26	0,77	0,43	3,49
sonar_all	2	0,144	1,02	6,00	0,06	0,03	0,06	0,97	0,46	5,85
transfusion	2	0,000	0,86	37,42	0,11	0,18	0,12	0,76	0,47	4,26
Haberman	2	0,000	0,98	8,36	0,06	0,06	0,08	0,93	0,48	5,43
Musk	2	0,111	0,95	7,37	0,01	0,01	-0,00	1,00	0,49	7,87
Spectf	2	0,100	0,85	14,82	-0,1	-0,07	-0,19	1,14	0,67	2,77
Iris	3	0,058	1,57	487,33	0,68	0,50	0,88	0,29	0,05	0,84
Wine	3	0,005	0,73	206,68	0,42	0,20	0,52	0,44	0,18	1,87
vertebral_column	3	0,007	0,56	97,71	0,21	0,11	0,38	0,72	0,29	2,36
Vehicle	4	0,009	0,87	72,72	0,11	-0,09	0,18	0,81	0,34	14,0
breast_tissue	6	0,000	0,02	6,73	0,04	-0,19	0,28	0,76	0,19	4,78
Glass	6	0,015	0,29	19,70	0,25	-0,09	0,38	0,64	0,27	4,26
Ecoli	8	0,049	0,45	81,18	0,61	0,24	0,80	0,50	0,11	1,70
vowel_context	11	0,060	0,67	54,20	0,22	0,01	0,44	0,76	0,25	4,51
movement_libras	15	0,040	0,60	15,21	0,24	0,02	0,46	0,74	0,29	4,06
Target		max	max	max	1	1	1	min	min	min

Figure 5a shows the first factorial plane. Figure 5b shows the 3-D projection over first three factorial axes. The indexes are represented as projected vectors over projection space. The analyzed datasets are represented by points.

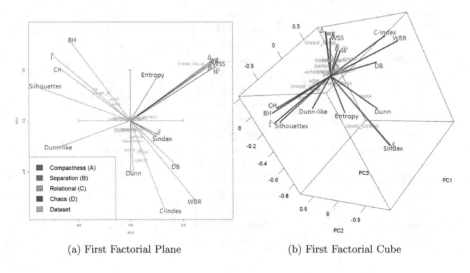

(a) First Factorial Plane   (b) First Factorial Cube

Fig. 5. Projection of the firsts factorial axis

It can be seen that indexes place grouped over 5 directions both over the 1st factorial plane and the 1st factorial cube. By interpreting the PCA results under classical approach, structural properties of indexes can be elicited by understanding what is common between the indexes related to each of these 5 directions of projection. On the one hand, all indexes of group A (compactness) place together and orthogonally most of the relational indexes (group C); on a third direction, we can find separation indexes (group B), except for $\overline{B}$ which behaves extremely related to $\overline{W}$ (this is normal because of the Hugges theorem); Entropy follows its own behavior; also the Dunn index behaves orthogonally of the other families, probably because it works with minimums and maximums. Finally, Dunn-like seems to follow inverse association with compactness indexes (group A).

Thus, by projecting any dataset on the factorial map one can determine whether the clusters of this dataset are more compact (vertebral) or have bigger gaps (breast_tissue), if classes are more separated (vowel_context) or seem to be overlapped (Transfusion).

In fact, as some packs of indexes behave similarly, they group over the factorial space according to the 5 projection directions, we propose to choose one representative index for every family and use the resulting reduced battery to evaluate new datasets in a more efficient way to learn about their class topology.

5   Class Evaluation Proposal

Thus, given a new dataset partitioned by an attribute P (either an expert-based or an induced clustering) the topology of classes might be understand by computing the following set of indexes: Diameter(Δ), Separation (δ), Calinski-Harabasz(CH), Dunn and Entropy.

From this battery, one can understand the following characteristics of the dataset:

1. Δ: Compact classes, without big gaps.
2. δ: Separated and non-overlapped classes.
3. CH: Compromise between compact and separated classes and if individuals are well-clustered.
4. Dunn: compact and well separated clusters.
5. Entropy: chaos.

Note that each index is interchangeable for any index of the same group (direction) since they measure the same characteristics.

6   Discussion

In this study, cluster validation through CVIs and indicators is faced. A joint multivariate evaluation of all indexes is proposed as a richer methodology than traditional and simple ranking according to indexes. The proposal provides information about the topology as well as the structure of the resulting partition.

Efforts have been invested to express all considered indexes by means of a common notation (Sect. 3.2); this permitted a deep understanding of the indexes themselves, and to realize that most of them refer to some upper category that represent different characteristics of the clusters from a structural point of view: whether clusters are more compact or more sparse, or whether there are at least two classes that are too close, or whether it seems to be more or less overlapping among clusters. In fact, from this conceptual analysis we identify 4 categories of indexes: those meaning compactness, separation, relation between compactness and separation or chaos.

With the analysis of the relationships among those indexes by means of PCA, the indexes group depending on its behavior in front of the different datasets that have been analyzed and, they group accordingly to the conceptual classification provided in previous section. Except for Dunn index that has its own behavior and the average Between-cluster distance ($\overline{B}$) that seems to approach closer the compactness indexes.

For the reason of efficiency, this would allow choosing a reduced battery of 5 indexes to evaluate the structure of a partition, one referred to each relevant characteristic.

7 Conclusions

This work has been motivated by the inherent difficulties of the cluster validation process. In most real applications, there is not prior information about the
number of clusters or about the structural characteristics of the existent clusters.

The main contribution of this research is that joint multivariate vision of
a complete set of indexes provides richer information about the topology and
structure of the clusters than traditional ranking analysis. A deep understanding
of what the 17 CVIS and indicators found in the literature are really measuring
is achieved through the analysis of their expressions under a common notation.
A higher conceptual hierarchy of indexes emerged from this analysis based on
the cluster characteristics targeted by each index. This explains why rankings
obtained are different depending on the index for a set of datasets. PCA analysis
confirms homogeneous behavior of indexes of same category in general trends.

Hence, from both the conceptual and the PCA analysis is possible to classify
the indexes into 5 groups. Eventually a dataset can be assessed using all of them
or a reduced battery containing a representative of each category. Then, for a
new dataset with one or more partitions, the global set of indexes might be used
to learn about the characteristics of each partition and this information support
the selection of the best one.

Acknowledgements. This work has been supported by the project Diet4You
(TIN2014-60557-R) funded by Spanish Government.

References

1. Duda, R.O., Hart, P.E., Stork, D.G.: Pattern Classification. Wiley, Hoboken (2012)
2. Arbelaitz, O., Gurrutxaga, I., Muguerza, J., Pérez, J.M., Perona, I.: An extensive
   comparative study of cluster validity indices. Pattern Recognit. **46**(1), 243–256
   (2013)
3. Brun, M., Sima, C., Hua, J., Lowey, J., Carroll, B., Suh, E., Dougherty, E.R.:
   Model-based evaluation of clustering validation measures. Pattern Recognit. **40**(3),
   807–824 (2007)
4. Dimitriadou, E., Dolnicar, S., Weingessel, A.: An examination of indexes for determining the number of clusters in binary datasets. Psychometrika **67**, 137–159
   (2002)
5. Maulik, U., Bandyopadhyay, S.: Performance evaluation of some clustering algorithms and validity indices. IEEE Trans. Pattern Anal. Mach. Intell. **24**, 1650–1654
   (2002)
6. Milligan, G.W., Cooper, M.C.: An examination of procedures for determining the
   number of clusters in a dataset. Psychometrika **50**, 159–179 (1985)
7. Dubes, R.C.: How many clusters are best? - an experiment. Pattern Recognit.
   20(6), 645–663 (1987)
8. Halkidi, M., Batistakis, Y., Vazirgiannis, M.: On clustering validation techniques.
   J. Intel. Inf. Syst. **17**(2), 107–145 (2001)
9. Halkidi, M., Batistakis, Y., Vazirgiannis, M.: Cluster validity methods: part I.
   ACM Sigmod Rec. **31**(2), 40–45 (2002)

10. Halkidi, M., Batistakis, Y., Vazirgiannis, M.: Clustering validity checking methods: part II. ACM Sigmod Rec. **31**(3), 19–27 (2002)
11. Bezdek, J.C., Pal, N.R.: Some new indexes of cluster validity. IEEE Trans. Syst. Man Cybern. Part B Cybern. **28**(3), 301–315 (1998)
12. Pearson, K.: On lines and planes of closest fit to systems of points in space. London Edinb. Dublin Philos. Mag. J. Sci. **2**(11), 559–572 (1901)
13. Benzécri, J.P.: L'analyse des données, 1st edn. Dunod, Paris (1973). Tome 1: La Taxinomie, Tome 2: L'analyse des correspondances
14. Kim, M., Ramakrishna, R.S.: New indices for cluster validity assessment. Pattern Recognit. Lett. **26**(15), 2353–2363 (2005)
15. Meilă, M.: Comparing clusterings? An information based distance. J. Multivar. Anal. **98**(5), 873–895 (2007)
16. Hennig, C., Liao, T.F.: Comparing latent class and dissimilarity based clustering for mixed type variables with application to social stratification. Technical report (2010)
17. Hennig, C.: How many bee species? A case study in determining the number of clusters. In: Proceedings of GfKl-2012, Hildesheim (2013)
18. Dunn, J.C.: Well separated clusters and optimal fuzzy partitions. J. Cybern. **4**(1), 95–104 (1974)
19. Halkidi, M., Vazirgiannis, M.: Clustering validity assessment using multi representatives. In: Proceedings of SETN Conference (2002)
20. Pal, N.R., Biswas, J.: Cluster validation using graph theoretic concepts. Pattern Recognit. **30**(6), 847–857 (1997)
21. Hennig, C.: fpc: Flexible procedures for clustering. R package version 2.1-5 (2013)
22. Caliński, T., Harabasz, J.: A dendrite method for cluster analysis. Commun. Stat.-Theor. Methods **3**(1), 1–27 (1974)
23. Rousseeuw, P.J.: Silhouettes: a graphical aid to the interpretation and validation of cluster analysis. J. Comput. Appl. Math. **20**, 53–65 (1987)
24. Baker, F.B., Hubert, L.J.: Measuring the power of hierarchical cluster analysis. J. Am. Stat. Assoc. **70**(349), 31–38 (1975)
25. Goodman, L.A., Kruskal, W.H.: Measures of association for cross classifications. J. Am. Stat. Assoc. **49**(268), 732–764 (1954)
26. Hubert, L.J., Levin, J.R.: A general statistical framework for assessing categorical clustering in free recall. Psychol. Bull. **83**(6), 1072–1080 (1976)
27. Gordon, A.D.: Classification, 2nd edn. Chapman and Hall/CRC, Boca Raton (1999)
28. Davies, D.L., Bouldin, D.W.: Cluster separation measure. IEEE Trans. Pattern Anal. Mach. Intell. **1**(2), 95–104 (1979)

Automated Spark Clusters Deployment for Big Data with Standalone Applications Integration

A.M. Fernández, J.F. Torres, A. Troncoso, and F. Martínez-Álvarez[✉]

Division of Computer Science, Universidad Pablo de Olavide, 41013 Seville, Spain
{amfergom,jftormal}@alu.upo.es, {ali,fmaralv}@upo.es

Abstract. The huge amount of data stored nowadays has turned big data analytics into a very trendy research field. Spark has emerged as a very powerful and widely used paradigm for clusters deployment and big data management. However, to get started is still a very tough task, due to the excessive requisites that all nodes must fulfil. Thus, this work introduces a web service specifically designed for an easy and efficient Spark cluster management. In particular, a service with a friendly graphical user interface has been developed to automate the deploying of clusters. Another relevant feature is the possibility of integrating any algorithm into the web service. That is, the user only needs to provide the executable file and the number of required inputs for a proper parametrization. Finally, an illustrative case study is included to show ad hoc algorithms usage (the MLlib implementation for k-means, in this case) across the nodes of the configured cluster.

Keywords: Big data · Spark · Algorithms · Automated deployment

1 Introduction

The era of Big Data has changed the way that data are stored and processed. Actually, the need of systems able to efficiently perform both actions has been dramatically increased recently.

Although Spark is an open source framework under the Apache 2.0 license, it was originally created and developed by the University of California. It provides an interface to program and deploy clusters parallelizing data, under the Map-Reduce paradigm.

Spark programming is focused on the use of a data structure called Resilient Distributed Dataset (RDD), which allows data distribution across the nodes of a cluster. It is also fault tolerant.

The main programming language supported by Spark is Scala, but it also supports Java, R or Phyton. Moreover, it can be used different operating systems, such as Linux, MAC OS or Windows.

For a proper clusters management, Spark can make use of Apache's own managers like Hadoop YARN o Mesos, or even it can make use of the native Spark manager (standalone). As for the distributed data storage, several implementations can be used, i.e. HDFS, Cassandra or Amazon S3.

O. Luaces et al. (Eds.): CAEPIA 2016, LNAI 9868, pp. 150–159, 2016.
DOI: 10.1007/978-3-319-44636-3_14

However, to the author's knowledge, there is no friendly application able to easily deploy and parameterize Spark clusters. And this is main goal of the developed approach: a web service that, by just few clicks and a graphical user interface, fully deploys and configure a cluster. That is, it aims at automating the cluster deploying thus avoiding tedious manual configuration.

The web service has also been designed in order to easily integrate new algorithms by just uploading executable files and configuring the inputs. That is, it is not only about to deploy the cluster, but also about integrating any application that needs to be launched the across nodes of the deployed cluster.

The rest of the paper is structured as follows. Section 2 provides a general overview on the state-of-the-art. Section 3 describes the proposed approach. A case study, showing how an algorithm can be added and launched in the cluster, is presented in Sect. 4. Finally, the conclusions drawn have been summarized in Sect. 5.

2   Related Works

In this section a review of the most recent parallel computing environments focused on massive data is provided.

Parallel processing approaches can be classified into compute-intensive and data-intensive [2,4]. In compute-intensive applications the major requirements are related to the computing and the volume of data usually is small. In this case, the applications are divided into separate tasks, which can be executed in a parallel way. Conversely, the processing time of the data-intensive applications is required for operations related to input/output and data management. Therefore, the strategy is to split the data into subsets, which can be processed by the same executable application in parallel.

Due to the available volume of information has grown considerably in the last years, much effort is being devoted to develop parallel computing platforms focussed on massive data and to enhance existing data mining techniques in order to process, manage and discover knowledge from big data [6].

In the last two decades several system architectures based on parallel and distributed relational database management systems have been implemented [7]. However, most data are unstructured and therefore new more flexible processing paradigms are needed nowadays.

One of the first platforms for data-driven parallel computing was proposed by the company LexisNexis Risk Solutions in the year 2000, although it was published in 2011 [5]. This platform includes the Thor cluster for typical tasks related to structured queries and data warehouse applications such as extract, transform and load, and the Roxie platform for online queries and data analysis. Its main disadvantage is the incapability to deal with unstructured data.

In 2004, Google publishes a modern systems architecture called MapReduce [1], which allows to the software developers to make programs based on a functional programming language. These programs basically are based on map functions processing key-value pairs and reduce functions that grouping the intermediate values by the same key. This system is now becoming attractive because splitting data and managing of the cluster, including the communications between nodes, is automatic. This reason promoted its implementation for Apache Software Foundation creating the open source software project called Apache Hadoop [10] in 2011. In addition to MapReduce, Apache Hadoop, inspired by Google, added the HDFS distributed filesystem to deal with unstructured data.

However, the limitations of the MapReduce paradigm for iterative algorithms development have led to new driven-data parallel computing platforms, such as Apache Spark [3]. Among its most important capabilities, multi-pass computations, high-level operators, diverse languages usage, in addition to its own language called Scala, are most notable.

Although Spark considerably reduces the software development cycles compared to Hadoop, it is not easy for programmers with no experience in parallel programming to configure and deploy a Spark cluster, which is one of the main purposes of this work.

3   The Application

Currently, the existing tools to manage clusters in the Spark framework do not allow full administration of the nodes included in a cluster.

The system used by Spark for clusters configuration is based on two files located at *conf* directory, as templates: *spark-env.sh* and *slaves*. These files are needed for the adequate cluster launching and functioning. A brief description of them can be found below:

1. *spark-env.sh*. This file contains all parameters related to the master node, as well as the minimum required configuration information, that is, number of cores, memory usage, number of instances per node, and so on.
2. *slaves*. This file is even simpler than the previous one. It only contains the list of worker nodes which will be launched in the cluster. In particular, IP addresses for each node can be here found.

Since the process previously described must be repeated for all the nodes forming the cluster, this configuration turns out to be a tedious and repetitive process, especially considering that the nodes can be geographically dispersed.

Once solved the configuration issue for all nodes, the cluster could be launched by means of any of the native Spark scripts in the master node, such as *start-all.sh, start-master.sh* or *start-slaves.sh*.

In case another cluster manager is used, e.g. Apache Mesos, its deployment and launching would be much easier under a different web interface. Nevertheless, this would not avoid that every node must be individually configured.

Given that it cannot be currently deployed a cluster without many initial configuration steps, a web application has been developed in order to automatize the entire configuration process.

The application can be divided into two different modules:

1. Communications. The main task of this module is to deploy and launch the cluster.
2. Algorithms. This module manages both parametrization and algorithm execution.

Figure 1 illustrates how the application is deployed. The node executing the application is denoted as master, and it hosts both databases and algorithms (repository of executable .jar files with the parametrization). Furthermore, different components and the way they are communicated with external resources and with the remaining nodes are also depicted.

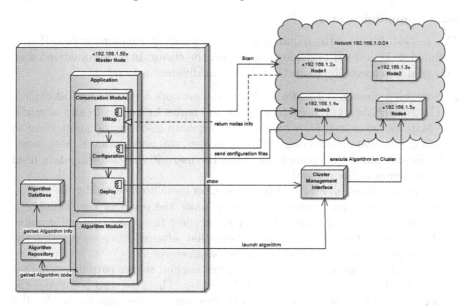

Fig. 1. Flowchart of the application deployment.

These modules, together with prerequisites, are described in subsequent sections.

3.1 Prerequisites

This section describes the prerequisites needed for a proper functioning of the proposed approach. In particular, the minimal prerequisites for the cluster launching can be summarized as follows:

1. Files repository. A shared files repository across all the nodes is needed. This is needed because the access to all datasets must be available for all the nodes composing the cluster.
2. NMap. This is, perhaps, the most important prerequisite. NMap must be installed in the master node in order to scan all accessible nodes in the network, in order to facilitate the cluster deployment when adding new slave nodes.

3. Same user. It is also needed that all nodes have the same credentials (user/pass), since ssh communications, shared keys and file access by absolute paths require the same user.
4. RSA ring. It is necessary to access to all nodes without typing the credentials. A RSA ring is used for such purpose.
5. Spark package. This package must be downloaded and unzipped in the user's root directory (/home/username).
6. Scala package. As happening with the Spark package, the Scala package must be downloaded and unzipped for a proper algorithms execution.

3.2 Communications

This section describes the required actions, in terms of communications. Hence, this module is devoted to deploy and launch the cluster in an automatized way. This goal is achieved by correctly taking four different actions:

1. Network scanning. All nodes visible in the network are found and identified. The NMap library is used to identify the nodes belonging to the network. NMap creates a .xml file which will subsequently used by the application to collect information from every node. Moreover, this information is later shown in the web interface. Figure 2 illustrates the user interface showing data from nodes found in the network.
2. IP filtering. From all available nodes, some of them are selected by the administrator to eventually create the cluster. Once the result of the scanning is shown in the web interface, the user must select the slaves that will eventually be part of the cluster. Figure 3 shows that, after selecting such nodes, the configuration file, *spark-env.sh,* can be parameterized.
3. Files configuration and sending. Configuration and cluster parameters are set and distributed across the nodes of the cluster. Thus, the next step, once the nodes have been chosen, consists in configuring and parameterizing the files related to the cluster deployment, i.e. *spark-env.sh* and slaves. Afterwards, a script is launched to replicate all files generated by the selected nodes. In short, the entire process is fully automatized in an easy and single step.
4. Cluster launching. The script that launches the cluster must be invoked. So, last, the web application invokes the Spark script *start-all.sh,* which is in charge of launching the nodes. Note that the configuration of such nodes is the one received in the previous step. The default configuration is set to one instance, four cores and 6.7 GB.

Finally, Fig. 4 depicts the entire flowchart that describes the steps followed by the application, in its communications module. It begins at the main page and ends by deploying the cluster.

3.3 Algorithms

One key function in clusters is the launching of algorithms to deal with big datasets. Again, with the idea in mind of simplifying the whole process, the proposed web application is designed to load and parameterize external algorithms,

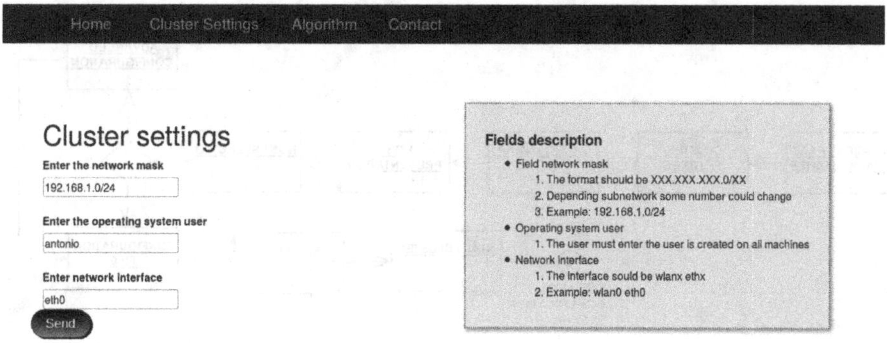

Fig. 2. Data from nodes found in the network.

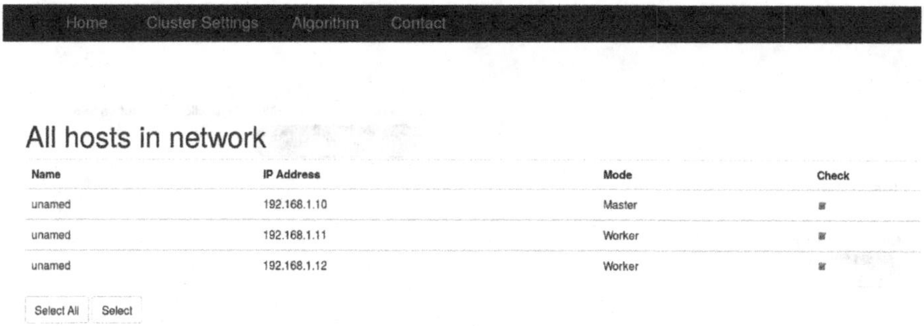

Fig. 3. Slaves selection, and spark-env.sh file parametrization.

by indicating the location (URL) of the target data and its input arguments. Figure 5 depicts the initial interface, in which the user can select the algorithm to be applied. In this case, the k-means (see Sect. 4), as well as its main parameters.

It can also be seen that users can add more algorithms (*Add algorithm* button), with automatic parametrization. Algorithms such as [9] could be easily integrated in this platform. In particular, the user must only provide the executable *.jar* file, which is stored in the web server. The algorithm's complete information, parameters and main class, is also stored in a relational database. Figure 6 shows the interface to upload the executable file and determine its possible parametrization.

Finally, Fig. 7 illustrates the whole flowchart for the modules related to algorithms, thus showing all the steps involved for both add and launch algorithms in the cluster.

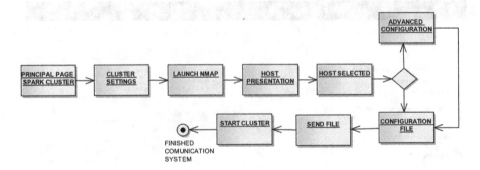

Fig. 4. Flowchart for the communications module.

Home   Cluster Settings   Algorithm   Contact

k-means

K

5

Number of iterations

50

Enter the dataset path SampledataSet.txt

Select

If you like to add an algorithm, please click in the button below

Add a new algorithm

Fig. 5. Initial interface for algorithms management.

Home   Cluster Settings   Algorithm   Contact

Complete the form to add a new algorithm

Name of the Algorithm

Genetic Algorithm

Principal Class

genetic

Select binary file

Browse... GeneticAlgorithm.jar

Number of parameters 3

Insert name and type

Number of populations   Integer

Insert name and type

Number of iterations   Integer

Insert name and type

Mutation probability   Double

Create   Cancel

Fields description

1. Name of the Algorithm
   ○ A descriptive name for your algorithm
2. Pricipal class
   ○ This is the main class of the algorithm
   ○ It does not need extension
   ○ Example: org.apache.spark.examples.SparkPi
3. Binary File
   ○ The File that you upload, should be a .jar packet
   ○ You do not upload anything
4. Number of parameters
   ○ This is the number of fields that will be created
   ○ Remember that you must complete all the fields

Fig. 6. Adding a new algorithm with parameters.

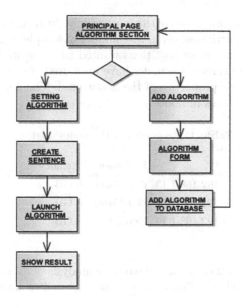

Fig. 7. Flowchart for the algorithms module.

3.4 System Architecture

For the development of the proposed application, the model–view–controller (MVC) architectural pattern for implementing user interfaces has been used. For each layer, different technologies have been used and are listed below:

1. Model. This layer is responsible for the access and management of the entities. In order to increase transparency, Hibernate framework has been used which makes use of data access object (DAO) design pattern.
2. View. This layer controls the user interaction. It has been developed with JSP, as well as CSS, JavaScript, JQuery y Ajax, all used for an optimized user interaction with dynamic forms.
3. Controller. User queries are managed by this layer. Hence, they are all distributed according to the required resource, delegating in the model and offering the results to the view. Servlets have been used for the development of this layer.

4 Case Study

Despite the goal of this application is not the algorithms integrated themselves, the well-known k-means algorithm has been integrated in the platform, in order to conduct a study on its performance, when used in a Spark cluster. What it is shown here is a simple case but proves that, indeed, any algorithm can be easily integrated in the proposed approach and easily launched.

The k-means algorithm is one of the most widely clustering algorithms used in order to create data partitions, given the number of samples (size of the dataset) and the number of clusters or partitions wanted to be created (k) [8]. For this illustrative test, up to three slave nodes have been used, and k has been set to 5. Table 1 summarizes the properties of the nodes used. The default configuration includes all available cores in nodes.

Table 1. Properties of the nodes used.

IP	Processor	Memory
192.168.1.13	i7 8 Cores	6 GB
192.168.1.12	i3 4 Cores	8 GB
192.168.1.14	Core2 Duo	8 GB

Additionally, Table 2 shows a comparative analysis of execution time for the k-means algorithm, when different size of data as well as number of slaves are used.

Table 2. Execution times, expressed in seconds, when varying the data size and number of nodes

Data size	One node	Two nodes	Three nodes
0.8 MB	18s	17s	17 s
20.9 MB	21s	18s	19 s
41.8 MB	22s	19s	22 s
62.7 MB	24s	21s	23 s
83.6 MB	24s	21s	23 s
104.4 MB	31s	43s	24 s
250.7 MB	33s	43s	38 s
501.4 MB	84s	60s	53 s
1024 MB	132s	84s	72 s
2048 MB	252s	156s	96 s

It can be seen that, for not particularly big datasets, execution times for two and three nodes are quite similar. However, as long as the size of the dataset becomes larger (>1 GB), the execution time for three nodes is much lower than those of using one or two nodes, respectively.

5   Conclusions

This paper introduces a platform for an easy and fast Spark cluster management. In this sense, this platform claims to be an essential tool for those programmers in Spark cluster context since it turns its deployment and configuration into a simple task, by means of its graphical user interface. Moreover, the platform has been conceived for an easy integration of new algorithms or programmes, since it allows to dynamically upload and integrate *.jar* files. In just a couple of steps, the user can determine the path of the big data as well as the algorithm that is desired to be applied on them. An illustrative case study has also been included in order to show the web service performance.

Acknowledgements. The authors would like to thank the Spanish Ministry of Economy and Competitiveness, Junta de Andalucía for the support under projects TIN2014-55894-C2-R and P12-TIC-1728 and PRY153/14, respectively.

References

1. Dean, J., Ghemawat, S.: Mapreduce: simplified data processing on large clusters. Commun. ACM **51**(1), 107–113 (2008)
2. Gorton, I., Greenfield, P., Szalay, A., Williams, R.: Computing in the 21st century. IEEE Comput. **41**(4), 30–32 (2008)
3. Hamstra, M., Karau, H., Zaharia, M., Knwinski, A., Wendell, P.: Learning Spark: Lightning-Fast Big Analytics. O' Really Media, Sebastopol (2015)
4. Kouzes, R.T., Anderson, G.A., Elbert, S.T., Gorton, I., Gracio, D.K.: The changing paradigm of data-intensive computing. Computer **42**(1), 26–34 (2009)
5. Middleton, A.M.: Data-Intensive Technologies for Cloud Computing. Springer, Heidelberg (2010)
6. Minelli, M., Chambers, M., Dhiraj, A., Data, B., Analytics, B.: Emerging Business Intelligence and Analytics Trends for Today's Businesses. Wiley, Hoboken (2013)
7. Pavlo, A., Paulson, E., Rasin, A., Abadi, D.J., Dewitt, D.J., Madden, S., Stonebraker, M.: A comparison of approaches to large-scale data analysis. In: Proceedings of the 35th SIGMOD International conference on Management of Data, pp. 165–178 (2009)
8. Pérez-Chacón, R., Talavera-Llames, R.L., Troncoso, A., Martínez-Álvarez, F.: Finding electric energy consumption patterns in big time series data. In: Proceedings of the International Conference on Distributed Computing and Artificial Intelligence, pp. 231–238 (2016)
9. Talavera-Llames, R.L., Pérez-Chacón, R., Martínez-Ballesteros, M., Troncoso, A., Martínez-Álvarez, F.: A nearest neighbours-based algorithm for big time series data forecasting. In: Martínez-Álvarez, F., Troncoso, A., Quintián, H., Corchado, E. (eds.) HAIS 2016. LNCS, vol. 9648, pp. 174–185. Springer, Heidelberg (2016). doi:10.1007/978-3-319-32034-2_15
10. White, T.: Hadoop: The definitive Guide. O' Really Media, Sebastopol (2012)

An Approach to Silhouette and Dunn Clustering Indices Applied to Big Data in Spark

José María Luna-Romera[✉], María del Mar Martínez-Ballesteros,
Jorge García-Gutiérrez, and José C. Riquelme-Santos

Department of Computer Science, Universidad de Sevilla, Seville, Spain
{jmluna,mariamartinez,jorgarcia,riquelme}@us.es

Abstract. K-Means and Bisecting K-Means clustering algorithms need the optimal number into which the dataset may be divided. Spark implementations of these algorithms include a method that is used to calculate this number. Unfortunately, this measurement presents a lack of precision because it only takes into account a sum of intra-cluster distances misleading the results. Moreover, this measurement has not been well-contrasted in previous researches about clustering indices. Therefore, we introduce a new Spark implementation of Silhouette and Dunn indices. These clustering indices have been tested in previous works. The results obtained show the potential of Silhouette and Dunn to deal with Big Data.

Keywords: Silhouette · Dunn · Clustering index · Big data · Spark

1 Introduction

Nowadays every device that surrounds us generates data. 90 % of the world data, around 10,000 exabytes, has been generated in the last three years and there exists an estimation to fourfold that amount of data by 2020 [10]. Big Data is mainly defined as a massive, heterogeneous and often-unstructured digital content that is difficult to process by using traditional tools and techniques [2]. From this scenario, old methodologies cannot be applied [9,16]. Apache Spark is an open source cluster computing framework in charged of working with Big Data [12] and it is based on Resilient Distributed Datasets, a type of structured data especially designed for parallel computing. This structure allows us to cache results in memory and reuse them to process huge amounts of data. Spark also includes a scalable machine learning library (MLlib) [14]. MLlib contains a set of common learning algorithms and utilities for classification, regression, clustering or filtering. In this paper, we are going to focus on clustering techniques, specifically on clustering indices.

K-Means and Bisecting K-Means clustering algorithms are included in MLlib. These clustering algorithms present an inconvenient: the number of clusters into which the dataset is going to be divided has to be known in advance. If the number of clusters is not known, different combinations may be tried until a good solution is reached. To solve this problem, there exists indices that help us define into how many clusters the dataset can be grouped.

© Springer International Publishing Switzerland 2016
O. Luaces et al. (Eds.): CAEPIA 2016, LNAI 9868, pp. 160–169, 2016.
DOI: 10.1007/978-3-319-44636-3_15

K-Means and Bisecting K-Means in MLlib include a measure that calculates the sum of squared distances between the centroids (WSSSE) [13]. Unfortunately, this measure neither calculates the cluster consistency nor the well-separated distance between clusters. In addition, the results of WSSSE may not be correct and they may mislead the clustering. Therefore, we introduce a new Spark implementation of Silhouette and Dunn indices.

First, Silhouette is an index that refers to a method of consistency interpretation within clusters of data. The measure of Silhouette sets how the example is fixed to its cluster compared to others [8,11,15]. Second, Dunn is a validity index whose aim is to identify clusters with a high inter-cluster distance and low intra-cluster distance [6,7]. These indices have been well-contrasted in previous work [1,4,17]. However, they have not been developed for Big Data to the best of our knowledge.

Hence, we propose in this paper a novel Spark implementation of Silhouette and Dunn indices as a solution for the calculation of the optimal number.

This paper is structured as follows. Section 2 describes the research methodology used in this work. Section 3 presents the detailed results of the experiments. Finally, Sect. 4 presents the conclusion of our experiments as well as future directions to follow in upcoming works.

2   Methods

In this section, we present the outlines of a new implementation of Dunn and Silhouette clustering indices based on Spark. We provide information about our Silhouette and Dunn indices (Sect. 2.1), the clustering algorithms that we have used for our experiments (Sect. 2.2) and the datasets that were used (Sect. 2.3). We also specify the hardware and software resources that have been used for our experiments (Sect. 2.4).

2.1   BD-Silhouette and BD-Dunn Indices

Our work is an approach of Silhouette and Dunn indices implemented in Spark. We will denote our indices as BD-Silhouette and BD-Dunn respectively. Our indices are approaches due to the limitations that Spark offers for applying quadratic complexity algorithms.

Let Ω be the space of the objects with $x \in \Omega$ with a given distance d.

Then $\{A_k\}_{k=1..N}$ is a set of clusters so that $\bigcup_k A_k = \Omega$, and $A_i \cap A_j = \emptyset$ $\forall i \neq j$.

C_k is the centroid of A_k, and C_o the centroid of Ω.

We suppose $X_i \in A_k$, then the distance from the object x_i to the cluster A_k is defined.

$$a_k(x_i) = \frac{1}{|A_k| - 1} \sum_{\substack{x_j \in A_k \\ x_j \neq x_i}} d(x_i, x_j) \tag{1}$$

The distance from x_i to the nearest cluster is defined $x_i \in A_k$

$$b_k(x_i) = min_{j=i..N}^{j \neq k}\{a_j(x_i)\} \tag{2}$$

interMean is defined as the average of the distances from centroids to the global center. *intraMean* is the average of the distances between each point to its centroid. With this *intracluster* calculation we avoid quadratic complexity, and it sets it as lineal order.

$$interMean = \frac{1}{N} \sum_{k=1}^{N} d(c_k, C_o) \tag{3}$$

$$intraMean = \frac{1}{|\Omega|} \sum_{x \in \Omega} d(x_i, C_k) \ with \ x_i \ in \ A_k \tag{4}$$

Formula 5 represents the BD-Silhouette that has been defined as the ratio between the difference of the interclusterMean and the intraclusterMean, and the maximum of them.

$$BD\text{-}Silhouette = \frac{interMean - intraMean}{max\{interMean, intraMean\}with \ x_i \in A_x} \tag{5}$$

BD-Silhouette returns a value from 0 to 1, depending on the consistence of the cluster and the separation between them. The higher the cluster number is, the lower intraclusterMean is because dataset's points tend to be more compacted which make BD-Silhouette tends to 1.

Furthermore, as it is specified in Formula 6, BD-Dunn is the ratio between the minimum of the distances from the centroids to the global center and the maximum of the distances from each point in the set to its centroid. This way BD-Dunn returns a value that seeks the best number of clusters attending to its consistency and as much separation as possible.

$$BD\text{-}Dunn = \frac{min_{k=1..N}\{d(C_k, C_0)\}}{max_{x_i \in \Omega}\{d(x_i, c_k)\}} \tag{6}$$

The implemented algorithms return all the values of these formulas from 2 to a given number. This number sets the maximum of the quantity of clusters we could suppose optimal. BD-Dunn results show a set of values whereby we have to keep the first maximum. It represents the best number of clusters whose inter-cluster and intra-cluster distances are optimized.

Algorithm 1 shows the pseudo-code of BD-Silhouette method with precise details of the functions utilized from Spark. In the following, we describe the most significant instructions, enumerated from 1 to 13.

As input, we receive the dataset *data*, the maximum number of cluster that we want to check *maxNumClusters* and the number of iterations for the algorithm *numIterations*.

Algorithm 1. BD-Silhouette implementation

Require: $data, maxNumClusters, numIterations$
1: $totalData = data.count()$
2: **for** $i = 2$ **to** $maxNumClusters$ **do**
3:    $clusters = Cluster.train(data, i, numIterations)$
4:    $intraMean = clusters.computeCost(data)/totalData$
5:    $centroides = sc.parallelize(clusters.clusterCenters)$
6:    $clusterCentroids = Cluster.train(centroides, 1, numIterations)$
7:    $interMean = clusterCentroids.computeCost(centroides)/i$
8:    **if** $interMean \geq intraMean$ **then**
9:       $max = interMean$
10:   **else**
11:       $max = intraMean$
12:   **end if**
13:   $Silhouette = (interMean - intraMean)/max$
14: **end for**

First, we create a cluster model from inputs (Instruction 3). In this way we get the *intraMean* by calculating the average of the distances between each point in the dataset to its centroid (Instruction 4). Next stage is the calculation of *interMean*. To this end we create a model from the centroids (Instruction 4) and we get the average of the distances between each centroid to the global center (Instruction 6–7). In this way we get the *interMean* value. The last step is to obtain the maximum between *intraMean* and *interMean* (Instruction 8–12) and get the silhouette value (Instruction 13). This sequence has to be done as many times as the *maxNumClusters* input is set (Instruction 2) for these instructions in order to calculate silhouette index for each number of clusters.

Below we present Dunn algorithm implementation. BD-Dunn algorithm receives the same input parameters: the dataset *data*, the maximum number of cluster that we want to check *maxNumClusters* and the number of iterations for the algorithm *numIterations*. Dunn algorithm implementation returns a set of values, one per number of cluster. Because of that it is in a loop and each iteration return one value of Dunn (Instruction 1).

The first step is to create a model from inputs (Instruction 2). With this model, we calculate the euclidean distance between each point and his centroid. And of all of these distances, we get the maximum one (Instruction 3). Next stage is to get the minimum distance between the centroids to global center (Instructions 4–6). To get this, the first step is to create a model with all the points (Instruction 5). With this model we can measure the distances between each centroid, and the global center. And with all of them, we get just the minimum one (Instruction 6). The last step is divide the minimum between the maximum (Instruction 7).

Algorithm 2. BD-Dunn implementation

Require: $data$, $maxNumClusters$, $numIterations$
1: **for** $i = 2$ **to** $maxNumClusters$ **do**
2:    $clusters = Cluster.train(data, i, numIterations)$
3:    $max = data.map\{x => Vectors.sqdist(x, clusters.predict(x))\}.max$
4:    $centroids = sc.parallelize(clusters.clusterCenters)$
5:    $clusterCent = Cluster.train(data, 1, numIterations)$
6:    $min = centroids.map\{x => Vectors.sqdist(x, clusterCent.clusterCenters)\}.min$
7:    $dunn = min/max$
8: **end for**

BD-Dunn method return a set of values, one for each iteration. From all the results the first maximum have to be chosen in order to choose the more compacted and well separated clusters.

2.2   Clustering Algorithms

As said above, machine learning algorithms from Spark library have been used for this study. In particular we have used K-Means (KM) and Bisecting K-Means (BKM). KM is a clustering algorithm commonly used that clusters the data into a predefined number of clusters. It splits data into k clusters in which each tuple belongs to the cluster with the nearest distance to the centroid. Moreover, BKM is a hierarchical clustering algorithm which seeks to build a hierarchy of clusters.

2.3   Datasets

In this experimental study we will use three synthetic Big Data (Table 1). These datasets have been specially generated for this task. We know the optimal number of cluster for each one in advance. The synthetic datasets have been specially generated for having well distinguished clusters. To achieve that objective, we have implemented an algorithm that receive the number of examples in each cluster and the number of features of the dataset. The algorithm generates an output file with random numbers in its columns and each column is in different range. After filling the cluster, the columns pivot, and it repeats the same operation. Between the ranges there is enough separation to not create overlaps between the clusters. With these conditions we make sure that the datasets have the number of clusters that we set.

Table 1. Description of used datasets

Dataset	#Examples	#Features	#Cluster
RandomSetN4	50,000,000	4	4
RandomSetN5	50,000,000	5	5
RandomSetN7	50,000,000	7	7

Table 1 summarizes the characteristics of these datasets. Table shows datasets dataset by rows, and by columns we can find the number of examples (#Examples), the number of features (#Features) and the number of cluster that has been established (#Cluster). As we said previously, we know the number of clusters for the datasets in advance. "RandomSetN4" has four clusters, "RandomSetN5" has five clusters and "RandomSetN7" is the largest dataset with seven clusters. We may say that we are talking about Big Data because all the datasets have fifty millions instances with different number of features.

2.4 Hardware and Software

All the experiments have been executed on Ubuntu Server 14.04 with the following features: Intel Xeon E7- 4820 processor with 8 cores (16 threads) and a clock speed of 2.00 GHz. Its cache was 18 MB and it counted with 64 GB of RAM. Spark 1.5.2 with Hadoop 2.6.0 was used with 20 GB for the driver memory.

3   Experimental Results

In this section we describe the results that were carried out to analyse the implementation of BD-Silhouette and BD-Dunn clustering indices applied to Big Data. In order to test our algorithms, we have applied two clustering methods, K-means(KM) and Bisecting K-means(BKM). For these executions we have set the maximum number of cluster as 10 and were applied on three different datasets in Sect. 2.3.

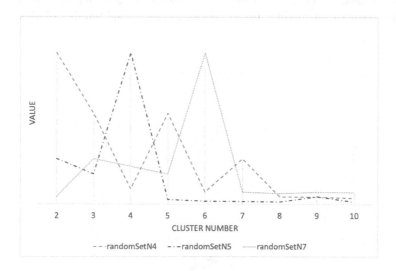

Fig. 1. BKM WSSSE

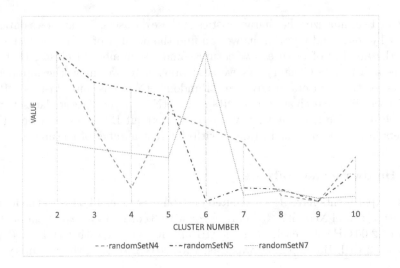

Fig. 2. KM WSSSE

Results of WSSSE are illustrated in Figs. 1 and 2. These results have been drawn in the same graph due to space problems in the paper. Figure 1 shows the results of WSSSE using BKM for each dataset. RandomSetN4 has four clusters, however the graph reports minimum values at four, six and eight. Random-SetN5 has five clusters and the graph reports minimums at three, five, and ten. Similarly, the dataset with seven groups, its graph illustrates minimum values in two, five and eight. The same situation is found in Fig. 2. Unfortunately, WSSSE provides results that might mislead choosing the optimal number of clusters.

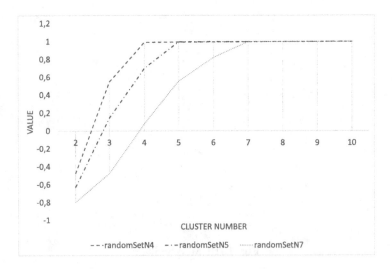

Fig. 3. BKM BD-Silhouette

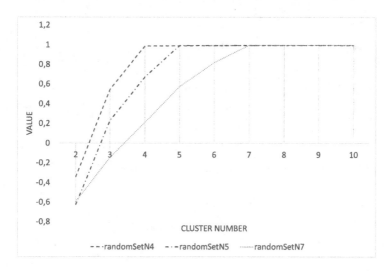

Fig. 4. KM BD-Silhouette

As we can see in Figs. 3 and 4, BD-Silhouette results for KM and BKM are represented. A well defined "elbow" is shown at the optimal number of cluster at each dataset. RandomSetN4 curve is increased until it reaches the maximum where it draws an elbow in the graph at four. Therefore, the optimal number of clusters for RandomSetN4 is four. The same situation happens for the other datasets. RandomSetN5 has its elbow at five, and RandomSetN7 has it at seven.

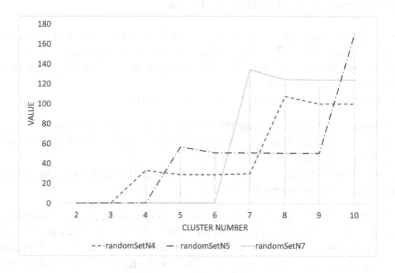

Fig. 5. BKM BD-Dunn results

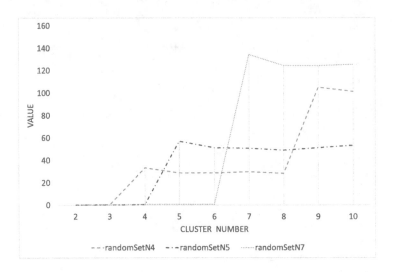

Fig. 6. KM BD-Dunn results

Furthermore, we have BD-Dunn index graphs results. The optimal number of clusters for the dataset is represented by the first maximum in the graph. Therefore, as we can see in Figs. 5 and 6, in the case of RandomSetN4, the first maximum is reached at four. For RandomSetN5 the first maximum is reached at five, and it is at seven for RandomSetN7.

4 Conclusions and Further Work

In this paper we have developed a solution to calculate the optimal number of clusters in Big Data. The use of Apache Spark has provided us a way to parallelize the processes to calculate the optimal number of Big Data through Silhouette and Dunn approaches.

The main achievements obtained are the following:

- An approach to Silhouette and Dunn indices applied to Big Data.
- These approaches allow us to calculate the optimal number of clusters for Big Data using traditional clustering indices.
- The source code of this technique can be found in the next repository: https://github.com/josemarialuna/ClusterIndex.

As future work, we aim to focus on the development of an implementation of Davies-Bouldin [3,5] index applied to Big Data. All the experiments have been tested in a single machine thus next experiments will be tested in a cluster in order to check the algorithms in terms of network efficiency, load balancing and data locality. We Another direction for future work is to enhance our Silhouette and Dunn approaches focused in computational time.

Acknowledgement. This work has been supported by the Spanish National Research Project TIN2014-55894-C2-1-R. J.M. Luna-Romera holds an FPI scholarship from the Spanish Ministry of Education.

References

1. Abdelkader, M., Abd-Almageed, W., Srivastava, A., Chellappa, R.: Silhouette-based gesture and action recognition via modeling trajectories on riemannian shape manifolds. Comput. Vis. Image Underst. **115**(3), 439–455 (2011)
2. Al-Jarrah, O.Y., Yoo, P.D., Muhaidat, S., Karagiannidis, G.K., Taha, K.: Efficient machine learning for big data: a review. Big Data Res. **2**(3), 87–93 (2015). http://www.sciencedirect.com/science/article/pii/S2214579615000271. Big Data, Analytics, and High-Performance Computing
3. Bezdek, J., Pal, N.: Some new indexes of cluster validity. IEEE Trans. Syst. Man Cybern. Part B: Cybern. **28**(3), 301–315 (1998)
4. Cane, J., O'Connor, D., Michie, S.: Validation of the theoretical domains framework for use in behaviour change and implementation research. Implementation Sci. **7**(1), 1 (2012)
5. Davies, D.L., Bouldin, D.W.: A cluster separation measure. Trans. Pattern Anal. Mach. Intell. **2**, 224–227 (1979)
6. Dunn, J.: Well-separated clusters and optimal fuzzy partitions. J. Cybern. **4**(1), 95–104 (1974)
7. Halkidi, M., Batistakis, Y., Vazirgiannis, M.: On clustering validation techniques. J. Intell. Inf. Syst. **17**(2–3), 107–145 (2001)
8. Jain, A., Murty, M., Flynn, P.: Data clustering: a review. ACM Comput. Surv. **31**(3), 264–323 (1999)
9. Katal, A., Wazid, M., Goudar, R.: Big data: issues, challenges, tools and good practices, pp. 404–409 (2013)
10. Lake, P., Drake, R.: Introducing big data. In: Lake, P., Drake, R. (eds.) Information Systems Management in the Big Data Era, pp. 1–18. Springer, Heidelberg (2014). http://dx.doi.org/10.1007/978-3-319-13503-8_1
11. Rousseeuw, P.: Silhouettes: a graphical aid to the interpretation and validation of cluster analysis. J. Comput. Appl. Math. **20**(C), 53–65 (1987)
12. Spark, A.: Lightning-fast cluster computing (2016). https://spark.apache.org/. Accessed 01 April 2016
13. Spark, A.: Clustering - spark.mllib (2016). http://spark.apache.org/docs/latest/mllib-clustering.html. Accessed 01 April 2016
14. Spark, A.: Machine Learning Library (MLlib) Guide (2016). http://spark.apache.org/docs/latest/mllib-guide.html/. Accessed 01 April 2016
15. Starczewski, A., Krzyżak, A.: Performance evaluation of the silhouette index. In: Rutkowski, L., Korytkowski, M., Scherer, R., Tadeusiewicz, R., Zadeh, L.A., Zurada, J.M. (eds.) Artificial Intelligence and Soft Computing. LNCS, vol. 9120, pp. 49–58. Springer, Heidelberg (2015)
16. Yang, C., Liu, C., Zhang, X., Nepal, S., Chen, J.: A time efficient approach for detecting errors in big sensor data on cloud. IEEE Trans. Parallel Distrib. Syst. **26**(2), 329–339 (2015)
17. Zhu, L., Du, T., Qu, S., Wang, K., Zhang, Y.: An improved clustering algorithm for big data based on k-means with optimized clusters' number (2015)

Multiagent Systems

Positioning of Geometric Formations in Swarm Robotics

Pilar Arques$^{(\boxtimes)}$, Fidel Aznar, and Mireia Sempere

Computer Science and Artificial Intelligence Department, University of Alicante,
San Vicente del Raspeig / Sant Vicent del Raspeig, Spain
{arques,fidel,mireia}@dccia.ua.es

Abstract. Nowadays, swarm robotics is presented as a solution for the collaboration between agents whose goal is the resolution of a common objective. One of the major challenges involved in the design of these algorithms is that they are expected to be distributed, scalable and fault tolerant. In this paper, we present an algorithm that, from random positions, gathers all the agents in an established geometric formation. This common formation is a preliminary step to teamwork and to achieve a common objective. The presented algorithm is distributed, scalable and fault tolerant.

Keywords: Swarm · Robustness · Fault-tolerance · Distributed

1 Introduction

As it occurs in nature with bees, ants and other insects and animals, as explained in [8–11]; colonies are grouped and positioned adopting an ordered structure from which they move as a single entity. In the natural world, formations adopted by swarms are diverse: birds fly in a V formation, ants form lines, fish shoal or form schools,... These formations are useful, among others, for migration, find food or protect themselves from predators. As in nature, in our work, agents that form the swarm gathers in an established formation to achieve an objective.

In security and surveillance tasks it is interesting to define a certain perimeter to be inspected by a swarm of autonomous robots. In this sense, it is essential that the robots be able to stand and move in a certain formation. In this paper, an algorithm that addresses this problem is presented, i.e., the formation of the swarm in different geometric shapes is defined, as a previous step to collaboration between agents to solve a problem or achieve an objective.

In this proposal, the user can determine the points that form the edges of the formation, so that the robots are positioned on the perimeter determined by the coordinates defined by the user. To ensure that the result is independent of the initial position of each robot, robots start at different random positions. As

This work has been carried out by the project "SISTEMAS DE ENJAMBRE INTELIGENTES DE VEHICULOS AEREOS NO TRIPULADOS PARA TAREAS DE SEGURIDAD Y VIGILANCIA" TIN2013-40982-R. Ministerio de Economía y Competitividad (Spain). Project co-financed with FEDER funds.

© Springer International Publishing Switzerland 2016
O. Luaces et al. (Eds.): CAEPIA 2016, LNAI 9868, pp. 173–182, 2016.
DOI: 10.1007/978-3-319-44636-3_16

the algorithm is distributed, all agents have the same information and all are equipped with the same sensors; no leader is defined; there is no communication between them; they should avoid any collision; and obviously, two robots cannot take up the same position.

This work has been divided into five sections. In Sect. 2 different works of other authors related to this problem are presented and the characteristics of different algorithms are studied, comparing it with the features of our work. Section 3 explains our proposal in detail. In Sect. 4 experimentation is presented and finally, Sect. 5 describes conclusions and future work.

2   State of the Art

In the literature there are different works dealing with the positioning of multiple robots forming geometric patterns; [3] formally describes the process of formation of robots, with local knowledge of the environment, however, more than one robot can be taking up the same position and it is assumed that the time for performing the process can be infinite.

In the work of [1] an algorithm in which robots must form a pattern is defined, these robots are aware of their direction and orientation and also have a global knowledge of the pattern to be formed, also, in this paper it is considered that each robot of the swarm has a global view of the rest of the swarm, knowing at all times where the other members that make up the swarm are located.

At [2,4] it is demonstrated that robots without information from previous movements can form the same geometric patterns that robots with such information, but as in [3], they work with robots that have global knowledge of the positions of the other members of the swarm, they need unlimited time for performing the formation and also they allow two or more robots take up simultaneously the same position, which cannot be extrapolated to a real swarm of robots.

In [7] a review of various algorithms for pattern formation is described, also a real practice with robots e-puck is presented, but this paper focus exclusively on the formation of a circle.

[5] works with 2D shapes, however, robots start from preset positions and each robot estimates the particular position to be placed, so that is totally dependent on the initial position of robots.

2.1   Comparison of Presented Algorithm with Other Proposals

Table 1 shows a comparison between different algorithms in which robot formations are defined and the proposed algorithm, also the features needed in each case to achieve each algorithm are described. These characteristics have been determined by the requirements that the robots must have in different tasks. In all these tasks, proposed algorithms are totally distributed, where all the robots of the swarm have the same features and all of them perform the same algorithm in which there is no communication between the robots and, therefore, information is collected by sensors.

We have studied the following characteristics:

- **Sensors.** This feature determines whether the robots with their sensors are able to capture information from all agents in the environment or only those closest to them.
- **Compass.** Whether robots have notion of the global orientation or not.
- **Obstacle Avoidance.** Whether the robots have to avoid obstacles or instead, they can take up the same position.
- **Coordinate System.** Whether robots have global or local knowledge of its position on the environment.
- **Initial Position.** Determines whether the initial positions of the robots are random or preset.

These characteristics have been chosen in order to study the feasibility of applying each case to a real system of autonomous robots.

Table 1. Comparison of features required in robots, in order to perform the algorithms.

	Algorithms [1–3]	Algorithm [5]	Algorithm [7]	Proposed algorithm
Sensors	Total	Partial	Partial	Partial
Compass	No	Yes	No	Yes
Obstacle avoidance	No	Yes	Yes	Yes
Coordinate system	Local	Global	Local	Global
Initial position	Random	Preset	Random	Radom

Of the various proposals under discussion, as shown in Table 1, our proposal is the appropriate algorithm for experimentation in real robots, since it follows the features that currently have autonomous robots. They are equipped with GPS, so they know their globlal position in any environment; they are equipped with a compass that tells them the orientation in their movements; and their sensors, infrared cameras, sonars, etc. provide partial information about the environment, never global information.

A swarm system must be fitted with an algorithm to avoid obstacles in order to avoid collisions between robots, also, using random initial positions, we ensure that the algorithm is performed automatically and swarm formation is totally emerging.

3 Proposed Algorithm

In rescue and surveillance tasks with autonomous robots it is interesting to position a swarm of robots around the perimeter of a given 2D shape. Our proposal places the members of the swarm on the perimeter of a predefined geometric formation. This geometric formation is defined by determining the vertices that configure the 2D shape. Thus, different formations are obtained depending on the vertices that are defined in each execution. This proposal is a distributed (all robots have the same information), scalable (the system should be able to operate under a wide range of group sizes), robust and fault tolerant algorithm (system should be able to continue to operate, despite failures in the individuals, or disturbances in the environment), all these concepts are widely explained in [12,13].

The premises from which we start to define the algorithm are the following:

- All the robots of the swarm have the same characteristics: they are equipped with a GPS, which lets them to know their position in the environment, a compass that tells them their orientation and a front sensor that allows them to detect obstacles at a certain distance within their field of vision.
- All robots have the same initial information of the formation to be carried out, they do not have a preset target position for each robot.
- In order to obtain the most general possible solution, initially the position, orientation and velocity vector of each robot are determined randomly.

In this way, the algorithm ensures that all members of the swarm have the same features and will perform the same behaviour.

Our proposal has two phases. In the first phase all members of the swarm are grouped around a particular position and in the second phase the agents move towards the formation that has been determined in each case.

- First phase: all robots are grouped around the central point of the environment. A random point within the environment could be also assigned, but we have chosen the central point to simplify the problem.
  The number of iterations of the algorithm is not unlimited. The number of iterations is equal to the maximum distance a robot can be of the meeting point. For this reason, the algorithm also takes into account the maximum speed that can reach a robot. That is, in this number of iterations, the algorithm ensures that the robot that is in the farthest position can reach the established meeting point.
  When second phase begins, it may be the case that there is a robot that has not reached the goal of the first phase. In this case, the robot also begins to execute the second phase, and try to reach one of the edges of the perimeter. It is more probable that these robots do not reach the final goal.
  Subsequently, the second phase will start.
- Second phase: robots move towards the perimeter defined by the vertices that indicate the specific segments in which robots must be stopped.
  This phase will result in the formation of the established shape.

3.1   Swarm Formation Algorithm

The macroscopic behaviour of the swarm will perform the same behaviour in each of the robots. The algorithm assigns each robot a random position (Pos) within the limits of the environment, having as a restriction that two robots cannot take up the same position. In this way, a safety distance between two robots is set, ensuring that the robots occupy a certain area in the environment. As well, it is assigned a velocity vector (Vel) and a random orientation (Vel_α). Additionally, a matrix ($PTOS$) with the coordinates of the points that define the vertices of the perimeter of the geometric formation is created. The algorithm runs for the preset number of iterations $Max\_Iterations$.

The microscopic behaviour of the swarm is shown in Algorithm 1 (on_Step) in which an execution step for each robot is described. In this algorithm the gradient of the velocity vector that is used to calculate the variation of the position and the orientation of each robot is obtained.

The Algorithm 1 is divided into two phases. In the first phase, when the number of iterations performed is less than the constant (It_C) the objective is to locate all members of the swarm around a position, in our case for simplicity, the centre of the environment, avoiding any possibility of collision. With this purpose, robots make a repulsion movement if their sensors ($S\_R(i)$) detect an object at a distance less than the safety distance (D_S). When a robot reaches the central position, it stops. When the value of the iteration is equals to (It_C), a random orientation and velocity vector is assigned to each robot (keeping the current position).

In the second phase, when the value of the iteration is greater than (It_C), each robot will try to reach a position on the established perimeter. This phase has the following characteristics:

- If there is possibility of collision: the velocity vector will be modified randomly but within a limited range, so that the robot does not change its direction abruptly.
- If the robot is on the delimited perimeter, it stops.
- If the robot is located in a coordinate greater than the farthest vertex of the center, both horizontally and vertically, then the robot should be directed towards the central area in order to reach a segment of the perimeter.
- In another case, the robot must maintain its velocity vector, because in some iteration it will reach the perimeter.

Finally, Algorithm 2 shows the function $is\_Perimeter$. This function determines if a robot is on the defined perimeter. The coordinate matrix ($PTOS$) containing the vertices of the desired shape and the specific position of a robot ($Pos(r)$) are used. This function will return a boolean value, true or false, depending on whether the robot is inside the delimited perimeter.

3.2 Circle Formation

It is worth mentioning separately circle formation, since it must be determined differently because it would be impossible to determine all vertices that form the perimeter. This can be addressed more easily and robustly if we consider that the only restriction that delimits the perimeter of a circle is its radius.

Algorithm 1. Calculation of the increase of the velocity vector at each step of execution.

```
1 Function on_Step(Pos(i) Vel(i) for each robot. PTOS Global points)
2      begin
3          while it < It_C do
4              if S_R(i) < D_max then /* possibility of collision        */
5              |   ΔVel(i) = −Vel(i)
6              else if Pos(i) < Γ then
7              |   ΔVel(i) ← (0,0)
8              else
9              |   Vel_d(i) ←| Vel(i) |
10             |   Vel_α(i) ← arctan(Pos(i)[1], Pos(i)[0])
11             |   Vel(i) ← (Vel_d(i), Vel_α(i))
12             end
13         end
14         if it == It_C then
15         |   Vel_d(i) ← 1 − random(0..1) · 2
16         |   Vel_α(i) ← random(0..1) · 2 · Π
17         |   Vel(i) ← (Vel_d(i) · cos(Vel_α(i)), Vel_d(i) · sin(Vel_α(i)))
18         end
19         while it > It_C do
20             if S_R(i) ≤ D_max then
21             |   Vel_d(i) ←| Vel(i) |
22             |   Vel_α(i) ← arctan(Vel(i)[1], Vel(i)[0])
23             |   β ← Vel_α(i) + Π/2 + random · Π
24             |   p ← (Vel_d(i) + random(0..1))%2
25             |   ΔVel(i) ← (p · cos(β), p · sin(β))
26             else if is_Perimeter(Pos(i)) then
27             |   ΔVel(i) = (0,0)
28             else if Pos(i)[0] > max PTOS[:, 0] ∨ Pos(i)[0] < min PTOS[:, 0]∨
                       Pos(i)[1] > max PTOS[:, 1] ∨ Pos(i)[1] < min PTOS[:, 1]) then
29             |   Vel_d(i) ←| Vel(i) |
30             |   Vel_α(i) ← arctan(Pos(i)[1], Pos(i)[0])
31             |   Vel(i) ← (Vel_d(i), Vel_α(i))
32             else
33             |   ΔVel(i) ← Vel(i)
34             end
35         end
36     end
37 end
```

Therefore, for the circle formation the position of the robot, the radius and the orientation angle of the robot are taken into account. Let $P_A(x, y)$ the position of the robot A, and r the radius of the circle we want to define, the restriction to satisfy is:

Algorithm 2. Determines if a robot is on the perimeter.

```
1  Function is_Perimeter()is
       input  : PTOS, Pos(r)
       output: Per
2      Per ← False
3      i ← 0
4      while i < PTOS.size − 1 do
5          P1 ← PTOS(i)
6          P2 ← PTOS(i + 1)
7          EC ← (Pos(r)[0] − P1[0])/(P2[0] − P1[0])−
8          (Pos(r)[1] − P1[1])/(P2[1] − P1[1])
9          if Pos(r)[0] > min(P1[0], P2[0])∧
10         Pos(r)[0] < max(P1[0], P2[0])∧
11         Pos(r)[1] > min(P1[1], P2[1])∧
12         Pos(r)[1] < max(P1[1], P2[1]) then
13             in_line ← True
14         else
15             in_line ← False
16         end
17         if | EC |< ε ∧ in_line then
18             Per ← True
19         end
20         i ← i + 1
21     end
22     P1 ← PTOS(1)
23     P2 ← PTOS(PTOS.size)
24     EC ← Pos(r)[0]−P1[0]/P2[0]−P1[0] − Pos(r)[1]−P1[1]/P2[1]−P1[1]
25     if Pos(r)[0] > min(P1[0], P2[0]) ∧ Pos(r)[0] < max(P1[0], P2[0]) ∧
       Pos(r)[1] > min(P1[1], P2[1]) ∧ Pos(r)[1] < max(P1[1], P2[1]) then
26         in_line ← True
27     else
28         in_line ← False
29     end
30     if | EC |< ε ∧ in_line then
31         Per ← True
32     end
33 end
```

$$EC \leftarrow \frac{Pos(r)[0]-P1[0]}{P2[0]-P1[0]} - \frac{Pos(r)[1]-P1[1]}{P2[1]-P1[1]}$$

If $r - \sqrt{x^2 + y^2} < \epsilon$ then the robot is on the perimeter of the circle and it stops.

4   Experimentation

In the experimentation the behaviour of the robots performing different geometric formations has been simulated. For the tests we selected the circle formation, as a special case, and three basic formations (triangle, square and star formation). In our case, we have worked with simple geometric figures, but varying the initial position of the vertices any closed geometric figure can be obtained.

Figure 1 shows the behaviour of the algorithm working with 25 robots performing a circle formation of radius 50. Also, this figure shows triangle and square formations. In this case, the initial data are the three or four vertices of the geometric figure, depending on each case.

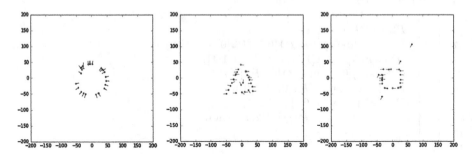

Fig. 1. Circle, triangle and square formation, it has been taken into account as initial data the coordinates of the three and four vertices respectively.

Figure 2 shows star formation, in this case the eight vertices that define this geometric shape has been defined. In the first picture, the initial random position is shown, in the second picture, all members of the swarm are located around the central point of the environment and in the third picture the star formation is achieved. Thus, we can extrapolate the algorithm to any other closed geometric shape. In order to achieve it, it is only necessary to define a larger or smaller number of vertices for robots to perform the desired geometric shape.

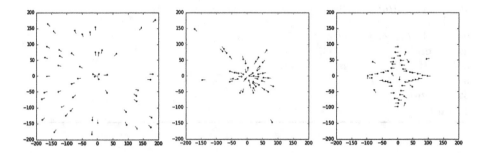

Fig. 2. Star formation, in this case it has been considered as initial data the coordinates of the eight vertices. First picture, random positions. Second picture, swarm members around a point. Third picture, star formation.

As generic data of these tests, the size of the environment on which we have worked, is in all tests the same, it is a square of side 400 pts. The number of iterations required to achieve the desired shape is variable, depending on the number of robots used and the shape. In this sense, with 25 robots, the circle has been achieved in 400 iterations; the square in 600; and triangle in 800 iterations. In the case of the star, the number of iterations required was 1500, due to in this case we have used 50 robots and many of the robots must rectify its trajectory to avoid possible collisions.

Additionally, different tests to demonstrate efficiency and scalability of the algorithm have been performed. Some tests have been also made to shown fault tolerance. The results of these tests are shown in Table 2. Efficiency and scalability tests have been performed with 10, 25 and 100 swarm members, 100 tests of each formation have been made. In Table 2 percentage of swarm members which achieved the formation is shown. As we can see in the table, percentage of robots that are in the defined formation is higher than 80 %. Robots are in the correct segment with an error position of ±0.005. In each formation, the values are practically independent of the number of robots employed. The results are similar for each formation. Thus, efficiency and scalability of our algorithm is proved.

In order to demonstrate fault tolerance, several tests with deliberate errors have been performed. These test have been made to simulate that some swarm members can crash or lost. Tests have been made with 100 swarm members and with 5 % and 10 % of error. As shown in Table 2, values of percentages of robots which get the final formation are similar to values in efficiency tests, so that partial loss of some swarm members is independent to final results. Thus, our algorithm is fault tolerant.

Table 2. Efficiency, scalability and fault tolerance proves, for the demonstrated formations. Eficiency and scalability with 10, 25 and 100 robots. Fault Tolerance with 100 robots, usign 5 % and 10 % of robots with error.

Shape	% Robots in formation			Fault tolerance	
	10	25	100	5	10
Circle	96	97.6	98	96	97
Square	90	84	91	88	91
Triangle	92	91	92	90	92
Star	86	81.6	82	80	82

5   Conclusions and Future Work

A swarm behaviour algorithm decentralized, robust, fault tolerant, scalable and totally distributed for the positioning of robots in geometric formations from random positions has been defined.

All the robots of the swarm have the same capabilities and perform the same behaviour, there is no leader nor need for communication between members of the swarm.

This algorithm is fault tolerant because although a robot does not reach the perimeter, the rest of the swarm is able to achieve the established geometric shape. So that the partial loss of an individual does not imply any problem in achieving the final goal.

With only the definition of certain points we can get the positioning of the swarm in the desired geometric shape and also, we can define any closed geometric formation.

Given the characteristics that defined the algorithm, its implementation is possible in real robotic systems.

As future work we propose the movement of the swarm without losing the formation and its implementation in real robots, both in UAV systems and Khepera robots.

References

1. Flocchini, P., Prencipe, G., Santoro, N., Widmayer, P.: Arbitrary pattern formation by asynchronous, anonymous, oblivious robots. Theor. Comput. Sci. **407**, 412–447 (2008)
2. Yamashita, M., Suzuki, I.: Characterizing geometric patterns formable by oblivious anonymous mobile robots. Theor. Comput. Sci. **411**, 2433–2453 (2010)
3. Suzuki, I., Yamashita, M.: Distributed anonymous mobile robots formation on geometric patterns. SIAM J. Comput. **28**(4), 1347–1363 (1999)
4. Fujinaga, N., Yamauchi, Y., Ono, H., Kijima, S., Yamashita, M.: Pattern formation by oblivious asynchronous mobile robots. SIAM J. Comput. **44**(3), 740–785 (2015)
5. Ani Hsieh, M., Kumar, V., Chaimowicz, L.: Decentralized controllers for shape generation. Robotica **26**, 691–701 (2008)
6. Balch, T., Arkin, R.C.: Behaviour-based formation control for multirobot teams. IEEE Trans. Robot. Autom. **14**(N6), 926–939 (1998)
7. Gautam, A., Umang, A., Mall, P., Mohan, S.: Positioning multiple mobile robots for geometric pattern formation: an empirical analysis. In: 2014 Seventh International Conference on Contemporary Computing (IC3), pp. 607–612 (2014)
8. Britton, N.F., Franks, N.R., Pratt, S.C., Seeley, T.D.: Deciding on a new home: how do honeybees agree? Proc. Biol. Sci. **269**(1498), 1383–1388 (2002)
9. Sumpter, D.J.T.: The principles of collective animal behaviour. Philos. Trans. R. Soc. B. (Biol. Sci.) **361**, 5–22 (2006)
10. Couzinnw, I.D., Krausew, J., Jamesz, R., Ruxtony, G.D., Franksz, N.R.: Collective memory and spatial sorting in animal groups. J. Theor. Biol. **218**, 1–11 (2002)
11. Reynolds, C.W.: Flocks, herds, and schools: a distributes behavioural model. Comput. Graph. **21**(4), 25–34 (1987)
12. Şahin, E.: Swarm robotics: from sources of inspiration to domains of application. In: Şahin, E., Spears, W.M. (eds.) Swarm Robotics 2004. LNCS, vol. 3342, pp. 10–20. Springer, Heidelberg (2005)
13. Mohan, Y., Ponnambalam, S.G.: An extensive review of research in swarm robotics. In: World Congress on Nature and Biologically Inspired Computing (2009)

ABT with Clause Learning for Distributed SAT

Jesús Giráldez-Cru and Pedro Meseguer[✉]

IIIA - CSIC, Universitat Autònoma de Barcelona, 08193 Bellaterra, Spain
{jgiraldez,pedro}@iiia.csic.es

Abstract. Transforming a planning instance into a propositional formula ϕ to be solved by a SAT solver is a common approach in AI planning. In the context of multiagent planning, this approach causes the *distributed* SAT problem: given ϕ distributed among agents –each agent knows a part of ϕ but no agent knows the whole ϕ–, check if ϕ is SAT or UNSAT by message passing. On the other hand, Asynchronous Backtracking (ABT) is a complete distributed constraint satisfaction algorithm, so it can be directly used to solve distributed SAT. Clause learning is a technique, commonly used in centralized SAT solvers, that can be applied to enhance ABT efficiency when used for distributed SAT. We prove that ABT with clause learning remains correct and complete. Experiments on several planning benchmarks show very substantial benefits for ABT with clause learning.

1 Introduction

Problem solving is often assumed as a *centralized* activity: the instance to solve is contained into a single agent, that has direct access to every detail of the instance to perform the solving process. However, in *distributed* problem solving the instance is distributed among several agents; each agent knows a part of the instance but no agent knows the whole instance. *Privacy* is a main motivation for distributed problem solving. When several agents collaborate for solving a problem, it may occur that some could see others as potential competitors. In this case, it is of the greatest importance to assure that the solving process is done without revealing more information than the strictly needed. This is essential for real-world applications, where companies by no means want to disclose sensitive information, of great interest for their business purposes.[1]

In the planning context, a common approach for classical planners when solving an instance is (i) translating the instance into a propositional formula which is SAT (satisfiable) iff the instance has a solution, (ii) solving the formula by an "off-the-shelf" SAT solver, and (iii) retranslating the solution into planning terms. In multiagent planning (MAP) [3,11,14], where privacy matters, this approach generates the *distributed* SAT problem: a propositional formula is distributed among several agents, each contains a part of the formula but

---

Partially funded by TIN2013-45732-C4-4-P and TIN2015-71799-C2-1-P.

[1] Privacy is not required in all distributed scenarios. But when present, it causes a major concern.

O. Luaces et al. (Eds.): CAEPIA 2016, LNAI 9868, pp. 183–193, 2016.
DOI: 10.1007/978-3-319-44636-3_17

none knows the whole formula.[2] Intense communication allows to synthesize a solution. This problem has been considered before [12,15].

ABT [18] –that stands for *asynchronous backtracking*– is a distributed algorithm that originally was presented for distributed CSP. Since SAT is a special case of CSP, the ABT algorithm can be used to solve distributed SAT. It is a correct and complete algorithm and offers a reasonable level of privacy, so ABT appears as a suitable candidate to solve MAP instances. We acknowledge the combination of distributed CSP algorithms with other solving techniques [8,14,19] in the MAP context. Using exclusively distributed constraint satisfaction algorithms has been explored [7]. In this paper, we use ABT as the only algorithm for MAP, assuming that each agent handles a single variable. The generalization to multiple variables per agent is later discussed.

The main contribution of this paper is to import clause learning –a very successful technique to solve industrial SAT instances in the centralized case– into ABT to solve distributed SAT. This is not trivial: one has to decide which clause to learn and who is the learning agent, for each learning episode. Our approach considers that each time an agent receives a backtracking it learns a new clause. This does not cause new messages with respect to the original algorithm. We prove that this new version of ABT remains correct and complete. In practice, it shows a much better performance than original ABT on several planning benchmarks. An instance with more than eight hundred variables have been solved, which is a novelty in the performance of distributed algorithms, often solving instances of more modest size (original ABT could not solve that instance in a timeout of 10 h).

2 Background

2.1 Definitions and Notation

A *centralized* CSP is defined by a tuple (X, D, C), where $X = \{x_1, x_2, ..., x_n\}$ is a set of n variables taking values in a collection of finite and discrete domains $D = \{D_1, D_2, ..., D_n\}$, such that x_i takes value in D_i, under a set of constraints C. A constraint indicates the combinations of permitted values in a subset of variables. A solution is an assignment of values to variables that satisfies all constraints. The goal is to find a solution or to prove that it does not exist. On the SAT problem, we recall the following concepts from propositional logic: a *literal* l is a variable x or its negation $\neg x$; a *clause* is a disjunction of literals; a *formula* ϕ in conjunctive normal form (CNF)[3] is a conjunction of clauses. A *centralized* SAT instance is defined by a formula ϕ in CNF, where variables may take the values *true* or *false*. The goal is determining if there exists an assignment that evaluates ϕ as *true*. Notice that to satisfy ϕ, each clause must be satisfied,

---

[2] This approach differs from an existing meaning in the SAT community, where "distributed" usually means "parallel", and the main goal is finding efficiency gains with respect to centralized SAT.

[3] Any propositional formula can be translated into CNF in linear time.

so at least one literal in each clause must be *true*. The *resolution* between clauses $A \vee x$ and $B \vee \neg x$ results into the clause $A \vee B$, where A and B are disjunctions of literals.

A *distributed* CSP is defined by (X, D, C, A, α) where (X, D, C) are as in the centralized case, A is a set of agents and α is a mapping that associates each variable with an agent. For simplicity, we assume that no agent controls more than one variable. Each agent knows all constraints in which its variable is involved. It is not possible to join all the information into a single agent. The solution is found by message passing. A *distributed* SAT instance is defined by a tuple (ϕ, A, α), where ϕ is as in centralized SAT, and A and α as in distributed CSP. Each agent knows the clauses where its variable appears.

Defined in a centralized context, a *nogood* is an assignment (a conjunction of variable-value pairs) that cannot be extended consistently into a solution [13]. A nogood ng is a justification to remove the value of the deepest variable in the search tree mentioned in ng. When all the values of such variable are removed by nogoods, one can perform *resolution* among them to produce a *new nogood* [2,13]. For example, let us assume that $D_y = \{a, b\}$ and both values are removed by the following nogoods,

$$(x_1 = v_1) \wedge (x_2 = v_2) \wedge (y = a)$$
$$(x_2 = v_2) \wedge (x_3 = v_3) \wedge (y = b)$$

If y is deeper in the search tree than x_1, x_2 and x_3, one can resolve them to obtain the new nogood,

$$(x_1 = v_1) \wedge (x_2 = v_2) \wedge (x_3 = v_3)$$

2.2   Centralized SAT Solving

Most of the modern (complete) SAT solvers are based on the DPLL procedure [10]. It is a depth-first search algorithm; its core idea is branching in each variable (*decisions*), assigning them a value, until all clauses are satisfied (then the formula is SAT), or until a conflict is found and it backtracks to a new assignment. A formula is UNSAT if a conflict is found for all assignments. It also includes the Unit Propagation (UP) rule. This rule is triggered when a certain clause has all its literals but one assigned and the clause is not satisfied. It forces this unassigned literal the value that satisfies such clause. This may occur after every assignment (by decisions or by other propagations).

The Conflict-Driven Clause-Learning (CDCL) SAT solvers are inspired in the DPLL algorithm, but they also include a wide variety of techniques [4]. One of them are the clause learning mechanisms [16], that summarize in new clauses the conflicts that were found in the past, in order to avoid them in the future. Empirically, it has been shown as a key technique to solve real-world SAT instances.

A *conflict* occurs when all literals of a clause are assigned but the clause is still unsatisfied. Hence, that (partial) assignment cannot satisfy the formula, and a new clause can be learnt to avoid the same conflict in the future. The new clause is found by analyzing the implication graph, i.e., the graph that represents the decisions and propagations that provoked the conflict. See an example in Fig. 1. A cut in the implication graph can be seen as a conjunction of the links it cuts. Any cut in the implication graph leaving the conflict in one side and all the decisions in the other side is an inconsistent assignment; its negation produces the new clause to learn. From a conflict, many clauses can be learnt. Experimentally, good performance has been found learning the 1-UIP clause [4] (see Sect. 3.2).

As a toy example, let us consider this formula with 3 clauses (c_i stands for the i-th clause): $\phi = (\neg x_2) \wedge (x_1 \vee x_2 \vee x_3) \wedge (x_1 \vee \neg x_3)$. Starting with the value false, $x_2 = false$ (by UP); decision $x_1 = false$ causes propagations $x_3 = true$ (by c_2), and $x_3 = false$ (by c_3). So there is a conflict; the implication graph finds that $x_1 = false$ is inconsistent, the clause to learn is simply (x_1). At this point, $x_1 = true$ and $x_2 = false$ (both by UP) satisfy the set of clauses, for any value of x_3. This is a solution for ϕ.

2.3   ABT

Asynchronous Backtracking (ABT) [18] was the pioneer asynchronous algorithm to solve distributed CSP. ABT is a distributed algorithm that is executed autonomously in each agent, which takes its own decisions and informs of them to other agents; no agent has to wait for decisions of others. When solving a problem instance, there are as many ABT executions as agents. A telegraphic description follows (for details, consult [18]).

ABT computes a global consistent solution or detects that no solution exists in finite time; it is correct and complete. ABT requires agents to be totally ordered. A binary constraint is translated into a directed link, from the higher to the lower agent that it connects.[4] An ABT agent keeps its agent view and nogood store. The agent view is the set of values it believes are assigned to higher agents connected with it. The nogood store keeps the nogoods received as justifications of inconsistent values. Agents exchange individual assignments and nogoods. When an agent cannot find any value consistent with its agent view, because of the original constraints or because of the received nogoods, a new nogood is generated from its agent view, and it is sent to the closest agent in the new nogood, causing backtracking. If an agent receives a nogood including another agent not connected with it, the receiver requires to add a link from that agent to itself. From this point on, a link from the other agent to itself will exist, receiving the values taken by that agent. ABT uses these messages:

1. *OK?*(*agent, value*). It informs *agent* that the sender has taken *value* as value.
2. *NGD*(*agent, ng*). It informs *agent* that the sender considers *ng* as a nogood.
3. *ADL*(*agent*). It asks *agent* to set a direct link to the sender.

---

[4] ABT can also deal with non-binary constraints; it is described in [5].

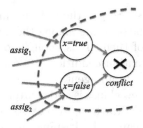

Fig. 1. The dotted line does the cut in the conflict graph.

3 ABT Enhanced with Clause Learning

ABT can solve distributed SAT. Clause learning, developed for centralized SAT, can also be applied to ABT for solving distributed SAT, causing very substantial gains.

3.1 Clause Learning

When ABT solves a distributed SAT instance, let us consider a Boolean variable x of ϕ with a conflict, as depicted in Fig. 1. A conflict appears when both possible values of x are forbidden, as effect of the assignments of previous variables in the total order: *false* is forbidden by $assig_1$, *true* is forbidden by $assig_2$. We say that,

$$assig_1 \wedge (x = false)$$
$$assig_2 \wedge (x = true)$$

are nogoods removing the values of x. In SAT terms $assig_1$ corresponds to the links pointing to $x = true$ in the implication graph, while $assig_2$ corresponds to the links pointing to $x = false$. Both assignments cause the conflict; their conjunction $assig_1 \wedge assig_2$ is the new nogood found by x. It corresponds to the cut that has in its right side the conflict variable only. It is easy to see that the negation of this conjunction $\neg(assig_1 \wedge assig_2)$ is a logical consequence of the original formula[5], so we can add the negation of this conjunction –that from now on we call *new learnt clause*– to the formula ϕ without altering its satisfiability.

Which agent has to learn this new clause? Let y be the agent to which x backtracks to, after discovering the conflict. We know that y is the closest agent to x in the new clause. In addition, y is connected (or it will be connected, after the reception of the *NGD* message by the use of *ADL* messages) with all the

---

[5] If the original formula is satisfiable, variable x in the satisfying assignment will take some value, either *true* or *false*. But that assignment necessarily has to satisfy $\neg assig_1 \vee \neg assig_2$, otherwise x will have no value. So $\neg assig_1 \vee \neg assig_2 = \neg(assig_1 \wedge assig_2)$ can be legally added to the formula without changing its satisfiability. If the original formula is unsatisfiable, any other clause can be added to it, because the resulting formula will remain unsatisfiable.

other agents in the new clause. So y is the right agent to store and evaluate the new clause: it is the last in the ordering among the new clause agents and it has direct connections with all of them. It is enough to store the new clause in a single agent: the ABT termination condition [18] cannot be achieved if there is at least one unsatisfied clause in an agent.

There is a drawback: if a new clause is added after each backtracking, memory may grow exponentially. This drawback also exists in centralized SAT solving. To avoid the extra overhead caused by keeping an increasing number of clauses in large formulas, some clauses deletion policies have been proposed [1,4,16]. However, in our experimentation we detected no memory overhead (each SAT instance was solved using a maximum of 4 GB of RAM). For this reason, we did not implement any clause deletion policy in our algorithm. The applicability of these policies to the proposed solution remains for future work.

In CDCL SAT solvers, clause learning is usually used jointly with non-chronological backtracking (the backjump destination and the learnt clause are related). In the distributed case, things are different because the agent that finds the conflict does not see the whole formula, only a subset of clauses. Then, it cannot do a complete conflict analysis to determine where to backjump. Since ABT agents have a limited view of the whole problem, the agent that finds a conflict backtracks to the closest agent in the nogood obtained from that conflict, following the backtracking policy of original ABT.[6]

Adding clause learning to ABT maintains its correctness and completeness, as we prove in the following theorem.

Theorem 1. *ABT enhanced with clause learning remains correct and complete.*

Proof. ABT is correct and complete [18]. ABT with clause learning on ϕ finds:

1. A satisfying assignment, which is a correct solution for ϕ' (the set of clauses in memory when the solution was found). This is also a solution for ϕ since $\phi \subseteq \phi'$;
2. There is no satisfying assignment (the two values of a variable have been unconditionally removed). Since all added clauses are logical consequences of ϕ, ABT on ϕ' would not remove any value that would not been removed by ABT on ϕ.

On completeness, the same argument (2) applies: the added clauses are logical consequences of ϕ, so they will never remove any value that would not have been finally removed by ϕ. So ABT with clause learning is correct and complete. ☐

In summary, we propose a new version of ABT that performs clause learning. Each time a *NGD* message reaches an agent, it learns the clause that is the negation of the nogood contained in that message. These learnt clauses can be

---

[6] In the toy example of Sect. 2.2 with lexicographic variable ordering, ABT executed on x_3 detects the conflict but it knows c_2 and c_3 only (the clauses where x_3 appears). It finds the nogood $\neg x_1 \wedge \neg x_2$. Then, x_3 backtracks to the deepest variable in the nogood, that is x_2.

seen as new constraints that summarize the conflicts found during the search. Each conflict is found after several *wrong* decisions, resulting in an inconsistency. Therefore, learning the reasons of a conflict allows us to detect it in the future in earlier stages, i.e., reducing the number of wrong decisions that lead to the same conflict. It is worth noting that this does not increase the number of messages used by normal ABT. To the best of our knowledge, it is first time that clause learning occurs in the distributed context. This novel approach keeps correctness and completeness of original ABT.

3.2 Learning 1-UIP Clause

Which is the right clause to learn? In centralized SAT solving, a 1-UIP clause seems to be the best practical choice. This clause is related to the decision level of each variable involved in the implication graph. A decision level contains a decision variable and all variables propagated by it (forced by UP), and it is increased in each new decision. Formally, a *1-UIP clause* is the first cut in the implication graph (from the conflict to the decision variables) that only contains one literal of the last decision level (i.e., the decision level of the conflict). Notice that the implication graph may contain several 1-UIP clauses. In ABT, the first learnt clause is not necessarily the 1-UIP. However, we show that in each conflict a 1-UIP clause is learnt by some agent.

Theorem 2. *For a single conflict, ABT with clause learning for distributed SAT learns exactly all possible clauses that can be derived from the implication graph of that conflict, if the total order of the variables in ABT is the same as in the implication graph.*

Proof. Each time a CDCL SAT solver finds a conflict, there exists in the last decision level at least one variable whose value was forced by UP, and (at least) an unsatisfied clause with no unassigned literals. This is the conflict clause. Notice that the implication graph of this conflict defines a total order among the variables involved. Applying resolution between this conflict clause and the clause that forced (by UP) the last variable in the ordering, we obtain a new clause (which is a logical consequence from the formula, and thus it can be added to the formula without altering its satisfiability). Using this resulting clause, this step can be repeated as many times as variables were assigned by UP, obtaining a new learnt clause at each step. The last possible learnt clause contains the decision variable of the last decision level.

Let us assume now an ABT algorithm whose agents order is the same as the one in the implication graph of a certain conflict. When an agent (variable) finds a conflict, there exists a pair of clauses that cannot be satisfied under its current agent view. The generated nogood ng is the resolvent between these two clauses, which is exactly the first possible learnt clause in the implication graph, and it is learnt by the highest priority agent in ng. If this agent has one of its values forbidden by another clause ω (it corresponds to a variable assigned by UP in a CDCL), it will apply resolution between ng and ω, and will send the resolvent to another agent, which will learnt this new clause. Hence, these clauses are exactly the cuts in the implication graph. This process will be repeated till the agent which receives the nogood has no forbidden values (it corresponds to the decision variable of the last decision level in a CDCL), and this is exactly the last clause that can be learnt by a CDCL. □

Assuming that the total order used by ABT is the same the the total order in the implication graph is a strong assumption, and reduces the effect of UP in ABT with respect to CDCL SAT solvers. However, this restriction is imposed in the original ABT.

Corollary 1. *ABT for distributed SAT with clause learning learns a 1-UIP clause.*

Proof. One of the derived clauses from a conflict is a 1-UIP clause. As ABT learns all possible clauses from a conflict (Theorem 2), one of them is precisely a 1-UIP clause. □

Therefore, after a conflict this approach assures that some agent has learnt a 1-UIP clause, although we do not know which agent has done it.

3.3   Example

Let us consider the following SAT formula ϕ:

$$(x_1 \lor \neg x_2) \land (x_2 \lor \neg x_3) \land (x_2 \lor \neg x_4) \land (x_3 \lor x_4 \lor x_5) \land (x_3 \lor x_4 \lor \neg x_5)$$

Let us summarize the performance of ABT with clause learning in ϕ, considering an initial lexicographical ordering of its variables; c_i stands for the i-th clause of ϕ. We also consider that it first assigns the value *false* to a variable if there is no nogood forbiding that value. We can deduce the following facts:[7]

1. Decision $x_1 = $ *false* causes the propagations $x_2 = $ *false* (by c_1), which in turn causes the propagations $x_3 = $ *false* (by c_2) and $x_4 = $ *false* (by c_3). There is a conflict in x_5, which triggers a cascade of backtrackings (from x_5 to x_4, from x_4 to x_3, from x_3 to x_2, from x_2 to x_1). In these backtrackings, the algorithm learns the following clauses: $c_{l_1} = (x_3 \lor x_4)$, $c_{l_2} = (x_2 \lor x_3)$, $c_{l_3} = (x_2)$, $c_{l_4} = (x_1)$.
2. Clause c_{l_4} is unit so $x_1 = $ *true* (by UP); the same occurs with $x_2 = $ *true*. Decision $x_3 = $ *false* causes the propagation $x_4 = $ *true* (by c_{l_1}). This satisfies clauses c_4 and c_5, with the decision $x_5 = $ *false*. The original clauses are satisfied, this assignment is a solution for the formula.

Observe that learnt clauses help to prune the search tree, avoiding traversing zones that do not contain any solution. Clause $c_{l_3} = (x_2)$ avoids exploring $x_2 = $ *false* which does not drive to any solution. After the propagation $x_2 = $ *true*

---

[7] For simplicity, we do not give the trace of ABT, which is quite long.

and the decision $x_3 = false$, clause $c_{l_1} = (x_3 \lor x_4)$ forces $x_4 = true$, avoiding $x_4 = false$ which does not drive to any solution. Clauses c_{l_1} and c_{l_3} have been learnt under $x_1 = false$, and they are used when exploring $x_1 = true$. Without clause learning, ABT would have to traverse a larger search tree. In addition to visiting more nodes, more messages were exchanged among the agents, messages that do not lead to any solution. It is worth noting that the nogood $(\neg x_3 \land \neg x_4)$ (that corresponds to the learnt clause c_{l_1}) was recorded as a justification of the removal of value $false$ for x_4. Original ABT would have removed that nogood after backtracking to x_3.

4 Experimental Results

We evaluate the performance of ABT with clause learning ($=\text{ABT}_{\text{CL}}$) against plain ABT, in terms of communication cost (total number of messages exchanged among agents) and computation effort (equivalent non-concurrent constraint checks, ENCCCs). Upon receipt of a message msg from another agent, the receiving agent ag updates its $ENCCC$ counter as: $ENCCC_{ag} = max\{ENCCC_{ag}, ENCCC_{msg}+1000\}$.[8] In a distributed scenario, exchanging messages among agents has a much higher cost than any other operation performed by an agent without communication.

We have used some planning benchmarks from the SAT Competition 2005 and from the SATLIB repository.[9] Moreover, we have generated a set of benchmark composed of 100 classical random 3-CNF formulas with 50 variables and 200 clauses. In Table 1, we present the results, on average, for each benchmark with lexicographic variable ordering. Each version of ABT was run in our simulator with a timeout of 10 h (to allow plenty of time for the execution of original ABT) with a limit of 4 GB of RAM memory per instance. Remark that we are only reporting the results for the instances that were solved by both ABT versions (original ABT and ABT with clause learning) discarding those that could not be solved by any of them in the established timeout of 10 h.[10] On all the planning instances, the benefits of ABT with clause learning are clear, in both #messages and ENCCCs (arriving to savings of orders of magnitude in some cases). It is worth mentioning that ABT with clause learning has solved an instance with more than one eight hundred variables (843 variables and 7301 clauses, found as `logistics/logistics.b.cnf`), while original ABT could not solve it in the timeout (because of that, it is not recorded in Table 1). To the best of our knowledge, it is first time that a distributed algorithm solves an instance of such size. Since all planning instances reported in Table 1 are satisfiable, we also experimented with unsatisfiable formulas, using classical random 3-SAT instances. We experimented with 100 random instances (51 satisfiable, 49 unsatisfiable) of 50 variables and

---

[8] Exchanging a message has a cost of 1000 $ENCCC$. We choose such $arbitrary$ value to emphasize that sending a message is much more costly than performing internal CPU operations.

[9] http://www.satcompetition.org/ and http://www.satlib.org/.

[10] Except in the Ferry benchmark, where we report one instance unsolved by ABT in the timeout.

Table 1. Results as the number solved instances, number of messages exchanged and ENCCCs, on average per each benchmark, solved by both algorithms in the timeout.

Benchmark	#inst	#solved		#messages		ENCCC	
		ABT	ABT$_{CL}$	ABT	ABT$_{CL}$	ABT	ABT$_{CL}$
Depots	8	5	5	120101314.60	**12953075.60**	98746867.40	**1578372.60**
DriverLog	20	11	11	56698280.45	**19969830.64**	49797937.36	**3761396.55**
Ferry	18	0	1	-	**625177269.00**	-	110158150.00
Rovers	11	9	9	21674815.78	**4720008.11**	33090165.44	**1724779.33**
Satellite	10	5	5	329448853.20	**103446296.00**	580921823.00	**10399030.00**
Blocksworld	7	5	5	24245647.40	**16771146.20**	16041447.80	**2328836.80**
Logistic	4	1	2	236392659.00	**7370661.00**	670032346.00	**5043248.00**
random	100	100	100	487734.01	**335262.44**	3692305.51	**1022613.69**

200 clauses. Results for this class also indicate that ABT enhanced with clause learning performs clearly better than original ABT.

5   Discussion and Conclusions

We have focused on ABT, while other efficient algorithms exist for distributed constraint solving. Why? We consider that clause learning is rather independent to the techniques used by existing algorithms, so it is expectable that, in the case that these algorithms were combined with clause learning, they would also increase their efficiency. Here we are using ABT as baseline, in order to show the benefits that clause learning may cause when included in a distributed constraint algorithm, although we believe that results of the same kind could be observed when clause learning is combined with other algorithms. A similar reasoning applies to heuristics.

We assumed the simplifying assumption of one variable per agent. Under this assumption we have shown how clause learning produces an important improvement in the communication cost among ABT agents. We are aware that the natural translation of a multiagent planning instance into a distributed propositional formula may assign several Boolean variables to the same agent. There are two classical reformulations, compilation and decomposition, that allows to comply with this assumption. We skip details because space limitations, the interested reader is addressed to [6,9,17]. However, these reformulations imply some drawbacks. As future work, we plan to extend this approach for agents with several variables without using any reformulation.

To conclude, we have presented ABT enhanced with clause learning, a new version of ABT for solving distributed SAT. We stress the inclusion of the powerful technique of clause learning. To the best of our knowledge, it is first time that clause learning is combined with a distributed algorithm. Interestingly, ABT with clause learning maintains the correctness and completeness of the original ABT. We have proved that a 1-UIP clause, the one most preferred in the centralized SAT, is learnt by some agent after a conflict. Experimentally, we observe that clause learning causes a substantial improvement in performance, with respect to the original algorithm when tested on planning benchmarks. ABT with clause learning can be useful for multiagent planning, and for other domains (as scheduling) where problems have to be solved distributedly.

References

1. Audemard, G., Simon, L.: Predicting learnt clauses quality in modern SAT solvers. In: Proceedings of IJCAI 2009, pp. 399–404 (2009)
2. Baker, A.: The hazards of fancy backtracking. In: Proceedings of AAAI 1994, pp. 288–293 (1994)
3. Benedetti, M., Aiello, L.C.: SAT-based cooperative planning: a proposal. In: Hutter, D., Stephan, W. (eds.) Mechanizing Mathematical Reasoning. LNCS (LNAI), vol. 2605, pp. 494–513. Springer, Heidelberg (2005)
4. Biere, A., Heule, M., van Maaren, H., Walsh, T.: Handbook of Satisfiability. IOS Press, Amsterdam (2009)
5. Brito, I., Meseguer, P.: Asynchronous backtracking for non-binary disCSP. In: ECAI-2006 Workshop on Distributed Constraint Satisfaction (2006)
6. Burke, D.A., Brown, K.N.: Efficient handling of complex local problems in distributed constraint optimization. In: Proceedings of ECAI 2006, pp. 701–702 (2006)
7. Castejon, P., Meseguer, P., Onaindia, E.: Multi-agent planning by distributed constraint satisfaction. In: Proceedings of CAEPIA 2015, pp. 41–50 (2015)
8. Dakota, K., Komenda, A.: Deterministic multi agent planning techniques: experimental comparison. In: Proceedings of DMAP (ICAPS Workshop), pp. 43–47 (2013)
9. Davin, J., Modi, P.J.: Hierarchical variable ordering for multiagent agreement problems. In: Proceedings of AAMAS 2006, pp. 1433–1435 (2006)
10. Davis, M., Logemann, G., Loveland, D.W.: A machine program for theorem-proving. Commun. ACM **5**(7), 394–397 (1962)
11. Dimopoulos, Y., Hashmi, M.A., Moraitis, P.: μ-SATPLAN: multi-agent planning as satisfiability. Knowl.-Based Syst. **29**, 54–62 (2012)
12. Hirayama, K., Yokoo, M.: Local search for distributed SAT with complex local problems. In: Proceedings of AAMAS 2002, pp. 1199–1206 (2002)
13. Katsirelos, G., Bacchus, F.: Unrestricted nogood recording in CSP search. In: Proceedings of CP 2003, pp. 873–877 (2003)
14. Nissim, R., Brafman, R., Domshlak, C.: A general, fully distributed multi-agent planning algorithm. In: Proceedings of AAMAS 2010, pp. 1323–1330 (2010)
15. Ruiz, E.: Distributed SAT. Artif. Intell. Rev. **35**, 265–285 (2011)
16. Silva, J.M., Sakallah, K.: GRASP - a new satisfiability algorithm. In: Proceedings of ICCAD, pp. 220–227 (1996)
17. Yokoo, M.: Distributed Constraint Satisfaction: Foundations of Cooperation in Multi-agent Systems. Springer, Berlin (2001)
18. Yokoo, M., Durfee, E., Ishida, T., Kuwabara, K.: The distributed constraint satisfaction problem: formalization and algorithms. IEEE Trans. Knowl. Data Eng. **10**, 673–685 (1998)
19. Zhang, Y., Kambhampati, S.: A formal analysis of required cooperation in multi-agent planning. In: Proceedings of DMAP 2014 (ICAPS Workshop), pp. 30–37 (2014)

Modeling Malware Propagation in Wireless Sensor Networks with Individual-Based Models

A. Martín del Rey$^{(\boxtimes)}$, J.D. Hernández Guillén, and G. Rodríguez Sánchez

Department of Applied Mathematics, University of Salamanca,
Calle del Parque 2, 37008 Salamanca, Spain
{delrey,diaman,gerardo}@usal.es

Abstract. The main goal of this work is to propose an individual-based model to simulate malware propagation over a wireless sensor network. Specifically, this is an improvement of the model proposed by Y. Song and G.P. Jiang in 2009 (see [11]) and based on a two-dimensional cellular automata whose cellular space is an homogeneous lattice where sensors are placed. In our model, different types of nodes are now considered (sensor nodes, router nodes and sink nodes) and heterogeneous topologies are used. The simulations computed lead to obtain more realistic scenarios for malware propagation over wireless sensor networks.

Keywords: Wireless sensor networks · Malware · Propagation · Individual-based models · Cellular automata

1 Introduction

The Internet of Things (IoT) is quickly becoming one of the most important ICT paradigms of the 21st century. This notion brings together both the people ubiquity and the physical objects ubiquity, that is, people and objects can be connected anytime and anywhere [13]. In this new paradigm, wireless sensor networks (WSNs) play a very important role because they serve as a useful tool to connect the physical infrastructure with the information and communication technologies [6].

A wireless sensor network is a network constituted by a large number of sensor nodes that cooperatively collect and transmit data from the environment, allowing interaction between individuals or computers and the surrounding environment [7]. A WSN usually includes sensor nodes, router nodes, sink nodes or gateways and task manager nodes (see Fig. 1). Sensor nodes are those whose objective is to sense the ambient, router nodes relay the data collected by sensors, sink nodes allow the exchange of data with other networks or Internet, and finally all monitored data reaches the task manager node. In addition, the user configures and manages the WSN and publishes monitoring missions by means of the management node [14].

Although initially WSNs were inspired and used for military purposes (surveillance in conflict zones, etc.), their applications are gradually expanding to other fields such as smart grids, smart water networks, intelligent transportation, smart homes, intelligent agriculture, e-health, etc. (see, for example, [3,8,10,12]).

© Springer International Publishing Switzerland 2016
O. Luaces et al. (Eds.): CAEPIA 2016, LNAI 9868, pp. 194–203, 2016.
DOI: 10.1007/978-3-319-44636-3_18

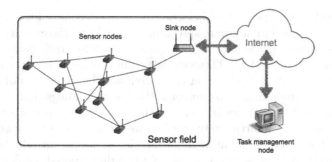

Fig. 1. Basic scheme of a wireless sensor network.

The deployment of a WSN is given by the following stages:

1. Placing sensors: The sensors are placed in the monitoring area (sensor field). This placement could be random (the sensors are dropped from air in random manner) or it could be in a deterministic manner such that exact locations are predetermined to deploy the sensors.
2. Waking up and detecting: Each sensor wake up and detect the other sensors in its neighborhood.
3. Connecting: The sensor nodes are organized into a connected network according to a fixed topology (linear, star, tree, mesh, etc.)
4. Routing and transmission: Connecting paths taking into account the network are computed to transmit the data collected.

The main goal of source nodes (simple sensor nodes) is to collect data from the environment (temperature, humidity, acoustic waves, vehicular movement, etc.) and send it to the sink node. During the transmission phase, the data is handle by multiple intermediate nodes (both sensor nodes and router nodes) to get the sink node after multihop routing.

The Multiple Access Control (MAC) protocol in WSNs specifies the way in which the wireless medium is shared by the nodes. This protocol allows to coordinate the transmissions of sensors in order to avoid collisions; this approach consists of sensing the physical medium for transmission, and when the medium is idle then the sensor node accesses it and transmits the data. Router nodes and sink nodes have advanced capacities and can receive multiple transmissions [14].

Considering the nature and characteristics of WSNs, security risks are unavoidable. Usually, sensor devices are deployed in hostile environments without human supervision. Although the data transmitted over these networks are normally encrypted [2,5], malicious actions can be implemented to compromise the data transmitted. These attacks can be classified into two types: passive attacks and active attacks. The main goal of passive attacks is to eavesdrop of data for the system without affecting the WSN performance, whereas active attacks aim to alter data or system resources. Of especial interest is this last kind of attacks and malware play an important role in its development. In this sense, it is very important to design efficient tools to detect the existence of malware in the network and to predict its behavior. Some models have been appeared in the literature to simulate malware spreading in WSN and the great majority are based on continuos mathematical tools such as ordinary differential equations (see, for example [1,4,9,15]). These models exhibit some drawbacks because of they do not take into consideration the individual characteristics of the nodes and their local interactions. To overcome these shortcomings, individual-based models based on AI techniques (such as cellular automata or agent-based models) could be considered. Unfortunately, as far as we know, there are few works based on these techniques and the most important is the model introduced by Song and Jian (see [11]). It is based on the use of a two-dimensional cellular automata such that the sensor field is tessellated as a square grid and each square area stands for a cell (memory unit) of the cellular automata. The sensor devices are placed in the monitoring area in such a way that there must be, at most, only one sensor per cell. The devices are endowed with a state (susceptible, infected, recovered or dead) at every step of time and it changes accordingly to some local transition rules which depend on some parameters.

Although this model considers the individual interactions, it also exhibits some drawbacks that make it unrealistic. Specifically, they are related to the main definition of the cellular automata and the topology derived. The main purpose of this work is to analyze in detail the last mentioned model in order to improve it. Furthermore, we will propose a novel model based on an alternative paradigm: an individual-based modeling based on a cellular automata whose cells stand for the individual nodes and the cellular space is defined by a graph. This allows us to consider different types on sensors and realistic topologies.

The rest of the paper is organized as follows: In Sect. 2 the model due to Song and Jian is shown, its critical analysis and the improved proposal are introduced in Sect. 3; in Sect. 4 some illustrative simulations are shown, and finally, the conclusions and further work are presented in Sect. 5.

2   Description of the Model by Song and Jian

As was mentioned above the model by Song and Jiang ([11]) is based on the use of a two-dimensional cellular automata whose cellular space is formed by an homogeneous array of $L \times L$ cells. Each of these cells represents an square area of the sensor field and can be occupied by, at most, only one sensor. As a consequence, the state of the cell (i, j) at the time step t is the three-dimensional vector $\mathbf{s}_{ij}^t = \left(p_{ij}^t, s_{ij}^t, m_{ij}^t\right)$, where:

$$p_{ij}^t = \begin{cases} 0, \text{ if the cell } (i, j) \text{ is empty at time } t \\ 1, \text{ if the cell } (i, j) \text{ is occupied at time } t \end{cases} \tag{1}$$

$$s_{ij}^t = \begin{cases} 0, \text{ if the sensor located in the cell } (i, j) \text{ is susceptible at time } t \\ 1, \text{ if the sensor located in the cell } (i, j) \text{ is infected at time } t \\ 2, \text{ if the sensor located in the cell } (i, j) \text{ is recovered at time } t \\ -1, \text{ if the sensor located in the cell } (i, j) \text{ is dead at time } t \\ \times, \text{ if } p_{ij}^t = 0 \end{cases} \tag{2}$$

$$m_{ij}^t = \begin{cases} 0, & \text{if the channel of the sensor located in } (i,j) \text{ is idle at time } t \\ 1, & \text{if the channel of the sensor located in } (i,j) \text{ is busy at time } t \quad (3) \\ \times, & \text{if } p_{ij}^t = 0 \end{cases}$$

Note that the information provided by the first coordinate of the state vector, p_{ij}^t, is related with the existence of a sensor node placed in the cell (i,j) at time step t. The second coordinate, s_{ij}^t, reflects the state of the sensor node in relation to malware (susceptible, infected, recovered or dead), and finally, the third coordinate of the state vector, m_{ij}^t, considers the impact of MAC protocol in WSNs.

The neighborhood of each occupied cell (i,j), V_{ij}, depends on the transmission range R of the sensor node placed in it. In this model three types of neighborhoods are considered: Von Neumann, Moore and extended Moore neighborhoods.

The vector state s_{ij}^t is updated according to some local transition functions. The first coordinate, p_{ij}^t, does not change due to the nature of the cellular automata considered and the fact that sensor nodes are not mobile. The transition functions governing the changes of s_{ij}^t are as follows:

- Transition from susceptible to infected: if the sensor node placed at the cell (i,j) is susceptible at time step $t-1$ ($s_{ij}^{t-1} = 0$) then it becomes infected at time step t ($s_{ij}^t = 1$) with probability $1 - (1 - \beta)^k$, where k is the number of infected neighborhoods of (i,j) whose channel is idle at time step $t-1$, and β is the probability to be infected when a malicious packet is received from a single (infected) sensor.
- Transition from infected to recovered: if the sensor node located in the cell (i,j) at time step $t-1$ is infected, then it becomes recovered at time step t with probability δ.
- Transition from susceptible, infected or recovered to dead: the sensor (susceptible, infected or recovered) node placed in the cell (i,j) at time $t-1$ becomes dead at step of time t with probability γ.

Finally, m_{ij}^t changes depending on the existence of connected neighbor sensors.

3 The Improved Proposed Model

3.1 Critical Analysis of the Model Due to Song and Jian

The model introduced in the last section exhibits the following drawbacks:

1. The specifications of the two-dimensional cellular automata state that each cell stands for an homogeneous square area of the monitoring area which can be occupied by, at most, only one sensor device. This assumption leads to consider unrealistic topologies: for example, topologies where the number of neighbor cells are limited to four (Von Neumann), eight (Moore) or twelve (extended Moore) cells. Consequently, this statement can be improved by supposing that each cell stands for a sensor node. Obviously, this new paradigm

implies changes in the notion of neighborhood of each cell/sensor. Specifically, it must be defined by all sensors that are located in the transmission range of such sensor and consequently, the topology of the network must be defined by means of an undirected graph whose nodes are the sensors and two sensors are neighbors (both are in the neighborhood of another) if they are adjacent by an edge.

2. In the model by Song and Jian all sensors have the same characteristics regardless to its role: source sensor, sink sensor, etc. In order to capture the particular specifications of each sensor device is more suitable to consider the cellular automata paradigm based on graphs instead of the homogeneous cellular automata paradigm. As a consequence, in the improved model it must be considered different types of cells (actors) standing for source nodes, router nodes and sink nodes (gateways). Each type will have different specifications in relation to the transmission range and the bandwidth (the number of active transmission at each step of time).

3. In the previous model the state "dead" is the same for all sensors (and, obviously, it is given by the same coefficient γ). Note that a sensor can be removed from the network either it has been damaged by virtue of the malicious action of malware, or by virtue of energy consumption (wireless sensor are battery driven devices and operate on an extremely frugal energy budget). Consequently, the initial assumption must be improved considering two new states: "damaged" sensors (due to the action of malware) and "out-of-order" sensors (their batteries are discharged).

4. Finally, the MAC protocol is not explicitly defined in the model introduced in the last section. Moreover, the local transition function of the coefficient m_{ij}^t was not given. This drawback must be overcome if we associate different transmission periods for each sensor. As in the model introduced in [11] a sensor node can transmit a data package during a step of time if all its neighbors are not transmitted; on the other hand, we will supposed that router nodes and sink nodes can receive and transmit without restriction (specifically, it is considered that sink nodes have greater bandwidth than router nodes).

3.2   Description of the Novel Model

Taking into account the considerations introduced in the last subsection, we can design an individual-based model to simulate the malware spreading in a WSN with the following main characteristics:

Specification of the Actors. Our model consists of the interaction of n actors denoted by $[i]$, $1 \leq i \leq n$, such that each sensor of the WSN stands for one of these actors. Consequently, three types of actors are considered: sensor nodes, router nodes and sink nodes. The sink nodes are permanently receiving data from sensors, whereas sensor nodes only transmit the data collected during an specific period of time –which differs from one sensor to other (as a consequence, collisions are avoided)–. In this sense, let $t_0[i]$ be the first step of time at which the sensor node $[i]$ transmits and receipts data, and set $t_e[i]$ the elapsed time between two consecutive wake-up periods. On the other hand, at every step of time t each actor (sensor node, router node or sink node) $[i]$ is endowed with one of the following states: susceptible, infected, recovered, damaged or out-of-order.

Topology of the Model. Once the sensor $[i]$ is deployed in the monitoring area, it broadcasts it status to the surroundings and receive the status from other nearby sensor devices. Those sensors that are placed in the transmission range R of $[i]$ constitute its neighborhood: $V[i]$. This approach allows us to model the WSN as an undirected graph whose nodes are the sensor/actors and the adjacent nodes are the neighbor nodes (see Fig. 2).

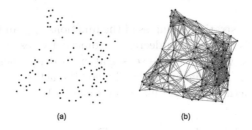

(a)   (b)

Fig. 2. (a) Random deployment of 100 sensors in a monitoring area of 50×50 m^2. (b) Graph defined using $R = 15$ m.

Transition Rules. The transition rules that govern the dynamic of the systems are the following:

- Transition from susceptible to infected: let $[i]$ be a susceptible node at step of time $t - 1$, and suppose that it receives transmissions from $k[i, t - 1]$ infected neighbor nodes during this step of time. Then $[i]$ will become infected at step of time t with probability $1 - (1 - \beta)^{k[i,t-1]}$, where $0 \leq \beta \leq 1$ is the probability to be infected when only one neighbor infected sensor sends it a malicious package.
- Transition from susceptible, infected or recovered to out-of-order: the susceptible/infected/recovered node $[i]$ at $t - 1$ will be out-of-order at step of time t with probability $\gamma_{out}(t) = b[i](t - t_0[i])$, where $b[i]$ is a specific coefficient for each sensor $[i]$ which depends on its characteristics, the environmental conditions, etc. In addition, it is supposed that:

$$b[\text{sink node}] \leq b[\text{router node}] \leq b[\text{sensor node}]. \qquad (4)$$

- Transition from infected to recovered: an infected node $[i]$ at sep of time $t - 1$ becomes recovered at step of time t with probability δ.
- Transition from infected to damaged: the infected node $[i]$ at sep of time $t - 1$ becomes damaged at step of time t with probability $\gamma_{dam}(t) = \frac{t^{1/a}}{c + t^{1/a}}$, with $a > 0, c > 0$.

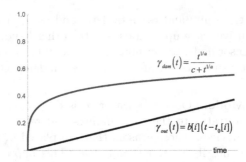

Fig. 3. (a) The function $\gamma_{out}(t)$ with $b[i] = 0.0015$. (b) The function $\gamma_{dam}(t)$ with $a = 3, c = 5$.

In Fig. 3 some illustrative examples of the functions γ_{out} and γ_{dam} are shown. The function γ_{out} is a linear non-decreasing function whose value is equal to 0 at $t = t_0[i]$ (the first wake up of the sensor after its deployment). On the other hand, the function γ_{dam} is only considered when the actor $[i]$ is infected. During this period, the function γ_{dam} gradually increases to 1.

4   Illustrative Simulations and Discussion

A simulation is shown now to illustrate the model introduced in the last section. We will consider a WSN formed by 200 nodes deployed at random in the sensor field (a square monitoring area of 10^4 m^2). It is supposed that the transmission range is $R = 15$ m and in Fig. 4 the graph defining the topology of this WSN is shown. There are 188 sensor nodes, 11 router nodes (the nodes [9], [51], [63], [67], [69], [111], [115], [117], [119], [166], and [199]), and one sink node (the node [21].0). Moreover, it is supposed that at time $t = 0$ there is only one infected node: the router node [199].

Moreover, the parameters used in the simulation are the following: $\beta = 0.9$, $\delta = 0.25$, $t_0[i] = i$ with $t_e[i] = 2$, $a = 3$, $c = 5$, and

$$b[i] = \begin{cases} 0.00015, & \text{if } [i] \text{ is a sensor node} \\ 0.000075, & \text{if } [i] \text{ is a router node} \\ 0.0000325, & \text{if } [i] \text{ is a sink node} \end{cases} \tag{5}$$

In Fig. 5-(a) the global evolution of the different compartments of the system (susceptible, infected, recovered, damaged and out-of-order) is shown, whereas the state of each sensor device at (for example) time step $t = 125$ is shown in Fig. 5-(b).

If we take into account the conditions considered in the work by Song and Jian (homogeneous topologies –Von Neumann, Moore and extended Moore neighborhoods– and the same characteristic for all devices) and we compare the simulations obtained with this one given by our model, the results are shown in Fig. 6. Note that, with independence of the neighbor considered, the original

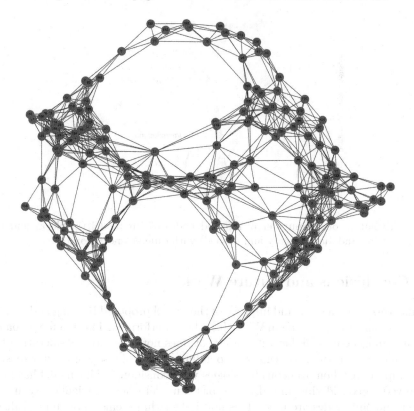

Fig. 4. Nodes deployed in the monitoring area.

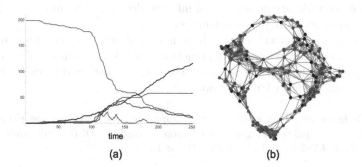

(a)   (b)

Fig. 5. (a) Global evolution of the different compartments of the model: susceptible (green), infected (red), recovered (blue), damaged (brown), and out-of-order (black). (b) States of all devices of the WSN at $t = 125$. (Color figure online)

model based on cellular automata overestimate the number of infected nodes and the outbreak appears before the novel model. Moreover, the improved model exhibits more than one isolated outbreaks.

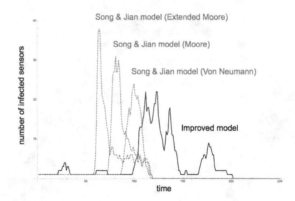

Fig. 6. Evolution of the number of infected nodes of our model (in black) and the model of Song and Jian (in gray and dashed) with different neighborhoods.

5   Conclusions and Future Work

In this work, the analysis and improve of the model proposed by Song and Jian to simulate malware spreading in WSNs have been performed. This is a model based on an homogeneous cellular automata that does not take into consideration the particular specifications of sensors depending on its role: sensor, router or sink nodes; moreover, homogeneous topologies were considered. This model has been improved by considering an individual-based model where particular features of router and sink nodes are used. This novel algorithm seems to be more realistic than the first one since because of heterogeneous topologies can be captured and it does not overestimate de number of infected devices. Moreover, some isolated outbreaks appears during the epidemic process.

Further work aims at defining in a more suitable way the functions and coefficients intimately related to the functioning of WSNs (out-of-order function, for example). Furthermore, it is also interesting to consider different behavioral patterns of the propagation of malware.

Acknowledgments. This work has been supported by Ministerio de Economía y Competitividad (Spain) and European Union through FEDER funds under grants TIN2014-55325-C2-2-R, and MTM 2015-69138-REDT.

References

1. Bahi, J.M., Guyeux, C., Hakem, M., Makhoul, A.: Epidemiological approach for data survivability in unattended wireless sensor networks. J. Netw. Comput. Appl. **46**, 374–383 (2014)
2. Cheikhrouhou, O.: Secure group communication in wireless sensor networks: a survey. J. Netw. Comput. Appl. **61**, 115–132 (2016)
3. Fadel, E., Gungor, V.C., Nassef, L., Akkari, N., Malik, M.G.A., Almasri, S., Akyildiz, I.F.: A survey on wireless sensor networks for smart grid. Comput. Commun. **71**(1), 22–33 (2015)

4. Feng, L., Song, L., Zhao, Q., Wanf, H.: Modeling and stability analysis of worm propagation in wireless sensor networks. Math. Probl. Eng. *2015*, 8 p. (2015). Article ID 129598 doi:10.1155/2015/129598

5. Ferng, H.W., Khoa, N.M.: On security of wireless sensor networks: a data authentication protocol using digital signature. Wireless Netw. (2016, in press). doi:10.1007/s11276-016-1208-0

6. Khan, S., Pathan, A.S.K., Alrajeh, N.A.: Wireless Sensor Networks: Current Status and Future Trends. CRC Press, Boca Raton (2013)

7. Obaidat, M.S., Misra, S.: Principles of Wireless Sensor Networks. Cambridge University Press, Cambridge (2014)

8. Ojha, T., Misra, S., Raghuwanshi, N.S.: Wireless sensor networks for agriculture: the state-of-the-art in practice and future challenges. Comput. Electron. Agric. **118**, 66–84 (2015)

9. Li, Q., Zhang, B., Cui, L., Fan, Z., Athanasios, V.V.: Epidemics on small worlds of tree-based wireless sensor networks. J. Syst. Sic. Complex **27**, 1095–1120 (2014)

10. Rashid, B., Rehmani, M.H.: Applications of wireless sensor networks for urban areas: a survey. J. Netw. Comput. Appl. **60**, 192–219 (2016)

11. Song, Y., Jiang, G.-P.: Model and dynamic behavior of malware propagation over wireless sensor networks. In: Zhou, J. (ed.) Complex 2009. LNICST, vol. 4, pp. 487–502. Springer, Heidelberg (2009)

12. Suciu, G., Suciu, V., Martian, A., Craciunescu, R., Vulpe, A., Marcu, I., Halunga, S., Fratu, O.: Big data, internet of things and cloud convergence - an architecture for secure E-health applications. J. Med. Syst. **39**, 141 (2015)

13. Whitmore, A., Agarwal, A., Xu, L.D.: The internet of things-a survey of topics and trends. Inf. Syst. Front. **17**(2), 261–274 (2015)

14. Yang, S.H.: Wireless Sensor Networks. Principles, Design and Applications. Springer, London (2014)

15. Zhu, L., Zhao, H., Wang, X.: Stability and bifurcation analysis in a delayed reaction-diffusion malware propagation. Comput. Math. Appl. **69**, 852–875 (2015)

Machine Learning

Tree-Structured Bayesian Networks for Wrapped Cauchy Directional Distributions

Ignacio Leguey$^{(\boxtimes)}$, Concha Bielza, and Pedro Larrañaga

Departamento de Inteligencia Artificial, Universidad Politécnica de Madrid, Campus de Montegancedo, 28660 Boadilla del Monte, Madrid, Spain
ig.leguey@upm.es, {mcbielza,pedro.larranaga}@fi.upm.es
http://cig.fi.upm.es

Abstract. Modelling the relationship between directional variables is a nearly unexplored field. The bivariate wrapped Cauchy distribution has recently emerged as the first closed family of bivariate directional distributions (marginals and conditionals belong to the same family). In this paper, we introduce a tree-structured Bayesian network suitable for modelling directional data with bivariate wrapped Cauchy distributions. We describe the structure learning algorithm used to learn the Bayesian network. We also report some simulation studies to illustrate the algorithms including a comparison with the Gaussian structure learning algorithm and an empirical experiment on real morphological data from juvenile rat somatosensory cortex cells.

Keywords: Directional statistics · Wrapped Cauchy distribution · Tree-structure · Bayesian networks

1 Introduction

Directional distributions are widely used in many areas such as geography, geology, geophysics, medicine, meteorology, oceanography or biology [1]. Traditional statistics methods are sometimes unequal to the task of dealing with directional data because data periodicity has to be taken into account. For example, whereas 0 and 360 are different points in non-directional data, dealing with angles, 0° and 360° are considered as the same point. Hence, the analysis of directional data is different and more challenging than non-directional data. There is substantial literature on directional data [6,8,18]. The von Mises distribution [20] is the best-known directional model and can be considered the directional analogue of the univariate normal distribution. Mardia [15,16] introduced a bivariate von Mises distribution and its extension to the multivariate case [17]. He showed that the conditional distributions are also von Mises distributions. However, the marginal distributions are either unimodal or bimodal, and only the unimodal case could be approximated to a von Mises distribution when the concentration parameter was large. The wrapped Cauchy distribution is another popular symmetric distribution on the circle introduced by Lévy [14]. It was studied

© Springer International Publishing Switzerland 2016
O. Luaces et al. (Eds.): CAEPIA 2016, LNAI 9868, pp. 207–216, 2016.
DOI: 10.1007/978-3-319-44636-3_19

by Wintner [25]. Further, it was shown that it could be obtained by mapping Cauchy distributions [19] onto the circle. Recently Kato and Pewsey [10] proposed a five-parameter bivariate wrapped Cauchy distribution for toroidal data, whose marginals and conditionals follow univariate wrapped Cauchy distributions. Their family is therefore said to be closed.

Probabilistic graphical models are widely used for non-directional data. These models, as a marriage between graph theory and probability theory, have some interesting properties that make them a useful and interesting tool for data modelling. For example they are easy interpretable, handle missing data nicely, treat inference and learning together or focus on conditional independence and computational issues. These models have been successfully applied in several different areas such as medicine, education or neuroscience [12], but, no directional probabilistic graphical models have yet been developed. One exception is Boomsma et al. [3], who modelled a specific part of the geometry of proteins called $C\alpha$ using a hidden Markov model that outputs amino acid symbols, secondary structure symbols and unit vectors. They used the directional five-parameter Fisher-Bingham distribution [11] on the unit sphere to represent the unit vectors. Also Razavian et al. [22] developed an undirected von Mises [20] graphical model using L_1 regularization for structure learning and Gibbs sampling for performing inference. They also compared their model with a Gaussian graphical model, demonstrating that the von Mises graphical model achieves higher accuracy than the Gaussian graphical model.

Our aim is to find a tree-structured model that reveals the relationship between several directional variables. A family distribution that is closed under conditionality and marginalization (marginals and conditionals belong to the same family) is necessary to make the modelling phase easier and simplify the subsequent inference process. In this paper we introduce a tree-structured Bayesian network for a five-parameter bivariate wrapped Cauchy, learning the structure from data using a directional mutual information criteria. The remainder of this paper is organized as follows. Section 2 reviews the univariate and bivariate wrapped Cauchy distributions. In Sect. 3 we explain the Bayesian network structure learning from data. Section 4 presents the simulation process for this model. Section 5 addresses a real data example using the proposed tree-structured Bayesian network. The paper ends in Sect. 6 with some concluding remarks and some proposals for future work.

2   Univariate and Bivariate Wrapped Cauchy

One of the best-known directional distributions is the wrapped Cauchy distribution [14]. A random variable Θ that follows a wrapped Cauchy distribution $wC(\mu, \varepsilon)$ has a density function

$$f(\theta) = \frac{1}{2\pi} \frac{1 - \varepsilon^2}{1 + \varepsilon^2 - 2\varepsilon \cos(\theta - \mu)}, \quad \theta, \mu \in (-\pi, \pi], \varepsilon \in [0, 1) \qquad (1)$$

where μ is the mean angle and ε the concentration parameter. Equation (1) is unimodal and symmetric about μ, unless $\varepsilon = 0$ which yields the directional uniform distribution. Data simulation from a $wC(\mu, \varepsilon)$ is already implemented in the "Circular"R package [21].

Kato and Pewsey [10] proposed a five-parameter bivariate wrapped Cauchy distribution, which is unimodal, pointwise symmetric around the mean and has a closed-form expression for the mode. A dependence parameter controls the correlation from total independence to perfect correlation. This distribution materializes as an appealing submodel of a six-parameter distribution obtained by applying a restricted version of the Möbius circle transformation to a random vector from a bivariate directional distribution previously proposed by Kato [9].

A random vector (Θ_1, Θ_2) is said to follow a bivariate wrapped Cauchy distribution $bwC(\mu_1, \mu_2, \varepsilon_1, \varepsilon_2, \rho)$ if its density function is given by

$$f(\theta_1, \theta_2) = c[c_0 - c_1 \cos(\theta_1 - \mu_1) - c_2 \cos(\theta_2 - \mu_2) - c_3 \cos(\theta_1 - \mu_1)\cos(\theta_2 - \mu_2) \\ -c_4 \sin(\theta_1 - \mu_1)\sin(\theta_2 - \mu_2)]^{-1}, \quad \theta_1, \theta_2 \in (-\pi, \pi]$$

(2)

where
$c = (1 - \rho^2)(1 - \varepsilon_1^2)(1 - \varepsilon_2^2)/4\pi^2$, $c_0 = (1 + \rho^2)(1 + \varepsilon_1^2)(1 + \varepsilon_2^2) - 8|\rho|\varepsilon_1\varepsilon_2$,
$c_1 = 2(1+\rho^2)\varepsilon_1(1+\varepsilon_2^2) - 4|\rho|(1+\varepsilon_1^2)\varepsilon_2$, $c_2 = 2(1+\rho^2)(1+\varepsilon_1^2)\varepsilon_2 - 4|\rho|\varepsilon_1(1+\varepsilon_2^2)$,
$c_3 = -4(1 + \rho^2)\varepsilon_1\varepsilon_2 + 2|\rho|(1 + \varepsilon_1^2)(1 + \varepsilon_2^2)$, $c_4 = 2\rho(1 - \varepsilon_1^2)(1 - \varepsilon_2^2)$, $\mu_1, \mu_2 \in (-\pi, \pi], \varepsilon_1, \varepsilon_2 \in [0, 1), \rho \in (-1, 1)$, and with ε_1 and ε_2 regulating the concentration of the marginal distributions and ρ being the correlation coefficient between Θ_1 and Θ_2. When $\varepsilon_1, \varepsilon_2 > 0$ Eq. (2) is unimodal and pointwise symmetric about (μ_1, μ_2).

As explained by McCullagh [19], computations are simplified in many wrapped Cauchy models by representing them in complex form. Let $Z = e^{i\Theta}$, where Θ is distributed as in Eq. (1), then the density function of Z is

$$f(z; \lambda) = \frac{1}{2\pi} \frac{|1 - |\lambda|^2|}{|z - \lambda|^2}, \quad z \in \Omega, \lambda \in \hat{\mathbb{C}} \setminus \Omega$$

(3)

where $\lambda = \varepsilon e^{i\mu}$, $\hat{\mathbb{C}} = \mathbb{C} \cup \{\infty\}$ and $\Omega = \{z \in \mathbb{C} : |z| = 1\}$. We use the notation $Z \sim C^*(\lambda)$ to denote that Z is distributed as in Eq. (3).

Similarly to Eq. (3), by representing random variables in complex form, let $(Z_1, Z_2) = (e^{i\Theta_1}, e^{i\Theta_2})$, where (Θ_1, Θ_2) is distributed as in Eq. (2), then the density of (Z_1, Z_2) is:

$$f(z_1, z_2) = \frac{(4\pi^2)^{-1}(1 - \rho^2)(1 - \varepsilon_1^2)(1 - \varepsilon_2^2)}{|a_{11}(\overline{z_1}\eta_1)^q z_2\overline{\eta_2} + a_{12}(\overline{z_1}\eta_1)^q + a_{21}z_2\overline{\eta_2} + a_{22}|^2}, \quad z_1, z_2 \in \Omega$$

(4)

where q is the sign of ρ, $\eta_k = e^{i\mu_k}$ with $k \in \{1, 2\}$, $\overline{z_n}$ is the complex conjugate of z_n, $a_{11} = \varepsilon_1\varepsilon_2 - |\rho|$, $a_{12} = |\rho|\varepsilon_2 - \varepsilon_1$, $a_{21} = |\rho|\varepsilon_1 - \varepsilon_2$, $a_{22} = 1 - |\rho|\varepsilon_1\varepsilon_2$, $\varepsilon_1, \varepsilon_2 \in [0, 1)$, $\rho \in (-1, 1)$ and $\eta_1, \eta_2 \in \Omega$.

Following the complex notation, we denote $(Z_1, Z_2) \sim bC^*(\eta_1, \eta_2, \varepsilon_1, \varepsilon_2, \rho)$ if (Z_1, Z_2) is distributed as in Eq. (4). This complex representation of a five-parameter bivariate wrapped Cauchy verifies the following result.

Theorem 1. *(Kato and Pewsey [10]) A random vector (Z_1, Z_2) with density given by Eq. (4) has marginals $Z_1 \sim C^*(\varepsilon_1\eta_1)$ and $Z_2 \sim C^*(\varepsilon_2\eta_2)$, and conditionals $Z_1|Z_2 = z_2 \sim C^*(-\eta_1[A \circ (z_2\overline{\eta_2})^q])$ and $Z_2|Z_1 = z_1 \sim C^*(-\eta_2[A^T \circ (z_1\overline{\eta_1})^q])$, where A is defined in Eq. (5), A^T is the transpose of A, and*

$$A \circ z = \frac{a_{11}z + a_{12}}{a_{21}z + a_{22}}.$$

$$A : \begin{bmatrix} a_{11} = \varepsilon_1\varepsilon_2 - |\rho| & a_{12} = |\rho|\varepsilon_2 - \varepsilon_1 \\ a_{21} = |\rho|\varepsilon_1 - \varepsilon_2 & a_{22} = 1 - |\rho|\varepsilon_1\varepsilon_2 \end{bmatrix}. \tag{5}$$

To the best of our knowledge, this is the first bivariate directional distribution for which marginal and conditional distributions are well-known, mathematically tractable and from the same family. Thus, we consider the wrapped Cauchy distribution to be suitable for developing our Bayesian network model, as we are using a tree structure that needs only bivariate and conditional densities.

2.1 Parameter Estimation

Working with the density given by Eq. (2), there is no closed-form expression for the maximum likelihood estimates, and numerical optimization methods must be used to find them. Although maximum likelihood estimation is the most common parameter estimation method, Kato and Pewsey [10] showed that method of moments is more efficient for our purpose. We use the method of moments, where all formulas for the estimates can be expressed in a closed form, as it is easier to implement and is computationally very fast.

Let $\{(\theta_{1j}, \theta_{2j}), j = 1, ..., n, \}$ be a random sample from a $bwC(\mu_1, \mu_2, \varepsilon_1, \varepsilon_2, \rho)$ as stated in Eq. (2). Then the method of moments estimators [4] of $\mu_1, \mu_2, \varepsilon_1, \varepsilon_2$ and ρ from [10] are

$$\begin{aligned}
&\tilde{\mu}_1 = Argument(\bar{R}_1) \quad with \quad \bar{R}_1 = \tfrac{1}{n}\sum_{j=1}^{n} e^{i\theta_{1j}}, \\
&\tilde{\mu}_2 = Argument(\bar{R}_2) \quad with \quad \bar{R}_2 = \tfrac{1}{n}\sum_{j=1}^{n} e^{i\theta_{2j}}, \\
&\tilde{\varepsilon}_1 = |\bar{R}_1|, \quad \tilde{\varepsilon}_2 = |\bar{R}_2|, \\
&\tilde{\rho} = \tfrac{1}{n}\left(|\sum_{j=1}^{n} e^{i(\Phi_{1j}-\Phi_{2j})}| - |\sum_{j=1}^{n} e^{i(\Phi_{1j}+\Phi_{2j})}|\right) \\
&with \quad \Phi_{rj} = 2\arctan\left(\tfrac{1+\tilde{\varepsilon}_r}{1-\tilde{\varepsilon}_r}\tan\left(\tfrac{\theta_{rj}-\tilde{\mu}_r}{2}\right)\right), \quad r = 1, 2
\end{aligned} \tag{6}$$

3 Wrapped Cauchy Tree-Structured Bayesian Network: Structure Learning

Assuming that the topology of the graph that we want to represent is unknown and not given, we must learn the structure of the model from our random sample. The so-called Bayesian networks structure learning has been studied at length for linear data. However, it is far from straightforward to adapt the structure learning algorithms to the directional domain. There are two different kinds of algorithms for structure learning in Bayesian networks. One kind of algorithm learns a network structure by capturing the conditional independences between the different triplets of variables used for the model. The best-known method for this kind of structure learning is the PC algorithm [23]. The other kind of algorithm, which we've chose for our structure learning problem, is based on score and search. It tackles the problem of structure learning as an optimization problem.

We use a maximum weight spanning tree structure learning algorithm. This is a variant of the algorithm introduced by Chow and Liu [5]. Instead of the mutual information measure, traditionally used for running this algorithm, for the first time we introduce circular mutual information (CMI) for directional variables.

Let Θ_i, Θ_j be wrapped Cauchy random variables, the CMI between a pair of variables is

$$CMI(\Theta_i, \Theta_j) = \int_0^{2\pi} \int_0^{2\pi} f(\theta_i, \theta_j) \log(\frac{f(\theta_i, \theta_j)}{f(\theta_i)f(\theta_j)}) d\theta_j d\theta_i. \tag{7}$$

where their marginal density functions $f(\theta_i), f(\theta_j)$ and the joint density function $f(\theta_i, \theta_j)$ have been previously estimated.

Since the resulting integral is intractable, it has to be approximated using numerical methods. We use the Cubature method [2,24]. Cubature is an adaptive multidimensional integration algorithm over hypercubes. It is the best method in terms of approximation error and computational cost. This method is also best suited for dimensions lower than seven. This applies to the tree structure, whose maximum dimension is two.

Like the traditional mutual information measure for linear variables, the CMI represents the weight of the edge that links Θ_i and Θ_j. To determine the parent of each node (only one parent per node), we select the root node and follow the structure learned by our algorithm (Algorithm 1) (i.e., in Fig. 1a, the selected root node is Θ_1, which is the parent of Θ_2 and Θ_3, Θ_2 is the parent of Θ_4 and Θ_3 is the parent of Θ_5 and Θ_6). Given a tree structure with N nodes, there are N possible resulting trees depending on the selected root node (see Fig. 1a).

Algorithm 1. Adaptation of Chow Liu algorithm

1: Given $\Theta_1, \Theta_2, ..., \Theta_N$ directional random variables, compute the joint distribution $f(\theta_i, \theta_j)$ for all variable pairs.
2: Using the pairwise distributions, compute all $N(N-1)/2$ edge weights and order them by CMI value.
3: Assign the largest two edges to the tree to be represented.
4: Examine the next-largest edge, and add it to the tree unless it forms a loop, in which case discard it and examine the next largest edge.
5: Repeat step 4 until $N-1$ edges have been selected (so the spanning tree is finished).

We use this algorithm for several reasons: (a) It uses only second-order statistics, which are easily and reliably measured from data, (b) we avoid the use

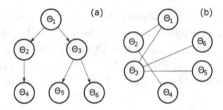

Fig. 1. (a) Wrapped Cauchy tree-structured network representation with $N = 6$. Each node $\Theta_i (i = 1, ..., 6)$ represents a wC random variable. The root node selected is Θ_1. (b) Wrapped Cauchy non-directed tree-structured network learned by Algorithm 1 from the structure of (a) created by simulation.

of conditional independence tests, which are often computationally expensive and only available by simulation [10] from wrapped Cauchy and (c) is a way of ensuring a tree-structure.

4   Simulation

In order to demonstrate the accuracy of the learning algorithm, we report the results of several simulation studies and the comparison with the Gaussian structure learning algorithm [7]. Note that we present only some selected results from a broader simulation study. For each simulation, we generated a tree-structured Bayesian network (i.e., the six-node network in Fig. 1a), assigning random parameters to the nodes ($0 < \mu < 2\pi, 0 < \varepsilon < 1$) and enforcing some dependence between parent and child nodes ($0.5 < |\rho| < 1$). From each node, we simulated n wrapped Cauchy samples using the "Circular" R package from [21]. Once we had completed the data simulation, we tested the algorithm by constructing the network from the created dataset (i.e., Fig. 1b) which we compared with the original network. In order to measure the accuracy of the method, we counted the number of edges that are misplaced in the created network with respect to the arcs of the original graph, therefore it wouldn't be necessary to direct the edges in the simulated network for measure accuracy. We simulated several networks changing the number of nodes from 3,6,10 (Fig. 3), 20 and 30 and simulating

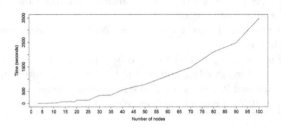

Fig. 2. Line chart that represents the increment of the computational time of our algorithm with the increment of the number of nodes in the network.

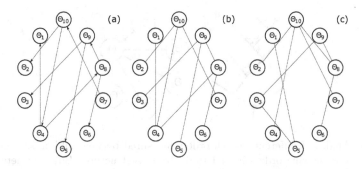

Fig. 3. Simulation output: wrapped Cauchy tree-structured network comparison in a 10-node network. (a) The original network. (b) Non-directed network, learned from data simulated from (a) using our algorithm. Accuracy is 9/9 (100 %). (c) Non-directed network, learned from the same dataset using the Gaussian structure learning algorithm. Accuracy is 6/9 (67 %).

100 observations per node for the dataset. The number of simulations differs for each network type due to the high computational cost of the biggest networks. For this reason, the maximum number of nodes used for simulation is 30. We have scaled our algorithm (Fig. 2) in order to show the computation complexity, as our algorithm has to perform $N * (N - 1)/2$ iterations.

The results (Table 1) show that of our method is highly accurate and the constructed graph is the same as the initial network in most cases, and outperforms the Gaussian method in terms of structure learning. Any cases where one or more than one edge is misplaced could probably be due to the randomization of the given parameters.

Table 1. Simulation results. Accuracy values are given by the mean of the non-misplaced edges in the total number of simulations.

			Wrapped Cauchy	Gaussian
Number of nodes	Simulations	Number of edges	Accuracy	Accuracy
3	1794	2	1.87	1.46
6	1764	5	4.37	2.61
10	1666	9	7.65	4.09
20	674	19	15.76	8.61
30	200	29	24.09	11.71

5   Real Data Example

Since our main application interest is in neuroscience, we applied our proposal to a real-world dataset of 3027 combinations of dendritic bifurcation angles composed by 288 3D pyramidal neurons from six different layers of the 14-day-old

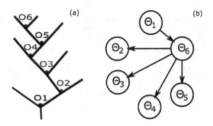

Fig. 4. (a) Angles of different branch orders measured between sibling segments in a dendritic arbor showing orders from 1 to 6. (b) Tree-structured Bayesian network for dendritic bifurcation angles from orders 1–6. Root node is Θ_1.

(P14) rat hind limb somatosensory (S1HL) neocortex recently published in [13]. Dendritic bifurcation angles are an important part of the geometry of pyramidal cell basal arbors. The comprehension and capability of modelling these angles is crucial for advances in neuroscience in order to replicate brain structure and functioning. Our purpose is to model the conditional relationship between the bifurcation angles of the whole neuron dataset in a tree-structured Bayesian network for wrapped Cauchy distributions. Each angle is generated by two sibling segments originating from the bifurcation of basal dendritic trees. Using the same notation as in [13], we denote the first bifurcation that takes place in a dendritic arbor path that starts from the soma and ends at the angle as O1, the second bifurcation would be O2, etc. (Fig. 4a). Bifurcation angles from orders higher than six are not included in the model because they are relatively few in number.

We fitted a wrapped Cauchy distribution for every set of angles of the same bifurcation order (Table 2). The resulting tree-structured Bayesian network learned from the dataset is the six-node directed graph shown in Fig. 4b. Looking at Fig. 4b, it is evident that the Θ_6 node has the highest CMI values for every pair of nodes. We have selected Θ_1 as the root node in order to finish the structure of our network and transform the undirected graph into a directed graph.

Table 2. Characteristics of the 6 different branch orders shown in Fig. 4a. Circular mean (μ) is measure in radians.

Bifurcation order	Variable	Number of angles	μ (radians)	ε
O1	Θ_1	1607	1.02	0.90
O2	Θ_2	2072	0.9	0.91
O3	Θ_3	1773	0.82	0.92
O4	Θ_4	998	0.78	0.92
O5	Θ_5	382	0.77	0.92
O6	Θ_6	106	0.81	0.92

6   Conclusions and Future Work

The main objective of this paper is to introduce the first Bayesian network that deals with directional wrapped Cauchy variables. We introduced the methods for learning and representing the model. The proposed model applied to real and simulated data is capable of representing the relationship between directional data nodes that fit wrapped Cauchy distributions.

In future work we intend to explore different distributions in order to extend this model to other directional families. This task is tough because the known directional family distributions are not closed. Another interesting possibility is to develop a supervised classification algorithm using wrapped Cauchy variables. An analogue of the tree-augmented naive Bayes would be rather straightforward, since we already developed the inference process.

This preliminary model is confined to tree structures. We hope to extend this model to a more general Bayesian network case, capable of accounting for more than one parent per node.

Acknowledgments. This work has been partially supported by the Spanish Ministry of Economy and Competitiveness through the TIN2013-41592-P and Cajal Blue Brain (C080020-09), by the Regional Government of Madrid through the S2013/ICE-2845-CASI-CAM-CM project. I.L. is supported by the Spanish Ministry of Education, Culture and Sport Fellowship (FPU13/01941). The authors thankfully acknowledge the Cortical Circuits Laboratory (CSIC-UPM) for the neurons dataset.

References

1. Batschelet, E.: Circular Statistics in Biology. Academic Press, London (1981)
2. Berntsen, J., Espelid, T.O., Genz, A.: An adaptive algorithm for the approximate calculation of multiple integrals. ACM Trans. Math. Softw. **17**(4), 437–451 (1991)
3. Boomsma, W., Kent, J.T., Mardia, K.V., Taylor, C.C., Hamelryck, T.: Graphical models and directional statistics capture protein structure. Interdisc. Stat. Bioinform. **25**, 91–94 (2006)
4. Bowman, K., Shenton, L.: Methods of moments. Encycl. Stat. Sci. **5**, 467–473 (1985)
5. Chow, C., Liu, C.: Approximating discrete probability distributions with dependence trees. IEEE Trans. Inf. Theory **14**(3), 462–467 (1968)
6. Fisher, N.I.: Statistical Analysis of Circular Data. Cambridge University, Cambridge (1995)
7. Geiger, D., Heckerman, D.: Learning gaussian networks. In: Proceedings of the Tenth International Conference on Uncertainty in Artificial Intelligence, pp. 235–243. Morgan Kaufmann Publishers Inc. (1994)
8. Jammalamadaka, S.R., Sengupta, A.: Topics in Circular Statistics. World Scientific, River Edge (2001)
9. Kato, S.: A distribution for a pair of unit vectors generated by Brownian motion. Bernoulli **15**(3), 898–921 (2009)
10. Kato, S., Pewsey, A.: A Möbius transformation-induced distribution on the torus. Biometrika **102**(2), 359–370 (2015)

11. Kent, J.T.: The Fisher-Bingham distribution on the sphere. J. Roy. Stat. Soc. Ser. B (Methodol.) **44**(1), 71–80 (1982)
12. Koller, D., Friedman, N.: Probabilistic Graphical Models: Principles and Techniques. MIT Press, Cambridge (2009)
13. Leguey, I., Bielza, C., Larrañaga, P., Kastanauskaite, A., Rojo, C., Benavides-Piccione, R., DeFelipe, J.: Dendritic branching angles of pyramidal cells across layers of the juvenile rat somatosensory cortex. J. Comp. Neurol. **524**(13), 2567–2576 (2016)
14. Lévy, P.: L'addition des variables aléatoires définies sur une circonférence. Bulletin de la Société Mathématique de France **67**, 1–41 (1939)
15. Mardia, K.V.: Statistics of directional data. J. Roy. Stat. Soc. Ser. B (Methodol.) **37**, 349–393 (1975)
16. Mardia, K.V.: Bayesian analysis for bivariate von Mises distributions. J. Appl. Stat. **37**(3), 515–528 (2010)
17. Mardia, K.V., Hughes, G., Taylor, C.C., Singh, H.: A multivariate von Mises distribution with applications to bioinformatics. Can. J. Stat. **36**(1), 99–109 (2008)
18. Mardia, K.V., Jupp, P.E.: Directional Statistics. Wiley, Hoboken (2009)
19. McCullagh, P.: Möbius transformation and Cauchy parameter estimation. Ann. Stat. **24**(2), 787–808 (1996)
20. von Mises, R.: Über die Ganzzahligkeit der Atomgewichte und verwandte Fragen. Zeitschrift für Physik **19**, 490–500 (1918)
21. R Development Core Team: R: A Language and Environment for Statistical Computing. R Foundation for Statistical Computing, Vienna, Austria (2008). ISBN 3-900051-07-0, http://www.R-project.org
22. Razavian, N., Kamisetty, H., Langmead, C.J.: The von Mises graphical model: regularized structure and parameter learning. Technical report CMU-CS-11-108. Carnegie Mellon University, Department of Computer Science (2011)
23. Spirtes, P., Glymour, C.N., Scheines, R.: Causation, Prediction, and Search. MIT Press, Cambridge (2000)
24. Van Dooren, P., de Ridder, L.: An adaptive algorithm for numerical integration over an N-dimensional cube. J. Comput. Appl. Math. **2**(3), 207–217 (1976)
25. Wintner, A.: On the shape of the angular case of Cauchy's distribution curves. Ann. Math. Stat. **18**(4), 589–593 (1947)

Enriched Semantic Graphs for Extractive Text Summarization

Antonio F.G. Sevilla, Alberto Fernández-Isabel[(✉)], and Alberto Díaz

Department of Software Engineering and Artificial Intelligence,
Universidad Complutense de Madrid, Madrid, Spain
{afgs,afernandezisabel}@ucm.es, albertodiaz@fdi.ucm.es

Abstract. Automatic extraction of semantic information from unstructured text has always been an important goal of natural language processing. While the best structure for semantic information is still undecided, graph-based representations enjoy a healthy following. Some of these representations are extracted directly from the text and external knowledge, while others are built from linguistic insight, created from the deep analysis of the surface text. In this document a combination of both approaches is outlined, and its application for extractive text summarization is described. A pipeline for this task has been implemented, and its results evaluated against a collection of documents from the DUC2003 competition. Graph construction is fully automatic, and summary creation is based on the clustering of conceptual nodes. Different configurations for the semantic graphs are used and compared, and their fitness for the task discussed.

Keywords: Semantic graph · Information extraction · Text summarization · Natural language processing

1 Introduction

Nowadays, information accessible through the Internet is always increasing. However, it is often present in the form of unstructured text. Applications that want to exploit this information have to face multiple problems related to knowledge extraction, and find a method to understand the true meaning of the data.

Either in a way parallel to human language understanding, or with alternative methods better suited for machine processing, the purpose of these applications is often to transform a text into a representation which can be further utilized. One of these representations is the conceptual graph. This graph is a semantic network which links the concepts present in the text using the relations that are deduced from it.

There are many alternatives for building a semantic graph. Some of them are focused on using the nouns in the sentences [12], while other proposals use verbs and other content words (e.g. adverbs or adjectives) [9] for representing the main concepts of the target text. This approach is closer to syntactical analysis

© Springer International Publishing Switzerland 2016
O. Luaces et al. (Eds.): CAEPIA 2016, LNAI 9868, pp. 217–226, 2016.
DOI: 10.1007/978-3-319-44636-3_20

and can often offer a richer structure. In both cases, concepts correspond to the nodes in the graph, while the links between them represent the implicit semantic information of the text.

In this document, a fully automatic process is described based on conceptual graphs. They are built from a previous dependency analysis of English text by Freeling [11]. These graphs are enriched with information based on both linguistic analysis [14] and external lexical knowledge. This knowledge extends the node structure with lexical information recovered from WordNet [8]. This provides a hypernym hierarchy which bridges related concepts from different sentences or paragraphs. The main entities in the graph are the concepts, nominal or otherwise, while the links are not limited to grammatical relations. Concept nodes are also linked to each other based on semantic similarity, in order to add implicit knowledge to the graph. This pipeline is implemented with an in-development conceptual graph library, code-named "Grafeno", which is to be released as open-source.

In this paper, the semantic graphs generated are used to perform text summarization, but the developed library is intended to be general enough. It can be used to create and manipulate concept graphs in different ways, and information (such as triplets, a description of relations as 3-tuples $relation$ $(concept_1, concept_2)$ [13]) can be extracted from it in text.

For the implemented summarization pipeline, clustering of the nodes based on a degree-based method [2] is performed, in order to identify the main topics of the target document. Text compression is achieved through an extractive method, where only a few sentences from the original document are selected. A heuristic based on selecting only the sentences related to the biggest cluster (main topic) is implemented [12].

For evaluation, eight documents from the DUC 2003 competition collection have been used. Summaries obtained with the extractive method are compared to a human-written summary, in order to measure the appropriateness of the approach.

The rest of the document is structured as follows: Sect. 2 situates the approach in the domain. Section 3 describes our semantic graph approach, its construction process where it is enriched with linguistic data, and the summarization process. Section 4 evaluates our proposal and discusses the results obtained. Finally, Sect. 5 discusses our conclusions and possible lines of future work.

2   Related Work

There are multiple forms of representing the semantic content of documents and extracting this information. One of the most common is related to conceptual graphs [5], where the topics of the text are identified and organised, keeping its general meaning linking them with edges.

There is not a standard approach to the structure of semantic graphs. One can situate the main verb of the target sentence as the root of the sub-graph that represent it, while the child nodes describe the nouns and other complements [9]. These graphs are often based on syntactical analysis and dependency identification, and store linguistic information and structures [14]. In contrast, others approaches use only the nouns in the sentence [12]. The first case is the one more closely followed by our proposal.

For building rich semantic graphs, syntactic analysis is needed. This process can be automatized using different tools. One of these tools is Freeling [11], which performs many different layers of linguistic analysis and can be easily integrated into a bigger pipeline.

Other automatic tools support lexical analysis and semantic information retrieval, for enriching the graphs with data not present in the text. WordNet [8] is an on-line knowledge base where related terms can be obtained for nouns, verbs, adjectives or adverbs. It also provides different types of lexical relations, such as *synonymy* or *hypernymy* among others.

Regarding automatic text summarization, its goal is to preserve the main topics of a document while reducing its complexity and size [10]. It presents two different approaches according to the sources from which the final text is obtained: *extraction* and *abstraction*. The former builds the summary from the sentences of the original text, linking them to the topics identified in the semantic graph [16]. The latter generates text using external resources, which leads to new sentences created from the semantic concepts extracted. These sentences preserve the original meaning and ideally avoid any loss of information [3].

There are various metrics that can be used to measure automatic summaries made by software. In this approach, one of the ROUGE metrics is used (Recall-Oriented Understudy for Gisting Evaluation) [6]. It compares the frequency of overlapping words in the human and the automatic summaries, and obtains a value from 0 to 1.

3   Methodology

3.1   Overview

Graphs are, in essence, a set of nodes and the edges between them. In our case, the main information that nodes need to represent is a concept. Concepts are defined as lexemes, and represented by its lemma. Nodes can store additional information, in a free-form set of attribute-value pairs associated to the particular concept. These attributes can capture surface information with semantic meaning, like tense or gender, or can be used to store information obtained from external sources (e.g. a WordNet synset name).

Linking the nodes in the graph there are edges, which connect pairs of concepts. Edges are directed, meaning there is a head or parent node and a tail or child one. The main information that edges represent is the concepts that they link, but also how they link them and what relation do they represent.

These relations can be of various types. Semantic ones associate verbal concepts with their arguments, like the agent or the theme of a predicative verb, or nominal entities with their modifying attributes. Discourse relations mark the succession of predicates in the text, and can potentially link anaphora to

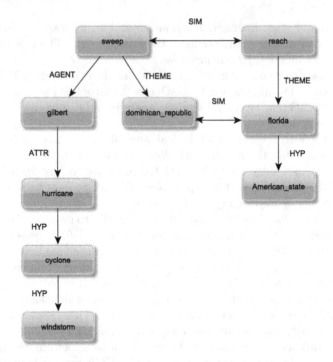

Fig. 1. Example extracted semantic graph for the text: *"Hurricane Gilbert swept the Dominican Republic Sunday evening. It then reached Florida."*

their antecedent. Knowledge relations link concepts with similar ones in terms of an external knowledge base (e.g. hypernyms and hyponyms from WordNet, or entailed predicates from ConceptNet [7]).

And just as nodes can have attributes, edges can have them too. These attributes serve to further specify the information conveyed by the relation. For instance, a complement relation to a verb can have an attribute discriminating duration, location, direction, or other types of adverbial modification. Additionally, the attributes can be used to store the confidence or relevance of the relation, in the cases where the original source of information is empirical data or heuristic operations.

An example extracted graph can be seen in Fig. 1. It features semantic edges, like AGENT and THEME, or ATTR for attribute. SIM edges link similar concepts, and HYP edges bring in the hypernym hierarchy from WordNet.

3.2   Enriched Semantic Graphs

The process of building the semantic graph must take a free-form text in the source language (in this case English), and output a conceptual representation of its meaning. The text input must already be pre-processed, in the sense of removing non-textual elements, such as html tags and other formatting structure, only the text proper remaining.

Before creating our deep-level representation of the text, the lower levels must be analyzed. We use the Freeling tool to perform these tasks. In particular, we ask the tool to extract a dependency representation of every sentence. In order to do this, the tool performs all previous steps of tokenization, phrase structure parsing, and even named entity recognition. The resultant parse is a dependency tree, with the words and their syntactic information as nodes.

After the syntax tree is obtained, it is transformed into a semantic graph. Different transformations can be used, ranging from simple extraction of content words based on part of speech information, to more complex rules that understand the different dependencies. Concepts are identified and added to the graph as nodes, and links between them are then found. These links can be based on syntactic information, such as adjective-noun modification or verbal arguments. Other links can also be added, relating concepts which are similar from an information-content point of view, or bridging anaphoric and co-referential nodes.

While the graph is being built, contextual information is also added to it. Lexical information is queried from WordNet, finding hypernyms for each term and linking them to their hyponyms. Since these hypernyms are added as nodes, but only once, they serve as a bridge between concepts which may appear far from each other in the text.

3.3 Using the Semantic Graph for Text Summarization

This graph-based semantic structure can then be used for different procedures, one of them being extractive text summarization [16]. To perform this task, two operations are required, and are presented below.

The first applies a clustering algorithm to the graph, with the purpose of identifying the main topics of the text. The second aligns the original sentences of the document to the clusters found, enabling the subsequent generation of the summary.

Clustering. This operation finds different groups (clusters) in the graph, which represent the topics of the original text. The grouping is based on connectivity, using a degree-based algorithm [2].

Clusters are created around the main concepts, which are found as the centroids of highly connected subgraphs. This is based on the assumption that documents written in English build a free scale network [1], and as a consequence the graph of target text is a network of this type. These networks present a few nodes highly connected between them (*Hub nodes*), while the rest of nodes have a relatively low connectivity.

Regarding the algorithm used to find the clusters, the fist step consists of locating and grouping the most connected nodes of the graph using the salience attribute [15]. A number between 2 % and 20 % of them are selected, called the *Hub nodes*. The exact number does not affect much the main clusters that are found. Since in this approach only the biggest one is used, the proportion is irrelevant, and so is fixed for the experiments. These vertices are then grouped in *Hub Vertex Sets (HVS)*. These are sets of nodes highly connected, and serve as the centroids of the clusters to be found. They are identified using the rule that the connectivity between the concepts of a cluster must be the highest, while the connectivity between different clusters should be minimal. Once the *HVS* are built, the last step involves linking the rest of nodes (i.e. those which are not *Hub nodes*) to the *HVS* to which they present most connectivity. Thus, the final clusters of nodes are obtained. Each cluster can be seen as a topic within the text, represented by the hub vertices in them.

Sentence Selection. After the clusters are identified, a score is computed for each sentence and cluster. The idea is to rank sentences as related to each topic, in order to extract the most relevant ones.

The scoring algorithm uses a voting mechanism [15]. During graph construction, the nodes corresponding to each sentence have been recorded. After clustering is performed, these nodes emit a vote for the cluster they belong to. This vote is qualified, counting double (i.e. 1 instead of 0.5) for those nodes belonging to the hub vertex set of each cluster.

Votes are then added, producing a function that for each sentence and cluster, gives a measure of how related the former is to the latter. This measure can be used to rank sentences as more or less relevant to each topic.

Finally, the most relevant sentences are extracted, until the desired length for the summary is reached.

4 Evaluation

Text summarization has been chosen to perform an evaluation on the extracted conceptual graphs. For this experiment, an approach similar to that in [12] is used, and eight documents from the DUC 2003 competition have been selected. These documents are news articles of variable length, for which a short summary of around a hundred words is provided. This summary has been written by a human, and serves as target of the evaluation.

The experiment uses as input the original article and creates a conceptual graph from the dependency analysis achieved by Freeling. Then, the topics of the texts are identified, applying the clustering algorithm from Sect. 3.3. For sentence selection, only the biggest cluster is used, since it represents the main topic. The sentences which best represent it are extracted from the original document, and concatenated (in the original order) to create a summary of the same length as the human-made one.

To have a baseline to compare to, another pipeline has been created, which creates the summary with the first sentences from the original text. For news articles this is a hard-to-beat baseline, since the most relevant information tends to appear at the beginning.

The created summaries are evaluated using the ROUGE recall-based metric, in particular ROUGE-N with unigram scores (ROUGE-1) [6]. This metric can

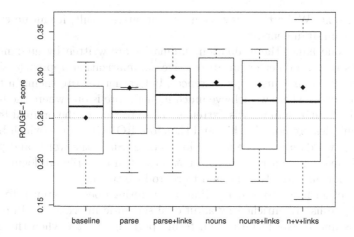

Fig. 2. Different graph configurations and their summary's Rouge scores. Boxplots show the median and interquartile range, and the diamonds mark the means. There is one outlier document, with scores of around 0.5, which is not shown.

be used in same-length summaries, computing the overlap of n-grams between the evaluated text and the gold standard. The values range from 0 (no overlap) to 1 (exact same sequences of words). The results are illustrated in Fig. 2.

Since the pipeline for graph construction is fully customizable, different configurations have been tried. All of them extract concepts from the text, and also add to them the lexical hierarchy queried from WordNet. Their main differences lie in what concepts are used as nodes and what links are then added.

The 'parse' experiment constructs the graph using all content words, and adds the semantic relations extracted from the dependency parse. 'parse+links' also links similar concepts according to the Jiang-Conrath Similarity measure [4]. 'nouns' does not use any sentence structure information, and just finds nominal entities in the text. 'nouns+links' again only uses nouns, but also adds the previously mentioned similarity links. 'n+v+links' is like the previous one, but also uses verbal entities as conceptual nodes.

4.1 Discussion of Results

The original idea for these experiments was to find a way to evaluate the more expressive concept graphs that we have created. Building on previous work, we expected that, since our concept graphs were richer than those used in previous approaches, they would improve performance in already existing and successful summarization methods. The more information there is in a graph, the better the summary that will be created from it.

As can be seen in Fig. 2, our results do slightly improve on the baseline. A few other experiments have been tried, with very similar results. However, this improvement is not statistically significant, and extremely dependent on the source text. While this may seem as a negative result, it can be explained with two main arguments.

On the one hand, the evaluation summaries are written by humans. These documents represent better an abstractive summarization approach, since the human writers do not just copy sentences, but rather rewrite them. In fact, the outlier document where we achieve much higher score is one where the language used by the human summary is extremely close to that of the original text. But most summaries are not like this, and therefore ROUGE scores, which take into account the words used, have a very low ceiling. Since the words and phrasing that the human summarizer uses are not present in the original document, it is impossible for an extractive method to reproduce them.

On the other hand, topic extraction by clustering does not appear to improve when the graphs are enriched by additional semantic information. In our opinion, this is due to the fact that clustering performs better when the graph is homogeneous. Thus, a graph composed solely of nominal entities will yield better clusters than one which includes verbs, adjectives or adverbs, and in which edges represent information of very heterogeneous nature.

On top of this, the loss of information from only using nouns does not actually hurt the extractive summarization method. Nouns represent the entities the text is talking about, and doing clustering on them accurately finds the main topics. And while the key information of what is being said about the topics is not present in the graph, it is put back by the extractive summarizer when selecting sentences from the original text.

This only works, however, when doing extractive summarization. If the conceptual graphs are to be used for further processing, leaving out all information but that of the entities present is unacceptable. This is precisely what we are trying to solve with our graphs, which include as much semantic information as possible.

Moreover, the enriched conceptual graphs manage to reach similar scores as those without the semantic enrichment. This means that they provide at least the same information as the previous ones, so what is being added is not noise. It just so happens that the additional data does not seem to improve extractive summarization via clustering.

5   Conclusions

This document has introduced a graph-based approach to extracting semantic information from text. It proposes a fully automatic graph building process, based on the result generated by a language processing tool such as Freeling. This tool takes a free-form text and generates a dependency parse, from which then the conceptual graph is created. Nodes in the graph represent concepts present or related to the text, and the edges describe their relations.

The graphs can then be clustered, and subgraphs extracted where the most important topics of the text are identified. These topics can then be used to score sentences for generating a short summary.

While we remain interested in using our richer concept graphs for semantic representations of texts, extractive summarization seems not to be the most appropriate application for them. Results are not conclusive, but exploration seems to indicate that there is not much room for improvement. An abstractive approach would probably be a better fit, and this leads to a possible line of future work in natural language generation based on concept graphs.

Another line of future work lies in creativity, an abstract step before this possible language generation. In this line, conceptual graphs can be merged or explored to find new pieces of information not present in the original text. This information can be deduced from the context added to the graph, or may be even created by observing and following patterns in the data.

Alongside further applications of concept graphs for processing, a clear line of work lies in the continuation of the enrichment effort. More semantic links can be found between the different concepts, understanding more complex dependency relations. Some function words that are now dropped as non-semantic, like determiners, can be interpreted to add nuances to the concepts found. Since the underlying dependency parser is able to give us a very complete description of the sentence, there is much information still waiting to be exploited.

In the same line of better linguistic enrichment, even more sophisticated relations can be found. Algorithms for endophora or even exophora resolution can be implemented, adding nodes and links, or merging co-referential nodes. Since the conceptual graph is not tied to the sentence or even the text structure, transformations can be performed to better convey the true meaning of the text. Other pragmatic relations can be found: discourse structure can be added between the different statements, or information structure in the sentence extracted. In this line, maybe clustering over the sub-graph of nominal nodes, as we already do for summaries, can be found to be a novel way of separating the topic and the focus of each sentence.

Acknowledgements. This work is funded by ConCreTe. The project ConCreTe acknowledges the financial support of the Future and Emerging Technologies (FET) programme within the Seventh Framework Programme for Research of the European Commission, under FET grant number 611733.

This research is funded by the Spanish Ministry of Economy and Competitiveness and the European Regional Development Fund (TIN2015-66655-R (MINECO/FEDER)).

References

1. Barabási, A.L., Albert, R.: Emergence of scaling in random networks. Science **286**(5439), 509–512 (1999)
2. Erkan, G., Radev, D.R.: LexRank: graph-based lexical centrality as salience in text summarization. J. Artif. Intell. Res. **22**, 457–479 (2004)
3. Fiszman, M., Rindflesch, T.C., Kilicoglu, H.: Abstraction summarization for managing the biomedical research literature. In: Proceedings of the HLT-NAACL Workshop on Computational Lexical Semantics, pp. 76–83. Association for Computational Linguistics (2004)

4. Jiang, J.J., Conrath, D.W.: Semantic similarity based on corpus statistics and lexical taxonomy (1997). arXiv preprint arXiv:cmp-lg/9709008
5. Leskovec, J., Grobelnik, M., Milic-Frayling, N.: Learning semantic graph mapping for document summarization. In: Proceedings of ECML/PKDD-2004 Workshop on Knowledge Discovery and Ontologies (2004)
6. Lin, C.Y.: Rouge: a package for automatic evaluation of summaries. In: Proceedings of the ACL 2004 Workshop on Text Summarization Branches Out, vol. 8 (2004)
7. Liu, H., Singh, P.: Conceptnet: a practical commonsense reasoning toolkit. BT Technol. J. **22**(4), 211–226 (2004)
8. Miller, G.A.: Wordnet: a lexical database for English. Commun. ACM **38**(11), 39–41 (1995)
9. Miranda, S., Gelbukh, A., Sidorov, G.: Generación de resúmenes por medio de síntesis de grafos conceptuales. Rev. Signos **47**(86), 463–485 (2014)
10. Moawad, I.F., Aref, M.: Semantic graph reduction approach for abstractive text summarization. In: 2012 Seventh International Conference on Computer Engineering and Systems (ICCES), pp. 132–138. IEEE (2012)
11. Padró, L., Stanilovsky, E.: Freeling 3.0: towards wider multilinguality. In: LREC 2012 (2012)
12. Plaza, L., Díaz, A., Gervás, P.: Concept-graph based biomedical automatic summarization using ontologies. In: Proceedings of the 3rd Textgraphs Workshop on Graph-Based Algorithms for Natural Language Processing, pp. 53–56. Association for Computational Linguistics (2008)
13. Rusu, D., Fortuna, B., Grobelnik, M., Mladenić, D.: Semantic graphs derived from triplets with application in document summarization. Informatica **33**(3), 357–362 (2009)
14. Sowa, J.F.: Conceptual Structures: Information Processing in Mind and Machine (1983)
15. Yoo, I., Hu, X., Song, I.Y.: A coherent graph-based semantic clustering and summarization approach for biomedical literature and a new summarization evaluation method. BMC Bioinform. **8**(9), 1 (2007)
16. Zhang, P.Y., Li, C.H.: Automatic text summarization based on sentences clustering and extraction. In: 2nd IEEE International Conference on Computer Science and Information Technology, ICCSIT 2009, pp. 167–170. IEEE (2009)

Optimization of MLHL-SIM and SIM Algorithm Using OpenMP

Lidia Sánchez[1]([✉]), Héctor Quintián[2], Hilde Pérez[1], and Emilio Corchado[2]

[1] Department of Mechanical, Computer and Aerospace Engineering,
University of León, León, Spain
{lidia.sanchez,hilde.perez}@unileon.es
[2] Departamento de Informática y Automática,
Universidad de Salamanca, Salamanca, Spain
{hector.quintian,escorchado}@usal.es

Abstract. In this research a parallel version of two existing algorithms that implement Maximum Likelihood Scale Invariant Map (MLHL-SIM) and Scale Invariant Map (SIM) is proposed. By using OpenMP to distribute the independent iterations of for-loops among the available threads, a significant reduction in the computation time for all the experiments is achieved. The higher the size of the considered map is, the higher the reduction of the computation time in the parallel algorithm is. So, for two given datasets, measured times are up to a 29.45 % and a 36.21 % of the sequential time for the MLHL-SIM algorithm. For the SIM algorithm it also reduces the computation time being a 42.09 % and a 36.72 % of the sequential version for the two datasets respectively. Results prove the improvement on the speed up of the parallel version.

Keywords: Parallel algorithms · OpenMP · Performance · Maximum Likelihood Hebbian Learning · Scale Invariant Map

1 Introduction

Neural networks have been widely used in artificial intelligence in order to predict or classify patterns that allows computers to behave with intelligence. Runtime efficiency is probably perceived as the most important topic when considering an efficient neural network implementation [3]. Being aware of that issue, many works provide solutions in order to optimize neural network implementations. In [3], a framework called Torch7 is presented which allows to develop flexible and fast code with high computation performance; high performance is obtained via efficient OpenMP/SSE (Streaming SIMD Extensions on Intel processors) and CUDA implementations of low-level numeric routines.

There are works that have proposed parallel versions of maximum likelihood fits using OpenMP and CUDA [13] in which they obtain an increase in its performance. There are numerous neural network implementations of different architectures [19], many of them have been implemented in parallel using

© Springer International Publishing Switzerland 2016
O. Luaces et al. (Eds.): CAEPIA 2016, LNAI 9868, pp. 227–236, 2016.
DOI: 10.1007/978-3-319-44636-3_21

CUDA and/or OpenMP. In [12], a combination of CUDA and OpenMP is used to speedup a feedforward neural network. They obtain 20-fold speedup with CUDA and OpenMP over sequential code, but using only CUDA the speedup is reduced to 5-fold. It seems that their neural network required sophisticated processing (they use it for image processing) and CUDA may not be ideal for sophisticated processing, but more for massive simple calculations [19]. There are other works that show how to reduce the computational cost when neural networks are used [20].

Among the great variety of tools for multidimensional data visualization, several of the most widely used are those belonging to the family of the topology preserving maps [9,15,22]. Two interesting models are the Scale Invariant Map (SIM) [1] and the Maximum Likelihood Scale Invariant Map (MLHL-SIM) [4]. Both are designed to perform their best with radial datasets due to the fact that both create a mapping where each neuron captures a pie slice of the data according to the angular distribution of the input data. The main difference between this mapping and the Self Organizing Maps (SOM) [15,16] is that this mapping is scale invariant. When the SOM is trained, it approximates a Moroni tessellation of the input space [15]. The SIM, however, creates a mapping where each neuron captures a pie slice of the data according to the angular distribution of the input data.

In this research the algorithms of MLHL-SIM and SIM and their parallel implementations are described. A study of the achieved performance between the parallel solutions and the sequential code is also carried out. Section 2 describes the algorithms optimized in this study. Section 3 explains the employed technique to run the code on parallel. In Sect. 4 the parallel version of the algorithms is presented. Experiments carried out to check the performance of the proposed code and obtained results are detailed in Sect. 5. Conclusions and future works are gathered in Sect. 6.

2   Maximum Likelihood Scale Invariant Map and Scale Invariant Map

The main target of the family of topology preserving maps [15] is to produce low dimensional representations of high dimensional datasets maintaining the topological features of the input space. The SIM [1,2] is an algorithm similar to SOM [15], but training uses a method based on negative feedback network [10,11]. SIM uses a neighborhood function and competitive learning in the same way as a SOM. SIM model is defined by Eqs. 1, 2 and 3.

$$Feedforward : y_i = \sum_{j=1}^{N} W_{ij} \cdot x_j, \tag{1}$$

$$Feedback : e = x - W_c y_c \quad (y_c = 1) \tag{2}$$

$$Weights \ \ update : \Delta W_i = h_{ci} \cdot \eta \cdot (x - W_c), \quad \forall i \in N_c, \tag{3}$$

where x is a N-dimensional input vector, and y an M-dimensional output vector, with W_{ij} being the weight linking input j to output i; e is the residual or error, η the learning rate, W_c is the weight connected to the output winner and h_{ci} represents the neighborhood function, which is a Gaussian function in this case. The input data x_j is feed forward through weights W_{ij} to the output neurons y_i, where a linear summation is performed to obtain the activation of the output neurons 1. Based on the previous obtained neurons activation, a winner neuron is selected using the minimum Euclidean distance (the neuron whose weight vector is closest to the input neuron wins) or using the maximum activation (the neuron with the highest activation wins). After selection of an output winner, the winner, c, is deemed to be firing ($y_c = 1$) and all other outputs are suppressed ($y_i = 0$, $\forall i \neq c$). The winners activation is then feed back through its weights and this is subtracted from the inputs, and simple Hebbian learning is used to update the weights of all nodes in the neighborhood of the winner.

The MLHL-SIM [4] is an extension of the SIM based on the application of the Maximum Likelihood Hebbian Learning (MLHL) [5]. The main difference with the SIM is that the MLHL is used to update the weights of all nodes in the neighborhood of the winner, once this has been updated. This can be expressed as in 4:

$$Weights\ update : \Delta W_i = h_{ci} \cdot \eta \cdot sign(e - W_c) \cdot |e - W_c|^{p-1}, \forall\ i \in N_c, \quad (4)$$

By giving different values to p the learning rule is optimal for different probability density functions of the residuals. h_{ci} is the neighborhood function as in the case of the SOM and SIM, and N_c is the number of output neurons. Finally, η represents the learning rate.

During the training of the SIM or the MLHL-SIM, the weights of the winning node are fed back as inhibition at the inputs, and then in the case of the MLHL-SIM, MLH learning is used to update the weights of all nodes in the neighborhood of the winner as explained above.

3   OpenMP

OpenMP [7,8] is a language extension to program shared-memory parallel computers. Although the most widely-used programming paradigm for highly-parallel systems or clusters is MPI [7], when just one computer is used, OpenMP provides the chance to reduce the execution time by employing the capacity of current processors of create threads that can be executed simultaneously. For that reason, the OpenMP library has been chosen to speed up the program since all computers nowadays have more than one core and they support several threads, so the application can be executed faster without needing either the use of a supercomputer or a cluster.

Basically the parallelization is achieved by running the iterations of the for-loops in parallel in different threads, instead of in a single thread. As each loop iteration is independent from each other, it can be executed simultaneously in a different thread.

4   Parallelization Strategy and Implementation

In this study a C version of the existing algorithms SIM [1, 2] and MLHL-SIM [4], has been written from scratch in order to exploit the parallel capabilities of the program. As the algorithms were written in MatLab there was no control over memory allocation [3], so C code is required in order to reduce overhead and manage memory allocation.

Firstly, the algorithms have been optimized and then have been parallelized using a data parallelism paradigm. OpenMP provides the functionality to deal with such kind of parallelism. Single precision is used to operate with all floating point numbers since neural networks usually do not require a high precision.

As the iterations in the loops for different calculations are independent, they can be parallelized using the `#pragma omp parallel for` directive. The scheduling of the iterations is static and each thread does a fixed number of iterations and accesses to consecutive elements of the arrays of input variables and obtain their corresponding results, allowing data vectorization of the loops as it is proposed in [13]. Arrays of input variables and results are shared among the threads, so that there is a negligible increment in the global memory footprint of the application when running it in parallel.

Due to the existing memory hierarchy, once you access to a given memory address, data that are nearby this address in memory are loaded into the various caches of the processor. This makes the access to nearby data available to the CPU much faster than it would be if it had to fetch it from memory. The most immediate consequence is that the innermost loops of any numerical computation should access to contiguous memory [20].

A parallel implementation of Neural PCA [10] and MLHL [5] for a GPU device using CUDA language has been also developed in [17]. Here, the kernels considered are: generation of the random weight matrix W, computation of the activation vector y, error calculation e, update of the error according to the MLHL learning and update of the weight matrix W.

After some analysis of the algorithms, two major classifications of operations were identified:

- Vector and Matrix operations: add, subtraction and vector-matrix multiplication. Each thread retrieves a subset of elements of each of the vector/matrices and add/subtract/multiply the corresponding ones as it can be done element-wise. The implementation is straightforward and coalescing memory calls are trivial [19].
- Matrix initialization: random number generation, distances between neurons and h_c. As the initialization is independent for each element, each thread computes a subset of elements of the final matrix.

The following for loops have been distributed among the available threads for the two considered algorithms:

- Initialization of the matrix of weights W with random numbers.
- Computation of the matrix of distances D between the neurons in the input space (map).
- Computation of the neighborhood function h_c.
- Computation of the activate function $y = x \cdot W$.
- Error computation $e = x - W$.
- Weights update: being $\Delta W = \eta \cdot h_c \cdot e$ for SIM algorithm and $\Delta W = \eta \cdot h_c \cdot sign(e) \cdot |e|^{p-1}$ for MLHL-SIM algorithm. And the new weights: $W = W + \Delta W$.

The sequential algorithm used to start is the one detailed in Algorithm 1. Variables means the following: N is the number of features, M is the map size, T is the number of iterations for training, η is the learning rate and $width$ is the step width.

Figure 1 shows a parallel implementation for both algorithms SIM and MLHL-SIM, following the same scheme proposed in [21]. After initializing connection weights with a small random numbers, the outer loop is executed until the network is trained or a number k is achieved, where k is the maximum number of epochs.

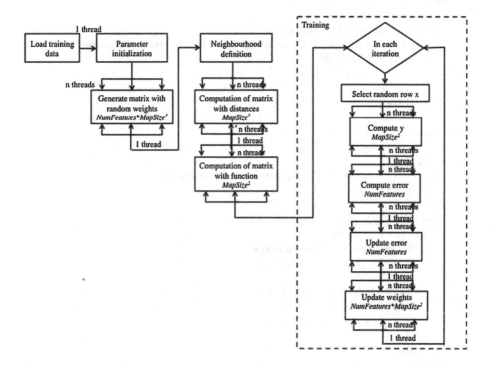

Fig. 1. Scheme of the parallel version for both SIM and MLHL-SIM algorithms.

Algorithm 1. Sequential algorithm of SIM. The for loops 1 to 6 have been distributed into threads

ParameterInitialization(lRateStep, widthStep)
for $i = 1 \rightarrow N$ **do** {**1. Computation of the matrix of weights**}
   for $j = 1 \rightarrow M$ **do**
      W(i,j)=rand()
   end for
end for
for $i = 1 \rightarrow M$ **do** {**2. Computation of the matrix of distances**}
   for $j = 1 \rightarrow M$ **do**
      $D(i,j) = \sqrt{(index(0,i) - index(0,j))^2 + (index(1,i) - index(1,j))^2}$
   end for
end for
for $i = 1 \rightarrow M$ **do** {**3. Computation of the neighborhood function**}
   for $j = 1 \rightarrow M$ **do**
      $h_c(i,j) = e^{-D(i,j)*D(i,j)/width}$
   end for
end for
for $t = 1 \rightarrow 10$ **do** {epochs}
   for $k = 1 \rightarrow T$ **do** {iterations}
     $x(:) = data(randomIndex, :)$
     if algorithm is MLHL-SIM **then**
        for $i = 1 \rightarrow M$ **do** {**4. Computation of the activate function**}
           for $j = 1 \rightarrow N$ **do**
              $y(i) = x(j) \cdot W(j,i)$
           end for
        end for
        $c = max(y)$
     else
        $c = min(distance(x, W))$
     end if
     for $i = 1 \rightarrow N$ **do** {**5. Computation of the error**}
        $e(i) = x(i) - W(i,c)$
     end for
     for $i = 1 \rightarrow N$ **do** {**6. Weights update**}
        for $j = 1 \rightarrow M$ **do**
           if algorithm is MLHL-SIM **then**
              $\Delta W(i,j) = \eta \cdot e(i) \cdot h_c(j,c) \cdot sign(e) \cdot |e|^{p-1}$
           else
              $\Delta W(i,j) = \eta \cdot e(i) \cdot h_c(j,c)$
           end if
           $W(i,j) = W(i,j) + \Delta W(i,j)$
        end for
     end for
   end for
   $\Delta\eta$
   $\Delta width$
end for

5   Experiments and Results

5.1   Computation Environment

Programs have been compiled by GCC 4.8.5 using the modifier -O3 and OpenMP 3.1. All the experiments have been run on a workstation with a Xeon Haswell Processor E5-2630 V3 at 2.4 Ghz with 8 cores and 16 threads, 20 MB of cache memory at 8GT/s and a memory of 32 GB of DDR4/2133 Mhz ECC Reg. Thus, up to 8 physical threads and up to 16 logical cores can be used.

Datasets considered to run the experiments are downloaded from the UCI Machine Learning Repository[1]. Two datasets have been used in the experiments. The first one consists of 1025010 samples of 10 features each that represent an example of a hand in a poker game[2] [18]. The second one has 434874 samples of 4 features each and represents information of 3D road network[3] [14].

Previously mentioned steps are distributed among the threads:

- Initialization of the matrix of weights with random numbers: the size is $N \times M$ being N the number of features of each sample and M the total map size (in this work, 10×10, 50×50 and 100×100). Element initialization is distributed among the threads ($M/numthreads$).
- Computation of the matrix of distances between the neurons in the input space (map): the size is $M \times M$ and rows are distributed among the threads ($M/numthreads$).
- Computation of the neighborhood matrix: the size is $M \times M$ and rows are distributed among the threads ($M/numthreads$).
- Computation of the activate function $y = x \cdot W$: the size is $1 \times M$. Computations of the elements of y are distributed among the threads ($M/numthreads$).
- Error computation $e = x - W$: the size is $1 \times N$ so it is distributed among the threads ($N/numthreads$).
- Weights update: being $\Delta W = \eta \cdot h_c \cdot e$ for SIM algorithm and $\Delta W = \eta \cdot h_c \cdot sign(e) \cdot |e|^{p-1}$ for MLHL-SIM algorithm.
- New weights: $W = W + \Delta W$: the size is $N \times M$. Rows are distributed among the threads ($N/numthreads$).

5.2   Performance Analysis/Evaluation

The evaluation setup consists of running data through the network on the previously mentioned system and using the configurations shown in Table 1. Each run was performed a minimum of 5 times and averaged using one thread (sequential) up to 8 since that is the maximum physical number of threads. A summary of the results for the MLHL-SIM algorithm is presented in column M in Tables 2 and 3. Results show how the map size affects to the reduction of the runtime.

---

[1] http://archive.ics.uci.edu/ml.

[2] https://archive.ics.uci.edu/ml/datasets/Poker+Hand.

[3] https://archive.ics.uci.edu/ml/datasets/3D+Road+Network+%28North+Jutland%2C+Denmark%29#.

Table 1. Configuration of the experiments run on the machine.

Map size	Number of iterations	Number of threads
10×10	10000	1–8
50×50	10000	1–8
100×100	10000	1–8

Table 2. Speed up $T_p/T_s\%$ obtained for both parallel MLHL-SIM algorithm (M) and parallel SIM algorithm (S) considering the poker dataset.

Map size	Number of threads															
	1		2		3		4		5		6		7		8	
	M	S	M	S	M	S	M	S	M	S	M	S	M	S	M	S
10×10	100	100	81.1	77.8	75.7	72.9	69.8	68.7	**61.2**	**62.5**	65.9	65.5	73.7	70.5	74.8	71.1
50×50	100	100	77.6	67.5	58.8	66.1	46.3	53.3	35.9	44.6	35.2	**43.5**	**33.5**	44.7	37.6	46.2
100×100	100	100	59.7	67.5	51.2	58.3	42.0	50.8	**29.5**	**42.1**	30.9	44.6	31.3	44.9	32.6	44.5

So whereas for a 10×10 map the execution time running on parallel T_p among 5 threads is up to the 61.24 % of the sequential time T_s in the case of the poker data and no improvement is achieved for the 3D road network dataset, for a 50×50 map is reduced to a 33.54 % of the sequential time with 7 threads in the case of the poker dataset or to a 36.21 % for the second dataset and 4 threads. Using a map size of 100×100 the computation time is reduced to a 29.45 % of the sequential time using 5 threads in the first dataset and to a 40.18 % of the sequential time for the 3D road network dataset running on 4 threads.

Parallelization of SIM algorithm also reduces the computation time as it is shown in column S in Tables 2 and 3. For the poker dataset, the higher optimization is achieved when 5 threads are used and the map size is 100×100, when the parallel time is just a 42.09 % of the sequential time. For 50×50 the best results are obtained with 6 threads (the computation time is the 43.45 % of the sequential time) and for 10×10 with 5 threads (62.47 % of the sequential time). For the 3D road network dataset, best results are obtained when 4 threads are used decreasing the computation time to a 91.18 % (map size of 10×10), 36.72 % (map size of 50×50) or 49.07 (map size of 100×100).

According to the results gathered in Tables 2 and 3, it is noticeable that the sequential time (expressed as 1 thread) is reduced when more threads are used.

Table 3. Speed up $T_p/T_s\%$ obtained for both parallel MLHL-SIM algorithm (M) and parallel SIM algorithm (S) considering the 3D road dataset.

Map size	Number of threads															
	1		2		3		4		5		6		7		8	
	M	S	M	S	M	S	M	S	M	S	M	S	M	S	M	S
10×10	100	100	57.9	92.1	65.5	103.6	**55.3**	**91.2**	60.4	95.8	64.5	103.8	71.9	110.0	70.5	108.6
50×50	100	100	51.9	64.9	62.7	54.9	**36.2**	**36.7**	37.3	38.6	38.1	40.1	38.3	41.3	37.8	40.2
100×100	100	100	66.6	70.6	64.3	77.0	**40.2**	**49.1**	41.6	50.5	45.3	51.9	45.9	53.1	44.9	53.4

The dataset size and the map size affect to the optimal number of threads that makes possible to achieve the best results. Typically this number is lower than the maximum number of possible threads since the operating systems keeps also running as well as the number of floating point units is not as high as the number of threads. Moreover, increasing the number of threads could be lowering cache reuse. It is also possible to cause overhead due to thread creation and synchronization. For all these reasons, the number of threads that is appropriate for a certain problem are established by running experiments with different configurations.

As it is shown in other works [21], rising of overheads is caused by the fact that the training algorithm is not parallel and requires synchronizations after each training iteration. Increasing the number of neurons in each layer should decrease the influence of overheads and leads to achieve a better performance of parallel application.

6 Conclusions and Further Works

In this study, a parallel version using OpenMP of two existing algorithms that compute the MLHL-SIM and SIM method is proposed. Using the `#pragma omp parallel for` directive, the independent loop iterations are distributed into the available threads in order to speed up the procedure. Experiments show that a reduction in the runtime up to 29.45 % for the poker dataset and 36.21 % for the 3D road dataset is achieved. The number of threads for which the higher reduction is achieved is dependent on the data set and the parameter configuration. In this case, best results are obtained for 4 or 5 threads.

Several techniques can be included in order to improve the obtained performance in further works, such as SSE instructions, use of BLAS package or CUDA implementation to run on a GPU. If the data size is big enough, parallel computation can speed up the network training in spite of the time wasted to thread creation and synchronization. Future work will also include the parallel version of other algorithms such as Beta Hebbian Learning or ensembles models such as WeVoS [6]. All these parallel versions should be viewed as powerful new tools for the Big Data community.

References

1. Baruque, B., Corchado, E.: A novel ensemble of scale-invariant feature maps. In: Kurzynski, M., Wozniak, M. (eds.) Computer Recognition Systems 3. AISC, vol. 57, pp. 265–273. Springer, Heidelberg (2009)
2. Baruque, B., Corchado, E.: WeVoS scale invariant map. Inf. Sci. **280**, 307–321 (2014)
3. Collobert, R., Kavukcuoglu, K., Farabet, C.: Implementing neural networks efficiently. In: Montavon, G., Orr, G.B., Müller, K.-R. (eds.) Neural Networks: Tricks of the Trade, 2nd edn. LNCS, vol. 7700, pp. 537–557. Springer, Heidelberg (2012)
4. Corchado, E., Fyfe, C.: The scale invariant map and maximum likelihood Hebbian learning, vol. 82, pp. 245–249. IOS Press (2002)

5. Corchado, E., MacDonald, D., Fyfe, C.: Maximum and minimum likelihood Hebbian learning for exploratory projection pursuit. Data Min. Knowl. Discov. **8**(3), 203–225 (2004)

6. Corchado, E., Baruque, B.: WeVoS-ViSOM: an ensemble summarization algorithm for enhanced data visualization. Neurocomputing **75**(1), 171–184 (2012)

7. Diaz, J., Muoz-Caro, C., Nio, A.: A survey of parallel programming models and tools in the multi and many-core era. In: IEEE Transactions on Parallel and Distributed Systems, pp. 1369–1386. IEEE (2012)

8. OpenMP Forum: OpenMP: a proposed industry standard API for shared memory programming. Technical report, October 1997

9. Fuertes, J.J., Dominguez, M., Reguera, P., Prada, M.A., Diaz, I., Cuadrado, A.A.: Visual dynamic model based on self-organizing maps for supervision and fault detection in industrial processes. Eng. Appl. Artif. Intell. **23**(1), 8–17 (2010)

10. Fyfe, C.: A neural network for PCA and beyond. Neural Process. Lett. **6**(1–2), 33–41 (1997)

11. Fyfe, C.: Hebbian Learning and Negative Feedback Networks. Advanced Information and Knowledge Processing. Springer, London (2005)

12. Jang, H., Park, A., Jung, K.: Neural network implementation using CUDA and OpenMP. In: Digital Image Computing: Techniques and Applications, pp. 155–161 (2008)

13. Jarp, S., Lazzaro, A., Leduc, J., Nowak, A., Pantaleo, F.: Parallelization of maximum likelihood fits with OpenMP and CUDA. In: CHEP Proceedings (2010)

14. Kaul, M., Yang, B., Jensen, C.: Building accurate 3D spatial networks to enable next generation intelligent transportation systems. In: Proceedings of International Conference on Mobile Data Management. IEEE (2013)

15. Kohonen, T.: The self-organizing map. Neurocomputing **21**(1–3), 1–6 (1998)

16. Kohonen, T.: Essentials of the self-organizing map. Neural Netw. **37**, 52–65 (2013)

17. Krömer, P., Corchado, E., Snášel, V., Platoš, J., García-Hernández, L.: Neural PCA and maximum likelihood Hebbian learning on the GPU. In: Villa, A.E.P., Duch, W., Érdi, P., Masulli, F., Palm, G. (eds.) ICANN 2012, Part II. LNCS, vol. 7553, pp. 132–139. Springer, Heidelberg (2012)

18. Lichman, M.: UCI machine learning repository (2013). http://archive.ics.uci.edu/ml

19. Ly, D.L., Paprotski, V., Yen, D.: Neural networks on GPUs: restricted Boltzmann machines. Technical report, MSU-CSE-00-2, Department of Electrical and Computer Engineering, University of Toronto (2008)

20. Vanhoucke, V., Senior, A., Mao, M.Z.: Improving the speed of neural networks on CPUs. In: Proceedings of the Deep Learning and Unsupervised Feature Learning Workshop (2011)

21. Volokitin, S.: Parallel implementation of a neural network learning algorithm. Int. J. Comput. Appl. **85**–**3**, 8–11 (2014)

22. Wu, Y., Doyle, T.K., Fyfe, C.: Multi-layer topology preserving mapping for K-means clustering. In: Yin, H., Wang, W., Rayward-Smith, V. (eds.) IDEAL 2011. LNCS, vol. 6936, pp. 84–91. Springer, Heidelberg (2011)

Incremental Contingency Planning for Recovering from Uncertain Outcomes

Yolanda E-Martín[1]($\boxtimes$), María D. R-Moreno[2], and David E. Smith[3]

[1] Centre for Automation and Robotics, CSIC-UPM, 28500 Madrid, Spain
yolanda.e.martin@csic.es
[2] Universidad de Alcalá, Ctra Madrid-Barcelona Km 33.6, 28871 Madrid, Spain
mdolores@aut.uah.es
[3] NASA Ames Research Center, Moffett Field, CA 94035, USA
david.smith@nasa.gov

Abstract. Incremental Contingency Planning is a framework that considers all potential failures in a plan and attempts to avoid them by incrementally adding contingency branches to the plan in order to improve the overall probability. The planner focuses its attempts on the higher probability outcomes. Precautionary planning is a form of incremental contingency planning that takes advantage of the speed of replanning for easy contingencies and only considers the unrecoverable outcomes in the plan. In this work, we present an approach to incrementally generating contingency branches to deal with uncertain outcomes. The main idea is to first generate a high probability non-branching seed plan, which is then augmented with contingency branches to handle the most critical outcomes. Any remaining outcomes are handled by runtime replanning.

1 Introduction

Incremental Contingency Planning (ICP) is a framework that considers all potential failures in a plan and attempts to avoid them by incrementally adding contingency branches to the plan in order to improve the overall probability [1]. The planner focuses its attempts on the higher probability outcomes. Precautionary planning [2] is a form of ICP that takes advantage of the speed of replanning for easy contingencies and only considers the unrecoverable outcomes in the plan. In this work, we present an approach to incrementally generating contingency branches to deal with uncertain outcomes. The main idea is to first generate a high probability non-branching seed plan, which is then augmented with contingency branches to handle the most critical outcomes. Any remaining outcomes are handled by runtime replanning. For the most critical outcomes, an attempt will be made to improve the chances of recovery by (1) finding a new plan that avoids or reduces the probability of getting to that outcome, (2) adding precautionary steps that allow recovery, if the failure occurs, or (3) adding a conformant solution that achieves the goal by using a different path. All three strategies can increase the overall probability of the plan. The process is repeated until (1) the resulting contingent plan achieves at least a given probability threshold, (2) the available time

O. Luaces et al. (Eds.): CAEPIA 2016, LNAI 9868, pp. 237–247, 2016.
DOI: 10.1007/978-3-319-44636-3_22

is exhausted, or (3) a certain number of branches are added. By critical outcomes, we mean those that are both likely and have poor chances of recovery.

Our incremental approach starts with a high probability seed plan that we generate using PIPSS[I] [3]. Section 2 defines the heuristic function used to identify points of failure that potentially improve the total probability of the plan. Section 3 details the different techniques we can apply to improve the chances of recovery, if the failure occurs. Section 4 presents an empirical evaluation. Section 5 discusses the drawbacks of our work and outlines some future work.

2   Recognizing Outcomes

Once a non-branching seed plan has been generated, we analyze all its potential unexpected outcomes to estimate how much utility could be gained by improving the chances of recovery for that outcome. We call this estimation *Gain* and it is the maximum probability that the plan could potentially be improved by precautionary planning. This measure is based on the Completion Probability Estimate (CPE)[1]. The CPE is computed by propagating probability and Interaction information through a plan graph [3] for a given state. This information is used to find relaxed plans, which then provide an estimate of the probability of reaching the goal from that state. To illustrate, consider the probabilistic planning problem shown in Fig. 1, where there is a package *pkg* and a truck *trk* at location *a*, and the package needs to be delivered to location *c*. The truck can move between different locations, and it may have a flat tire during the trip with 0.4 probability. Locations *a* and *d* have a spare tire.

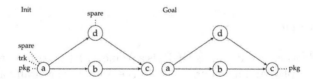

Fig. 1. Initial and goal states for a simple probabilistic Logistics problem.

Figure 2 shows the non-branching seed plan generated by the planner using all-outcomes determinization [4]. Action (drive trk a b) has an alternative outcome o_1 with probability 0.4 and CPE = 0. This means that there is no chance of completing the objective if this outcome actually happens – the tire goes flat and the truck cannot reach the goal. Action (drive trk b c) has an alternative outcome, o_2, with probability 0.4 and CPE = 1 because even though the tire goes flat, the truck still arrives at location c, and the remainder of the plan succeeds. For an alternative outcome (or branch) x of action a, the optimistic possible gain from precautionary planning will be the difference between the *estimated reward with repair* and the *estimated reward without repair*. We compute the latter using

---

[1] CPE is essentially the same as CCE [3], but expressed in terms of probability instead of in terms of cost.

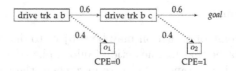

Fig. 2. Example of a non-branching seed plan with potential outcomes to be repaired

the CPE estimation. That is, the probability of reaching the goal from that state. On the other hand, to compute the *estimated reward with repair*, we propagate probability and Interaction in the plan graph only considering the outcome x, but allowing other actions in the plan to change. By doing this, we force x to be in the plan and, therefore, the new probability and Interaction information can be used to construct a relaxed plan. We call this estimation *Optimistic Probability Estimation* (OPE). More formally, for a branch x, the gain is a measure of how much the total plan probability could potentially be increased by precautionary planning and is computed by the difference between the OPE of branch x and the CPE of x:

$$\text{Gain}(x) = \text{OPE}(x) - \text{CPE}(x) \tag{1}$$

Following the previous example, for branches o_1 and o_2, the gains from precautionary planning are:

$$\text{Gain}(o_1) = \text{OPE}(o_1) - \text{CPE}(o_1) = 0.36 - 0 = 0.36$$
$$\text{Gain}(o_2) = \text{OPE}(o_2) - \text{CPE}(o_2) = 0.36 - 1 = -0.64$$

This means that by repairing branch o_1, the total plan probability will improve more than through branch o_2. Therefore, we would prefer to recover o_1 since it seems that it is possible to gain more probability mass, and o_2 might be recoverable by using runtime replanning.

The calculation of gains allows us to create a ranking to start the recovery of alternative paths.

3   Repairing Outcomes

Given the recognized undesirable outcomes ranking, the next step is to repair the plan in order to increase the overall probability of success. For each outcome, the idea is to look for the best improvement. In the next subsections, we present three methods to do that. The first method is called *Confrontation*, which tries to find a plan that avoids the problematic action's outcome when its execution depends on a condition. The second method is called *Precautionary Steps*, which adds precautionary actions before the problematic action to increase the probability of recovery in case it happens. The third method is called *Conformant Augmentation*, which increases the total probability by adding conformant steps to the contingency plan solution.

3.1   Confrontation

A probabilistic outcome of an action may be subject to different conditions. In our example, it might be that for the action (unload pkg trk c), proposition ¬(at c pkg) occurs when, for instance, the store in c where the package needs to be delivered is closed. Confrontation on this condition will avoid ¬(at c pkg) by ensuring that the store is open before the start of driving.

The idea is to find a new plan that avoids or reduces the probability of getting to that branch, and then replace the old seed plan with the new plan. More precisely, suppose that a is the action in the seed plan with an unrecoverable outcome conditioned by c. We force the planner to find a new seed plan that achieves ¬c to prevent the failure from occurring. The way we do that is by creating a new version of the action a, a', that keeps its original preconditions plus a new additional precondition ¬c, and its original effects plus an additional unique effect. The unique effect is also added to the set of goals. We then add the new action to the set of operators and call the deterministic planner to find a plan for the goals. If a new plan is found and it has higher probability than the old seed plan, the new plan replaces the old seed plan.

3.2   Precautionary Steps

Precautionary Steps consists of repairing an undesirable action's outcome by adding precautionary actions to the plan before the problematic action. For example, picking up a spare tire before driving in case you have a flat tire. This method improves the chance of recovery, if the seed plan fails, and makes it possible to reach the goal when the unexpected outcome of the problematic action happens during runtime. The idea is to force the planner to find a plan that uses each alternative outcome, but does not lose any precondition needed to reach the goal when the action has the desired outcome. In other words, for each alternative outcome o of action a, the method:

1. Divides the initial seed plan into two parts: a *prefix*, which contains all actions preceding a, and a *suffix*, which contains all actions following a.
2. Creates a new action a' that keeps its original preconditions and effects except for the new predicate (unique-effect), which is added to its effects.
3. Analyzes the causal structure of the suffix to collect all the preconditions needed by the suffix, and adds them to the set of preconditions of a'.
4. Adds the predicate (unique-effect) to the goal state to force a' into the plan.
5. Adds a' to the set of operators and calls the deterministic planner to find a plan for the new goal state. If a plan is found and the overall probability of the plan is higher, the prefix is replaced with the prefix of the new plan and the suffix is added to it.

3.3   Conformant Plan

It is possible that there are several plans that reach the goal, which are not initially generated because they have lower probability. In some cases, one or more of these plans may be executable with the original seed plan and will raise the probability of the plan. Conformant plans may happen when the Precautionary Steps method is applied. This is the case when the plan that is generated contains action a' (the one forced to be in the plan), but it is only in the plan to achieve the unique effect.

4 Experimental Evaluation

We conducted an experiment on IPPC-06 and IPPC-08 fully observable probabilistic planning domains, as well as on the *probabilistically interesting domains* (PID) [5]. The test consists of running the planner and using the resulting plan in the MDP Simulator [6]. The planner and the simulator communicate by exchanging messages. The simulator first sends the planner the initial state. Then, the interaction between planner and simulation consists of the planner sending an action and the simulator sending the next state to the planner.

The planners used for this test were FPG [7], FF-Replan [4], FHH [8], FHH$^+$ [9], and RFF [10]. We compare these with two variants of our planner:

- PIPSS$_r^I$ [3], which generates a high-probability non branching seed plan and does runtime replanning to deal with unexpected states at execution time.
- C-PIPSS$_r^I$, a modified PIPSS$_r^I$ planner that incrementally augments the plan solution using confrontation, precautionary steps, and conformant augmentation. It does runtime replanning to deal with unexpected states at execution time.

The experiments were conducted on a 2.4 GHz Pentium dual core processor. For the rest of the planners, given that we were not able to obtain and run them ourselves, data were collected from work done by Yoon et al. [9]. For all the planners, 30 trials per problem were performed with a total time limit of 30 min for the 30 trials. There are 15 problems for each domain, except for the 2-Tireworld domain that has 10, and the PID domains that have one each. Therefore, the maximum number of successful rounds for each domain is $15 \times 30 = 450$, $10 \times 30 = 300$, and 30 respectively.

Table 1 (left panel) shows the number of successful rounds for each planner in each IPPC-06 domain. C-PIPSS$_r^I$ gets good results in two of the three domains. The highest success rates are obtained in Exploding-Blocks and Tireworld domains. In fact, C-PIPSS$_r^I$ is the planner that achieves the highest rate in the Exploding-Blocks domain. We expected that C-PIPSS$_r^I$ would perform better than PIPSS$_r^I$. However, in the Elevator domain, C-PIPSS$_r^I$ performs much poorer than PIPSS$_r^I$, and it is only slightly better in the Tireworld domain. Figure 3 shows data on the plan solution after applying ICP to the initial nonbranching seed plan. The left column presents a plot for each domain in the IPPC-06 that shows the increase in probability after repairing the plan outcomes, and if a conformant branch has been added on the plan solution. The right column presents a scatter plot for each domain in the IPPC-06, where each dot in the plot represents the relationship between the *total number of outcomes in the plan* and the number of *recoverable outcomes*, and the *total number of outcomes in the plan* and the number of *unrecoverable outcomes*.

Table 1. Total number of successful rounds on the IPPC-06 and IPPC-08 using ICP.

	PLANNERS						PLANNERS				
IPPC-06	FFH	FFH$^+$	FPG	PIPSS$_r^I$	C-PIPSS$_r^I$	IPPC-08	FFH	FFH$^+$	RFF	PIPSS$_r^I$	C-PIPSS$_r^I$
Exploding-Blocks	205	**265**	193	239	262	Exploding-Blocks	131	**214**	58	171	176
Elevators	214	292	342	**396**	382	2-Tireworld	**420**	**420**	382	21	68
Tireworld	343	**364**	337	360	356	TOTAL	551	**634**	440	192	244
TOTAL	762	921	872	995	**1000**						

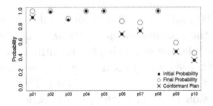

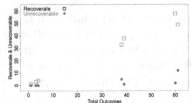

(a) Probability difference in the Exploding-Blocks Domain

(b) Recoverable and unrecoverable outcomes in the Exploding-Blocks Domain

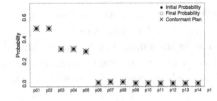

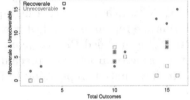

(c) Probability difference in the Elevator Domain

(d) Recoverable and unrecoverable outcomes in the Elevator Domain

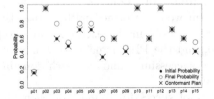

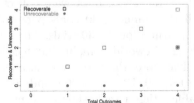

(e) Probability difference in the Tireworld Domain

(f) Recoverable and unrecoverable outcomes in the Tireworld Domain

Fig. 3. Comparison between initial and final plan probability (left column), and recoverable and unrecoverable plan outcomes (right column) of IPPC-06.

Figure 3(a) shows that for the Exploding-Blocks domain the overall probability of the plan increases in all the problems. The reason is the high number of recoverable outcomes, which is shown in Fig. 3(b). Therefore, the performance of C-PIPSS$_r^I$ is better than the performance of PIPSS$_r^I$. Figure 3(c) shows that for the Elevator domain the overall probability of the plan does not increase in any of the problems, but a conformant plan is added to each of them. Figure 3(d) shows that the number of unrecoverable outcomes is higher than the number of recoverable outcomes. This is why the overall probability does not increase. Although each problem has a conformant plan added, this additional plan has lower probability than the initial plan. Therefore, the chances of failure during execution are higher. However, the success rate of C-PIPSS$_r^I$ is higher than FFH and close to FFH$^+$. Figure 3(e) shows that for the Tireworld domain the overall probability of the plan increases in half of the problems, and a conformant plan is added to each of them. Figure 3(d) shows that the number of recoverable outcomes is higher than the number of unrecoverable outcomes. However, C-PIPSS$_r^I$ performs just a bit better than PIPSS$_r^I$, where we expected better performance. The success rate of C-PIPSS$_r^I$ is higher than FFH and FPG. FFH$^+$ performs slightly better.

Table 1 (right panel) shows the number of successful rounds for each planner in each IPPC-08 domain. C-PIPSS$_r^I$ has a lower success rate than we expected. For the Exploding-Blocks domain, even though from Fig. 4(a) we can see the overall probability increase for some of the problems, the success rate of C-PIPSS$_r^I$ does not improve. For the 2-Tireworld domain, the success rate of C-PIPSS$_r^I$ increases considerably compare to PIPSS$_r^I$, but it is still very low.

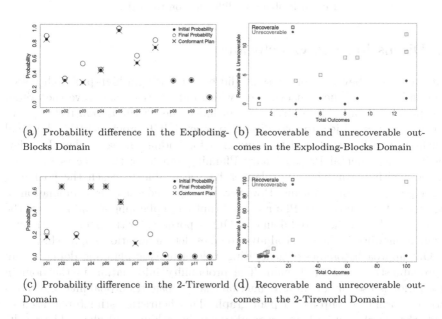

(a) Probability difference in the Exploding-Blocks Domain

(b) Recoverable and unrecoverable outcomes in the Exploding-Blocks Domain

(c) Probability difference in the 2-Tireworld Domain

(d) Recoverable and unrecoverable outcomes in the 2-Tireworld Domain

Fig. 4. Comparison between initial and final plan probability, and recoverable and unrecoverable plan outcomes of IPPC-08.

Table 2 shows the number of successful rounds for each planner in each PID domain. Figure 5 shows that surprisingly there is no improvement in the overall probability for any of the tested domains. PIPSS$_r^I$, and C-PIPSS$_r^I$ have relatively high success rates in the Climb and River domains. However, we expected some improvement in the Tire1 and Tire10 domains after ICP was applied.

Table 2. Total number of successful rounds on the PID using ICP.

DOMAINS	PLANNERS					
	FF-Replan	FFH	FFH$^+$	FPG	PIPSS$_r^I$	C-PIPSS$_r^I$
Climb	19	**30**	**30**	**30**	**30**	**30**
River	20	20	20	20	**23**	20
Tire1	15	**30**	30	30	21	19
Tire10	0	6	**30**	0	0	0
TOTAL	54	86	**110**	80	74	69

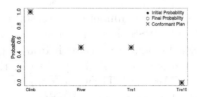

Fig. 5. Probability difference on the PID.

5   Discussion and Conclusions

This work goes beyond what Foss [2] did by computing a high-probability seed plan and a *Gain* value that evaluates which outcomes will improve the overall seed plan probability. In addition, we included the *Confrontation* technique to repair outcomes subject to a condition. In general, ICP provides little additional benefit using all-outcomes determinization for finding the seed plan. In a few domains, Incremental Precautionary Planning can help; the success rates are higher, which means that the planner has been able to reach the goal in a larger percentage of problems. However, we expected that the combination of Incremental Precautionary Planning and runtime replanning would increase the success rate for all the tested domains. Our hypothesis for the poor performance of our framework is the classical all-outcomes determinization approach.

Our approach consists of generating a deterministic planning domain from a probabilistic planning domain. The probability information in the domain description is used in a heuristic function that propagates probability and Interaction information through a plan graph. This heuristic estimator is used to guide the search toward high probability non-branching seed plans. The resulting plans are then analyzed to find potential points of failure that can be identified as recoverable or unrecoverable. Recoverable failures will be left in the plan and will be repaired through replanning at execution time. For each unrecoverable failure, we attempt to incrementally improve the chances of recovery by applying confrontation, adding precautionary steps, and adding conformant plans. The final plan is a contingency plan that has a highest probability of success during execution time. However, we observed that the probability and Interaction information underestimates the actual probability of propositions and actions in the plan graph, and therefore, the probability of each state in the search space. To illustrate, consider the simple probabilistic Logistics domain defined in Fig. 1. Assume we use all-outcomes determinization, then the probabilistic domain results in a deterministic domain with two deterministic actions created from the probabilistic action *drive*. Figure 6 shows that determinization process. The most likely outcome of the action implies that the car successfully drives between locations with probability 0.6. This results in action *drive-1*. For the other outcome, the car achieves the destination, but it gets a flat tire with a probability of 0.4. This results in action *drive-2*.

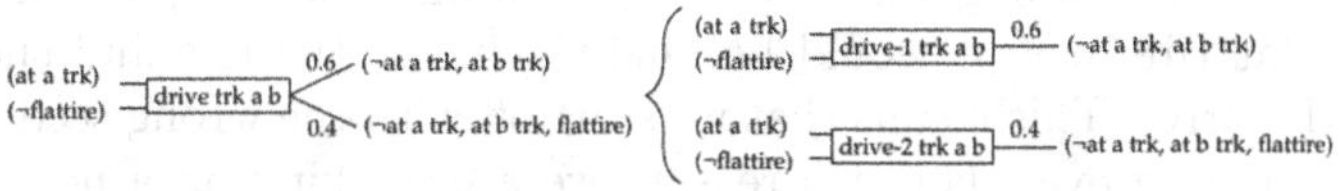

<figure>
(at a trk)
(¬flattire) ——[drive trk a b]⟨ 0.6 (¬at a trk, at b trk)
                              0.4 (¬at a trk, at b trk, flattire)

⎧ (at a trk)
⎪ (¬flattire) —[drive-1 trk a b]— 0.6 (¬at a trk, at b trk)
⎨
⎪ (at a trk)
⎩ (¬flattire) —[drive-2 trk a b]— 0.4 (¬at a trk, at b trk, flattire)
</figure>

Fig. 6. Example of all-outcomes determinization of a probabilistic action.

Figure 7 shows the plan solution that is generated by our planner. If we compute the probability of the resulting state after performing (drive-1 trk a b), the probability of (at b trk) and ¬(flattire) is 0.6. As a result, the probability of performing (drive b c) is equal to the product of the probability of its preconditions. That is, pr(at b trk) pr(¬flattire) $= 0.6(0.6) = 0.36$. As a consequence, the probability of (at c trk) is the product of the probability of performing (drive b c) and the probability of achieving (at c trk) through (drive b c). That is, $0.36(0.6) = 0.216$. This means that the probability of success of the plan is 0.216. However, both outcomes of the probabilistic action (drive trk a b) result in the car at the next location. This means that, the probability of achieving (at b trk) is dependent on the outcome. The all-outcomes determinization technique does not consider the dependence between propositions and outcomes since it does not consider the overall probability of those propositions that are common in all the outcomes. Therefore, by considering propositions individually instead of as a result of an action's outcome, we can compute more accurate probability estimates.

Fig. 7. Plan solution probability using determinization.

To illustrate, consider the example in Fig. 8 that shows the same plan solution as before. In this case, the probability for each state is computed by considering probabilistic actions and propositions individually. Therefore, after (drive trk a b) is performed, there is a probabilistic state where ¬(at a trk) and (at b trk) have a probability of 1 – since both propositions are in both outcomes of the action; ¬(flattire) has a probability of 0.6 and (flattire) has a probability of 0.4. Consequently, the probability of (drive trk b c) is 0.6, instead of 0.36 for the all-outcomes determinization. This results in (at c trk) having a probability of 0.6. Consequently, the probability of success of the plan is 0.6 where before it was 0.216. The underestimation that is caused by all-outcomes determinization is, therefore, harmful to our probability propagation, yielding seed plans that do not have high probability of success. To illustrate this, consider the simple probabilistic Logistic problem in Fig. 1. It has two possible paths that achieve the goal (1) driving from a to b and from b to c, which has a probability of 0.6 of reaching the goal, and (2) driving from a to d and from d to c, which has a probability of 1 of reaching the goal since location d has a spare tire – if the truck got a flat tire in d, it would be able to change the tire and successfully continuing the drive. This means that we start off with the wrong seed plan and, therefore, do not recover. For this reason, we are working on a new approach that computes estimates of probability, which consider the overall probability of each proposition across all of the action's outcomes, and the dependence between those propositions. These estimates will generate high probability seed plans.

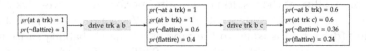

Fig. 8. Plan solution probability considering the overall probability of propositions across action outcomes.

Acknowledgments. This work was supported by the NASA Safe Autonomous Systems Operations (SASO) project, the MINECO project EphemeCH TIN2014-56494-C4-4-P, and UAH project 2015/00297/001.

References

1. Dearden, R., Meuleau, N., Ramakrishnan, S., Smith, D.E., Washington, R.: Incremental contingency planning. In: Proceedings of ICAPS 2003 Workshop on Planning under Uncertainty, Trento, Italy (2003)
2. Foss, J., Onder, N., Smith, D.E.: Preventing unrecoverable failures through precautionary planning. In: Proceedings of the ICAPS 2007 Workshop on Moving Planning and Scheduling Systems into the Real World, Providence, RI, USA (2007)
3. E-Martín, Y., R-Moreno, M.D., Smith, D.E.: Progressive heuristic search for probabilistic planing based on interaction estimates. Expert Syst. **31**(5), 421–436 (2014)
4. Yoon, S., Fern, A., Givan, R.: Ff-replan: a baseline for probabilistic planning. In: Proceedings of the International Conference on Automated Planning and Scheduling, Providence, RI, USA (2007)
5. Little, I., Thiébaux, S.: Probabilistic planning vs replanning. In: Proceedings of the ICAPS 2007 Workshop on Planning Competitions, Providence, RI, USA (2007)
6. Younes, H.L.S., Littman, M.L., Weissman, D., Asmuth, J.: The first probabilistic track of the international planning competition. JAIR **24**, 841–887 (2005)

7. Buffet, O., Aberdeen, D.: The factored policy-gradient planner. Artif. Intell. **173**, 722–747 (2009)
8. Yoon, S., Fern, A., Givan, R., Kambhampati, S.: Probabilistic planning via determinization in hindsight. In: Proceedings of AAAI, Chicago, IL, USA (2008)
9. Yoon, S., Ruml, W., Benton, J., Do, M.: Improving determinization in hindsight for on-line probabilistic planning. In: Proceedings of ICAPS, Toronto, Ontario, Canada (2010)
10. Teichteil-Königsbuch, F., Kuter, U., Infantes, G.: Incremental plan aggregation for generating policies in MDPs. In: Proceedings of AAMAS, Toronto, Canada (2010)

Applications

Clinical Decision Support Using Antimicrobial Susceptibility Test Results

Bernardo Cánovas-Segura[1]([✉]), Manuel Campos[1], Antonio Morales[1],
Jose M. Juarez[1], and Francisco Palacios[2]

[1] Computer Science Faculty, University of Murcia, Murcia, Spain
{bernardocs,manuelcampos,morales,jmjuarez}@um.es
[2] University Hospital of Getafe, Madrid, Spain
franciscodepaula@gmail.com

Abstract. Prescribing the proper antibiotic against an infectious agent
is crucial not only for the patient's health but also for the community,
due to fast development of new resistances in bacteria. To ensure the
efficacy of the treatment, laboratory tests are performed on cultures of
samples obtained from the patient, analysing the resistance patterns of
the infectious microorganism against some antibiotics. In order to assist
clinical microbiologists, the European Committee on Antimicrobial Susceptibility Testing proposes a catalogue of clinical rules to identify resistance patterns and clinical recommendations from the results of previous
antibiotic susceptibility tests. The aim of our proposal is to automatise
and evaluate this source of biomedical knowledge. To this end, we have
implemented a knowledge module combining ontologies and production
rules. This module was included in a clinical decision support system
and evaluated using test results of 365 days. After its execution, 20.9 %
of the final antibiograms were new resistance patterns not covered by
the laboratory tests, having 44 % of them a high clinical evidence grade.
These results could help clinicians to prescribe more efficient treatments
against infections in the future.

Keywords: Clinical decision support systems · Antimicrobial susceptibility testing · Ontologies · Production rules · Knowledge representation
and reasoning

1 Introduction

The rise of multidrug-resistant bacteria along with the lack of new antibiotics
is one of the most relevant health issues at the present time. Several health
organisations, such as the Centers of Disease Control and Prevention and the
European Centre for Disease Prevention and Control, are already warning about
this problem, being the cause of thousands of deaths per year [4,5].

A proper use of current available antibiotics is one of the major defences
against this global threat. The use of a wrong antibiotic for resistant bacteria
might aggravate an infection or deteriorate the patient's health unnecessarily.

© Springer International Publishing Switzerland 2016
O. Luaces et al. (Eds.): CAEPIA 2016, LNAI 9868, pp. 251–260, 2016.
DOI: 10.1007/978-3-319-44636-3_23

Furthermore, some bacteria are known to be able to develop new resistances under certain antibiotic therapies, becoming a threat to the entire community.

To avoid these problems, a sample of the infectious agent is taken when possible and its antibiogram is performed to check whether it is resistant or susceptible to some antibiotics. The antibiogram, defined by the Clinical and Laboratory Standards Institute (CLSI) as an overall profile of antimicrobial susceptibility results to a battery of antibiotics [17], is sent to clinicians to assist them in selecting the best treatment against the infection. However, these tests are not performed against all the available antibiotics, and sometimes the resistance patterns may be different in *in-vitro* and *in-vivo* scenarios.

Other works focused on supporting clinicians when dealing with infectious diseases and susceptibility tests results. The MERCURIO system [8] was designed for the validation of microbiological data and the creation of a real time epidemiological information system, incorporating knowledge from different sources. The HASIS information system [10] implements guidelines for hospital-acquired infections and includes algorithms for the detection of suspicious cases, using Service-Oriented Architecture (SOA) to integrate surveillance data. Finally, the COSARA platform [14] focuses on infection surveillance in intensive-care units, providing alerts to alarming trends among other functionalities.

In this paper we propose an implementation of part of the expert rules [9] developed by the European Committee on Antimicrobial Susceptibility Testing (EUCAST) to help clinicians to avoid improper antibiotic prescription, inferring new resistance patterns from basic laboratory test results. Our approach is based on an ontology model and production rules due to the nature of the EUCAST clinical rules. Furthermore, we have included this development into a clinical decision support system (CDSS) called WASPSS [3] and tested against infectious episodes that happened during a whole year, analysing the new resistance patterns obtained and their overlapping with previous laboratory test results.

The remainder of this paper is as follows: Sect. 2 describes the expert knowledge selected and how ontologies and production rules are used to model and implement it, ending with some details about its inclusion into a broader CDSS. In Sect. 3 we present the evaluation of the results obtained after inferring test results from a whole year's data. Section 4 provides a summary of our work and our future related research lines.

2   Methods

2.1   Knowledge Source

The EUCAST clinical rules in antimicrobial susceptibility testing [9] are the main expert knowledge source of our proposal. These rules were developed to assist microbiologists with the susceptibility test results in several ways, such as including inferred susceptibilities for non-tested agents and recommending actions on reporting to clinicians. They are based on clinical and/or microbiological evidence, with some rules having attached an evidence degree, exceptions or comments. These meta-data play a key role when deciding over a treatment.

There are three kinds of EUCAST rules: intrinsic resistances, exceptional resistances and interpretive resistances. Intrinsic resistance rules indicate which antibiotics are clinically useless against bacteria species as a result of their innate characteristics. Exceptional resistance rules associate microorganisms with very rare or never reported antibiotic resistances, which might indicate a mistake during bacteria identification if they are present in the performed tests. Finally, interpretive rules suggest resistances or susceptibilities depending on the results of the susceptibility tests performed over a concrete microorganism. EUCAST clinical rules are grouped in 13 tables. Since each rule is displayed in the row of a table, we denote by $X.Y$ the rule in table X row Y.

In this work we focus on the interpretive rules (rules 8.* to 13.*). On the one hand, most of the intrinsic resistance rules are well known by clinicians and microbiologist, and exceptional rules might not be useful for clinicians. On the other hand, interpretive rules are based on recent studies and have different evidence grade, therefore they might be not known in detail by many professionals.

2.2 Knowledge Modelling Techniques

Our main knowledge source is essentially in the form of production rules. However, this domain presents different types of knowledge that must be also modelled. Resistance rules are defined over species of bacteria mostly (i.e. *IF Streptococcus pneumoniae is resistant to ... THEN ...*), but also over families, classes and other groups of bacteria. In a similar way, these rules might be defined over a concrete antibiotic or over a group of them. The relationships between antibiotics, bacteria and resistances are exposed using *if-then* statements, complemented with comments, exceptions and their evidence grade.

Antibiotics and bacteria domains are modelled by ontologies. In particular, public available taxonomies have been used as basis for our ontologies. The Anatomical Therapeutic Chemical Classification (ATC) hierarchy [16], published by the Word Health Organization (WHO), and the National Center for Biotechnology Information (NCBI) taxonomy [6] have been used as initial taxonomies of antibiotics and microorganisms respectively. Both taxonomies have been trimmed to contain only our domain related concepts for performance reasons. Moreover, some additional concepts, such as Gram negative/positive bacteria, Non-fermentative bacteria or ureidopenicillins antibiotic group have been added.

For modelling the rules themselves we have chosen production rules. Although using ontologies could predispose to use another rule modelling options such as the Semantic Web Rule Language (SWRL) [7], production rules are more flexible when defining the action to be taken if the conditions are met. Our intention is to incorporate these rules into a broader expert system; therefore this flexibility becomes a fundamental requisite in our scenario. Furthermore, the interoperability between production rules and ontologies has been achieved in several works [1,2,13], and others consider this fusion as an interesting research topic [15].

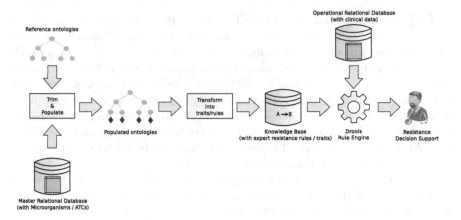

Fig. 1. Approach used to combine the ontologies into the production rules system.

Concretely, we have based our development in OWL 2 [11] as ontology language and Drools [12] as production rules engine. Complementing them, we have used OWL API and Protégé.

The steps performed to incorporate the ontological concepts into the rule engine, shown in Fig. 1, can be summarized as follows: The original ontologies are populated with individuals representing the most concise concepts used in our domain (i.e. the antibiotics and microorganisms available in the master tables of our institutional database), typing them as the most concise class available (i.e. the *Escherichia coli* individual is typed as *Escherichia coli* instead of *Bacteria*). Afterwards, a Drools source file is generated defining all the classes as hierarchical traits, and containing rules for assigning the fact representing each individual to its lower trait in the hierarchy. When used, the result is an initial knowledge base with all the concepts needed to define the resistance rules directly.

This initial knowledge base consists of 1845 concepts, 1884 relations between them and an overall of 1377 rules to associate facts to their basic concepts. From the original 36 interpretive clinical rules we chose to implement 25 of them due to its clinical relevance. Figure 2 shows a simplified example of how an interpretive rule would be implemented in our knowledge base.

2.3 CDSS Integration

This work is pretended to be a new module for the CDSS of the Wise Antimicrobial Stewardship Program Support System (WASPSS) project. The aim of this CDSS, in collaboration with the Antimicrobial Stewardship Program (ASP) team of the Hospital of Getafe (Spain), is to assist clinicians in a proper use of antibiotics.

Rule no.	Organism	Rule	Exceptions, scientific basis, and comments	Evidence grade
13.5	*Enterobacteriaceae*	IF resistant to ciprofloxacin, THEN report as resistant to all fluoroquinolones	Acquisition of at least two target mutations ...	B

(a)

```
rule "Interpretive EUCAST Table 13 Rule 13.5"
    @id ("RPEUT13.R5")
    @altName("Interpretive rules for quinolones - Rule 13.5")
    @note1 ("Acquisition of at least two target mutations ...")
    @evidenceGrade("B")
when
    $c:          Culture(microorganism isA Enterobacteriaceae)
    $abgR1:      Antibiogram (culture == $c,atc isA Ciprofloxacin,isResistant)
    $atcResult:  Atc (this isA Fluoroquinolones)
then
    InterpretiveEUCASTResult r = new InterpretiveEUCASTResult(
        $c, $abgR1, $atcResult, drools.getRule(),
        new Explanation($c.getMicroorganism(), "is a Enterobacteriaceae"),
        new Explanation($abgR1, "indicates resistance to Ciprofloxacin"),
        new Explanation($actResult, "is a fluoroquinolone antibacterial")
    );
    insert(r);
end
```

(b)

Fig. 2. Example of a rule as explained in the reference paper (a) and its implementation in Drools (b)

The outcome of the module is a set of (inferred) antibiograms using the laboratory test results available. These new antibiograms can be used by the system in the same way it uses the results of real laboratory tests. Furthermore, the inferred antibiograms contain all the traceability information that the clinician need to support his/her decision such as the EUCAST rule that generated the antibiogram, the original facts that launched the rule, the evidence grade and the scientific basis.

A graphical and simplified view of the process can be shown in Fig. 3. First, a battery of tests is performed in the laboratory to study how the microorganism found in a patient reacts to several antibiotics. In Fig. 3a, we represent a common used technique, called disc diffusion, which consist on placing different antibiotics over an agar plate in which the bacteria have let to grown. The clear disc indicates in which zone the bacteria have not grown, with a bigger disc indicating a bigger susceptibility to the antibiotic. The results are interpreted by an expert, who performs a report to the clinician with the resistance patterns (Fig. 3b). This report includes the taxonomical identification of the microorganism (family, genus, species, etc.) and the antibiogram, which is the set of the interpretations of each laboratory test, indicating to which antibiotics should be considered the microorganism as resistant or susceptible by the clinician. With our proposal, the CDSS could then apply the EUCAST rules to enhance this antibiogram (Fig. 3c), adding inferred resistance patterns not covered by the laboratory tests. The kind of inferred results and their relevance are discussed in the next section.

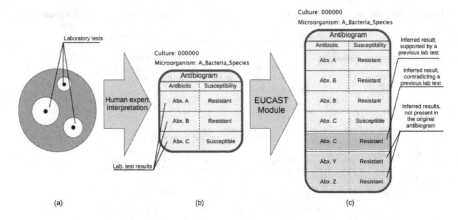

Fig. 3. Simplified process of obtaining an inferred antibiogram. First, laboratory test are performed (a) and the traditional antibiogram (b) is introduced into our system, which is able to apply part of the EUCAST rules to infer new lab test results (c).

3   Experiments and Discussion

3.1   Experimental Objectives

Our main intention is to estimate the quantity and quality of the new inferred knowledge, as a first step to evaluate whether our solution might be interesting to clinicians. The more new knowledge generated, the better support might be given. Furthermore, the implemented rules have an attached evidence grade, which may allow us to assess the quality of the generated knowledge. Testing other technical issues, such as performance and time consumption, have been delayed until having a more mature solution, with more implemented rules.

As is graphically explained in Fig. 3c, the new inferred results may be classified depending on their relationship with the previous available results. A new inferred test result may overlap with a previous one, i.e. it refers to an antibiotic that was already tested in the laboratory, or it may indicate a non-tested antibiotic (shadowed as green). If it overlaps, the inferred resistance pattern may be similar (shadowed as yellow) or different (shadowed as red) from the one obtained in the laboratory.

Despite our main interest is on the not-overlapping inferred results, the overlapping ones might be also interesting. If the system infers a different resistance pattern for an antibiotic, it might communicate this discrepancy to the clinician. Thanks to the use of production rules, we are able to identify the rule that generated the contradiction and show the experimental arguments attached to it. With this additional information, the clinician might be able to evaluate whether to use the conflicting antibiotic in the treatment.

3.2   Experimental Results

The knowledge base with the interpretive rules has been tested over the antibiograms of 365 days of data (121727 susceptibility test results). This set of antibiograms was inserted as facts into the Drools working memory. Afterwards, all the interpretive rules were fired, inferring new susceptibilities and resistances (inferred antibiograms).

The final output was a set of susceptibility test results containing both the initial antibiograms and the inferred ones (Fig. 4). 20.9 % of them were new (inferred) test results, not present in the original set. 4.1 % of the facts were inferences over already available test results (i.e. we had a previous laboratory result indicating a resistance/susceptibility of a microorganism to an antibiotic, and a clinical rule, basing on other facts, supported or contradicted it). Finally, 75 % of the facts corresponded to the original test results not affected by the inference process.

As expected, some of the inferred tests results did not support the previous results obtained in the laboratory. In these 4.1 % facts with two different origins, 88 % of them (3.6 % of total) were supporting the resistance pattern found in laboratory, but in 12 % of them (0.5 % of total) the predicted resistance pattern differed. These differences are depicted by rule in the normalized stacked bar chart of the Fig. 5, which shows the proportion of supported and contradicted facts by rule in this overlapping subset. Differences in rules 11.5, 12.7, 12.8, 12.9, 13.1, 13.3 and 13.6 might be due to the fact that these rules predict a clinical overcome instead of a concise resistance test result, alerting for a possible reduced bactericidal activity of the antibiotic despite of its in-vitro results. Our rule system reports them as resistant or intermediately resistant to discourage clinicians to use the antibiotic in these cases in spite of resulting effective in the microbiological test. Contradictions found for rules 8.6, 11.1, 12.2, 13.2 and 13.5 are more difficult to understand, and should be studied by microbiologists in the future. The rest of overlapping results produced by rules 8.1, 10.1, 10.2, 12.3, 12.6, 13.4 and 13.8 are almost completely coincidences.

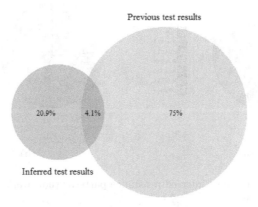

Fig. 4. Overview of the susceptibility test results after executing the implemented rules.

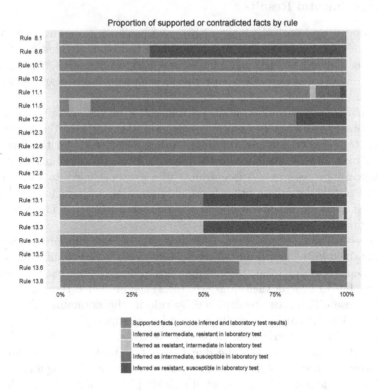

Fig. 5. Overview of the supports and contradictions between the inferred resistances and the previous laboratory tests results.

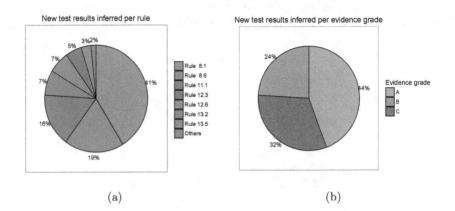

Fig. 6. Overview of the new inferred resistance patterns (not overlapping) by rule (a) and by evidence grade (b).

Relating to the new test results inferred and not present before, 44 % of them have the highest evidence grade (A), which is defined in [9] as having "... good clinical evidence that reporting the test result as susceptible leads to clinical failures." Very few of the EUCAST rules have this evidence grade (7 of 36, some of them even for special cases only). Fortunately, some of these clinical rules, like rule 8.1, are defined over common families of microorganisms and/or antibiotics, being able to be applied in many situations. A summary of these new resistance patterns is shown in Fig. 6.

4   Conclusions

In this work we propose the automation of the clinical rules described by the European Committee in Antimicrobial Susceptibility Testing in a clinical decision support system.

Our approach is based on a knowledge base that combines ontologies and production rules, trying to obtain the best of each technology.

We evaluate our proposal checking the laboratory test results of 365 days of data in a hospital. According to the results we obtained a set of new resistance patterns, not covered by the standard tests results, which might have helped clinicians in selecting the best treatment for a patient. In addition, many of these new patterns have a high grade of clinical evidence.

In the future, we plan to check whether these inferred test results might have been used to generate improper treatment alerts, and their clinical relevance if so. In addition, we plan to implement both intrinsic and exceptional EUCAST rules to increase the number of new generated antibiograms.

Acknowledgments. This work was partially funded by the Spanish Ministry of Economy and Competitiveness under the WASPSS project (Ref: TIN2013-45491-R) and by the European Fund for Regional Development (EFRD, FEDER).

References

1. Bragaglia, S., Chesani, F., Ciampolini, A., Mello, P., Montali, M., Sottara, D.: An hybrid architecture integrating forward rules with fuzzy ontological reasoning. In: Graña Romay, M., Corchado, E., Garcia Sebastian, M.T. (eds.) HAIS 2010, Part I. LNCS, vol. 6076, pp. 438–445. Springer, Heidelberg (2010)
2. Busto, J., Varas, J.: Knowledge enabled services (KES) for decision support in control rooms. CESADS (KES) case study at ESA/ESOC. In: 10th International Conference on Accelerator and Large Experimental Physics Control Systems (ICALEPCS), pp. 10–14, Geneva (2005)
3. Cánovas-Segura, B., Campos, M., Morales, A., Juarez, J.M., Palacios, F.: Development of a clinical decision support system for antibiotic management in a hospital environment. Prog. Artif. Intell. 1–17 (2016). doi:10.1007/s13748-016-0089-x
4. Centers for Disease Control, Prevention: Antibiotic Resistance Threats in the United States (2013)

5. European Centre for Disease Prevention and Control, European Medicines Agency: The bacterial challenge: time to react (2009)

6. Federhen, S.: The NCBI taxonomy database. Nucleic Acids Res. **40**(Database issue), D136–D143 (2012)

7. Horrocks, I., Patel-schneider, P.F., Boley, H., Tabet, S., Grosof, B., Dean, M.: SWRL: a semantic web rule language combining OWL and RuleML. In: W3C Member Submission, 21 May 2004 (2004). https://www.w3.org/Submission/SWRL/

8. Lamma, E., Mello, P., Nanetti, A., Riguzzi, F., Storari, S., Valastro, G.: Artificial intelligence techniques for monitoring dangerous infections. IEEE Trans. Inform. Technol. Biomed. **10**(1), 143–155 (2006)

9. Leclercq, R., Cantón, R., Brown, D.F.J., Giske, C.G., Heisig, P., Macgowan, A.P., Mouton, J.W., Nordmann, P., Rodloff, A.C., Rossolini, G.M., Soussy, C.J., Steinbakk, M., Winstanley, T.G., Kahlmeter, G.: EUCAST expert rules in antimicrobial susceptibility testing. Clin. Microbiol. Infect. **19**(2), 141–160 (2013)

10. Lo, Y.S., Liu, C.T.: Development of a hospital-acquired infection surveillance information system by using service-oriented architecture technology. In: 2010 3rd International Conference on Computer Science and Information Technology, vol. 4, pp. 449–453. IEEE (2010)

11. W3C OWL Working Group: OWL 2 web ontology language document overview (Second Edition). In: Online, pp. 1–7 (2012). http://www.w3.org/TR/owl2-overview/

12. Proctor, M., Neale, M., Lin, P., Frandsen, M.: Drools documentation. Technical report, pp. 1–297 (2008)

13. Sottara, D., Bragaglia, S., Mello, P., Pulcini, D., Luccarini, L., Giunchi, D.: Ontologies, rules, workflow and predictive models: knowledge assets for an EDSS. In: 6th International Congress on Environmental Modelling and Software, iEMSs 2012 Proceedings, Leipzig, Germany, pp. 204–211 (2012)

14. Steurbaut, K., Colpaert, K., Gadeyne, B., Depuydt, P., Vosters, P., Danneels, C., Benoit, D., Decruyenaere, J., De Turck, F.: COSARA: integrated service platform for infection surveillance and antibiotic management in the ICU. J. Med. Syst. **36**, 3765–3775 (2012)

15. Van Hille, P., Jacques, J., Taillard, J., Rosier, A., Delerue, D., Burgun, A., Dameron, O.: Comparing Drools and ontology reasoning approaches for telecardiology decision support. Stud. Health Technol. Inf. **180**, 300–304 (2012)

16. WHO Collaborating Centre for Drug Statistics Methodology: Guidelines for ATC classification and DDD assignment 2013. Oslo (2012)

17. Zapantis, A., Lacy, M.K., Horvat, R.T., Grauer, D., Barnes, B.J., O'Neal, B., Couldry, R.: Nationwide antibiogram analysis using NCCLS M39-A guidelines. J. Clin. Microbiol. **43**(6), 2629–2634 (2005)

Proposal of a Big Data Platform for Intelligent Antibiotic Surveillance in a Hospital

Antonio Morales[1]([⊠]), Bernardo Cánovas-Segura[1], Manuel Campos[1], Jose M. Juarez[1], and Francisco Palacios[2]

[1] Computer Science Faculty, University of Murcia, Murcia, Spain
{morales,bernardocs,manuelcampos,jmjuarez}@um.es
[2] University Hospital of Getafe, Madrid, Spain
franciscodepaula@gmail.com

Abstract. From a technological point of view two kinds of requirements must be taken into account when implementing Clinical Decision Support Systems (CDSSs) for antibiotic surveillance in a hospital. First, Artificial Intelligence (AI) technologies are usually applied to represent and reason about existing clinical knowledge, but also to discover new one from raw data. Second, at a global decision level, representative applications of Business Intelligence (BI) must be also considered. The present work introduces the design and implementation of a CDSS platform that integrates both AI and BI technologies to assist clinicians in the rational use of antibiotics in a hospital. The choice of a Hadoop based Big Data architecture provides a suitable solution for the problem of integrating, processing and analysing large sets of clinical data. The platform facilitates the daily follow-up of antibiotic therapies and infections while offering various decision support modules at both patient and global level. The system is being tested and evaluated in a university hospital.

Keywords: Clinical decision support systems · Antibiotic surveillance · Big data · Knowledge representation and reasoning · Business intelligence

1 Introduction

Infections caused by bacteria and other microorganisms are one of the most relevant health issues at the present time. The best clinical solutions to this problem are antibiotics, which are unique drugs owing to their high efficacy in terms of the reduction of morbidity and mortality resulting from this kind of affections. However, the rise of multi-drug resistant bacteria along with the lack of new antibiotics require the development of policies and initiatives that supervise the appropriate use of antibiotics [12,14].

Computer-based information systems and particularly Clinical Decision Support Systems (CDSSs) may be a key issue for the success of antibiotic surveillance initiatives. Some recent studies suggest that the combination of Electronic Medical Records and CDSSs have a positive impact on appropriate antimicrobial

© Springer International Publishing Switzerland 2016
O. Luaces et al. (Eds.): CAEPIA 2016, LNAI 9868, pp. 261–270, 2016.
DOI: 10.1007/978-3-319-44636-3_24

use [1,3]. When implementing a CDSS for antibiotic surveillance there are two kinds of intelligence technologies that can help in the decision-making process. On the one hand, Artificial Intelligence (AI) and knowledge based technologies are required not only to formally represent and reason with medical knowledge but also to learn new one from raw data. On the other hand, Business Intelligence (BI) related technologies provide a powerful set of analytical tools that can assist clinicians in the global surveillance and monitoring of antibiotic use and resistance. However, traditional BI solutions have problems when dealing with what is known as *Big Data*: vast amounts of structured, unstructured or semi-structured data which are generated and flow rapidly. Actually, healthcare data meet these basic characteristics of Big Data. Moreover, Big Data analytics in healthcare is evolving into a promising field for providing insight from very large data-sets and improving outcomes while reducing costs [6,13]. Open source initiatives such as the Apache Hadoop project are facilitating the implementation of Big Data solutions at different organisational levels.

This paper introduces a Big Data platform for decision support that integrates AI and BI technologies with the purpose to assist clinicians in the rational use of antibiotics in a hospital, providing decision support tools and solving the problem of integrating and managing large sets of clinical data.

The reminder of the paper is structured as follows. Section 2 presents an overview of previous systems related to antibiotic and infection stewardship. The overall architecture of the platform, its design and implementation details are introduced in Sect. 3. Section 4 details different decision support modules of the platform. A pilot deployment in a university hospital is described in Sect. 5. Finally, Sect. 6 outlines the main conclusions and identifies future research work.

2   Related Work

There have been several CDSS developments focused on similar scenarios, but few of them are dedicated to the global problem of antibiotic stewardship or infection management.

The MERCURIO system [10] was designed for the validation of microbiological data and the creation of a real time epidemiological information system. The HASIS system [16] implements the guidelines for hospital-acquired infections published by the Centers for Disease Control and Prevention and includes algorithms for detection of suspicious cases. The MONI-ICU system [9] offers automatic surveillance for the detection of Intensive Care Unit (ICU) nosocomial infections where infection guidelines are represented in Arden Syntax and uncertainty of medical data is represented using fuzzy logic. COSARA [15] is another ICU platform for infection surveillance and antibiotic management that automatically integrates data from different sources and provides a visually presentation of infections, antibiotics and clinical results. Regarding the use of Big Data technologies it is worth mentioning the Artemis project [8] which was proposed to support the acquisition and storage of patients' physiological data for the purpose of online real-time analytics and retrospective data mining.

Our proposal has been conceived taking into account several aspects that have been overlooked by the aforementioned systems and that we consider essential when developing CDSSs for antibiotic stewardship: (*i*) CDSSs must be multidisciplinary, (*ii*) must integrate multiple knowledge sources, (*iii*) must promote and ease communication between all the participants, (*iv*) must provide the most suitable information at the most appropriate moment to each specific user, and (*v*) must help in the education of clinical staff members in the management of antibiotics. Furthermore, most of these cited systems focus their attention on a single department within the hospital and few of them deal with the problem of managing large sets of clinical data.

3   Big Data Architecture

For the platform design a Big Data oriented architecture was chosen due to the advantages of scalability, cost-effective storage and flexibility. Figure 1 shows an schematic view of the platform's components.

3.1   Sources of Information and Knowledge

The platform allows integration of data coming from multiple *source systems* within the hospital (Pharmacy and Microbiology databases, Hospital Information System (HIS), etc.). Clinical data may be available in different forms and formats such as plain text files, XML documents, spreadsheets, images or records stored in a relational database management system (RDBMS).

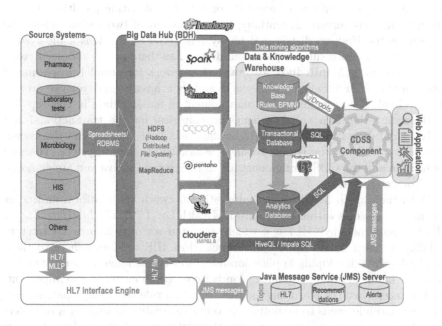

Fig. 1. Design of the Big Data platform with data flow between different components

The *Big Data Hub* (BDH) is the component that allows for the distributed storage and processing of large sets of clinical data. It behaves as a data 'refinery' [7], i.e. it stores, aggregates and transforms multi-structured raw data into usable formats so that the refined data could be analysed either directly by the decision support modules (using specific Big Data query languages or machine learning algorithms) or indirectly having preloaded them into the transactional and analytics databases.

The *Data and Knowledge Warehouse* is a repository that includes specific dedicated storage systems. The *knowledge base* contains clinical knowledge modelled as production rules or business process models (BPMs) representing clinical guidelines (CGs) or internal protocols. The *transactional database* is a standard RDBMS where clinical data is stored in a normalized way allowing efficient insert, update and delete operations. The *analytics database* is a read-only database which stores data in a suitable format for consultation by the decision support modules.

Additionally, the CDSS *component* includes several modules which help in the decision-making process for antibiotic surveillance. This component is described in further detail in Sect. 4. Finally, the *web application* provides a multi-user web interface that allows clinicians to interact with the CDSS component.

3.2   Big Data Layout

The platform has been implemented using a very disparate set of open source languages, tools and frameworks. The most significant alternative to implement the BDH is the open source distributed data platform Hadoop. Hadoop has the potential to process enormous amounts of data by allocating partitioned datasets to numerous servers. Essentially, it is composed of two technologies. The first one is the Hadoop distributed file system (HDFS) which is a file system that divides data into smaller parts and distributes them across various servers. The second one is MapReduce, a software framework for parallel processing of data stored in HDFS. Several frameworks and tools have been developed around these technologies to facilitate the management of massive data in Hadoop [5].

Regarding the data and knowledge repositories, for the transactional and analytics databases the PostgreSQL database has been chosen, and the knowledge base is built on the Drools Business Rules Management System. The web application and the CDSS component are implemented in Java and are deployed on a Tomcat server.

With the aim to facilitate the integration between the platform and other information systems within the hospital a Health Level 7 (HL7) *Interface Engine* (IE) has been included. HL7 is a widely accepted set of standards for interoperability between healthcare organisations. Most HIS vendors adhere to these standards when developing application interfaces to exchange patient data. On the other hand, internal communication between components is also important. For instance, when the reasoning module triggers a rule reporting a patient risk, the alerts module needs to be notified in order to create and register a new alert entry in the database. For this reason the platform includes a *Java Message*

Service (JMS) server. JMS allows Java application components to create, send, receive, and read messages using reliable, asynchronous and loosely coupled communication. The combination of both JMS and the HL7 IE provides a flexible and comprehensive solution for the notification of clinical events between the Big Data platform and external information systems.

4   Decision Support

This section describes the different decision support modules that constitute the CDSS component of the platform. Figure 2 shows an schematic diagram.

4.1   Knowledge Representation and Reasoning

Clinical knowledge is mainly modelled as production (*if-then*) rules. The knowledge base consists of basically two kinds of rules: *alert rules* and EUCAST *expert rules* [11]. On the one hand, alert rules are used to notify users when certain abnormal conditions are met in a patient. Alert rules for detecting inappropriate use of antibiotics, dose adjustment, microbiological surveillance or detecting pathogens resistant to certain antibiotics are defined. On the other hand, EUCAST expert rules includes rules for intrinsic resistances of isolated bacterial species and rules with which to infer other susceptibilities and resistances from tests. Ontologies are used to model the hierarchical relationships of microorganisms and antibiotics when implementing EUCAST rules.

The *reasoning module* executes an instance of the rules engine with all the rules in the knowledge base. Then, all clinical facts available in the transactional database are also asserted into the working memory of the rules engine. Finally, when all rules are fired, the inferred alerts are stored in the transactional database so that clinicians can check them.

Definition of complex alert rules and EUCAST rules require the intervention of a knowledge engineer. However, the platform provides a simple tool to create custom alert rules. With this tool, platform's users enter different search criteria to be met for a patient along with the attributes of the alert that has to be

Fig. 2. Decision support modules included in the CDSS component

created when these criteria are met. Before the reasoning module instantiates the rules engine all the alert rules created with this tool are translated into the native rule language supported by the rules engine and subsequently are added to the knowledge base.

4.2 Antibiotic Prescription

Selecting an appropriate antibiotic treatment is a key decision task for clinicians because it implies important health and economic consequences. An antibiotic treatment is *empiric* or *targeted* depending on whether it is given to a patient before or after the specific microorganism causing the infection is known.

The *antibiotic prescription module* provides wizard and visual tools to assist platform's users in the prescription of appropriate empiric or targeted antibiotic treatments. This module uses the cumulative antibiogram of the hospital in order to compute a general measure of efficacy of antibiotics. This measure is based on the probabilities of occurrence of microorganisms (prevalence) and the probabilities that the microorganisms are resistant to antibiotics.

On the one hand, the wizard tool allows filtering antibiogram data by different criteria. The result is a list of antibiotics ranked by efficacy and confidence interval. On the other hand, the visual tool (see Fig. 3) uses the *Bipartite* model [4], which is a type of graphic that allows the amount of relationships between two set of separate elements (in this case the microorganisms and antibiotics) to be represented by means of a channel of different width. In this model the clinical concepts and their relationships have been represented through the use of visual properties, such as colour, intensity, area, width, length, position and sorting.

4.3 Global Surveillance

The monitoring of both clinical and process outcomes is important for proposing new clinical actions, and also for reviewing the impact of measures or policies on patient safety, economy or antibiotic resistance. Global surveillance and monitoring in the proposed platform is achieved by four modules. First, the *epidemiology module* visualises the evolution of statistical measures such as prevalence and incidence of microorganisms, antibiotics, microbiological sample types and alerts. It is also used to show measures of antibiotic consumption such as the defined daily dose (DDD) and the number of days of therapy (DOT). Second, the *dashboarding module* provides interactive charts that summarise global measures related to antibiograms, alerts and antibiotic recommendations over a specified time interval. Third, actionable reports are generated using the *reporting module*. Last, the *indicators module* computes several process indicators (see Fig. 4) whose results are presented in two forms: (i) as a run sequence plot showing the evolution of the indicator over time; and (ii) as a control table showing results of the current month and year, labelled with colour codes indicating the goodness of the result.

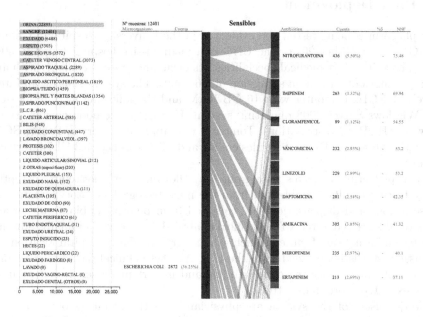

Fig. 3. Screenshot of the visual tool (bipartite model) for antibiotic prescription

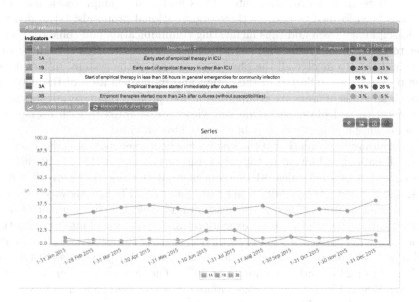

Fig. 4. Screenshot of the indicators module with control table (top) and run sequence plot (bottom)

5   Pilot Deployment

The platform is being tested and evaluated in the University Hospital of Getafe (UHG) since October 2014. The UHG is a medium-size hospital (approx. 500 beds), covering most medical specialities. Its occupancy rate is 83.35 %, with an average length of stay upon admission of 6.64 days. The system runs on an Intel Core i7 3.5 GHz computer with 16 GB RAM and the following installation set up: Windows Server 2008 operating system, Hadoop single-node cluster (Hortonworks HDP 2.4 distribution), Tomcat 8 web application server, PostgreSQL 9.4 database server, Drools 6.4 rules engine and MirthConnect 3.3 HL7 interface engine.

The platform integrates data from the following source systems: susceptibility testing results are obtained from the microbiology laboratory; treatment prescriptions and dispensations are collected from pharmacy; blood and other tests results are requested to the clinical analysis laboratory; and finally, administrative information of patients such as demographic data, hospital location or admission status is obtained from the HIS. All these clinical data are available at 24 h intervals, hence reasoning module and import processes do not require to be executed more frequently.

Major users of the system are physicians and the members of a recently implanted programme for antibiotic surveillance named PAMACTA (Programme for Multidisciplinary Assistance and Control of Antimicrobial Therapy). The PAMACTA team is composed of 9 members: 1 pharmacist, 2 microbiologists, 1 surgeon, 2 internists, 2 intensivists and 1 infectionpreventionist. This team has been formed to address three organisational proposals: (i) to define a multidisciplinary team and thus facilitating communication and collaboration in order to improve antibiotic use, (ii) to include a representative of each department, and (iii) to involve all the physicians as part of the system. In fact, these three proposals are reflected in the design and implementation of the platform in which all kinds of users are grouped into three profiles (manager, department-representative and physician). Different views are adapted to each user profile and messaging and feedback capabilities are also provided.

A performance evaluation of the system has been executed using data belonging to all patients admitted in the UHG during February 2015. The knowledge base consisted of 1465 rules: 91 of them were alert rules, 530 were EUCAST rules, and the rest were initialization or support rules. Figure 5 shows daily measures of the execution times of the reasoning module and the number of facts inserted in the rules engine. Total execution time is subdivided into initialization of the knowledge base, insertion of facts, execution of rules and storage of generated alerts. The average total execution time during this period was 314 s, with a minimum of 243 s and a maximum of 365 s. The average number of inserted facts was 52851. Finally, the average number of active alerts and new fired alerts per day were 441 and 71 respectively.

In the light of these results and in the case that clinical data were available more frequently, the reasoning module could run even every hour and therefore could generate alerts in near real time.

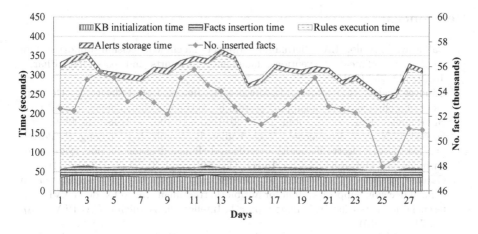

Fig. 5. Performance evaluation of the system during a month

6   Conclusions and Future Work

In this paper we have presented a CDSS platform for antibiotic surveillance in a hospital that integrates knowledge based and business intelligence technologies. Unlike other related systems, our proposal is focused in the whole hospital and deals with the problem of managing large sets of clinical data. For the design of the platform we have proposed a Big Data oriented architecture, based on the Hadoop distributed platform. Several decision support modules have been implemented. A reasoning module uses expert knowledge, which is represented as production rules, to generate daily alert notifications. Based on the cumulative antibiogram of the hospital, a wizard tool and a visual tool have been implemented to assist clinicians in the prescription of empiric and targeted antibiotic treatments. Modules for reporting, epidemiology, dashboarding and indicators have also been included in order to provide global monitoring and surveillance of both clinical and process outcomes. A pilot deployment in a university hospital shows that the system is valuable for antibiotic stewardship and surveillance.

Regarding future work, there are some issues still open. Clinical guidelines and mined rules might be included into the knowledge base (a first approach is shown in [2]). Moreover, a further exhaustive evaluation of the platform in terms of scalability, usability and utility will be considered. Finally, due to the advantages of the Big Data platform we will study to scale up the system to manage several hospitals. This will introduce interoperability challenges such as how to share and reuse the clinical knowledge (rules and CGs) and how to deal with different coding systems.

Acknowledgments. This work was partially funded by the Spanish Ministry of Economy and Competitiveness under the WASPSS project (Ref: TIN2013-45491-R) and by European Fund for Regional Development (EFRD, FEDER).

References

1. Calloway, S., Akilo, H.A., Bierman, K.: Impact of a clinical decision support system on pharmacy clinical interventions, documentation efforts, and costs. Hosp. Pharm. **48**(9), 744–752 (2013)
2. Cánovas-Segura, B., Campos, M., Morales, A., Juarez, J.M., Palacios, F.: Development of a clinical decision support system for antibiotic management in a hospital environment. Prog. Artif. Intell. 1–17 (2016). doi:10.1007/s13748-016-0089-x
3. Forrest, G.N., Van Schooneveld, T.C., Kullar, R., Schulz, L.T., Duong, P., Postelnick, M.: Use of electronic health records and clinical decision support systems for antimicrobial stewardship. Clin. Infect. Dis. **59**(Suppl. 3), S122–S133 (2014)
4. Garcia-Caballero, H., Campos, M., Juarez, J.M., Palacios, F.: Visualization in clinical decision support system for antibiotic treatment. In: Actas de la XVI Conferencia de la Asociación Española para la Inteligencia Artificial (CAEPIA 2015), pp. 71–80 (2015)
5. Grover, M., Malaska, T., Seidman, J., Shapira, G.: Hadoop Application Architectures. O'Reilly, Beijing (2015)
6. Groves, P., Kayyali, B., Knott, D., Kuiken, S.V.: The 'big data' revolution in healthcare: accelerating value and innovation. Center for US Health System Reform, Business Technology Office (2013)
7. Hopkins, B.: The patterns of big data. Technical report, Forrester Research, Inc. (2013)
8. Khazaei, H., McGregor, C., Eklund, M., El-khatib, K., Thommandram, A.: Toward a big data healthcare analytics system: a mathematical modeling perspective. In: 2014 IEEE World Congress on Services (SERVICES), pp. 208–215 (2014)
9. Koller, W., Blacky, A., Bauer, C., Mandl, H., Adlassnig, K.P.: Electronic surveillance of healthcare-associated infections with MONI-ICU - a clinical breakthrough compared to conventional surveillance systems. Stud. Health Technol. Inform. **160**(PART 1), 432–436 (2010)
10. Lamma, E., Mello, P., Nanetti, A., Riguzzi, F., Storari, S., Valastro, G.: Artificial intelligence techniques for monitoring dangerous infections. IEEE Trans. Inf. Technol. Biomed. **10**(1), 143–155 (2006)
11. Leclercq, R., Cantón, R., Brown, D.F.J., Giske, C.G., Heisig, P., Macgowan, A.P., Mouton, J.W., Nordmann, P., Rodloff, A.C., Rossolini, G.M., Soussy, C.J., Steinbakk, M., Winstanley, T.G., Kahlmeter, G.: EUCAST expert rules in antimicrobial susceptibility testing. Clin. Microbiol. Infect. **19**(2), 141–160 (2013)
12. Piddock, L.J.V.: The crisis of no new antibiotics–what is the way forward? Lancet. Infect. Dis. **12**(3), 249–253 (2012)
13. Raghupathi, W., Raghupathi, V.: Big data analytics in healthcare: promise and potential. Health Inf. Sci. Syst. **2**(1), 3 (2014)
14. Spellberg, B.: The antibiotic crisis: can we reverse 65 years of failed stewardship? Arch. Intern. Med. **171**(12), 1080–1081 (2011)
15. Steurbaut, K., Colpaert, K., Gadeyne, B., Depuydt, P., Vosters, P., Danneels, C., Benoit, D., Decruyenaere, J., De Turck, F.: COSARA: integrated service platform for infection surveillance and antibiotic management in the ICU. J. Med. Syst. **36**, 3765–3775 (2012)
16. Lo, Y.-S., Liu, C.-T.: Development of a hospital-acquired infection surveillance information system by using service-oriented architecture technology. In: 2010 3rd International Conference on Computer Science and Information Technology, pp. 449–453. IEEE (2010)

Predictive Analysis Tool for Energy Distribution Networks

Pablo Chamoso[1(✉)], Juan F. De Paz[1], Javier Bajo[2],
Gabriel Villarrubia[1], and Juan Manuel Corchado[1]

[1] Departamento de Informática y Automática,
Universidad de Salamanca, Plaza de la Merced, s/n, 37008 Salamanca, Spain
{chamoso, fcofds, gvg, corchado}@usal.es
[2] Department of Artificial Intelligence, Polytechnic University of Madrid,
Campus Montegancedo s/n, Boadilla del Monte, 28660 Madrid, Spain
jbajo@fi.upm.es

Abstract. There has been multiple research in the energy distribution sector over the last years because of the significant impact in societies. However, the use of aerial high voltage power lines involves some risks that may be avoided with periodic reviews. The objective of this work is to reduce the number of these reviews to reduce the maintenance cost of power lines. So the work is focused on the periodic review of transmission towers (TT). A virtual organization of agents in conjunction with different artificial intelligence methods and algorithms are proposed in order to reduce the number of TT to be reviewed. The proposed system is able to provide a sample of TT from a set of them, a whole line for example, to be reviewed and to ensure that the set will have similar values without needing to review all the TT. The result is a web application to manage all the review processes and all the TT of a country (Spain in this case). This allows the review companies to use the application either when they initiate a new review process for a whole line or area of TT, or when they want to place an entirely new set of TT, in which case the system would recommend the best place and the best type of structure to use.

1 Introduction

High voltage power lines maintenance is a problem that has generated a variety of research lines [3, 4, 9]. TT supporting that high voltage power lines have to be reviewed on a regular basis depending on their characteristics, specially if they are in urban places. In the reviews it is necessary to measure the ground resistance, the resistance of the TT, and also the step and touch potentials. These reviews are really expensive. However, many of the reviews could be predicted, as most of the TT share the same features and are located on terrain with similar characteristics. Therefore, the possibility of reducing the costs associated to this kind of maintenance is not only attractive, but quite reasonable.

As technology has continued to advance, there have been different approaches that attempt to apply innovations both in the review and the maintenance processes, resulting in a common need to reduce costs. Indeed, this is precisely the reason for having created the proposed predictive maintenance system.

© Springer International Publishing Switzerland 2016
O. Luaces et al. (Eds.): CAEPIA 2016, LNAI 9868, pp. 271–279, 2016.
DOI: 10.1007/978-3-319-44636-3_25

There are 4 common maintenance types for TT: (1) corrective, to solve existing problems; (2) preventive, to prevent the system from failures; (3) predictive, to predict possible irregularities; (4) proactive, which is a combination of preventive and predictive maintenances. The present work is focused on the predictive maintenance, where different techniques are already being used. Some authors have used artificial neural networks to model the environment, including [11], while other authors use neural networks to set failure times of the devices [13]. In addition, data mining or machine learning techniques are used to model different systems.

This study proposes a virtual organization of agents to predict the maintenance of TT by selecting only a sample for review which results in reducing that costs. The selection is autonomous and is based on different TT parameters that make it possible to determine the status of the analyzed lines of the TT. The system has built-in statistical sampling techniques combined with neural networks to estimate the ground resistance, as well as the step and touch potentials. In addition, the system provides different geopositioning tools to facilitate the search and selection of the TT and lines to be sampled.

The paper is organized as follows: Sect. 2 includes a revision of related work, Sect. 3 describes our proposal, Sect. 4 provides the preliminary results, and finally Sect. 5 shows the conclusions obtained and the future work.

2 Background

There are different kinds of maintenance types [1]: corrective, preventive, predictive and proactive.

Predictive maintenance refers to the capacity of generating assumptions or estimations about the status of a component. When predicting well-known processes, especially in process control [10], it is possible to generate a mathematical model which represents reality in a reliable way [7]. However, in other processes experimental techniques are needed, for example classification algorithms [6] or artificial neural networks [11]. This approach tries to extract and model the system features from historical data.

Support vector machines are used in [14] to predict the amount of ice that will be accumulated in aerial power lines. This is a serious problem that can interrupt the electrical service for a significant time, and the solution could be really expensive. Because of that proposed work, it is possible to estimate the level of ice (with a minimum error) by using historical meteorological data.

Another point to take into account is the machine performance (generators and current transformers). Due to the natural deterioration or machines over time, reviews are required over their useful lifespan. Periodic maintenance can be carried out, so machine performance is evaluated regularly, regardless of their status. This solution is not optimal when the review period is short and the machines are in perfect working condition. An alternative is based on monitoring the status of the equipment and evaluating some of their parameters. From the combination of these two options, a new model is presented in [15], where performance loss is predicted by the using failure rate and the performance degradation in conjunction with their derivatives and a Weibull distribution [13].

In other works such as [1], current transformer failures are analysed by Dissolved Gas Analysis (DGA). The currently existing methods are based on monitoring every substance ratio in oil; limit values are then established to determine all the possible failures [2]. The possibility of applying artificial neural networks and similar techniques to try to predict values is also presented in [1]. [12] applies Principal Component Analysis (PCA) and back-propagation artificial neural networks (BP-ANN) to obtain a discrete transformer status (normal, waiting for confirmation, abnormal). The accuracy levels reached are between 92 % and 96 % largely due to the input data PC treatment. Without this technique, the accuracy varies from 69 % to 75 %.

3 Proposal

The objective of this study is twofold: first, to predict the resistance of existing TT with unknown values, and second, to reduce the number of TT to be reviewed with samples. To carry out these tasks, we propose a multi-agent system (MAS), which follows the structure shown in Fig. 1. The organization data processing includes agents to process the information. In this organization there are 4 agents to predict the resistance, resistivity, Kp (step potential) and Kc (touch potentials). An additional agent provides a MLP to carry out these predictions. The Kp and Kc are calculated according to the Kr with the MLP and resistance and resistivity are calculated with the algorithm in Sect. 3.1.

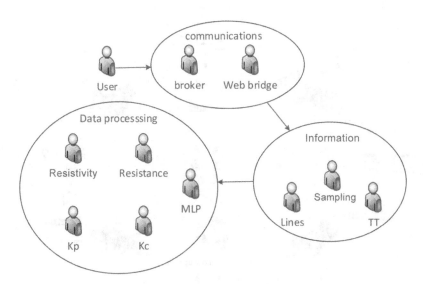

Fig. 1. Virtual organizations of agents

Other virtual organizations have less importance in the system. The information virtual organization contains three agents that manages the date related to the lines (set of connected TT), to the TT and the sample of towers to be revised. The communications virtual organization includes agents to receive and send messages to the web application (represented by the agent "User") and the delivery of the received messages to the system. That messages are first sent to the information virtual organization that will use the agents allocated in the data processing virtual organization when needed.

These agent system has been developed by using a modification of PANGEA, that uses FIPA ACL for the message structure specification [8].

3.1   Resistance and Resistivity Estimation

To estimate resistance as related to the different measured parameters, the only parameters used are those that were shown to influence the final value. To determine what the most influent parameters are, the correlation analysis and Kruskal Wallis methods were used. Once these parameters were known, the estimation was carried out by a CBR system, as shown in Fig. 2. The cases memory is grouped by the TT types as defined by their Kr value. To group them by their Kr value, PAM (Partitioning Around Medoids) is applied; the Henning and Liao [5] proposal is then used to determine the number of clusters. More specifically, three clusters are generated from a list of approximately 60000 TT in Spain, and we only have values for the location and the Kr value. In these three clusters, the cases base is organized whereby every case contains: resistivity, temperature, humidity, Kr and resistance values.

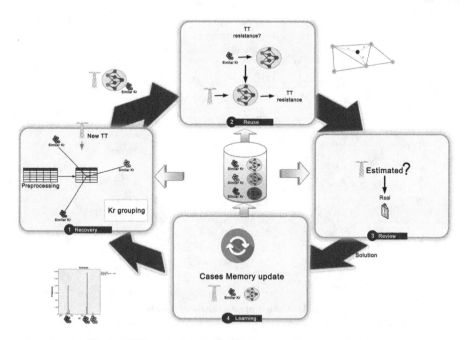

Fig. 2.   CBR cycle for the resistivity and resistance estimation.

Every cluster has a trained multi-layer perceptron (MLP) where the inputs are resistivity, humidity, temperature and Kr, and the output is the resistance. In the recovery phase, the system recovers the previously trained network associated to the new Kr value. In the adaptation phase the network is used to generate the prediction. Finally, the data and training are updated in the revise phase.

With regards to the proposed CBR algorithm, its input is based either on the known information about a TT that already exists in the system, or a fictitious TT to be placed in a determined location. The only difference for the algorithm is the evaluation of the nearest neighbors.

First, the nearest neighbors have to be found and identified depending on different established parameters such as the maximum distance to be considered a neighbor, or the maximum number of neighbors to use.

Once determined, if the TT resistivity is unknown, it is estimated by the Inverse Distance Weighting (DW) method by applying this equation:

$$\bar{\rho} = \sum_1^n \rho(TT_i) * \frac{D_{max}/d_i}{\sum_1^n D_{max}/d_i} \tag{1}$$

Where: $\rho(TT_i)$ is the resistivity of the ith TT, D_{max} is the largest distance, d_i is the distance of the ith TT.

The equation provides the resistivity value with an estimated deviation of σ^2, where:

When the resistivity value and range of the TT are obtained, the value of the resistance can be estimated. In order to estimate the resistance, an artificial neural network is used, specifically, an MLP with four inputs: resistivity, Kr value, ground humidity and temperature. The hidden layer consists of 9 neurons and provides a single output with the value of the estimated resistance.

3.2   Sampling

One of the objectives of this work is to reduce the number of reviews in order to reduce the TT maintenance cost. To attain this objective, a new algorithm was proposed. It uses several TT parameters as inputs, such as the Kr value, which determines the type of the TT, and the TT resistivity value to create stratums which are defined based on both parameters. The proposed algorithm follows these steps:

1. The sample provided as an algorithm input is analyzed to determine how many Kr intervals will be generated. For every interval, a list with the corresponding TT is created, so TT are now grouped by type (Kr value).
2. All lists are sorted in ascending order according to TT resistivity.
3. Once the lists are sorted, the deciles are calculated for each of the lists created according to the resistivity of similar Kr TT groups (step 2). The lowest and highest resistivity values of every list are also stored.
4. For every list of Kr groups (step 2) there are 10 sublists (step 3) containing TT with similar structure (associated to the Kr value) and similar resistance. The algorithm

will now contain n lists (equal to the number of Kr intervals selected in step 1), which are in turn divided into 10 sublists, which are generated after calculating the deciles in the lists found at the first level.

5. Variance is calculated and stored for every sublist created in step 4.
6. The maximum error e is calculated and stored for every sublist from step 4. This error is considered as the maximum between 0.1 mid-point of two consecutive deciles and 0.1 distance between two consecutive deciles:

$$e = Max[0.1 * \frac{d[i] + d[i+1]}{2}, 0.1 * (d[i+1] - d[i])] \tag{2}$$

7. From the sublists generated in 4, the variance calculated in 5, and the maximum error calculated in 6, the number of TT to be reviewed for every sublist n is defined by the following equation:

$$n = N * z^2 * \sigma^2 / ((N-1) * e^2 + z^2 * \sigma^2)) \tag{3}$$

where: N is the size number of TT, n: Number of TT to review for every sublist, $z = 1.9599$, σ deviation, e is maximum error allowed

8. The output of the algorithm, n is provided for every sublist.
   If the output number is too high the interval is divided recursively to reduce the elements in the sample.

4 Results

The system offers a web application with a series of tools for companies in charge of reviewing the TT. For example, the user can select a set of lines of an area to be reviewed and the system will show the user a subset of TT to review that would ensure that the system works fine with a confidence level of 95 % (this percentage is directly related to the value of z). This makes it possible to reduce the number of TT to be reviewed, with the added benefit of improving efficiency and reducing costs.

Figure 3 shows the process to execute the algorithm and obtain the result. In the figure some TT in the South-East coast of Spain are selected, as seen in "2. Selected towers are shown on the map". When the algorithm is run, the system proposes the review of 42 TT from the initial 119 ("4a. Number of towers to review") and shows exactly which TT have to be reviewed in "4b. Towers to be reviewed". Finally, the user can see where the proposed TT are on the map or the output, as well as the details of every algorithm step in "5. Algorithm details, steps and outputs can be shown".

The web application provides an additional tool. Since one part of the required calculations is already included in the previously implemented sample algorithm, it would be worthwhile to include a tool that could determine the best structure to use in each location. In addition, unknown resistivity and resistance values of existing TT can be estimated. This is a very frequent situation because there is no information of most TT throughout Spain. Figure 4 shows an example of this functionality, where values

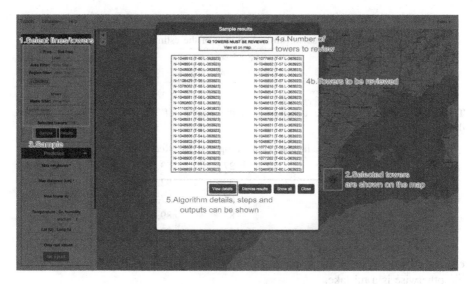

Fig. 3. Web application, sampling process

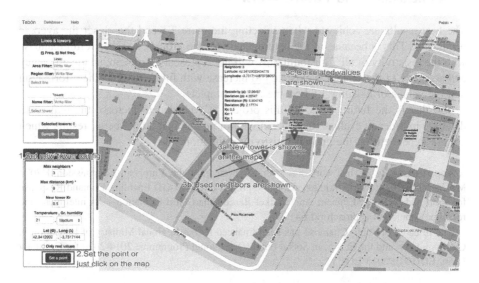

Fig. 4. Web application, new or existing TT values prediction process.

for a new TT are estimated by taking into consideration just 3 neighbors (this is just for demonstration purposes, 3 neighbors is a really poor number for real cases).

In general, the efficiency on of the algorithm is evaluated according to the accuracy of the estimation and the proposed reduction percentage, which can be seen in Tables 1 and 2. To evaluate the system, 1600 TT have been reviewed so we have real data and them we have applied the algorithms over them. When the real value is inside the range

Table 1. Accuracy percentage on the estimation according to the mean distance.

Average distance (km)	Accuracy of the estimation (%)
~1	98.85 %
~5	97.74 %

Table 2. Reduction percentage depending on the number of selected TT and the average distance.

TT	Average distance (km)	Proposed TT	Reduction (%)
100	~50	27	73 %
200	~50	35	82.5 %
500	~50	64	87.2 %
800	~50	83	89.625 %
800	~300	154	80.75 %

estimated by the system (the proposed value ± the deviation value), we consider it as a hit, otherwise is a mistake.

5   Conclusions and Future Work

The best results are achieved when selecting the more TT and the closer the average distance is. This is because of the heterogeneity of the ground, so when a full database with the resistivity of all TT is built, this will not represent a problem, so the efficiency and accuracy of the system is expected to increase with future work as the information and the values of existing TT become more complete.

So that is the future work for this project. It's needed to increase the real cases database in order to evaluate the system with more real data to get better results which are not dependent on the ground resistivity estimation.

Acknowledgments.   This work has been supported by the European Commission H2020 MSCA-RISE-2014: Marie Skłodowska-Curie project DREAM-GO Enabling Demand Response for short and real-time Efficient And Market Based Smart Grid Operation - An intelligent and real-time simulation approach ref 641794.

The research of Pablo Chamoso has been financed by the Regional Ministry of Education in Castilla y León and the European Social Fund (Operational Programme 2014-2020 for Castilla y León, EDU/310/2015 BOCYL).

References

1. de Faria, H., Costa, J.G.S., Olivas, J.L.M.: A review of monitoring methods for predictive maintenance of electric power transformers based on dissolved gas analysis. Renew. Sustain. Energy Rev. **46**, 201–209 (2015)
2. Duval, M., DePabla, A.: Interpretation of gas-in-oil analysis using new IEC publication 60599 and IEC TC 10 databases. IEEE Electr. Insul. Mag. **17**(2), 31–41 (2001)

3. Eltawil, M.A., Zhao, Z.: Grid-connected photovoltaic power systems: technical and potential problems—a review. Renew. Sustain. Energy Rev. **14**(1), 112–129 (2010)
4. Gonçalves, R.S., Carvalho, J.C.M.: Review and latest trends in mobile robots used on power transmission lines. Int. J. Adv. Robot. Syst. (Print) **10**, 1–14 (2013)
5. Hennig, C., Liao, T.: How to find an appropriate clustering for mixed-type variables with application to socio-economic stratification. J. Roy. Stat. Soc. Ser. C Appl. Stat. **62**, 309–369 (2013)
6. Krishnanand, K.R., Dash, P.K., Naeem, M.H.: Detection, classification, and location of faults in power transmission lines. Int. J. Electr. Power Energy Syst. **67**, 76–86 (2015)
7. Na, M.G.: Auto-tuned PID controller using a model predictive control method for the steam generator water level. IEEE Trans. Nucl. Sci. **48**(5), 1664–1671 (2001)
8. Sánchez, A., Villarrubia, G., Zato, C., Rodríguez, S., Chamoso, P.: A gateway protocol based on FIPA-ACL for the new agent platform PANGEA. In: Pérez, J.B., et al. (eds.) Trends in Practical Applications of Agents and Multiagent Systems. AISC, vol. 221, pp. 41–51. Springer, Heidelberg (2013)
9. Singh, J., Gandhi, K., Kapoor, M., Dwivedi, A.: New approaches for live wire maintenance of transmission lines. MIT Int. J. Electr. Instrum. Eng. **3**(2), 67–71 (2013)
10. Lipták, B.G. (ed.): Process Control: Instrument Engineers' Handbook. Butterworth-Heinemann, Burlington (2013)
11. Taher, S.A., Sadeghkhani, I.: Estimation of magnitude and time duration of temporary overvoltages using ANN in transmission lines during power system restoration. Simul. Model. Pract. Theory **18**(6), 787–805 (2010)
12. Trappey, A.J., Trappey, C.V., Ma, L., Chang, J.C.: Intelligent engineering asset management system for power transformer maintenance decision supports under various operating conditions. Comput. Ind. Eng. **84**, 3–11 (2015)
13. Weibull, W.: Wide applicability. J. Appl. Mech. **103**, 33 (1951)
14. Zarnani, A., Musilek, P., Shi, X., Ke, X., He, H., Greiner, R.: Learning to predict ice accretion on electric power lines. Eng. Appl. Artif. Intell. **25**(3), 609–617 (2012)
15. Zhou, D., Zhang, H., Weng, S.: A novel prognostic model of performance degradation trend for power machinery maintenance. Energy **78**, 740–746 (2014)

Quantifying Potential Benefits of Horizontal Cooperation in Urban Transportation Under Uncertainty: A Simheuristic Approach

Carlos L. Quintero-Araujo[1,2]([envelope]), Aljoscha Gruler[1], and Angel A. Juan[1]

[1] IN3 - Department of Computer Science, Universitat Oberta de Catalunya,
Av. Carl Friedrich Gauss 5, 08860 Castelldefels, Spain
{cquinteroa,agruler,ajuanp}@uoc.edu
[2] International School of Economics and Administrative Sciences,
Universidad de La Sabana, Autopista Norte Km 7, Chía, Colombia

Abstract. Horizontal Cooperation (HC) in transportation activities has the potential to decrease supply chain costs and the environmental impact of delivery vehicles related to greenhouse gas emissions and noise. Especially in urban areas the sharing of information and facilities among members of the same supply chain level promises to be an innovative transportation concept. This paper discusses the potential benefits of HC in supply chains with stochastic demands by applying a simheuristic approach. For this, we integrate Monte Carlo Simulation into a metaheuristic process based on Iterated Local Search and Biased Randomization. A non-cooperative scenario is compared to its cooperative counterpart which is formulated as multi-depot Vehicle Routing Problem with stochastic demands (MDVRPSD).

Keywords: Horizontal cooperation · Simheuristics · MDVRPSD · Biased randomization · Iterated local search

1 Introduction

Driven by fierce competition, rapidly changing customer demands, and the need for high service levels, efficient transportation activities are of major importance for companies [5]. However, transportation activities should not only be viewed from a cost- and customer satisfaction point of view. Especially in urban areas freight transportation yields consequences related to the environment, society, and economy that impact a range of different stakeholders. As such, transportation accounts for over a quarter of total greenhouse gas emissions in the USA [27], while 41 % of Europeans are affected by extensive noise levels through freight transportation vehicles in cites [7]. Furthermore, urban areas account for 85 % of total Gross Domestic Product (GDP) in the European Union (EU), leading to increased interest of municipalities in efficient transportation systems to fortify their cities economic attractiveness [6].

© Springer International Publishing Switzerland 2016
O. Luaces et al. (Eds.): CAEPIA 2016, LNAI 9868, pp. 280–289, 2016.
DOI: 10.1007/978-3-319-44636-3_26

In recent years, Horizontal Cooperation (HC) has been increasingly discussed in theory and practice as transportation model to decrease the negative impacts of transportation. In HC scenarios, companies on the same supply chain level—e.g. suppliers, manufacturers, retailers—cooperate by sharing information and resources. For example by using the same warehouses or transportation vehicles, the aim is to decrease overall transportation costs through economies-of-scale and higher resource utilization [2,22]. HC is defined by [1] as "a business agreement between two or more companies at the same level in the supply chain or network in order to allow ease of work and co-operation towards achieving a common objective".

To show the potential benefits of HC in Logistics and Transportation (L&T), we solve different variants of the well-known Vehicle Routing Problem (VRP) [26]. In the non-cooperative case, each company plans the optimal routing plans, which can be formulated as capacitated VRP (see Fig. 1, *left*). In a cooperative scenario (*right*), better overall routing solutions (in terms of monetary and environmental aspects) can be obtained by sharing customers and some resources. In the Figure below, the difference between both cases can be intuitively observed.

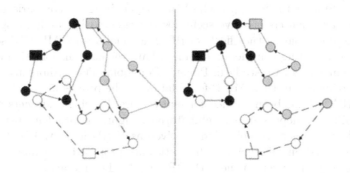

Fig. 1. HC example

Considering that HC often involves the cooperation of competitors, the potential micro and macro benefits of the concept need to be quantified in order to convince company decision makers of its implementation. In this paper we will show the potential benefits of HC by comparing a non-cooperative scenario in which each company individually optimizes their routes with its cooperative counterpart which we solve as MDVRP. Our metaheuristic approach is based on Biased Randomization (BR) [16] and Iterated Local Search (ILS) [19], which we combine with Monte Carlo Simulation in a simheuristic framework [17]. Like this we are able to solve the MDVRP with stochastic demands (MDVRPSD) as additional contribution of this work.

In the following, this paper is structured as follows: Sect. 2 reviews related work regarding HC, the MDVRP, and simheuristic applications; the problem setting is formalized in Sect. 3; Sect. 4 outlines the applied metaheuristic and its combination with simulation; the results of a set of experiments that were run to quantify our approach are presented and discussed in Sect. 5; finally, Sect. 6 summarizes the highlights of this paper.

2   Literature Review

2.1   Horizontal Cooperation

HC is often discussed in the context of City Logistics development, which is based on the collaboration of different supply chain actors in urban areas. As such, [8] present a methodology to study the impact of collaborative transportation networks, especially the case of Urban Consolidation Centers in a case study in France. Their approach is based on Game Theory and the GRASP metaheuristic for the resulting routing problems. In [11], the authors develop a decision support system based on simulation to evaluate collaborative demand pooling.

One of the main advantages of HC lies in the global optimization of transportation activities in supply chains. In contrast to that, optimization of vehicle routes that focus on different individual companies cannot reach the same overall benefits. Similar to the approach of this paper, in [21] a comparison among cooperative and non cooperative scenarios is presented by solving single VRP instances and comparing the effects of HC in a collaborative MDVRP scenario. Their problem setting considers last-mile urban freight transportation and collection schemes in a case study in Bogota, Colombia. The authors also address stochastic demands in their MILP formulation of the problem.

The MDVRP has been studied for many years. Hereby, customers are allocated to different depots in a combinatorial assignment problem, before each depot-node assignment combination is solved as VRP. Some MDVRP solution approaches based on different metaheuristics are proposed for example by [23] or [28]. For a good review on the MDVRP see [20]. The metaheuristic approach used in this paper is based to the one proposed by [18], where the deterministic MDVRP is solved by combining ILS with BR.

2.2   Simheuristics for COPs Under Uncertainty

Many COPs experience a certain level of uncertainty concerning different input parameters in real-life applications. In the development of solution algorithms to such stochastic problems, the stochastic information is typically included in the objective function or the constraints of the mathematical problem formulation [3]. Simheuristics can be characterized as so called *a priori* stochastic optimization. That is, random variables are modeled according to a probability function during the planning process, which is later not changed during the execution [25].

Simheuristics allows the consideration of stochastic objective functions and constraints by including simulation in a metaheuristic based framework [17]. Given a stochastic problem setting, the random variables are transformed into their deterministic counterpart by considering expected values, which can be solved using efficient metaheuristics for deterministic COPs. In the following the constructed a priori solution is evaluated in a stochastic scenario by running several simulation runs in which the stochastic variable is depicted from a given (theoretical or empirical) probability distribution.

Different simheuristic implementations have been presented. Stochastic demands in routing problems are for example addressed by [13], who investigate the effect of safety stocks in routing under uncertainty. The Arc Routing Problem with stochastic demands is discussed by [10]. Furthermore, simheuristics have been applied to tackle the complex Inventory Routing Problem (IRP) with stochastic demands [15], in which centralized decisions about inventory management and routing activities are taken. Other applications of simheuristics can be found in the field of flow shop problems [12] or in dynamic home-service routing with synchronized ride-sharing [9].

3 Problem Description

We present two different HC decision-making scenarios related to urban distribution with stochastic demands: *(i)* a non-cooperative scenario which is equivalent to solve m Capacitated Vehicle Routing Problems (where m represents the number of companies involved in the cooperation agreement); and *(ii)* a cooperative scenario which can be modeled as MDVRP.

3.1 Non-Cooperative Scenario

To represent a non-cooperative scenario, we assume that each company serves its own customer set $I = n_1, n_2, ..., n_n$ from their central depot n_0 with their available (capacitated) vehicles. That is, the vehicles deliver the demand of each customer i (with $d_i > 0$), whereas the depot capacity is unlimited and travel costs c_{ij} (e.g. distance, time, NOx-emissions) between any two clients are known. While the objective function is to minimize total costs, problem constraints include that every customer is only served by one vehicle, all routes start and end at the central depot, and that no vehicle can stop twice at the same customer.

3.2 Cooperative Scenario

In this scenario, different companies cooperate in the execution of tasks linked to the final distribution of goods to serve different customers. We assume that the cooperation agreement includes the sharing of *(i)* storage areas inside the facilities; and *(ii)* vehicle capacities, in order to facilitate joint distribution tasks. As a first step, each customer needs to be assigned to a depot. Then, a set of routes is planned in order to satisfy customer demands. In terms of optimization problems, this scenario corresponds to a MDVRP.

4 Solution Approach

Our solution approach to the MDVRPSD consists of two main phases. First, we create different customer-depot allocation maps which we evaluate using the randomized version of the CWS to solve the deterministic counterpart of the stochastic problem. This process is integrated into an ILS framework to create numerous allocation maps. Then, we apply MCS to evaluate the behavior of the most promising allocation maps in a stochastic environment.

To create different customer-depot allocation maps we use a biased round-robin criterion. That is, a distance based priority list of potential customers for depot k is created based on the marginal savings μ_i^k of serving a customer i from each depot $k \in V_d$, compared to serving it from the best alternative depot k^* (such that $\mu_i^k = c_i^{k^*} - c_i^k$). Next, the nodes are randomly assigned. Each depot iteratively 'chooses' an unassigned customer to serve from its priority list. At each step, the probability of adding the customer with the highest potential savings to the map is defined by parameter $\alpha(0 \leq \alpha \leq 1)$. This parameter defines the specific geometric distribution used to assign the diminishing probability distributions for each edge, whereby all edges are potentially eligible.

Once all customers have been assigned, the created map is evaluated using the extended version of the CWS based on biased randomization as described by [14]. In order to test different customer-depot allocation maps, we implement the described procedure into an ILS framework. Hereby, we consider the deterministic counterpart of the stochastic problem by using expected demands at each customer. After finding an initial solution (which is set as $currentBest$) and the corresponding allocation map, the map is perturbed by applying a destroy-and-repair strategy, in which $p\%$ of customers are exchanged among the depots. The resulting allocation map is evaluated again using the extended CWS algorithm. Accordingly, the current best solution is updated when necessary. Furthermore, we include an acceptance criterion which allows a solution worsening of $currentBest$ in some cases. More specifically, we accept the current best solution to worsen to a certain extend when the last iteration from x to x^* was an improvement $(f(x) > f(x^*))$, and the difference between the current best solution and the new solution x^{**} is not bigger than the last improvement step $(|f(x) - f(x^*)| < f(x^{**}) - f(x^*))$. This increases the solution search space and avoids the algorithm running into local minima. The described ILS procedure is run for $pertubTime$ seconds, during which the m most promising (deterministic) solutions are defined. See Algorithm 1 for an overview over the applied approach.

This solution set is then evaluated in a stochastic scenario. Hereby, we assume a positive correlation between high-quality deterministic solutions and their stochastic counterpart with relatively low-variances. By simulating only the most promising deterministic customer-depot allocation maps we keep the computational effort manageable. To test the behavior of each solution considering stochastic demands, we repeatedly sample random demands using MCS [24]. That is, during each of a total of $nIter$ simulation runs, the demand d_i of each customer i is sampled from a probability function using the expected demands as mean and considering a demand variance $Var[d_i]$. In our case we use a log-normal

Inputs: V_d; I; α; p
//Depots, customers, distribution parameter, customers to be exchanged
$M \leftarrow \emptyset$
//Set of Promising Solutions
Priority List $\leftarrow$ establish customer priorities $\forall d \in V$
establish customer-depot allocation map(α)
initSol $\leftarrow$ solve map using randomized CWS
initSol = *currentBest*
while *pertubtime not reached* **do**
    pertubate current map(p)
    newSol $\leftarrow$ solve map using randomized CWS
    if *newSol* < *currentBest*|| *acceptance criterion is met* **then**
    | *newSol* = *currentBest*
    end
end
return Set M of promising deterministic solutions

Algorithm 1. Establishment of Promising Solutions

distribution, but any other theoretical (e.g. Weibull) or empirical probability distribution providing positive values could have also been used.

Through the repeated simulation of customer demands, the stochastic costs can be estimated. As vehicle capacities are limited, a higher-than-expected overall demand will lead to route failures. That is, the vehicle has to return to the depot to fill up its stock before continuing its route. Accordingly, we penalize a route failure by adding additional costs for a round trip from the current customer to the depot and back. The overall stochastic solutions are estimated by summing the costs of all round trip failures during each simulation run n and dividing it by the total number of simulation runs, so that *expectedStochCosts* $= \frac{\sum_{n=0}^{nIter} RouteFailCost_n}{nIter}$. Route failures also affect the reliability of the solution. For each route, we estimate its reliability using the following formula: $RouteReliability = (1 - \frac{\sum_{n=0}^{nIter} RouteFailuresCount}{nIters}) * 100\,\%$. Therefore, the reliability of the solution is obtained by multiplying the reliabilities of the corresponding routes.

The simulation allows for a reliable estimate of the expected total costs of each suggested MDVRP solution by summing the deterministic costs and *expectedStochCosts*. At this stage we suggest the use of short and long simulation runs. By applying a short simulation with *nIterShort* iterations to each promising solution a first estimate of the overall stochastic solution can be obtained. After this first simulation, the promising solutions are re-ranked to define e elite solutions through a more reliable simulation by using more simulation runs *nIterLong*. Finally our approach returns a list of MDVRPSD solutions. See Algorithm 2 for a description of the simulation procedure.

Input: M; $nIter$; $Var[d_i]$
//*Set of promising deterministic Solutions, number of Simulation runs (short and long), demand variance level*
$E \leftarrow \emptyset$
//*Set of Elite Solutions*
for *each solution* $\in M$ **do**
| run short simulation ($nIterShort$)
| estimate *expectedStochCosts*
| **if** *solution among best e stochastic solutions* **then**
| | include solution in E
| **end**
end
for *each solution* $\in E$ **do**
| run long simulation ($nIterLong$)
end
return Set reliable stochastic MDVRPSD solutions

Algorithm 2. Simulation of Stochastic Demands

5   Experiments and Discussion of Results

In order to allow the assessment of the aforementioned scenarios, we have carried out preliminary tests using five benchmark instances proposed by [4] for the MDVRP. The algorithm was implemented as Java application and run on a Macbook Pro Core i5-2.4 GHz processor with 8 GB RAM. Each instance was transformed to fit the non-cooperative scenario by using a greedy distance-based heuristic (round robin tournament) which iteratively assigns each customer to its closest facility. Both scenarios were tested using biased randomization-based algorithms already available in the literature. The non-cooperative scenario was solved by using the SR-GCWS-CS proposed in [14], whereas the cooperative case was solved by means of the BR-ILS algorithm explained in Sect. 4.

The following values were used for the different parameters during the execution of tests:

– $nIterShort$ (short simulation runs): 30
– $nIterLong$ (long simulation runs): 5000
– α (geometric distribution parameter for customer allocation) : 0.05–0.8
– p (percentage of customers allocated to new depots): 10 %–50 %
– m (number of promising solutions): 10
– e (number of elite solutions): 5

In Table 1 we can see the comparative results among non-cooperative (NC) and cooperative (HC) scenarios in a deterministic environment ($Var[d_i] = 0\,\%$). Next to the instance specifications, this table reports the deterministic costs of scenario as well as the benefits generated by implementing HC. On average, HC leads to route savings of 3.93 % with values rising up to 7.3 %.

Table 2 shows the results for a low-variance demand ($Var[d_i] = 5\,\%$). For each scenario, we include the expected stochastic costs (which are the estimated

Table 1. Results for the deterministic scenario

Instance name	Depots	Customers	Vehicles/ depots	Vehicle capacity	NC costs	HC costs	Delta cost
P01	4	50	4	500	624.74	582.34	7.28 %
P07	4	100	4	100	963.17	898.97	7.14 %
P10	4	249	8	500	3876.16	3765.49	2.94 %
P15	4	160	5	60	2617.26	2570.54	1.82 %
P23	9	360	5	60	6145.58	6117.74	0.46 %
Average							**3.93 %**

Table 2. Results with $Var[d_i] = 5\%$

Instance name	NC det. costs	NC stochas-tic costs	NC expected total costs	NC expected reliability	HC det. costs	HC stochastic costs	HC expected total costs	HC expected reliability
P01	624.74	2.37	627.11	91.02 %	582.34	1.99	584.33	92.75 %
P07	963.17	5.03	968.20	82.41 %	898.97	2.97	901.95	89.80 %
P10	3876.16	22.39	3898.56	69.13 %	3765.49	22.20	3787.69	69.99 %
P15	2617.26	0.00	2617.26	100.00 %	2570.54	0.46	2571.00	98.36 %
P23	6145.58	0.00	6145.58	100.00 %	6117.74	0.00	6117.74	100.00 %

costs for corrective actions), the expected total costs and the expected reliability of the solution. It can be seen that the cooperative scenario outperforms the non-cooperative case in all considered instances. Expected stochastic costs and reliabilities show similar values in both scenarios.

6 Conclusion

This paper discusses possible savings through the implementation of HC strategies in problem settings under uncertainty. It is shown that HC can lead to a reduction of distribution costs by considering two different scenarios which represent alternative degrees of cooperation by identifying and solving the corresponding optimization problems. Moreover, a realistic situation is considered by adding uncertainty to customer demands.

The developed simheuristic approach includes Biased Randomization, Iterated Local Search and Monte Carlo Simulation. According to the preliminary tests carried out using instances from a well-known benchmark set for the MDVRP, a cooperative strategy can contribute to reduction in total costs for all the considered instances. The average costs reduction is around 4 % with values rising up to 7.3 %. Future research could evaluate further routing aspects, e.g. the impact of HC on environmental and social issues. Also, the stochastic component could be extended to consider stochastic travel times or other input variables under uncertainty.

Acknowledgements. This work has been partially supported by the Spanish Ministry of Economy and Competitiveness (TRA2013-48180-C3-P and TRA2015-71883-REDT), and FEDER. Likewise, we want to acknowledge the support received by the Department of Universities, Research & Information Society of the Catalan Government (2014-CTP-00001), the Special Patrimonial Fund from Universidad de La Sabana and the doctoral grant of the UOC.

References

1. Bahinipati, B., Kanada, A., Deshmukh, S.: Horizontal collaboration in semiconductor manufacturing industry supply chain: an evaluation of collaboration intensity index. Comput. Ind. Eng. **57**, 880–895 (2009)
2. Ballot, E., Fontane, F.: Reducing transportation CO2 emissions through pooling of supply networks: perspectives from a case study in french retail chains. Prod. Plan. Control **21**(6), 640–650 (2010)
3. Bianchi, L., Dorigo, M., Gambardella, L.M., Gutjahr, W.J.: A survey on metaheuristics for stochastic combinatorial optimization. Nat. Comput. **8**(2), 239–287 (2009)
4. Cordeau, J.F., Gendreau, M., Laporte, G.: A tabu search heuristic for periodic and multi-depot vehicle routing problems. Networks **30**, 105–119 (1997)
5. Ehmke, J.F.: Integration of Information and Optimization Models for Routing in City Logistics. Springer Science+Business, New York (2012)
6. European Commission: Cities of tomorrow - challanges, visions, ways forward. Publications Office of the European Union (2011)
7. European Environment Agency: Eea draws the first map of Europe's noise exposure (2009). http://www.eea.europa.eu/media/newsreleases/eea-draws-the-first-map-of-europe2019s-noise-exposure
8. Faure, L., Battaia, G., Marquès, G., Guillaume, R., Vega-Mejía, C.A., Montova-Torres, J.R., Muñoz-Villamizar, A., Quintero-Araújo, C.L.: How to anticipate the level of activity of asustainable collaborative network: the case of urban freight delivery throughlogistics platforms. In: IEEE International Conference on Digital Ecosystems and Technologies, pp. 126–131 (2013)
9. Fikar, C., Juan, A., Martinez, E., Hirsch, P.: A discrete-event driven metaheuristic for dynamic home service routing with synchronised trip sharing. Eur. J. Ind. Eng. **10**(3), 323–340 (2016)
10. González, S., Riera, D., Juan, A., Elizondo, M., Fonseca, P.: SIM-RandSHARP: a hybrid algorithm for solving the Arc routing problem with stochastic demands. In: Proceedings of the 2012 Winter Simulation Conference, pp. 1–11 (2012)
11. Gonzalez-Feliu, J., Routhier, J.: Sustainable Urban Logistics: Concepts, Methods and Information Systems. Springer, Heidelberg (2014)
12. Juan, A.A., Barrios, B.B., Vallada, E., Riera, D., Jorba, J.: A simheuristic algorithm for solving the permutation flow shop problem with stochastic processing times. Simul. Model. Pract. Theor. **46**, 101–117 (2014)
13. Juan, A.A., Faulin, J., Grasman, S., Riera, D., Marull, J., Mendez, C.: Using safety stocks and simulation to solve the vehicle routing problem with stochastic demands. Transp. Res. Part C: Emerg. Technol. **19**(5), 751–765 (2011)
14. Juan, A.A., Faulin, J., Jorba, J., Riera, D., Masip, D., Barrios, B.: On the use of monte carlo simulation, cache and splitting techniques to improve the clarke and wright savings heuristics. J. Oper. Res. Soc. **62**(6), 1085–1097 (2011)

15. Juan, A.A., Grasman, S.E., Caceres-Cruz, J., Bektaş, T.: A simheuristic algorithm for the single-period stochastic inventory-routing problem with stock-outs. Simul. Model. Pract. Theor. **46**, 40–52 (2014)
16. Juan, A.A., Faulin, J., Ferrer, A., Lourenço, H.R., Barrios, B.: MIRHA: multi-start biased randomization of heuristics with adaptive local search for solving non-smooth routing problems. Top **21**(1), 109–132 (2013)
17. Juan, A.A., Faulin, J., Grasman, S.E., Rabe, M., Figueira, G.: A review of simheuristics: extending metaheuristics to deal with stochastic combinatorialoptimization problems. Oper. Res. Perspect. **2**, 62–72 (2015)
18. Juan, A.A., Pascual, I., Guimarans, D., Barrios, B.: Combining biased randomization with iterated local search for solving the multidepot vehicle routing problem. Int. Trans. Oper. Res. **22**(4), 647–667 (2015)
19. Lourenço, H.R., Martin, O.C., Stützle, T.: Iteratedlocal search: framework and applications. In: Gendreau, M., Potvin, J. (eds.) Handbook of Metaheuristics, 2nd edn, pp. 363–397. Springer, New York (2010)
20. Montoya-Torres, J.R., Franco, J.L., Isaza, S.N., Jiménez, H.F., Herazo-Padilla, N.: A literature review on the vehicle routing problem with multiple depots. Comput. Ind. Eng. **79**, 115–129 (2015)
21. Muñoz-Villamizar, A., Montoya-Torres, J., Vega-Mejía, C.A.: Non-collaborative versus collaborative last-mile delivery in urban systems with stochastic demands. Procedia CIRP **30**, 263–268 (2015)
22. Pérez-Bernabeu, E., Juan, A.A., Faulin, J., Barrios, B.B.: Horizontal cooperation in road transportation: a case illustrating savings in distances and greenhouse gas emissions. Int. Trans. Oper. Res. **22**(3), 585–606 (2015)
23. Pisinger, D., Ropke, S.: A general heuristic for vehicle routing problems. Comput. Oper. Res. **34**, 2403–2435 (2007)
24. Raychaudhuri, S.: Introduction to monte carlo simulation. In: Proceedings of the 2008 Winter Simulation Conference, pp. 91–100 (2008)
25. Ritzinger, U., Puchinger, J., Hartl, R.F.: A survey on dynamic and stochastic vehicle routing problems. Int. J. Prod. Res. **54**(1), 215–231 (2016)
26. Toth, P., Vigo, D. (eds.): Vehicle Routing - Problems, Methods and Applications, 2nd edn. SIAM - Society for Industrial and Applied Mathematics, Philadelphia (2014)
27. United States Environmental Protection Agency: Greenhouse Gas Emissions 1990–2013 (2013). http://www3.epa.gov/otaq/climate/documents/420f15032.pdf
28. Vidal, T., Crainic, T., Gendreau, M., Lahrichi, N., Rei, W.: A hybrid genetic algorithm for multi-depot and periodic vehicle routing problems. Oper. Res. **60**(3), 611–624 (2012)

Short-Term Traffic Congestion Forecasting Using Hybrid Metaheuristics and Rule-Based Methods: A Comparative Study

Pedro Lopez-Garcia[1,2(✉)], Eneko Osaba[1,2], Enrique Onieva[1,2], Antonio D. Masegosa[1,2,3], and Asier Perallos[1,2]

[1] DeustoTech-Fundacion Deusto, Deusto Foundation, 48007 Bilbao, Spain
{p.lopez,e.osaba,enrique.onieva,ad.masegosa,perallos}@deusto.es
[2] Faculty of Engineering, University of Deusto, 48007 Bilbao, Spain
[3] IKERBASQUE, Basque Foundation for Science, 48011 Bilbao, Spain

Abstract. In this paper, a comparative study between a hybrid technique that combines a Genetic Algorithm with a Cross Entropy method to optimize Fuzzy Rule-Based Systems, and literature techniques is presented. These techniques are applied to traffic congestion datasets in order to determine their performance in this area. Different types of datasets have been chosen. The used time horizons are 5, 15 and 30 min. Results show that the hybrid technique improves those results obtained by the techniques of the state of the art. In this way, the performed experimentation shows the competitiveness of the proposal in this area of application.

Keywords: Genetic algorithms · Cross entropy · Classification · Machine learning · Hybrid optimization · Fuzzy rule-based systems · Intelligent transportation systems

1 Introduction

According to the Eurobarometer [2], road congestions are one of the problems that citizenship are more worried about regarding road transport. Therefore, traffic congestion prediction is a fundamental issue in the field of Intelligent Transportation Systems (ITSs). If congestion is predicted successfully, it could help to take decisions can result in noise reduction and energy savings. Also, it could increase the effectiveness and the performance of transport systems, and lead to savings in public infrastructure.

While two of the most frequently used methods for this task in the last decade are the Kalman Filter and the Autoregressive Integrated Moving Average (ARIMA), other alternatives have been developed in recent years. Among them, Soft Computing techniques as Support Vector Machines (SVM), Neural Networks (NN), Genetic Algorithms (GA) or Fuzzy Rule-Based Systems (FRBS) have been used in traffic forecasting tasks in particular [22], and in ITS field in general [17,18].

© Springer International Publishing Switzerland 2016
O. Luaces et al. (Eds.): CAEPIA 2016, LNAI 9868, pp. 290–299, 2016.
DOI: 10.1007/978-3-319-44636-3_27

The research developed in this paper aim at extending the analysis done in [13] by comparing the method presented in that paper with state of the art classification algorithms in order to evaluate the competitiveness of our proposal versus high-performance methods for traffic congestion prediction over different scenarios in terms of data available. In this way, we intend to offer an analysis about the advantages of our method depending on the characteristics of the data at hand. For this purpose, a hybrid algorithm which combines a Genetic Algorithm and a Cross Entropy, called GACE, is used with the aim of optimizing the different parts of a hierarchy of Fuzzy Rule-Based Systems (FRBS). This hierarchy was applied for predicting the congestion in several points and sectors of a road. The article is structured as follows. In Sect. 2, we give some background information about GA, cross entropy and hybrid metaheuristics. The definition of the proposed algorithm is detailed in Sect. 3. Then, the experimentation, the datasets used, and the comparative study are described in Sect. 4. Finally, conclusions are pointed out in Sect. 5.

2   Background

In this section, a brief summary about recent literature related to the different algorithms that compose the proposal is done, i.e. GA (Sect. 2.1) and Cross Entropy (CE) (Sect. 2.2). Besides, some examples about hybrid algorithms are shown in Sect. 2.3.

2.1   Genetic Algorithm

GA is a well-known metaheuristic introduced by Holland in [8]. Their objective is to mimic some of the processes observed in natural evolution. They have widely used since their proposal. For example, in [23], GA optimizes a fuzzy controller in order to improve the regenerative braking energy recovery rate of an electric vehicle. In that study, several road conditions are simulated and analysed. Results indicated that the use of a fuzzy logic control strategy based on the GA could improve the energy recovery and prolong the endurance mileage of the electric vehicle. Another example can be found in [6], where a GA is introduced to optimize the signal cycle length, split ratio, and phase difference for a traffic signal control in a district of Shangai. Interested readers are referred to [10,11] for extensive reviews of GAs in the literature.

2.2   Cross Entropy

CE method is an adaptive method proposed by Rubinstein [20] for rare-event probabilities and combinatorial optimization. The technique is divided in three phases:

1. Generate random samples from a normal distribution with given mean and standard deviation.

2. Select the best individuals from the previous samples.
3. Update mean and standard deviation according to the best individuals.

The aim of this algorithm is to focus the search in the area that contains the best samples found. CE has been used in the last years in different fields.

In the field of ITS, CE has been used in [19] to solve a Vehicle Routing Problem with weight coefficients and stochastic demands. In [16], CE is applied to optimize fuzzy logic controllers. These controllers are designed to command the orientation of an unmanned aerial vehicle to modify its trajectory for avoiding collisions.

2.3 Hybrid Algorithms

The hybridization of different metaheuristics is an important topic in the literature [7]. In hybridization, two or more techniques are combined in order to create synergies among them and cover the lacks that they can have separately. The combination is made with the aim of obtaining a good performance, improving the results obtained by the techniques for its own. Metaheuristics and their hybridizations have been widely used in the literature for different problems. In [1], a GA with a restricted search is hybridized with Extreme Learning Machine for reducing traffic noise and improve ITS. A method to design an intelligent suspension system with the objective of overcoming the trade-off barrier using the smallest actuator is presented in [9]. A hybrid genetic algorithm is used to tune the system, and performed good scenarios previously used in literature.

3 GACE: Genetic Algorithm with Cross Entropy

The method used in this study is an hybridization of the two methods described in Sect. 2, and it has been called GACE (Genetic Algorithm with Cross Entropy). The lack of exploitation ability in population-based algorithms as GA and the high probability of CE to become stuck in local optima, especially when a high learning rate is assigned, motivated the creation of this hybridization. The proposed technique tries to cover the lack of exploitation of GA using CE, focusing the search in the promising areas. On the other hand, the low exploration balance of CE is compensated by GA. Therefore, GACE is created with the aim of taking advantage of the exploration ability of GA and the exploitation ability of the CE. GACE works as follows: first of all, the initial population is created randomly with a given number of individuals $Size_{POP}$. The population is divided into two sub-populations in each generation. These sub-populations are POP_{GA} with $Size_{GA}$ individuals and POP_{CE} with a size of $Size_{CE}$ individuals.

In this application of the algorithm, $Size_{GA}$ and $Size_{POP}$ are established by the user, while $Size_{CE}$ is calculated as $Size_{CE} = Size_{POP} - Size_{GA}$. While the individuals that form POP_{GA} are chosen by the given selection method, POP_{CE} individuals are the best individuals in the current population POP_t. After the creation of both sub-populations, each one is used in a different way:

– In POP_{GA}, GA operators are applied in order to create $Size_{GA}$ new individuals with p_c and p_m as crossover and mutation probability respectively.
– In case of POP_{CE}, a total of $Size_{CE}$ individuals are randomly generated applying a normal distribution $\mathcal{N}(\overline{M}, S)$, where $\overline{M}$ is the mean and S the standard deviation. Both parameters, $\overline{M}$ and S, are updated employing the CE method with the n_{up} best individuals of POP_{CE}, and a parameter called Learning Rate L_r, used to update $\overline{M}$ and S during the execution of the algorithm with the means and deviations of the new selected samples.

After both algorithms are applied to its sub-population, POP_{t+1} is created using the offsprings generated in the last two steps, i.e. POP_{t+1} is formed by the GA_{size} individuals generated with POP_{GA} and the $Size_{CE}$ individuals created using CE method. Therefore, the total population size is the sum of the number of individuals in each sub-populations, i.e. $POP_{size} = Size_{GA} + Size_{CE}$. In addition, elitism is applied, i.e. if the best individual found so far is not part of the actual population, it is inserted on it, replacing the worst individual. The whole process is presented in Algorithm 1.

Data: $Size_{POP}$, $Size_{GA}$, p_c, p_m, L_r, n_{up}, T_{max}
Result: *Best individual found*
1 $Size_{CE} \leftarrow Size_{POP} - Size_{GA}$
2 $t \leftarrow 0$
3 $POP_0 \leftarrow$ Initialize($Size_{POP}$)
4 $\overline{M} \leftarrow$ Initialize Means vector
5 $S \leftarrow$ Initialize Standard Deviation vector
6 Evaluate POP_0
7 **while** $t < T_{max}$ **do**
8 $\quad POP_{GA} \leftarrow$ SelectionOperator($POP_t, Size_{GA}$)
9 $\quad POP_{CE} \leftarrow$ SelectBestSamples($POP_t, Size_{CE}$)
10 $\quad Offspring_{GA} \leftarrow$ Crossover(POP_{GA}, p_c)
11 $\quad Offspring_{GA} \leftarrow$ Mutation($Offspring_{GA}, p_m$)
12 $\quad Offspring_{CE} \leftarrow$ Generate($POP_{CE}, Size_{CE}, \overline{M}, S$)
13 $\quad \overline{M} \leftarrow UpdateMeans(L_r, \overline{M}, Offspring_{CE}, n_{up})$
14 $\quad S \leftarrow UpdateDeviation(L_r, S, Offspring_{CE}, n_{up})$
15 $\quad POP_{t+1} \leftarrow Offspring_{GA} \bigcup Offspring_{CE}$
16 $\quad$ Evaluate POP_{t+1}
17 $\quad$ Add the best individual found to POP_{t+1} if it is not in the population
18 $\quad t \leftarrow t + 1$
19 **end**

Algorithm 1. Pseudocode of the workflow followed by the proposed method GACE

Focusing on congestion forecasting, the algorithm was used to optimize the different parts of a hierarchical FRBS. In this work, we extend the experimentation done in [13] by comparing our proposal with state of the art classification algorithms for traffic congestion prediction over different scenarios in terms of data available. In this way, we intend to offer an analysis about the advantages of our method depending on the characteristics of the data at hand.

3.1 Application of the Proposal to Optimize FRBS Hierarchy

In this section, we explain the structure and the parts used for optimizing the Hierarchical Fuzzy Rule-Based Systems (HFRBS). First of all, the HFRBS counts with three parts:

1. Hierarchy ($C_{hierarchy}$): the subset of variables selected to be used by the HFRBS and the order in which they are included in the system. An ending character is included in this part. After this point, no more variables are used.
2. Membership Functions (C_{label}): codification of the location of the labels used to encode each variable for each FRBS in the hierarchy.
3. Rules (C_{rules}): positions of the singletons used as consequence of the rule bases of the FRBSs in the hierarchy.

These three parts are optimized by the proposed algorithm. These variables are used by the HFRBS as showed in Fig. 1. As it can be seen in this figure, systems are structured in a parallel way. The reason to use this organization is to consider each variable at the same time and with similar relevance. Also, a constraint is imposed: each FRBS has only two inputs. For more details, the interested reader is referred to [13].

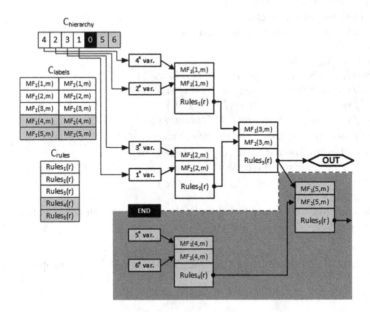

Fig. 1. Example of a hierarchy with six variables. The variables after the ending character (remarked as 0) have not count for its use in the hierarchy.

4 Experimentation and Results

In this section, information about the datasets used in the experimentation is showed in Sect. 4.1, which also includes the configuration used by the algorithm in this experimentation. Besides, the results of the performend tests are showed in Sect. 4.2.

4.1 Datasets and Configuration

With the aim of forecasting traffic congestion in a road, different types of datasets are considered in the present experimentation. These datasets represent a 9-km sector from the I5 highway in California, and they can be downloaded from the link[1]. The data is taken from the platform PeMS[2]. There are a total of 13 sensors in the road which take three values: flow (number of vehicles), occupancy (percentage of time during which the sensor was switched on) and speed (in miles per hour). Besides these values, a congestion variable is added using the intervals applied in the previous work and showed in Table 1. Density is also calculated using the values of the flow and the speed: $density = flow/speed$. In addition, there are a total of 8 ramps (4 in-ramps and 4 out-ramps) in the section of the road. These ramps provide flow values, which is the number of vehicles that get in (or out) the road. Following the levels showed in the table, congestion can take Free, Slight, Moderate or Severe values. These values are presented as universal units of the metric system (km). The different types of congestion are replaced by numbers in order to provide proper forecasting measures. Therefore, congestion states will be changed to use them for the calculation of the error: {Free = 1, Slight = 2, Moderate = 3 and Severe = 4}.

Table 1. Values of congestion and their calculus.

Level of congestion	Traffic density (ve/km/ln)	Vehicle speed (km/h)
Slight	[29–37]	[48–80]
Moderate	[37–50]	[24–64]
Severe	>50	<40
Free	Other cases	

Figure 2 shows a schema with the section of road used as well as the sensors located on it. Two types of datasets have been used: Point (PD) and Sector (SD) datasets. In the first one, the point of interest (S7), that is, the point in which the congestion is predicted, is found in the middle of the road, while in the second one, the point of interest is the complete road segment. A total of 49 variables are contained in PD and SD datasets (39 variables for the sensors in

---

[1] https://www.researchgate.net/publication/287771448_I5_Congestion_Datasets_GACE2015.

[2] http://pems.dot.ca.gov/.

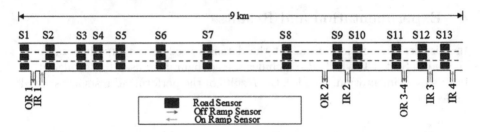

Fig. 2. Sector of the I5 highway used in this work. Sensors are denoted by S. Off and On Ramps are denoted by OR and IR respectively

the road, 8 variables in ramps, and one congestion variable). The time-horizons used are 5, 15, and 30 min, and they are indicated as a subscript in each dataset.

For the GA part of the proposal, binary tournament is used as the selection operator. In case of crossover operator, BLX-α has been applied to C_{labels} and C_{rules} parts, while a variant of the order crossover has been chosen for $C_{hierarchy}$. In case of mutation operators, BGA has been used for C_{labels} and C_{rules} and a swap mutation operator has been applied to $C_{hierarchy}$.

About the configuration used by GACE, the values are summarized in Table 2. The number of labels and rules of each system of the hierarchy are defined as six (three per input variable) and nine respectively. Besides, a 10-fold cross validation method for testing the model is used.

Table 2. Values of the parameters used in the experimentation

Parameter	Value
T_{max}	500
$Size_{pop}$	50
$Size_{GA}$	{35,40,45}
p_c	0.8
p_m	0.2
L_r	0.7
n_{up}	$Size_{CE}$

4.2 Comparative and Results

In this experimentation, we compare the combination of GACE and HFRBSs for congestion prediction, with six other state-of-the-art data mining techniques in order to get more insights about the performance and competitiveness of this method. KEEL software[3] has been used for the execution of the algorithms with their default values:

---

[3] http://sci2s.ugr.es/keel/.

- **Adaboost** [3] is a boosting algorithm, which repeatedly invokes a learning algorithm to successively generate a committee of simple, low-quality fuzzy classifiers. Each time these classifiers are added to the compound one, the weights of the examples in training set are changed, and a voting strength, which depends on its accuracy, is given to the classifier. In this algorithm, each of the weak hypothesis is a fuzzy rule extracted from data.
- **Grammar-Based Genetic Programming Algorithm** (GP) [21] is used to learn a fuzzy classifier by means of learning fuzzy rules throught Genetic Programming algorithms.
- **INNER** [14] tries to extract a small set of suitable rules to represent the training set, achieving an aceptable accuracy.
- **PART** [4] is a classification model by covering rules based on decision trees. The aim is to determine a decision list of rules that predicts correctly the value of the target attribute. PART is based on C4.5 algorithm, due to in each iteration, a partial C4.5 Tree is generated and its best rule is extracted. The method ends when all the examples are covered.
- **Real Encoding - Particle Swarm Optimization** (REPSO) [12] is a PSO-based classifier that perform a classification task by means of a PSO algorithm. It uses a real encoding approach.
- **Tree Analysis with Randomly Generated and Evolved Trees** (Target) [5] is a hybrid decision tree with the aim of obtain a forest of rules that better suits the training data by means of a GA search.

The error used for the comparative is the symmetric mean absolute percentage error (sMAPE) [15]. The calculation of sMAPE is showed in Eq. 1, where $\bar{Y}$ is the expected value, Y the predicted one, and n is the number of examples. The aim of using SMAPE is to take into account that the error between two close types of congestion is smaller than the error between two values of congestion. For example, the error between $Y = Free$ and $\bar{Y} = Severe$ is greater than the error between $Y = Free$ and $\bar{Y} = Slight$.

$$sMAPE = \frac{1}{n} \sum_{i=1}^{n} \frac{|\bar{Y}_i - Y_i|}{(|\bar{Y}_i| + |Y_i|)/2} \tag{1}$$

Experimentation is made with these techniques and the best configurations obtained in [13], i.e. $GACE_{45-5}$, $GACE_{40-10}$ and $GACE_{35-15}$. Subscript indicates the size of both subpopulations, i.e. $GACE_{45-5}$ means that $Size_{GA} = 45$ while $Size_{CE} = 5$. The results obtained and the comparison between them are showed in Table 3. Bold values indicate the two best techniques in each dataset.

Results show that GACE obtains one of the two best values in all the datasets, and the two best values so far in 4 out 6. The best configuration, $GACE_{45-5}$, achieves one of the best sMAPE value in all datasets. $INNER$ and $Target$, together with GP are the techniques that obtain an error closer to the proposal.

Table 3. Average errors of the different techniques in each dataset

Dataset	GACE			AdaBoost	GP	INNER	PART	REPSO	Target
	45–5	40–10	35–15						
PD_5	**0.009**	**0.009**	**0.010**	0.042	0.014	0.028	0.032	0.013	0.016
PD_{15}	**0.013**	**0.013**	**0.013**	0.042	0.017	0.027	0.042	0.020	**0.016**
PD_{30}	**0.017**	**0.016**	**0.016**	0.042	0.020	0.036	0.043	0.022	0.021
SD_5	**0.149**	0.184	0.195	0.433	0.333	**0.169**	0.409	0.386	0.176
SD_{15}	**0.130**	0.182	**0.169**	0.386	0.2539	0.227	0.392	0.386	0.397
SD_{30}	**0.123**	**0.140**	0.169	0.392	0.409	0.205	0.394	0.387	0.404

5   Conclusions

In this paper, we aimed at studying more in depth the performance of Fuzzy Rule-Based Systems evolved by GACE to predict traffic congestion. The goal of this study is to check the competitiveness of this approach when it is used for this purpose. To this end, we compared this method versus other six literature techniques with data obtained in a 9-km stretch of highway. In this new comparative, the best configurations obtained previously have been used. The results confirm the good performance of GACE and HFRBS against well-known techniques of the state of the art in this kind of problems. In future works, other datasets are planned to be used. Besides, new time horizons can be interesting to use. Also, a exhaustive study about computational time of the proposal and the literature methods would be interesting to make. Finally, congestion datasets from other sources could be created, or found, in order to prove the performance of different metaheuristics in this theme.

Acknowledgments. Authors work was supported by TIMON Project. This project has received funding from the European Unions Horizon 2020 research and innovation programme under grant agreement No. 636220.

References

1. Alexandre, E., Cuadra, L., Salcedo-Sanz, S., Pastor-Snchez, A., Casanova-Mateo, C.: Hybridizing extreme learning machines and genetic algorithms to select acoustic features in vehicle classification applications. Neurocomputing **152**, 58–68 (2015)
2. European Commission: Special Eurobarometer 422a, Quality of Transport (2014)
3. del Jesus, M.J., Hoffmann, F., Junco, L., Sánchez, L.: Induction of fuzzy-rule-based classifiers with evolutionary boosting algorithms. IEEE Trans. Fuzzy Syst. **12**(3), 296–308 (2004)
4. Frank, E., Witten, I.H.: Generating accurate rule sets without global optimization. In: Proceedings of the Fifteenth International Conference on Machine Learning, pp. 144–151 (1998)
5. Gray, J.B., Fan, G.: Classification tree analysis using target. Comput. Stat. Data Anal. **52**(3), 1362–1372 (2008)

6. Han, Y., Xing, B., Yao, J., Liu, J.: Optimal model of regional traffic signal control under mixed traffic flow condition. Jiaotong Yunshu Gongcheng Xuebao/J. Traffic Transp. Eng. **15**(1), 119–126 (2015)

7. Hernández, S.A., Leguizamón, G., Mezura-Montes, E.: Hybridization of differential evolution using hill climbing to solve constrained optimization problems. Revista Iberoamericana de Inteligencia Artificial **16**(52), 3–15 (2013)

8. Holland, J.H.: Adaptation in Natural and Artificial Systems: An Introductory Analysis with Applications to Biology, Control, and Artificial Intelligence. University of Michigan Press, Ann Arbor (1975)

9. Kanarachos, S., Kanarachos, A.: Intelligent road adaptive suspension system design using an experts' based hybrid genetic algorithm. Expert Syst. Appl. **42**(21), 8232–8242 (2015)

10. Karakatic, S., Podgorelec, V.: A survey of genetic algorithms for solving multi depot vehicle routing problem. Appl. Soft Comput. **27**, 519–532 (2015)

11. Lim, T.Y.: Structured population genetic algorithms: a literature survey. Artif. Intel. Rev. **41**(3), 385–399 (2014)

12. Liu, Y., Qin, Z., Shi, Z., Chen, J.: Rule discovery with particle swarm optimization. In: Chi, C.-H., Lam, K.-Y. (eds.) AWCC 2004. LNCS, vol. 3309, pp. 291–296. Springer, Heidelberg (2004)

13. Lopez-Garcia, P., Onieva, E., Osaba, E., Masegosa, A.D., Perallos, A.: A hybrid method for short-term traffic congestion forecasting using genetic algorithms and cross entropy. IEEE Trans. Intell. Trans. Syst. **17**(2), 557–569 (2016)

14. Luaces, O.: Inflating examples to obtain rules. Int. J. Intel. Syst. **18**, 1113–1143 (2003)

15. Makridakis, S., Hibon, M.: The M3-competition: results, conclusions and implications. Int. J. Forecast. **16**(4), 451–476 (2000)

16. Olivares-Mendez, M.A., Fu, C., Kannan, S., Voos, H., Campoy, P.: Using the cross-entropy method for control optimization: a case study of see-and-avoid on unmanned aerial vehicles, pp. 1183–1189 (2014)

17. Onieva, E., Milanes, V., Villagra, J., Perez, J., Godoy, J.: Genetic optimization of a vehicle fuzzy decision system for intersections. Expert Syst. Appl. **39**(18), 13148–13157 (2012)

18. Osaba, E., Diaz, F., Onieva, E.: Golden ball: a novel meta-heuristic to solve combinatorial optimization problems based on soccer concepts. Appl. Intell. **41**(1), 145–166 (2014)

19. Qiu, Y.: Vehicle routing problem with weight coefficients and stochastic demands based on the cross-entropy method, pp. 159–162 (2009)

20. Rubinstein, R.Y.: Optimization of computer simulation models with rare events. Eur. J. Oper. Res. **99**(1), 89–112 (1997)

21. Sánchez, L., Couso, I., Corrales, J.A.: Combining GP operators with SA search to evolve fuzzy rule based classifiers. Inf. Sci. **136**(1–4), 175–192 (2001)

22. Vlahogianni, E., Karlaftis, M.: Testing and comparing neural network and statistical approaches for predicting transportation time series. Transp. Res. Rec. J. Transp. Res. Board **2399**, 9–22 (2013)

23. Zhou, M., Bi, S., Dong, C., He, C.: Regenerative braking system for electric vehicles based on genetic algorithm fuzzy logic control. ICIC Express Lett. Part B: Appl. **5**(3), 689–695 (2014)

Multiclass Prediction of Wind Power Ramp Events Combining Reservoir Computing and Support Vector Machines

Manuel Dorado-Moreno[1]($\boxtimes$), Antonio Manuel Durán-Rosal[1],
David Guijo-Rubio[1], Pedro Antonio Gutiérrez[1], Luis Prieto[2],
Sancho Salcedo-Sanz[3], and César Hervás-Martínez[1]

[1] Department of Computer Science and Numerical Analysis,
Universidad de Córdoba, Córdoba, Spain
i92domom@uco.es
[2] Department of Energy Resources, Iberdrola, Madrid, Spain
[3] Department of Signal Processing and Communications,
Universidad de Alcalá, Alcalá de Henares, Spain

Abstract. This paper proposes a reservoir computing architecture for predicting wind power ramp events (WPREs), which are strong increases or decreases of wind speed in a short period of time. This is a problem of high interest, because WPREs increases the maintenance costs of wind farms and hinders the energy production. The standard echo state network architecture is modified by replacing the linear regression used to compute the reservoir outputs by a nonlinear support vector machine, and past ramp function values are combined with reanalysis data to perform the prediction. Another novelty of the study is that we will predict three type of events (negative ramps, non-ramps and positive ramps), instead of binary classification of ramps, given that the type of ramp can be crucial for the correct maintenance of the farm. The model proposed obtains satisfying results, being able to correctly predict around 70 % of WPREs and outperforming other models.

Keywords: Wind ramp events · Reservoir computing · Echo state networks · Support vector machines

1 Introduction

The prediction of wind power ramp events (WPREs) in wind farms is one of the current hot topics in wind energy research. WPREs increase the management cost of wind farms, because of their potential damage effect in wind turbines [1,2]. WPREs consist of important fluctuations of wind power in a short period of time (within a few hours), leading to a significant increase or decrease of the power produced in the wind farm. The origin of WPREs are specific meteorological processes (usually crossing fronts, local fast changes in the wind, etc.).

M. Dorado-Moreno—This work has been subsidized by the TIN2014-54583-C2-1-R project of the Spanish Ministerial Commission of Science and Technology (MICYT), FEDER funds and the P11-TIC-7508 project of the "Junta de Andalucía" (Spain).

O. Luaces et al. (Eds.): CAEPIA 2016, LNAI 9868, pp. 300–309, 2016.
DOI: 10.1007/978-3-319-44636-3_28

Currently, the most effective way of dealing with WPREs in wind farms is the correct prediction of these events, as has been recently reported [3,4].

Recurrent artificial neural networks (RNNs) represent a large set of computing models that have been designed imitating the connections of the biological brain. RNNs consist of processing units called neurons, which are interconnected among them. After receiving a specific signal, these neurons are activated (or not), allowing the signal to propagate to other neurons. Unlike other artificial neural networks (ANNs), RNNs present cycles in their connections, which means:

- Even with no inputs at a given instant, an old input (propagated through the cycles of the network links) may activate some neurons. This makes them dynamical systems instead of static, like ANNs.
- When receiving an input, these networks keep them (nonlinearly transformed) in their neurons during a certain amount of time (depending on the size of the cycles), i.e., they are models with dynamical memory, so they are able to process temporal information.

This paper proposes the use of RNN architectures, as their features make them highly suitable for the treatment of time series. However, RNNs have some already known problems, such as the gradient vanishing, which, generally, makes the training algorithm convergence very difficult. Moreover, when a network weight changes, several cycles are needed for this change to be reflected in the output neurons, which implies a high computational cost for training large size RNNs, greatly limiting the memory of the RNN.

In 2001, different models of RNNs were proposed, including echo state networks (ESNs) [5] and Liquid State Machines [6]. These proposals are grouped into a paradigm known as reservoir computing (RC) [7], which aims to alleviate the above mentioned disadvantages. All these proposals have some characteristics to overcome the disadvantages of standard RNNs:

- They are created randomly and are not modified during the training process.
- They keep a dynamical memory with non-linear transformations of the inputs. This part of the model is known as Reservoir in the literature.
- The network output is calculated as a linear combination of the outputs of the reservoir. However, in our case, we will apply a nonlinear classifier, the support vector machine (SVM) [8].

The training approach for these networks is based on creating the Reservoir randomly and only adjusting the output weights to approximate the target variable. These models have been tested in several renewable energy-related problems [9–13], showing good performance.

The main idea of the present paper is to use ESNs for merging real ramp function measures with numerical model data from the ERA-Interim (a global atmospheric reanalysis from 1979, continuously updated) in order to perform WPRE prediction in three different classes (negative ramp, non-ramp and positive ramp). The inclusion of reanalysis data has been successfully tested in several previous studies on wind speed prediction, including WPRE estimation cases [14,15]. Specifically, we propose a novel RC architecture to exploit the temporal structure of the ramp function values and reanalysis data. Several variables from the ERA-Interim reanalysis are considered, and the resolution of these reanalysis is 0.75×0.75 Km, giving us the possibility of covering any location with good quality predictive variables. The real performance of the proposed WPRE prediction system based on RC methodology has been tested in three different wind farms distributed in the Spanish geography, by means of a complete comparison with alternative prediction models.

The remainder of the paper is structured in the following way: next section describes the database used in this paper. Section 3 presents the main characteristics of the RC methodology and the architecture used in this paper for WPRE prediction. Section 4 evaluates the performance of the proposed RC system in data from three different wind farms in Spain. Finally, Sect. 5 gives some conclusions on the work carried out.

2 Database

In this section, the different data used to build the dataset is explained. Two datasets have been considered. In the first one, the data is obtained hourly from three wind farms in Spain (see Fig. 1). The other dataset contains reanalysis data from the ERA-Interim project [16], where the data is obtained every 6 hours. Both datasets were merged, calculating a ramp function 1 to detect ramps in 6 hours intervals.

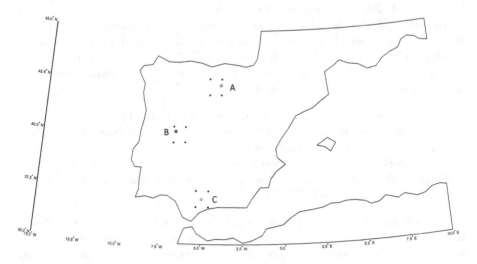

Fig. 1. Location of the three wind farms and the reanalysis nodes considered in the study.

2.1 Wind Farm Data

Let $S_t : \mathbb{R}^k \to \mathbb{R}$ be a ramp function evaluated to decide whether there is a WPRE or not. There are several definitions of S_t [1], all them involving power production (P_t) criteria at the wind farm or wind turbine. In this paper, we have used the following one in order to detect negative ramps (NRs), non-ramps (NoRs) and positive ramps (PRs):

$$S_t = P_t - P_{t-\Delta t_r}, \tag{1}$$

where Δt_r is the time interval considered (6 h in our case).

Using S_t, the classification problem can be stated by defining a threshold value S_0, in the following way:

$$y_t = \begin{cases} \text{NR}, & \text{if } S_t \leq -S_0, \\ \text{NoR}, & \text{if } -S_0 < S_t < S_0, \\ \text{PR}, & \text{if } S_t \geq S_0. \end{cases} \tag{2}$$

In this case, we have considered S_0 as a percentage of the wind farm rated power (specifically, 50 % of the wind farm rated power [1]). The WPRE prediction problem also involves a vector of predictive variables. In our case, we will use meteorological data from reanalysis as input data ($\mathbf{z}$) (which are defined in the next section), together with the past values of the ramp function $(S_{t-1}, S_{t-2}, \ldots)$, considering t with 6-hour resolution.

2.2 Reanalysis Data

For each of the three wind farms, we have 40 predictors, corresponding to 10 variables per reanalysis node. These variables are computed each 2.5° all around the globe(latitude and longitude) through a physical model and contain wind speed, pressure and temperature measures at different heights. In order to avoid dealing with so many variables, which in many cases can be highly correlated, introducing noise in the model, we perform a weighted average depending on the distance from each reanalysis node to the wind farm center. This reduces the total number of reanalysis variables at each wind farm to 10, without losing the relative information from each node. First, the distance from each reanalysis node to the wind farm is calculated as follows:

$$d(p_0, p_j) = \arccos(\sin(lat_0) \cdot \sin(lat_j) \cdot \cos(lon_0 - lon_j) + \cos(lat_0) \cdot \cos(lat_j)), \tag{3}$$

where p_0 is the wind farm geographical position, p_j stands for the location of each reanalysis node, and lat and lon are the latitude and longitude of the points, respectively. Once the distance from each of the four reanalysis nodes (four black points containing the wind farm) to the wind farm is calculated (see Fig. 1), these distances are inverted and normalized, considering that the shorter the distance, the greater the weight that reanalysis node should have:

$$w_i = \frac{\sum_{j=0}^{4} d(p_0, p_j)}{d(p_0, p_i)}, \quad i = 1, \ldots, 4. \tag{4}$$

After calculating these weights, they are applied to obtain a weighted average for each of the 10 variables.

3   Reservoir Computing Proposal

The paper proposes a RC model which follows the standard ESN architecture, replacing the regression of the output layer with a SVM model, and combining the reservoir with the reanalysis data. The objective is the classification of each future event as a NR, NoR or PR event.

3.1   Architecture

As previously stated, we focus on ESNs [5]. ESNs are based on (i) feeding a fixed, random, large reservoir with the inputs, producing a nonlinear response signal for each neuron of this reservoir, and (ii) estimating the desired output signal by using a simple linear model combining all of these response signals. Specifically, we now describe a novel ESN architecture which includes WPRE measured data and ERA-Interim reanalysis. Figure 2 shows the structure proposed.

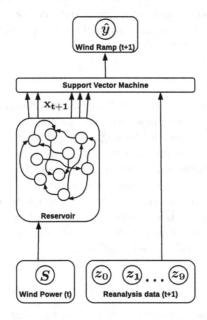

Fig. 2. Novel ESN architecture proposed

Some symbols of the figure must be explained: in the input layer, S_t and $\mathbf{z}_{t+1}$ are the input vectors (ramp function and 10 reanalysis variables in time t and $t+1$, respectively). The use of $\mathbf{z}_{t+1}$ in the input layer for predicting y_{t+1} is plausible, given that the vector $\mathbf{z}_{t+1}$ is given by meteorological models which can produce reliable estimations for 6 hours ahead. In the hidden layer, there are M neurons randomly interconnected among them, and the inputs are connected to these neurons with a random weight. Finally, we have an output layer that will classify each event in its corresponding class.

This architecture is a variant of the standard ESN, in such a way that the reservoir is constructed similarly, but the standard regression method (ridge regression) is replaced by a SVM approach. Moreover, another novelty of this architecture is that we consider not only the reservoir outputs but also the reanalysis variables as direct inputs of the SVM model.

3.2   Training Algorithm

The methodology proposed to adjust the weights of the previously presented architecture is the following:

1. Create a random reservoir of size M, interconnecting neurons randomly and generating weights $\mathbf{W}$ by a Gaussian probability distribution. The weights of the connections that link the inputs with the reservoir neurons ($\mathbf{W}^{in}$) are generated using the same distribution.
2. Harvest the reservoir states, feeding the reservoir inputs from time $t = 1$ to $t = M$, so that all the network connections would have received a signal, allowing to obtain the full vector $\mathbf{x}_t$.
3. Compute the output weights by training a SVM model, maximizing the margin of the discriminant functions for each class $\{0, 1, 2\}$ (NR, NoR and PR) in the next time instant. The strategyr for tackling SVM multiclass classification is the *one-versus-all* approach [17]. Once the network is trained, it can be used for real-time prediction of ramps, discarding the pattern corresponding to $t = 0$ since there would be no information from an earlier instant.

4   Experiments

This section describes the experiments considered for validating the architecture proposed in Sect. 3 (RCSVM).

4.1   Other Methods Evaluated

Four alternative models will be evaluated in order to compare their results with the ones obtained by RCSVM:

Persistence. This method, in order to predict ramps, returns the output value observed 6 hours earlier. Thus, if there occurs any kind of state change between instants t and $t+1$, a classification error will be made. However, when the output is constant, the persistence model would work correctly. The performance of this method is established as the minimum threshold for good classification.

LogReg and SVM. These models are trained by directly using all the inputs available at time t (i.e. S_t and $\mathbf{z}_{t+1}$) to predict S_{t+1}. The standard logistic regression method (LogReg) and SVM models are trained and configured as described in Sect. 4.3.

Table 1. Characteristics of the different datasets considered in the experimentation, including the periods used for training and test and the number of WPREs

Farm	#NR	#NoR	#PR	Train interval	Test interval
A	602	13852	706	11/1/2002-29/10/2011	30/10/2011-29/10/2012
B	1077	12463	1074	1/1/2002-17/2/2012	18/2/2012-17/2/1013
C	617	13857	649	2/3/2002-30/6/2012	11/7/2012-30/6/2013

RCLogReg. This method follows the same architecture proposed for RCSVM but, in this case, the classifier is a LogReg linear model. In this way, we are comparing the results of a non-linear classifier in the output layer, to the ones obtained by standard linear models.

Due to the imbalanced nature of the database (as shown in Table 1), for all SVM and LogReg models, specific weights are applied to the patterns, according to their class. The weights are inversely proportional to the number of patterns of each class:

$$w_i = \frac{N}{N_i}, \quad i = 0, \ldots, 2, \tag{5}$$

where N_i is the number of patterns in class i, N is the total number of patterns in the training set and w_i is the weight for each class. In this way, we avoid obtaining a trivial classifier (i.e. a classifier predicting all patterns as belonging to the majority class).

4.2   Evaluation Metrics

The goal of this paper is to obtain good classifiers, which are able to detect most of the WPREs. Several measures can be considered for evaluating multiclass classifiers, but we have considered the following ones:

- The **sensitivities** of each class (S_{NR}, S_{NoR} and S_{PR}), which represent the model ability to correctly predict each type of event:

$$S_{\mathrm{NR}} = \frac{CC_{\mathrm{NR}}}{N_0}, \quad S_{\mathrm{NoR}} = \frac{CC_{\mathrm{NoR}}}{N_1}, \quad S_{\mathrm{PR}} = \frac{CC_{\mathrm{PR}}}{N_2}, \tag{6}$$

where CC_{NR}, CC_{NoR} and CC_{PR} are the number of NR, NoR and PR events correctly classified by the evaluated classifier, respectively, and N_0, N_1 and N_2 are the total number of NR, NoR and PR events, respectively.
- The **geometric mean of the sensitivities** (GMS) of each class is a geometric average of the correct classification percentages per class:

$$GMS = \sqrt[3]{S_{\mathrm{NR}} \cdot S_{\mathrm{NoR}} \cdot S_{\mathrm{PR}}}. \tag{7}$$

We include this measure because we are dealing with a highly unbalanced prediction problem, so trivial classifiers ignoring one of the classes are characterized by $GMS = 0$.

4.3   Experimental Design

To evaluate the results, the three databases have been split in the same way: the last 365 days will be used as the test set, and the rest of the database as the training set (the specific dates for each dataset are shown in Table 1).

The regularization coefficient (C) and the radius width of the RBF kernel (γ) of the SVM model have been adjusted using a nested 5-fold cross-validation in the set $\{10^{-3}, 10^{-2}, ..., 10^{3}\}$. For LogReg, C has been adjusted in the same way, using the set $\{10^{1}, 10^{2}, ..., 10^{15}\}$

The parameters of the reservoir have been configured as follows: $M = 50$, assuming this is a sufficient number of neurons to address the problem, and it does not represent a high computational cost. On the other hand, reservoir neurons were given a bias, which is interconnected with all the neurons with a value on the range $[-1, 1]$ following a uniform distribution.

To obtain more robust results, as the reservoir methods are stochatic, each of the experiments was run with 30 different seeds, allowing us to calculate the mean and standard deviation for each of the methods evaluated.

4.4   Results

This section discusses the results shown in Table 2. We first analyse the sensitivities individually obtained for each class, although they have to be carefully interpreted, given that a very good result for one class can be obtained at the

Table 2. Results of the different methods evaluated for wind farms A, B and C.

Farm	Model	GMS $Mean \pm SD$	S_{NR} $Mean \pm SD$	S_{NoR} $Mean \pm SD$	S_{PR} $Mean \pm SD$
A	Persistence	0.0000	0.00 %	**90.86 %**	0.00 %
	LogReg	0.5507	56.25 %	54.57 %	54.43 %
	SVM	0.5615	51.56 %	58.99 %	58.22 %
	RCLogReg	*0.6361 ± 0.0318*	*70.31 ± 1.64* %	56.58 ± 1.51 %	**64.81 ± 2.58** %
	RCSVM	**0.6516 ± 0.0109**	**77.13 ± 2.92** %	*59.06 ± 0.87* %	*60.80 ± 2.10* %
B	Persistence	0.0000	1.03 %	**87.14 %**	0.00 %
	LogReg	0.4593	54.63 %	26.60 %	**66.66 %**
	SVM	*0.5861*	71.13 %	46.70 %	60.60 %
	RCLogReg	0.5827 ± 0.0072	*73.81 ± 1.63* %	42.98 ± 1.14 %	*62.42 ± 1.57* %
	RCSVM	**0.6167 ± 0.0231**	**76.28 ± 2.25** %	*50.96 ± 3.37* %	60.40 ± 1.95 %
C	Persistence	0.0000	0.00 %	**91.96 %**	0.00 %
	LogReg	0.5411	0.6935	42.33 %	53.96 %
	SVM	0.5799	66.12 %	46.46 %	*63.49 %*
	RCLogReg	*0.5930 ± 0.0101*	**78.70 ± 1.97** %	45.77 ± 1.68 %	57.98 ± 2.83 %
	RCSVM	**0.6171 ± 0.0159**	*70.64 ± 3.37* %	*50.87 ± 2.09* %	**65.39 ± 2.75** %

The best result is shown in bold face and the second one in italics.

expense of misclassifying the rest. The Persistence results show that it is impossible to predict these events just looking at the previous state: all sensitivities related to the classes of interest, NR and PR, are 0 % or close to 0 %. Observing standard SVM and LogReg results (without considering a reservoir), they obtain quite good performance, correctly classifying nearly 65 % of WPREs in B and C wind farms, with a sightly better performance for SVM. Finally, when adding the reservoir, these results are improved, being able to correctly predict from 74 to 79 % of the negative ramps.

The GMS results are now analysed, taking into account that this metric is able to evaluate the global performance of the model. RCSVM obtains the most balanced results, with the highest GMS for all the databases. Moreover, it is the only method able of classifying more than 50 % of NoR events without losing accuracy on predicting ramp events, even obtaining better results in most of the cases.

5   Conclusions

This paper evaluates a novel ESN architecture for predicting WPREs considering the nature of the ramps and differentiating between negative and positive ramps. The architecture is based on combining data from past values of the ramp function and reanalysis data. Additionally, a nonlinear SVM is considered in the output layer, instead of using a linear model. The problem is tackled as a three-class classification problem (NR, NoR and PR events) and three wind farms in Spain are used for evaluating the performance of the new architecture. The results obtained show that all models are better than a simple persistence prediction, that the reservoir is able to improve the classification performance of a standard classification model and that the SVM method results in more robust prediction than a linear LogReg classifier.

Given that the considered classes can be naturally ordered (NR$\prec$ NoR$\prec$ PR), a future research line is to evaluate the performance of ordinal regression methods [18] for this problem, with the hope of exploiting this natural order for obtaining better models.

References

1. Gallego-Castillo, C., Cuerva-Tejero, A., López-García, O.: A review on the recent history of wind power ramp forecasting. Renew. Sustain. Energy Rev. **52**, 1148–1157 (2015)
2. Ouyang, T., Zha, X., Qin, L.: A survey of wind power ramp forecasting. Energy Power Eng. **5**, 368–372 (2013)
3. Cui, M., Ke, D., Sun, Y., Gan, D., Zhang, J., Hodge, B.M.: Wind power ramp event forecasting using a stochastic scenario generation method. IEEE Trans. Sustain. Energy **6**(2), 422–433 (2015)
4. Foley, A.M., Leahy, P.G., Marvuglia, A., McKeogh, E.J.: Current methods and advances in forecasting of wind power generation. Renew. Energy **37**, 1–8 (2012)

5. Jaeger, H.: The "echo state" approach to analysing and training recurrent neural networks. GMD report 148, German National Research Center for Information Technology, pp. 1–43 (2001)
6. Natschlaeger, T., Maass, W., Markram, H.: The "liquid computer": a novel strategy for real-time computing on time series. TELEMATIK **8**(1), 39–43 (2002)
7. Lukosevicius, M., Jaeger, H.: Reservoir computing approaches to recurrent neural network training. Comput. Sci. Rev. **3**(3), 127–149 (2009)
8. Cortes, C., Vapnik, V.: Support-vector networks. Mach. Learn. **20**, 273–297 (1995)
9. Jayawardene, I., Venayagamoorthy, G.K.: Reservoir based learning network for control of two-area power system with variable renewable generation. Neurocomputing **170**, 428–438 (2015)
10. Crisostomi, E., Gallicchio, C., Micheli, A., Raugi, M., Tucci, M.: Prediction of the Italian electricity price for smart grid applications. Neurocomputing **170**, 286–295 (2015)
11. Galle de Aguiar, B.C., Silva-Valencia, M.J.: Using reservoir computing for forecasting of wind power generated by a wind farm. In: Proceedings of the Sixth International Conference on Advanced Cognitive Technologies and Applications, pp. 184–188 (2014)
12. Basterrech, S., Buriánek, T.: Solar irradiance estimation using the echo state network and the flexible neural tree. In: Pan, J.-S., Snasel, V., Corchado, E.S., Abraham, A., Wang, S.-L. (eds.) Intelligent Data Analysis and Its Applications, Volume I. AISC, vol. 297, pp. 475–484. Springer, Heidelberg (2014)
13. Liu, D., Wang, J., Wang, H.: Short-term wind speed forecasting based on spectral clustering and optimised echo state networks. Renew. Energy **78**, 599–608 (2015)
14. Cannon, D.J., Brayshaw, D.J., Methven, J., Coker, P.J., Lenaghan, D.: Using reanalysis data to quantify extreme wind power generation statistics: a 33 year case study in Great Britain. Renew. Energy **75**, 767–778 (2015)
15. Gallego-Castillo, C., García-Bustamante, E., Cuerva-Tejero, A., Navarro, J.: Identifying wind power ramp causes from multivariate datasets: a methodological proposal and its application to reanalysis data. IET Renew. Power Gener. **9**(8), 867–875 (2015)
16. Dee, D.P., Uppala, S.M., Simmons, A.J., Berrisford, P., Poli, P., et al.: The ERA-interim reanalysis: configuration and performance of the data assimilation system. Q. J. R. Meteorol. Soc. **137**, 553–597 (2011)
17. Hsu, C.W., Lin, C.J.: A comparison of methods for multi-class support vector machines. IEEE Trans. Neural Netw. **13**(2), 415–425 (2002)
18. Gutiérrez, P.A., Pérez-Ortiz, M., Sánchez-Monedero, J., Fernández-Navarro, F., Hervás-Martínez, C.: Ordinal regression methods: survey and experimental study. IEEE Trans. Knowl. Data Eng. **28**, 127–146 (2016)

Genetic Fuzzy Modelling of Li-Ion Batteries Through a Combination of Theta-DEA and Knowledge-Based Preference Ordering

Yuviny Echevarría[1,3(✉)], Luciano Sánchez[1], and Cecilio Blanco[2]

[1] Department of Computer Science, University of Oviedo, Gijón, Spain
yuviny@gmail.com, luciano@uniovi.es
[2] Department of Electrical Engineering, University of Oviedo, Gijón, Spain
cecilio@uniovi.es
[3] Department of Informatics, University of Cienfuegos, Cienfuegos, Cuba

Abstract. Learning semi-physical fuzzy models of rechargeable Li-Ion batteries from data involves solving a complex multicriteria optimization task where the accuracies of the approximations of the different observable variables are balanced. The fitness function of this problem depends on the recursive evaluation of a set of differential equations, where fuzzy rule-based systems are embedded as nonlinear blocks. Evaluating this function is a time consuming process, thus algorithms that efficiently promote diversity and hence demand a low number of evaluations of the fitness function are preferred. In this paper, a comparison is carried out between some recent genetic algorithms, whose performances are assessed in this particular modelling problem. It is concluded that the combination of the recent θ-Dominance Evolutionary Algorithm (θ-DEA) with a Knowledge-based precedence operator, that improves the selection, is a sensible choice. Dominance relations between the Pareto fronts are assessed in terms of binary additive ϵ-quality indicators.

Keywords: Genetic fuzzy systems · Li-Ion battery model · Multi-objective genetic algorithms · Preference orderings

1 Introduction

Li-Ion batteries are complex and unstable dynamical systems with multiple inputs and outputs [1]. Learning a multi-output dynamical system is intended to minimize the Mean Squared Error (MSE) between each of the observed output variables and the model. In addition to this, there are also latent variables that cannot be observed but influence the dynamical behavior of the system. In the particular case of batteries, these latent variables are often referred to as the State of Charge (SoH) and the State of Health (SoH). The most relevant observable variables are Voltage, Current and Temperature.

According to the amount of expert knowledge included in the definition of the model, there is a wide range of alternatives that range from the pure black

© Springer International Publishing Switzerland 2016
O. Luaces et al. (Eds.): CAEPIA 2016, LNAI 9868, pp. 310–320, 2016.
DOI: 10.1007/978-3-319-44636-3_29

box, where there is no expert knowledge, to the electrochemical definition of the state equations that define the speed of the diffusion of Lithium in the electrodes, that is the "first principles" model. Both extremes of the catalog of alternatives are impractical: on the one hand, the battery is a so complex system that black boxes would need an impossibly large number of training examples to cover all situations. In addition, the electrochemical model depends on battery-dependent physical parameters that are also unknown, and fitting these parameters from data is also unfeasible [2]. An intermediate point of view is often used where simplified models cover the useful part of the state space for a particular application, say for instance the prediction of the remaining charge of an automotive battery on the basis of its voltage, current and temperature. The semi-physical model that will be used in this paper [3] falls into this class, and comprises a set of differential equations, whose structure reflects the knowledge about the domain, and Fuzzy Rule-Based Systems (FRBS) are embedded as nonlinear blocks in these equations, to model the battery-specific parts. The fitness function of this problem depends on the recursive evaluation of this set of differential equations over a training path.

Learning semi-physical fuzzy models of rechargeable Li-Ion batteries from data involves therefore the solution of a complex multicriteria optimization task where the accuracies of the approximations of the different observable variables along the training path are balanced. Observe that the learning process of the semi-physical battery model here described can be regarded as a Genetic Fuzzy System (GFS) because the learning task include, among other parts, obtaining the antecedents and consequents of the fuzzy rule-based systems embedded in the model. This is, however, a non-standard GFS were the fitness function is a very time consuming process, thus learning algorithms that efficiently promote diversity and hence demand a low number of evaluations of the fitness function are preferred.

Empirical observations suggest that the fitness landscape of this problem contains many local minima, reaffirming the complexity of the learning process. Also, the preciseness of the model with respect to the MSE demands a high accuracy in order to obtain a well-fitted output curve (at least three-four significant figures for each parameter, according to our own experimentation).

The convergence in problems with complex fitness landscapes is deeply influenced by the selection approach and the subsequent promotion of diversity in a given population. Studies about ordinary selection processes that are based in Pareto Non-Dominance levels show an excellent performance in at least one of the objectives, but poor performance in the rest of objectives. In this respect, optimization problems with hard restrictions, many local minima or with more than four objectives inspired many alternatives in preference relations to the selection process. To mention some, Favor Relation [4], ϵ-dominance [5], Fuzzy Pareto Dominance [6] and preference order ranking [7]. In this paper, an empirical comparison is carried out between some recent genetic algorithms, whose performances are assessed in this particular modelling problem. This study has two purposes: First, state-of-the-art multi-criteria optimization algorithms are assessed and it is determined whether they are suitable for performing multi-criteria modelling of semi-physical battery models. The Multi-Objective

Optimization Algorithms (MOOAs) were chosen for this study are: SPEA2 [8], NSGA-II [9], OMOPSO [10], NSGA-III [11], MOEA/D [12], in addition to the Ad-hoc hybrid algorithms in the original model [3] and the recently proposed θ-DEA [13]. Second, a minor modification has been introduced into the selection stage of the most recent algorithm (θ-DEA) that makes use of Preference Ordering (PO) in the ranking procedure. It is concluded that this modification is advantageous for this particular modelling problem. Lastly, it is remarked that a comparison between multi-criteria algorithms has certain technical difficulties on its own, as the assessment of the Pareto Fronts (PF) from different MOOAs is by itself a current research topic [14]. This study is based on Zitzler's binary additive ϵ-indicator to assess the different dominance relations between PFs [15].

The structure of the present paper is as follows: in Sect. 2, the battery model is outlined for the convenience of the reader. Section 3 introduces the proposed algorithm and put it into context. Section 4 contains experimental tests and discuss the obtained results. The paper concludes in Sect. 5.

2   Semi-physical Model for Li-Ion Battery

The semi-physical model studied in this work can be depicted as an electrical equivalent circuit comprising non-linear impedances described by means of FRBSs [3]. This semi-physical model implement the methodology described in [16]. The inputs of the model are: (i) the current i_B applied to the battery, positive or negative in charge or discharge process respectively; (ii) the ambient temperature T_A. On the other hand, the outputs are the battery voltage v_B and the battery temperature T_B. The model outputs are defined by the following differential equations:

$$v_B = i_B R_1 + \text{OCV}(Q) + \eta(Q, T_B, i_B) \tag{1}$$

$$\dot{T}_B = (\alpha(Q, i_B) + \beta T_B) \cdot i_B^2 + \gamma \cdot (T_B - T_A) \tag{2}$$

In the voltage output Eq. 1, R_1 is the series resistance in the RC equivalent circuit. The Open-Circuit Voltage (OCV) is a FRBS that depends of the stored charge in the battery Q which is time-dependent. (OCV) is an internal battery electrochemical characteristic defined as the difference in voltage between the terminals of a cell, in other words, voltage when the circuit is open [17]. The nonlinearity of the Eq. 1, the function $\eta(Q, T_B, i_B)$ represents the over-potential in the charge/discharge process and the time evolution of the system is described by the following nonlinear differential equation:

$$\dot{\eta} = -\tau(i_B) \cdot (\eta - f(Q, T_B, i_B) \cdot i_B) \tag{3}$$

$$f(Q, T_B, i_B) \cdot i_B = \begin{cases} f^+(Q, T_B) \cdot i_B & \text{when charging} \\ f^-(Q, T_B) \cdot i_B & \text{when discharging} \end{cases} \tag{4}$$

where f^+ and f^- are FRBS that depend of the charge and the battery temperature. The limited speed of the electrochemical process is modeled by a dependence between charge and capacity which is governed by an exponential decay with a time constant τ (that depends on i_B). The second output of the model represent the heat balance by the dynamical Eq. 2. The FRBS α depends on SoC and current.

$$\alpha(Q, i_B) = \begin{cases} \alpha^+(Q, i_B) \cdot i_B & \text{when charging} \\ \alpha^-(Q, i_B) \cdot i_B & \text{when discharging} \end{cases} \tag{5}$$

β and γ are constants, related with heating and cooling rates. The term $(\alpha(Q) + \beta T_B) \cdot i_B^2$ models the internal heating when charging/discharging the battery. The differential Eqs. 1, 2 and 3 are integrated by means of the implicit Euler's method (backward Euler's method), which is adequate for a slow system like this. The obtained discretized equations are:

$$v_B(t) = i_B(t) R_1 + \text{OCV}(Q_{(t)}) + \eta(t) \tag{6}$$

$$\eta(t + \Delta t) = \frac{\eta(t) + \Delta t \cdot \tau(i_{B_{(t+\Delta t)}}) \cdot i_B \cdot f(Q_{t+\Delta t}, T_{B_{t+\Delta t}}, i_{B_{t+\Delta t}})}{1 + \tau(i_{B_{t+\Delta t}}) \Delta t} \tag{7}$$

$$T_B(t + \Delta t) = \frac{T_B(t) + \Delta t \cdot (\alpha(Q_{(t+\Delta t)}, i_{B_{t+\Delta t}}) i_B^2(t + \Delta t) - \gamma T_B(t + \Delta t))}{1 - \Delta t \cdot (\beta i_B^2(t + \Delta t) - \gamma)} \tag{8}$$

The fuzzy rules in the model are zeroth-order Takagi-Sugeno-Kang type in which the antecedents are AND combinations of statements. For example, the following rule is part of the knowledge base of the forcing function $f^-(Q, T_B)$:

$$\text{If } Q \text{ is LOW and } T_B \text{ is HRT, then } f^-(Q, T_B) = 0.8$$

where Q and T_B are described by eight linguistic terms with triangular fuzzy sets joined to left and right trapezoidal for the extremes. The values of the linguistic variable Q (SoC) are: "VERY LOW (VL) CHARGE", "LOW (L) CHARGE", "QUASI LOW (QL) CHARGE", "MEDIUM LOW (ML) CHARGE", "MEDIUM HIGH (MH) CHARGE", "QUASI HIGH (QH) CHARGE", "HIGH (H) CHARGE", and "VERY HIGH (VH) CHARGE". The linguistic terms for the variable T_B is based on the rise of temperature (RT): ("VL-RT", "L-RT", "QL-RT", "ML-RT", "MH-RT", "QH-RT", "H-RT", "VH-RT"). Moreover, the current i_B use three terms: "POSITIVE", "ZERO" and "NEGATIVE". All fuzzy memberships in this model are part of strong fuzzy partitions.

3   Learning the Studied Model

Learning the semi-physical battery model consists in finding the unknown parameters of the discretized Eqs. 6, 7 and 8 by means of a multi-objective optimization algorithm. In the present study, a list of relevant state-of-the-art MOOAs has been build, albeit the list is by no means complete. It is highlighted that the recent proposed θ-Dominance Evolutionary Algorithm (θ-DEA) has been included, as it seems to be particularly well suited to the problem at hand.

The algorithms being studied include the well-known Zitzler's Strength Pareto Evolutionary Algorithm (SPEA2) [8] and Deb's Nondominated Sorting Genetic Algorithm (NSGA-II) [9]. In addition, the third version of this last algorithm (NSGA-III) is also included. NSGA-III replaces the crowding distance operator of the second version with a clustering operator aided by a set of well-distributed reference points [11]. In the same spirit, a Multi-Objective Evolutionary Algorithm based on Decomposition (MOEA/D) proposed by Zhang and Li in [12], is also included in this study. MOEA/D is based on conventional aggregation approaches in which the multi-criteria problem is decomposed into a number of scalar objective optimization problems. Lastly, the same authors of NSGA-III and MOEA/D jointly proposed a new algorithm named MOEA/DD [18]. The new approach exploits the merits of dominance and decomposition to obtain a balance between convergence and diversity. MOEA/DD is suitable for problems with a high number of objectives and therefore it is not suitable for the model proposed in this paper. In addition to this, Sierra and Coello Coello propose OMOPSO [10], is an improving of Particle Swarm Optimization for Multi-Objective Problems based on Pareto dominance and using the crowding factor for the selection of leaders.

The θ-DEA recently proposed by Yuan [13] merge the fitness evaluation scheme of MOEA/D and the strength of NSGA-III preserving the diversity. The θ-dominance is based in nondominated sorting scheme, the solutions are clustered around distributed reference points. The parameters $H1$ and $H2$ make a proportion between the population size and the divisions of boundary and inner layers with linear hyperplane respect to the reference points. The environmental selection procedure prefers solutions with better fitness value in the competitive relationship in each cluster preserving the diversity. The chosen aggregation fitness function similar to penalty-based boundary intersection function [18] based on the distance $d1$, $d2$ and the penalty parameter θ (see reference [13] for details).

$$F_j(x) = d_{j,1}(x) + \theta d_{j,2}(x) \qquad j \in 1, 2, ..., N \qquad (9)$$

The fitness function $F_j(x)$ is the evaluation scheme of the solution x in a given cluster where N represent the number of reference point.

In this paper it is proposed that domain specific knowledge is incorporated into the evolutionary process by means of a preference ordering that sorts nondominated solutions. In this particular case, the proposed preference ordering in the individuals selection introduce knowledge respect to the Open-Circuit Voltage of the battery. In other words, a framework of θ-DEA modifying the ranking fitness function is used, Eq. 10.

$$F_j(x) = (d_{j,1}(x) + \theta d_{j,2}(x)) * E_{OCV} \qquad (10)$$

where $E_{OCV} = 1/24 \sum_{Q_i=1}^{24} \{V_B(\mathrm{OCV}(Q_i) - \mathrm{OCV}(Q_i)^{TRUE}\}^2$. The Battery Test Laboratory at Oviedo University (Spain) provided us with the real OCV each ten percent of the State of Change $SoC = f(Q)$, with a total of twenty-four pairs of (SoC, Q). All in all, is understood that in the preference order approach the individuals in each cluster change slightly the ranking order respect θ-dominance. The next section discuss the results of the proposed algorithm.

4   Experimental Results and Discussion

Collected data in the Battery Test Laboratory is divided in three files with one charge-discharge cycles (DS-C/3, DS-C/2 and DS-C)[1], one per discharge currents 14A, 21A and 42A. The present section begin describing the methodology that was used to compare the different Pareto Fronts. A subsection is added showing numerical results and discussing the proposed algorithm and the state-of-the-art of the multi-objectives optimization algorithms in the studied problems.

4.1   Statistical Experimental Design

Different operators exist that can be used for examining the different dominance relations between Pareto Fronts in the experiments. Following [15], unary quality indicators were not the best choice, because they oversimplify the comparisons. Statistical studies with unary quality indicators as Generational Distance (GD), Inverted Hypervolume Indicator, among other, required the true Pareto of the problem. The binary additive ϵ-indicator measure was selected to assess the different techniques instead. This metric is defined as follows [19]: $I_{\epsilon+}(A, B) = \inf \{\varepsilon \in \mathbb{R} \mid \forall b \in B \, \exists a \in A : a \succeq_{\varepsilon+} b\}$ where $A, B \in X$, ϵ express the minimum factor that we can add to each objective value in $b \in B$ and the resulting objective is still weakly dominated by $a \in A$.

When $I_{\epsilon+}(A, B) < 0$, A strictly dominates B ($A \succ\succ B$). If $I_{\epsilon+}(A, B) = 0$ and $I_{\epsilon+}(B, A) = 0$, then A and B represent the same PF. Otherwise, if $I_{\epsilon+}(A, B) \leq 0$ and $I_{\epsilon+}(B, A) > 0$ then A is better than B ($A \triangleright B$). If both epsilon are greater than zero A and B are incomparable ($A \parallel B$).

In the present study each assessment algorithm was launched ten times. The Pareto front was built by combining all non-dominated models that were found by each algorithm at these ten iterations.

4.2   Assessment of Multi-Objective Optimization Algorithms

According to the experimentation with the state-of-the-art MOOAs in three different datasets the Pareto Fronts obtained are depicted in Fig. 1. The solutions in Fig. 1(a), (b) and (c) (from left-to-right and top-to-bottom) correspond to the input datasets DS-C, DS-C2 and DS-C3 respectively. Note that the precision of solutions are different in therm of significant figures for each objective. This phenomenon is related with the unit of measurement, the maximum model

---

[1] Data publicly available at http://www.unioviedo.es/batterylab/.

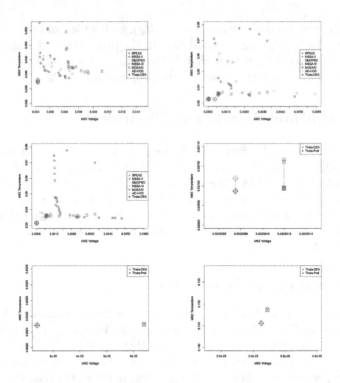

Fig. 1. From upper to lower, left to right: outcomes of the MOOAs (a) Resulting PFs with dataset DS-C as input; (b) DS-C2 as input and (c) DS-C3 as input. (d), (e) and (f): outcomes of the second experiment with θ-DEA and the proposed algorithm.

voltage curves error are twenty millivolts while the maximum temperature curve error are less than zero point five Celsius degrees. All in all, the solutions are reasonable from a practical point of view.

The poor performance of NSGA-II is remarked, for the particular cases of Fig. 1b and c. It is improved by NSGA-III and even by SPEA2 but with a higher consumption of memory and time for the last one. Notice also that, in the resulting PF from MOEA/D in the particular case of the datasets DS-C (Fig. 1a) is the worst, whereas that, in the rest of the datasets shows good performance.

The main conclusions of the Fig. 1 is the graphical evidence that the recently proposed θ-dominance relationship improve the leaning process of the studied Li-Ion battery model. θ-DEA outperforms the Ad-Hoc hybrid algorithm and the rest of the MOOAs. The Tables 1 and 2 depict the dominance relationships based on the selected binary additive indicator for all the studied algorithms across the three datasets above mentioned. The lower triangular matrix for each dataset dimension shows the relationships based on the indicators $I_{\epsilon+}(A, B)$ and $I_{\epsilon+}(B, A)$. Notice that the superiority of the θ-DEA is reaffirmed numerically for the studied problem.

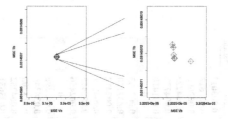

Fig. 2. PF accuracy of the proposed algorithm with dataset DS-C/3 as input.

4.3   Assessment of the Proposed Preference Order

The last three drawings in Fig. 1(d); (e) and (f) depict the resulting PFs from
θ-DEA and the proposed algorithm with a low number of evaluations.

Table 1. Binary additive epsilon indicator between θ-DEA and the proposed algorithm.

		A = θ-DEA		A = Partial preferences	
		$I_{\epsilon+}(A, B)$	Relation	$I_{\epsilon+}(A, B)$	Relation
DS-C	B = θ-DEA	0	=	7.104480E-6	
	B = Partial pref.	-4.465794E-7	◁	0	=
DS-C2	B = θ-DEA	0	=	8.135880E-6	
	B = Partial pref.	-3.458562E-6	◁	0	=
DS-C3	B = θ-DEA	0	=	6.658846E-7	
	B = Partial pref.	-4.685980-7	◁	0	=

This result clearly signals that the new ranking based on domain specific
knowledge preference improve the original θ-DEA in the particular case of the
complex studied problem. One criticism that can be made about the proposed
algorithms, is caused by the preferences of solutions, that are directly related
with the voltage output of the model (Eq. 1) and the domain of the voltage
variable. The effect is that the error of the voltage objective is lower than the
temperature objective. On the other hand, observe that in figures in this section
PFs are collapsed to points in the feasible area. This is an effect of the scale of
the variables; for a best understanding, the PF of the proposed algorithms with
dataset DS-C3 as input (Fig. 1(f)) is zoomed in Fig. 2.

Table 2. Binary additive epsilon indicator relations between the multi-objective optimization algorithms.

		A = SPEA2		A = NSGA-II		A = OMOPSO		A = NSGA-III		A = MOEA/D		A = AD-HOC		A = θ-DEA	
		$I_{\epsilon+}(A,B)$	relation	$I_{\epsilon+}(A,B)$	relation	$I_{\epsilon+}(A,B)$	relation	$I_{\epsilon+}(A,B)$	relation	$I_{\epsilon+}(A,B)$	relation	$I_{\epsilon+}(A,B)$	relation	$I_{\epsilon+}(A,B)$	relation
DS-C	B = SPEA2	0	=	-0.001092	=	0.000532		0.000558		-0.001456		0.001601		0.003011	
	B = NSGA-II	0.006690	△	0	=	0.005207	=	0.007084		0.004785		0.007207		0.007812	
	B = OMOPSO	0.002396	=	0.001137	=	0	△	0.002274		-0.000422		0.002000		0.002605	
	B = NSGA-III	0.001583	△	-0.000259	▽	0.001617	△	0	△	-0.000232	=	0.003054	=	0.004223	=
	B = MOEA/D	0.003939	△	0.002679	=	0.002127	▽	0.003817	▽	0	▽	0.004127	▽	0.004732	
	B = AD-HOC	-0.001396	▽	-0.000137	▽	-0.001000	▽	-0.001274	▽	-0.002422	▽	0	=	0.001410	
	B = θ-DEA	-0.000014	▽	-0.001273	▽	-0.002410	▽	-0.000136	▽	-0.003027	▽	-0.000605	▽	0	=
DS-C2	B = SPEA2	0	=	-0.000215	=	0.001087	=	-0.000127	=	0.001572	=	0.001570		0.002283	
	B = NSGA-II	0.035407	△	0	=	0.034758	=	0.034171		0.034715		0.034714		0.037170	
	B = OMOPSO	0.000835	=	0.000620	=	0	=	0.000581		0.000620		0.000802		0.002412	
	B = NSGA-III	0.002588	△	0.000041	=	0.002907	▽	0	▽	0.003107	=	0.003289	=	0.004871	=
	B = MOEA/D	0.000691	▽	-4.6E-07	▽	0.000043	▽	-0.000039	▽	0	▽	0.000207	▽	0.002455	
	B = AD-HOC	-0.000693	▽	-0.000182	▽	-0.000044	▽	-0.000117	▽	-0.000001	▽	0	=	0.002456	
	B = θ-DEA	-0.000297	▽	-0.000512	▽	-0.001132	▽	-0.000551	▽	-0.000511	▽	-0.000330	▽	0	=
DS-C3	B = SPEA2	0	=	0.000437	=	0.000626	=	0.001225	=	0.001539	=	0.001839		0.003396	
	B = NSGA-II	0.035424	=	0	▽	0.024038	▽	0.034108	=	0.034715		0.035714		0.038346	
	B = OMOPSO	0.011514	=	-0.000085	▽	0	▽	0.010075	▽	0.010677		0.011676		0.014308	
	B = NSGA-III	0.001444	=	-0.000301	△	-0.000216	▽	0	▽	0.000645	=	0.001635	=	0.004252	=
	B = MOEA/D	0.000836	=	-0.000020	△	0.000065	▽	0.000281	▽	0	▽	0.000999	▽	0.003631	
	B = AD-HOC	-0.000162	▽	-0.000152	▽	-0.000067	▽	-0.000149	▽	-0.000132	▽	0	=	0.002632	
	B = θ-DEA	-0.000960	▽	-0.000524	▽	-0.000439	▽	-0.000223	▽	-0.000504	▽	-0.000372	▽	0	=

5   Conclusion

An empirical study has been presented where different multicriteria optimization algorithms have been applied to a specific learning of a semi-physical battery model. It is remarked that the θ-dominance favor the convergence of learning process. A minor change has been proposed to the selection stage of θ-DEA algorithm has been proposed where domain specific knowledge was used to alleviate the computational burden. In this paper it has been shown that knowledge based preference ordering of individuals found a very accurate solution of the complex studied model. Future work will focus on adaptive Multi-Objective Memetic Algorithms where local optimizers fine-tune the definition of the fuzzy rules in the last stages of the learning.

Acknowledgements. This work funded by the Eureka SD project (agreement number 2013-2591), that is supported by the Erasmus Mundus programme of the European Union. In addition, was supported by the Spanish Ministry of Science and Innovation (MICINN) and the Regional Ministry of the Principality of Asturias under Grants TIN2014-56967-R, DPI2013-46541-R and FC-15-GRUPIN14-073.

References

1. Cuma, M.U., Koroglu, T.: A comprehensive review on estimation strategies used in hybrid and battery electric vehicles. Renew. Sustain. Energy Rev. **42**, 517–531 (2015)
2. Waag, W., Fleischer, C., Sauer, D.U.: Critical review of the methods for monitoring of lithium-ion batteries in electric and hybrid vehicles. J. Power Sources **258**, 321–339 (2014)
3. Sanchez, L., Blanco, C., Anton, J.C., Garcia, V., Gonzalez, M., Viera, J.C.: A variable effective capacity model for LiFePO4 traction batteries using computational intelligence techniques. IEEE Trans. Industr. Electron. **62**(1), 555–563 (2015)
4. Drechsler, N., Drechsler, R., Becker, B.: Multi-objective optimisation based on relation favour. In: Zitzler, E., Thiele, L., Deb, K., Coello, C.A.C., Corne, D. (eds.) EMO 2001. LNCS, vol. 1993, pp. 154–166. Springer, Heidelberg (2001)
5. Laumanns, M., Thiele, L., Deb, K., Zitzler, E.: Combining convergence and diversity in evolutionary multiobjective optimization. Evol. Comput. **10**(3), 263–282 (2002)
6. Farina, M., Amato, P.: A fuzzy definition of "optimality" for many-criteria optimization problems. IEEE Trans. Syst. Man Cybern. Part A: Syst. Hum. **34**(3), 315–326 (2004)
7. di Pierro, F., Khu, S.T., Savic, D.A.: An investigation on preference ordering ranking scheme in multiobjective evolutionary optimization. IEEE Trans. Evol. Comput. **11**(1), 17–45 (2007)
8. Zitzler, E., Laumanns, M., Thiele, L.: SPEA2: improving the strength pareto evolutionary algorithm, pp. 95–100 (2001)
9. Deb, K., Pratap, A., Agarwal, S., Meyarivan, T.: A fast and elitist multiobjective genetic algorithm: NSGA-II. IEEE Trans. Evol. Comput. **6**(2), 182–197 (2002)

10. Sierra, M.R., Coello, C.A.C.: Improving PSO-based multi-objective optimization using crowding, mutation and ϵ-dominance. In: Coello Coello, C.A., Hernández Aguirre, A., Zitzler, E. (eds.) EMO 2005. LNCS, vol. 3410, pp. 505–519. Springer, Heidelberg (2005)

11. Deb, K., Jain, H.: An evolutionary many-objective optimization algorithm using reference-point-based nondominated sorting approach, part I: solving problems with box constraints. IEEE Trans. Evol. Comput. 18(4), 577–601 (2014)

12. Zhang, Q., Li, H.: MOEA/D: a multiobjective evolutionary algorithm based on decomposition. IEEE Trans. Evol. Comput. 11(6), 712–731 (2007)

13. Yuan, Y., Xu, H., Wang, B., Yao, X.: A new dominance relation based evolutionary algorithm for many-objective optimization. IEEE Trans. Evol. Comput. PP(99), 1 (2015)

14. Tutum, C.C., Deb, K.: A multimodal approach for evolutionary multi-objective optimization (MEMO): proof-of-principle results. In: Gaspar-Cunha, A., Antunes, C.H., Coello, C.C. (eds.) EMO 2015. LNCS, vol. 9018, pp. 3–18. Springer, Heidelberg (2015)

15. Zitzler, E., Laumanns, M., Thiele, L., Fonseca, C.M., da Fonseca, V.G.: Why quality assessment of multiobjective optimizers is difficult. In: GECCO 2002: Proceedings of the Genetic and Evolutionary Computation Conference, pp. 666–674. Morgan Kaufmann Publishers Inc., July 2002

16. Sánchez, L., Couso, I., González, M.: A design methodology for semi-physical fuzzy models applied to the dynamic characterization of LiFePO4 batteries. Appl. Soft Comput. 14, 269–288 (2014)

17. Linden, D.: Linden's Handbook of Batteries, 4th edn. McGraw-Hill, New York (2011)

18. Li, K., Deb, K., Zhang, Q., Kwong, S.: An evolutionary many-objective optimization algorithm based on dominance and decomposition. IEEE Trans. Evol. Comput. 19(5), 694–716 (2015)

19. Zitzler, E., Thiele, L., Laumanns, M., Fonseca, C., da Fonseca, V.: Performance assessment of multiobjective optimizers: an analysis and review. IEEE Trans. Evol. Comput. 7(2), 117–132 (2003)

Using Evolutionary Algorithms to Find the Melody of a Musical Piece

Enrique Alba and Andrés Camero[(⊠)]

Departamento de Lenguajes y Ciencias de la Computación,
Universidad de Málaga, Andalucía Tech, Málaga, Spain
eat@lcc.uma.es, andrescamero@uma.es

Abstract. The melody of a piece of music contains the essence of that piece. Its study has been done for centuries, evolving side by side with other concepts and notions of music. However, musical analysis techniques are known to be analyst dependent (i.e., subjective), thus we propose a mathematical approach for characterizing the melody by fitting a curve to the pitch contour. This melody fitting will be calculated by an evolutionary algorithm, and we will use a wide set of musical pieces of many different styles to ground our claims. As a conclusion, we not only compute melodies out of a piece of music, but we also offer a new way of encapsulating components of this melody, what could lead to future applications in music composition and understanding.

Keywords: Evolutionary algorithm · Pitch contour · Curve-fitting

1 Introduction

The term *melody* is a musical aspect related to the combination of pitch and rhythm. Since pitch and rhythm are related to the perception of sound [1], the term is often used in different manners. The music information retrieval (MIR) community widely adopted the definition given by Poliner et al. [12]: "the melody is the single (monophonic) pitch sequence that a listener might reproduce if asked to whistle or hum a piece of polyphonic music, and that a listener would recognize as being the 'essence' of that music when heard in comparison". But, how can we formally characterize a melody?

The traditional approach to melody characterization is given by *musical analysis*. Musical analysis is concerned with the overall form and with the melodic, harmonic, and rhythmic contents of music. Analytic methods chop up a musical piece into components and try to figure out how these components relate to each other and what relations are more important. Mathematics and computer science have provided tools to aid the process of analyzing music [10], however most of these techniques are an extension or automation of traditional methods: deriving the music from some rules [4]. Furthermore, it is widely accepted that there is no authoritative explanation of how components are related to each other [10], i.e. the analysis is subjective.

© Springer International Publishing Switzerland 2016
O. Luaces et al. (Eds.): CAEPIA 2016, LNAI 9868, pp. 321–330, 2016.
DOI: 10.1007/978-3-319-44636-3_30

The objective of this work is to demonstrate that the characterization of a melody can be done by describing it with mathematical functions. An evolutionary algorithm (EA) that fits Legendre polynomials and Trigonometric-polynomial functions to melodies, extracted from audio, is presented in this paper, along with performance results of the algorithm when analyzing a wide set of musical pieces. Section 2 outlines related work; Sect. 3 introduces the EA for approximating the melody; Sect. 4 shows the results obtained, and Sect. 5 presents the conclusions and proposes future work.

2   Background

Although there is much work related to interpolation [2], very few has been done up to date regarding melody approximation by mathematical functions. In order to address the problem we propose to begin by dividing the problem into components: (i) extracting the melody from a musical piece and (ii) finding a suitable set of functions for approximating the melody.

2.1   Melody Extraction and Segmentation

There are many different methods to extract the melody either from score or audio [14]. In *musical analysis context*, it is common to extract the melody from the audio, since the score is considered to be already *filtered* [10].

State of the art algorithms may extract the melody from a polyphonic audio source with an accuracy higher than 70 % [14] and some of these algorithms, for example *SG* proposed by Salamon and Gómez [13], are available as *Vamp* plugins (dynamic link libraries that process sampled audio data).

In the middle of the 18th century Mattheson [9] introduced the concept of *musical phrases*. A musical phrase is a sequence of consecutive notes that act as a unit and are described by the caesura (a complete pause). Then, the melody is made of a set of consecutive phrases. The detection of such pauses or phrase boundaries has been further studied and many rules and techniques have been defined [11]. Thom et al. [15] benchmarked automatic phrase segmentation techniques against human expert segmentation, concluding that musical phrases are ambiguous or rule dependent. Thus, in this work we will consider pauses (silences) as phrase boundaries.

2.2   Pitch Contour Approximation

As said before, the approach explored in this work does not extend musical analysis methods. Instead, we propose to use mathematical functions to approximate the *pitch contour*. Pitch contour is defined as the function that tracks the pitch over time, and according to Poliner et al. [12] definition of melody, we might consider that the pitch contour is a good approximation to the melody.

In speech processing we might find a similar problem within the analysis of *prosody*. Indeed the main attributes of prosody (in auditory terms) are the pitch of the voice, the length of the sounds, the loudness and the timbre. Those are the same parameters that are used to describe the perception of sound in music [1].

Among the prosodic parameters, the pitch contour is considered to be especially important when processing speech, thus there are several studies that approximate the pitch contour of the voice by fitting mathematical function. For example, Gu and Yiang [7] introduced a pitch contour generator for synthesizing speech, where the pitch contour was approximated by a discrete cosine transform (DCT). Lin and Wang [8] also proposed an automatic language identification technique based on the pitch contour, where the pitch contour was approximated by a set of Legendre polynomials. Thus, our hypothesis is that fitting is a good tool, and we will approach it with an EA.

3   Proposed Method

The goal of this work is to characterize the melody of a musical piece by fitting the pitch contour with basic mathematical functions, particularly Legendre polynomials and Trigonometric-polynomial. However, since there is a gap in the literature related to melody approximation by functions, the objective is narrowed to compare the two approaches in terms of performance and to outline the feasibility (quality) of using these approaches for characterizing the melody in a formal way.

The main idea is to extract the melody from a polyphonic audio, break it up into phrases and approximate the melody using mathematical functions, where the parameters of this functions will be calculated by an EA.

Figure 1 shows a high level view of the proposed system, that we call *Bio-inspired Music Approximation and Composition* (BMAC). The input of the system is a musical piece (in audio format). First, the melody is extracted from the audio, generating the pitch contour. Then the pitch contour is segmented into phrases, using pauses in the melody (silences) as phrase boundaries. Next, for each phrase a curve is fitted with an EA. Finally the output is a set of *vectors*, where each vector contains the parameters of the fitted function.

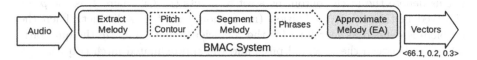

Fig. 1. High level view of the proposed system (BMAC) for approximating the melody of a musical piece by fitting mathematical functions with an evolutionary algorithm.

3.1   Legendre Polynomials Approximation

As proposed by Lin and Wang [8], the pitch contour may be approximated by a set of Legendre polynomials (see Fig. 2). Let us denote the pitch contour approximation as a temporal function $g(t)$, as described in Eq. 1:

$$g_L(t) = \sum_{i=0}^{N} \alpha_i P_i(t), \qquad (1)$$

where $P_i(t)$ denotes the i-th order Legendre polynomial and $\alpha_i \in \mathbb{R}$ the coefficients to be determined. Figure 2 shows the Legendre polynomials up to order 5. Note that $P_0(t) = 1$ and $P_1(t) = t$, thus simple pitch changes over time are easy to track.

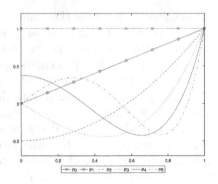

Fig. 2. Legendre polynomials up to order 5.

3.2 Trigonometric-Polynomial Approximation

Using the main idea proposed by Gu and Yiang [7], of approximating the pitch contour by applying DCT, and the proposal of Eubank and Speckman [6] of curve-fitting by trigonometric functions and low-order polynomial terms (in order to alleviate boundary problems), we define a Trigonometric-polynomial approximation as in Eq. 2:

$$g_T(t) = \kappa + \alpha t + \beta t^2 + \sum_{i=1}^{p} \gamma_i \sin i\omega t + \sum_{j=1}^{q} \delta_j \cos j\omega t, \qquad (2)$$

where $p, q \in \mathbb{N}$ are known parameters (the number of oscillators), $\omega \in \mathbb{R}^+$ is the frequency of the interpolant and $\kappa, \alpha, \beta, \gamma_i, \delta_i \in \mathbb{R}$ are the coefficients to be determined.

3.3 Search: Evolutionary Algorithm

The determination of the coefficients is modeled as a minimization problem. Let us denote the pitch contour as a set of points (t_i, f_i), where f_i is the *pitch* observed in time t_i. By definition (monophony) all t_i are distinct. Then the problem is defined as searching for the coefficients that minimize the quadratic difference between the observed pitch and the approximated pitch (Eq. 3).

$$F(t) = \sum_{i=1}^{L} (g(t_i) - f_i)^2, \qquad (3)$$

where L is the length of the sample, and $g(t) = g_L(t)$ and $g(t) = g_T(t)$ are the approximated pitch contour.

This measurement equals L times the mean square error [5], and intends to find the function that is closest to the observed pitch contour (i.e., maximum sound quality). To perform the search we define an evolutionary algorithm, briefly described in Algorithm 1.

Algorithm 1. Evolutionary algorithm for approximating the melody.

Data: Piece of music (in audio format), maximum number of evaluations (E_{max}), crossover probability P_c and mutation probability P_m.

Result: Set of functions that approximate the melody

begin

    extractMelody ; // **Convert from audio to MIDI samples**

    segmentMelody ; // **Chop up the melody into** *phrases*

    for *each phrase* **do**

        Calculate *mean* and *stdv* of the pitches f_i of the phrase ;

        Initialize population ;

        Evaluate population using fitness function ;

        while *Fitness* > 0 *or Number of evaluations* $< E_{max}$ **do**

            Generate the offspring using binary tournament selection and single point crossover with probability P_c ;

            Mutate each individual with P_m ;

            Evaluate the offspring using fitness function ;

            Replacement of the population ; // **Truncate, elitism or rank**

Each individual corresponds to a possible solution (vector of the parameters defined in Eqs. 1 and 2) and is encoded into a chromosome that contains GN genes, where $||GN_L|| = N + 1$ the maximum order of the Legendre polynomial plus one (there is an order zero Legendre polynomial); and $||GN_T|| = 3 + p + q$ the total number of coefficients to be determined in Trigonometric-polynomial approach. Each gene is of length $GL = 1$ and is encoded as a real number. For example, a Legendre individual (order 2) may be represented by the vector $l = <66.1, 0.2, 0.3>$, where the coefficients correspond to $<\alpha_0, \alpha_1, \alpha_2>$.

Since the initialization of the population in EAs affects the convergence speed, we defined two algorithms based on the distribution of the notes (refer to Sect. 4.1) and on the form of the mathematical functions used (Eqs. 1 and 2). The function $init_L$ (Algorithm 2) initializes an individual for the Legendre approach. The value of α_0 (associated with P_0, constant in time) is set near the *mean* tone, i.e. with a normal distribution having a mean equal to the *mean* of the phrase and a standard deviation equal to the standard deviation (*stdv*) of the phrase being processed. The subsequent coefficients are initialized with a standard normal distribution. The motivation is to use the Legendre polynomials of order greater than zero to model the changes of the pitch over time.

Note that the function $randomGaussian(mean, stdv)$ returns a real number with a normal distribution (with a given mean and standard deviation).

The initialization of individuals for the Trigonometric-polynomial approach is defined by the $init_T$ function, which is described in Algorithm 3.

The mutation of an individual (for both approaches) is defined in Algorithm 4. The mutated gene is assigned with a normally distributed value with a mean equal to the original value of the gene and a standard deviation equal to

---

Algorithm 2. Function $init_L$, for initializing a 'Legendre' individual.

Data: Number of genes GN_L, *mean* and *stdv* of the phrase.
Result: Individual initialized using the statistics of the phrase.
begin

$\quad gene_1 = randomGaussian(mean, stdv)$; // α_0 `parameter`
$\quad$**for** $i = 3$ **to** $N + 1$ **do**
$\quad\quad gene_2 = randomGaussian(0, 1)$; // α_i `parameters`

Algorithm 3. Function $init_T$, 'Trigonometric-polynomial' individual init.

Data: *Mean* and *stdv* of the phrase, p and q (number of sine and cosine).
Result: Individual initialized using the statistics of the phrase.
begin

$\quad gene_1 = randomGaussian(mean, stdv)$; // `Set` κ `with value near the`
$\quad\quad$ `mean tone`
$\quad gene_2 = randomGaussian(0, stdv)$; // `Parameter` α, `used to alleviate`
$\quad\quad$ `boundary problems`
$\quad gene_3 = randomGaussian(0, stdv)$: // `Parameter` β
$\quad$**for** $i = 4$ **to** $p + q$ **do**
$\quad\quad gene_i = randomGaussian(0, stdv)$; // `Set parameters` γ_j `and` δ_j,
$\quad\quad\quad$ `associated with p sines and q cosines. The initial values`
$\quad\quad\quad$ `are set to track the max and min pitch`

---

stdv (standard dev. of the phrase). In order to generate smaller perturbations as the number of evaluations increases, the *stdv* value is adjusted by $\epsilon \leq 1$.

The selection of the individuals for creating the offspring is made by a binary tournament, while the offspring is created using two individuals (parents) that are crossed using single point crossover (SPX) with a probability P_c. SPX is defined as selecting n genes from the first parent and $GN - n$ genes from the second, where $0 \leq n \leq GN$ and n is randomly selected. Note that with $1 - P_c$ probability one of the parents is returned unmodified (with uniform probability).

We defined three variants for replacing the population: (i) *truncate*, generate one offspring and replace the worst individual of the population with it; (ii) *elitism*, generate $O_s = pop - 1$ offspring, where *pop* is the size of the population, and preserve the best individual of the original population; and (iii) *rank*, generate $O_s > pop$ offspring, rank the offspring along with the original population and select the fittest individuals to generate the new population (of size *pop*).

4   Results

We tested the proposed algorithm using 1000 musical pieces (30 s of audio each) from various genres: blues, classical, country, disco, hip-hop, jazz, metal, pop, reggae and rock. This dataset was defined by Tzanetakis and Cook [16].

Algorithm 4. Function *mutate*, for mutating and individual.

Data: Individual, mutation probability (P_m) and *stdv* of the phrase.
Result: Mutated individual.
begin
    for $i = 1$ **to** *NumberofGenes* **do**
        if $random(0, 1) \leq P_m$ **then**
            // One gene mutated per individual on average
            $gene_i = randomGaussian(gene_i, stdv)$;
        $stdDev = stdDev * \epsilon$; // Smaller perturbations over time

---

The melody of each musical piece was extracted using the software *Sonic Annotator* [3] and the Vamp plugin *Melodía*, an implementation of the algorithm SG proposed by Salamon and Gómez [13]. The approximation of each melody is repeated 30 times (independent executions) for each approach (Legendre and Trigonometric-polynomial), in order to enable statistical analysis.

4.1 Preprocessing and Tuning

We analyzed the extracted melodies to set the parameters of the algorithm. Figure 3 shows the probabilistic distribution of the notes (MIDI notation) of a subset of the melodies of the dataset and the normal curve fitted to the histogram.

The W value of Shapiro-Wilk normality test is equal to 0.98. We concluded that the normal distribution is a good approximation to the distribution of the notes of the melodies; thus the initialization of the algorithm will be made by using the *mean* and *stdv* of each phrase.

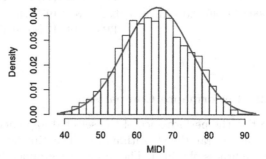

Fig. 3. Histogram of notes (MIDI) in dataset.

Several combinations of the parameters of the algorithm were tested using a subset of the musical pieces (a summary is presented on Table 1), concluding that the best results are obtained for a $pop = 50$, $O_s = 49$, $E_{max} = 10000$, $P_c = 0.8$ and $P_m = 1/GN$. Regarding the approach of Legendre polynomials, the best results in terms of fitness were obtained by polynomials up to order 3 $(GN = 4)$. Polynomials up to order 5 $(GN = 6)$ were also tested, but because of the rapid increments (noise) produced by higher order polynomials the results showed a higher variance and mean error. Lin and Wang [8] also stated that, for speech processing using Legendre polynomials, up to order 3 is good enough. In the case of Trigonometric-polynomial approach, the best results were obtained with $p = q = 6$ (the number of oscillators) and $\omega = 16$.

Table 1. Overall comparison of the EA performance over the *tuning* dataset using Legendre of order 3 approach and Trigonometric-polynomial approach with $p = q = 6$ and $\omega = 16$ (TP 6-6-16).

Configuration							Mean	
E_{max}	pop	O_s	P_c	P_m	ϵ	Approach	Fitness	Time [s]
20000	50	1	0.8	1/GN	1.00	Legendre 3	20496.85	16.63
						TP 6-6-16	17517.30	88.57
10000	50	1	0.8	1/GN	1.00	Legendre 3	20661.08	8.39
						TP 6-6-16	17914.52	45.01
10000	10	1	0.8	1/GN	1.00	Legendre 3	25295.54	8.58
						TP 6-6-16	17877.87	45.50
10000	50	1	0.2	1/GN	1.00	Legendre 3	20902.93	8.81
						TP 6-6-16	17939.47	45.77
10000	50	49	0.8	1/GN	1.00	Legendre 3	19787.03	8.06
						TP 6-6-16	17522.05	47.24
10000	10	9	0.8	1/GN	1.00	Legendre 3	23563.03	7.39
						TP 6-6-16	17493.27	47.08
10000	10	50	0.0	1/GN	1.00	Legendre 3	21345.29	7.56
						TP 6-6-16	18162.28	44.04
10000	50	49	0.8	1/GN	0.99	Legendre 3	18833.71	8.20
						TP 6-6-16	17751.09	45.51
10000	50	49	0.0	1/GN	0.99	Legendre 3	19738.45	8.18
						TP 6-6-16	17880.60	43.92

Table 2. L3 parameters.

Parameter	Value
pop	50
0_s	49
GN	4
P_c	0.80
P_m	0.25
ϵ	0.99
E_{max}	10000

Table 3. TP 6-6-16 parameters.

Parameter	Value
pop	50
O_s	49
GN	15
P_c	0.80
P_m	0.07
ϵ	0.99
E_{max}	10000
ω	16

4.2   Performance Comparison

To test the performance of the selected approaches (refer to Tables 2 and 3 for details) we ran the algorithm over the entire dataset. Figure 4 shows a summary of the fitness obtained. The results are grouped by the method used to approximate the pitch contour, where *L3* stands for the Legendre approach using poly-

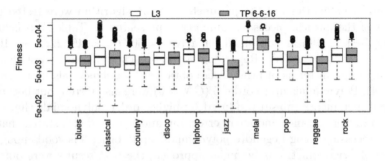

Fig. 4. Fitness comparison by musical genre. The Legendre approach is presented in white and the Trigonometric-polynomial approach in gray.

nomials up to order 3 and *TP 6-6-16* for Trigonometric-polynomial approach with $p = q = 6$ (the number of oscillators) and $\omega = 16$.

Considering the overall results, *TP 6-6-16* was a 5 % better than *L3* on average, however *L3* proved to be 6x faster than *TP 6-6-16*. In terms of fitness, the results by genre are similar for both approaches, thus the differences (quality of the approximation) between genres may be related to the intrinsic form of the melodies, rather than to the set of functions.

We selected a musical piece (randomly) and used the best solution given by the algorithm (for both approaches) to reconstruct the pitch contour[1] extracted by SG algorithm. Figure 5 shows the approximated pitch contour for a *pop* melody (fragment). The shaded areas (in gray) of the plots correspond to approximation errors. There is a clear mathematical suitability of the approximation (relative small error). From the audio point of view, these approximations allowed the regular human recognition of the melody, and *sounds* like someone learning a musical piece (there are few notes out of tune).

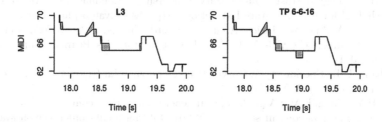

Fig. 5. Melody reconstruction of a *pop* melody (fragment). The approximation relative error is equal to 18 % for L3 approach and 21 % for TP 6-6-16 approach.

5 Conclusions

In this work we have introduced an approach for characterizing the melody of a musical piece by approximating the pitch contour by basic mathematical functions: Legendre polynomials and Trigonometric-polynomial, and we proposed a fitting method based on an evolutionary algorithm.

The results show that a mathematical approximation of the pitch contour is feasible for both methods presented. While the Legendre approximation proved to be faster than the Trigonometric-polynomial, this last showed a slightly better performance in terms of numerical fitting.

Despite that the fitted curve may not be as accurate as other state of the art methods, the results obtained (approximation vectors) may be useful for the further understanding of melodies, because of their simplicity. We are planning to perform a vector analysis on the results to spot patterns. We are also planning to test splines as an alternative approximation method, but we envision a problem there in order to analyze the meaning of the parameters worked out.

---

[1] For audio samples please refer to http://neo.lcc.uma.es/staff/acamero.

We propose as a future work to use other concepts introduced for automatic music composition. The idea is to generate original melodies by using the functions introduced in this paper, a set of parameters (that may be extracted or not from the approximation vectors obtained), and *time* vectors (the range and regularity of t, the input of the function). We also plan to use a still larger dataset (including more genres, like Flamenco) to improve the analysis.

Acknowledgments. This work has been partially funded by the Spanish MINECO and FEDER project TIN2014-57341-R (http://moveon.lcc.uma.es).

References

1. ANSI, ASA: Acoustics: ANSI/ASA S1 (2013)
2. Bergh, J., Lofstrom, J.: Interpolation Spaces: An Introduction. Grundlehren der mathematischen Wissenschaften. Springer, Heidelberg (2012)
3. Centre for Digital Music, Queen Mary, University of London: Sonic Annotator: A Batch Tool for Audio Feature Extraction. http://www.vamp-plugins.org/
4. Cook, N.: A Guide to Musical Analysis. Oxford University Press, Oxford (1994)
5. DeGroot, M.H., Schervish, M.J.: Probability and Statistics. Pearson, Upper Saddle River (2011)
6. Eubank, R.L., Speckman, P.: Curve fitting by polynomial-trigonometric regression. Biometrika **77**(1), 1–9 (1990)
7. Gu, H.Y., Jiang, K.W.: A pitch-contour generation method combining ANN, global variance, and real-contour selection. In: 2015 International Conference on Machine Learning and Cybernetics, pp. 396–402. IEEE, Guangzhou (2015)
8. Lin, C.Y., Wang, H.C.: Language identification using pitch contour information. In: Proceedings of International Conference on Acoustics, Speech and Signal Processing I, pp. 601–604 (2005)
9. Mattheson, J.: Kern Melodischer Wissenschafft (Nachdruck der Ausgabe Hamburg) (1976). (Original work published 1737)
10. Meredith, D.: Computational Music Analysis. Springer, Heidelberg (2015)
11. Neuhaus, C., Knösche, T.R., Friederici, A.D.: Effects of musical expertise and boundary markers on phrase perception in music. J. Cogn. Neurosci. **18**(3), 472–493 (2006)
12. Poliner, G.E., Ellis, D.P.W., Ehmann, F., Gómez, E., Steich, S., Ong, B.: Melody transcription from music audio: approaches and evaluation. IEEE Trans. Audio Speech Lang. Process. **15**(4), 1247–1256 (2007)
13. Salamon, J., Gomez, E.: Melody extraction from polyphonic music signals using pitch contour characteristics. IEEE Trans. Audio Speech Lang. Process. **20**(6), 1759–1770 (2012)
14. Salamon, J., Gomez, E., Ellis, D.P.W., Richard, G.: Melody extraction from polyphonic music signals: approaches, applications, and challenges. IEEE Signal Process. Mag. **31**, 118–134 (2014)
15. Thom, B., Spevak, C., Höthker, K.: Melodic segmentation: evaluating the performance of algorithms and musical experts. In: Proceedings of the International Computer Music Conference, 2002(12), pp. 65–72 (2002)
16. Tzanetakis, G., Cook, P.: Musical genre classification of audio signals. IEEE Trans. Speech Audio Process. **10**(5), 293–302 (2002)

Optimizing Airline Crew Scheduling Using Biased Randomization: A Case Study

Alba Agustín[1], Aljoscha Gruler[2(✉)], Jesica de Armas[2], and Angel A. Juan[2]

[1] Public University of Navarra, Pamplona, Spain
albamaria.agustin@unavarra.es
[2] Open University of Catalonia, Barcelona, Spain
{agruler,jde_armasa,ajuanp}@uoc.edu

Abstract. Various complex decision making problems are related to airline planning. In the competitive airline industry, efficient crew scheduling is hereby of major practical importance. This paper presents a metaheuristic approach based on biased randomization to tackle the challenging Crew Pairing Problem (CPP). The objective of the CPP is the establishment of flight pairings allowing for cost minimizing crew-flight assignments. Experiments are done using a real-life case with different constraints. The results show that our easy-to-use and fast algorithm reduces overall crew flying times and the necessary number of accompanying crews compared to the pairings currently applied by the company.

Keywords: Biased randomization · Airline planning · Metaheuristics · Crew pairing problem · Crew scheduling

1 Introduction

The airline industry is highly competitive, leading to constant pressure on commercial airlines to reduce costs wherever possible. After fuel, flight crew expenses are hereby the second highest source of costs. Thus, efficient crew scheduling and the resulting operational challenges are of major practical importance [6].

Airline planning consists of a number of consecutive steps, each related to different operational challenges: *(i)* the schedule design, during which the company decides which airports to serve and the corresponding connections and their frequencies, *(ii)* the fleet assignment problem in which the aircraft type for each connection is defined, *(iii)* aircraft maintenance routing to ensure an efficient flight schedule considering different maintenance requirements, and *(iv)* crew scheduling [5]. Optimization problems concerning the efficient scheduling of cockpit and cabin crews to reach cost minimizing crew-flight assignments can be further divided. On the one hand, a sequence of flights (so called *pairings*) to be served by a single crew is defined in the Crew Pairing Problem (CPP). On the other hand, the Crew Assignment Problem arises in the so called rostering process, during which individual crews are assigned to one of the established pairings. This paper addresses the CPP, whose intermediate position in the complete planning process can be seen in Fig. 1.

© Springer International Publishing Switzerland 2016
O. Luaces et al. (Eds.): CAEPIA 2016, LNAI 9868, pp. 331–340, 2016.
DOI: 10.1007/978-3-319-44636-3_31

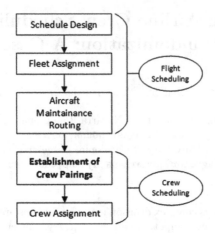

Fig. 1. Position of the CPP in the complete airline planning process

In this paper, a metaheuristic approach based on biased randomization to solve the CPP is presented. The algorithm is tested using a real-life data set provided by a commercial airline (which will not be named due to the existing agreement with the company). Results show that the pairings established by the applied metaheuristic decreases overall crew flying times as well as the necessary number of crews to serve all scheduled flights. Hereby different solutions are provided in only a few seconds, making the algorithm adaptable to short term flight schedule changes and allowing for more decision making flexibility.

This work is structured as follows: the CPP and biased randomization are reviewed and discussed in Sect. 2. Our solution approach is outlined in Sect. 3. In Sect. 4, the suggested algorithm (implemented as C++ application) is tested on a set of real-life data. Finally, the work concludes and discusses possible future work in Sect. 5.

2   Biased Randomization as CPP Solution Approach

2.1   The Crew Pairing Problem

Problem Description. Given a timetable with all the flight legs that must be carried out by an airline during the next few days, the goal is to generate round-trip routes (pairings) of minimum cost that cover all these legs. Each pairing is assigned to a different crew (hence the name crew pairing) and spans over a number of working days (duties). On the one hand, the complexity of the CPP is driven by the problem size which increases exponentially with a growing number of flight legs that need to be scheduled [21]. On the other hand, various problem constraints for both, flights and crew, need to be considered as shown in Fig. 2. As such, established flight schedules defining the date and time of flights need to be considered. Furthermore, labor regulations and internal company rules need to be adhered to: each pairing must start and end at the same airport (the base location of the crew), a minimum transfer time between flight connections must be met, and a limit in daily crew working hours as well as consecutive working days cannot be exceeded.

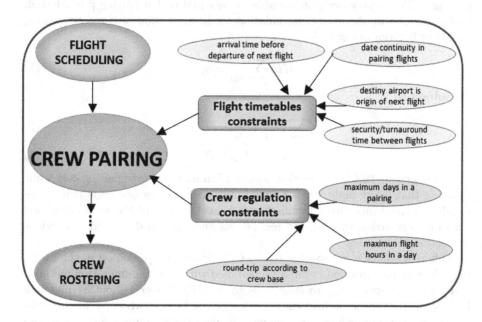

Fig. 2. Flight constraints and crew constraints of the CPP

To illustrate the CPP, a simple example with flight legs between three Cities (A, B, C) on a three day planning horizon can be seen in Table 1. The proposed solution (when considering airport A as crew base) shows that the scheduled flights can be completed by two crews (see Table 2).

Table 1. Simple flight scheduling example

Day	Day 1			Day 2			Day 3	
Flight	A-B	A-C	B-A	A-B	C-A	B-A	A-C	C-A
Departure	10:00	10:00	13:00	8:00	15:00	16:00	9:00	13:00
Arrival	11:35	13:05	14:35	9:35	18:05	17:35	12:05	16:05

Table 2. Possible crew pairings

Pairing	Day	Flight Sequence
X	1	A-B, B-A
	2	A-B, B-A

Pairing	Day	Flight Sequence
Y	1	A-C
	2	C-A
	3	A-C, C-A

Mathematical Formulation. Given a set F of all flights legs (or segments) the aim of the CPP is to establish sequences of flight legs i from a set P of all possible crew pairings in such a way that the sum of crew pairing cost c_p is minimized. In this article we consider c_p as the overall crew flying times in pairing p. The binary decision variables y_p is equal to 1 if pairing p is selected, 0 otherwise. A mathematical formulation for basic version of the crew pairing problems is given below [11].

$$Min \sum_{p \in P} c_p y_p \tag{1}$$

Subject to

$$\sum_{p:i \in P} y_p = 1; i \in F \tag{2}$$

$$y_p \in 0, 1; p \in P \tag{3}$$

Summarizing this mathematical model minimizes the crew pairing cost while ensuring that every flight leg is covered only once, i.e. by one crew pairing. In real-life applications, this simplified model must be completed with additional constraints referring to workload regulations and rules as described in previous subsection.

Different solution approaches to the CPP have been presented in the literature. A large neighborhood search is combined with exact enumeration methods and integer programming to solve a large scale CPP over a monthly planning horizon in [4]. Another hybrid approach is discussed by [1], who present three different solution approaches based on genetic algorithms, column generation, and a knowledge based random algorithm. Case studies in which the CPP is applied in practical problem settings have also been investigated in the past. In [22], column generation for the improvement of crew pairings of a commercial Taiwanese airline is proposed. Furthermore, [14] establish a robust CPP model considering the short term integration of new flights for small local Turkish airlines. For an extensive overview over the robust CPP, see [20]. While the CPP is discussed as individual optimization issue in the works mentioned in this paragraph, some approaches to integrate the CPP with other airline planning problems exist. An integrated approach over all planning steps is discussed in [16,18]. Furthermore, [15] combine the aircraft routing problem with crew scheduling, while the CPP and the crew assignment problem is solved globally by [13].

2.2 Metaheuristics Based on Biased Randomization

By trading the guarantee for optimality against faster computation times, approximate metaheuristic methods are often the method of choice for large scale optimization problems [19]. Hereby the use of randomization techniques in the construction and/or local search phase is a common approach to tackle combinatorial optimization problems (COPs) [2,3]. Randomization techniques are often included in multi-start methods, which use multiple algorithm iterations to increase the considered COP solution search space [12].

Biased randomization can be seen as extension of the well-known Greedy Randomized Search Procedure (GRASP) introduced by [17]. A COP typically consists of a finite ground set of elements $E = \{1, \ldots, n\}$, a set of feasible solutions $F \subseteq 2^E$, and an objective function $f : 2^E \to \mathbb{R}$. GRASP uses various algorithm iterations to build a feasible COP solution using a randomized construction process. At each construction step a new solution element is added, according to the myopic costs of including the element in the currently constructed solution. However, instead of always choosing the element with the highest potential benefits, a list with the most promising elements is created. In the original GRASP, the element to add to the currently constructed solution is chosen from this list according to a uniform distribution.

When using biased randomization, the elements are added according to a skewed probability distribution. Hereby, all available solution elements are eligible at each step. Their probability of being included in the current solution is based on a bias function calculated according to some criteria (e.g., ranking in a list, heuristic value, etc.) [9]. While the element on the first position of the list has the highest chances of being included in the current COP solution, all elements are potentially eligible. Note that the figure shows a geometric distribution, but other theoretical (e.g. triangular) or empirical probability distributions could also be used. For some application examples of biased randomized approaches the reader is referred to [7,8,10].

3   Solution Approach for the CPP

To solve the CPP we suggest the use of a multi-start metaheuristic based on biased randomization. A pseudo-code for the algorithm illustrating the following descriptions can be seen in Algorithm 1.

Step 1: Given the flight schedule—i.e., the destinations, days, and exact times of the flights—an initial solution (*initSolution*) is created by assigning one crew per flight. This CPP solution (the worst solution possible) is set as *bestSolution* found so far. Furthermore, the transfer times between any two flights i and j are calculated. If the connection time for $transfer_{ij}$ does not break any flight constraints as specified in 2, the corresponding transfer is added to the *transferlist* of possible flight connections. Once all possible flights have been checked, the created list is ordered from lowest to highest transfer time.

Step 2: Once *transferlist* is established it is sorted using a skewed probability distribution, assigning higher probabilities of being on the top of the list to segments composed of a larger number of waypoints. In our case, a Geometric distribution with $\alpha = 0.25$ was employed to induce this biased randomization behavior [9,10]. So, we always select the $transfer_{ij}$ in the top to be the flights which merge two different pairings. Next, the algorithm checks if the flights are on the same day and that no further constraints are broken. Once a transfer is selected, *transferList* is updated. Step 2 ends when *transferlist* is empty.

Algorithm 1. MultiStart (allFlights, alpha, maxIter1, maxIter2)

// Create list of possible tranfers and initial solution
1 transferList ← readData(allFlights)   // step 1
2 initSolution ← createInitialSol(allFlights)   // step 1
3 bestSolution ← initSolution   // step 1
  // Generate daily parings
4 **for** *(0 to maxIter1)* **do**
5   dailyPairing ← initSolution
6   dailyPairing ← createDailyParing(dailyPairing, tranferList, alpha)
                                                        // step 2
     // Create pairing over given time horizon
7   **for** *(0 to maxIter2)* **do**
8   newSolution ← combineDailyPairings(dailyPairings)   // step 3
        // Ensure that flights return to crew base location
9   newSolution ← complete(newSolution, allFlights)   // step 4
10   solutionsList ← update(newSolution)   // step 5
11   **if** *(crewFlightHours(newSolution) < crewFlightHours(bestSolution))*
        then
12   bestSolution ← newSolution   // step 5

        end
     end
                                                  // step 6

  end
13 **return** bestSolution

Step 3: The daily crew pairings are merged in the next step to establish a complete crew pairing solution over the considered time period (see Procedure 3). According to a uniform distribution, the daily pairings are hereby randomly combined on a single crew duty period when feasible.

Step 4: Until now, constraints concerning the crew base location have not been considered. For each constructed crew pairing solution the base location is therefor included as the first and final destination of the flight sequence to complete the crew pairings. In practice, this is referred to as so called 'deadheading'. Note that this additional flight connection counts as working time for the crew, leading to scheduled flights can appear more than once in the final crew pairing solution.

Step 5: Finally, the constructed solution is included in the solution list (giving decision takers a range of solutions to choose from). The current *bestSolution* is updated when necessary.

Step 6: The stopping criteria in this multi-Start algorithm is set as $maxIter1$ and $maxIter2$ iterations at step 2 and step 3 respectively. Therefore a total of $maxIter1 * maxIter2$ solutions is evaluated.

Procedure 2. createDailyPairings(dailyPairing, transferList, alpha)

1 transferList ← randomSelection (transferList, alpha)
2 **while** *(transferList not empty)* **do**
3     $flight_i$ ← select $flight_i$ of transferList[0]
4     $flight_j$ ← select $flight_j$ of transferList[0]
5   iP ← associatedPairing(dailyPairing, $flight_i$)
6   jP ← associatedPairing(dailyPairing, $flight_j$)
7   **if** *((time $flight_i$ + time $flight_j$ < max dailyTime) and (iP day = jP day) and (iP ≠ jP) and ($flight_i$ last in iP) and ($flight_j$ first in jP))* **then**
8 | dailyPairings ← linkSequences(iP, jP)
   end
9   updateList(transferList)
  end
10 **return** dailyPairings

Procedure 3. combineDailyPairings(dailyPairings)

1 RandomSort(dailyPairings)
2 **for** pos_i = 0 to dailyPairings.size() **do**
3   iP ← dailyPairings[pos_i]
4   **for** pos_j = 0 to dailyPairings.size() **do**
5   jP ← dailyPairings[pos_j]
6   **if** *(iP destination airport = jP origin airport) and (last day iP + 1 = first day jP) and (total days iP + total days jP < max pairing days)* **then**
7   currentPairings ← combinePairings(iP,jP)
8   pos_j ← 0
      end
   end
  end
9 **return** currentPairings

4 Computational Experiments

The real life case with which we show the potential of our algorithm consists of 41 flight legs that have to be paired over a five day time period. According to company regulations, the maximum daily flight time per crew is eight hours, while the maximum consecutive working days is limited to three days. Furthermore the minimum transfer time between two flights is 45 min. The base location of the flight crews is in Madrid (MAD). Note that deadheading is possible. The set of flights for which the pairings have to be established can be seen in Table 3. The current pairings used by the company to schedule their crews on the flights is outlined in Table 4. With the current pairings, the scheduled flights are accompanied by six crews, with an overall flight time of 69 hours 40 min. Moreover, there are three deadheading flights.

Table 3. Set of scheduled flights

Day 1		Day 2		Day 3		Day 4		Day 5	
Flight	*Time*	*Flight*	*Time*	*Flight*	*Time*	*Flight*	*Time*	*Flight*	*Time*
MAD-BCN	7.00-8.00	BCN-ORY	6.25-8.05	BCN-PMI	5.50-6.30	BRU-MAD	7.15-9.35	LPA-MAD	11.20-13.50
BCN-FCO	8.45-10.25	ORY-BCN	8.55-10.30	MAD-BCN	7.00-8.00	BCN-FCO	8.45-10.25	MAD-FRA	15.05-17.35
FCO-BCN	11.40-13.20	MAD-SCQ	17.45-18.55	PMI-BCN	7.15-8.00	BCN-MAD	8.55-9.55	BCN-MUC	15.15-17.15
				SCQ-MAD	8.10-9.15	MAD-NCE	10.50-12.30	MUC-MAD	18.00-20.35
				BCN-FCO	8.45-10.25	FCO-BCN	11.40-13.20	FRA-MAD	18.25-20.55
				BCN-MAD	8.55-9.55	BCN-ORY	13.15-14.55	AMS-MAD	18.40-21.05
				BCN-BRU	9.00-11.05	NCE-MAD	13.20-15.05		
				MAD-NCE	10.50-12.30	MAD-SCQ	15.05-16.15		
				MAD-BCN	11.30-12.30	BCN-MXP	15.10-16.40		
				FCO-BCN	11.40-13.20	ORY-BCN	15.45-17.20		
				NCE-MAD	13.20-15.05	MAD-LPA	16.35-19.25		
				BCN-SCQ	15.05-16.40	SCQ-MAD	17.05-18.10		
				MAD-BCN	16.00-17.00	MXP-BCN	17.35-19.20		
				SCQ-BCN	17.35-19.05	BCN-MAD	18.45-19.45		
						MAD-AMS	19.10-21.30		

Table 4. Currently used pairings (*deadheading flights)

Pairing	Day	Flight Sequence					Transfer Time	Total Time
A	4	MAD-SCQ	SCQ-MAD	MAD-AMS			1h30m	6h25m
	5	AMS-MAD					0h00m	2h25m
B	2	MAD-SCQ					0h00m	1h10m
	3	SCQ-MAD	MAD-BCN	BCN-SCQ	SCQ-BCN		5h45m	10h55m
	4	BCN-ORY	ORY-BCN	BCN-MAD			1h55m	6h30m
C	3	MAD-BCN	BCN-FCO	FCO-BCN			2h00m	6h20m
	4	BCN-FCO	FCO-BCN	BCN-MXP	MXP-BCN		4h00m	10h35m
	5	BCN-MUC	MUC-MAD				0h45m	5h20m
D	3	MAD-BCN*	BCN-MAD	MAD-NCE	NCE-MAD	MAD-BCN	3h35m	10h00m
	4	BCN-MAD	MAD-NCE	NCE-MAD	MAD-LPA		3h15m	10h30m
	5	LPA-MAD	MAD-FRA	FRA-MAD			2h05m	9h35m
E	3	MAD-BCN*	BCN-BRU				1h00m	4h05m
	4	BRU-MAD					0h00m	2h20m
F	1	MAD-BCN	BCN-FCO	FCO-BCN			2h00m	6h20m
	2	BCN-ORY	ORY-BCN				0h50m	4h05m
	3	BCN-PMI	PMI-BCN	BCN-MAD*			1h40m	4h05m

To test our algorithm, we use a geometric distribution algorithm α of 0.25. Furthermore, we apply 250 iterations for the daily pairing construction phase ($maxIter1$). Each time a daily solution is constructed, they are then combined in an iterative process using 25 iterations ($maxIter2$). The algorithm was implemented with C++ on a personal computer with a Intel Core i5-2400 (3,1 GHz) processor and 3 GB RAM. Our results as outlined in Table 5 show that the biased randomization metaheuristic is able to reduce total flight time by two hours to 67 h and 40 min, as only one deadheading flight is necessary. Moreover, the proposed solution only needs five crews to serve all flights in the considered period (instead of the six in the current solution).

Another important attribute of our metaheuristic are the short calculation times. As the complete process can be completed in only a few seconds (approximately 20 s considering the parameters and CPU used to obtain the presented results), the algorithm is adaptable to short term flight schedule changes as they

Table 5. Our solution (*deadheading flights)

Pairing	Day	Flight Sequence					Transfer Time	Total Time
A	2	MAD-SCQ					0h00m	1h10m
	3	SCQ-MAD	MAD-BCN				2h05m	6h45m
	4	BCN-ORY	ORY-BCN	BCN-MAD			2h15m	4h15m
B	3	MAD-BCN	BCN-SCQ	SCQ-BCN			3h30m	4h05m
	4	BCN-FCO	FCO-BCN	BCN-MXP	MXP-BCN		4h00m	6h35m
	5	BCN-MUC	MUC-MAD				0h45m	4h35m
C	3	MAD-BCN	BCN-FCO	FCO-BCN			2h00m	4h20m
	4	BCN-MAD	MAD-NCE	NCE-MAD	MAD-LPA		3h15m	7h20m
	5	LPA-MAD	MAD-FRA	FRA-MAD			2h05m	7h20m
D	3	MAD-BCN*	BCN-BRU				1h00m	3h05m
	4	BRU-MAD	MAD-SCQ	SCQ-MAD	MAD-AMS		7h20m	6h55m
	5	AMS-MAD					0h00m	2h25m
E	1	MAD-BCN	BCN-FCO	FCO-BCN			2h00m	4h20m
	2	BCN-ORY	ORY-BCN				0h50m	3h15m
	3	BCN-PMI	PMI-BCN	BCN-MAD	MAD-NCE	NCE-MAD	3h25m	5h50m

regularly occur in the airline industry. Moreover, the multi-start procedure leads to a list of promising solutions, enabling decision takers to choose from more than one option according to individual preferences and necessities.

5   Conclusion

In this paper a multi-start metaheuristic based on biased randomization to tackle the complex CPP is presented. Computational results on a real-life scenario show that our approach leads to improvements concerning overall flying times due to less necessary deadheading and the overall number of crews to accompany the scheduled flights. The very fast calculation times make the algorithm applicable to short term schedule changes. Furthermore, the range of solutions created in the multi-start procedure gives decision takers more flexibility in the decision taking process.

Future research will include a more detailed analysis of the algorithm's robustness. Furthermore, an integrated approach together with other decision making problems in the airline planing phase (e.g. concerning aircraft routing) could be done.

References

1. Aydemir-Karadag, A., Dengiz, B., Bolat, A.: Crew pairing optimization based on hybrid approaches. Comput. Ind. Eng. **65**(1), 87–96 (2013)
2. Clerc, M.: Guided Randomness in Optimization, vol. 1. Wiley-ISTE, London (2006)
3. Collet, P., Rennard, J.P.: Stochastic optimization algorithms. In: Rennard, J.P. (ed.) Handbook of Research on Nature Inspired Computing for Economics and Management, pp. 28–44. Idea Group Inc., Hershey (2006)
4. Erdogan, G., Haouari, M., Matogl, M.O., Özener, O.O.: Solving a large-scale crew pairing problem. J. Oper. Res. Soc. **66**, 1742–1754 (2015)

5. Gao, C.: Airline integrated planning and operations. Ph.D. dissertation, Georgia Institute of Technology (2007)
6. Gopalakrishnan, B., Johnson, E.: Airline crew scheduling: state-of-the-art. Ann. Oper. Res. **140**(1), 305–337 (2005)
7. Gruler, A., Juan, A.A., Contreras-Bolton, C., Gatica, G.: A biased-randomized heuristic for the waste collection problem in smart cities. In: Proceedings of the 2015 International Conference of the Forum for Interdisciplinary Mathematics (FIM 2015) (2015)
8. Juan, A.A., Lourenço, H., Mateo, M., Luo, R., Castella, Q.: Using iterated local search for solving the flow-shop problem: parallelization, parameterization, and randomization issues. Int. Trans. Oper. Res. **21**(1), 103–126 (2014)
9. Juan, A.A., Faulin, J., Ferrer, A., Lourenço, H.R., Barrios, B.: MIRHA: multi-start biased randomization of heuristics with adaptive local search for solving non-smooth routing problems. Top **21**(1), 109–132 (2013)
10. Juan, A.A., Pascual, I., Guimarans, D., Barrios, B.: Combining biased randomization with iterated local search for solving the multidepot vehicle routing problem. Int. Trans. Oper. Res. **22**(4), 647–667 (2015)
11. Klabjan, D., Lee, Y.C., Stojković, G.: Crew management information systems. In: Barnhart, C., Smith, B. (eds.) Quantitative Problem Solving Methods in the Airline Industry, pp. 237–282. Springer, New York (2012)
12. Martí, R., Resende, M., Ribeiro, C.C.: Multi-start methods for combinatorial optimization. Eur. J. Oper. Res. **226**(1), 1–8 (2013)
13. Medard, C.P., Sawhney, N.: Airline crew scheduling from planning to operations. Eur. J. Oper. Res. **38**(3), 1013–1027 (2007)
14. Muter, I., Birbil, S.I., Bülbül, K., Şahin, G., Yenigün, H., Taş, D., Tüzün, D.: Solving a robust airline crew pairing problem with column generation. Comput. Oper. Res. **40**(3), 815–830 (2013)
15. Mohamed, N.F., Zainuddin, Z.M., Salhi, S., Mohamed, N.H., Mohamed, N.A.: A heuristic and exact method: integrated aircraft routing and crew pairing problem. Mod. Appl. Sci. **10**(4), 128–136 (2016)
16. Papadakos, N.: Integrated airline scheduling. Comput. Oper. Res. **36**, 176–195 (2009)
17. Resende, M.G.C., Ribeiro, C.C.: GRASP: greedy randomized adaptive search procedures. In: Glover, F., Kochenberger, G. (eds.) Handbook of Metaheuristics, pp. 219–249. Springer, New York (2003)
18. Salazar-González, J.J.: Approaches to solve the fleet-assignment, aircraft-routing, crew-pairing and crew-rostering problems of a regional carrier. Omega **43**, 71–82 (2014)
19. Talbi, E.-G.: Metaheuristics: From Design to Implementation. Wiley, London (2006)
20. Tekiner, H.: Robust crew pairing for managing extra flights. Master's thesis (2006)
21. Vance, P.H., Barnhart, C., Johnson, E.L., Nemhauser, G.L.: Airline crew scheduling: a new formulation and decomposition algorithm. Oper. Res. **45**(2), 183–200 (1997)
22. Yan, S., Tung, T.T., Tu, Y.P.: Optimal construction of airline individual crew pairings. Comput. Oper. Res. **29**, 341–363 (2002)

Estimating the Spanish Energy Demand Using Variable Neighborhood Search

Jesús Sánchez-Oro[1(✉)], Abraham Duarte[1], and Sancho Salcedo-Sanz[2]

[1] Department of Computer Science, Universidad Rey Juan Carlos, Móstoles, Spain
{jesus.sanchezoro,abraham.duarte}@urjc.es
[2] Department of Signal Processing and Communications,
Universidad de Alcalá, Madrid, Spain
sancho.salcedo@uah.es

Abstract. The increasing of the energy demand in every country has lead experts to find strategies for estimating the energy demand of a given country for the next year. The energy demand prediction in the last years has become a hard problem, since there are several factors (like economic crisis, industrial globalization, or population variation) that are not easy to control. For this reason, it is interesting to propose new strategies for efficiently perform this estimation. In this paper we propose a metaheuristic algorithm based on the Variable Neighborhood Search framework which is able to perform an accurate prediction of the energy demand for a given year. The algorithm is supported in a previously proposed exponential model for estimating the energy, and its input is conformed with a set of macroeconomic variables gathered during the last years. Experimental results show the excellent performance of the algorithm when compared with both previous approaches and the actual values.

Keywords: Energy demand · VNS · Metaheuristics · Estimation

1 Introduction

The estimation of the energy demand for a given country has become a relevant problem that needs to be tackled each year in every country [4]. Furthermore, the energy demand is constantly increasing, mainly due to the global industrialization experienced in the last decades. It is worth mentioning that approximately 50 % of the total energy demand of a given country is performed by the industry, which clearly shows the importance of this sector in the energy demand estimation. The variation in the population as well as the globalization are two additional key factors in the estimation of the energy demand of a country.

This problem has been previously addressed using different heuristic approaches. Most of the previous works have been devoted to predict the energy demand in developing countries like Turkey [1,4,7–9,14–16]. However, several algorithms have been proposed to perform a similar task in China [17–19], Iran [12], Korea [5], and Spain [13], among others. The algorithms proposed in these

O. Luaces et al. (Eds.): CAEPIA 2016, LNAI 9868, pp. 341–350, 2016.
DOI: 10.1007/978-3-319-44636-3_32

works base their effectiveness on the use of socio-economic variables. This fact can be illustrated with the Genetic Algorithm (GA) proposed in [1], which introduces a model based on four macroeconomic variables: Gross Domestic Product (GDP), population, import and export size. These variables are used again in a Multilayer Perceptron Neural Network [5] proposed for estimating the energy demand in Korea.

More bio-inspired heuristic algorithms have been used for solving this task. For instance, Particle Swarm Optimization (PSO) has been used as a stand-alone algorithm [9,16] and hybridized with other bio-inspired algorithms, as Ant Colony Optimization (ACO) and GA, for estimating the energy demand in several countries [8,17–19]. Several prediction models based on logarithmic and exponential functions have been proposed [12], supported by a GA for energy demand estimation in Iran. Finally, the prediction of the energy demand in Spain has been recently tackled with a Harmony Search algorithm combined with Extreme Learning Machine [13].

This work is intended to solve the estimation of the Spanish energy demand one-year-ahead, selecting the most relevant set of socio-economic variables, among the ones used in previous works. The prediction is performed by using a previously proposed exponential model [13], where a Variable Neighborhood Search (VNS) algorithm is responsible of selecting the best parameters for the model.

The remainder of the paper is structured as follows: Sect. 2 presents the exponential model used for estimating the energy demand. The algorithmic proposal is introduced in Sect. 3, while the experiments performed to test the VNS method are described in Sect. 4. Finally, the conclusions derived from the experiments are discussed in Sect. 5.

2   Prediction Model

The estimation of the energy demand in a given country can be represented by different models that try to fit a function to the real energy demand. We can find in the literature several models, based on different mathematical functions, but most of works concludes that the exponential model fits better to the real energy demand of the country [12]. Furthermore, in this paper we focus on estimating the energy demand of Spain, where the best results have been found by using the exponential model [13]. For that reason, our algorithmic proposal is intended to optimize this model.

The exponential function to estimate the energy demand $\hat{E}(t)$ for a given year t is defined based on the values X_i of the considered macroeconomic variables in the previous year $t - 1$. In mathematical terms,

$$\hat{E}(t) = \epsilon + \sum_{i=1}^{|X|} \alpha_i X_i(t-1)^{\beta_i}$$

where ϵ, α_i and β_i are the parameters that need to be fitted in order to improve the energy demand prediction. Specifically, ϵ represents a bias in order to obtain a better fit, while α_i, β_i represent the weight of the macroeconomic variable X_i.

Unlike the original model [13], we do not fix the macroeconomic variables that are included in the model. Therefore, this model requires two different optimizations: (i) select the best subset of macroeconomic variables, and (ii) find the best values for the model parameters.

A solution $\mathcal{M}$ for the problem is given by both the subset of macroeconomic variables and the values for the parameters of the model. Let us define $X^\star$ as the set of all available macroeconomic variables. The solution is divided in two well-differenced sets: $X = \{X_1, X_m\} \in X^\star$ for the selected macroeconomic variables and $W = \{\epsilon, \alpha_1, \ldots, \alpha_m, \beta_1, \ldots, \beta_m\}$ for the bias and variable weights.

For the sake of clarity, we describe the evaluation of an example solution by using the proposed representation. We consider the solution $\mathcal{M} = (X, W)$, with $X = \{ME1, ME3, ME4\}$ and $W = \{4.1, 0.4, 0.1, 0.2, -0.05, 0.3, -0.1\}$. In this solution, we have selected the macroeconomic variables $X_1 = ME1, X_2 = ME3, X_3 = ME4$, where each one (*ME1, ME3, ME4*) represents a different value (i.e., GDP, import and export size, etc.). In order to estimate the energy demand for a given year t, we first need to obtain the variable values for the previous year $t - 1$. For this example, we set $X_1 = 0.1, X_2 = 0.4, X_3 = 0.2$. Notice that for each variable X_i (see for instance $\alpha_1 = 0.4, \beta_1 = 0.1$ for X_1) we provide a pair of coefficients α_i, β_i, plus the first bias coefficient ϵ (4.1 in the example).

The estimation of the energy demand for the current year is performed as follows:

$$\hat{E}(t) = \epsilon + \alpha_1 \cdot X_1(t-1)^{\beta_1} + \alpha_2 \cdot X_2(t-1)^{\beta_2} + \alpha_3 \cdot X_3(t-1)^{\beta_3}$$
$$= 4.1 + 0.4 \cdot 0.1^{0.1} + 0.2 \cdot 0.4^{-0.05} + 0.3 \cdot 0.2^{-0.1}$$
$$= 4.98$$

Each solution is evaluated using an objective function to analyze the similarity of the solution when compared with the real energy demand. In this work we minimize the mean squared error (MSE) between prediction and real value. The MSE is defined as follows:

$$f(\mathcal{M}) = \sum_{j=1}^{n} \left(E(j) - \hat{E}(j) \right)^2$$

where n is the number of samples used to test the quality of the solution. We use the same error measure previously considered in the related works [1,13] in order to ease the comparison among different proposals. Therefore, the objective is to find the solution $\mathcal{M}^\star$ with the minimum f-value. In mathematical terms,

$$\mathcal{M}^\star = \arg\min_{\mathcal{M} \in \mathbb{M}} f(\mathcal{M})$$

where $\mathbb{M}$ is the set of all possible solutions for the problem.

It is worth mentioning that all variable values and parameters are normalized in a traditional manner. Specifically, the value of each macroeconomic variable and each α, β parameter is normalized in the range $[-1, 1]$. However, the bias parameter considers a larger range $[-5, 5]$, as recommended in previous works [13], in order to obtain better results.

3   Variable Neighborhood Search

Variable Neighborhood Search (VNS) is a metaheuristic framework designed for solving hard optimization problems. VNS relies on systematic changes of neighborhood structures for finding high quality solutions, without guaranteeing their optimality. Several VNS strategies have been proposed during the study of this metaheuristic. Specifically, we can emphasize Variable Neighborhood Descent (VND), Reduced VNS (RVNS), Basic VNS (BVNS), Skewed VNS (SVNS), General VNS (GVNS), Variable Neighborhood Decomposition Search (VNDS), and Variable Formulation Search (VFS) among others (see [6] for a thoroughly review of the metaheuristic and its variants). This methodology has lead to several successfull research in recent years [3,10,11].

This paper is focused on the Basic VNS (BVNS) variant, which combines deterministic and stochastic changes of neighborhood during the search. Algorithm 1 shows the pseudocode of BVNS. The algorithm requires two parameters: an initial solution $\mathcal{M}$ and the maximum number of iterations. The procedure starts by exploring the neighborhoods from the first one (step 1). For each neighborhood, it randomly perturbs the current solution (step 4), with the shake procedure described in Sect. 3.1. Then, the perturbed solution is improved with the local search method presented in Sect. 3.2 (step 5). Finally, BVNS selects the next neighborhood to be explored (step 6). Specifically, if the search has found a new best solution, i.e., $f(\mathcal{M}'') < f(\mathcal{M})$, the method starts again from the first neighborhood ($k = 1$). Otherwise, it continues with the next neighborhood ($k = k + 1$). These three steps are repeated until the maximum predefined neighborhood $k_{\max}$ is reached (steps 3–7). The VNS framework usually considers two different stopping criterion: time horizon or number of iterations. In this work the algorithm is executed a fixed number of iterations (steps 1–8).

Algorithm 1. Basic VNS($\mathcal{M}$, iterations)

1: **for** $i \in 1 \ldots$ iterations **do**
2:    $k \leftarrow 1$
3:    **while** $k \leq k_{\max}$ **do**
4:       $\mathcal{M}' \leftarrow$ Shake($\mathcal{M}, k$)
5:       $\mathcal{M}'' \leftarrow$ LocalSearch($\mathcal{M}'$)
6:       $k \leftarrow$ NeighborhoodChange($\mathcal{M}, \mathcal{M}'', k$)
7:    **end while**
8: **end for**

The initial solution for the BVNS algorithm can be generated either with a specific constructive procedure or with a random method. We have decided to use a random procedure since we do not have *a priori* information about the problem that can be useful during the constructive phase. Therefore, for the initial solution we select a subset of macroeconomic variables (each one is selected with a probability of 0.5). Then, we select a random bias in the range $[-5, 5]$ and, for each variable, random values for its α and β parameters. The resulting solution (improved with the local search method) is used as the initial solution for the BVNS algorithm.

The representation of the solution selected splits it into two parts: the variables selected and the associated weights. Regarding the BVNS algorithm, each of the main procedures are devoted to modify a different part of the solution. In particular, the shake procedure focuses in the selected variables, while the local search method is intended to improve the values of their ϵ, α and β parameters.

3.1 Shake

In the context of VNS, the shake procedure consists of perturbing the incumbent solution in the corresponding neighborhood in order to diversify the search. Regarding the energy demand estimation problem, the shake procedure is intended to modify the macroeconomic variables selected in the solution. Given a solution $\mathcal{M}$, X represents the set of selected macroeconomic variables ($X \subseteq X^*$). The current neighborhood k represents the perturbation size.

The shake procedure selects k variables from X^* at random. Then, for each selected macroeconomic variable X_i, the method includes it in the solution ($X \leftarrow X \cup \{X_i\}$) if it is not yet included ($X_i \notin X$). Otherwise ($X_i \in X$) the shake procedure removes that variable from the solution ($X \leftarrow X \setminus \{X_i\}$).

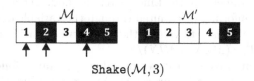

$$\texttt{Shake}(\mathcal{M}, 3)$$

Fig. 1. Example of performing the shake procedure in a solution $\mathcal{M}$ with $k = 3$.

Figure 1 represents the shake procedure executed over a solution $\mathcal{M}$ where the macroeconomic variables selected are represented in with solid black color. Before executing the shake procedure, $\mathcal{M}$ includes the variables 2, 4, and 5. Since the neighborhood in the example is 3, the method selects three variables at random (1, 2 and 4, highlighted with an arrow). The first variable selected, is included in the new solution $\mathcal{M}'$, since it did not originally belong to $\mathcal{M}$. Variables 2 and 4 are removed from the new solution $\mathcal{M}'$ since they were already included in $\mathcal{M}$. Therefore, the resulting solution after executing the shake procedure only contains variables 1 and 5.

3.2   Local Search

Unlike the shake procedure, the local search procedure proposed in this paper is intended to improve a solution by modifying the value of the bias and the weights associated to each macroeconomic variable. Since these values belong to the real domain (i.e., $\{\epsilon, \alpha_i, \beta_i\} \in \mathbb{R}, \forall i \in 1 \ldots |X|$), the local search considers global optimization techniques. One of the most extended strategy for improving solutions in global optimization is the Line Search method, which has lead to several successful works in the recent years [2].

The Line Search method iterates over every parameter of the solution (including ϵ, α and β), trying to improve the quality of the solution by modifying one parameter at a time.

The improvement of a parameter $w \in \{\epsilon, \alpha_1 \ldots \alpha_{|X|}, \beta_1, \ldots, \beta_{|X|}\}$ whose available range is $[MIN, MAX]$ starts by performing a discretization of the search space in h different points. Then, the method iterates over each generated point, assigning its value to the current weight, and evaluating the resulting solution. If the new solution outperforms the previous best one, it is updated, and the search starts again.

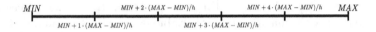

Fig. 2. Discretization of the search space with $h = 5$

Figure 2 shows the discretization of the search space for a parameter w in the range $[MIN, MAX]$. Since w belongs to the real domain, the search would need to explore infinite points in order to perform an exhaustive search for the best value. Let h be a parameter of the Line Search method. The algorithm generates h different values uniformly distributed through the variable domain. Therefore, in order to generate h discrete values, the gap between each pair of consecutive values is evaluated as $(MAX - MIN)/h$.

The search then traverses the set of values generated following a random order. If the method finds an improvement in a given value, then it is updated in the solution and the search starts again (first improvement strategy). Once all values generated have been evaluated without finding an improvement (local optimum), the search continues with the next parameters of the solution. It is worth mentioning that the next parameter to be explored is selected at random. The Line Search method ends when no improvement is found in any parameter, returning the best solution found during the search.

4   Computational Experiments

The problem addressed in this paper is completely focused in solving an actual problem. Therefore, the data used in the experiments needs to be real, in order to analyze the applicability of the proposed algorithm to real-world data, which often include high level of noise. In particular, we have used the same data used in a previous work [13], related with the energy demand estimation in Spain. Specifically, the data contains information about several macroeconomic variables that were analyzed from 1980 to 2011.

For each year, the dataset contains information about 14 different macroeconomic variables, namely: Gross Domestic Product (GDP), population, export, import, energy production (kilotonne of oil equivalent, kTOE), electricity power transport (kW/h), electricity production (kW/h), GDP per unit of energy use, energy imports net (% of use), fossil fuel consumption (kW/h), electric power consumption (kW/h), CO_2 total emissions (Mtons), unemployment rate, and diesel consumption in road (kTOE).

The data have been split in two different sets in order to avoid overtraining. The training set contains data for 15 years, while the test set contains data for the remaining 16 years. Both sets have been generated at random, but considering the years related with the economic crisis (2010 and 2011) in the test set, with the aim of analyzing if the algorithm is able to predict these behaviors. It is worth mentioning that we have considered the same error measure, MSE, for the preliminary experimentation, in order to have comparable results.

Both, VNS (feature selection) and ELM (training) are executed only once. After that, a decision maker will only need to feed the trained algorithm in order to immediately obtain the energy demand prediction associated to the input data used, without requiring computing time. The computing time for training is 10 s per VNS iteration and 5 s for ELM.

The main objective of the first experiment is to select the best parameters for the BVNS algorithm proposed. In particular, it requires two different parameters: the number of iterations and the maximum neighborhood number to explore (k_{max}). Notice that the maximum neighborhood to be explored represents the maximum number of variations in the macroeconomic variables that will be performed. On the one hand, it is easy to see that both, quality and computing time, increase with the number of iterations, so we have selected 25 in order to maintain reasonable computing times. On the other hand, we have tested the following values for $k_{max} = \{2, 4, 6, 10\}$. Table 1 shows the results obtained for each variant in terms of the mean squared error obtained in the test set when considering the parameters selected by the algorithm in the training set. It is worth mentioning that the h parameter for the Line Search method has been experimentally set to 1000 during the whole experimentation.

Notice that those macroeconomic variables selected in all variants are highlighted in bold, since they seem to be relevant features. In particular, the common macroeconomic variables are import, energy imports net, and CO_2 total emissions. From these results we can extract that $k_{max} = 4$ presents the best results in terms of MSE, emerging as the best BVNS variant. It can be seen that the MSE increases with the size of the maximum neighborhood. However, the worst results are obtained when considering $k_{max} = 2$, which may reveal that it is a small maximum neighborhood to be used in this kind of problems. Therefore, BVNS with $k_{max} = 4$ is selected for the remaining experiments.

The next experiment is intended to compare the results obtained by our proposal when compared with the best previous works. Table 2 shows the results obtained by our BVNS compared with a Harmony Search algorithm isolated (HS) and combined (HS+ELM) with a neural network [13], and, finally, a Genetic Algorithm (GA) [1]. The bad performance of Genetic Algorithm can be partially motivated by its design, in which the algorithm is only able to consider 4 joint macroeconomic variables. The remaining algorithms are more versatile, since they consider a variable number of macroeconomic variables, increasing the explored region of the search space. We can also see an improvement of 0.20 % in HS+ELM with respect to HLM isolated, which reveals the relevance of the neural network in the algorithm. Finally, our BVNS emerges as the best algorithm, improving the combination of HS with ELM.

The final experiment is intended to test how the best results obtained by BVNS fit with the real energy demand values for each year available in the dataset. Figure 3 presents these results in a line graph where the x-axis represents the year evaluated and the y-axis indicates the total energy demand, measured in kilotonne of oil equivalent (kTOE). The line with triangle markers for each year represents the real measure, while the one with rectangle markers represents the estimation given by BVNS.

Table 1. Performance of BVNS with the proposed values of k_{max}. Common features selected in all cases are highlighted in bold font.

k_{max}	MSE (%)	Selected variables
2	3.40	{**4**, 7, **9**, **11**, 13, 14}
4	2.10	{3, **4**, 8, **9**, **11**, 13}
6	2.59	{1, 3, **4**, 5, 8, **9**, **11**}
10	2.86	{2, 3, **4**, 6, 7, **9**, **11**, 12}

Table 2. Results obtained by BVNS when compared with the best previous algorithms: Harmony Search (HS), Harmony Search with neural network (HS+ELM), and Genetic Algorithm (GA).

Algorithm	MSE (%)	Selected variables
BVNS	2.10	{3, 4, 8, 9, 11, 13}
HS+ELM	2.16	{1, 2, 3, 7, 8, 9, 12}
HS	2.36	{1, 2, 3, 7, 8, 9, 12}
GA	2.89	{1, 2, 3, 4}

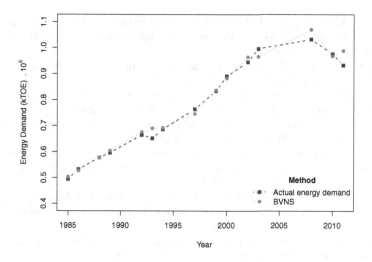

Fig. 3. Comparison of the BVNS prediction when compared with the real values

5   Conclusions

This paper has introduced a new metaheuristic algorithm, based on the Variable Neighborhood Search framework, for estimating the energy demand of a country. The experiments has been performed using a dataset which contains macroeconomic information about Spain for the last years. The thoroughly experimentation presented has been used for selecting the best parameters for the algorithms, as well as for comparing the best results obtained with respect to the actual energy demand of the years in which the data is available. The obtained results have shown the superiority of our proposal, reducing the error obtained when compared to the best previous approach, based on a Harmony Search method. We do believe that this algorithm can become a precise tool for helping decision makers.

Acknowledgments. This work has been partially supported by the projects TIN2014-54583-C2-2-R and TIN2015-65460-C2-2-P of the Spanish Ministerial Commission of Science and Technology (MICYT), and by the Comunidad Autónoma de Madrid, under project numbers S2013ICE-2933_02 and S2013ICE-2894.

References

1. Ceylan, H., Ozturk, H.K.: Estimating energy demand of Turkey based on economic indicators using genetic algorithm approach. Energy Convers. Manag. **45**(1516), 2525–2537 (2004)
2. Duarte, A., Martí, R., Glover, F., Gortázar, F.: Hybrid scatter tabu search for unconstrained global optimization. Ann. Oper. Res. **183**(1), 95–123 (2009)

3. Duarte, A., Pantrigo, J.J., Pardo, E.G., Sánchez-Oro, J.: Parallel variable neighbourhood search strategies for the cutwidth minimization problem. IMA J. Manag. Math. **27**(1), 55–73 (2016)
4. Ediger, V.S., Akar, S.: ARIMA forecasting of primary energy demand by fuel in Turkey. Energy Policy **35**(3), 1701–1708 (2007)
5. Geem, Z.W., Roper, W.E.: Energy demand estimation of South Korea using artificial neural network. Energy Policy **37**(10), 4049–4054 (2009)
6. Hansen, P., Mladenović, N.: Variable neighborhood search: principles and applications. Eur. J. Oper. Res. **130**(3), 449–467 (2001)
7. Kankal, M., Akpinar, A., Kömürcü, M.I., Özsahin, T.S.: Modeling and forecasting of Turkeys energy consumption using socio-economic and demographic variables. Appl. Energy **88**(5), 1927–1939 (2011)
8. Kiran, M.S., Özceylan, E., Gündüz, M., Paksoy, T.: A novel hybrid approach based on particle swarm optimization and ant colony algorithm to forecast energy demand of Turkey. Energy Convers. Manag. **53**(1), 75–83 (2012)
9. Kiran, M.S., Özceylan, E., Gündüz, M., Paksoy, T.: Swarm intelligence approaches to estimate electricity energy demand in Turkey. Knowl.-Based Syst. **36**, 93–103 (2012)
10. Sánchez-Oro, J., Sevaux, M., Rossi, A., Martí, R., Duarte, A.: Solving dynamic memory allocation problems in embedded systems with parallel variable neighborhood search strategies. Electron. Notes Discrete Math. **47**, 85–92 (2015)
11. Sánchez-Oro, J., Pantrigo, J.J., Duarte, A.: Combining intensification and diversification strategies in VNS. An application to the Vertex Separation problem. Comput. Oper. Res. **52**(Part B), 209–219 (2014)
12. Piltan, M., Shiri, H., Ghaderi, S.F.: Energy demand forecasting in Iranian metal industry using linear and nonlinear models based on evolutionary algorithms. Energy Convers. Manag. **58**, 1–9 (2012)
13. Salcedo-Sanz, S., Muñoz-Bulnes, J., Portilla-Figueras, J., Del Ser, J.: One-year-ahead energy demand estimation from macroeconomic variables using computational intelligence algorithms. Energy Convers. Manag. **99**, 62–71 (2015)
14. Toksari, M.D.: Estimating the net electricity energy generation and demand using the ant colony optimization approach: case of Turkey. Energy Policy **37**(3), 1181–1187 (2009)
15. Toksari, M.D.: Ant colony optimization approach to estimate energy demand of Turkey. Energy Policy **35**(8), 3984–3990 (2007)
16. Ünler, A.: Improvement of energy demand forecasts using swarm intelligence: the case of Turkey with projections to 2025. Energy Policy **36**(6), 1937–1944 (2008)
17. Yu, S., Wei, Y.M., Wang, K.: A PSOGA optimal model to estimate primary energy demand of China. Energy Policy **42**, 329–340 (2012)
18. Yu, S., Zhu, K.: A hybrid procedure for energy demand forecasting in China. Energy **37**(1), 396–404 (2012)
19. Yu, S., Zhu, K., Zhang, X.: Energy demand projection of China using a path-coefficient analysis and PSOGA approach. Energy Convers. Manag. **53**(1), 142–153 (2012)

Evolutionary and Genetic Algorithms

Evolutionary Image Registration in Craniofacial Superimposition: Modeling and Incorporating Expert Knowledge

Oscar Gómez[1(✉)], Oscar Ibáñez[2], and Oscar Cordón[2]

[1] Departamento de Ciencias de la Computación e Inteligencia Artificial, CITIC-UGR (Centro de Investigación en Tecnologías de la Información y las Comunicaciones), Granada, Spain
ogomez@decsai.ugr.es

[2] Departamento de Ciencias de la Computación e Inteligencia Artificial, University of Granada, Granada, Spain
{oscar.ibanez,ocordon}@decsai.ugr.es

Abstract. Craniofacial superimposition involves the process of overlaying a skull with a number of ante-mortem images of an individual and the analysis of their morphological correspondence. This research focused on the skull-face overlay stage with the aim of modeling the expert knowledge that is related to the existing anthropometric differences among landmarks and incorporating it into this stage. Consequently, we have moved from a single-objective optimization problem to a multiobjective optimization one aimed to reduce the distances between pairs of landmarks from each group independently. To tackle it, two classic approaches from the area of multicriteria decision making were used: weighted sum and lexicographical order. The results, which were obtained over a Ground Truth dataset, are promising in those cases where the forensic expert has located a large number of landmarks, and worse results than the state of the art method in cases with few landmarks.

1 Introduction

Craneofacial superimposition (CFS) [1] is one of the most relevant skeleton-based identification techniques. It involves the process of overlaying a skull image (or a skull 3D model) with a number of ante-mortem images of an individual and the analysis of their morphological correspondence to try to establish whether they correspond to the same individual. Three consecutive stages for the whole CFS process have been distinguished in [2]:

- Acquisition and processing of the face and the skull photographs/models. In some approaches, this step also involves the location of anatomical landmarks on the skull and the face.
- Skull-face overlay (SFO), which focuses on achieving the best possible superimposition of an image, video-frame or a 3D model of a physical skull, and a single ante-mortem image of a missing person.
- Skull-face overlay assessment and decision making, in which the degree of support (strong support, moderate support, limited support, and undetermined [3]) that the skull and the available photograph belong to the same person or not (exclusion) is determined.

© Springer International Publishing Switzerland 2016
O. Luaces et al. (Eds.): CAEPIA 2016, LNAI 9868, pp. 353–362, 2016.
DOI: 10.1007/978-3-319-44636-3_33

From the Computer Vision (CV) point of view, there is a clear relation between the SFO procedure and an Image Registration (IR) problem [4]. SFO can be tackled following an IR approach in order to superimpose the skull onto the facial photograph. To do so, the most convenient procedure is to guide the IR process by matching the corresponding cranial and facial landmarks.

Concerning soft computing, this matching process involves a really complex optimization task. There is incomplete and vague information guiding the process (matching of two different objects, a skull and a face). Thus the resulting search space is huge and presents many local minima, especially when a skull 3D model is considered. Due to it, exhaustive search methods are not useful. Furthermore, forensic experts demand highly robust and accurate results. IR approaches based on Evolutionary Algorithms (EA) are a promising solution for facing this challenging optimization problem. Thanks to their global optimization nature, EAs are capable to perform a robust search in complex and ill-defined problems as IR [5].

However one drawback of the existing EA-based proposals dealing with the SFO problem is that they consider all landmarks equally important when they are not. For instance, landmarks located in the teeth represent the most confident source of information since it is the only bony part visible in the face. Thus, there is a need to properly model the different relative importance of the pairs of landmarks used to perform SFO as a 3D-2D image registration problem.

To overcome these problems, we modeled the expert knowledge related to the differences among landmarks based on anthropometric's characteristics into the existing automatic SFO method. This has been modeled with two classic approaches from the area of multicriteria decision making [6]: Weighted sum and Lexicographic order. In addition, the obtained results have been compared with the state-of-the-art approach (rcga-mc45) [7] using a "ground truth" dataset [8].

This paper is structured as follows. Section 2 reviews the current state of the art and introduces the automatic CFS system. Section 3 describes our proposals for modeling and incorporating expert knowledge within the optimization process. Section 4 presents the experiments and results. The final conclusions are detailed in Sect. 5.

2　Craniofacial Superposition

The diverse CFS approaches evolved as new technologies became available on foundations laid previously [1]. Although several authors had made different classifications of the technique, all of them recognize three different categories: photographic superimposition, video superimposition and computer-aided superimposition [1,9]. Another one was proposed by Damas et al. [2] classifying them into two groups: non-automatic computer-aided methods and automatic computer-aided methods. Those later approaches deal with the SFO task within CFS and drastically reduce the time taken for SFO. Those proposals are based either on photograph to photograph comparison [10] or on skull 3D model to photograph comparison [7,11–14].

2.1   Skull-Face Overlay as a Computer Vision Problem

Skull-face overlay requires positioning the skull in the same pose as the face of the photograph. From a pure CV point of view, the ante-mortem photograph is the result of the 2D projection of a real (3D) scene that was acquired by a particular (unknown) camera [15]. In such a scene, the living was somewhere inside the camera field of view with a given pose.

The most natural way to face the SFO problem is to replicate the original scenario. The goal is thus to adjust its size and orientation of the skull 3D model with respect to the head in the photograph through geometric transformations in the camera coordinate [1]. The specific characteristics of the camera must also be replicated to reproduce the original as far as possible and hence the perspective projection of the skull 3D model onto the facial photograph.

2.2   Our Automatic Skull-Face Overlay Procedure

The 3D-2D IR approach is guided by the cranial and facial landmarks previously assigned by a forensic expert in the skull 3D model and the facial photograph.

Hence, given two sets of cranial and facial landmarks, $C = \{cl^1, ..., cl^n\}$ and $F = \{fl^1, ..., fl^n\}$, the process has to solve a system of equations with 12 unknowns [12]: the direction of the rotation axis $d = (d_x, d_y, d_z)$, the location of the rotation axis with respect to the center of coordinates $r = (r_x, r_y, r_z)$, the rotation angle θ, the factor s that scales the size of the skull 3D model as the face in the photograph, the translation $t = (t_x, t_y, t_z)$ that places the origin of the skull 3D model in front of the camera to replicate the moment of the photograph, and the camera angle of view ϕ. Although rotation parametrization with only 3–4 parameters are also possible, and usually employed in the literature, we used 7 in order to increase the interpretability of the corresponding transformation and the definition of its constrains. Those parameters determine the geometric transformation f that projects every cranial landmark cl^i of the skull 3D model onto its corresponding facial landmark fl^i of the photograph:

$$F = C \cdot R \cdot S \cdot T \cdot P \qquad (1)$$

where R S, T, and P are rotation, scaling, translation and perspective projection matrices, respectively [12]. In addition, it modeled two sources of uncertainty.

Firstly, the location of facial landmarks refers to the difficult task of placing landmarks on a photograph [16]. The definition of many anthropometric landmarks is imprecise in nature [17]. Using precise landmarks, forensic anthropologists can only place the facial landmarks that they clearly identify in the facial photograph. The fuzzy approach developed in [13] allows experts to enclose a region where the facial landmark is placed without any doubt by using variable-size ellipses (fuzzy landmarks) instead of locating a precise point as usual. The number of landmarks placed by the expert can thus increase when those landmarks are considered. This leads to a better description of the skull-face correspondence thanks to the new pairs of cranial points and fuzzy landmarks in the face. The performance of the automatic SFO method is thus improved.

Secondly, facial soft tissue depth varies for each landmark correspondence and for different groups of people. It produces a mismatch among cranial and facial landmarks. Thus, the correspondence of a particular landmark on the surface of the skull and on the surface of the skin may not be symmetrical and perpendicular. This variability has been widely studied in many populations and considering different age and gender subgroups. The first and unique proposal tackling this uncertainty within an automatic SFO process has been recently published in [7]. This directly incorporates the corresponding landmark spatial relationships and distances within the automatic SFO procedure. To do this, they model the minimum (min), mean ($mean$) and maximum (max) distances between a pair of cranial and facial landmarks. These distances can be obtained from any anthropometric study looking at the specific population group considered. They used two alternative approaches to deal with the landmark matching imprecision in SFO (using Spheres or Cones).

Using the cranial and facial landmarks together with the previous consideration, an EA iteratively searches for the best geometric transformation f, i.e. the optimal combination of the 12 parameters that minimizes the mean error (ME) fitness function [7]:

$$
FME = \frac{\sum_{i=1}^{Ncrisp} (d'(x_i, f(\tilde{C}^i)) + \sum_{j=1}^{Nfuzzy} (d''(\tilde{F}^j, f(\tilde{C}^j)))}{N}, \tag{2}
$$

where $Ncrisp$ is the number of 2D facial landmarks precisely located (crisp points), $Nfuzzy$ is the number of 2D facial landmarks imprecisely located and defined as bi-dimensional fuzzy sets, N is the total number of landmarks considered ($N = Ncrisp + Nfuzzy$), x_i corresponds to a 2D facial landmark defined as a crisp point ($x_i \in F$), $\tilde{C}^i$ and $\tilde{C}^j$ are fuzzy sets modeling each 3D cranial landmark and the soft tissue distance to the corresponding 3D facial landmark i or j; f is the function that determines the 3D-2D perspective transformation that properly projects every 3D skull point onto the 2D photograph; $f(\tilde{C}^i)$ and $f(\tilde{C}^j)$ are two fuzzy sets, corresponding to the result of applying the perspective transformation f to the 3D volume (either sphere or cone), which model the landmark matching uncertainty; $\tilde{F}^j$ represents the fuzzy set of points of the imprecise 2D facial landmark; $d'(x_i, f(\tilde{C}^i))$ is the distance between a point and a fuzzy set of points, and $d''(\tilde{F}^j, f(\tilde{C}^j))$ is the distance between two fuzzy sets.

3   Modeling Anthropometric Landmarks Relative Importance Within the Automatic SFO Process

3.1   Anthropometric Differences Among Landmarks for SFO Purposes

The rationale behind differentiating or grouping landmarks could be multiple. However since not all of them can be tested to find the best way of grouping them for every particular scenario, there is a need to choose among them. In this work, we focused on their anthropometric differences in order to differently consider them within the SFO optimization process. In particular, we modeled the three following scenarios:

Landmark Classification I: According to Their Anatomical Definition. It has long been recognized that not all landmarks are equally identifiable. This way, distinguishes three types of landmarks in [17] named type 1, 2, and 3 according to the decreasing precision of their anatomical location. Type 1 includes landmarks at which three different tissues meet. Type 2 defines points of maximum curvature or other local morphogenetic processes, usually with a biomechanical implication like a muscle attachment site. Finally, type 3 refers to external landmarks, which belong to a curve or surface. In addition there is a good reason to suspect that the identification precision differs among landmarks. Related with the previous classification, a recent study analyzing the spatial distribution/precision of forensic experts while locating landmarks in facial photographs concluded that there is a significant correlation between the type of landmark and the precision in their location.

Landmark Classification II: According to the Rigid or Mobile Nature of the Region. The jaw is the only articulated part on the skull, hence slightly or even large differences in the articulation of the mandible in the available facial photographs and in the 3D skull model are always expected. In fact, CFS practitioners call this region "terra incognita", in the sense that they can not precisely assess craniofacial correspondence in this region due to its mobile nature. Although jaw articulation has been widely studied and mathematically modeled, there is not a single CFS method or practitioner reproducing jaw articulation in ante-mortem images in a reliable and objective manner. Another alternative to address this source of error/uncertainty will be thus to introduce a mathematical modeling of the jaw articulation into the automatic SFO process so it could be estimated for each particular ante-mortem image. However, even if the latter is successfully performed, there will always be a margin of error justifying the need of considering the landmarks within this region in a more suspicious way.

Landmark Classification III: According to the Presence or Absence of Soft Tissue. Most of landmarks do not have an exact match between their position in the skull and in the face due to the facial soft tissue thickness. Contrary to them, a few landmarks (located in the teeth) have a direct matching relation since they are located in a bony region. Thus, it seems quite obvious to consider this group of landmarks as the most representative to study craniofacial anatomical correspondence, something recently corroborated by an experimental study developed with the framework of the European project MEPROCS. However, it has not been analytically modeled or tested this higher importance within an automatic SFO procedure, which in any case will need the guidance of other landmarks due to the mostly coplanar region represented by teeth.

3.2   Modeling the Differences Among Landmarks

As a result of distinguishing different groups of landmarks with a different relative importance with the two previously mentioned approaches from the area of multicriteria decision making [6]: Weighted sum and Lexicographical order.

Weighted Sum. In this approach, all landmarks will always contribute to the final fitness, however not all of them will contribute equally. Depending on the relative importance of a particular group of landmarks and the number of marked landmarks per group in each case (to be able to fairly compare the results of different cases with a different number of marked landmarks per group). More formally, the fitness of each individual of the Genetic Algorithm (GA) population will be calculated according to Eq. (3):

$$Fitness = \frac{\sum_{i=1}^{n} w_i * fitnessLevel_i * nLevel_i}{\sum_{i=1}^{n} nLevel_i} \tag{3}$$

where $nLevel_i$ is the number of pairs of corresponding landmarks of group i located in a particular SFO case. w_i, that ranges from 0 to 1, is the weight of group i, and $\sum_{i=1}^{n} w_i$ is equal to 1. $FitnessLevel_i$ is the result of calculating the fitness with just the landmarks of the group i.

Once this proposal has been defined, the last point is to establish the value of the free parameters of this approach, i.e., the number of groups and landmarks included in them, and the weight w_i of each particular group (their relative importance). While the three different and independent landmarks grouping approaches have an anthropometric motivation, the values for weighting them could be any possible combination adding 1.

Lexicographical Order. This approach lexicographically minimizes the fitness of each individual of the GA population. The first group of landmarks is the most important and it always contributes to the final fitness. However the information of a following group is only used when two individual are "similar" in all the previous groups. Two individual are considered "similar" when the differences between their fitness is lower than an ϵ. However since the marked landmarks and the distance between them are different in each case, this epsilon has thus to be adaptive to each case, group and generation.

$$\epsilon_i^{it} = k * |bestFitness_i^{it} - worstFitness_i^{it}| \tag{4}$$

where i is the group, it is the generation number, ϵ_i^{it} is the adaptive ϵ of the group i at generation it, $bestFitness_i^{it}$ is the best value of the fitness at generation it calculated only using the landmarks of the group i, $worstFitness_i^{it}$ is the worst value of the fitness at generation it calculated only using the landmarks of the group i, K is a parameter that define how severe is the epsilon.

The variable k modulates how easily two individual are considered "similar". A high value of k will produce more ties at each lexicographical level and thus, the information of the less important group of landmarks will be considered more frequently.

Table 1. Experimental design for Landmark classification I, II and III

Modeling approach	Parametrization	Landmark classification	Acronym
Weighted sum	(Group 1:0,7; Group 2:0,2; Group 3: 0,1)	Bookstein anatomical definition	G1W1
Weighted sum	(Group 1:0,6; Group 2:0,25; Group 3: 0,15)	Bookstein anatomical definition	G1W2
Weighted sum	(Group 1:0,5; Group 2:0,3; Group 3: 0,2)	Bookstein anatomical definition	G1W3
Lexicographical order	K = 0,05	Bookstein anatomical definition	G1L1
Lexicographical order	K = 0,1	Bookstein anatomical definition	G1L2
Lexicographical order	K = 0,2	Bookstein anatomical definition	G1L3
Weighted sum	(Group 1:0,9; Group 2:0,1)	Mobile or rigid nature	G2W1
Weighted sum	(Group 1:0,75; Group 2:0,25)	Mobile or rigid nature	G2W2
Weighted sum	(Group 1:0,6; Group 2:0,4)	Mobile or rigid nature	G2W3
Lexicographical order	K = 0,05	Mobile or rigid nature	G2L1
Lexicographical order	K = 0,1	Mobile or rigid nature	G2L2
Lexicographical order	K = 0,2	Mobile or rigid nature	G2L3
Weighted sum	(Group 1:0,9; Group 2:0,1)	Bone or soft tissue	G3W1
Weighted sum	(Group 1:0,75; Group 2:0,25)	Bone or soft tissue	G3W2
Weighted sum	(Group 1:0,6; Group 2:0,4)	Bone or soft tissue	G3W3
Lexicographical order	K = 0,05	Bone or soft tissue	G3L1
Lexicographical order	K = 0,1	Bone or soft tissue	G3L2
Lexicographical order	K = 0,2	Bone or soft tissue	G3L3

4   Experiments

A total of 324 different experiments were carried out. These involved 18 SFO problem instances corresponding to nine cases of live people (from Spain and Italy), three different parametrizations for both weighted sum and lexicographical order approaches, and the three different landmark classifications. Table 1 shows a summary of the experiments that have been carried out, along with the configuration of their parameters. Since all the approaches tested are based on stochastic processes, 10 independent runs were performed for each problem instance to compare the robustness of the methods and to avoid any possible bias.

Table 2 shows the average error distance of our approaches for all the SFO cases. The error of each experiment was calculated by measuring the euclidean distance from the GT to the closest point of the backprojection line for the obtained geometric transformation f (see [7] for a detailed explanation of this validation metric). Weighted sum performs slightly better when the differences of weights is small (W3). Similarly, lexicographical order performs better when the similarity function is relaxed (larger k values, L3). This similar behaviour is more evident in the first and second group of landmarks, and it does not apply for the third group probably because of the limited number of bony landmarks. In fact, both approaches also reach very similar average errors when considering the latter group of landmarks. However, weighted sum performs better in the remaining two cases. The best parametrization for each particular approach and landmark group are marked in bold. G3W2 and G3L1 resulted to be the best performing approaches with similar average distance error. Notice that, the third group of landmarks (G3) could be only tested on a small subset (four cases) due to the impossibility to locate landmarks in the teeth. Then, within those approaches that could have been applied over the entire data set, the weighted sum with parametrization W3 is the best approach (G1W3 and G2W3).

Table 2. Mean error in mm regarding the ground truth of all the SFO cases (18 in total) for each particular approach, landmarks classification and parametrization

Experiment	Average	Experiment	Average	Experiment	Average
MC45	0,56765				
G1W1	0,80423	G2W1	0,7629887	G3W1	0,69053726
G1W2	0,7495467	G2W2	0,7226197	G3W2	**0,63774209**
G1W3	**0,7293624**	G2W3	**0,7134323**	G3W3	0,66171256
G1L1	0,9095235	G2L1	0,786698	G3L1	**0,64084892**
G1L2	0,9260042	G2L2	0,7905109	G3L2	0,6575175
G1L3	**0,881676**	G2L3	**0,7776824**	G3L3	0,6659166

For all cases, there is not statistical significance difference between the MC45 and the two proposals when they model the differences according to the presence or absence of soft tissue (G3W2, G3L1). However this way of classifying is only formed in our dataset for frontal poses and it could be misleading. With the rest of approaches the MC45 is significantly better than the obtained results.

For lateral cases, our results are always significantly worse than the MC 45. However for frontal cases, G2W3, G3W2 and G3L1 have shown a performance as good as the MC45 and sometime it is slightly better although not significant differences have been found.

Once it is clear that there is a completely different behaviour of the two proposals in frontal and lateral poses, the following is to study in depth the reason behind it.

It is crucial to facilitate the location of a significant number of facial landmarks in order to properly determine the geometric transformation. Thus, the performance of those cases that did not have enough landmarks was unsatisfactory. We also performed a Pearson test in order to measure the correlation between the number of landmarks and its final performance. This shown that the performance is not just related to the number of landmarks but also with which landmarks are located.

5 Conclusion

This paper addressed the SFO stage and the problem of the relative importance of landmarks according to their anthropometric differences. Therefore, we modeled it using two classic approaches (weighted sum and lexicographical order) from multicriteria decision making [6] into the current SFO stage with three different ways of classifying landmarks.

The weighted sum obtained better results than the lexicographical order in almost all the experiments. At first sight, the performance of both approaches was significantly worse than the state of the art method. However analyzing the performance of the cases separately depending on the facial pose of the subject in the ante-mortem photographs, they showed very different behaviors. On the one hand in lateral pose cases, the performance was significantly worse than the state-of-the-art. This poor performance appears to be closely related to the small number of landmarks in the first groups. On the other hand in frontal pose cases, the performance was slightly better than the state of the art proposal although no significant differences were achieved. In summary although more future testing seems necessary, promising results were obtained in those cases where the forensic expert has located a large number of landmarks, and worse results in those cases with few landmarks.

Promising research lines for future work include the study of other ways of classificate landmarks as well as modeling other relationships among landmarks such as their correlation due to face symmetry. Another future work will focus on progressively reducing the uncertainty in fuzzy landmarks. Lastly, another interesting research line is to use the idea of using memetic algorithms [18] in the current proposal as a means of local refinement of the chromosomes.

Acknowledgments. This research was supported by the Spanish *Ministerio de Economía y Competividad* under NEWSOCO project TIN2015-67661-P, and the Andalusian Dept. of *Innovación, Ciencia y Empresa* under project TIC2011-7745, including European Development Regional Funds (EDRF). Mr. O. Gomez's work was supported by Spanish MECD FPU grant FPU14/02380. Dr. Ibañez's work was supported by Spanish MINECO *Juan de la Cierva* Fellowship JCI-2012-15359.

References

1. Yoshino, M.: Craniofacial superimposition. In: Wilkinson, C., Rynn, C. (eds.) Craniofacial Identification, pp. 238–253. Cambridge University Press, Cambridge (2012)
2. Damas, S., Cordón, O., Ibáñez, O., Santamaría, J., Alemán, I., Botella, M.: Forensic identification by computer-aided craniofacial superimposition: a survey. ACM Comput. Surv. **43**, 27 (2011)
3. Damas, S., Wilkinson, C., Kahana, T., Veselovskaya, E., Abramov, A., Jankauskas, R., Jayaprakash, P.T., Ruiz, E., Navarro, F., Huete, M.I., Cunha, E., Cavalli, F., Clement, J., Lestón, P., Molinero, F., Briers, T., Viegas, F., Imaizumi, K., Humpire, D., Ibáñez, O.: Study on the performance of different craniofacial superimposition approaches (II): best practices proposal. Forensic Sci. Int. **257**, 504–508 (2015)

4. Zitovà, B., Flusser, J.: Image registration methods: a survey. Image Vis. Comput. **21**, 977–1000 (2003)
5. Damas, S., Cordón, O., Santamaría, J.: Medical image registration using evolutionary computation: an experimental study. IEEE Comput. Intell. Mag. **6**, 26–42 (2011)
6. Chankong, V., Haimes, Y.: Multiobjective Decision Making Theory and Methodology. North-Holland, Amsterdam (1983)
7. Campomanes-Alvarez, B., Ibanez, O., Campomanes-Alvarez, C., Damas, S., Cordon, O.: Modeling facial soft tissue thickness for automatic skull-face overlay. IEEE Trans. Inf. Forensics Secur. **PP**(99), 1 (2015)
8. Ibáñez, O., Cavalli, F., Campomanes-Álvarez, B.R., Campomanes-Álvarez, C., Valsecchi, A., Huete, M.I.: Ground truth data generation for skull-face overlay. Int. J. Leg. Med. **129**, 569–581 (2015)
9. Huete, M.I., Ibáñez, O., Wilkinson, C., Kahana, T.: Past, present, and future of craniofacial superimposition: literature and international surveys. Leg. Med. **17**(4), 267–278 (2015)
10. Ghosh, A.K., Sinha, P.: An economised craniofacial identification system. Forensic Sci. Int. **117**, 109–119 (2001)
11. Nickerson, B.A., Fitzhorn, P.A., Koch, S.K., Charney, M.: A methodology for near-optimal computational superimposition of two-dimensional digital facial photographs and three-dimensional cranial surface meshes. J. Forensic Sci. **36**, 480–500 (1991)
12. Ibáñez, O., Ballerini, L., Cordón, O., Damas, S., Santamaría, J.: An experimental study on the applicability of evolutionary algorithms to craniofacial superimposition in forensic identification. Inf. Sci. **79**, 3998–4028 (2009)
13. Ibáñez, O., Cordón, O., Damas, S., Santamaría, J.: Modeling the skull-face overlay uncertainty using fuzzy sets. IEEE Trans. Fuzzy Syst. **16**, 946–959 (2011)
14. Ibáñez, O., Cordón, O., Damas, S.: A cooperative coevolutionary approach dealing with the skull face overlay uncertainty in forensic identification by craniofacial superimposition. Soft Comput. **18**, 797–808 (2012)
15. Faugeras, O.: Three-Dimensional Computer Vision. A Geometric Viewpoint, 1st edn. The MIT Press, Cambridge (1993)
16. Cummaudo, M., Guerzoni, M., Marasciuolo, L., Gibelli, D., Cigada, A., Obertová, Z., Ratnayake, M., Poppa, P., Gabriel, P., Ritz-Timme, S., Cattaneo, C.: Pitfalls at the root of facial assessment on photographs: a quantitative study of accuracy in positioning facial landmarks. Int J. Leg. Med. **127**, 699–706 (2013)
17. Bookstein, F.L.: Morphometric Tools for Landmark Data: Geometry and Biology, 1st edn. Cambridge University Press, New York (1991)
18. Krasnogor, N., Smith, J.: A tutorial for competent memetic algorithms: model, taxonomy, and design issues. IEEE Trans. Evol. Comput. **9**(5), 474–488 (2005)

Studying the Influence of Static API Calls for Hiding Malware

Alejandro Martín[1](✉), Héctor D. Menéndez[2], and David Camacho[1]

[1] Universidad Autónoma de Madrid, 28049 Madrid, Spain
{alejandro.martin,david.camacho}@uam.es
[2] University College London, London WC1E 6BT, UK
h.menendez@ucl.ac.uk

Abstract. Malware detection has become a challenging task over the last few years. Different concealment strategies such as packing compression, polymorphic encryption and metamorphic obfuscation have produced that malware Analysts need to find more original techniques to discriminate whether a file is malware or not. One of the current benchmark techniques is static analysis of API Calls. This technique aims to detect malware using the API Calls information extracted from the malware files. In this work, we aim to show a complete study of this technique using a behavioural model, built through an evolutionary process, in order to define possible limitations. For this analysis we will use a benchmark dataset to study the discrimination between malware and benignware and evaluate how malware writers are trying to imitate benign behaviour in order to defeat this technique.

Keywords: Malware · Genetic algorithms · Evolutionary computation · Behavioural models · Clustering

1 Introduction

In the malware arms race, static and dynamic analysis are the main research fields to detect and analyse new malicious software [5]. Static analysis is based on identifying malware according its disassembly information (such as analysing the Control Flow Graph, Opcodes order, etc.). Dynamic Analysis aims to study malware execution and is focused on registers, network traces, memory variations, etc. These processes are usually complementary and combined (hybrid analysis) in order to improve the detection of new malware and generate a deep understanding of its behaviour.

Both approaches are limited in different ways, but according to timing, dynamic analysis suffers the trigger limitation problem, which consists on waiting until the malicious code activates its payload. Normally, malware is able to detect debugging, emulation and virtual machines systems, and it uses this information to hide this payload, making dynamic analysis useless.

On the other hand, there is also an extensive literature in static analysis. The main fields are based on syntactic and semantic comparisons [3], control

O. Luaces et al. (Eds.): CAEPIA 2016, LNAI 9868, pp. 363–372, 2016.
DOI: 10.1007/978-3-319-44636-3_34

flow analysis [4] and API calls [9]. However, there are two main strategies used by malware to conceal from static analysis: polymorphism and metamorphism. Besides, malware designers are able to cheat these methodologies using not just these classical concealment strategies, but also behavioural concealment.

There are several analytical examples that aim to overcome these concealment methodologies. Recent examples of static analysis are focused on avoiding the obfuscation process using semantics methodologies [3]. Other examples are focused on thef application of machine learning techniques to different representations of the program such as the Control Flow Graph or the Data Flow Graph [4]. Besides, the information extracted from the program body can provide a behavioural profile of the malware based on the Opcodes or the API Calls imported [13]. There are also similar studies based on the PE (Portable Executable) header of the binary file [11]. However, as Moser et al. [10] studied, Static Analysis has several limitations such as the detection of zero-day malware, or new obfuscation techniques. In order to overcome these limitations Jacob et al. [6] propose to apply dynamic analysis techniques based on malware behavioural patterns.

Behavioural patterns have been widely studied in dynamic analysis, focusing specially on different traces that the program execution generates. One of the first relevant steps, once these behavioural features are extracted, is to determine a good similarity metric. In [1], Apel et al. study different similarity metrics that can help to develop a malware comparison. Other approaches aim to detect malicious software based on behavioural reports [12] or general malware reports [2]. These studies apply classifiers to discriminate the malicious behaviour. Other approaches aim to simplify the detection process using API system calls [7]. Although the study of dynamic API Calls is out of the scope of this work, in benign programs, they are strong correlated with static API Calls.

During the disassembly process of static analysis, it is usual to wait until malware makes its first system call to consider that it has finished with the decompression/decryption process (applied in packed and polymorphic malware). Malware authors usually include useless system calls to avoid the body detection process. Extending this idea, this paper aims to show that they are also improving this technique to avoid static API Calls detection including extra API calls that simulate benign behaviour. In order to prove this statement, we have created a simple behavioural model based on Multi-Objective algorithms and we have applied it on a benchmark static API Calls dataset (introduced by Sami et al. [13] in 2010). The main idea is to show that this data is also biased.

This paper aims to study the search space generated by static API calls in order to identify overlapping regions. In this space, the API calls define the dimensions and each point represents a program. We will consider similar behaviour when two programs are closed in this space. Due to the data provided is large enough to require different granularity levels, we will combine a multi-objective approach with clustering cost function to find optimal groups where the elements share similar behaviours, and we use the parameters of the groups to describe different granularity levels.

The paper is structured as follows: next section describes the behavioural model, Sect. 3 introduces the experimental setup, which is followed by the experiments in Sect. 4. Finally, the last section summarises the conclusions.

2   Genetic Behavioural Model

This section presents the Genetic Behavioural Model (GBM), a semi-supervised algorithm focused on studying the static API calls space. The algorithm is divided in three parts: the encoding (which defines the chromosomes), the operations (used during the evolutionary process) and the fitness function (used to guide the search). In this case the algorithm has been designed using a Multi-Objective Genetic Algorithm (MOGA) to guide the search.

In order to describe the search space, we will use different granularity levels. On the one hand, this approach is based on clustering, then one of the granularity parameters will be the number of clusters. On the other hand, the approach also aims to generalise in a semi-supervised way, then the other granularity factor is a percentage of supervised information provided to the algorithm.

The method evolves a population of possible groups that are defined as a sample-cluster assignation. When the execution ends the algorithm defines a space partitions (the clusters). However, the labels of such groups –i.e. malware or benignware, are unknown. To tackle the label allocation problem, a subset of the elements (or samples) represented in the individual are marked as *fixed items*, whose labels are known. During the evolution, these samples move between clusters in the same way as the other elements. At the end, the clusters generated are analysed separately and the majority class between fixed items is used to decide the label of the whole cluster. The algorithm has been designed as follows:

1. It takes the whole zoo of programs which aims to group. The algorithm randomises the data and marks a subset as *Fixed Elements*, according to a percentage previously defined.
2. The individuals are randomly initialised. They are represented by an array where each position represents a sample and its value the assigned cluster (the encoding of the individual is described below in depth). The first f items are flagged as fixed (items related to samples whose labels are known).
3. The algorithm runs and evolve the population to achieve the best possible separation of samples into different clusters, minimising the internal distance of the clusters (*intracluster distance*) on one hand and maximising the distance between them (*intercluster distance*) on the other.
4. When the evolution ends, the fixed items in each cluster are analysed and the majority label found between them is designated as the whole cluster label. This creates the *tagging list*, which links clusters and their tags. If there are no fixed items, the set is flagged as invalid and no label is assigned to its examples.

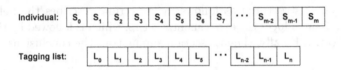

Fig. 1. Individual and tagging list representation

2.1 Encoding

The encoding which has been chosen for the algorithm is a integer encoding where each allele of the chromosome represents an example and its value determines the assigned cluster. A secondary list is used to set the clusters labels. Figure 1 shows these two structures. The individual is defined as an array of m positions or samples. Each value lies within the range of 0 to $(n-1)$, where n defines the number of clusters (n is fixed before the algorithm execution). The *tagging list* contains n positions (one for each cluster) with a binary value representing when the cluster (and its samples) is considered as benignware or malware. This value is defined in accordance with the majority labels founded amongst the fixed elements for each cluster (so the maximum number of malware or benignware labels will define the final value for L_i).

2.2 Operations

The operations chosen for the algorithm are the classical operations for an integer encoding. First, we have performed an Elitism **selection** where the l best individuals of a population past to the next generation. The chromosomes which are chosen for the **reproduction** are selected using a Tournament operator. The **crossover** applied is a uniform crossover, where two string are exchanged between two parents and finally, the **mutation** is a random based operator where any allele is randomly assigned to a different cluster.

2.3 Fitness Function

The fitness function has been defined as a multi-objective fitness. Clustering is usually described related to two clear objectives: to guarantee the separation among clusters and to ensure the cohesion of every cluster. Due to these two objectives might generate opposite solutions, we use a multi-objective approach. In this case, the internal metric (J_i) ensures the cohesion and the external distance (J_e) the separation. They are defined as the following cost functions:

$$J_i = \min_{c_i} \sum_j ||x_j - c_i||, \quad J_e = \max_{c_i} \sum_j ||c_j - c_i||$$

Where c_i defines the centroid of the cluster defined by the metric $|| \cdot ||$, and $x_j \in X$ represents a data instance, i.e., a program. These two objectives define a Pareto Front which provides a solutions space. With these solutions we have a whole range of discrimination where different properties of malware and benignware behaviours are highlighted.

In order to get representative clusters in the space and to avoid disparity between the size of the clusters (which could cause a distortion in the relation of the objectives with the real accuracy), a multiplication factor is applied in the calculation of the internal distance of each cluster. This factor is the number of samples belonging the cluster, which penalises the larger ones with the objective of having similar density in all clusters with respect to the number of samples.

3   Experimental Setup

In order to provide some experimental evidences using the Genetic Behavioural Model, we aim to answer to the following Research Questions:

- **RQ1: How is the discrimination in the search space?** Modifying the granularity level according to the algorithm parameters (fixed elements and number of clusters) we aim to describe the similarity between malware and benignware in the search space using evaluation metrics.
- **RQ2: What is the overlapping level inside the space?** To study the correctness of the hypothesis, we use visualisation techniques to show how the overlapping is presented in specific areas of the search space.

3.1   Datasets

We have analysed three datasets extracted from [13]. The former authors recovered and analysed samples consisting of 31,860 malware and 2,951 benignware Microsoft Windows executables. A report of each example was generated with information about the use of different API calls. These data are raw and need to be processed before the analytical process. The authors summarized their data information in three datasets:

- **"DLL" Dataset**: The API calls are grouped by the DLLs they are related, composed by 178 attributes.
- **"Close" Dataset**: In this dataset, attributes represent combinations of API calls, calculated with the Clospan algorithm.
- **"Cat+" Dataset**: The first 95 attributes of each sample represent categories in which the most used API calls are classified. These values are integers showing the number of API calls imported of every category. The rest of the attributes (more than 44,000) are a selection of the top discriminative particular API calls.

The large number of features defined in this problem implies the necessity of a dimensionality reduction, which has been performed with Principal Component Analysis (PCA). PCA transforms an input space into a smaller set of variables (or components), minimising the information loss. The basic idea of this method is to find those directions that maximise the data variance, without taking into account labels, and project the original data in these new directions [8]. With this process we ensure that the projective search space contains the same variance than the original, in order to guarantee that the system is no biased.

3.2   Genetic Algorithm Parameterisation

In order to execute the genetic algorithm proposed, different parameters have to be fixed. First, with the aim ob reducing the execution time of each experiment, the number of generations has been set as a dynamic value, depending on the algorithm convergence. This condition is satisfied when the last 10 generations produce the same minimum or maximum value for the minimisation or maximisation objective, respectively. The selection of the rest of parameters has been decided testing different configurations to find the most appropriate. Each generation produces 1000 individuals, after testing values between 100 and 10,000 individuals. From these individuals, the 30 best individuals are selected to generate the new population, a decision taken after testing values between 5 and 200. Regarding the mutation and crossover rates, different settings were tested in the range of 5 % to 50 % for both parameters, where the best configuration was found using a crossover rate of 15 % and a mutation rate of 0.5 %.

4   Experiments

In order to answer the research questions and due to the random nature of the initialisation process and operations in genetic algorithms, 20 executions with the configuration previously stated were run.

In order to choose a good solution from the Pareto Front, we have performed different evaluations based on the accuracy value for all the datasets (see Fig. 2). We have discovered that the two objectives (inter and intra cluster distances) obtain similar results, but the Pareto normally provide the best accuracy to the

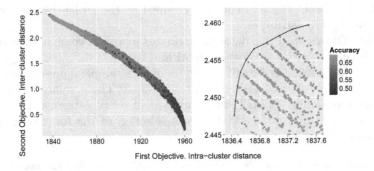

Fig. 2. (a) Representation of all the solutions of one execution. (b) Pareto frontier with the best solutions

inter cluster objective, therefore this solution has been used for the description, specially because of our interest in the behavioural discrimination process.

The data used to perform the experiments is formed by the three datasets listed above. In the research of the authors that built these datasets, the executions were performed with an unbalanced number of labels. Due to it is needed a balanced dataset to properly describe the search space, we have extracted a representative balanced subset of 1200 programs, containing 600 malware and 600 benignware from each dataset. They have been randomly selected.

4.1   Space Description Based on Granularity

The high dimensionality description of the projective space defined by the static API calls data makes us need to use different granularity levels, in order to understand the space and be able to evaluate whether the malware and benignware behaviour is similar. In this case, we use the Genetic Behavioural Model, whose goals are known, to guide us in this descriptive task.

The two granularity parameters that are used to provide a deeper knowledge of the space are: the number of clusters and the percentage of fixed elements. The former will zoom from a general definition of the space (divided in two cluster of malware and benignware) to some specific regions defined by the Voronoi Tesselation (where the number of clusters in incremented). The later will measure the discrimination quality according to the information provided to the space, incrementing or decrementing the fixed elements. The more fixed elements in the space, the more information the model can use to describe it. In order to be able to understand the results according to the modification of the two parameters, we will calculate the Accuracy varying the granularity.

Figure 3 shows the results for the three datasets. When the number of clusters influence has been evaluated, the number of Fixed Elements has been fixed to 15 % because it provides the best Accuracy values. These results show that when the number of clusters is incremented, the accuracy is initially reduced, and it is incremented again when the number of clusters is close to 200 (which supposes average granularity of 6 elements per cluster). This shows that there are regions of the space where malware and benignware behaviour is extremely similar, but from a general perspective (2 clusters) or a low level perspective, they can be discriminated with a limited accuracy of 60–70%, depending on the dataset. We can see that this happens in all benchmark datasets.

Modifying the information provided to the space through the number of fixed elements (see Fig. 3), and fixing the number of clusters to the best accuracy of the previous case, we can see that there are almost no variances in the discrimination quality. This means that, although we provide more information to define better sets, this information does not provide any variance for any of the datasets. However, it influences to worse accuracy values. When the number of clusters is increased notoriously, for example, to 100, the percentage of fixed elements takes importance as it is shown in Fig. 4. With this number of clusters, the overall Accuracy decreases substantially, but it allows us to evaluate how it is affected by the number of fixed items. As noted in the graphic, the Accuracy

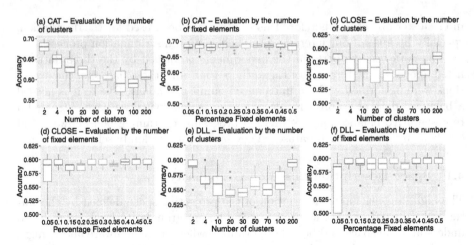

Fig. 3. Accuracy using different numbers of clusters and fixed elements for Cat+, close and DLL datasets

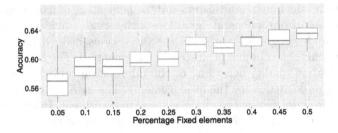

Fig. 4. Accuracy with different numbers fixed elements for 100 clusters and the Cat+ dataset

increases linearly with the number of fixed elements. An increment in the number of clusters needs to go hand-in-hand with an increase in the percentage of fixed elements, since it is necessary a good quantity of labelled items in each set to determine the set nature –malware or benignware.

> Research question 1 asks about the discrimination in the search space. The granularity study has shown that malware authors conceal their behaviour in order to prevent a clear discrimination through static API calls. They limit the Voronoi Tesselation restricting its discrimination accuracy to 60–70%.

4.2 Overlapping Visualization Based on Projections

In order to support the hypothesis of the behavioural models, we aim to visualise the overlapping levels of the two classes. Figure 5 shows the separation in the Cat+ dataset. Samples of both labels are widely spread and mixed in the space.

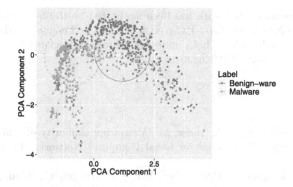

Fig. 5. Representation of the Cat+ dataset balanced with 1200 samples of each label in a 2-dimensional projection

While it is true that there are areas with groups of samples of a single label, many samples overlap, as is evidenced in the lower left hand corner.

Considering the fact that the model does not take into account labels to allocate samples into a cluster, there are clear intentions to overlap the behaviours, supported by these and all previous evidences. This means that, although learning processes can help to identify the patterns, this will be useless when these two classes will totally overlap. Therefore, it is important to complement this approach with more knowledge or it will be probably discarded in a few years.

Research question 2 asks about the overlapping level. The previous two sections have shown how several regions easily overlap making difficult to summarize the information of the search space, following a **behavioural imitation strategy**.

---

5 Conclusions

Malware has evolved dramatically in the last years to very complex forms. Obfuscation techniques are increasing its complexity, making more difficult to analyse and predict their behaviour, and this process is unlikely to diminish in a short space of time. As has occurred repeatedly in the past, when malware has changed towards new shapes, it is necessary to find new techniques to detect and classify malware, whatever its nature is.

In this work, we have shown that malware writers have performed a step forward in malware evolution, using a behavioural imitation strategy, based on static API calls. Our approach, based on behavioural models, identifies general overlapping according to different granularity levels, showing that the discrimination process becomes more difficult using only this information. This supposes another important step forward for Black Hats in the malware arms race, forcing White Hats to use dynamic analysis (whose cost is higher) to be able to identify the malware with API Calls information.

Acknowledgements. This work has been supported by the next research projects: EphemeCH (TIN2014-56494-C4-4-P) Spanish Ministry of Economy and Competitivity, CIBERDINE S2013/ICE-3095, both under the European Regional Development Fund FEDER, and SeMaMatch EP/K032623/1.

References

1. Apel, M., Bockermann, C., Meier, M.: Measuring similarity of malware behavior. In: Proceedings - Conference on Local Computer Networks, LCN, pp. 891–898 (2009)
2. Bayer, U., Comparetti, P.M., Hlauschek, C., Kruegel, C., Kirda, E.: Scalable, behavior-based malware clustering. Sophia **272**(3), 51–88 (2009)
3. Christodorescu, M., Jha, S., Seshia, S.A., Song, D., Bryant, R.E.: Semantics-aware malware detection. In: IEEE Symposium on Security and Privacy (S&P 2005), pp. 32–46. IEEE (2005)
4. Gheorghescu, M.: An automated virus classification system. In: Virus Bulletin Conference (2005)
5. Idika, N., Mathur, A.P.: A survey of malware detection techniques. Purdue University (2007)
6. Jacob, G., Debar, H., Filiol, E.: Behavioral detection of malware: from a survey towards an established taxonomy. J. Comput. Virol. **4**(3), 251–266 (2008)
7. Li, J., Xu, J., Xu, M., Zhao, H., Zheng, N.: Malware obfuscation measuring via evolutionary similarity. In: 1st International Conference on Future Information Networks, ICFIN, pp. 197–200 (2009)
8. Jolliffe, I.: Principal Component Analysis. Wiley Online Library, New York (2002)
9. Martín, A., Menéndez, H.D., Camacho, D.: Genetic boosting classification for malware detection. In: IEEE Congress on Evolutionary Computation (CEC). IEEE (2016)
10. Moser, A., Kruegel, C., Kirda, E.: Limits of static analysis for malware detection. In: Twenty-Third Annual Computer Security Applications Conference (ACSAC 2007), pp. 421–430. IEEE, December 2007
11. Ramadass, S.: Malware detection based on evolving clustering method for classification. Sci. Res. Essays **7**, 2031–2036 (2012)
12. Rieck, K., Trinius, P., Willems, C., Holz, T.: Automatic analysis of malware behavior using machine learning. J. Comput. Secur. **19**(4), 639–668 (2011)
13. Sami, A., Yadegari, B., Peiravian, N., Hashemi, S., Hamze, A.: Malware detection based on mining API calls. In: Proceedings of the 2010 ACM Symposium on Applied Computing, SAC 2010, p. 1020. ACM Press, New York, March 2010

Feature Selection with a Grouping Genetic Algorithm – Extreme Learning Machine Approach for Wind Power Prediction

Laura Cornejo-Bueno, Carlos Camacho-Gómez, Adrián Aybar-Ruiz,
Luis Prieto, and Sancho Salcedo-Sanz(✉)

Department of Signal Processing and Communications,
Universidad de Alcalá, Alcalá de Henares, Madrid, Spain
sancho.salcedo@uah.es

Abstract. This paper proposes a hybrid algorithm for feature selection in a Wind Power prediction problem, based on a Grouping Genetic Algorithm-Extreme Learning Machine (GGA-ELM) approach. The proposed approach follows the classical wrapper method where a global search algorithm looks for the best set of features which minimize the output of a given predictors. In this case a GGA searches for several subsets of features and the ELM provides the fitness of the algorithm. Moreover, we propose to use variables from atmospheric reanalysis data as predictive inputs for the system, which opens the possibility of hybridizing numerical weather models with Machine Learning (ML) techniques for wind power prediction in real systems. The ERA-Interim reanalysis from the European Center for Medium-Range Weather Forecasts has been the one used in this paper. Specifically, after the process of feature selection, we have tested the ELM and Gaussian Processes (GPR) to solve the problem. Experimental evaluation of the prediction system in real data from three wind farms in Spain has been carried out, obtaining excellent prediction results when the ELM is applied after the feature selection but not enough in the case of the GPR algorithm.

Keywords: Grouping genetic algorithm (GGA) · Wind power prediction · Extrem learning machines (ELM) · Gaussian processes (GPR)

1 Introduction

The growing demand of sustainable resources energy, position the wind energy at the top of the most important green energies in the World [1]. However, the main inconvenient of wind energy is its intermittent generation, since this renewable source depends on the weather conditions, which makes difficult its integration in the system. Wind power forecasting has been reported as a key point to improve this integration [2], maximizing the value of wind energy in system operation [3].

Wind power forecasting techniques can be classified into two major families: statistical approaches and classical physical models. Statistical techniques include

O. Luaces et al. (Eds.): CAEPIA 2016, LNAI 9868, pp. 373–382, 2016.
DOI: 10.1007/978-3-319-44636-3_35

different methodologies such as autoregressive moving average (ARMA) algorithms, or based on computational intelligence such as neural networks (NNs) or kernel methods [4], etc. There is a third alternative, consisting the combination of physical and statistical models. The main characteristic of these hybrid physical-statistical models is that the meteorological variables produced by the physical models can be used as inputs for the statistical methods. We can find some previous works about wind power or wind speed forecast problems [5–7].

In this paper we present a novel algorithm for feature selection in a context of wind power prediction problem. Specifically, we propose a system for Wind Power prediction based on Machine Learning regression techniques, in which predictive variables are obtained from the ERA-Interim reanalysis data. ELM and GPR has been tested combined with the GGA-ELM approach. The latter is also used in a previous step of feature selection [8] in order to improve the following predictions with the regressions techniques. The reason for this is that irrelevant features, used as part of a training procedure in a classification or regression machine, can unnecessarily increase the cost and running time of a prediction system, as well as degrade its generalization performance [9,10].

The rest of the paper is organized as follows: next section details the main characteristics of the GGA, the encoding for this problem, operators and fitness function implemented. Section 3 presents the experimental part of the paper, where the hybrid GGA-ELM approach is tested in a real problem of wind power prediction in three different wind farms. The Sect. 4 summarize the results obtained, and finally, Sect. 5 closes the paper with some final conclusions and remarks on this research.

2   GGA-ELM

The grouping genetic algorithm (GGA) is a class of evolutionary algorithm especially modified to tackle grouping problems, i.e., problems in which a number of items must be assigned to a set of predefined groups (subsets of features, in this case). It was first proposed by Falkenauer [11,12], who realized that traditional genetic algorithms had difficulties when they were applied to grouping problems (mainly, the standard binary encoding increases the space search size in this kind of problem). The GGA has shown very good performance on different applications and grouping-related problems [13,14]. In the GGA, the encoding, crossover and mutation operators of traditional GAs are modified to obtain a compact algorithm with very good performance in grouping problems. In this paper we show how to apply the GGA to solve a feature selection problem in a context of wind power prediction. We structure the description of the GGA in Encoding, Operators and Fitness Function calculation.

2.1   Problem Encoding

The encoding is carried out by separating each individual in the algorithm into two parts: the first one is an *assignment* part that associates each item to a given group. The second one is a *group* part, that defines which groups must be taken into account for the individual. In problems where the number of groups is not previously defined, it is easy to see why this is a variable-length algorithm: the group part varies from one individual to another. An example of an individual in the proposed GGA for a feature selection problem, with 10 features and 3 groups, is the following:

$$1\ 1\ 2\ 3\ 1\ 2\ 1\ 3\ 3\ 2\mid 1\ 2\ 3$$

where the group 1 includes features $\{1, 2, 5, 7\}$, group 2 features $\{3, 6, 10\}$ and finally group 3 includes features $\{4, 8, 9\}$.

2.2 Genetic Operators

In this paper we use a tournament-based selection mechanism, similar to the one described in [15]. The crossover operator is applied in the following way:

1. Choose two parents from the current population, at random.
2. Randomly select two points for the crossover, from the "Groups" part of parent 1, then, all the groups between the two cross-points are selected.
3. Insert the selected section of the "Groups" part into the second parent. After the insertion the assignment of the nodes of the offspring individual will be those of parent 1, while the rest of the nodes' assignment are those of parent 2. The "Groups" part of the offspring individual is that of parent 2 plus the selected section of parent 1.
4. Modify the "Groups" part of the offspring individual with their corresponding number. Modify also the assignment part accordingly.
5. Remove any empty groups in the offspring individual and rearrange the rest. The final offspring is then obtained.

Regarding mutation operator, a swapping mutation in which two items are interchanged is taken into account. This procedure is carried out with a very low probability ($P_m = 0.01$), to avoid increasing of the random search in the process.

2.3 Fitness Function

In this work we consider *wrapper* feature selection [16], which means that the GGA evolves (minimizes) direct output of a regressor. The regressor chosen must be as accurate as possible, and also very fast in its training process, in order to avoid high computational cost for the complete algorithm. The ELM [17] is a fast learning method based on the structure of MLPs. This is used as the fitness of the algorithm, and regressor method applied after feature selection and with all features. The ELM algorithm can be summarized as follows:

Given a training set $\mathbb{T} = (\mathbf{x_i}, p_i)|\mathbf{x_i} \in \mathbb{R}^n, p_i \in \mathbb{R}, i = 1, \cdots, l$, an activation function $g(x)$ and number of hidden nodes ($\tilde{N}$), which are calculated by means of a validation process for each group of individuals, in order to optimize the accuracy and CPU time,

1. Randomly assign inputs weights $\mathbf{w}_i$ and bias b_i, $i = 1, \cdots, \tilde{N}$.
2. Calculate the hidden layer output matrix $\mathbf{H}$, defined as

$$\mathbf{H} = \begin{bmatrix} g(\mathbf{w}_1\mathbf{x}_1 + b_1) & \cdots & g(\mathbf{w}_{\tilde{N}}\mathbf{x}_1 + b_{\tilde{N}}) \\ \vdots & \cdots & \vdots \\ g(\mathbf{w}_1\mathbf{x}_l + b_1) & \cdots & g(\mathbf{w}_{\tilde{N}}\mathbf{x}_N + b_{\tilde{N}}) \end{bmatrix}_{l \times \tilde{N}} \tag{1}$$

3. Calculate the output weight vector β as

$$\beta = \mathbf{H}^\dagger \mathbf{P}, \tag{2}$$

where $\mathbf{H}^\dagger$ stands for the Moore-Penrose inverse of matrix $\mathbf{H}$ [17], and $\mathbf{P}$ is the training output vector, $\mathbf{P} = [\mathbf{p}_1, \cdots, \mathbf{p}_l]^t$.

There are different ways of calculating the final fitness associated with each individual ($\mathbf{x}$). In this case we considered the fitness functions specified below, using a measure of the root mean squared error (RMSE) of the prediction:

$$f(\mathbf{x}) = \sqrt{\frac{1}{N} \sum_{k=1}^{N} \left(P(k) - \hat{P}^b(k) \right)^2} \tag{3}$$

where $P(k)$ stands for the wind power measured for sample k, and $\hat{P}^b(k)$ stands for the wind power estimated by the ELM in the group of the individual with less error, for sample k. Note that N stands for the number of training samples.

3   Experimental Part

In order to test the proposed method, we have carried out a number of experiments, which use real data from three wind farms in Spain, whose location is shown in Fig. 1. Our goal is to get the estimation of wind power by means of the ELM

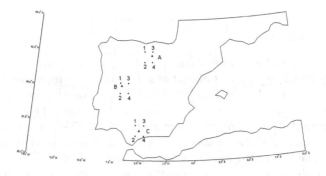

Fig. 1. Wind farms considered for the experiments. The four closest nodes from the Era-Interim reanalysis (where predictive variables are calculated) are also displayed in the picture.

and GPR [18] approaches without feature selection method, and to compare the results with the approaches after a feature selection by means of the GGA-ELM. We pretend to demonstrate the importance of features in the predictive process. To this end, in the following subsection we present the data description and how the characteristics are processed to train the different models.

3.1   Data Description and Methodology

The peculiarity of the predictive variables considered for this problem of wind power prediction (Table 1) is that these predictors are *reanalysis* predictive variables. That means that these variables come from a *reanalysis* project, which consists of combining past observation with a modern meteorological forecast model. In this way, the information registered in the past is improved, producing regular gridded datasets of many atmospheric and oceanic variables, with a temporal resolution of few hours. The reanalysis projects usually extends over several decades and cover the entire planet. There are several current reanalysis projects at global scale, but maybe the most important one is the *ERA-Interim reanalysis project*, produced by the European Centre for Medium-Range Weather Forecasts (ECMWF), and which is used in this work. The main characteristics of the model are that the spatial resolution of the data set is approximately 15 km, on 60 vertical pressure levels from the surface up to 0.1 hPa. Moreover, Era-Interim provides 6-hourly atmospheric fields on model levels, pressure levels, potential temperature and potential vorticity. In order to tackle the wind power prediction in this paper, we consider wind and temperature variables from ERA-Interim at four points around the three different wind farms under study. The predictive variables presented in the Table 1 are taken at different pressure levels (surface, 850 hPa, 500 hPa). As a result, we have 12 predictive variables

Table 1. Predictive variables considered at each node from the ERA-Interim reanalysis.

Variable name	ERA-Interim variable
skt	Surface temperature
sp	Surface pression
u_{10}	Zonal wind component (u) at 10 m
v_{10}	Meridional wind component (v) at 10 m
temp1	Temperature at 500 hPa
up1	Zonal wind component (u) at 500 hPa
vp1	Meridional wind component (v) 500 hPa
wp1	Vertical wind component (ω) at 500 hPa
temp2	Temperature at 850 hPa
up2	Zonal wind component (u) at 850 hPa
vp2	Meridional wind component (v) at 850 hPa
wp2	Vertical wind component (ω) at 850 hPa

per four point around the wind farm considered, at time t. This give a total of 48 predictive variables per wind farm.

Different number of data are available for each wind farm: in wind farm A, data from 11/01/2002 to 29/10/2012, in wind farm B, data from 23/11/2002 to 17/02/2013 and in wind farm C, data from 02/03/2002 to 30/06/2013. Note that we only kept data every 6 h (00 h, 06 h, 12 h and 18 h), to match the predictive variables from the ERA-Interim to the objective variables. These data are divided into training set (80 %) and test set (remaining 20 %) to evaluate the performance of the different algorithms. The methodology followed consists of running the ELM and GPR methods, and once the results are obtained, we run the GGA-ELM algorithm. This is initialized with a total of 50 individuals all of them with a random group part between 2 and 10 (after the crossover operator, the group part can increase or not). The number of evaluations are 100. In this way, we choose the best set of features for the problem, which will be in the group of the individual with less error. This final set of features is then tested using the ELM and GPR methods. Thanks to this procedure we can compare the results obtained by the ELM and GPR with the total of 48 features and only with the selected features, given by the GGA-ELM algorithm. We consider 3 error measurements to evaluate the performance of the proposed approaches, the Root Mean Square Error (RMSE) [MW], the Mean Absolute Error (MAE) [MW] and also the Pearson's correlation coefficient (r^2) [%].

4   Results

Table 2 shows the results obtained in the process to get the prediction of wind power prediction. First of all, the results by the ELM and GPR with all the available features (48 in this case, no feature selection applied) at the three wind farms, is shown. As can be seen, the GPR obtains better results than the ELM, in the three cases, and in general, the performance of the ELM algorithm is far from good, with values of r^2 of 58,56 % and MAE around 4,9755 MW, in the best case that is wind farm C; whereas in the GPR method the values of r^2 is 71,13 % and the measure of MAE is 3,9902 MW. Figures 2(a) and (c) show the time performance of the ELM and GPR in this case without feature selection applied, for the 300 first samples of the test set.

Table 2. Comparative best results of the wind power estimation by the ELM and GPR approaches after the feature selection by the GGA-ELM.

	A			B			C		
	RMSE	MAE	r^2	RMSE	MAE	r^2	RMSE	MAE	r^2
All features-ELM	6.03	4.61	0.63	7.87	6.49	0.41	6.46	4.98	0.59
All features-GPR	5.31	3.97	0.73	5.86	4.41	0.67	5.44	3.99	0.71
GGA-ELM	5.83	4.30	0.63	6.28	4.72	0.63	5.81	4.42	0.67
GGA-GPR	5.61	4.17	0.68	6.05	4.57	0.66	5.44	3.99	0.72

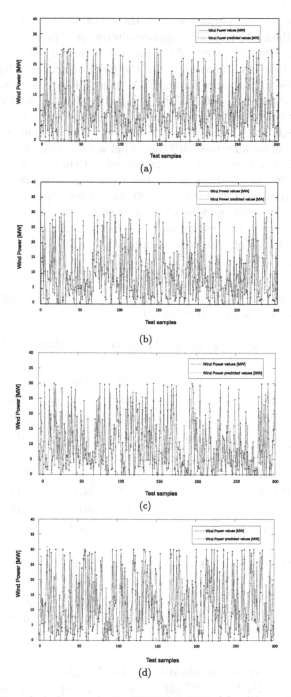

Fig. 2. Estimation of wind power by the ELM and GPR; (a) y (b) are the ELM method with all features and features selection, respectively. (c) y (d) are the GPR method with all features and features selection, respectively.

We can also see the performance of the GGA-ELM approach for feature selection, with the ELM and GPR applied after it. It is possible to see that the GGA-ELM improves the quality of the prediction carried out by the ELM, but it does not produce any improvement in the GPR algorithm. Figures 2(b) and (d) show the time performance for the ELM and GPR approaches, respectively, after the application of the GGA-ELM, also for the 300 first samples of the test set, in the best case that is wind farm C. Again, the GPR approach presents better results than the ELM method, but at this point we must choose between accuracy or speed, because the GPR algorithm obtains more precision than the ELM method, but it is more slow in its execution than the ELM. Whereas the ELM method takes 195 to 198 s in the execution, depending on the wind farm, the GPR algorithm can take between 43000 and 48000 s, also depending on the wind farm (with the same number of training samples).

Table 3 summarizes the performance of the algorithms in terms of *mean* and *variance* (Var) at each of measurements proposed (RMSE, MAE, and r^2), after 10 runs of the algorithms.

Table 3. Comparative of the model's performance in the ELM and GPR approaches after the feature selection by the GGA-ELM.

	Mean RMSE	Mean MAE	Mean r^2	Var RMSE	Var MAE	Var r^2
A						
All features-ELM	6.22	4.67	0.60	0.01	0.01	3.19E-04
All features-GPR	5.65	4.17	0.68	0.04	0.01	6.43E-04
GGA-ELM	6.00	4.42	0.63	0.01	0.01	1.37E-04
GGA-GPR	5.80	4.27	0.66	0.02	0.01	2.50E-04
B						
All features-ELM	8.13	6.74	0.38	0.04	0.05	4.36E-04
All features-GPR	6.08	4.55	0.65	0.02	0.01	1.69E-04
GGA-ELM	6.41	4.84	0.60	0.01	0.01	2.52E-04
GGA-GPR	6.27	4.72	0.64	0.02	0.01	2.20E-04
C						
All features-ELM	6.57	5.11	0.57	0.01	0.01	1.69E-04
All features-GPR	5.57	4.10	0.69	0.02	0.01	2.35E-04
GGA-ELM	6.12	4.64	0.63	0.03	0.01	5.77E-04
GGA-GPR	5.71	4.18	0.68	0.03	0.02	3.89E-04

Regarding the variables obtained by the GGA-ELM as the best set for wind farm A, are [9, 11, 15, 16, 22, 27, 33, 34] which correspond to variables temp2 (point 1), vp2 (point 1), u10 (point 2), v10 (point 2), up2 (point 2), u10 (point 3), temp2 (point 3), up2 (point 3). For wind farm B, the selected features are [11, 22, 23, 47] which correspond to variables vp2 (point 1), up2 (point 2), vp2 (point 2), vp2 (point 4). Finally, for wind farm C, the features are [3, 16, 34, 35, 37, 39, 45] which correspond to variables u10 (point 1), v10 (point 2), up2 (point 3), vp2 (point 3), skt (point 4), u10 (point 4), temp2 (point 4). Note that in the three wind farms the variables up2 and vp2 are always selected in different point. In this regard, it seems that the influence of wind components at 850 hPa is decisive to obtain an accurate wind power prediction.

5   Conclusions

In this paper we have proposed a novel wrapper feature selection approach for a problem of wind power prediction in wind farms. Specifically, the proposed approach is formed by a Grouping Genetic Algorithm as global search, and an ELM as regressor. The GGA allows obtaining different groups of features which can be useful for the search. The results obtained show a good performance of this regressors (ELM and GPR with or without feature selection) with the ERA-Interim reanalysis data in this problem, showing that the proposed algorithm is a good alternative to deal with this problem that arise in the management of wind farms.

Acknowledgement. This work has been partially supported by the project TIN2014-54583-C2-2-R of the Spanish Ministerial Commission of Science and Technology (MICYT), and by Comunidad Autónoma de Madrid, under project number S2013ICE-2933_02.

References

1. Kumar, Y., Ringenberg, J., Depuru, S.S., Devabhaktuni, V.K., Lee, J.W., Nikolaidis, E., Andersen, B., Afjeh, A.: Wind energy: trends and enabling technologies. Renew. Sustain. Energ. Rev. **53**, 209–224 (2016)
2. Tascikaraoglu, A., Uzunoglu, M.: A review of combined approaches for prediction of short-term wind speed and power. Renew. Sustain. Energ. Rev. **34**, 243–254 (2014)
3. Cutler, N.J., Outhred, H.R., MacGill, I.F., Kay, M.J., Kepert, J.D.: Characterizing future large, rapid changes in aggregated wind power using numerical weather prediction spatial fields. Wind Energ. **12**(6), 542–555 (2009)
4. Li, G., Shi, J.: On comparing three artificial neural networks for wind speed forecasting. Appl. Energ. **87**(7), 2313–2320 (2010)
5. Salcedo-Sanz, S., Prez-Bellido, A.M., Ortiz-Garcia, E.G., Portilla-Figueras, A., Prieto, L., Paredes, D.: Hybridizing the fifth generation mesoscale model with artificial neural networks for short-term wind speed prediction. Renew. Energ. **34**(6), 1451–1457 (2009)
6. Landberg, L.: Short-term prediction of the power production from wind farms. J. Wind Eng. Ind. Aerodyn. **80**, 207–220 (1999)
7. Salcedo-Sanz, S., Pastor-Snchez, A., Prieto, L., Blanco-Aguilera, A., Garca-Herrera, R.: Feature selection in wind speed prediction systems based on a hybrid coral reefs optimization - extreme learning machine approach. Energ. Convers. Manag. **87**, 10–18 (2014)

8. Weston, H., Mukherjee, S., Chapelle, O., Pontil, M., Poggio, T., Vapnik, V.: Feature selection for SVMs. In: Advances in NIPS, pp. 526–532. MIT Press (2000)
9. Blum, A., Langley, P.: Selection of relevant features and examples in machine learning. Artif. Intell. **97**, 245–271 (1997)
10. Salcedo-Sanz, S., Prado-Cumplido, M., Pàrez-Cruz, P.F., Bousono-Calzón, C.: Feature selection via genetic optimization. In: International Conference on Artificial Neural Networks, pp. 547–552 (2002)
11. Falkenauer, E.: The grouping genetic algorithm-widening the scope of the GAs. Belg. J. Oper. Res. Stat. Comput. Sci. **33**, 79–102 (1992)
12. Falkenauer, E.: Genetic Algorithms for Grouping Problems. Wiley, New York (1998)
13. Agustìn-Blas, L.E., Salcedo-Sanz, S., Vidales, P., Urueta, G., Portilla-Figueras, J.A.: Near optimal citywide WiFi network deployment using a hybrid grouping genetic algorithm. Expert Syst. Appl. **38**(8), 9543–9556 (2011)
14. Agustìn-Blas, L.E., Salcedo-Sanz, S., Ortiz-García, E.G., Portilla-Figueras, J.A., Pàrez-Bellido, A.M.: A hybrid grouping genetic algorithm for assigning students to preferred laboratory groups. Expert Syst. Appl. **36**, 7234–7241 (2009)
15. Yao, X., Liu, Y., Lin, G.: Evolutionary programming made faster. IEEE Trans. Evol. Comput. **3**(2), 82–102 (1999)
16. Kohavi, R., John, G.H.: Wrappers for features subset selection. Int. J. Digit. Libr. **1**, 108–121 (1997)
17. Huang, G.B., Zhu, Q.Y.: Extreme learning machine: theory and applications. Neurocomputing **70**, 489–501 (2006)
18. Rasmussen, C.E., Williams, K.H.: Gaussian Processes for Machine Learning. MIT Press, Cambridge (2006)
19. Skamarock, W.C., et al.: A Description of the Advanced Research WRF Version 2. National Center for Atmospheric Reserach, Technical Note (2005)

Genetic Algorithms Running into Portable Devices: A First Approach

Christian Cintrano[✉] and Enrique Alba

Departamento de Lenguajes y Ciencias de la Computación,
University of Málaga, Andalucía Tech, Málaga, Spain
{cintrano,eat}@lcc.uma.es

Abstract. Nowadays, smartphones and tablets are essential parts of our daily life. In research, lines of work in advanced algorithms are always wanted to explore the advantages and difficulties of new computing platforms. As an obvious combination of these two facts, analyzing the performance of intelligent algorithms (such as metaheuristics) on these portable devices is both interesting for science and for building new high-impact apps. Thus, we here design and evaluate a genetic algorithm executed over two kinds of portable devices (smartphone and tablet), as well as we compare its results versus a traditional desktop platform. Among several contributions, we mathematically model the running time to analyze the numerical performance of the three devices. Also, we identify weak and strong issues when running an intelligent algorithm on portable devices, showing that efficiency and accuracy can also come out of such computing limited systems.

Keywords: Genetic algorithm · Smartphone · Tablet · Performance · Numerical study

1 Introduction

The use of smartphones and tablets has become commonplace in our daily life [12]. Health, management, living, and energy are just some examples of applications (apps) that we can find in this kind of platforms. Portable devices have grown on sales in the last few years because of their many functionalities (handy, sensors, connectivity, ...) and the large wealth of apps that fit the needs of every single user. However, the limited computational power of smartphones and tablets have yet caused that the core computing work is done in remote servers [10]. It is our belief that, given the advances in hardware (e.g., multi-core CPUs and large memories) and the recent results in building very efficient algorithms (micro-algorithms, specialized operators, simplifications coming from

This research was partially funded by the University of Málaga, Andalucía Tech, and the Spanish Ministry of Science and Innovation and FEDER (TIN2014-57341-R) and Christian Cintrano's grant BES-2015-074805.

O. Luaces et al. (Eds.): CAEPIA 2016, LNAI 9868, pp. 383–393, 2016.
DOI: 10.1007/978-3-319-44636-3_36

theoretical studies, ...), we could start offering optimization and learning techniques on the portable device itself.

Metaheuristics are algorithms designed to solve general optimization problems [1–3]. This kind of algorithms are very used in medicine, smart cities, management, energy control, etc. Running these algorithms on a smartphone would lead to offer independent computing for experts in these domains, either coupled or not with other platforms through Wi-Fi or 4G/5G links.

This research continues the previous work did in [11]. Our goal is to test the strengths and weaknesses of software techniques to solve a complex problem using a metaheuristic algorithm such as a genetic algorithm (GA) [8] over a smartphone and a tablet. Questions like any limitations in the running time or battery, special needs of the implementation, and actual problem reporting/solving will be addressed in the following sections. We will also quantitatively characterize the behavior of this type of portable devices as optimization platforms, and use them as standalone devices which could help users make decisions to solve real NP-hard problem when need it in an uncontrolled (no lab) general scenario.

In summary, we will answer the following research questions:

- *RQ1: Are there specific considerations on portable platforms that, if not taken into account, would lead to inefficient algorithms?*
- *RQ2: Can GAs solve known problems when running on a such limited memory and computing devices?*
- *RQ3: How can we get competitive results (in some way) between traditional and portable platforms?*

This article is organized as follows: Sect. 2 presents the devices used in the analysis. Section 3 describes two example problems to test the performance. Section 4 explains the implemented GA. Section 5 presents some previous details of the experiments. Section 6 analyzes and discusses the experimental results. Finally, Sect. 7 draws the main conclusions and the future work research.

2   Devices

In this work several devices are used. On the one hand, a desktop computer, which serves as a basis to compare the results obtained. On the other hand, we use two portable devices: a Samsung Galaxy ALPHA smartphone and a Samsung Galaxy Tab GT-P7510 tablet. They represent reasonably modern devices commonly found in practice. We could have made a more sophisticated choice, but we want to avoid any bias towards a very powerful and specialized portable device that would hinder the generalization of our conclusions. Table 1 shows the technical specifications of these three platforms. They are of course of varied features, since in practice we will face heterogeneous systems like these.

Table 1. Main technical specifications of the three devices used

Feature	Desktop	Smartphone	Tablet
Operating system	Ubuntu 14.04 LTE	Android 4.4.4	Android 4.0.4
Cores	4xIntel i5-4460	4xARM Cortex-A15[a]	2xARM Cortex-A9
Frequency	3.2 GHz	1.9 GHz	1.0 GHz
Cache L1	64 KB	16 KB + 16 KB	64 KB
Cache L2	256 KB + 6 MB (L3)	2048 KB	1024 KB
Memory	8 GB DDR3	2 GB DDR3	1 GB DDR2
Battery	—	1860 mAh	7000 mAh

[a] Also it has 4xARM Cortex-A7 (1.3 GHz), but they were not used in this work.

3   Problems Used for This Study

We will use two common problems found in the scientific literature to measure the performance of metaheuristic algorithms: OneMax [13] and Frequency Modulation Sounds (FMS) [15]. The first one represents a very common and simple problem serving as a link between our new scenarios of research and the well-known results in the previous literature. The second problem is a hard real problem with applications in the sound industry and in electronic assets like CD players and similar stuff. They two are easy to understand, a desired feature for this article where the focus is in running algorithms on new platforms (not really in solving complex problems).

OneMax seeks to maximize the number of ones in a bit vector, i.e. to find a vector $x = \{x_1, x_2, \ldots, x_n\}$, with $x_i \in \{0, 1\}$ that maximizes the equation:

$$f(x) = \sum_{i=1}^{n} x_i \tag{1}$$

The problem FMS tries to find six real parameters $\{a_1, w_1, a_2, w_2, a_3, w_3\}$ that minimize the mean square error, with $t \in [0, 100]$, between two equations:

$$y(t) = a_1 \sin(w_1 t\theta + a_2 \sin(w_2 t\theta + a_3 \sin(w_3 t\theta))) \tag{2}$$

$$y(t) = 1.0 \sin(5.0t\theta + 1.5 \sin(4.8t\theta + 2.0 \sin(4.9t\theta))) \tag{3}$$

If a solution has a error $E_{FMS} < 10^{-3}$, we will assume that it is acceptable.

4   Algorithm

A genetic algorithm (GA) is a good example of current powerful intelligent techniques. This algorithm is able to find the optimal solution of a problem from an initial (random) set of them (the population). The basic pseudocode of a GA is well-known and so we just briefly present it in the Algorithm 1.

Algorithm 1. A steady-state genetic algorithm pseudocode

```
1 initialize(P(0)) // Create and evaluate the initial population P(0)
2 step ← 0
3 while not stop_condition do
4     parent₁ ← selection-tour2(P(step))
5     parent₂ ← selection-tour2(P(step))
6     individual ← crossover-2points(parent₁, parent₂, prob_cross)
7     mutation(individual, prob_mut)
8     individual.fitness ← evaluation(individual)
9     P(step + 1) ← replacement-ifbetter(P(step), individual)
10    step ← step + 1
11 end
12 return Best solution found
```

The operators selected for running our experiments are quite common: binary tournament selection, two point crossover with probability 0.8, *bit-flip* (OneMax) and normal distribution (FMS) mutations with same probability 0.5, and an *if-better* elitist replacement. The crossover and mutation probabilities are similar to those used in [6] just to get sure we are using reasonable values for them. Same operators and parameters have been kept for all platforms to ensure fairness.

The main stop condition is to find an acceptable solution or run a maximum number of iterations (ten millions). A solution is acceptable if the error between the value of their fitness and the fitness of the optimal solution is less than 10^{-3} for real problems (FMS) or the optimal solution for discrete problems (OneMax).

5 Implementation

Before explaining the experiments it is necessary to present some implementation details to correctly understand the results. For the sake of fairness, We have used the same implementation of the algorithm and problems in the three devices. For taking actual results on portable and desktop platforms we used a simple representation for both problems. We represent the OneMax problem like a bit vector and FMS problem with six different real variables. Also, we have implemented the GA described before in Java [9], which is popular and easily portable to devices having Android as operating system [7].

Android is a common young operative system based on Unix for portable devices. Limited hardware resources in this kind of platforms justify its own *Java Virtual Machine*, which is expected to improve the memory and CPU efficiency.

We need to take spacial care to program algorithms for Android for the dynamic life cycle and one single thread of the apps. Libraries and mechanisms such as *AsyncTask* or *Services*, to cite a few, are useful for running pieces of code in different threads in order to not affect the user experience. We used the first one in our experiments for their easy way to program. This is an important detail of our implementation that answer the RQ1.

6   Experimental Analysis

For a comprehensive view of the behavior on these devices we defined three different dimensions of problems $\{100, 500, 1000\}$, FMS problem has this value fixed in six by the nature of the problem, and for the population size $\{10, 100, 1000\}$. These ranges were selected after an initial analysis to have a trade-off between a fast answer to the user and a long enough execution of algorithms so as to study their properties with statistical meaning. Hence, we have always performed 30 independent runs of each of the GA executions. A different seed was selected within a fixed set of prime numbers between $[0, 1000]$ for each repetition.

As to the type of our studies, we have compared the performance obtained from the desktop computer, smartphone, and tablet on different aspects: *speed*, *memory*, and *battery*. Also, we applied a Kruskal-Wallis statistical test to analyze the confidence on the results. We must say that we always obtained statistical differences between all devices ($p\text{-}value < 2.2 \cdot 10^{-16}$), so the findings in next sections are not due to random fluctuations, but truly represent different behavior.

6.1   Computational Performance

In this section we present results of speed, memory, and battery obtained in the experiments. Table 2 has all the results from our experiments, including the maximum number of iterations performed and the percentage of optimal solution found for each configuration of the experiments.

Let us start by analyzing the memory consumption. Figure 1 reports how many times the portable devices consumes more memory than the desktop machine ($m_{portable}/m_{desktop}$) if we see the results from the perspective of the population sizes. Results are very stable and show a similar trend. Furthermore, both problems offer a similar profile, thus more linked to the algorithm than to the problem itself. FMS has an expected lower consumption due to its number of variables. Please note that for a population size of 1000 individuals, portable devices use less memory than the desktop. This is a fantastic feature of portable devices that seems to need less memory for running this kind of algorithms. Furthermore, this feature is even more noticeable if we look at the results from the perspective of the size of the problem. Figure 2 shows the memory consumption for OneMax across different sizes of problem.

A conclusion is that the memory management in the desktop is less efficient compared to portable devices. The latter ones, given their small memory size, need to optimize its use, and thus algorithms are running smoothly on them.

After the previous memory consumption analysis, we will now study running times. Even if we need less memory, its access on smartphones and tablets is very slow compared to the desktop. We show in Fig. 3 the relation between the running times for the execution (ms) in the two kinds of devices ($t_{portable}/t_{desktop}$).

In the case of the FMS problem, running times are very similar to the desktop (mean factors $\times 1.64$ in the smartphone). This is noticeable: for a normal problem (not a hard one but not easy) we could find similar behavior in the performances offered by the portable platforms. Without these results we should probably keep

Table 2. Performance data obtained in the experiments

	Problem size	Population size	Device	Iterations	Percentage of hits	Time (s)	Memory (MB)	Battery (%)
OneMax	100	10	desktop	1463	100%	0.01	0.94	—
	100	10	smartphone	1463	100%	0.01	4.83	0.00
	100	10	tablet	1463	100%	0.02	7.13	0.00
	100	100	desktop	3508	100%	0.01	1.01	—
	100	100	smartphone	3508	100%	0.04	5.19	0.00
	100	100	tablet	3508	100%	0.05	7.44	0.00
	100	1000	desktop	18571	100%	0.01	3.45	—
	100	1000	smartphone	18571	100%	0.39	5.73	0.00
	100	1000	tablet	18571	100%	0.68	7.56	0.00
	500	10	desktop	10550	100%	0.01	6.14	—
	500	10	smartphone	10550	100%	0.16	5.74	0.00
	500	10	tablet	10550	100%	0.32	7.54	0.00
	500	100	desktop	23003	100%	0.02	12.76	—
	500	100	smartphone	23003	100%	0.35	5.54	0.00
	500	100	tablet	23003	100%	0.80	7.58	0.00
	500	1000	desktop	81567	100%	0.09	35.18	—
	500	1000	smartphone	81567	100%	1.87	6.38	0.00
	500	1000	tablet	81567	100%	4.45	8.22	0.00
	1000	10	desktop	22067	100%	0.03	23.04	—
	1000	10	smartphone	22067	100%	0.49	5.55	0.00
	1000	10	tablet	22067	100%	1.40	7.59	0.00
	1000	100	desktop	48528	100%	0.06	47.42	—
	1000	100	smartphone	48528	100%	1.15	5.79	0.03
	1000	100	tablet	48528	100%	3.43	7.75	0.03
	1000	1000	desktop	170340	100%	0.28	164.60	—
	1000	1000	smartphone	170340	100%	5.32	7.65	0.03
	1000	1000	tablet	170340	100%	14.09	8.58	0.03
FMS	6	10	desktop	2485470	93.3%	95.38	11.40	—
	6	10	smartphone	2485470	93.3%	158.57	5.11	1.03
	6	10	tablet	2485470	93.3%	417.57	7.49	1.10
	6	100	desktop	5425421	83.3%	213.54	12.69	—
	6	100	smartphone	5425421	83.3%	346.15	5.04	2.40
	6	100	tablet	5425421	83.3%	884.34	7.55	2.23
	6	1000	desktop	10000000	0%	392.37	21.86	—
	6	1000	smartphone	10000000	0%	652.83	5.24	2.90
	6	1000	tablet	10000000	0%	1643.10	7.42	3.07

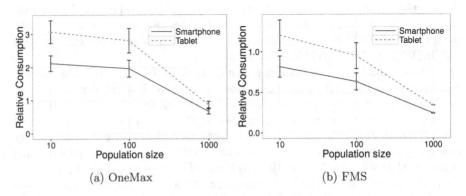

(a) OneMax   (b) FMS

Fig. 1. Memory consumed on portable devices versus desktop, by population size

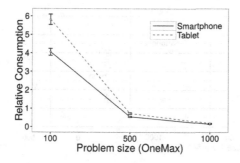

Fig. 2. Memory consumed on portable devices versus desktop, by problem size

on thinking that portable devices are too slow or wrong platforms for intelligent techniques. Much on the contrary, we are giving some hints here that they can do it: RQ1 is then answered positively. However, having a large number of variables, as OneMax has in this study, provokes some differences between traditional and portable platforms. That was somehow expected, and needs to be addressed carefully when designing an algorithm for such light computing devices.

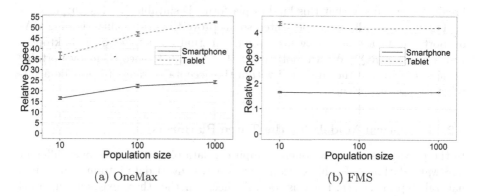

(a) OneMax   (b) FMS

Fig. 3. Execution times of desktop versus portable devices, by population size

If we now observe the behavior of OneMax from the perspective of the size of the problem, we see a difference in the trend of the speed between the two portable devices (see Fig. 4). Nowadays, the gap of performance between traditional and portable desktops has come to a minimum in many cases, and we can only notice small differences in (e.g.) the manipulation of large data vectors.

The third part of our performance analysis is the battery consumption in portable devices. As we saw previously in the experimental results, the OneMax problem has not made any significant power consumption because the running time is too small (even for 1000 bits), but FMS consumes more energy.

Battery consumption in this last problem largely depends on execution time, as Fig. 5 shows. The battery consumption in each case was calculated

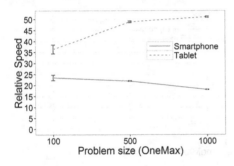

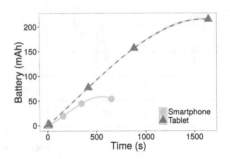

Fig. 4. Execution times of desktop versus portable devices, by problem size

Fig. 5. Battery consumption by running time for all executions of FMS

by averaging the percentage of battery consumed out of thirty executions of the same instance. We can observe that the smartphone is more energy efficient than the tablet. The reason is that A15 cores are faster than A9 cores, so that the first ones can sleep sooner so that they consume less energy. Even if this is true, based in our experiments, the worst tablet computing time in our performance test allows us for almost fifteen hours of computing if we run our GA without a break, so we can say that this kind of platforms is suitable for this purpose.

Furthermore, all results presented so far prove the practicality running GAs on portable devices (showing even some punctual advantages over desktops!), which answers RQ2. We are not saying that we can replace them by portable devices, but overall the times fall within the acceptable range to provide a satisfactory user experience.

6.2   Numerical Models for the Three Platforms

In the previous sections we offered empirical data of performance over different hardware platforms. In this section we will now convert data into information, a natural step in science. For this, we will check whether there exists a numerical model fitting the previously presented data. If we can offer a formula describing our numerical results we could use it for future applications, and hopefully will enlarge the methodological knowledge to build other algorithms and apps [5].

To provide an objective base for comparing running times obtained in our experiments we will use two different existing computing benchmarks: one based on *performance puzzler* [4] and a stochastic simulation algorithm made by us. These tests will allow us calculate the theoretical speed of the three devices as computers. As a result, the portable devices had worse times by factors ×160 for the smartphone and ×568 for the tablet versus the desktop when running the first benchmark. This was a surprisingly bad result that we never found in our previous experimental analysis. It seems that GAs can be run much more optimistically than what standard benchmarks predict.

Because of this weird result, we made our own benchmark based on a Java stochastic simulation algorithm, something that looks nearer a GA. Now, as expected, we got smaller factors for these portable devices: ×28.49 for the smartphone and ×29.94 for the tablet. These results are more reasonable than the previous ones, but our previous tests indicate that an actual GA can run still faster than benchmarks could predict, what again is a good news for developments on this kind of devices. Also, this proves that standard benchmarks must be taken with caution when judging a computing platform.

When we go to the actual values themselves, we can see that a certain relationship exists between the distinct running times in the devices. After a curve fitting step we can get the equations presented in Table 3.

Table 3. Fitting the running times of the devices for every problem and the error

Problem	Device	Problem size	Curve fitting ($x = population\ size$)	R^2
OneMax	Desktop	100	$f(x) = 0.98 + 0.01x$	0.9330
		500	$f(x) = 7.25 + 0.08x$	0.9942
		1000	$f(x) = 32.85 + 0.24x$	0.9928
	Smartphone	100	$f(x) = 4.32 + 0.39x$	0.9829
		500	$f(x) = 159.23 + 1.71x$	0.9959
		1000	$f(x) = 49.74 + 4.78x$	0.9945
	Tablet	100	$f(x) = -2.46 + 0.68x$	0.9952
		500	$f(x) = -331.94 + 4.12x$	0.9964
		1000	$f(x) = 1712.16 + 12.42x$	0.9912
FMS	Desktop	6	$f(x) = -63234 + 64492\log(x)$	0.9726
	Smartphone	6	$f(x) = -108404 + 107326\log(x)$	0.9620
	Tablet	6	$f(x) = -243862 + 266121\log(x)$	0.9629

Both problems are predictable in terms of running time when the size of the problem instances is increased: as we expected there is a behavioral pattern. The data fit well to a linear model ($y = a + bx$), with the exception that FMS problem has a logarithmic behavior ($y = a + b\log(x)$).

In our desire to offer a complete theoretical review of the behavior of these hardware platforms, we have calculated the relation between the factors found in every equation of the previous fitting. We presented two factors: one dividing the parameter b of the previous fitting ($b_{portable}/b_{desktop}$); and another normalized previously the b parameter multiply it by the frequency of its processor ($b \times f$), thus we reduce the impact of hardware on these kinds of devices. All these information can be seen in Table 4.

Once normalized, the fittings still predict greater running times than the obtained in the experimentation, but now they are very close: we have a good mathematical model now. The larger the problem size, the more similar the speed ratios. An exception is for the tablet, we suspect is due to its old technology.

In the normalized equations, the speed factor between portable devices and desktop platform become very similar and small factors. Even in the smartphone,

Table 4. Relative speed factors of portable devices versus desktop for different problems and sizes

Device	Data source	OneMax			FMS
		100	500	1000	
Smartphone	Fitting	39.00	21.38	19.91	1.66
	Empirical	23.45	21.91	18.02	1.64
	Normalized	23.16	12.69	11.82	0.99
Tablet	Fitting	68.00	51.50	51.75	4.13
	Empirical	36.31	48.84	51.08	4.23
	Normalized	21.25	16.09	16.17	1.29

when running the FMS problem, we obtain a slightly faster run than in the desktop (factor less than one). This is a amazing result, as it shows that both platforms would offer the same performance if their processors had the same speed rate. This shows that the hardware design is a primary factor in the performance of algorithms developed on this kind of portable platforms. The fast technological growth on smartphones and tablets suggests that this difference will be reduced in the coming years.

In conclusion, the hardware advances in portable devices made them increasingly closer in performance to desktops, opening a way to use algorithms on then, thus answering RQ3. Please note that although the theoretical model and the real experiments have some differences, we have approached close enough a mathematical model for the GA behavior in portable platforms.

7   Conclusions

In this article we have analyzed the performance of a genetic algorithm on different types of portable devices. We have found that they can actually be used to run optimization algorithms, thus opening a new line of research. Even if this conclusion could seem common sense, we here offer fresh numerical and actual evidence of it.

We have offered a methodology to compare the empirical versus theoretical efficiency of algorithms running over heterogeneous devices (RQ3), which again is beneficial for future works in this area.

We have tested the efficiency itself in terms of time and memory consumption for portable devices to run a GA (RQ2), obtaining equivalent results in the smartphone to those of the desktop: same trends and similar results.

We have also discussed some of the technical constraints in portable devices, such as the limited memory size and the impact of speed on the battery (RQ1).

As a future work we will analyze other metaheuristic algorithms, like simulated annealing, to know whether our results hold for trajectory based techniques. Additionally, we plan to measure the behavior of the performance of the algorithm while running other common applications: chat, play music, calls, etc. It would also be interesting to study the use of parallelism and JNI [14] to improve the running times and check the impact of multithreading on memory and power consumption.

References

1. Alba, E., Blum, C., Asasi, P., Leon, C., Gomez, J.A.: Optimization Techniques for Solving Complex Problems. Wiley, Hoboken (2009)
2. Back, T., Fogel, D.B., Michalewicz, Z. (eds.): Handbook of Evolutionary Computation, 1st edn. IOP Publishing Ltd., Bristol (1997)
3. Blum, C., Roli, A.: Metaheuristics in combinatorial optimization: overview and conceptual comparison. ACM Comput. Surv. **35**(3), 268–308 (2003)
4. Boyer, B.: Robust Java Benchmarking (2008). http://www.ibm.com/developerworks/java/library/j-benchmark1.html
5. Domínguez, J., Alba, E.: A methodology for comparing the execution time of metaheuristics running on different hardware. In: Hao, J.-K., Middendorf, M. (eds.) EvoCOP 2012. LNCS, vol. 7245, pp. 1–12. Springer, Heidelberg (2012)
6. D'Addona, D.M., Teti, R.: Genetic algorithm-based optimization of cutting parameters in turning processes. Procedia CIRP **7**, 323–328 (2013). Forty Sixth CIRP Conference on Manufacturing Systems 2013
7. Goadrich, M.H., Rogers, M.P.: Smart smartphone development: iOS versus Android. In: Proceedings of the 42nd ACM Technical Symposium on Computer Science Education, SIGCSE 2011, pp. 607–612. ACM, New York (2011)
8. Holland, J.H.: Adaptation in Natural and Artificial Systems. MIT Press, Cambridge (1992)
9. IEEE Spectrum: The Top Programming Languages 2015 (2015). http://spectrum.ieee.org/static/interactive-the-top-programming-languages-2015
10. Juntunen, A., Kemppainen, M., Luukkainen, S.: Mobile computation offloading - factors affecting technology evolution. In: International Conference on Mobile Business, ICMB 2012, 21–22 June 2012, Delft, The Netherlands, p. 9 (2012)
11. Matos, J., Alba, E.: Benchmarking metaheuristics on portable devices. Technical report UMA
12. Page, T.: Smartphone technology, consumer attachment and mass customisation. Int. J. Green Comput. (IJGC) **4**(2), 38–57 (2013)
13. Schaffer, J.D., Eshelman, L.J.: On crossover as an evolutionarily viable strategy. In: Belew, R.K., Booker, L.B. (eds.) Proceedings of the 4th International Conference on Genetic Algorithms, July 1991, San Diego, CA, USA, pp. 61–68 (1991)
14. Sheng, L.: Java Native Interface: Programmer's Guide and Reference (1999)
15. Tsutsui, S., Ghosh, A., Corne, D., Fujimoto, Y.: A real coded genetic algorithm with an explorer and an exploiter populations. In: Bäck, T. (ed.) Proceedings of the 7th International Conference on Genetic Algorithms, 19–23 July 1997, East Lansing, MI, USA, pp. 238–245. Morgan Kaufmann (1997)

Metaheuristics

GRASP for Minimizing the Ergonomic Risk Range in Mixed-Model Assembly Lines

Joaquín Bautista[✉], Rocío Alfaro-Pozo, and Cristina Batalla-García

Research Group OPE-PROTHIUS,
Dpto. de Organización de Empresas,
Universitat Politècnica de Catalunya BarcelonaTech (UPC),
Avda. Diagonal, 647, 08028 Barcelona, Spain
{joaquin.bautista,rocio.alfaro,
cristina.batalla}@upc.edu

Abstract. This research examines an assembly line balancing problem and compares the linear programing with a Greedy Randomized Adaptive Search Procedure (GRASP). The problem focuses on minimizing the absolute average deviation for the ergonomic risk between the set of workstations of the line, considering a fixed cycle time and an available space per station. However, the final objective is to obtain line configurations with the lowest possible ergonomic risk, and the lowest discrepancy for the risk level between all stations. Although GRASP does not win linear programing, in all cases, it shows competitive.

Keywords: GRASP · MILP · Assembly line balancing problem · Ergonomic risk

1 Introduction

Ergonomics is the scientific study of the relationship between man and his working environment (including tools, materials, methods of work and organization). Applying ergonomic principles to workplaces can reduce the likelihood of accidents and the potential for ill health at work.

Currently, a lot of jobs require repetitive movements, awkward positions, and manual material handling that may lead to Work-related Musculoskeletal Disorders (WMSDs). The WMSDs constitute an important and expensive occupational problem, because they may suppose a rising costs by wage compensation and medical expenses, and they may reduce productivity and the quality of products.

The latter may occur in mixed-model assembly lines whether the ergonomic attribute is not taken into account in the design of the line. Usually, the processors of workstations from an assembly line are human resources. Therefore, it is important to consider, at the balancing of the line, not only technological and managerial attributes, but also the social issues that can derive from ergonomic risks.

Some authors have already incorporated ergonomics into the Simple Assembly line Balancing Problems (SALBPs) [1, 2]. Others have included ergonomic attributes into the Time and Space Assembly Line Balancing Problems (TSALBPs), the spatial

© Springer International Publishing Switzerland 2016
O. Luaces et al. (Eds.): CAEPIA 2016, LNAI 9868, pp. 397–407, 2016.
DOI: 10.1007/978-3-319-44636-3_37

required by jobs or tasks is also considered in [3–5]. Indeed, we base this work on a mathematical model proposed by [5].

We evaluate a variant for the TSALBP_erg problem that focuses on balancing workstations in regard with the comfort of workers, and thus, all workers will be submitted to a similar ergonomic risk level. The problem also includes the spatial limitation for workstations; and the production rate is fixed by the cycle time, c.

The aim of this evaluation is in line with the work presented by the authors [6] and it consists of comparing two different resolution procedures. On the one hand, we use the Mixed Integer Linear Programming (MILP); and, on the other hand, we use a Greedy Randomized Adaptive Search Procedure (GRASP). Unlike the previous work [6], now the problem does not aim at minimizing the maximum ergonomic risk, but minimizes the average absolute deviation for the ergonomic risk from the set of workstations. However, both researches, this one and [6], seek to maximize indirectly the comfort of an assembly line, by means of considering the area and the time limitations. This comfort of the assembly line supposes minimizing, as far as possible, the maximum ergonomic risk of the line and minimizing the range or, in other words, the difference between the worst and the best workstation in regard with their ergonomic risk values.

In accordance with the purpose of this research, we describe the problem under study in Sect. 2, and we also formulate the mathematical model. Section 3 presents the resolution procedures. Section 4 shows the computational experience and the obtained results, given a case study linked with the Nissan's engine plant in Barcelona (NMISA, Nissan Motor Ibérica – BCN). Finally we conclude in Sect. 5.

2   Balancing the Ergonomic Risk in the TSALBP_erg

The TSALBP_erg can be characterized by three different groups of elements: The first one (1) is the set of operations or tasks $(J : j = 1, \ldots, |J|)$, which are associated with temporal attributes (i.e. the processing time of each task, $t_j : j = 1, \ldots, |J|$), spatial requirements (necessary area for each task $a_j : j = 1, \ldots, |J|$) and ergonomic stress levels (i.e. ergonomic risk of each task: $R_j : j = 1, \ldots, |J|$); the second one (2) is the set of workstations $(K : k = 1, \ldots, |K|)$ with finite or infinite elements; and the third one (3) is the set of sequencing restrictions and precedence relationships between tasks, restrictions of incompatibility, and constraints that affect the stations in regard with their assignable time, their available area, and their admissible risk.

The problem attempts to assign all tasks to workstations in a way that all constraints and limitations are observed, and the system achieves its maximum efficiency regarding some of the considered attributes.

This study aims to find a line configuration that balances all workstations regarding the ergonomic risk besides to fulfill the spatial and temporal limitations. Therefore, tasks will be assigned to a specific set of workstations in order to reduce range of values for the ergonomic risk of the line, and without exceeding the maximum available space and the cycle time per workstation.

To this purpose, we use a specific case from a general mathematical model proposed by [5]. The objective of the model is to minimize the average absolute deviation around the ideal ergonomic risk for the line, considering simultaneously a maximum work time per station and product (c, cycle time), a maximum linear area per workstation (A) and the ergonomic risk of tasks. In this case, the ideal value corresponds with the average risk of the line, considering a number m of workstations. The discrepancy is measured considering the rectangular distance.

Before the mathematical formulation of the so-called *min AAD_R* model, we define the parameters and variables thereof.

Parameters	
J	Set of elemental tasks ($j = 1, \ldots, |J|$)
K	Set of workstations ($k = 1, \ldots, |K|$)
Φ	Set of ergonomic risk factors ($\phi = 1, \ldots, |\Phi|$)
t_j	Processing time of elemental task j ($j = 1, \ldots, |J|$) at normal activity
a_j	Linear area required by the elemental task j ($j = 1, \ldots, |J|$)
$\chi_{\phi,j}$	Category of task j ($j = 1, \ldots, |J|$) associated with the risk factor ϕ ($\phi = 1, \ldots, |\Phi|$).
$R_{\phi,j}$	Ergonomic risk of task j ($j = 1, \ldots, |J|$) associated with the risk factor ϕ ($\phi = 1, \ldots, |\Phi|$). Here: $R_{\phi,j} = t_j \cdot \chi_{\phi,j}$
P_j	Set of direct precedent tasks of task j ($j = 1, \ldots, |J|$)
c	Cycle time. Standard time assigned to each station to process its workload (S_k)
m	Number of workstations, $m = |K|$, that is known and fixed
A	Available space or linear area assigned to each workstation
R_ϕ^{med}	Average ergonomic risk present at each workstation regarding the risk factor $\phi \in \Phi$. That is: $R_\phi^{med} = (1/|K|) \cdot \sum_{j=1}^{|J|} R_{\phi,j}, \ \forall \phi \in \Phi$

Variables	
$x_{j,k}$	Binary variable equal to 1 if the elemental task j ($j = 1, \ldots, |J|$) is assigned to the workstation k ($k = 1, \ldots, |K|$), and to 0 otherwise
R_ϕ	Maximum ergonomic risk for the risk factor ϕ ($\phi = 1, \ldots, |\Phi|$)
$\bar{R}(\Phi)$	Average maximum ergonomic risk associated with the set of factors Φ
S_k	Workload of station k. Set of tasks assigned to the station $k \in K$: $S_k = \{j \in J : x_{j,k} = 1\}$
$R_\phi(S_k)$	Ergonomic risk for the factor $\phi \in \Phi$ associated with the workload: $S_k : R_\phi(S_k) = \sum_{j \in S_k} R_{\phi,j}$
$\delta_{\phi,k}^+(R)$	Ergonomic risk excess at workstation $k \in K$ depending on the factor $\phi \in \Phi$ with respect to its average value, $\delta_{\phi,k}^+(R) = [R_\phi(S_k) - R_\phi^{med}]^+$
$\delta_{\phi,k}^-(R)$	Ergonomic risk defect at workstation $k \in K$ depending on the factor $\phi \in \Phi$ with respect to its average value, $\delta_{\phi,k}^-(R) = [R_\phi^{med} - R_\phi(S_k)]^+$

The *min AAD_R* mathematical formulation is the following:

$$min\ AAD(R(\Phi)) = \frac{1}{m \cdot |\Phi|} \cdot \sum_{\phi=1}^{|\Phi|} \sum_{k=1}^{|K|} \left| R_\phi(S_k) - R_\phi^{med} \right| \equiv$$

$$\frac{1}{m \cdot |\Phi|} \cdot \sum_{\phi=1}^{|\Phi|} \sum_{k=1}^{|K|} \left(\delta_{\phi,k}^+(R) + \delta_{\phi,k}^-(R) \right) \tag{1}$$

Subject to:

$$\sum_{k=1}^{|K|} x_{j,k} = 1 \quad \forall j \in J \tag{2}$$

$$\sum_{j=1}^{|J|} t_j \cdot x_{j,k} \leq c \quad \forall k \in K \tag{3}$$

$$\sum_{j=1}^{|J|} a_j \cdot x_{j,k} \leq A \quad \forall k \in K \tag{4}$$

$$R_\phi(S_k) - \sum_{j=1}^{|J|} R_{\phi,j} \cdot x_{j,k} = 0 \quad \forall k \in K \wedge \forall \phi \in \Phi \tag{5}$$

$$R_\phi(S_k) - \delta_{\phi,k}^+(R) + \delta_{\phi,k}^-(R) = R_\phi^{med} \quad \forall k \in K \wedge \forall \phi \in \Phi \tag{6}$$

$$\sum_{k=1}^{|K|} k\left(x_{i,k} - x_{j,k}\right) \leq 0 \quad \forall \{i, j\} \subseteq J : i \in P_j \tag{7}$$

$$\sum_{k=1}^{|K|} k \cdot x_{j,k} \leq m \quad \forall j \in J \tag{8}$$

$$\sum_{j=1}^{|J|} x_{j,k} \geq 1 \quad \forall k \in K \tag{9}$$

$$R_\phi(S_k), \, \delta_{\phi,k}^+, \, \delta_{\phi,k}^-(R) \geq 0 \quad \forall k \in K \wedge \forall \phi \in \Phi \tag{10}$$

$$x_{j,k} \in \{0, 1\} \tag{11}$$

The objective function (1) expresses the average absolute deviation of ergonomic risk around the mean ergonomic risk of the line. Constraint (2) force the assignment of all tasks. Constraints (3) and (4) impose the maximum limitation of the workload time and the maximum linear area allowed by station. Constraint (5) determine the real ergonomic risk associated with the workload at each workstation. Constraint (6) define the ergonomic risk discrepancies, both positive and negative, between the average and real values. Constraint (7) correspond to the precedence task bindings. Constraints (8) and (9) limit the number of workstations and force that there is no empty workstation, respectively. Finally, constraints (10) and (11) necessitate that variables be non-negative and the assigned variables be binary.

3   Resolution Procedure: GRASP Algorithm

The hardness of balancing problems and the high computational cost in regard with the time required to solve them by exact procedures have given rise to other non-exact procedures such as heuristic applications. We can find numerous heuristic procedures, in literature, with the aim at solving single [7] and multi-objective [8, 9] balancing problems. Indeed, this paper is addressed to compare the results obtained by linear programming with those obtained by a GRASP algorithm, like the research [6].

Given the *min AAD_R* model features we must use the Mixed Integer Linear Programming (MILP) as exact procedure because some of the problem variables are constrained to be integers while other variables are allowed to be non-integers.

On the other hand, we use a metaheuristic procedure as non-exact procedure to solve the combinatorial optimization problem. Specifically, we use a multi-start metaheuristic, in which two phases are repeated iteratively. These phases are (1) the construction phase that builds progressively an initial solution by means of a greedy algorithm; and (2) the local search phase that investigates the neighborhood of the solution built in the first phase until a local minimum is found. Finally, the best overall solution is kept as the result.

Briefly, GRASP requires the following: (1) the greedy randomized algorithm and the greedy evaluation function; (2) the neighborhood and the procedure to explore it; (3) the maximum number of performed iterations or the stopping criterion. All must be defined according the objective of the problem that is to minimize the average absolute deviation (*min AAD_R*) for the ergonomic risk of the assembly line.

3.1 Constructive Phase: Greedy Procedure

In this phase a sequence of tasks $\pi(N) = (\pi_1, \ldots, \pi_N)$ is progressively built by adding a task from the candidate list $RCL(n)$ at stage associated with the position $n (n = 1, \ldots, N)$ of the sequence $\pi(N)$.

At each stage, the $RCL(n)$ is formed by all tasks that can be incorporated into the partial solution under construction without destroying feasibility. That means that tasks must satisfy:

1. Not be assigned to the sequence $\pi(n - 1) = (\pi_1, \ldots, \pi_{n-1})$.
2. Have all the precedent tasks assigned and, therefore, incorporated into the sequence $\pi(n - 1) = (\pi_1, \ldots, \pi_{n-1})$. That is $\forall j \in RCL(n) \Rightarrow P_j \subseteq \pi(n - 1)$.

Once the $RCL(n)$ is formed, all candidate tasks are evaluated according four hierarchical priority indices. The (12) and (13) allow for ordering the $RCL(n)$ and generating the $\pi(N)$ sequence, and the last two, (15) and (16), allow for obtaining another candidate list, $RCL'(n)$, and therefore, another sequence, $\pi'(N)$. Specifically the $f_j^{(n)}$ index denotes the ergonomic risk generated by the task $j \in RCL(n)$ and the set of its following tasks, F_j^*; the $g_j^{(n)}$ index is used to break ties and serves to measure the non-regularity of the sequence in terms of ergonomic risk; the $f_j^{'(n)}$ index denotes the linear area required by the task $j \in RCL'(n)$ and the set of its following tasks F_j^*; and finally the $g_j^{'(n)}$ index is analogous to the $f_j^{(n)}$ index.

$$f_j^{(n)} = \sum_{\phi \in \Phi} t_j \cdot \chi_{\phi,j} + \sum_{\phi \in \Phi} \sum_{h \in F_j^*} t_h \cdot \chi_{\phi,h} \quad (\forall j \notin \pi(n - 1) \wedge P_j \subseteq \pi(n - 1)) \quad (12)$$

$$g_j^{(n)} = \sum_{\phi \in \Phi} \left(t_j \cdot \chi_{\phi,j} + \sum_{h=1}^{n-1} t_{\pi_h} \cdot \chi_{\phi,\pi_h} - n \cdot r_\phi(J) \right)^2 \quad (\forall j \notin \pi(n - 1) \wedge P_j \subseteq \pi(n - 1))$$

$$(13)$$

Where $r_\phi(J)$ is the ergonomic risk rate of factor $\phi \in \Phi$ for the set of tasks J:

$$r_\phi(J) = \frac{1}{|J|} \cdot \sum_{j=1}^{J} t_j \cdot \chi_{\phi,j} \quad (\forall \phi \in \Phi) \tag{14}$$

$$f_j^{'(n)} = a_j + \sum_{h \in F_j^*} a_h \quad (\forall j \notin \pi'(n-1) \wedge P_j \subseteq \pi'(n-1)) \tag{15}$$

$$g_j^{'(n)} = \sum_{\phi \in \Phi} t_j \cdot \chi_{\phi,j} + \sum_{\phi \in \Phi} \sum_{h \in F_j^*} t_h \cdot \chi_{\phi,h} \quad (\forall j \notin \pi'(n-1) \wedge P_j \subseteq \pi'(n-1)) \tag{16}$$

Indices lead to the creation of restricted candidate lists that are composed by the best tasks, i.e., those tasks with the best values for the indices and, therefore, with smallest impact in the solution. The $RCL(n)$ list is restricted through sorting the tasks according to the value of the $f_j^{(n)}$ index (in descending order) and according to the $g_j^{(n)}$ index (in ascending order) in case of ties. Similarly, the $RCL'(n)$ list is reduced after sorting the tasks by the $f_j^{'(n)}$ index (in descending order) and by the $g_j^{'(n)}$ index (in descending order) whether it is necessary to break any tie.

Both lists are reduced by the admission factor Λ, which determines the percentage of tasks that will be sorted among the best candidates. The new lists are called restricted candidate lists, $\overline{RCL}(n, \Lambda)$ and $\overline{RCL}'(n, \Lambda)$.

This phase allow for generating two feasible sequences. The $\pi(N)$ sequence without delays and with regular ergonomic risk and the $\pi'(N)$ sequence without delays in required linear area and ergonomic risk. Furthermore, the procedure makes sure the sequences are consistent with both precedent and succession constraints, and they do not accumulate the ergonomic risk (for $\pi(N)$ case) or the required linear area (for $\pi'(N)$ case) at the end of the assembly line.

The line configurations are generated by dividing the sequences $\pi(N)$ and $\pi'(N)$ into a number of segments equal than the number of workstations m $(m > 1)$. Obviously, the segments must keep the following features: (1) the total processing time assigned to any segment cannot be greater than the cycle time, c; (2) the total space required by the tasks assigned to any segment cannot be greater than the available linear area at each workstation, A; (3) the segments must be formed by adjacent tasks of the sequence; (4) no segment must be empty; and (5) the segments are disjoint between them and their union corresponds with the set J of tasks.

3.2   Local Search Phase

This phase focuses on iteratively improving the solutions generated by the greedy algorithm, replacing the current solutions by better solutions in a neighborhood of the current solutions. Specifically, to improve the starting solution, our local search procedure consists of applying four algorithms with different neighborhood structure, sequentially. Each one of these algorithms tries to improve the given solution by means of task exchanges between different neighborhoods of workstations.

Although all algorithms explore a different neighborhood, all of them must meet the same condition to consolidate a new solution: for replacing the current solution by a better one, the constraints linked with the cycle time, linear area and precedence rules, must be satisfied and the average absolute deviation of the ergonomic risk of the line must improve.

Additionally, if there is tie, and different solutions meet the constraints and the average absolute deviation is the same, at each neighborhood structure a different condition will be evaluated.

The algorithms and the neighborhoods defined in order to improve the current solution are the following:

1. Inserting tasks from the station with the greatest ergonomic risk into any other station: the workstation with the greatest ergonomic risk inserts all its tasks, one by one, into any previous station and then into any next station. The insertion will only be consolidated, in case of tie, if the ergonomic risk at the receiving station is greater than the current minimum ergonomic risk.
2. Inserting a task from any station into the station with the lowest ergonomic risk: the workstation with the lowest ergonomic risk increases its workload with the last task from any previous station and/or the first task from any next station. The conditions of this algorithm to consolidate an insertion, in case of tie, are: (1) the ergonomic risk at the emitting station is greater than the minimum ergonomic risk and (2) the ergonomic risk at the receiving station is less than the current maximum ergonomic risk.
3. Exchanging tasks from the station with the greatest ergonomic risk to any other station: this consists of performing exchanges between the tasks from the station with the greatest ergonomic risk, one by one, and the first task from the following workstations and, after, the last task from previous stations. The ergonomic risk at both stations must be greater than the current minimum ergonomic risk and less than the current maximum ergonomic risk to consolidate the exchange in case of tie.
4. Switching task between workstations: the last step consists of exchanging tasks between two stations. Obviously, the exchanges besides meet the cycle time, linear area and precedence constraints and improve the average absolute deviation of ergonomic risk, must reduce the Euclidean discrepancies of the ergonomic risk in both stations, in case of tie.

Finally, the best solution found is returned.

4 Computational Experience

Once the mathematical model, *min AAD_R*, and the GRASP algorithm for the problem have been explained, we continue this research with a computational experience. This allows us to compare and evaluate the procedures.

Specifically, we have chosen a case study that corresponds to an assembly line from the Nissan's engine plant in Barcelona, whose main features are the following:

- Daily production of 270 engines with a cycle time of 180 s.
- Engines divided into three families: crossovers (p_1, p_2, p_3), Vans (p_4, p_5) and medium tonnage trucks (p_6, p_7, p_8, p_9), with equivalent partial demands.
- An engine requires 140 tasks (related to the 378 elementary tasks) [10].

On the other hand, considering the line features we have fixed the values for other necessary parameters. Indeed, we have defined value ranges for some parameters, such as the number of workstations, the available area and the admission factor; this allows for measuring the effect of these parameters on the ergonomic risk of the line.

- Number of workstation (length of the line): $m = \{19, 20, 21, 22, 23, 24, 25\}$.
- Available linear area per workstation: $A = \{4, 5, 10\}$ m.
- Number of iterations for the GRASP algorithm: $Iter_{max} = 10000$.
- Admission factor for the candidate lists: $\Lambda = \{25\ \%, 50\ \%, 100\ \%\}$.

To solve the *min AAD_R* model by MILP we have used the CPLEX (v11.0) software, running on a Mac Pro computer with an Intel Xeon, 3.0 GHz CPU and 2 GB RAM memory under the Windows XP operating system, given a CPU time limit of 2 h

Table 1. Maximum ergonomic risk and ergonomic risk range given by the CPLEX solver with the *min AAD_R* model; ergonomic values are measured in ergo-seconds[a].

Maximum ergonomic risk of the line/m						
A	19	20	21	22	23	24	25
4	-	-	450	420	375	345	285
5	440	390	320	300	275	265	255
10	360	315	300	285	275	265	255

Ergonomic risk range of the line/m						
A	19	20	21	22	23	24	25
4	-	-	320	274	215	185	125
5	240	162	92	50	25	15	19
10	75	30	15	15	17	15	15

[a]Time unit measured in seconds and used to assess the ergonomic risk of a task, with a processing time of 1 s at normal work pace, bearing a risk category of 1. Time spent by a worker to perform a task (at normal pace) considering the level of the ergonomic risk of the task.

for each instance. The GRASP has been run on an iMac with an Intel Core i7 2.93 Ghz, 8 GB of RAM, and MAC OS X 10.6.8 operating system. The results given by both procedures are shown in Tables 1 and 2, respectively.

As we can see in Tables 1 and 2, both procedures, MILP and GRASP, do not find a feasible solution when the number of workstations is 19 and 20 and the maximum area per workstation is 4 m.

Table 2. Best results (considering all admission factor values, $\Lambda = \{25\ \%,\ 50\ \%,\ 100\ \%\}$) given by GRASP regarding the maximum ergonomic risk of the line and the ergonomic risk range.

Maximum ergonomic risk of the line/m							
A	19	20	21	22	23	24	25
4	-	-	450	350	330	300	270
5	420	345	325	300	285	270	260
10	360	330	310	295	280	270	255
Ergonomic risk range of the line/m							
A	19	20	21	22	23	24	25
4	-	-	290	235	170	150	120
5	205	125	115	90	65	40	40
10	83	60	35	30	30	25	25

Table 3. Absolute gain of GRASP against MILP considering the maximum ergonomic risk and the range between the best ergonomic risk of the line and the worst one.

Maximum ergonomic risk of the line/m							
A	19	20	21	22	23	24	25
4	-	-	0.00	0.20	0.14	0.15	0.06
5	0.05	0.13	-0.02	0.00	-0.04	-0.02	-0.02
10	0.00	-0.05	-0.03	-0.04	-0.02	-0.02	0.00
Ergonomic risk range of the line/m							
A	19	20	21	22	23	24	25
4	-	-	0.10	0.17	0.26	0.23	0.04
5	0.17	0.30	-0.25	-0.80	-1.60	-1.67	-1.11
10	-0.11	-1.00	-1.33	-1.00	-0.76	-0.67	-0.67

Considering the found solutions and the CPU times, GRASP is more competitive than MILP. Indeed, GRASP uses, on average, a CPU time of 136.02 s, while MILP reaches the CPU limit (2 h) at all the executions.

On the other hand, if we calculate the absolute gain of GRASP versus MILP (see Table 3) in accordance with Eq. (17), we can state that:

1. In regard with the maximum ergonomic risk of the line, MILP gives better results than GRASP in 9 executions, gives the same results in 4 executions and gives worse results in 6 executions. However, the average gain of GRASP facing of MILP is higher than the average gain of MILP versus GRASP (12 % vs 2.71 %, respectively).
2. In regard with the ergonomic risk range of the line, MILP gives better results than GRASP in 12 executions and gives worse results in 6 executions. Similarly, the average gain of MILP (91.33 %) is better than the average gain of GRASP (18.23 %).

3. On average, the winner procedure in the basis of maximum ergonomic risk is GRASP by an average gain of 2.51 %; nevertheless, considering the ergonomic risk range the winner is MILP with a gain of 51 %.

$$\Delta(GRASPvsMILP) = \frac{S_{MILP}(m,A) - S_{GRASP}(m,A)}{min\{S_{MILP}(m,A), S_{GRASP}(m,A)\}} \quad (m = 19, \ldots, 25), \ (A = 4, \ 5, \ 10)$$

$$(17)$$

5 Conclusions

We address a TSALBP_erg problem through MILP and GRASP. The problem explicitly focuses on minimizing the average absolute deviation of the ergonomic risk, and implicitly, it minimizes the range of the ergonomic risk, i.e., it minimizes the difference between the ergonomic risk of the least comfortable workstation and the most comfortable one.

In order to compare the procedures, we have used a case study linked with an assembly line from the Nissan's engine plant in Barcelona and we have used two metrics to analyze the performance of the procedures: (1) the maximum ergonomic risk and (2) the ergonomic risk range.

In accordance with the average value of all solutions, GRASP is more competitive than MILP in CPU time and maximum ergonomic risk of the line. However, MILP wins GRASP in ergonomic risk range.

Acknowledgment. This work was funded by the Ministerio de Economía y Competitividad (Spanish Government) through the FHI-SELM2 (TIN2014-57497-P) project.

References

1. Otto, A., Scholl, A.: Incorporating ergonomic risks into assembly line balancing. Eur. J. Oper. Res. **212**(2), 277–286 (2011). doi:10.1016/j.ejor.2011.01.056
2. Battini, D., Delorme, X., Dolgui, A., Sgarbossa, F.: Assembly line balancing with ergonomics paradigms: two alternative methods. IFAC-PapersOnLine **48**(3), 586–591 (2015). doi:10.1016/j.ifacol.2015.06.145
3. Bautista, J., Batalla, C., Alfaro, R.: Incorporating ergonomics factors into the TSALBP. In: Emmanouilidis, C., Taisch, M., Kiritsis, D. (eds.) Advances in Production Management Systems. IFIP AICT, vol. 397, pp. 413–420. Springer, Heidelberg (2013)
4. Batalla, C.: Métodos para la incorporación del riesgo ergonómico en líneas de montaje de productos mixtos. Thesis for Ph.D. in Industrial Engineering - Universitat Politècnica de Catalunya BarcelonaTech (2015). https://www.researchgate.net/publication/280235683
5. Bautista, J., Batalla-García, C., Alfaro-Pozo, R.: Models for assembly line balancing by temporal, spatial and ergonomic risk attributes. Eur. J. Oper. Res. **251**(3), 814–829 (2016). doi:10.1016/j.ejor.2015.12.042

6. Bautista, J., Alfaro-Pozo, R., Batalla-García, C.: GRASP approach to a min-max problem of ergonomic risk in restricted assembly lines. In: Puerta, J.M., et al. (eds.) CAEPIA 2015. LNCS, vol. 9422, pp. 278–288. Springer, Heidelberg (2015). doi:10.1007/978-3-319-24598-0_25

7. Battaïa, O., Dolgui, A.: A taxonomy of line balancing problems and their solution approaches. Int. J. Prod. Econ. **142**(2), 259–277 (2013). doi:10.1016/j.ijpe.2012.10.020

8. Chica, M., Cordón, O., Damas, S., Bautista, J.: Multiobjective constructive heuristics for the 1/3 variant of the time and space assembly line balancing problem: ACO and random greedy search. Inf. Sci. **180**(18), 3465–3487 (2010). doi:10.1016/j.ins.2010.05.033

9. Chica, M., Cordón, O., Damas, S., Bautista, J.: A multiobjective GRASP for the 1/3 variant of the time and space assembly line balancing problem. In: García-Pedrajas, N., Herrera, F., Fyfe, C., Benítez, J.M., Ali, M. (eds.) IEA/AIE 2010, Part III. LNCS, vol. 6098, pp. 656–665. Springer, Heidelberg (2010). http://dx.doi.org/10.1007/978-3-642-13033-5_67

10. Chica, M., Cordón, O., Damas, S., Bautista, J.: Including different kinds of preferences in a multiobjective and algorithm for time and space assembly line balancing on different Nissan scenarios. Expert Syst. Appl. **38**(1), 709–720 (2011). doi:10.1016/j.eswa.2010.07.023

A Simheuristic for the Heterogeneous Site-Dependent Asymmetric VRP with Stochastic Demands

Laura Calvet[1(✉)], Adela Pagès-Bernaus[1], Oriol Travesset-Baro[2], and Angel A. Juan[1]

[1] Computer Science Department, Open University of Catalonia - IN3, Castelldefels, Spain
{lcalvetl,apagesb,ajuanp}@uoc.edu
[2] Observatori de la Sostenibilitat d'Andorra (OBSA), Sant Julià de Lòria, Andorra
otravesset@obsa.ad

Abstract. Rich Vehicle Routing Problems (RVRPs) refer to complex and realistic extensions of the classical Vehicle Routing Problem. They constitute a hot topic in logistics due to their high number of relevant applications. This work focuses on a RVRP with the following characteristics: *(a)* heterogeneous fleet of vehicles, *(b)* site-dependency, i.e., not all types of vehicle can reach all customers, *(c)* asymmetric costs, and *(d)* stochastic demands. We formally define the problem and describe real-life applications. Our main contribution is a simheuristic-based methodology including a Successive Approximations Method for solving it. A computational experiment is carried out to illustrate the proposed methodology. Moreover, the suitability of considering a simheuristic approach is analyzed.

Keywords: Simheuristics · Successive approximations method · Heterogeneous VRP · Site-dependent VRP · Metaheuristics · Stochastic optimization problems

1 Introduction

In our globalized and dynamic economy, transport constitutes the backbone of complex and large supply chains that require the fast, economical and reliable flow of goods. In most countries, road transport is the most used system. In addition to contribute to Gross Domestic Product and employment, the correct functioning of this sector is essential for other sectors, having an important effect on company competitiveness. While the activity of this sector is growing due to the increase of good demands (as a consequence of the increase of population and purchasing power), infrastructures are limited. Moreover, road transport causes congestion, accidents, noise, pollution, environmental impacts, and dependency on imported fossil fuels. Therefore, the development of efficient optimization methods is required.

© Springer International Publishing Switzerland 2016
O. Luaces et al. (Eds.): CAEPIA 2016, LNAI 9868, pp. 408–417, 2016.
DOI: 10.1007/978-3-319-44636-3_38

The delivery of goods has always been a challenging problem for the Operations Research community. The popular Vehicle Routing Problem (VRP) (where routes are built to visit a set of customers with uncapacitated vehicles, minimizing distance-based costs) is the most basic example. This problem has been extended in many directions to introduce realistic characteristics. A classification and review on these rich problems can be found in [4].

We study the Heterogeneous Site-dependent Asymmetric VRP with Stochastic Demands (HSAVRP-SD). Its main goal is to minimize the costs associated to the distribution of goods in such a way that all demands are satisfied. It considers a number of vehicles that may have different loading capacities (i.e., a heterogeneous fleet). This diversity usually comes from two facts: different customers and locations may require different types of vehicle (e.g., due to narrow roads, available parking spaces, and vehicle weight restrictions), and the vehicle acquisitions may be made in different times and places. Related to this characteristic, the HSAVRP-SD describes a scenario where some customers cannot be accessed with all types of vehicle, which is known as site-dependency. Regarding the cost matrix, we relax the classical assumption about its symmetry, since there can be cost differences associated to the direction of a route (for instance, differences between driving uphill or downhill in mountainous regions). Finally, we account for uncertainty in demands by modeling them as random variables following specific probability distributions (either empirical or theoretical ones).

The HSAVRP-SD has several real-life applications. A typical example is the fuel oil distribution which can be associated to petrol station replenishment or to the delivery of domestic heating oil. Generally, in these cases, the exact demand required by a customer is not known until the time of the delivery, and cost between nodes (based on energy consumption) is asymmetric due to the presence of important road grades. A review of the petrol station replenishment problem is presented in [8]. The optimization of domestic heating oil distribution has been less studied, even though the high dependence on heating oil of some isolated regions. Once again, it could be of particular interest in mountainous regions where in absence of a gas pipeline, domestic oil is frequently the predominant fuel for heating.

Being the analyzed problem a NP-hard and Stochastic Combinatorial Optimization Problem (SCOP) [3], we propose a simheuristic-based methodology for addressing it. Simheuristics [15] is a relatively new approach for solving SCOPs in a natural way by combining metaheuristics and simulation techniques. While the former search for promising solutions, the latter assess their performance in a stochastic environment. We apply an Iterated Local Search (ILS) metaheuristic [19], which employs the Successive Approximations Method (SAM) [14] for creating solutions, and Monte Carlo Simulation (MCS) techniques. The main contributions of this paper are: *(1)* a simple yet powerful methodology for solving the HSAVRP-SD; and *(2)* a computational experiment carried out to illustrate the methodology and assess the need of a simheuristic approach.

2 Literature Review

2.1 Heterogeneous Site-Dependent Asymmetric VRPs

Nag et al. [20] is the first work to analyze site-dependencies, which propose simple heuristics. Other authors [5,7,21] also address this characteristic by applying metaheuristics. Regarding asymmetric costs, [12] present a hybrid algorithm including biased randomization techniques and several local searches for solving the Asymmetric and Heterogeneous VRP. In [25] the authors suggest a three-phase heuristic for the Multi-depot Heterogeneous, Site-dependent and Asymmetric VRP. The characteristic of heterogeneity has been much more studied than the others; [13] provide a comprehensive review.

2.2 Stochastic VRPs (SVRPs)

Despite the fact that SVRPs have not been so extensively studied as the deterministic counterparts, there are some interesting works related to this article. For instance, Tillman [23] is considered the first work. It expands the CWS heuristic [6] to address the Multi-Depot Vehicle Routing Problem with Stochastic Demands, which follow Poisson distributions. The concept of route failure (i.e., when the demand of the customer being visited by a given vehicle exceeds its remaining capacity) is proposed in [9]. A review of the main works on SVRPs [10] classifies them according to the stochasticity source (customers, demands and/or times). [24] propose anticipating potential route failures by incorporating preventive breaks in the design of routes. [2] compare the performance of a few metaheuristics (Simulated Annealing, Tabu Search, ILS, Ant Colony Optimization and Evolutionary Algorithm) for solving the VRP with Stochastic Demands (VRP-SD). It is also worthwhile mentioning the work of [3], which provides a comprehensive survey on metaheuristics for SCOPs.

Many works have tackled SVRPs using simheuristics. The VRP-SD is addressed in [16], which introduces the use of safety stocks. It consists of reducing the vehicle capacities, multiplying them by a number between 0 and 1, only for designing the routes. Thus, the remaining capacity is kept as a reserve in case real demands are higher than expected. An improved version is presented in [17], where the benefits of parallel and distributed computing are studied.

3 Definition of the Problem

The HSAVRP-SD is defined over a complete graph $G = (N, A)$, where $N = 0, 1, ..., n$ is a set of nodes representing the depot (node 0) and the n customers (nodes 1 to n). Each node $i \in N$ has associated a demand D_i, which is a random variable following a given probability distribution. The actual demand of a specific customer is only known when a vehicle visits her/him. It is assumed that the depot has no demand. The set $A = (i, j) : i, j \in N, i \neq j$ contains the arcs connecting each pair of nodes. Moreover, there is a set $F = 1, ..., m$ referring to the types of vehicle. For each type $o \in F$, there are p_o available vehicles, the parameter Q_o represents the maximum load that a vehicle can carry, and U_o ($U_o \subseteq N \setminus 0$) denotes the set of customers that can be served. Each arc has associated a cost c_{ij}^o that depends on the type of vehicle. The cost of a route is the sum of the costs of its arcs and a fixed cost for using a vehicle (f_o).

The goal is to design routes that satisfy all demands and minimize the total costs while satisfying the constraints previously introduced and the following ones: *(a)* each vehicle starts and ends its route at the depot; and *(b)* each customer is visited by just one vehicle.

4   Our Methodology

The methodology we propose is a simheuristic procedure combining the ILS metaheuristic and MCS techniques. Simheuristics efficiently solve SCOPs in a natural way by extending competitive metaheuristics for the deterministic problem (usually much more studied) with simulation techniques. The ILS metaheuristic is highly popular for addressing a wide range of problems in routing, scheduling, finance, etc. It is relatively easy to understand and to implement because of its modularity. MCS enables the assessment of solutions in a stochastic environment by following these steps: *(1)* simulate a set of scenarios (where each scenario is created by generating a value for each random variable); and *(2)* compute the mean value of a performance measure. For building solutions, the SAM procedure is used. The description of our methodology is explained below and summarized in Fig. 4 and Algorithm 1.

Algorithm 1. The SAM procedure

1: **procedure** BUILDSOLUTION(*customers, vehicles*)
2:     *globalSol* ← *empty*
3:     *nonServedCust* ← *customers*
4:     **while** *nonServedCust* ≠ *empty* **do**
5:         *vehType* ← *selectType(vehicles)*
6:         *compatCust* ← *getCompatibleCust(nonServedCust, vehType)*
7:         *sol* ← *solveHoSAVRP(compatCust, vehType)*
8:         *routes* ← *getRoutes(sol)*
9:         *numVehOfTypeK* ← *numberOfVehicle(vehType)*
10:        **if** *numberOfRoutes* > *numVehOfTypeK*
11:            *routes* ← *SelectRoutes(numVehOfTypeK, Random)*
12:        **end if**
13:        *globalSol* ← *addRouteToSol(routes, globalSol)*
14:        *vehicles* ← *deleteUsedVehicles(vehicles)*
15:        *nonServedCust* ← *extractCustomers(nonServedCust, globalSol)*
16:    **end while**
17:    **return** *globalSol*
18: **end procedure**

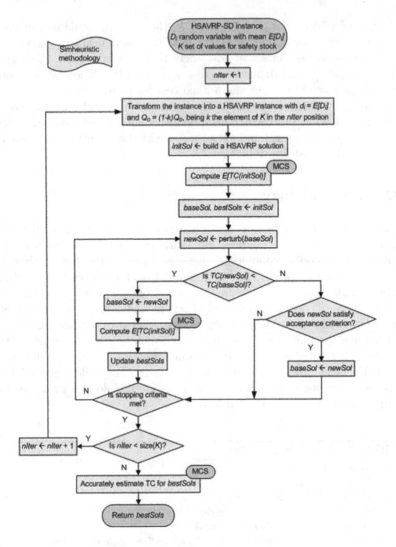

Fig. 1. Flowchart of our methodology.

The inputs are the HSAVRP-SD instance, where each demand is modeled as a random variable following a specific probability distribution, and a set K of values used to determine safety stocks. Their use leads to lower costs due to route failures (which are the costs of going from the customer being served to the depot to refill and come back to complete the delivery). However, it may also increase the number of routes needed, increasing the deterministic costs (those obtained considering that demand variances are 0). Consequently, it is required to test different values and compare expected total costs.

The algorithm starts by selecting the first value $k \in K$ and transforming the original instance into a deterministic one replacing stochastic demands by their means. Additionally, the capacities are reset to: $Q_o = (1 - k)Q_o$ ($\forall o \in F$). The next step consists in building an initial solution (*initSol*) for the new instance and estimating the associated total costs using MCS techniques with a short number of scenarios. Afterwards, a base solution (*baseSol*) is constructed by cloning *initSol*, and a list of solutions (*bestSols*) is created, which will store the best stochastic solutions (i.e., those with the lowest expected total cost). Initially, the list includes (*initSol*). Then, a new solution (*newSol*) is obtained by perturbing *baseSol*, which involves removing a random number of routes and repairing it. If the former has lower total costs (i.e., costs in the deterministic environment), it replaces *baseSol*, the total costs in the stochastic environment are estimated with a short MCS, and *bestSols* is updated. On the other hand, if (*newSol*) is not better than (*baseSol*), an acceptance criterion is checked to decide whether the base solution is replaced. We use a Demon-like acceptance criterion [22], which allows the base solution to be deteriorated if no consecutive deteriorations take place and the degradation does not exceed the value of the last improvement. By doing this, the algorithm avoids getting stuck in a local optima. This procedure is repeated to visit different solutions until a stopping criteria is met. At this point, the algorithm is re-initialized with another value of K. When all values have been tested, the total costs of *bestSols* are accurately estimated using MCS with a larger number of scenarios. Finally, the list is returned.

Regarding the building of solutions, the SAM procedure is implemented. It can be described as follows. The procedure receives one list of customers and one of available vehicles. First, an empty global solution is created, and the list of customers is copied into a list of non-served customers. While this list is not empty, the next steps are taken. A vehicle type not used yet is selected and those customers not compatible with the selected vehicle are removed from the list. Then the problem is transformed into an Homogeneous SAVRP (HoSAVRP) with no limitation on the number of vehicles that is solved with a state-of-the-art algorithm. If the solution provided reports more routes than the number of available vehicles of the current type, some routes are discarded. This partial solution is included in the global solution. The last instructions inside the while loop update the list of available vehicles and the list of non-served customers. This process ends when all customers are assigned to a route. Finally, the global solution is returned.

The procedure for repairing solutions is exactly the same but receiving as inputs only those customers that remain to be included in a route and copying the perturbed solution into the global one when this is created.

Each HoSAVRP solution is constructed using the SR-GCWS-CS algorithm described in [18]. It is based on the CWS heuristic and incorporates biased randomization techniques and cache and splitting techniques, which contribute to reduce computational times. We have adapted this algorithm in order to consider asymmetric costs. For this, the easy procedure of computing savings as the mean of the two savings associated to each pair of nodes [11] has been applied.

5 Computational Experiments

In order to test the simheuristic approach presented in the previous section, we have generalized a (randomly chosen) set of 4 classical CVRP instances. The original data can be downloaded from [1]. The same location of the nodes and demand is used. To include all the characteristics of the rich VRP, the instances have been modified in the following aspects.

Given that a cost perspective is taken as objective function, a fixed cost for using vehicle, f_o, and a variable cost, v_o, that multiplies the distance have been established. Therefore, the cost of arc $(i, j) \in A$, $c_{ij}^o = v_o d_{ij}$, where d_{ij} is the Euclidean distance. In order to account for asymmetric costs, the cost of an edge (i, j) is incremented by 10 % if the y-coordinate of the destination node j is greater than the y-coordinate of the origin node j.

An heterogeneous fleet has been proposed, with three type of vehicles. Large vehicles have a capacity equal to the one used in the benchmark, and medium and small vehicles have a reduced capacity of 75 % and 50 % respectively. All vehicles can serve all customers except for customers belonging to a randomly selected sub-area in which we assume that large vehicles cannot access.

Without loss of generality we have chosen the demand of a particular customer, D_i, to follow a logNormal distribution, with expected value as the demand of the benchmark instance (d_i) and variance proportional to the expected value (κd_i). The results presented next are obtained with $\kappa = 0.1$.

All the assumptions were made considering realistic situations. The resulting instances can be provided to the interested reader.

Several measures will be computed for each solution. When a solution is evaluated with deterministic demands, the cost (Z^{det}) and the distance $(dist)$ are shown. When a solution is assessed with stochastic demands, route failures may happen which increase the cost. Therefore, the expected cost (Z^{stoch}) and the percentage of expected route failures (r^{fail}) is displayed. Given that our strategy for searching alternative solutions with better performance in the stochastic world is to define safety stocks, this value is also included.

Test cases were run on a laptop with 4 cores at 2.6 GHz. Experiments were run over 5 random seeds for 60 s except for instance A-n80-k10 which run for 300 s. The name of the instances indicate the number of nodes (after the letter n). Short MCS were run for 100 scenarios, and long simulations consisted of a sample of 10000.

Table 1 compares the solution of the original CVRP instance with the current version HSAVRP with deterministic demands. When the SAM method is employed to solve the CVRP, Our Best Solution (OBS) shows to be competitive compared with the optimal (OPT) solution reported in the literature, with an average gap of 0.52 %. With the solution of the HSAVRP we also report the composition of the fleet for each solution. We can observe that a mix fleet is used, motivated by the fact that some vehicles cannot access some customers. The performance of the deterministic solution is tested in the operational level with stochastic demands in Table 2.

Table 1. Test instances - Comparison between the original CVRP distance-based solution and the HSAVRP cost-based solution

Instance	Original instance (CVRP)				Deterministic HSAVRP - OBS							
	Veh. capac.	OPT	OBS	Gap	Veh. used	Avail. vehicles			Z^{det}	dist	Δ dist	Used vehicles		
					L	L	M	S				L	M	S
P-n40-k5	140	458	461.7	0.81	5	4	2	3	2318.3	559.5	21.18	3	2	1
B-n41-k6	100	829	833.7	0.56	6	5	6	6	3656.7	1075.2	28.97	4	4	0
B-n45-k5	100	751	754.0	0.39	5	4	3	3	2907.6	802.2	6.40	4	2	0
A-n80-k10	100	1763	1768.7	0.32	10	8	6	6	6809.2	2040.9	15.39	6	5	0

A particular solution is tested under stochastic demands using MCS techniques, the same routine that we used in the simheuristic with a large sample. In Table 2 we can observe how the expected cost of the deterministic solution increases on average a 4 % and experiences a high percentage of route failures. This is mainly due to the fact that some routes has a filling rate of 99 %, and small variations of the demand induce route failures. On the other hand, stochastic solutions show a filling rate more balanced among the routes, and the route failures decrease dramatically. Figure 2 illustrates such situation for test case P-n40-k5. The expected cost of the stochastic solution outperforms that of the

Table 2. Comparison of solution under stochastic demand

Instance	Deterministic HSAVRP				Stochastic demands HSAVRP					
	Z^{det}	dist	Z^{sto} (1)	r^{fail}	Z^{det}	dist	Z^{sto} (2)	r^{fail}	Safety stock	Gap ((2)-(1))/(2)
P-n40-k5	2318.3	559.5	2320.7	3 %	2318.3	560.5	2318.4	0 %	100 %	0.10 %
B-n41-k6	3656.7	1075.2	4054.9	68 %	3667.1	1078.6	3678.6	21 %	99 %	10.23 %
B-n45-k5	2907.6	802.2	2972.9	56 %	2912.4	804.1	2912.6	0 %	99 %	2.07 %
A-n80-k10	6809.2	2040.9	7334.5	82 %	6964.2	2063.0	7004.7	14 %	98 %	4.71 %

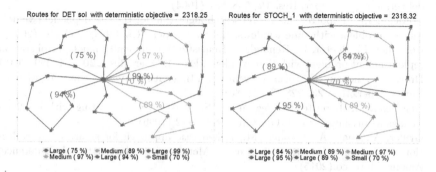

Fig. 2. Delivery routes for instance Pn40k5 - deterministic and stochastic solution

deterministic solution with an average of 4.28 %, and results in lower variability of the costs (given the low percentage of route failures).

6   Conclusions

Road transport is increasingly relevant in our globalized economies, contributing to Gross Domestic Product and employment. On the other hand, it may lead to congestion, pollution, etc. In this work, we have focused on the Heterogeneous Site-dependent Asymmetric Vehicle Routing Problem with Stochastic Demands, which constitutes a complex and realistic problem. A solving methodology based on the simheuristic approach has been described. It employs a Successive Approximations Method. Results show that our methodology is able to solve the problem, and quantify the benefit of using simheuristics in stochastic environments.

Acknowledgments. This work has been partially supported by the Spanish Ministry of Economy and Competitiveness (TRA2013-48180-C3-P and TRA2015-71883-REDT), FEDER, the Catalan Government (2014-CTP-00001) and the Government of Andorra (ACTP022-AND/2014).

References

1. Branch and Cut. http://www.coin-or.org/SYMPHONY/branchandcut/VRP/data/
2. Bianchi, L., Birattari, M., Chiarandini, M., Manfrin, M., Mastrolilli, M., Paquete, L., Rossi-Doria, O., Schiavinotto, T.: Hybrid metaheuristics for the vehicle routing problem with stochastic demands. J. Math. Modell. Algorithms **5**, 91–110 (2006)
3. Bianchi, L., Marco, D., Gambardella, L.M., Gutjahr, W.J.: A survey on metaheuristics for stochastic combinatorial optimization. Nat. Comput. **8**, 239–287 (2009)
4. Caceres, J., Arias, P., Guimarans, D., Riera, D., Juan, A.: Rich vehicle routing problem: a survey. ACM Comput. Surv. **47**(2), 1–28 (2014)
5. Chao, I.M., Liou, T.S.: A new tabu search heuristic for the site-dependent vehicle routing problem. Next Wave Comput. Optim. Decis. Technol. **29**, 107–119 (2005)
6. Clarke, G., Wright, J.: Scheduling of vehicles from a central depot to a number of delivering points. Oper. Res. **12**, 568–581 (1964)
7. Cordeau, J.F., Laporte, G.: A tabu search algorithm for the site dependent vehicle routing problem with time windows. Inf. Syst. Oper. Res. **39**(3), 292–298 (2001)
8. Cornillier, F., Boctor, F., Renaud, J.: Heuristics for the multi-depot petrol station replenishment problem with time windows. Eur. J. Oper. Res. **220**, 361–369 (2012)
9. Dror, M., Trudeau, P.: Stochastic vehicle routing with modified savings algorithms. Eur. J. Oper. Res. **23**, 228–235 (1986)
10. Gendreau, M., Laporte, G., Séguin, R.: Stochastic vehicle routing with modified savings algorithms. Eur. J. Oper. Res. **88**, 3–12 (1996)
11. Gruler, A., Juan, A., Steglich, M.: A heuristic approach for smart waste collection management. In: Proceedings of the Metaheuristics International Conference, Agadir, Morocco (2015)

12. Herrero, R., Rodriguez, A., Caceres-Cruz, J., Juan, A.: Solving vehicle routing problems with asymmetric costs and heterogeneous fleets. Int. J. Adv. Oper. Manag. **6**(1), 58–80 (2014)
13. Hoff, A., Andersson, H., Christiansen, M., Hasle, G., Løkketangen, A.: Industrial aspects and literature survey: fleet composition and routing. Comput. Oper. Res. **37**(9), 2041–2061 (2010)
14. Juan, A., Faulin, J., Caceres, J., Barrios, B., Martinez, E.: A successive approximations method for the heterogeneous vehicle routing problem: analyzing different fleet configurations. Eur. J. Ind. Eng. **8**(6), 762–788 (2014)
15. Juan, A., Faulin, J., Grasman, S., Rabe, M., Figueira, G.: A review of simheuristics: extending metaheuristics to deal with stochastic optimization problems. Oper. Res. Perspect. **2**, 62–72 (2015)
16. Juan, A., Faulin, J., Grasman, S., Riera, D., Marull, J., Mendez, C.: Using safety stocks and simulation to solve the vehicle routing problem with stochastic demands. Transp. Res. Part C: Emerg. Technol. **19**(5), 751–765 (2011)
17. Juan, A., Faulin, J., Jorba, J., Caceres, J., Marques, J.M.: Using parallel & distributed computing for real-time solving of vehicle routing problems with stochastic demands. Ann. Oper. Res. **207**(1), 43–65 (2013)
18. Juan, A., Faulin, J., Jorba, J., Riera, D., Masip, D., Barrios, B.: On the use of monte carlo simulation, cache and splitting techniques to improve the clarke and wright savings heuristics. J. Oper. Res. Soc. **62**, 1085–1097 (2011)
19. Lourenço, H.R., Martin, O.C., Stützle, T.: Iterated local search: framework and applications. In: Gendreau, M., Potvin, J.-Y. (eds.) Handbook of Metaheuristics. International Series in Operations Research & Management Science, vol. 146, pp. 363–397. Springer, US (2010)
20. Nag, B., Golden, B., Assad, A.: Vehicle routing with site dependencies. In: Vehicle Routing: Methods and Studies, pp. 149–159. Elsevier, Amsterdam (1988)
21. Pisinger, D., Ropke, S.: A general heuristic for vehicle routing problems. Comput. Oper. Res. **34**(8), 2403–2435 (2007)
22. Talbi, E.: Metaheuristics: From Design to Implementation. Wiley, New Jersey (2009)
23. Tillman, F.A.: The multiple terminal delivery problem with probabilistic demands. Transp. Sci. **3**, 192–204 (1969)
24. Yang, W.H., Mathur, K., Ballou, R.H.: Stochastic vehicle routing problem with restocking. Transp. Sci. **34**, 99–112 (2000)
25. Yusuf, I.: Solving multi-depot, heterogeneous, site dependent and asymmetric VRP using three steps heuristic. J. Algorithms Optim. **2**(2), 28–42 (2014)

On the Use of the Beta Distribution
for a Hybrid Time Series Segmentation
Algorithm

Antonio M. Durán-Rosal[✉], Manuel Dorado-Moreno, Pedro A. Gutiérrez,
and Cesar Hervás-Martínez

Department of Computer Science and Numerical Analysis, Rabanales Campus,
University of Córdoba, Albert Einstein Building, 14071 Córdoba, Spain
{i92duroa,i92domom,pagutierrez,chervas}@uco.es

Abstract. This paper presents a local search (LS) method based on
the beta distribution for time series segmentation with the purpose of
correctly representing extreme values of the underlying variable studied. The LS procedure is combined with an evolutionary algorithm (EA)
which segments time series trying to obtain a given number of homogeneous groups of segments. The proposal is tested on a real problem of
wave height estimation, where extreme high waves are frequently found.
The results show that the LS is able to significantly improve the clustering quality of the solutions obtained by the EA. Moreover, the best
segmentation clearly groups extreme waves in a separate cluster and
characterizes them according to their centroid.

Keywords: Time series segmentation · Evolutionary algorithms ·
Clustering · Extreme value distributions

1 Introduction

The relevance of temporal data has currently led to various research efforts
in the field of data mining and machine learning. Specifically, time series are
major sources of temporal databases and can be easily obtained from several real
problems. Time series data are characterized by their numerical and continuous
nature and their inherent difficulty to be processed, analyzed and mined.

"Numeric-to-symbolic" (N/S) conversion is considered one of the most important processes before mining the time series, where a continuous time series is
discretized into a set of significant symbols [1,2]. In this context, time series
segmentation can be used as a first step to provide a more compact representation of the series data by dividing data into segments and using a simple model

This work has been subsidized by the project TIN2014-54583-C2-1-R of the Spanish Ministry of Economy and Competitiveness (MINECO), FEDER funds and the
P11-TIC-7508 project of the Junta de Andalucía (Spain). Antonio M. Durán-Rosal's
research has been subsidized by the FPU Predoctoral Program of the Spanish Ministry of Education, Culture and Sport (MECD), grant reference FPU14/03039.

© Springer International Publishing Switzerland 2016
O. Luaces et al. (Eds.): CAEPIA 2016, LNAI 9868, pp. 418–427, 2016.
DOI: 10.1007/978-3-319-44636-3_39

to approximate each segment. According to Lin, Orgun and Williams [3], time series segmentation algorithms can be applied in time series databases with two main objectives: matching of sequence patterns and recognition of periodical patterns.

Time series clustering has been used by many researchers for grouping time series [4,5] by using clustering methods such as k-means, hierarchical clustering and expectation maximization. In this way, after segmenting the time series, N/S conversion can accomplished by these algorithms with the objective of discovering the similarities between the segments and grouping them [6,7]. One of the possible applications of the joint application of segmentation and clustering is the detection of interesting events in the time series. In this field, previous researchers such as Guralnik et al. proposed an event detection algorithm [8] to detect events from time series, or Himberg et al. proposed a context recognition algorithm to recognize significant activities of mobile devices [9].

One of the approaches for segmenting time series is the application of evolutionary algorithms (EAs) [10], which can also be combined with clustering algorithms [6,7]. However, several researchers [11,12] have shown that EAs perform well for global searching because they are capable of quickly finding and exploiting promising regions of the search space, but they take a relatively long time to converge to a local optimum. This lack of precision can be tackled by the combination of EAs with local search (LS) procedures, which are good at finding local optima. These algorithms are commonly known as hybrid algorithms.

In this paper, we propose a hybrid EA method combined with a local search method (EA-LS). The LS is a statistical procedure based on the maximization of the logarithmic likelihood-ratio. This LS is able to improve the performance of the EA in time series segmentation and it is applied to the final solution obtained by the EA, allowing the precise local optimum around the final solution to be found. The results of the algorithm are compared when run with and without the LS process.

To test the performance of the proposed hybrid algorithm, it is applied to a real-world time series of significant wave height at the Gulf of Alaska. Our objective is the detection of wave height extreme values, grouping them in a separated cluster. Because of this, we assume a beta distribution [13] for the LS step, which is able to better represent the distribution of extreme values of a population.

The rest of the paper is organized as follows. Section 2 includes the characteristics of the algorithm proposed, while Sect. 3 shows the description of the time series, the experiments performed and the discussion about the results. Finally, Sect. 4 presents the conclusions.

2   Hybrid Segmentation Algorithm

2.1   Summary of the Algorithm

The algorithm presented in this paper extends that proposed in [7], including a final step of LS. Given a time series $Y = \{y_i\}_{i=1}^{N}$, the objective is to divide Y

into m consecutive segments. These segments should be associated to homogeneous behaviours of the time series. Time indexes ($i = 1, \ldots, N$) are divided according to the segments: $s_1 = \{y_1, \ldots, y_{t_1}\}, s_2 = \{y_{t_1}, \ldots, y_{t_2}\}, \ldots, s_m = \{y_{t_{m-1}}, \ldots, y_N\}$. The ts are the different cut points indexed in order ($t_1 < t_2 < t_{m-1}$). All cut points belong to two segments (the one before and the one after). The algorithm determines the number of segments m and the values of the cut points $t_i, i = 1, \ldots, m - 1$. Then, segments have to be grouped into k different clusters (where $k < m$ is a parameter to be defined by the user). Each segment will be associated to a class label, from k different possible labels, $\{\mathcal{C}_1, \ldots, \mathcal{C}_k\}$.

2.2   Evolutionary Algorithm

The characteristics of the EA are summarized in this section[1]. First of all, the initial population consists on a set of binary vectors of length N, where the cut points are randomly selected and set to 1, and the rest are set to 0. The length of the chromosome is the time series length, N.

The evaluation of a candidate segmentation (fitness evaluation) consists of three steps:

1. **Obtaining the Characteristics of the Segments**: Because of the different lenght of the segments of the chromosome, they are projected into the same five dimensional space to compare and group them, where the used metrics are the Variance (S_s^2), the Skewness (γ_{1s}), the Kurtosis (γ_{2s}), the Slope of a linear regression over the points of the segment (a_s) and the Autocorrelation coefficient (AC_s).

2. **Clustering Process**: After projecting all segments to the same five dimensional space, a clustering process is applied to group them. All metrics are previously scaled to the range $[0, 1]$, and the algorithm chosen for clustering is a modified k-means, where the initial centroids are deterministically chosen based on the variability of the characteristics.

3. **Evaluating the Quality of the Clustering Process**: To evaluate the quality of the clustering, the Caliński and Harabasz index (CH) [15] is considered as fitness measure, which is defined as:

$$CH(C) = \frac{m - k}{k - 1} \frac{\sum_{c_k \in C} |c_k| d_e(\overline{\mathbf{c_k}}, \overline{\mathbf{X}})}{\sum_{c_k \in C} \sum_{\mathbf{x_i} \in c_k} d_e(\mathbf{x_i}, \overline{\mathbf{c_k}})}, \tag{1}$$

where m is the number of segments, k is the number of clusters, $|c_k|$ is the number of segments of cluster k, $\overline{\mathbf{c_k}}$ is the centroid of cluster k, $\overline{\mathbf{X}}$ is the average value of all segments, and $d_e(\mathbf{x}, \mathbf{y})$ is the Euclidean distance between vector $\mathbf{x}$ and vector $\mathbf{y}$.

The reproduction and the generation of the offspring is performed considering the whole population. This selection process promotes diversity, while a roulette wheel selection is used for the replacement process, which promotes elitism. Two kinds of reproduction operators are included:

---

[1] For extended information about the EA see [7,14].

- A probability p_m of performing a mutation is decided by the user. Four mutation operators can be used with the same probability: add, remove, move to the left or move to the right a percentage of the cut points of the segmentation.
- The crossover probability is p_c. When applied to a parent, the operator randomly selects the other parent and a point of the genotype. Then, the right and the left parts with respect to this point are interchanged.

2.3   Likelihood-Based Segmentation Algorithm

This section describes a hierarchical segmentation procedure, which is applied to each segment of the best segmentation of the time series obtained in the last generation of the evolutionary algorithm.

Likelihood Ratio Test. We may assume that each segment $s_s = (x_{t_s}, \ldots, x_{t_{s+1}})$ is sampled from a Beta(α_s, β_s) distribution with different α_s and β_s coefficients $(s = 1, \ldots, m)$, considering that the values of the time series for each segment are normalized between 0 and 1. The beta distribution is a distribution specifically designed for correctly representing extreme values.

Under this hypothesis and taking into account the best segmentation obtained by the EA, a recursive segmentation scheme is used in this work, based on that introduced in [16]. Let s_s be a random sample drawn from a X_t distribution, then the segmentation scheme is fundamentally based on the likelihood ratio test under an i.i.d. Beta null hypothesis model for the whole series, $H_0 \equiv X_t \in B(\alpha, \beta)$, and a alternative hypothesis consisting on assuming two different Beta models for the right and the left parts of a possible cut point t, $H_1 \equiv \begin{cases} X_{t_L} \in B(\alpha_L, \beta_L) \\ X_{t_R} \in B(\alpha_R, \beta_R) \end{cases}$, where $X_{t_L} \equiv \begin{cases} X_t, & \text{if } t_L \leq t, \\ 0, & \text{in other case,} \end{cases}$ and

$X_{t_R} \equiv \begin{cases} X_t, & \text{if } t_R \geq t, \\ 0, & \text{in other case.} \end{cases}$

Supposing $n = t_{s+1} - t_s$ observations for the s_s segment and assuming that the observations should be segmented at a new cut point $t_s + u$, we define the likelihood functions as:

$$L_1 = \prod_{t=t_s}^{t_{s+1}} f(x_t; \alpha, \beta), \qquad (2)$$

$$L_2(u) = \prod_{t=t_s}^{t_s+u} f(x_t; \alpha_L, \beta_L) \prod_{t=t_s+u+1}^{t_{s+1}} f(x_t; \alpha_R, \beta_R).$$

where $f(x_t; \alpha, \beta)$ represents the probability density function, pdf, which can be defined based on different parameters for the whole segment (α, β) and for the left and right parts with respect to t $(\alpha_L, \beta_L, \alpha_R$ and $\beta_R)$. Then, the discriminator $\Delta(u)$ is defined as:

$$\Delta(u) = \log \frac{L_2(u)}{L_1} = \log L_2(u) - \log L_1. \tag{3}$$

Substituting (2) in (3):

$$\Delta(u) = \sum_{t=t_s}^{t_s+u} \log f(x_t; \alpha_L, \beta_L) + \sum_{t=t_s+u+1}^{t_{s+1}} \log f(x_t; \alpha_R, \beta_R) - \sum_{t=t_s}^{t_{s+1}} \log f(x_t; \alpha, \beta). \tag{4}$$

Assuming Beta(α, β) pdfs, Eq. (4) can be rewritten using maximum likelihood estimators, ML, for $\boldsymbol{\theta} = (\alpha, \alpha_L, \alpha_R, \beta, \beta_L, \beta_R)$:

$$\Delta(u) = -n \int_0^1 f(x_t; \hat{\alpha}, \hat{\beta}) \log f(x_t; \hat{\alpha}, \hat{\beta}) dx_t \tag{5}$$

$$+ u \int_0^1 f(x_t; \hat{\alpha}_L, \hat{\beta}_L) \log f(x_t; \hat{\alpha}_L, \hat{\beta}_L) dx_t$$

$$+ (n-u) \int_0^1 f(x_t; \hat{\alpha}_R, \hat{\beta}_R) \log f(x_t; \hat{\alpha}_R, \hat{\beta}_R) dx_t,$$

where $\hat{\boldsymbol{\theta}} = (\hat{\alpha}, \hat{\alpha}_L, \hat{\alpha}_R, \hat{\beta}, \hat{\beta}_L, \hat{\beta}_R)$ are ML estimators of $\boldsymbol{\theta}$. The calculation of these estimates is obtained iteratively [17]. Then $\Delta(u)/n$ is equivalent to:

$$\frac{\Delta(u)}{n} = H\left[f(x_t; \hat{\alpha}, \hat{\beta})\right] - \frac{u}{n} H\left[f(x_t; \hat{\alpha}_L, \hat{\beta}_L)\right] - \frac{n-u}{n} H\left[f(x_t; \hat{\alpha}_R, \hat{\beta}_R)\right], \tag{6}$$

where $H\left[f(x_t; \hat{\alpha}, \hat{\beta})\right]$ is the Shannon entropy associated to a Beta distribution [18], whose expression is defined as:

$$H\left[f(x; \hat{\alpha}, \hat{\beta})\right] = -(\hat{\alpha}-1)\left\{\Gamma(\hat{\alpha})\left(\ln \hat{\alpha} - \frac{1}{2\hat{\alpha}}\right) - \Gamma(\hat{\alpha}+\hat{\beta})\left(\ln(\hat{\alpha}+\hat{\beta}) - \frac{1}{2(\hat{\alpha}+\hat{\beta})}\right)\right\}$$

$$-(\hat{\beta}-1)\left\{\Gamma(\hat{\beta})\left(\ln \hat{\beta} - \frac{1}{2\hat{\beta}}\right) - \Gamma(\hat{\alpha}+\hat{\beta})\left(\ln(\hat{\alpha}+\hat{\beta}) - \frac{1}{2(\hat{\alpha}+\hat{\beta})}\right)\right\}$$

$$+ \ln \Gamma(\hat{\alpha}) + \ln \Gamma(\hat{\beta}) - \ln \Gamma(\hat{\alpha}+\hat{\beta}), \tag{7}$$

where $\Gamma(x)$ is the Gamma Euler function defined as:

$$\Gamma(x+1) = \sqrt{2\pi x}(x^x)\exp(-x). \tag{8}$$

To start the recursive ML estimation procedure, it is necessary to have initial estimates of the parameters $\hat{\boldsymbol{\theta}}$, which have been obtained by the method of moments. $\Delta(u)$ can be used as a score to evaluate the best new cut point $t_s + u$ of the segment s_s, by maximizing its value:

$$u^* = \arg\max_u \Delta(u). \tag{9}$$

The procedure is recursive, i.e., after a first segmentation, this procedure is also applied for each sub-segment. The stopping condition of the recursive process is the following one: if $\Delta(u^*)$ is lower than a threshold value Δc, then the segmentation should be terminated.

Decision Rule. The possible treatment-induced location differences between the two samples associated to X_t and $X_{t_L} \cup X_{t_R}$ are analized by testing the null hypothesis against the alternative hypothesis proposed in the previous section.

If the parameter space is $\boldsymbol{\theta}_0 = \{\alpha, \beta\}$ for H_0 and $\boldsymbol{\theta}_1 = \{\alpha_L, \alpha_R, \beta_L, \beta_R\}$ for H_1 and the corresponding estimates are $\hat{\boldsymbol{\theta}}_0$ and $\hat{\boldsymbol{\theta}}_1$, then the approximated sample distribution of the likelihood ratio test statistic given by $2\Delta(u)$ is a χ^2 distribution with $4 - 2 = 2$ degrees of freedom [19] (χ_2^2). The cumulative distribution of a χ_k^2 is given by the regularized incomplete Gamma Function $F(x) = \gamma\left(\frac{k}{2}, \frac{\Delta c}{2}\right)$. Therefore, under a given level of significance p, the threshold for the stopping condition is calculated as $\gamma\left(\frac{k}{2}, \frac{\Delta c}{2}\right) = p$, and for $k = 2$, $F(x) = 1 - \exp\left(-\frac{\Delta c}{2}\right)$, and the threshold is given by $\Delta c = -2\ln(1 - p)$.

Then, for the Beta distribution, the decision rule to divide a segment is:

IF $\max(\Delta(u)) > -2\ln(1 - p)$,
THEN the initial segment s_s must be split at u^*. Continue dividing the resultant left subsegment s_{sL}, provided that $u^* > 2s_{\min}$, and/or the resultant right subsegment s_{sR}, if $(n - u^*) > 2s_{\min}$,
ELSE Stop the division procedure,
where $s_{\min}$ is the minimum length of a segment, specified by the user.

3   Experimental Results and Discussion

The experiments performed and the results obtained are analysed in this section.

3.1   Wave Height Time Series

The time series used in our experiments is the wave significant height of one buoy at the Gulf of Alaska: specifically, it is a buoy belonging to the National Buoy Center of the USA [20], with registration number 46001. In the proposed experiment, data from 1st January 2008 to 31st December 2013 (6 h resolution) are considered. The complete time series used in the experiments can be seen in Fig. 1(a). Our objective is to group the extreme values of wave height in one separate cluster, without using any "a priori" information. These extreme values can be defined as waves with a very high absolute height or those which can be considered to be high in relation to other waves close in time. In Fig. 1(b), extreme waves have been manually marked with circles.

3.2   Experimental Setting

A *trial and error* procedure was used for the configuration of the EA parameters: the population size is set to $P = 100$; crossover and mutation probabilities are $p_c = 0.8$ and $p_m = 0.2$, respectively; a 20 % of the current number of cut points is modified during each mutation; the algorithm is run until $g = 100$ generations; k-means clustering process is allowed a maximum of 20 iterations; the likelihood-based segmentation algorithm was configured with a $p = 0.05$. The most three decisive parameters were set by the experts: the initial minimum and maximum

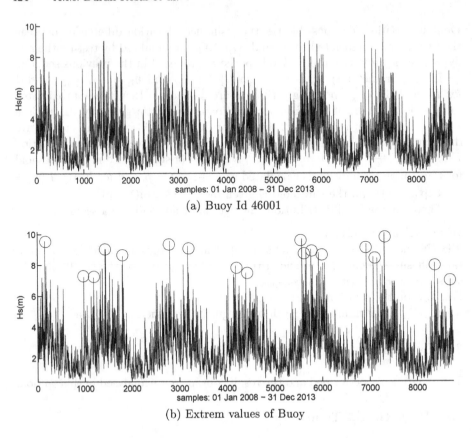

(a) Buoy Id 46001

(b) Extrem values of Buoy

Fig. 1. Buoy id 46001 time series at the Gulf of Alaska.

size of the segments are $s_{min} = 20$ and $s_{max} = 120$, respectively; the number of clusters or groups is $k = 5$. Finally, given the stochastic nature of GAs, our algorithm was run 30 times with different seeds.

3.3 Discussion

The results of our experiments in the 30 executions are shown in Table 1. As can be seen, the LS segmentation proposal is able to significantly improve the results of the EA. In this way, the LS method based on detecting extreme values obtains good results for this time series, improving the quality of the clusters obtained by the EA.

Furthermore, we can analyse the best seed in terms of the fitness function, which is seed 50 with a fitness of 12433.7574 for EA+LS (which means an improvement of a 235.38 % with respect to the original EA). This segmentation is included in Fig. 2, where all the extreme values are grouped in the red cluster. These results can be justified in the sense that the time series shows a

Table 1. Fitness values (CH metric) for the 30 runs of the original EA and its combination with the beta LS procedure (EA+LS)

Seed	EA	EA+LS	Seed	EA	EA+LS
10	5091.8828	9104.4274	160	4409.2212	7078.6426
20	4984.3820	9612.9151	170	3833.2169	8256.2235
30	4970.3533	5626.7425	180	4387.8613	8477.7797
40	5329.7515	7896.7463	190	5655.1356	3079.6018
50	5284.6638	**12433.7574**	200	5839.9101	9351.9910
60	5146.7390	8938.1999	210	4093.2253	4505.3476
70	5396.0051	5014.5036	220	4776.6194	5208.3407
80	3162.4078	2334.7366	230	8367.4085	9970.3690
90	4461.4372	4704.4004	240	5343.6356	8211.0237
100	5334.5933	7047.9172	250	4891.4332	3144.5291
110	4795.5042	5720.7451	260	4687.0542	7382.3472
120	4754.1631	3054.0858	270	4709.2985	8680.5507
130	4368.4020	3103.5328	280	4243.3546	4949.5414
140	5008.9391	8964.9285	290	5380.5474	9864.4764
150	5244.3656	5029.9157	300	5066.7178	7399.4439
Mean		4967.2743			**6804.9254**
±	EA	±		**EA+LS**	±
Std		854.0110			**2573.0280**

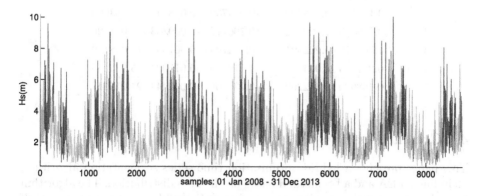

Fig. 2. Buoy Id 46001 Segmentation (Online version in colour)

histogram very similar to the synthetic beta distribution, so the recursive partition of the time series using this criteria can improve the results (both histograms are shown and compared in Fig. 3).

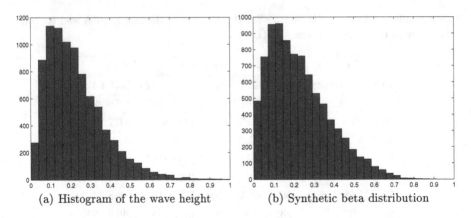

(a) Histogram of the wave height   (b) Synthetic beta distribution

Fig. 3. Comparison of the real histogram with the synthetic beta histogram.

Finally, the statistical characteristics of the centroids of the clustering process for this best segmentation are shown in Table 2. The cluster which groups the extreme values is cluster 1 (red colour) and a kurtosis near zero. The segments of this cluster have the highest variance. The distribution is the second highest asymmetric one (to the right). The slope is slightly negative (almost negligible), and it has the second highest autocorrelation.

Table 2. Buoy id 46001 centroids of clusters

Cluster	Variance	Asymmetry	Kurtosis	Slope	Autocorrelation
1	3.157554	0.903020	−0.014730	−0.028944	21.483000
2	0.836559	1.129722	0.706716	−0.000353	20.021126
3	1.369518	0.202591	−0.864793	0.007332	18.028179
4	0.232093	0.044508	−1.179249	−0.015024	5.934155
5	0.498620	0.452262	−0.738666	0.000444	24.217147

4   Conclusions

This paper presents a hybrid optimisation time series segmentation algorithm, including an EA and a LS method based on the beta distribution. The algorithm is used to detect extreme values of wave height in a real case of one buoy at Gulf of Alaska. Results show that the LS improve the results of the EA. The segments obtained are used for a posterior clustering-based analysis (where these segments are mapped to a 5-dimensional space representing their statistical properties and grouped according to their similarity). This clustering-based analysis shows that the most important characteristics to detect extreme wave height are high variance and autocorrelation. A future research line is the prediction of future segments, using the temporal patterns identified in the segmentation/clustering phase.

References

1. Das, G., ip Lin, K., Mannila, H., Renganathan, G., Smyth, P.: Rule Discovery From Time Series. AAAI Press, Menlo Park, pp. 16–22 (1998)
2. Yang, O., Jia, W., Zhou, P., Meng, X.: A new approach to transforming time series into symbolic sequences. In: Proceedings of the 1st Joint Conference Between the Biomedical Engineering Society and Engineers in Medicine and Biology, p. 974 (1999)
3. Lin, W., Orgun, M., Williams, G.: An overview of temporal data mining (2002)
4. Wang, X., Smith, K.A., Hyndman, R.J.: Dimension reduction for clustering time series using global characteristics. In: Sunderam, V.S., van Albada, G.D., Sloot, P.M.A., Dongarra, J. (eds.) ICCS 2005. LNCS, vol. 3516, pp. 792–795. Springer, Heidelberg (2005)
5. Rani, S., Sikka, G.: Recent techniques of clustering of time series data: a survey. Int. J. Comput. Appl. 52(15), 1–9 (2012)
6. Tseng, V.S., Chen, C.H., Huang, P.C., Hong, T.P.: Cluster-based genetic segmentation of time series with DWT. Pattern Recogn. Lett. 30(13), 1190–1197 (2009)
7. Nikolaou, A., Gutiérrez, P.A., Durán, A., Dicaire, I., Fernández-Navarro, F., Hervás-Martínez, C.: Detection of early warning signals in paleoclimate data using a genetic time series segmentation algorithm. Clim. Dyn. 44(7), 1919–1933 (2015)
8. Guralnik, V., Srivastava, J.: Event detection from time series data. In: Proceedings of the Fifth ACM SIGKDD International Conference on Knowledge Discovery and Data Mining, KDD 1999, pp. 3–42. ACM, New York (1999)
9. Himberg, J., Korpiaho, K., Mannila, H., Tikanmaki, J., Toivonen, H.: Time series segmentation for context recognition in mobile devices. In: Proceedings IEEE International Conference on Data Mining, ICDM 2001, pp. 203–210 (2001)
10. Chung, F.L., Fu, T.C., Ng, V., Luk, R.W.: An evolutionary approach to pattern-based time series segmentation. IEEE Trans. Evol. Comput. 8(5), 471–489 (2004)
11. Houck, C.R., Joines, J.A., Kay, M.G.: Comparison of genetic algorithms, random restart and two-opt switching for solving large location-allocation problems. Comput. Oper. Res. 23(6), 587–596 (1996)
12. Joines, J.A., Kay, M.G., King, R.E., Culbreth, C.T.: A hybrid genetic algorithm for manufacturing cell design. J. Chin. Inst. Ind. Eng. 17(5), 549–564 (2000)
13. Evans, M., Hastings, N., Peacock, B.: Statistical Distributions. Wiley Series in Probability and Statistics. Wiley, Hoboken (2000)
14. Durán-Rosal, A.M., de la Paz-Marín, M., Gutiérrez, P.A., Hervás-Martínez, C.: Applying a hybrid algorithm to the segmentation of the Spanish stock market index time series. In: Rojas, I., Joya, G., Catala, A. (eds.) IWANN 2015. LNCS, vol. 9095, pp. 69–79. Springer, Heidelberg (2015)
15. Calióski, T., Harabasz, J.: A dendrite method for cluster analysis. Commun. Stat. 3(1), 1–27 (1974)
16. Sato, A.H.: A comprehensive analysis of time series segmentation on Japanese stock prices. Procedia Comput. Sci. 24, 307–314 (2013). 17th Asia Pacific Symposium on Intelligent and Evolutionary Systems, IES 2013
17. El-Sagheer, R.: Inferences for the generalized logistic distribution based on record statistics. Intell. Inf. Manag. 6, 171–182 (2014)
18. Menendez, M.: Shannon's entropy in exponential families: statistical applications. Appl. Math. Lett. 13(1), 37–42 (2000)
19. Wilks, S.S.: Mathematical Statistics. John Wiley, New York (1963)
20. National Buoy Data Center. National Oceanic and Atmospheric Administration of the USA (NOAA) (2015). http://www.ndbc.noaa.gov/

A Heuristic-Biased GRASP for the Team Orienteering Problem

Airam Expósito[✉], Julio Brito[✉], and José A. Moreno[✉]

Department of Computer Engineering and Systems, University of La Laguna,
38206 Santa Cruz de Tenerife, Spain
{aexposito,jbrito,jamoreno}@ull.edu.es

Abstract. This paper introduces a route-planning problem in the sector of tourism. The Tourist Trip Design Problem seeks to maximize the number of points of interest to visit. This paper also proposes an optimization approach for a multi-day planning problem for sightseeing. In order to solve this optimization problem, an efficient Greedy Randomized Adaptive Search Procedure is developed to obtain high-quality solutions. Enhanced solution construction mechanisms and bias functions used in construction mechanism have been proposed. The computational experiments indicate the solving scheme is able to report competitive solutions by using short computational times.

Keywords: Tourist Trip Design Problem · Team Orienteering Problem · Greedy Randomized Adaptive Search Procedure

1 Introduction

Deciding what tourist attractions to visit is an optimization problem that arises when a tourist visits a destination for one or several days. Generally, the destination of the tourist has multiple points of interests (POIs) or tourist attractions. POIs are the main reason why tourists visit the destination either by historical, beauty or cultural values. The reality is that as a rule the tourist has a limited time to visit the POIs; only one day or even a few hours. In short, tourists have the problem of selecting what POIs are most interesting to visit and determining a travel route per day at the destination. This problem involves a series of constraints such as the visiting time required for each POI, the traveling distance among POIs, the time available for sightseeing each day and the satisfaction associated with the visit to each POI, termed score. Given this problem, the design and development of tourist trip planning systems is an interesting area of research in computer engineering.

Designing tourist routes has been addressed as an optimization problem mainly associated with the route generation and termed as Tourist Trip Design Problem (TTDP) in the literature [20]. Concerning the TTDP there is a wide range of topics covered in the literature, the main one focuses on the solving of TTDP through optimization methods. In general terms, TTDP model considers a number of basic parameters such as the candidate set of POIs to be

© Springer International Publishing Switzerland 2016
O. Luaces et al. (Eds.): CAEPIA 2016, LNAI 9868, pp. 428–437, 2016.
DOI: 10.1007/978-3-319-44636-3_40

visited by the tourist, number of routes to be generated based on the period of tourist stay in the destination, travel time between all POIs using multi-modal routing information among POIs (it is assumed that tourists can take any kind of transport available at the destination), score or interest related to each POI as a weighted function of the objective (a high score implies a high degree of interest and vice-versa), the visiting time of the tourists at each POI, and the time available for sightseeing each day or daily route maximum time, termed T (daily route time should be less than T). The feasible solutions for the optimization problem must contemplate maximizing the score of POIs visited by the tourist, and the best possible optimization for scheduling routes. Besides, there are different variants of the optimization problem resulting of modifying different constraints and parameters.

Depending on the routes number to be considered in the TTDP, it is possible to establish a basic classification. Single-tour-based approaches can be considered with the aim of designing a single tour that maximizes the score holding certain constraints, or multiple-tour-based approaches can be considered with the aim of designing multiple tours based on the number of days that the tourist stays in the destination. Most of the operational research literature dealing with TTDP modeling as the Orienteering Problem (OP) and the Team Orienteering Problem (TOP) depending on whether it considers single or multiple tour, respectively. TOP can be considered as a version of the well-known Vehicle Routing Problem (VRP) [17] in which the aim is to maximize the total amount of collected profits from visiting customers while not exceeding the predefined travel time limit of each vehicle. The name Orienteering Problems and Team Orienteering Problem are inspired in outdoor competitive games. In these games you have to carry out routes through a number of locations where certain scores are obtained and the winner is whoever gets the highest score. OP only considers one route whereas TOP takes into account multiple tours. The OP has been shown to be $\mathcal{NP}$-hard by [10]. Therefore, the TOP is $NP - hard$. This paper proposes a multiple tour TTDP modeled as TOP.

The first TOP is introduced by [7]. However, this problem had previously appeared in the literature as the High School Athlete Recruitment Problem or Multiple Tour Maximum Collection Problem [5]. One of the most extensive reviews in the literature include models, formulations, solution methods, applications and main benchmark instances. This paper is developed by [19]. Concerning resolution methods, different exact methods have been proposed to solve the TOP, using column generation [3,6] and branch and cut algorithm [8]. However, as mentioned above, this problem is $\mathcal{NP}$-hard, this implies that heuristics and metaheuristics are suitable methods to be applied to obtain high-quality solutions. It is possible to find several heuristic and metaheuristic approaches based on local search, population-based methods, and trajectory-based methods in the literature, a sample of these methods are listed below. A Tabu Search (TS) is used to solve a routing problem of technicians to service customers and compared against the heuristic proposed by [7] in [16]. Two variants of a Tabu Search (TS) algorithm and a Variable Neighbourhood Search (VNS) algorithm is presented by [1]. An Ant Colony Optimization (ACO) approach is proposed by [11]. A Guided Local Search (GLS) is developed in [18]. A Path Relinking (PA) metaheuristic approach is introduced by [15]. A Memetic Algorithm based on an optimal split procedure for chromosome evaluation and a local search techniques for mutation is proposed by [2]. A Large Neighbourhood Search (LNS) method with a Local Search (LS) improvement, is proposed by [12]. An effective multi-start Simulated Annealing (SA) is used by [13].

In order to get high-quality solutions, the solution approach proposed in this paper uses an algorithm based on the Greedy Randomized Adaptive Search Procedure (GRASP). This metaheuristic is an iterative process composed of two phases: construction and local search. GRASP, proposed by [9], has been successfully applied to a wide variety of combinatorial optimization problems, including route planning [14]. This paper also included alternative solution construction mechanisms and techniques to improve the search in the GRASP. Some of these mechanisms introduce several probability distributions to guide the candidates selection in the construction phase of the GRASP. And these consider differents techniques to sort the list of candidates.

The rest of the paper is organized as follows. The subsequent section presents the problem description and model formulation. Section 3 explains optimization solution approach to solve the TOP variant. In Sect. 4 computational experiments and results are described. Finally, some concluding remarks and future works are included in the last section.

2   Problem Description

The Tourist Trip Design Problem (TTDP) addressed in this paper is modelled as a multiple route-planning problem. It is aimed at designing a set of routes in a given tourist destination where the number of routes corresponds to the number of days of the stay at the destination. The problem addressed in this paper is modeled through TOP. In the TOP, a set of n POIs is given, each with a given score s_i. The starting point and the end point are fixed. The travel time is known for each pair of POIs i, j and it is denoted by t_{ij}. Not all POIs can be visited. The goal is to determine m routes, limited in time by a given time budget T_{max}, that visits some of the POIs in order to maximise the total collected score.

The POIs are identified by an index i, $i = 1, 2, ..., n$ where 1 and n represent the starting and end POI. Each route is represented by an index k, $k = 1, 2, ..., m$. The score obtained in each location is s_i. r_i is the time spent by the tourist when visiting POI i. The travel time from location i to location j is denoted by t_{ij}. The time limit for each route is T_{max}^k.

The model contains three sets of decision variables u_i^k, x_{ij}^k and y_i^k , $i, j = 1, ..., n$, $k = 1, 2, ..., m$. The position of location i in the route k is given by an integer variable u_i^k. $x_{ij}^k = 1$ if and only if route k goes from location i to j and $x_{ij}^k = 0$ otherwise. $y_i^k = 1$ if location i is visited in route k and $y_j^k = 0$ otherwise.

This variant of the TOP is formulated as a linear programming problem as follows:

Maximize:

$$\sum_{k=1}^{m}\sum_{i=2}^{n-1} s_i y_i^k \tag{1}$$

Subject to:

$$\sum_{k=1}^{m}\sum_{j=2}^{n-1} x_{1j}^k = \sum_{k=1}^{m}\sum_{i=2}^{n-1} x_{in}^k = m \tag{2}$$

$$\sum_{k=1}^{m} y_i^k \leq 1 \quad i = 2, ..., n - 1 \tag{3}$$

$$\sum_{j=1}^{n-1} x_{ji}^k = \sum_{j=2}^{n} x_{ij}^k = y_i^k \quad i = 2, ..., n - 1, \; k = 1, ..., m \tag{4}$$

$$\sum_{i=1}^{n-1}(r_i y_i^k + \sum_{j=2}^{n} t_{ij} x_{ij}^k) \leq T_{max}^k \quad k = 1, ..., m \tag{5}$$

$$u_i^k - u_j^k + 1 \leq (n - 1)(1 - x_{ij}^k) \quad k = 1, 2, ..., m, \; i, j = 2, ..., n \tag{6}$$

$$u_i^k \in \{2, ..., n - 1\} \quad i = 2, ..., n - 1, \; k = 1, ..., m \tag{7}$$

$$x_{ij}^k, y_i^k \in \{0, 1\} \quad k = 1, 2, ..., m, \; i, j = 1, 2, ..., n. \tag{8}$$

Equation (1) represents the objective function, which is the total collected score. Constraints (2) guarantees that each route starts at location 1 and ends at location n. The set of constraints (3) establishes that every location is visited at most once. Constraints (4) ensure that, if a location is visited in a given tour, it is preceeded and followed by exactly one other visit in the same tour. Constraints (5) ensure the limited time for each tour. Constraints (6) avoid subtours. Finally (7) and (8) establish the ranges of the variables.

3   Optimization Approach

We propose a solution algorithm based on the GRASP to solve the optimization problem introduced in Sect. 2. GRASP is a multistart two-phase metaheuristic for combinatorial optimisation proposed by [16]. It consists basically of a construction phase and a local search improvement phase. A feasible solution is obtained in the construction phase. Subsequently, the neighborhood of the solution is explored until a local minimum is found in the local search phase. The pseudocode shown in Algorithm 1 illustrates the main phases of a GRASP where *maxIterations* is the maximum number of iterations in the procedure.

Algorithm 1. GRASP

1: **function** GRASP$maxIterations$
2: readInput()
3: **for** $it = 1$ **to** maxIterations **do**
4:     **begin**
5:         $solution$ = GRASPConstructPhase()
6:         $solution$ = localSearch($solution$)
7:         updateSolution($solution$, $bestSolution$)
8:     **end**

Algorithm 2. GRASP - Construction phase

1: **function** GRASPConstructPhase($maxIterations$)
2: Let x_0 be an initial empty partial solution. Set $j = 0$.
3: **repeat**
4:     **begin**
5:         Construct the restricted candidate list RCL with the nearest available POIs to the last element POI_j
6:         Choose at random an element POI_{j+1} from RCL
7:         Update the partial solution by $x_{j+1} = x_j + \{POI_{j+1}\}$
8:         Set $j = j + 1$
9:     **end**
10: **until** there is no element to include in the partial solution

---

The construction phase of the GRASP is shown in Algorithm 2. The solution construction mechanism builds a solution step-by-step by adding a random new element from a candidate list (the restricted candidate list, RCL) to the current partial solution under construction without losing feasibility.

The candidate list is generated from the selection of the next element, which is determined by ordering of all candidate elements in a candidate list according to a greedy evaluation function. The list of candidates is sorted in two ways in order to compare alternatives. It is sorted in descending order according to the score or ascending order according to the travel time so that the candidates with the highest score or lowest travel time are placed at the top of the candidate list. The RCL is generated by limiting the candidate list size, forming a list of the best candidates.

When a candidate is selected, it is incorporated into the partial solution. In its conception, the GRASP assigns equal probabilities of being chosen to candidates in the RCL. Nevertheless, it is possible use any probability distribution to bias the candidate selection mechanism towards some particular candidates. A slection procedure using several biased probability distributions based on the ranking of candidates by the greedy function is presented in [4]. In this paper we use four bias functions, specifically random bias $bias(r_i) = 1$ (used by standard GRASP), logarithmic bias $bias(r_i) = log^{-1}(r + 1)$, polynomial bias $bias(r_i) = r^{-n}$ of order n and linear bias $bias(r_i) = 1/r$, being r_i the rank of candidate i. In order to assign a probability to each element of the RCL we evaluate the bias values for each of the elements. Thereafter, the probability of selecting the candidate i is calculated as follows:

$$P(i) = \frac{bias(r_i)}{\sum_{i' \in RCL} bias(r_{i'})}$$

Using any of these probability distributions, the candidate is excluded from the candidate list and added to the current partial solution under construction without losing feasibility. In order to add the selected candidate and minimize the total travel time, the algorithm locates the best position in which to insert the selected candidate for all routes for the partial solution. The construction phase ends with a feasible current solution and empty RCL.

Subsequently, the local search phase is applied with the aim of improving the solution. Usually a local search algorithm works iteratively replacing the current solution by a better solution obtained in the neighborhood. The procedure ends when a no better solution is found in the neighborhood. Algorithm 3 shows a basic local search algorithm. Our local search uses exchange movements between POIs of different routes in order to reduce the total travel time. This neighborhood search uses a best improvement strategy. That is, all the neighbors are explored and the current solution is replaced by the best neighbor. If the first steps in the local search are able to reduce the route travel time, then the local search tries to insert a new location in the solution in order to maximize the total score.

Algorithm 3. GRASP - Local Search Improvement Phase

1: **function** localSearch(*solution*)
2: **repeat**
3:     **begin**
4:     Find the best *neighbor* of *solution*
5:     If $f(neighbor) < f(solution)$ do *solution* = *neighbor*
6:     **end**
7: **until** no better neighbor is found
8: **return** *solution*

In general terms, the construction phase and the local search try to maximize the total score of the solution. This two-phase process is iterated, continuing until the user termination criteria is met.

4   Experimentations and Results

This section describes the results from the computational experiments that were carried out in our study. The aim of the experiments is to evaluate the performance of the proposed approach and assess its behavior when it is used to solve the TTDP modeled as a TOP.

Two types of instances were used in the experiments for comparative purposes. The instances are part of the group of Tsiligirides instances for Team Orienteering Problem. Specifically in this experimentation, instances of set 1 were chosen. The data provide the position of a set of locations with a given score which can be visited on a specific day. The maximum number of routes of the solution is also included. The selected instances contain 32 locations. The maximum number of routes and the maximum time per route varies according to the specific instance. For more details concerning the used instances, see Table 1.

Table 1. Tsiligirides instances used in experimentation

Instances	Size	Routes	Max. time
Set1			
p1.4.r	32	4	21.2
p1.3.r	32	3	28.3
Set2			
p2.3.k	21	3	15.0
p2.2.j	21	2	20.0

The experimentation is divided depending on the configuration of the different parameters of GRASP. Among which can be found; the size of the restricted candidate list, sort candidate list by distance or score and if the probability of candidate selection at random or using a probability associated with each candidate proportional to the candidate position in RCL. The GRASP was run 100 times for each of the instances and parameter combinations used in experimentation.

Experimental results are shown in Table 2 that contains the results for set1. Regarding the results, in general terms, it can be seen that random and linear functions bias performs best average score. On the matter of the size of the RCL, the value with better average score is 5. In reference to the sorting, clearly it shows that sorting by score gives better results with respect to the score.

In Table 3 shows the average value and standard deviation for each instance regardless of the combination of parameters. In the case of Table 3, two new instances were included for calculation of average and standard deviation. These instances are the p2.3.k and p2.2.j instance described in Table 1.

5   Conclusions

In this study, we present optimization approach to study and solve the TTDP modeled as TOP. In order to solve the problem to get quality solutions in reasonable time GRASP metaheuristic has been used. The computational experiment confirms that approach proposed is feasible to solve this model. The application of this methodology generates a set of different solutions.

Table 2. Results of set 1 instances

Instances/ bias/RCL size	Sorting by travel time				Sorting by score			
	Best		Average		Best		Average	
	Score	Travel time	Score	Travel time	Score	Travel time	Score	Travel time
p1.4.r								
Random								
Size = 3	160	61.22	151.50	70.27	220	62.59	192.50	71.38
Size = 5	175	69.97	161.00	74.36	225	66.52	190.50	72.10
Size = 7	175	66.91	156.00	72.59	205	58.25	187.50	69.92
p1.4.r								
Logarithmic								
Size = 3	165	67.48	145.00	69.92	200	66.21	179.50	72.12
Size = 5	170	63.13	148.00	70.48	215	61.13	194.00	71.14
Size = 7	170	64.59	157.00	72.52	220	65.82	184.00	70.97
p1.4.r								
Polynomial								
Size = 3	160	64.43	140.00	69.83	220	67.33	195.00	71.37
Size = 5	160	68.35	143.50	72.28	220	69.79	195.50	73.18
Size = 7	170	62.60	152.00	68.36	200	71.14	191.50	74.19
p1.4.r								
Linear								
Size = 3	155	64.97	144.50	69.71	210	73.80	195.00	69.134
Size = 5	180	65.31	153.00	72.13	210	69.16	195.50	72.29
Size = 7	180	59.51	153.45	70.95	225	66.67	199.50	72.84
p1.3.r								
Random								
Size = 3	145	66.91	130.00	71.76	195	67.83	178.50	72.62
Size = 5	140	63.84	129.50	70.06	220	62.55	182.50	71.55
Size = 7	145	69.04	133.00	73.92	195	61.35	177.00	69.87
p1.3.r								
Logarithmic								
Size = 3	145	64.96	129.50	70.34	200	60.98	178.00	71.00
Size = 5	150	66.00	138.00	72.27	200	66.14	179.00	72.56
Size = 7	155	66.86	138.50	71.76	215	63.73	177.50	72.57
p1.3.r								
Polynomial								
Size = 3	140	66.45	128.00	72.63	200	66.22	169.50	70.56
Size = 5	140	68.97	130.50	74.19	210	68.94	179.50	73.05
Size = 7	140	67.04	129.00	71.93	200	67.14	177.50	72.04
p1.3.r								
Linear								
Size = 3	140	64.32	129.00	74.16	210	69.96	186.00	73.80
Size = 5	145	64.79	131.50	71.99	200	63.08	175.50	69.47
Size = 7	145	64.77	130.00	68.12	190	63.94	169.00	71.97

Table 3. Average and standard deviation

Instances	Average	Standard deviation
p1.4.r	170.95	24.57
p1.3.r	154.41	26.54
p2.3.k	287.85	31.06
p2.2.j	249.50	37.61

Future work will extend experimentation with other instances, among which some can be real cases. The behavior of other metaheuristics. Specifically the multiobjective problem will be one of the first lines of research to be studied. Although the objective function is to maximize the score obtained in the locations, we have found that by minimizing the time of the routes it is possible to add more locations to the routes and thus maximize the total score obtained in the locations. This multiobjective version will consider the score obtained in the locations and route time in the objective function.

Acknowledgment. This paper has been partially funded by the Spanish Ministry of Economy and Competitiveness (TIN2012-32608 and TIN2015-70226-R projects). Contributions by Airam Expósito are supported by the research training program of University of La Laguna and La Caixa. Thanks to IUDR (Instituto Universitario de Desarrollo Regional) for its support provided.

References

1. Archetti, C., Hertz, A., Speranza, M.G.: Metaheuristics for the team orienteering problem. J. Heuristics **13**(1), 49–76 (2007)
2. Bouly, H., Dang, D.C., Moukrim, A.: A memetic algorithm for the team orienteering problem. 4OR **8**(1), 49–70 (2010)
3. Boussier, S., Feillet, D., Gendreau, M.: An exact algorithm for team orienteering problems. 4OR **5**(3), 211–230 (2007)
4. Bresina, J.L.: Heuristic-biased stochastic sampling. In: AAAI 1996, pp. 271–278 (1996)
5. Butt, S.E., Cavalier, T.M.: A heuristic for the multiple tour maximum collection problem. Comput. Oper. Res. **21**(1), 101–111 (1994)
6. Butt, S.E., Ryan, D.M.: An optimal solution procedure for the multiple tour maximum collection problem using column generation. Comput. Oper. Res. **26**(4), 427–441 (1999)
7. Chao, I.M., Golden, B.L., Wasil, E.A.: The team orienteering problem. Eur. J. Oper. Res. **88**(3), 464–474 (1996)
8. Dang, D.-C., El-Hajj, R., Moukrim, A.: A branch-and-cut algorithm for solving the team orienteering problem. In: Gomes, C., Sellmann, M. (eds.) CPAIOR 2013. LNCS, vol. 7874, pp. 332–339. Springer, Heidelberg (2013)
9. Feo, T.A., Resende, M.G.C.: Greedy randomized adaptive search procedures. J. Glob. Optim. **6**, 109–133 (1995)

10. Golden, B., Levy, L., Vohra, R.: The orienteering problem. Nav. Res. Logistics **34**, 307–318 (1987)
11. Ke, L., Archetti, C., Feng, Z.: Ants can solve the team orienteering problem. Comput. Ind. Eng. **54**(3), 648–665 (2008)
12. Kim, B.I., Li, H., Johnson, A.L.: An augmented large neighborhood search method for solving the team orienteering problem. Expert Syst. Appl. **40**(8), 3065–3072 (2013)
13. Lin, S.W.: Solving the team orienteering problem using effective multi-start simulated annealing. Appl. Soft Comput. **13**, 1064–1073 (2013)
14. Resende, M.G., Ribeiro, C.C.: Greedy randomized adaptive search procedures: advances, hybridizations, and applications. In: Gendreau, M., Potvin, J.Y. (eds.) Handbook of Metaheuristics. International Series in Operations Research and Management Science, vol. 146, pp. 283–319. Springer, Heidelberg (2010)
15. Souffriau, W., Vansteenwegen, P., Berghe, G.V., Oudheusden, D.V.: A path relinking approach for the team orienteering problem. Comput. Oper. Res. **37**(11), 1853–1859 (2010)
16. Tang, H., Miller-Hooks, E.: A tabu search heuristic for the team orienteering problem. Comput. Oper. Res. **32**(6), 1379–1407 (2005)
17. Toth, P., Vigo, D.: An overview of vehicle routing problems. In: The Vehicle Routing Problems. Monographs on Discrete Mathematics and Applications, vol. 9, pp. 1–26. SIAM (2002)
18. Vansteenwegen, P., Souffriau, W., Berghe, G.V., Oudheusden, D.V.: A guided local search metaheuristic for the team orienteering problem. Eur. J. Oper. Res. **196**(1), 118–127 (2009)
19. Vansteenwegen, P., Souffriau, W., Oudheusden, D.V.: The orienteering problem: a survey. Eur. J. Oper. Res. **209**(1), 1–10 (2011)
20. Vansteenwegen, P., Van Oudheusden, D.: The mobile tourist guide: an or opportunity. OR Insight **20**(3), 21–27 (2007)

Optimization

A Note on the Boltzmann Distribution and the Linear Ordering Problem

Josu Ceberio[1(✉)], Alexander Mendiburu[2], and Jose A. Lozano[3,4]

[1] Department of Computer Languages and Systems,
University of the Basque Country UPV/EHU, 48013 Bilbao, Spain
josu.ceberio@ehu.eus
[2] Department of Computer Architecture and Technology,
University of the Basque Country UPV/EHU, 20018 Donostia, Spain
[3] Department of Computer Science and Artificial Intelligence,
University of the Basque Country UPV/EHU, 20018 Donostia, Spain
[4] Basque Center for Applied Mathematics (BCAM), 48009 Bilbao, Spain

Abstract. The Boltzmann distribution plays a key role in the field of optimization as it directly connects this field with that of probability. Basically, given a function to optimize, the Boltzmann distribution associated to this function assigns higher probability to the candidate solutions with better quality. Therefore, an efficient sampling of the Boltzmann distribution would turn optimization into an easy task. However, inference tasks on this distribution imply performing operations over an exponential number of terms, which hinders its applicability. As a result, the scientific community has investigated how the structure of objective functions is translated to probabilistic properties in order to simplify the corresponding Boltzmann distribution. In this paper, we elaborate on the properties induced in the Boltzmann distribution associated to permutation-based combinatorial optimization problems. Particularly, we prove that certain characteristics of the linear ordering problem are translated as conditional independence relations to the Boltzmann distribution in the form of $L - decomposability$.

Keywords: Boltzmann distribution · Combinatorial optimization · L-decomposability · Linear ordering problem · Permutation

1 Introduction

In the last decades, the Boltzmann distribution has been a recurrent research topic in the field of combinatorial optimization as it constitutes on of the bridges between this field and that of probability [5]. Basically, given an objective function f, the associated Boltzmann distribution assigns higher probabilities to those solutions with better objective values. Formally, under this distribution, the probability of a solution x is defined as

$$P(x) = \frac{\exp(\beta f(x))}{Z_f(\beta)} \quad x \in \Omega \tag{1}$$

© Springer International Publishing Switzerland 2016
O. Luaces et al. (Eds.): CAEPIA 2016, LNAI 9868, pp. 441–446, 2016.
DOI: 10.1007/978-3-319-44636-3_41

where Ω denotes the set of all candidate solutions (which is usually of exponential size), β is the Boltzmann constant, and $Z_f(\beta)$ stands for the partition function. When β equals 0, the distribution becomes uniform. In contrast, when β is large, the probability concentrates around the global optimal solutions.

Due to its ideal properties (the better the solution, the higher its probability), if it were possible to efficiently sample the Boltzmann distribution for any β, optimization would be an easy task [7]. However, in general, there is no closed form expression for $Z_f(\beta)$, and therefore, any inference on this distribution usually implies performing a sum over exponentially many terms:

$$Z_f(\beta) = \sum_{y \in \Omega} \exp(\beta f(y)) \tag{2}$$

In spite of these difficulties, the scientific community has researched how the structural properties of the objective function are translated to the probability properties of the corresponding Boltzmann distributions, and how this helps in the optimization process. In this sense, Muhlenbein et al. [7] showed that, in the case of combinatorial problems, it is possible to simplify the representation of the Boltzmann distribution. Particularly, they translated properties of additively decomposable functions into conditional independence assertions between variables that, finally, produced (efficient, in some cases) factorizations of the associated Boltzmann distribution. Motivated by such results, the authors proposed a novel estimation of distribution algorithm based on the Boltzmann distribution.

Nonetheless, the work by Muhlenbein et al. [7] is not applicable to any search space. For instance, when solving permutation-based combinatorial optimization problems, the set of all permutations (of a given size n) constitutes the search space of candidate solutions. In this case, due to the *mutual exclusivity constraints* associated with the codification of solutions, the previous conditional independence assertions between variables do not provide information. However, numerous works on permutations probabilistic modelling have defined independence properties that do consider the nature of permutations [2–4,8], and therefore, allow to factorize the distribution. The most recurrent of these properties is the *L-decomposability* [2].

According to Csizar [3], a probability distribution P over the space of permutations $\mathbb{S}_n$ is said to be *L-decomposable*, if there are choice probabilities $P_C(i)$ for all subsets $C \subseteq \{1, \ldots, n\}$ and $i \in C$, such that

$$P(\sigma) = \prod_{r=1}^{n} P_{\{\sigma(r),\ldots,\sigma(n)\}}(\sigma(r)) \qquad \forall \sigma \in \mathbb{S}_n \tag{3}$$

where n denotes the size of the permutations and the choice probability $P_C(i)$ is the probability that item i is chosen as the best preferred from the subset C of items. This property implies that the choice probabilities at the r-th step depend only on the set of items remaining at that step and are independent of the ordering of the previously selected items.

As carried out in Muhlenbein et al. [7], in this paper we aim to set the basis to also use the Boltzmann distribution to optimize permutation-based optimization problems. To this end, we show that the structure of these problems can be interpreted in the domain of probability as specific properties of the associated Boltzmann distribution. In this manuscript, we take the Linear Ordering Problem (LOP) [6] as a case of study, and demonstrate that its associated Boltzmann distribution is *L-decomposable*.

Nonetheless, it is worth mentioning that this research may be extended to other permutation problems with different structures than that of LOP given rise to other independence properties on the corresponding Boltzmann distribution.

Given a matrix $B = [b_{k,l}]_{n \times n}$ of numerical entries, the LOP consists of finding a simultaneous permutation σ of the rows and columns of B, such that the sum of the entries above the main diagonal is maximized (see Fig. 1). The equation below formalizes the LOP function:

$$f(\sigma) = \sum_{k=1}^{n-1} \sum_{l=k+1}^{n} b_{\sigma(k),\sigma(l)} \qquad (4)$$

where $\sigma(k)$ and $\sigma(l)$ denote the items ranked at positions k and l in the solution σ.

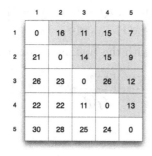

Fig. 1. Example of an LOP instance of $n = 5$.

In the LOP, the influence of locating a given item at position r ($r \in \{1,\ldots,n\}$) to the quality of the solution σ depends on the distribution of the items in the previous $\{1,\ldots,r-1\}$ and posterior $\{r+1,\ldots,n\}$ positions. However, it does not change for any ordering of the items within the subsets [1]. In the following section, we demonstrate that such a notion of independence between the items is interpreted as *L-decomposability* of the associated Boltzmann distribution.

2   Main Result

In this section, the main result of the manuscript is introduced: Theorem 1, the *L-decomposability* of the Boltzmann distribution associated to the LOP.

Theorem 1. *The Boltzmann distribution associated to the linear ordering problem is L-decomposable.*

Proof. In order to verify that a probability distribution $P(\sigma)$ is *L-decomposable*, it is a necessary and sufficient condition that, for each $r = 3, \ldots, n$ and for each $i_1, \ldots, i_r$, the conditional probability

$$P(\sigma(r) = i_r | \sigma(1) = i_1, \ldots, \sigma(r-1) = i_{r-1}) \tag{5}$$

is a symmetric function of $i_1, \ldots, i_{r-1}$ [2]. Therefore, without loss of generality, by proving the equality below for every permutation π of the items $\{i_1, \ldots, i_{r-1}\}$

$$\begin{aligned}
P(\sigma(r) = i_r | \sigma(1) = i_1, \ldots, \sigma(r-1) = i_{r-1}) = \\
P(\sigma(r) = i_r | \sigma(1) = \pi(1), \ldots, \sigma(r-1) = \pi(r-1))
\end{aligned} \tag{6}$$

where $\forall j, k \in \{1, \ldots, r-1\}, \pi(j) \in \{i_1, \ldots, i_{r-1}\}$ and $\pi(j) \neq \pi(k)$, unless $j = k$, we prove that $P(\sigma)$ is *L-decomposable*.

So, from (6), by applying the Bayes' theorem, we obtain

$$\begin{aligned}
\frac{P(\sigma(1) = i_1, \ldots, \sigma(r-1) = i_{r-1}, \sigma(r) = i_r)}{P(\sigma(1) = i_1, \ldots, \sigma(r-1) = i_{r-1})} = \\
\frac{P(\sigma(1) = \pi(1), \ldots, \sigma(r-1) = \pi(r-1), \sigma(r) = i_r)}{P(\sigma(1) = \pi(1), \ldots, \sigma(r-1) = \pi(r-1))}
\end{aligned} \tag{7}$$

and, by replacing the terms with the Boltzmann distribution of the LOP (8),

$$P(\sigma) = \frac{\exp(\beta \sum_{k=1}^{n-1} \sum_{l=k+1}^{n} b_{\sigma(k),\sigma(l)})}{Z_f(\beta)} \qquad \sigma \in \mathbb{S}_n \tag{8}$$

we rewrite (7) as follows[1]:

$$\frac{\sum_{\sigma \in S_r} \exp(\sum_{k=1}^{n-1} \sum_{l=k+1}^{n} b_{\sigma(k),\sigma(l)})}{\sum_{\sigma \in S_{r-1}} \exp(\sum_{k=1}^{n-1} \sum_{l=k+1}^{n} b_{\sigma(k),\sigma(l)})} = \frac{\sum_{\sigma \in T_r} \exp(\sum_{k=1}^{n-1} \sum_{l=k+1}^{n} b_{\sigma(k),\sigma(l)})}{\sum_{\sigma \in T_{r-1}} \exp(\sum_{k=1}^{n-1} \sum_{l=k+1}^{n} b_{\sigma(k),\sigma(l)})} \tag{9}$$

where S_r and S_{r-1} denote the set of permutations that agree with $i_1, \ldots, i_r$ and $i_1, \ldots, i_{r-1}$ orderings in the first r and $r-1$ positions. T_{r-1} denotes the set of permutations that agree with π in the first $r-1$ positions, and T_r restricts, even more, the previous set by fixing item i_r at position r.

Let us first focus on the left-hand side of the equality in (9). Taking into account the positions in which items are already known, we decompose the exponent terms in the numerator and denominator (10) as illustrated in Fig. 2.

---

[1] Note that partition functions $Z(\beta)$ and the Boltzmann constant β are cancelled.

$$\frac{\sum_{\sigma \in S_r} \exp \left(\sum_{k=1}^{r-1} \sum_{l=k+1}^{r} b_{i_k,i_l} + \overbrace{\sum_{k=1}^{r} \sum_{l=r+1}^{n} b_{\sigma(k),\sigma(l)}}^{X_1(\sigma)} + \overbrace{\sum_{k=r+1}^{n-1} \sum_{l=k+1}^{n} b_{\sigma(k),\sigma(l)}}^{Y_1(\sigma)} \right)}{\sum_{\sigma \in S_{r-1}} \exp \left(\sum_{k=1}^{r-2} \sum_{l=k+1}^{r-1} b_{i_k,i_l} + \underbrace{\sum_{k=1}^{r-1} \sum_{l=r}^{n} b_{\sigma(k),\sigma(l)}}_{X_2(\sigma)} + \underbrace{\sum_{k=r}^{n-1} \sum_{l=k+1}^{n} b_{\sigma(k),\sigma(l)}}_{Y_2(\sigma)} \right)}$$ (10)

For readability purposes, we replace the terms related to $\sigma(r), \ldots, \sigma(n)$ with X_1, X_2, Y_1 and Y_2.

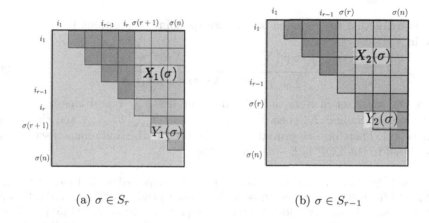

(a) $\sigma \in S_r$ (b) $\sigma \in S_{r-1}$

Fig. 2. Decomposition of $f(\sigma)$ for the solutions in S_r and S_{r-1}.

Note that for the solutions in S_r and S_{r-1}, the items in the first $r-1$ positions are equal, i.e. $i_1, \ldots, i_{r-1}$. Thus, we extract the common factor from the numerator and denominator (the terms that correspond to the computation of items $i_1, \ldots, i_{r-1}$), and the equation is simplified to

$$\frac{\sum_{\sigma \in S_r} \exp \left(\sum_{k=1}^{r-1} b_{i_k,i_r} + X_1(\sigma) + Y_1(\sigma) \right)}{\sum_{\sigma \in S_{r-1}} \exp \left(X_2(\sigma) + Y_2(\sigma) \right)}$$ (11)

Now, we perform a similar procedure on the right-hand side of the equality in (9) by following the decomposition of the objective function in Fig. 3:

$$\frac{\sum_{\sigma \in T_r} \exp \left(\sum_{k=1}^{r-2} \sum_{l=k+1}^{r-1} b_{\pi(k),\pi(l)} + \sum_{k=1}^{r-1} b_{\pi(k),i_r} + X_1(\sigma) + Y_1(\sigma) \right)}{\sum_{\sigma \in T_{r-1}} \exp \left(\sum_{k=1}^{r-2} \sum_{l=k+1}^{r-1} b_{\pi(k),\pi(l)} + X_2(\sigma) + Y_2(\sigma) \right)}$$ (12)

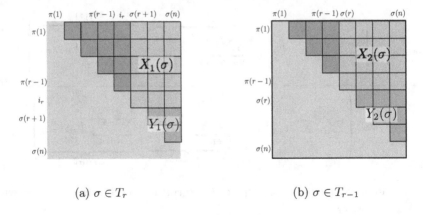

(a) $\sigma \in T_r$ (b) $\sigma \in T_{r-1}$

Fig. 3. Decomposition of $f(\sigma)$ for the solutions in T_r and T_{r-1}.

By extracting the common factor corresponding to positions $1, \ldots, r-1$ we obtain

$$\frac{\sum_{\sigma \in T_r} \exp\left(\sum_{k=1}^{r-1} b_{\pi(k),i_r} + X_1(\sigma) + Y_1(\sigma)\right)}{\sum_{\sigma \in T_{r-1}} \exp\left(X_2(\sigma) + Y_2(\sigma)\right)} \tag{13}$$

Since the same set of items is ordered in the first $r-1$ positions in the permutations in S_r and T_r, then $\sum_{k=1}^{r-1} b_{i_k,i_r}$ equals $\sum_{k=1}^{r-1} b_{\pi(k),i_r}$, and thus, (13) equals (11). Therefore, we proved that (6) is true and the Boltzmann distribution associated to the LOP is $L - decomposable$.

Acknowledgements. This work has been partially supported by the Research Groups 2013-2018 (IT-609-13) programs (Basque Government) and TIN2013-41272P (Ministry of Science and Technology). Jose A. Lozano is also supported by BERC 2014-2017 and Elkartek programs (Basque government) and Severo Ochoa Program SEV-2013-0323 (Spanish Ministry of Economy and Competitiveness).

References

1. Ceberio, J., Mendiburu, A., Lozano, J.A.: The linear ordering problem revisited. Eur. J. Oper. Res. **241**(3), 686–696 (2014)
2. Critchlow, D.E., Fligner, M.A., Verducci, J.S.: Probability models on rankings. J. Math. Psychol. **35**(3), 294–318 (1991)
3. Csiszar, V.: On L-decomposability of random orderings. J. Math. Psychol. **53**, 294–297 (2009)
4. Duncan, L.R.: Individual Choice Behavior. Wiley, New York (1959)
5. Kirkpatrick, S., Gelatt, C.D., Vecchi, M.P., et al.: Optimization by simulated annealing. Science **220**(4598), 671–680 (1983)
6. Martí, R., Reinelt, G.: The Linear Ordering Problem: Exact and Heuristic Methods in Combinatorial Optimization, vol. 175. Springer, Heidelberg (2011)
7. Muhlenbein, H., Mahnig, T., Ais, F.: Evolutionary algorithms and the Boltzmann distribution. In: FOGA 7, pp. 525–556 (2003)
8. Plackett, R.L.: The analysis of permutations. J. R. Stat. Soc. **24**(10), 193–202 (1975)

A Binary Fisherman Search Procedure for the 0/1 Knapsack Problem

Carlos Cobos[1(✉)], Hernán Dulcey[1], Johny Ortega[1],
Martha Mendoza[1], and Armando Ordoñez[2]

[1] Information Technology Research Group (GTI),
Universidad del Cauca, Popayán, Colombia
{ccobos, dulcey.hernan, johnyortega,
mmendoza}@unicauca.edu.co
[2] Intelligent Management Systems Group,
Foundation University of Popayán, Popayán, Colombia
jaordonez@unicauca.edu.co

Abstract. The 0/1 Knapsack Problem is a widely studied problem of binary discrete optimization that has applications in a number of diverse, real-world applications. From existing algorithms for solving this problem, the three best meta-heuristics in the state of the art were selected, namely: Modified discrete shuffled frog-leaping, Soccer league competition, and Simplified binary harmony search. These algorithms were compared with a new binary algorithm of fisherman search procedure. In order to perform this comparison, instances of the 0/1 knapsack problem with low and medium dimensionality (100 and 200 items) were used. Medium instances have three levels of complexity (uncorrelated, weakly correlated, and strongly correlated). Used instances were generated previously by other authors (in order to avoid bias). The results were analyzed using three criteria: success rate in reaching the global optima, execution time, and number of fitness function evaluations. The results enable it to be seen that the proposed algorithm is the best meta-heuristic for solving these types of 0/1 knapsack problem.

Keywords: Fisherman search procedure · 0/1 knapsack problem · Modified discrete shuffled frog-leaping algorithm · Simplified binary harmony search algorithm · Soccer league competition algorithm

1 Introduction

The 0/1 Knapsack problem is an optimization problem in which a set of items and one knapsack are given, each item has a value and a weight and the knapsack has a maximum capacity. The goal of this problem is to find a subset of items of maximum value such that they may be packaged in the knapsacks without exceeding its capacity. The 0/1 knapsack problem may be defined mathematically as shown in Eq. (1).

Several real-world applications of the 0/1 knapsack problem can be found. These include business decision making, project selection, The network-interdiction problem, as well as the problem of filling containers for storage and transportation [1]. At present, there are a range of algorithms available for solving this problem. However,

© Springer International Publishing Switzerland 2016
O. Luaces et al. (Eds.): CAEPIA 2016, LNAI 9868, pp. 447–457, 2016.
DOI: 10.1007/978-3-319-44636-3_42

complexity (dimensions) of these problems increases continually, as well as the need to solve them quickly. The main objective of this work is to define the most effective meta-heuristic to date in the state of the art for solving 0/1 knapsack problems.

$$Max f(x) = \sum_{k=1}^{n} v_k \times x_k$$

Subject to :

$$\sum_{k=1}^{n} w_k \times x_k \leq w_{max} \; x_k \in \{0, 1\}, k = 1, 2, \ldots, n \tag{1}$$

Where x is the set of decision variables or items. x_k represents the state of each item in the knapsack, where 0 means that item k must not be included in the knapsack and 1 that the item must be included in the knapsack. v_k is the value of the item k, w_k is the weight of the item k, w_{max} is the knapsack capacity, and n is the problem dimension (total number of items or objects).

The rest of this paper is structured as follows. Section 2 briefly describes the meta-heuristics selected as well as the modifications made to these meta-heuristics in order to perform the comparison. Section 3 depicts the proposed Binary Fisherman Search Procedure (BFSP). Section 4 analyzes the experimental results. Finally, Sect. 5 gives the conclusion and outlines future work.

2   State of the Art Meta-Heuristics for the 0/1 Knapsack Problem

Meta-heuristics were selected according to the following criteria: (i) Novelty: selected approaches must be in the state of the art within the observation period of 5 years (2010–2015). (ii) Diversity: selected algorithms must be based on diverse meta-heuristic techniques to solve the problem (e.g. Particle Swarm Optimization, Harmony Search, among others). (iii) Effectiveness: selected algorithms must report the best results for solving 0/1 knapsack problems; specifically problems with a high number of data were considered. The three selected meta-heuristics are:

Modified Discrete Shuffled Frog-Leaping Algorithm (MDSFL). In this algorithm, the population is made of a set of frogs (solutions) which is partitioned into subsets known as memeplexes. These memeplexes represent different cultures of frogs, each of them performing a local search. Within each memeplex, the individual frogs have ideas that can be influenced by the ideas of other frogs, and evolve following a process of memetic evolution. After a concrete number of memetic evolution steps, ideas are passed among memeplexes in a shuffling process [1]. This algorithm has reported successful results in diverse optimization problems [2, 3]. Unfortunately, the paper [1] does not describe the repair procedure for infeasible solutions and the genetic mutation operator. For this reason, in the present work the repair procedure of infeasible solutions of the simplified harmonic search algorithm was used (see below) [4]; likewise, for the genetic mutation operator, the one-bit mutation was selected. Despite this algorithm being published recently in a leading journal, the paper does not present any comparison with other meta-heuristics: only a comparison with variations of the same algorithm.

A Simplified Binary Harmony Search Algorithm (SBHS). SBHS is an improvement of the harmony search algorithm for the 0/1 knapsack problem. In this new version, only two parameters need to be tuned (HMS and HMCR). In addition, the PAR parameter is no longer required, since a new method for tuning the tone is included. The new tuning method performs a crossover between the best harmony and another harmony randomly selected from the harmony memory. It uses an HMCR that grows linearly with the size of the problem, which optimizes the algorithm for different problems. A greedy two-stage procedure was implemented to repair infeasible solutions within the memory [4]. This algorithm was compared with 14 other algorithms (9 continuous and 5 binary), including Adaptive Binary Harmony Search, (ABHS) [5] and Novel Discrete Global-Best Harmony Search (DGHS) [6]. On completion of the comparison, the SBSH was found to return better results.

Soccer League Competition Algorithm (SLC). SLC was initially used for optimizing the design of water distribution networks [7]. SLC is inspired by professional soccer league and the search process is based on the competitions among teams and players. In SLC, teams (subsets) with different players (solutions) face each other, and the winning team (determined by a random event) has the possibility of mutating its players. Two mutation operators aim for improving solutions from a global scope (Enhanced Imitation Operator) and a local scope (Provocation Operator). At the end of the season, new teams are assembled and players are assigned to different teams in order to expand the search space [8]. However, in this research a modification was made to the objective function due to the fact that unlike previous algorithms, this algorithm does not use a repair method but instead penalizes infeasible solutions. Penalization is described in the objective function based on Eq. (2), where λ value penalizes infeasible solutions in order to reduce the probability that these solutions are selected. In [8] the original value of λ was constant and very high, penalizing all the instances of the problem in the same way. To correct this, a variable λ was included, this variable penalizes in proportion to the total sum of the weights in each problem.

Equation (2) was used for comparing SLC with other meta-heuristics because the objective function described in [8] showed very low performance when used in problems with a higher dimension number ($> = 100$). This algorithm was compared with 4 other algorithms, 3 based on Harmony Search and one binary version of PSO [5].

$$F(x) = \sum_{k=1}^{n} x_k \times v_k - \lambda * P(x)$$
$$\lambda = \sum_{k=1}^{n} v_k$$
$$P(x) = \left(\frac{\sum_{k=1}^{n} x_k \times w_k}{w_{max}} - 1 \right) > 0? \frac{\sum_{k=1}^{n} x_k \times w_k}{w_{max}} : 0 \tag{2}$$

Repair Procedure. Optimization problems with constraints may be solved using two strategies: (i) by exploring the entire search space and penalizing the value of the objective function of infeasible solutions; this strategy is implemented in the algorithm

SLC. And (ii) by exploring only feasible solution space, this involves using a repair procedure to ensure that solutions are within the feasible search space; this strategy is implemented by the BFSP, MDSFL and SBHS algorithms. Kong et al. [4] define a greedy two-stage procedure to repair infeasible solutions. This is described in [4]. The procedure repairs solutions using the relative profit density of each item according to Eq. (3), where u_k indicates the most valuable objects, according to their value and weight.

$$u_k = \frac{v_k}{w_k} \tag{3}$$

The repair procedure can be summarized as follows: (i) calculate the volume of the items chosen by the infeasible solution, (ii) Define S1 as a sequence of items sorted by density u_k expressed by Eq. (3) in ascending order and remove items from S1 until the volume is smaller than the knapsack capacity, (iii) Define S2 as a sequence of items sorted by volume w_k in ascending order and store in S3 the item positions with a volume smaller than the remaining volume of the knapsack, and (iv) Get the corresponding tab sequence S4 of those positions contained in S3 based on their relative profit density in ascending order and insert the items into the knapsack following the tab sequence S4 until there is no space in the knapsack.

3 Binary Fisherman Search Procedure (BFSP)

The Fisherman Search Procedure (FSP) is a meta-heuristic used for solving continuous optimization problems [9]. FSP is inspired by the knowledge and skills of fishermen. FSP uses a combination of guided search and local search. In the present work, a binary version of the algorithm is proposed (see Fig. 1). This algorithm was also adapted to solve the 0/1 knapsack problem and includes a HUX [10] crossover in order to exploit with a certain probability around the best-found solution (Similar to PSO).

BFSP uses 6 parameters: T is the number of iterations of the algorithm, N is the number of capture points, L is the number of throws of the fishing network in each capture point, M is the number of knots (network position vectors) representing the fishing network, p_{best} is the probability of finding the best-found solution (g_{best}) and $p_{diversity}$ is the probability of getting out of a local optima. A capture point x_i based in Eq. (4) is an n-size vector, where n is the dimension of the problem instance and $x_{i,k}$ represent the k decision variable (item/object).

$$x_i = \{x_{i,1}, x_{i,2}, \ldots, x_{i,k}, \ldots, x_{i,n}\}$$
$$where \ x_{i,k} \in \{0,1\}, i = 1, 2, \ldots, N \ and \ k = 1, 2, \ldots, n \tag{4}$$

In order to represent the fishing network, M, knots $y_{i,j}$ are used based on Eq. (5). Knots are n-size vectors representing a possible better solution for p_i.

```
Input: T, N, L, M, pbest, pdiversity
for i ← 1 to N do
    Initialize xi;  Repair and Evaluate xi
    Update gbest        // if fitness(xi) > fitness(gbest) then gbest ← Copy(xi)
    pi ←Copy(xi);  ci ← 2
end for
for t ← 1 to T do                    // maximum number of iterations
    for i ← 1 to N do                 // for each capture point on search space
        for l ← 1 to L do              // throws L times the fishing network
            for j ← 0 to M do          // for each node in the fishing network
                if U(0, 1) <= pbest then
                    Update yij based on HUX crossover between xi and gbest        //Similar to PSO
                else
                    Update yij based on random mutation of ci bits and current values of xi
                end if
                Repair and Evaluate yij
                Update pi              // if fitness(yij) > fitness(pi) then pi ←yij
            end for
            if fitness (pi) > fitness (xi) then break
        end for
        if U(0, 1) <= pdiversity then    // pdiversity: diversity parameter
            Bit string mutation xi
            Repair and Evaluate xi
        end if
        Update xi                     // if fitness(pi) > fitness(xi) then xi ← Copy(pi)
        Update ci                     // if fitness(pi) > fitness(xi) then ci ← 1 else ci ← 2
        Update gbest                  // if fitness(xi) > fitness(gbest) then gbest ← Copy(xi)
    end for
end for
return gbest
```

Fig. 1. Binary fisherman search procedure

$$y_{i,j} = \{y_{i,j,1}, y_{i,j,2}, \ldots, y_{i,j,k}, \ldots, y_{i,j,n}\}$$
$$where\ y_{i,j,k} \in \{0,1\}, i = 1, 2, \ldots, N, j = 1, 2, \ldots, M,\ and\ k = 1, 2, \ldots, n \tag{5}$$

A capture point p_i is the best solution found for the current x_i. After throwing the fishing network in the capture point and the updates of p_i with the $y_{i,j}$, the capture point x_i is moved to p_i if any improvement is achieved.

Creation of the Fishing Network Knots. The local search is done with the network knots ($y_{i,j}$). In FSP the $y_{i,j}$ are generated using Eq. (6) where A_j is an n-dimensional vector whose elements are random numbers in the range [-c, c], where c is a real number known as width coefficient.

$$y_{i,j} = x_i + A_j \tag{6}$$

In BFSP the creation of $y_{i,j}$ is done using the parameter p_{best}. This parameter determines the probability of creating the knots $y_{i,j}$ around the best-found solution (g_{best}) using the Half Uniform Crossover (HUX), or using a random mutation of c_i bits. In order to create the knots $y_{i,j}$ based on HUX, g_{best} is taken as a first father and x_i as a second father. The present approach (HUX operator to create the network knots) works similarly to Particle Swarm Optimization (PSO).

Width Coefficient. In the BFSP the width coefficient (c_i) is used to determine the number of bits to mutate in the current capture point. A c_i has a value of 1 (exploitation) or 2 (exploration). After performing the throws and updating p_i, the value of c_i is set to 1 if the capture point p_i is better than x_i; otherwise, this value is set to 2. In this way, exploitation is performed if the previous exploitation was successful. Otherwise, exploration must be initiated. Finally, if the exploration was carried out and it was successful, then the exploitation mode is initiated. Otherwise, the exploration mode continues.

4 Experimentation and Evaluation

This section shows the experimental results of comparing the optimization capabilities of the four meta-heuristics: BFSP, MDSFL [1], SBHS [4], and SLC [8]. Experiments were carried out using C++ over Microsoft Visual Studio Ultimate 2012 on an Intel(R) Core(TM) i5 PC, CPU 650 @ 3.20 GHz with 8 GB of RAM and Windows 8 using a designed framework to achieve a fair environment.

Instances of 0/1 Knapsack Problem. In order to compare the meta-heuristics, 10 test instances were used (easy problems) along with 6 experimentation instances (available in http://goo.gl/M6vSGr). The first 10 test problems have been used in diverse works [1, 4, 8] to estimate the robustness of meta-heuristics. A detailed description of the origin of these instances can be found in [8]. For the experimentation instances, 3 instances of 100 and 200 items were defined, these instances had different types of complexity (uncorrelated, weakly correlated, and strongly correlated). In [11] 16 types of complexity types are reported. However, in this work, only the first 3 types were selected as these were the most commonly employed in performing comparisons [1, 4, 8]. The original files of these instances are available at http://www.diku. dk/~pisinger/codes.html.

Parameter Tuning. In order to perform the comparison most similar to the results previously presented in [1, 4, 8], the parameter tuning followed the recommendation of the authors of each algorithm (see Tables 1 and 2); in the case of BFSP the values correspond to an initial process of parameter tuning according to the recommendations of [9]. However, the stop criterion of the algorithm was modified for the comparison. Two stop criteria were used for the algorithms: the first one is to stop when the optimal solution for the current problem instance is found, and the second is to stop when a maximum execution time is reached. The maximum execution time was defined considering that all meta-heuristics had the same chance of finding the optimal. For the 10 test instances the maximum execution time was 5 s. For the 6 experimentation instances

Table 1. Parameters for each algorithm over low dimensionality 0/1 knapsack problems

Algorithm	Parameters tuning
BFSP	T = n/a; N = 20; L = 5; M = 10; pbest = 0.4, pdiversity = 0.25
MDSFL	P = 200; m = 10; it = 10; iMax = n/a; α = 0.4; pm = 0.06; Δ = n/a, iMax > 50
SBHS	NI = n/a; HMS = 5; HMCR = 0.95
SLC	seasons = n/a; nT = 10; nF = 10; nS = 10; HMCR = 0.1; PAR = 0.05; λ = n/a

Table 2. Parameters for all algorithms over medium dimensionality 0/1 knapsack problems

Algorithm	Parameters tuning
BFSP	T = n/a; N = 400, 60; L = 5; M = 10; pbest = 0.4, pdiversity = 0.25
MDSFL	P = 400, 60; m = 20; it = 10; iMax = n/a; α = 0.4; pm = 0.06; Δ = n/a, iMax > 50
SBHS	NI = n/a; HMS = 5; HMCR = 1 – 1/n, n ≥ 100
SLC	seasons = n/a; nT = 10; nF = 10; nS = 10; HMCR = 0.1; PAR = 0.05; λ = n/a

the maximum execution time was 120 s (2 min). In accordance with the above, in Tables 1 and 2 there exist parameters with a value of n/a to indicate that they are not used due to the stop criteria modifications. In SLC, the parameter λ is calculated based on the specific values of the problem instance to be solved, as presented in Eq. (2).

Results. The results of the 10 test instances are presented below in Table 3 shows the problem dimension (n), the maximum capacity of the knapsack (w_{max}), the optimal value, and the results of the experiments for the meta-heuristics. In addition, Table 3 presents the success rate (SR) of the algorithm in finding the global optima, the best value found in 50 independent executions of each algorithm (Best), the worst value found (Worst), the medium value (Median), the average value (Mean) and finally, the standard deviation of the values found (Std).

The results indicate that only BFSP have a success rate of 100 % for all test instances, MDSFL and SLC has a success rate of 100 % in 9 instances. SBHS, for its part, produced the lowest performance with a success rate of 100 % in only 8 instances, and 98 %, and 96 % in the other instances.

The relatively low success rate in MDSFL can be explained by the fact that after one iteration of the algorithm, approximately 40 % of the population mutates. This mutation is done in order to provide higher diversity. However, due to the small size of the problems, this operation has a negative impact [1]. In summary, the results described in Table 3 demonstrate that the best meta-heuristics are BFSP and SLC, with similar results; these are followed by MDSFL, with SBHS taking last place.

The following is a summary of the results obtained for the 6 experimentation instances with 100 and 200 dimensions and 3 types of complexity. These results, shown in Table 4, were obtained by executing the algorithms separately 30 times. The optimal shown in this table corresponds to the solution found (this is not necessarily the global optimum) using the algorithm called Combo [11], which is based on dynamic programming and tighter upper and lower bounds.

Table 4 presents in addition to the data in Table 3, the average execution time (Mean), as well as the standard deviation of the execution time (Std) of 30 independent executions of the algorithms. Furthermore, Table 4 shows information on the execution of the MDSL and BFSP algorithms with different population sizes - for the first algorithm (MDSFL) the number of frogs, and for the second algorithm, the number of capture points. The latter was done in order to evaluate the impact of the initial exploration in solving each problem.

Table 4 also shows that BFSP, with N = 400 and N = 60, finds the global optimum in all instances. On the other hand, MDSFL with P = 400 and P = 60 finds the global optimum only in 4 instances. Regarding effectiveness, BFSP is better than other

Table 3. Results obtained for test instances of 0/1 knapsack problems

n	w_{max}	Optimum	Algorithm	SR	Best	Worst	Median	Mean	Std
10	269	295	**BFSP**	**1**	**295**	**295**	**295**	**295**	**0**
			MDSFL	0,66	295	294	295	294,66	0.4737
			SBHS	**1**	**295**	**295**	**295**	**295**	**0**
			SLC	1	295	295	295	295	0
20	878	1024	**BFSP**	**1**	**1024**	**1024**	**1024**	**1024**	**0**
			MDSFL	**1**	**1024**	**1024**	**1024**	**1024**	**0**
			SBHS	0,98	1024	1018	1024	1023,88	0,84
			SLC	1	1024	1024	1024	1024	0
4	20	35	**BFSP**	**1**	**35**	**35**	**35**	**35**	**0**
			MDSFL	**1**	**35**	**35**	**35**	**35**	**0**
			SBHS	**1**	**35**	**35**	**35**	**35**	**0**
			SLC	1	35	35	35	35	0
4	11	23	**BFSP**	**1**	**23**	**23**	**23**	**23**	**0**
			MDSFL	**1**	**23**	**23**	**23**	**23**	**0**
			SBHS	**1**	**23**	**23**	**23**	**23**	**0**
			SLC	1	23	23	23	23	0
15	375	481,069	**BFSP**	**1**	**481,069**	**481,069**	**481,069**	**481,069**	**0**
			MDSFL	**1**	**481,069**	**481,069**	**481,069**	**481,069**	**0**
			SBHS	**1**	**481,069**	**481,069**	**481,069**	**481,069**	**0**
			SLC	1	481,069	481,069	481,069	481,069	0
10	60	52	**BFSP**	**1**	**52**	**52**	**52**	**52**	**0**
			MDSFL	**1**	**52**	**52**	**52**	**52**	**0**
			SBHS	**1**	**52**	**52**	**52**	**52**	**0**
			SLC	1	52	52	52	52	0
7	50	107	**BFSP**	**1**	**107**	**107**	**107**	**107**	**0**
			MDSFL	**1**	**107**	**107**	**107**	**107**	**0**
			SBHS	**1**	**107**	**107**	**107**	**107**	**0**
			SLC	0,98	107	105	107	106,96	0,28
23	10000	9767	**BFSP**	**1**	**9767**	**9767**	**9767**	**9767**	**0**
			MDSFL	**1**	**9767**	**9767**	**9767**	**9767**	**0**
			SBHS	**1**	**9767**	**9767**	**9767**	**9767**	**0**
			SLC	1	9767	9767	9767	9767	0
5	80	130	**BFSP**	**1**	**130**	**130**	**130**	**130**	**0**
			MDSFL	**1**	**130**	**130**	**130**	**130**	**0**
			SBHS	**1**	**130**	**130**	**130**	**130**	**0**
			SLC	1	130	130	130	130	0
20	879	1025	**BFSP**	**1**	**1025**	**1025**	**1025**	**1025**	**0**
			MDSFL	**1**	**1025**	**1025**	**1025**	**1025**	**0**
			SBHS	0,96	1025	1019	1025	1024,76	1,1758
			SLC	1	1025	1025	1025	1025	1

Table 4. Results obtained for experimentation instances of 0/1 knapsack problems

n	w_{max}	Algorithm	Global optima					Total time	
			SR	Best	Worst	Mean	Std	Mean	Std
100	995	**BFSP (400)**	**1**	**9147**	**9147**	**9147**	**0**	**0,0076**	**0,0054**
		BFSP (60)	**1**	**9147**	**9147**	**9147**	**0**	**0,0048**	**0,0048**
		MDSFL (400)	**1**	**9147**	**9147**	**9147**	**0**	**0,0551**	**0,0341**
		MDSFL (60)	**1**	**9147**	**9147**	**9147**	**0**	**0,6993**	**1,46**
		SBHS	0,9333	9147	8900	9131,5	58,1164	13,9198	35,1836
		SLC	1	9147	9147	9147	0	0,6354	0,3689
200	1008	**BFSP (400)**	**1**	**11238**	**11238**	**11238**	**0**	**0,0142**	**0,0088**
		BFSP (60)	**1**	**11238**	**11238**	**11238**	**0**	**0,0071**	**0,0045**
		MDSFL (400)	0,9667	11238	11227	11237,63	1,9746	4,1958	21,4866
		MDSFL (60)	0,7667	11238	11227	11235,43	4,6525	34,7069	50,1269
		SBHS	0,6	11238	10900	11185,97	90,8436	52,9280	56,915
		SLC	1	11238	11238	11238	0	3,241	2,9058
100	995	**BFSP (400)**	**1**	**1514**	**1514**	**1514**	**0**	**0,0519**	**0,0097**
		BFSP (60)	**1**	**1514**	**1514**	**1514**	**0**	**0,0161**	**0,0141**
		MDSFL (400)	**1**	**1514**	**1514**	**1514**	**0**	**0,0416**	**0,0102**
		MDSFL (60)	**1**	**1514**	**1514**	**1514**	**0**	**0,0433**	**0,0875**
		SBHS	0,1	1514	1481	1505,73	10,3921	107,9252	35,9577
		SLC	0,9333	1514	1501	1513,13	3,2428	19,6362	29,7198
200	1008	**BFSP (400)**	**1**	**1634**	**1634**	**1634**	**0**	**0.0136**	**0,0129**
		BFSP (60)	**1**	**1634**	**1634**	**1634**	**0**	**0,0234**	**0,0449**
		MDSFL (400)	**1**	**1634**	**1634**	**1634**	**0**	**0,0834**	**0,0694**
		MDSFL (60)	**1**	**1634**	**1634**	**1634**	**0**	**0,1414**	**0,2565**
		SBHS	0,7667	1634	1604	1630,63	7,2777	28,1271	50,6354
		SLC	0,1333	1634	1590	1619,53	8,7587	113,6445	21,5741
100	997	**BFSP (400)**	**1**	**2397**	**2397**	**2397**	**0**	**0,1251**	**0,413**
		BFSP (60)	**1**	**2397**	**2397**	**2397**	**0**	**1,5784**	**2,4347**
		MDSFL (400)	0,8	2397	2396	2396,8	0,4	0,0481	47,9396
		MDSFL (60)	0,5	2397	2396	2396,5	0,5	59,9563	59,9439
		SBHS	0,9333	2397	2381	2396,23	3,095	8,7503	29,7425
		SLC	0,4	2397	2297	2356,8	48,83	84,6571	47,0546
200	997	**BFSP (400)**	**1**	**2697**	**2697**	**2697**	**0**	**0,0079**	**0,006**
		BFSP (60)	**1**	**2697**	**2697**	**2697**	**0**	**0,0031**	**0,0023**
		MDSFL (400)	**1**	**2697**	**2697**	**2697**	**0**	**0,045**	**0,0373**
		MDSFL (60)	**1**	**2697**	**2697**	**2697**	**0**	**0,9284**	**3,1125**
		SBHS	**1**	**2697**	**2697**	**2697**	**0**	**0,4610**	**0,6365**
		SLC	0,6667	2697	2597	2683,47	33,9173	53,3342	48,8563

meta-heuristics at solving these problems. The average success rates for SBHS and SLC in all instances are 72 % and 68 % respectively. These rates are low compared with the rates for BFSP and MDSFL. It can be concluded that the best meta-heuristic is BFSP, followed by MDSFL, SBHS and SLC.

Regarding execution time, MDSFL obtained good results. However, its speed and effectiveness are closely related to the size of the initial exploration (P = 400). When this number decreases, its success rate is also reduced. This indicates that the evolution process (generation of new solutions) requires improvement. It can also be appreciated that BFSP obtains the best results and is scalable and very stable even when the problem complexity (the number of items and knapsack capacity) is increased. Execution time values are affected directly by algorithm effectiveness; this is due to the fact that if the algorithm does not find the global optima, the whole maximum time set for its execution is spent during execution of the algorithm.

In addition to the two aforementioned comparison criteria, one last comparison criterion was analyzed: the number of fitness function evaluations (FFE). Although the results are not displayed, MDSFL showed an increase in FFE as the number of frogs decreases. In the case of BFSP, the number of FFE is lower than other three algorithms. Finally, using the number of FFE criteria, the best algorithm is BFSP followed by MDSFL, SLC and SBHS.

5 Conclusions and Future Work

This paper presented a binary version of the Fisherman Search Procedure (BFSP) adapted for solving 0/1 knapsack problems and with an initial parameter tuning process. The following modifications were introduced to the original version (FSP): (i) continuous representation was changed to a binary representation, (ii) a reinterpretation of the width coefficient c parameter was carried out in order to support binary operations that would allow exploitation and exploration, (iii) the pbest parameter was added to determine the probability of using HUX crossover and to exploit the neighborhood of the best-found solution (gbest), thus using a behavior similar to the PSO approach, and finally, (iv) the parameter pdiversity was added to mutate the capture point and to escape from local optima.

Experimental results using success rate in achieving the global optimum in the 10 test instances indicate that BFSP and SLC are the best algorithms and that these algorithms present similar behavior. Experimentation also makes it possible to deduce that these problem instances are easy to solve, and the algorithms present a relatively high success rate. Experimental results using success rate in finding the global optimum and maximum execution time in the 6 experimentation instances indicate that BFSP followed by MDSFL are the best meta-heuristics. Equally, the results demonstrate that when different population sizes (capture points or frogs) are used, the BFSP algorithm performs a better search process in the solution space and although it takes longer there is a higher probability that this algorithm finds the optimum value.

As future work, the research group visualizes conducting a detailed process of parameter tuning for the BFSP algorithm. Equally, the comparison of meta-heuristics selected for high-dimensional instances of the 0/1 knapsack problem (500, 1000, 2000, 3000, 5000 and 10000 dimensions) will be continued. This comparison will include a non-parametric statistical test (Friedman and Wilcoxon) to analyze the results and define their statistical significance. Finally, parallel versions (based on CUDA) of all studied meta-heuristics will be compared.

References

1. Bhattacharjee, K.K., Sarmah, S.P.: Shuffled frog leaping algorithm and its application to 0/1 knapsack problem. Appl. Soft Comput. **19**, 252–263 (2014)
2. Eusuff, M., Lansey, K., Pasha, F.: Shuffled frog-leaping algorithm: a memetic meta-heuristic for discrete optimization. Eng. Optim. **38**, 129–154 (2006)
3. Pan, Q.K., Wang, L., Gao, L., Li, J.: An effective shuffled frog-leaping algorithm for lot-streaming flow shop scheduling problem. Int. J. Adv. Manufact. Technol. **52**, 699–713 (2011)
4. Kong, X., Gao, L., Ouyang, H., Li, S.: A simplified binary harmony search algorithm for large scale 0–1 knapsack problems. Expert Syst. Appl. **42**, 5337–5355 (2015)
5. Wang, L., Yang, R., Xu, Y., Niu, Q., Pardalos, P.M., Fei, M.: An improved adaptive binary harmony search algorithm. Inf. Sci. **232**, 58–87 (2013)
6. Wan-li, X., Mei-qing, A., Yin-zhen, L., Rui-chun, H., Jing-fang, Z.: A novel discrete global-best harmony search algorithm for solving 0-1 knapsack problems. Discrete Dyn. Nat. Soc. **2014**, 12 (2014)
7. Moosavian, N., Roodsari, B.K.: Soccer league competition algorithm: a novel meta-heuristic algorithm for optimal design of water distribution networks. Swarm Evol. Comput. **17**, 14–24 (2014)
8. Moosavian, N.: Soccer league competition algorithm for solving knapsack problems. Swarm Evol. Comput. **20**, 14–22 (2015)
9. Alejo-Machado, O.J., Fernández-Luna, J.M., Huete, J.F., Morales, E.R.C.: Fisherman search procedure. Prog. Artif. Intell. **2**, 193–203 (2014)
10. Eshelman, L.J.: The CHC adaptive search algorithm: how to have safe search when engaging in nontraditional genetic recombination. In: Rawlins, G.J.E. (ed.) Foundations of Genetic Algorithms, pp. 265–283. Morgan Kaufmann Publishers, San Mateo (1991). ISBN: 1-55860-170-8
11. Pisinger, D.: Where are the hard knapsack problems? Comput. Oper. Res. **32**, 2271–2284 (2005)

Estimating Attraction Basin Sizes

Leticia Hernando[1(✉)], Alexander Mendiburu[1], and Jose A. Lozano[1,2]

[1] Intelligent Systems Group, University of the Basque Country (UPV/EHU),
Donostia 20018, Spain
{leticia.hernando,alexander.mendiburu,ja.lozano}@ehu.eus
[2] Basque Center for Applied Mathematics (BCAM), Bilbao 48009, Spain

Abstract. The performance of local search algorithms is influenced by the properties that the neighborhood imposes on the search space. Among these properties, the number of local optima has been traditionally considered as a complexity measure of the instance, and different methods for its estimation have been developed. The accuracy of these estimators depends on properties such as the relative attraction basin sizes. As calculating the exact attraction basin sizes becomes unaffordable for moderate problem sizes, their estimations are required. The lack of techniques achieving this purpose encourages us to propose two methods that estimate the attraction basin size of a given local optimum. The first method takes uniformly at random solutions from the whole search space, while the second one takes into account the structure defined by the neighborhood. They are tested on different instances of problems in the permutation space, considering the swap and the adjacent swap neighborhoods.

1 Introduction

Local search algorithms have been proved as efficient methods for solving hard permutation-based COPs. These methods rely on a neighborhood structure over the search space. The properties of this neighborhood can cause dramatic differences in the performance of those local search methods [9,10,12]. Thus, the same local search algorithm can produce different results in the same instance depending on the neighborhood chosen, because different neighborhoods draw different shapes (ruggedness) in the landscapes.

One of the features imposed by the neighborhood is the number of local optima. This number of local optima has commonly been taken as a complexity measure of an instance when solving it with a local search algorithm, and many authors have tried to estimate it [1–6]. One of the results found when developing these techniques for predicting the number of local optima was that their accuracy is highly affected by the variance of the attraction basin sizes of the local optima. In general, the more uniform the attraction basin sizes are, the better the prediction. However, there are methods that are able to provide good estimations for instances where the variance of the attraction basin sizes is extremely large [6]. Looking at these methods, we can observe that their estimations rely

O. Luaces et al. (Eds.): CAEPIA 2016, LNAI 9868, pp. 458–467, 2016.
DOI: 10.1007/978-3-319-44636-3_43

on the concept of sample coverage, that is, the sum of the relative sizes of the attraction basins of the local optima observed in the sample. Inspired by this finding, our interest lies in finding methods that calculate the attraction basin size of any given local optimum. Unfortunately, in the literature there is a lack of studies fulfilling this aim.

The most intuitive way of obtaining the exact attraction basin of a local optimum would be by exhaustively applying the local search algorithm starting from each solution of the search space, and taking those solutions that finish at such local optimum. Of course, this is useless because if we were able to perform this process, we would be able to solve the optimization problem. Hence, another method for calculating the attraction basin of a local optimum is by considering, as the starting point, this local optimum. Then, applying a recursive procedure that checks at each time whether the neighbors of the current solution belong to the attraction basin. This procedure finishes when there are no more possible solutions to add to the attraction basin. In this last method we do not need to evaluate all the solutions of the search space. However, in general, the number of solutions to evaluate grows exponentially with respect to the problem size. Therefore, for large problem sizes, there could be local optima for which it becomes computationally intractable to exactly calculate their attraction basins.

The fact that there is no known method that calculates, in polynomial time, the exact attraction basins of the local optima, or at least, their sizes, leads us to focus on methods that estimate the attraction basin sizes. An easy and simple method for estimating the sizes of the attraction basins consists of applying a local search to a sample of solutions, estimating each proportion of the size of the attraction basin of the local optima as the proportion of times that it has been reached in the sample [7,11]. However, this method has a major weakness: it is supposed that there are no more local optima in the search space except just those encountered in the sample. Of course, in general, this is not true.

Given a local optimum, we propose in this paper two methods for estimating its attraction basin size. Both methods start from the local optimum for which we want to estimate the attraction basin size. The first method consists of taking solutions uniformly at random from the whole search space. In the second method, the search space is divided in different subsets, which correspond to the sets of permutations at different distances. Three different sample strategies are used to sample these subsets. The way of choosing the sample sizes for the different chunks of the search space could help in the estimation, as well as could disorientate it, because, once chosen the sample strategy, the performance of this proposal will depend on the landscape properties. Considering the adjacent swap and swap neighborhoods, we test the methods on instances of two permutation-based combinatorial optimization problems: Permutation Flowshop Scheduling Problem (PFSP) and Linear Ordering Problem (LOP).

The rest of the paper is organized as follows. In Sect. 2, we explain in detail both methods and, in Sect. 3, we compare their accuracy when they are applied to the instances using the different neighborhoods. Finally, in Sect. 4, we review the main conclusions obtained.

2   Methods for Estimating the Attraction Basin Sizes

A **neighborhood** $\mathcal{N}$ in a search space Ω is a mapping that assigns to each solution $\pi \in \Omega$ a set of neighboring solutions $\mathcal{N}(\pi)$. Particularly, we work with instances where Ω is the space of permutations of size n, so $|\Omega| = n!$. Two examples of neighborhoods in the space of permutations are the adjacent swap and the swap operators. The **adjacent swap neighborhood** considers two neighboring solutions if one is generated by swapping two adjacent elements of the other. While two solutions are neighbors under the **swap neighborhood** if one is the result of swapping any two elements of the other, not necessarily adjacent.

Supposing a minimization problem, a solution $\pi^* \in \Omega$ is a **local optimum** if $f(\pi^*) \leq f(\pi)$, $\forall \pi \in \mathcal{N}(\pi^*)$. Each local optimum π^* has associated its attraction basin $\mathcal{B}(\pi^*)$, that is, the set composed of all the solutions that, after applying a local search algorithm starting with those solutions, finishes in π^*. Particularly, we use a deterministic best-improvement local search (the steps followed by this algorithm are specified in Algorithm 1). Denoting by $\mathcal{H}$ the operator that associates to each solution π the local optimum π^* obtained after applying the algorithm, we can formally define the **attraction basin of a local optimum** as: $\mathcal{B}(\pi^*) = \{\pi \in \Omega \mid \mathcal{H}(\pi) = \pi^*\}$. Notice that the neighbors are evaluated in a specific order, so that, in the case of two neighbors having the same function value, the algorithm will always choose that which was encountered first (the neighbor that is the result of swapping the smallest items $\pi(i)$ and $\pi(j)$).

We propose two estimators to calculate the size of the attraction basin of a given local optimum π^*. This estimation will be denoted by $|\hat{\mathcal{B}}(\pi^*)|$.

Algorithm 1. Deterministic best-improvement local search algorithm

---
1: Choose an initial solution $\pi \in \Omega$
2: **repeat**
3:     $\pi^* = \pi$
4:     **for** $i = 1 \rightarrow |N(\pi^*)|$ **do**
5:         Choose $\sigma_i \in N(\pi^*)$
6:         **if** $f(\sigma_i) < f(\pi)$ **then**
7:             $\pi = \sigma_i$
8:         **end if**
9:     **end for**
10: **until** $\pi = \pi^*$

2.1   Uniformly at Random Method (UM)

Given a local optimum π^*, we sample solutions uniformly at random from the search space counting those that belong to its attraction basin. That is, we take a sample of size M of random initial solutions: $S = \{\pi_1, \pi_2, \ldots, \pi_M\} \subseteq \Omega$. The number of those solutions that belong to the attraction basin of π^* divided by the total number of solutions evaluated (M) is the estimated proportion of the attraction basin size of π^* over the size of the search space $|\Omega|$. So, the attraction basin size of π^* is this proportion multiplied by the size of the search space $(n!)$. In Algorithm 2, we specify these steps to follow.

Algorithm 2. Uniformly at random Method (UM) to estimate the size of the attraction basin of a local optimum π^*

1: Input: M
2: Initialize $InAB = 0$
3: **for** $i = 1 \rightarrow M$ **do**
4:     take a random permutation $\pi_i \in \Omega$
5:     $\sigma = \mathcal{H}(\pi_i)$
6:     **if** $\sigma == \pi^*$ **then**
7:         $InAB + +$
8:     **end if**
9: **end for**
10: $|\hat{\mathcal{B}}(\pi^*)| = \frac{InAB}{M} \cdot n!$
11: Output: $|\hat{\mathcal{B}}(\pi^*)|$

2.2 Distance-Based Method (DM)

In this second proposal, we do not take a random sample directly from the whole search space Ω. Instead, given a local optimum π^*, we choose the solutions from different subsets of Ω related to π^*. That is, we consider the different subsets $D_i = \{\pi_1^i, \pi_2^i, \ldots, \pi_{|D_i|}^i\} \subseteq \Omega$ that are composed of those solutions at distance i from the local optimum π^*. We say that two permutations π_1 and π_2 are at distance i if, starting from π_1, and moving from neighboring to neighboring solutions, the length of the smallest path until reaching π_2 is i. Particularly, two neighboring permutations are at distance one.

Notice that any permutation in $\Omega \setminus \{\pi^*\}$ should belong to one, and just one, of these subsets D_i. That is:

$$\text{(i)}\ \ D_i \cap D_j = \emptyset, \forall i \neq j.$$
$$\text{(ii)}\ \ \bigcup_i D_i \cup \{\pi^*\} = \Omega.$$

So, given the local optimum π^*, we take samples $S_1, S_2, \ldots$, of uniformly at random solutions at distances $1, 2, \ldots$, respectively, from π^*:

$$S_1 = \{\pi_1^1, \pi_2^1, \ldots, \pi_{M_1}^1\} \subseteq D_1;\ \ S_2 = \{\pi_1^2, \pi_2^2, \ldots, \pi_{M_2}^2\} \subseteq D_2;\ \cdots$$

We use the methods described in [8] to obtain these uniformly at random solutions π_j^i for the different distances. In order to estimate the attraction basin size of π^*, we proceed in a similar way to the previous method but, we work with the different subsets D_i independently. That is, we record the number of solutions that belong to the attraction basin of π^* in each sample set S_i, divided by the sample size considered for each distance M_i, and multiplied by the total number of permutations that exist in each subset D_i. Therefore, the sum of these quantities obtained for each distance plus one (π^* itself is in its attraction basin and has not been considered in any subset) is the resultant attraction basin size of the local optimum π^*. This process is detailed in Algorithm 3, where $MaxDist$ denotes the maximum distance between two permutations and $|D_{dist}|$ refers to the number of permutations at distance $dist$. Both the maximum distance and the number of permutations at a given distance depend on the problem size and the neighborhood used. The input parameter of the algorithm is $\mathbf{M} = \{M_1, \ldots, M_{MaxDist}\}$, that is, we need to set in advance the sample size used at each distance $dist$. On the one hand, different subsets D_i have different sizes, which could lead us to change the sample size taking values proportional to $|D_i|$. On the other hand, the closer a permutation to the optimum, the more probable it belongs to its attraction basin. Thus, we could consider the possibility of taking more random solutions in the subsets D_i than D_j, with $i < j$, or even, to stop taking solutions from a certain distance on.

Algorithm 3. Distance-based Method (DM) to estimate the size of the attraction basin of a local optimum π^*.

1: Input: $\mathbf{M} = \{M_1, \ldots, M_{MaxDist}\}$
2: $|\hat{\mathcal{B}}(\pi^*)| = 1$
3: **for** $dist = 1 \to MaxDist$ **do**
4:     Initialize $InAB = 0$
5:     **for** $j = 1 \to M_{dist}$ **do**
6:         take a random permutation $\sigma \in D_{dist}$
7:         $\pi = \mathcal{H}(\sigma)$
8:         **if** $\pi == \pi^*$ **then**
9:             $InAB + +$
10:        **end if**
11:    **end for**
12:    $|\hat{\mathcal{B}}(\pi^*)| = |\hat{\mathcal{B}}(\pi^*)| + \frac{InAB}{M_{dist}} \cdot |D_{dist}|$
13: **end for**
14: Output: $|\hat{\mathcal{B}}(\pi^*)|$

---

3   Experiments

We analyze and compare the two proposed methods for estimating the sizes of the attraction basins of the local optima for instances of different problems and considering different neighborhoods. We work with instances of the PFSP and the LOP, and we focus on the adjacent swap and swap neighborhoods. For the PFSP we consider 5 instances with 10 jobs and 5 machines, obtained from the well-known benchmark proposed by Taillard. The 5 instances of the LOP have been obtained from the xLOLIB benchmark, and the matrix size considered is 10×10. So, in both problems the size of the search space is 10!. Notice that the problem size is quite small. The reason is that, in order to measure the accuracy of the methods, we calculate the exact attraction basin size of each of the local optima of the instances, and thus, working with large permutation sizes is computationally unaffordable. Regarding the parameters of the algorithms, we specify the sample sizes used. For the first method (UM) we choose samples of sizes: $M = \{1125, 2250, 4500\}$. For the second method (DM), we need to fix different sample sizes M_i according to the distance. In order to study different possibilities, for the second method we consider three different cases:

1. **Equal Sample sizes for each distance (ES):** $M_i = M_j, \forall i \neq j$.
2. **Sample sizes Proportional to the number of permutations at each distance (SP):** $M_i \propto |D_i|$.
3. **Sample sizes Decreasing as the distance increases (SD):** $M_i \propto \frac{1}{i}$, and $M_i = 0, i > MaxDist/2$.

We should use the same (or almost similar) total sample size, when comparing the second method (DM) with the first one (UM). So, we need to choose, in this case, M_i such that

$$M \approx \sum_{i=1}^{MaxDist} M_i \approx \begin{cases} 1125 \\ 2250 \\ 4500 \end{cases} \qquad (1)$$

We show in Table 1 the sample sizes used at each distance according to the neighborhood, in order to fulfill Eq. (1). In Table 2, the number of solutions of size 10 at each distance from a given permutation for the adjacent swap and swap neighborhoods is facilitated. Both algorithms UM and DM are applied 10 times to each local optimum for each sample size, and the average estimations of the attraction basin sizes are recorded. From now on, instead of considering just two methods, we will refer to four: UM, DM-ES, DM-SP and DM-SD.

Table 1. Sample sizes used in the methods.

	ADJACENT SWAP			SWAP		
UM	DM-ES	DM-SP	DM-SD ($i \leq 22$)	DM-ES	DM-SP	DM-SD ($i \leq 4$)
1125	25	$\frac{|D_i|}{3300}$	$\lceil \frac{302}{i} \rceil$	125	$\frac{|D_i|}{3240}$	$\lceil \frac{540}{i} \rceil$
2250	50	$\frac{|D_i|}{1630}$	$\lceil \frac{608}{i} \rceil$	250	$\frac{|D_i|}{1616}$	$\lceil \frac{1080}{i} \rceil$
4500	100	$\frac{|D_i|}{811}$	$\lceil \frac{1217}{i} \rceil$	500	$\frac{|D_i|}{807}$	$\lceil \frac{2160}{i} \rceil$

In Table 3, the average relative error (in absolute value), $\frac{||\hat{\mathcal{B}}(\pi^*)| - |\mathcal{B}(\pi^*)||}{|\mathcal{B}(\pi^*)|}$, and the variance (in brackets) given by each method for all the local optima of each instance from the 10 repetitions, are reported, for the UM, the DM-ES, the DM-SP and the DM-SD, and according to the problem and neighborhood considered. As we can appreciate, when estimating the attraction basin sizes, there is not a best overall method. We observe that, clearly, on average terms, the method

Table 2. Number of permutations of size 10 at different distances from a given solution.

ADJACENT SWAP										SWAP	
dist	#perms	dist	#perms	dist	#perms	dist	# perms	dist	# perms	dist	# perms
1	9	10	21670	19	211089	28	162337	37	8095	1	45
2	44	11	32683	20	230131	29	135853	38	4489	2	870
3	155	12	47043	21	243694	30	110010	39	2298	3	9450
4	440	13	64889	22	250749	31	86054	40	1068	4	63273
5	1068	14	86054	23	250749	32	64889	41	440	5	269325
6	2298	15	110010	24	243694	33	47043	42	155	6	723680
7	4489	16	135853	25	230131	34	32683	43	44	7	1172700
8	8095	17	162337	26	211089	35	21670	44	9	8	1026576
9	13640	18	187959	27	187959	36	13640	45	1	9	362880

that provides the best results for the instances of the PFSP considering the adjacent swap neighborhood is DM-SD, where we find the lowest errors and very small variances. For the instances of the LOP considering the adjacent swap neighborhood, the DM-SD performs well, but we also find good results for the DM-ES. For both problems, when using the swap neighborhood, the results given by DM-SD are really bad (high errors and variances). This is because the DM-SD takes a lower number of solutions as the distance to the local optima increases, and it stops taking solutions at $MaxDist/2$. The bad performance of this method indicates that, when using the swap neighborhood, the attraction basins of the local optima are composed by a high number of solutions that are far from them, but this does not happen when using the adjacent swap. Of course, even if we increase the sample size with this method, as we stop considering solutions at certain distance, for both neighborhoods we do not obtain better results. The best method on average for almost all instances for the swap is DM-ES. So, for this neighborhood it seems convenient to take the same number of solutions at different distances. As a general rule, the higher the sample size the lower the average relative errors and variances. Except for DM-SD with the swap neighborhood, that the results are almost similar for all sample sizes.

We carry out a statistical analysis to compare the estimations obtained for the different methods. A nonparametric Friedman's test with level of significance $\alpha = 0.05$ is used to test if there are statistical significant differences between the estimations provided by the 4 methods in the different scenarios (according to problem and neighborhood). As we find statistical differences in all the cases, we proceed with a post-hoc test which carries out all pairwise comparisons. Particularly, we use the Holm's procedure fixing the level of significance to $\alpha = 0.05$. In the case of the PFSP with the adjacent swap neighborhood, we find that the best method is the DM-SD with significant differences. When using the swap neighborhood, the best method is the DM-ES but with no significant differences with the DM-SP. For the LOP and the adjacent swap, the best methods are the DM-SD and the DM-ES with no significant differences, while for the swap

Table 3. Average relative errors (and variances) of the attraction basin sizes of the local optima.

		M = 1125				M = 2250				M = 4500			
		UM	DM-ES	DM-SP	DM-SD	UM	DM-ES	DM-SP	DM-SD	UM	DM-ES	DM-SP	DM-SD
PFSP ADJACENT S.	1	1.16(5.13)	0.19(0.03)	0.56(0.33)	**0.16(0.03)**	0.90(1.77)	0.14(0.02)	0.49(0.25)	**0.12(0.02)**	0.75(1.08)	0.10(0.01)	0.40(0.14)	**0.09(0.01)**
	2	1.30(4.61)	0.15(0.02)	0.55(0.30)	**0.12(0.01)**	1.06(2.16)	0.11(0.01)	0.50(0.22)	**0.09(0.01)**	0.84(1.06)	0.11(0.01)	0.43(0.14)	**0.07(0.00)**
	3	1.33(5.26)	0.14(0.01)	0.51(0.25)	**0.10(0.01)**	1.11(2.95)	0.10(0.01)	0.47(0.21)	**0.08(0.00)**	0.83(1.27)	0.08(0.00)	0.42 (0.14)	**0.07 (0.00)**
	4	1.49(8.77)	0.14(0.02)	0.54(0.31)	**0.11(0.01)**	1.17(3.05)	0.11(0.01)	0.51(0.24)	**0.08(0.01)**	1.02(2.27)	0.12(0.01)	0.45(0.15)	**0.07(0.00)**
	5	0.60(0.46)	0.24(0.05)	0.46(0.22)	**0.23(0.04)**	0.45(0.24)	0.18(0.03)	0.35(0.13)	**0.17(0.03)**	0.34(0.15)	**0.13(0.01)**	0.26(0.07)	**0.13(0.01)**
SWAP	1	0.08(0.01)	**0.05(0.00)**	0.07(0.00)	0.43(0.05)	0.06(0.01)	**0.04(0.00)**	0.05(0.01)	0.43(0.05)	**0.03(0.00)**	**0.03(0.00)**	0.04(0.00)	0.42(0.05)
	2	0.30(0.13)	**0.13(0.02)**	0.25(0.10)	0.24(0.03)	0.24(0.11)	**0.09(0.01)**	0.20(0.09)	0.21(0.02)	0.19(0.06)	**0.07(0.00)**	0.14(0.03)	0.21(0.02)
	3	0.22(0.10)	**0.10(0.01)**	0.17(0.03)	0.24(0.03)	0.15(0.05)	**0.08(0.00)**	0.13(0.02)	0.25(0.03)	0.10(0.01)	**0.05(0.00)**	0.10(0.02)	0.23(0.03)
	4	0.40(0.52)	**0.13(0.01)**	0.29(0.11)	0.21(0.02)	0.22(0.12)	**0.10(0.01)**	0.20(0.06)	0.18(0.02)	0.19(0.07)	**0.07(0.00)**	0.15(0.04)	0.17(0.02)
	5	**0.04(0.00)**	0.05(0.00)	0.05(0.00)	0.55(0.05)	0.03(0.00)	0.03(0.00)	**0.02(0.00)**	0.54(0.05)	**0.02(0.00)**	0.03(0.00)	0.02(0.00)	0.55(0.05)
LOP ADJACENT S.	1	0.93(2.51)	0.21(0.03)	0.56(0.44)	**0.18(0.03)**	0.79(1.81)	0.15(0.02)	0.48(0.25)	**0.13(0.01)**	0.55(0.77)	0.11(0.01)	0.37(0.14)	**0.10(0.01)**
	2	1.37(10.99)	0.20(0.03)	0.65(0.48)	**0.16(0.02)**	1.02(2.29)	0.15(0.02)	0.57(0.29)	**0.12(0.01)**	0.79(1.36)	0.11(0.01)	0.48(0.22)	**0.10(0.01)**
	3	1.64(28.06)	0.24(0.05)	0.73(0.80)	**0.20(0.04)**	1.50(16.84)	0.18(0.03)	0.68(0.57)	**0.16(0.02)**	1.26(6.72)	0.15(0.01)	0.61(0.36)	**0.14(0.01)**
	4	0.44(0.19)	**0.26(0.09)**	0.36(0.15)	0.27(0.07)	0.34(0.21)	**0.20(0.04)**	0.27(0.12)	**0.20(0.04)**	0.26(0.11)	**0.13(0.01)**	0.21(0.08)	**0.13(0.01)**
	5	0.33(0.13)	**0.23(0.05)**	0.26(0.10)	0.27(0.07)	0.19(0.05)	**0.17(0.04)**	0.19(0.04)	0.19(0.03)	0.14(0.02)	**0.11(0.01)**	0.14(0.03)	0.13(0.02)
SWAP	1	0.18(0.03)	**0.10(0.01)**	0.15(0.03)	0.33(0.07)	0.13(0.03)	**0.09(0.01)**	0.12(0.02)	0.32(0.07)	0.11(0.01)	**0.05(0.00)**	0.09(0.01)	0.31(0.07)
	2	0.32(0.91)	**0.12(0.02)**	0.23(0.09)	0.33(0.05)	0.16(0.05)	**0.08(0.01)**	0.18(0.07)	0.30(0.04)	0.13(0.06)	**0.06(0.00)**	0.12(0.02)	0.29(0.04)
	3	0.43(0.27)	**0.19(0.03)**	0.33(0.12)	0.23(0.02)	0.32(0.13)	**0.13(0.01)**	0.25(0.07)	0.20(0.02)	0.19(0.04)	**0.09(0.01)**	0.18(0.04)	0.17(0.02)
	4	**0.02(0.00)**	0.03(0.00)	0.05(0.01)	0.60(0.03)	**0.04(0.00)**	**0.04(0.00)**	**0.04(0.00)**	0.60(0.03)	0.02(0.00)	0.02(0.00)	**0.01(0.00)**	0.59(0.04)
	5	**0.06(0.00)**	0.09(0.01)	0.10(0.02)	0.49(0.04)	**0.05(0.00)**	0.06(0.00)	0.07(0.01)	0.47(0.05)	**0.04(0.00)**	**0.04(0.00)**	0.05(0.01)	0.46(0.05)

the UM, the DM-ES and the DM-SP are the best methods without significant differences among them. Of course, for both problems using the swap, the worst performing one is the DM-SD with significant differences.

4   Conclusions

The estimation of the attraction basin sizes of the local optima helps in the understanding of the landscapes and is a useful information when analyzing the complexity of the instances for local search algorithms. For example, the knowledge about the attraction basin sizes becomes essential for the prediction of the number of local optima. On the one hand, knowing the relative attraction basin sizes facilitates the choice of a suitable method for estimating the number of local optima. On the other hand, if we have information about the proportion of the search space occupied by the attraction basins of those local optima observed in a sample, we would know the proportion of the search space that has not yet been explored. Consequently, this would be a valuable information to estimate the number of not seen local optima.

We present two methods for estimating the attraction basin size of a given local optimum. In the first method proposed (UM), the proportion of the attraction basin size of the local optimum is estimated as the proportion of solutions of a random sample that belong to it. The second method (DM), which is more computationally demanding, consists of taking random solutions at different distances and estimating the total size considering the sum of the estimations of the sizes that are related to each distance. In the DM, the sample size taken at each distance is of high relevance. We notice differences in considering different ways of choosing the samples for different neighborhoods. First, we consider the case where, for each distance, the same sample size is taken (DM-ES). Then, we take samples of sizes proportional to the number of permutations that are at the different distances (DM-SP). Finally, the samples are chosen with sizes that decrease as the distance to the local optimum increases, and we stop taking solutions further than $MaxDist/2$ (DM-SD).

The main result observed is that for the swap neighborhood, the DM-SD provides bad estimations. We have concluded that this is due to the fact that, for this neighborhood, the attraction basins of the local optima must have a high number of solutions far from it. The methods perform similar for instances of both problems. However, we observe differences in the estimations provided for the different instances considering the same problem. Another important observation derived from this analysis is that the sample size does not have a high influence on the three versions of the DM, while it has to be taken into account if we use the UM. Of course, the higher the sample size considered in the UM, the more accurate the estimations. After observing the statistical analysis, we recommend the following:

- Working under the adjacent swap neighborhood, apply DM-SD
- Considering the swap neighborhood, use DM-ES or DM-SP

We plan to study the estimations provided by these methods considering other different neighborhoods. The performance of the methods, of course, depends on some properties of the landscapes, above all, the distributions of the attraction basins all along the search space. So, we could think of other ways of sampling according to the different distances. This sampling way, should be designed focusing on the specific operator considered, as it is the most important aspect that influences the behavior of these methods. Thus, in order to obtain good results, it is essential to have knowledge beforehand about the properties of the landscape.

Acknowledgements. This work has been supported in part by the Saiotek and Research Groups 2013–2018 (IT-609-13) Programs (Basque Government) and in part by the Spanish Ministry of Science and Innovation under Grant TIN2013-41272P.

References

1. Albrecht, A., Lane, P., Steinhofel, K.: Combinatorial landscape analysis for k-SAT instances. In: Proceedings of IEEE Congress on Evolutionary Computation, pp. 2498–2504. IEEE Press, Hong Kong, June 2008
2. Albrecht, A., Lane, P., Steinhofel, K.: Analysis of local search landscapes for k-SAT instances. Math. Comput. Sci. **3**(4), 465–488 (2010)
3. Eremeev, A.V., Reeves, C.R.: Non-parametric estimation of properties of combinatorial landscapes. In: Cagnoni, S., Gottlieb, J., Hart, E., Middendorf, M., Raidl, G.R. (eds.) EvoIASP 2002, EvoWorkshops 2002, EvoSTIM 2002, EvoCOP 2002, and EvoPlan 2002. LNCS, vol. 2279, pp. 31–40. Springer, Heidelberg (2002)
4. Eremeev, A.V., Reeves, C.R.: On confidence intervals for the number of local optima. In: Raidl, G.R., et al. (eds.) EvoIASP 2003, EvoWorkshops 2003, EvoSTIM 2003, EvoROB/EvoRobot 2003, EvoCOP 2003, EvoBIO 2003, and EvoMUSART 2003. LNCS, vol. 2611, pp. 224–235. Springer, Heidelberg (2003)
5. Grundel, D., Krokhmal, P., Oliveira, C., Pardalos, P.: On the number of local minima for the multidimensional assignment problem. J. Comb. Optim. **13**(1), 1–18 (2007)
6. Hernando, L., Mendiburu, A., Lozano, J.A.: An evaluation of methods for estimating the number of local optima in combinatorial optimization problems. Evol. Comput. **21**(4), 625–658 (2013)
7. Hernando, L., Pascual, J.A., Mendiburu, A., Lozano, J.A.: A study on the complexity of TSP instances under the 2-exchange neighbor system. In: 2011 IEEE Symposium on Foundations of Computational Intelligence (FOCI), pp. 15–21, April 2011
8. Irurozki, E., Calvo, B., Lozano, J.A.: An R package for permutations, mallows and generalized mallows models. J. Stat. Softw. (2016)
9. Mattfeld, D.C., Bierwirth, C.: A search space analysis of the job shop scheduling problem. Ann. Oper. Res. **86**, 441–453 (1999)
10. Reeves, C.R., Eremeev, A.V.: Statistical analysis of local search landscapes. J. Oper. Res. Soc. **55**(7), 687–693 (2004). doi:10.1057/palgrave.jors.2601611
11. Tayarani-Najaran, M.H., Prügel-Bennett, A.: On the landscape of combinatorial optimization problems. IEEE Trans. Evol. Comput. **18**(3), 420–434 (2014)
12. Tomassini, M., Vérel, S., Ochoa, G.: Complex-network analysis of combinatorial spaces: the NK landscape case. Phys. Rev. E **78**(6), 66–114 (2008)

Multi-Objective Memetic Algorithm Based on NSGA-II and Simulated Annealing for Calibrating CORSIM Micro-Simulation Models of Vehicular Traffic Flow

Carlos Cobos[1($\boxtimes$)], Cristian Erazo[1], Julio Luna[1], Martha Mendoza[1], Carlos Gaviria[2], Cristian Arteaga[2], and Alexander Paz[2]

[1] Universidad del Cauca, Popayán, Colombia
{ccobos, camiloerazo, jcluna, mmendoza}@unicauca.edu.co
[2] University of Nevada, Las Vegas, USA
{cgaviria, carteaga, apaz}@unlv.edu

Abstract. This paper proposes a multi-objective memetic algorithm based on NSGA-II and Simulated Annealing (SA), NSGA-II-SA, for calibration of microscopic vehicular traffic flow simulation models. The NSGA-II algorithm performs a scan in the search space and obtains the Pareto front which is optimized locally with SA. The best solution of the obtained front is selected. Two CORSIM models were calibrated with the proposed NSGA-II-SA whose performance is compared with two alternative state-of-the-art algorithms, a single-objective genetic algorithm which uses simulated annealing (GASA) and a simultaneous perturbation stochastic approximation algorithm (SPSA). The results illustrate the superiority of the NSGA-II-SA algorithm in terms of both runtime and convergence.

Keywords: Multi-objective optimization · NSGA-II · Memetic algorithm · Pareto front · Simulated annealing

1 Introduction

Parameter identification is still a difficult task for microscopic vehicular traffic flow simulations [1] for reasons including: the parameters are not directly observable from common traffic data, data are not transferable to other situations (e.g. different places and times of day), and there are significant nonlinear and stochastic interdependencies among parameters and across model inputs. Hence, optimization models have been proposed for decades to determine adequate model parameters to represent the actual system as realistic as possible [2]. A significant challenge is to determine the combination of values, for selected parameters, that enables convergence and stability of the solution. Hence, simultaneous search for the values of all the selected parameters has been proposed by multiple authors. In addition, each parameter can have different ranges, which makes the calibration process very complicated and time-consuming. Optimization algorithms enable this simultaneous search and allow to define constraints to stablish boundary or any other type of conditions required by the problem [3]. In [4],

© Springer International Publishing Switzerland 2016
O. Luaces et al. (Eds.): CAEPIA 2016, LNAI 9868, pp. 468–476, 2016.
DOI: 10.1007/978-3-319-44636-3_44

traditional optimization techniques including Tabu search and Simulated Annealing algorithms were used. In general, the goal of these techniques is to find a good enough solution efficiently with the characteristics of the problem. However, they do not guarantee that such a solution is a global optimum. Recently, memetic algorithms have begun to be used to solve various optimization problems, showing that the strategy of combining exploration, exploitation and specific knowledge of the problem can achieve better solutions in a shorter time [5]. Thus, in [6] a memetic algorithm, GASA (Genetic algorithm with simulating annealing), was able to perform better than a Simultaneous Perturbation Stochastic Approximation (SPSA) algorithm. However, GASA has not shown adequate results for complex networks.

Most of complex real-world optimization problems require a multi objective approach. The optimal sought in these problems is a set of solutions rather than a single one [7]. In [8], the authors argue that it is preferable for decision makers to be able to explore and visualize different solutions among several conflicting objectives because this helps to consider a range of the potential solutions that are available.

Multi-objective algorithms continue to grow in popularity in many fields of engineering because of their ability to handle problems with different types of decision variables [8]. NSGA-II [9] is considered one of the most widely used and most competitive multi-objective optimization algorithms [7]. NSGA-II is known in the literature for its great performance and easy implementation [10]. Multi-objective algorithms are known to better enable the use of knowledge of the problem to define the problem objectives compared with single-objective algorithms that use a weighting function.

Considering the advantages of both multi-objective and memetic algorithms, the algorithm proposed in this paper for the calibration of microsimulation traffic flow models, NSGA-II-SA, uses NSGA-II to perform a comprehensive search of the best areas in the solution space (exploration) and simulated annealing to perform a more detailed local search in areas with potentially superior solutions (exploitation). Previous experience using memetic algorithms for the same problem context suggest that mutation be applied to more than one gene because minor mutations are unlikely to provide reasonable changes to the solution.

The rest of this paper is structured as follows. Section 2 depicts the proposed NSGA-II-SA algorithm. Section 3 includes experiments and analyzes of results. Finally, Sect. 4 provides conclusion and outlines future work.

2 Proposal

2.1 Formulation of the Calibration Problem

Two objectives are proposed in this study for the calibration of microscopic vehicular traffic flow simulation models: (1) the minimization of the difference between actual and simulated volumes (formally expressed by Eq. (1)), and (2) the minimization of the difference between actual and simulated speeds (formally expressed by Eq. (2)) as suggested in [11]. The formulas proposed for each objective are an adaptation of the function of error proposed in [6] called Root Mean Squared Normalized Error (RMSNE) where the two functions are grouped into a single function.

$$Volume = \frac{1}{\sqrt{N}} \sum_{t=1}^{T} \sqrt{\sum_{i=1}^{N} \left(\frac{V_{i,t} - \tilde{V}_{(\theta)i,t}}{V_{i,t}} \right)^2} \tag{1}$$

Where $V_{i,t}$ is the count of actual links for link i in time t, $\tilde{V}_{(\theta)i,t}$ is the count of simulated links for link i in time t, N is the total number of links in the model and T is the total number of periods of time t.

$$Speed = \frac{1}{\sqrt{N}} \sum_{t=1}^{T} \sqrt{\sum_{i=1}^{N} \left(\frac{S_{i,t} - \tilde{S}_{(\theta)i,t}}{S_{i,t}} \right)^2} \tag{2}$$

Where $S_{i,t}$ is the actual speeds for link i in time t, $\tilde{S}_{(\theta)i,t}$ is the simulated link for link i in time t, N is the total number of links in model and T is the total number of periods of time t.

The RMSNE is formally expressed by Eq. (3) and it was used in this study in order to make a comparison with other single-objective algorithms proposed in the state of the art.

$$RMSNE = (W * Volume + (1 - W) * Speed) \tag{3}$$

Where W is a weight used to assign more or less value to counts (volume) and speeds.

Calibration criteria: The Federal Highway Administration (FHWA) guidelines for CORSIM models were used in this study. The difference between the count for real and simulated links ought to be less than 5 % for all the links; to do this, statistical GEH [12] was used, which should be less than 5 in at least 85 % of the links. The formula used to calculate the GEH statistic was the same as used in [6] and shown in Eq. (4).

$$GEH = \sum_{i=1}^{N} \sqrt{\frac{2(V_i - \tilde{V}_{(\theta)i})^2}{V_i + \tilde{V}_{(\theta)i}}} \tag{4}$$

Where V_i is the count of actual links for link i and $\tilde{V}_{(\theta)i}$ is the count of simulated links for link i.

2.2   NSGA-II-SA Algorithm for Calibration

NSGA-II is a multi-objective genetic algorithm based on sorting by non-dominance frontiers. This sorting consists of assigning a ranking to each solution, equal to the frontier number in which it is located. For example, a solution dominated by only one other solution is set in the second frontier of non-dominance and have a ranking of 1.

This approach introduces the concept of elitism. Crowding distance is another concept used by NSGA-II to introduce diversity in solutions. Thus, when deciding between solutions that have the same non-dominance frontier ranking values, solutions that are less crowded in the solution space are preferred, that is, a solution that differs most from the others would allow a better exploration of the search space.

In NSGA-II-SA, an individual represents a parameter vector containing a solution for the optimization problem (in this work, the calibration problem). Each individual has a measure of overall fitness as well as a fitness value for each objective. The algorithm seeks to create a population through the generation and selection of appropriate individuals (exploration). The best individuals are used to generate new populations through iterative steps. Furthermore, after the best individuals are selected, the process of exploitation based on simulated annealing refines the Pareto front solutions, in order to obtain improved solutions [13]. After the stop criteria is met, the Pareto front of the latest generation as well as the solution that is considered to be better are expected to be obtained. The proposed algorithm performs the following steps:

Step 0: The first population of individuals P_0 is randomly generated. The first population of descendants, denoted by Q_0 and size N, is generated from P_0. The descendants are achieved by the methods of selection, crossover, and mutation. In this study, selection based on elitism was used - according to front number (or Rank) and crowding distance - as well as uniform crossover and multi-gene mutation.

Step 1: The populations of parents and offspring, P_t and Q_t are grouped in a global population R_t. Using the concept of fronts or non-dominance ranking, the different individuals are grouped in the fronts: F1 for the individuals that form the Pareto front (rank = 0), F2 for those with rank = 1, etc. The fast sort method defined in [9] based on non-dominance and crowding distance are used to generate the fronts.

Step 2 (exploitation with simulated annealing): For each of the individuals in the Pareto Front (Ranking = 0) do the following:

- **Step A:** A neighbor is built around the individual. A parameter is mutated if a random number is less than one probability of mutation. If the parameter needs to be mutated, it is modified by a value generated randomly in a Mutation Radius of the current value (uniform mutation). The Mutation Radius is calculated according to the range of possible values for each parameter.

- **Step B:** If the neighbor has a value of RMSNE less than the current value, the neighbor becomes the best result and the algorithm moves on to step C. If the neighbor is not better, the temperature and evaluation of the objective function are used to calculate the probability of selecting or not the neighbor as a starting point for the following iteration of simulated annealing. The temperature in the next iteration decreases according to the given cooling rate. The equation used to establish the probability of selecting the neighbor is the same used in [6].

- **Step C:** If the stopping criteria have been met (maximum number of optimizations), complete Step 2. If not, return to step A.

Step 3: All fronts (ranking) are recalculated using the method defined in [9]. Then, the next population P_{t+1} is created. In the new population individuals from R_t are included, front by front, starting with the front with rank equal to 0, until the N elements in the new population are filled, or a number close to N (while $|P_{t+1}| + |F_i| \leq N$, to give $P_{t+1} = P_{t+1} \cup F_i$; $i = i + 1$).

Step 4: The population is completed. If it has not been possible to fully complete the new population P_{t+1} with exact fronts, the $N - |P_{t+1}|$ required individuals from F_i front. To do this, the front is sorted using the crowding operator and the most diverse are included.

Step 5: The population of descendants Q_{t+1}, is obtained by applying to the population P_{t+1} the operators of selection, crossover and mutation. A generation is advanced: t = t + 1.

Step 6: If the stopping criterion is not met (maximum number of iterations), return to step 1. Otherwise, return the front 0 of the last population. If you want to get automatically the best solution that is chosen by the value of RMSNE.

3   Experiments and Results

NSGA-II-SA was tested using CORSIM, a tool that integrates FreSim (Freeway Simulation) and NetSim (Network Simulation) to represent the whole traffic environment. The calibration parameters used in this study were those outlined in [6].

Experimental configuration: The experimentation was performed on two COR-SIM models, one of the Pyramid Highway in Reno, Nevada and another provided by McTrans. To implement the calibration algorithm, the tool developed in [6] was used. System specifications: The algorithm was run on a computer with the following operating system characteristics: Windows Server, Standard Edition, 2007, Service Pack 2 - 64 bits. System: Intel Xeon CPU E7450 2.4 GHz (2 processors). RAM memory: 32 GB.

Algorithm parameters: Initial population (N) = 40, Percent Selection = 50, Probability of mutation = 40, Radius of mutation = 1 %, Initial temperature = 0.045, Final temperature = 0, and Cooling rate = 0.92.

Experiments: In the first experiment, the Reno model was calibrated by counting vehicles (volume) and speeds as field measurements. This model includes a total of 126 arterial links and actual data are available for 45 of these. For the second experiment, on the McTrans model, the default parameters were taken as field data. All calibration parameters were initialized randomly and used as a starting point for the calibration. This model includes a total of 20 arterial links.

The initial value of RMSNE for the Reno model was 0.22. After 32 iterations the RMSNE value decreased to 0.08. This represents an improvement of 64 %. The initial RMSNE value for McTrans model was 0.29. After 20 iterations, the RMSNE decreased to 0.015. This represents a 95 % improvement.

Figure 1 represents the vehicle count (volume) for the Reno and McTrans models before and after calibration. The 45° line represents the state in which the counts from the model and the field measurements match perfectly for each link. For Reno, the initial values were some distance from the 45° line, especially for the higher counts, but after calibration the counts improved for all the links and the model represented showed more accuracy. For McTrans it can be seen that after calibration it was close to meeting the calibration criteria. It can therefore be said that the proposed algorithm improves the results for all network links.

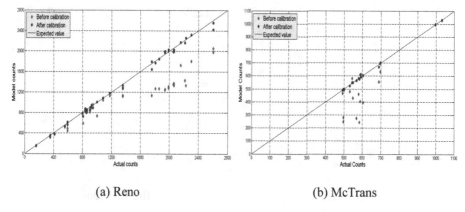

(a) Reno   (b) McTrans

Fig. 1. Vehicle count (volume) before and after calibration process, (A) Reno, (b) McTrans.

Similarly, Fig. 2 shows the values of speed before and after calibration process. The speed values in the Reno experiment improved only slightly particularly for the lowest values, while in the McTrans experiment, speed values were improved considerably. This improvement is due to the precision of the proposed algorithm.

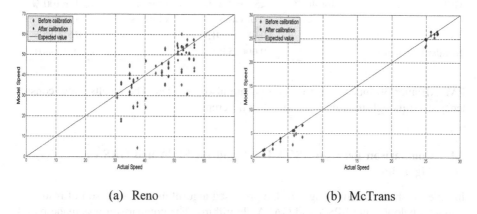

(a) Reno   (b) McTrans

Fig. 2. Speed values before and after calibration process, (A) Reno, (b) McTrans.

Figure 3 shows the GEH statistic for the two models, before and after the calibration process. The red line represents the initial condition of the model (before). For the Reno model, the initial GEH value was less than 5 for approximately 40 % of the links. For the McTrans model, the initial GEH value was less than 5 for approximately 50 % of the links. The blue line represents the condition of the model after calibration. GEH improved considerably for both experiments, since the GEH value fell to a value less than 5 for 100 % of the links (all links).

Table 1 provides a summary of results using NSGA-II-SA. RMSNE and GEH values were improved considerably. The average value and standard deviation of the

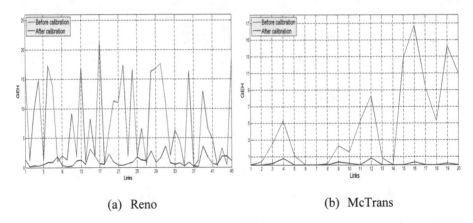

(a) Reno   (b) McTrans

Fig. 3. GEH statistics for the two models, before and after calibration

Table 1. Summary of results of the first experiment.

Experiments/criteria	Reno		McTrans	
	Before	After	Before	After
RMSNE	0.22	0.08	0.29	0.015
GEH	<5 for 40 % of cases	<5 for 100 % of cases	<5 for 50 % of cases	<5 for 100 % of cases
Average		0.089037013		0.026759498
Standard deviation		0.006254651		0.005414801

RMSNE after 30 independent executions are also provided. The results show consistency even though the initial values were different.

3.1 Comparison Between NSGA-II-SA and the SPSA and GASA Algorithms

In order to show the advantages of the proposed algorithm, a comparison of results is provided below using SPSA and GASA algorithms. The comparison was made based on runtime and the best result obtained by the three algorithms in the two models previously presented, using the best results from each of these. Figure 4 shows the convergence curve for each algorithm and each model. When comparing the values achieved by RMSNE in runtime, it is observed that NSGA-II-SA in the two experiments converges faster to the best solution, that is, the NSGA-II-SA curve falls faster and at no time is it bettered by the other algorithms.

Table 2 provides a summary of runtime, RMSNE and GEH values achieved by the three algorithms. The NSGA-II-SA algorithm required 49 min less (36.5 % less) than SPSA and 55 min less (39.28 % less) than GASA to calibrate the Reno model. In the McTrans model, NSGA-II-SA required 4 and 8 min less than SPSA (26.6 % less) and

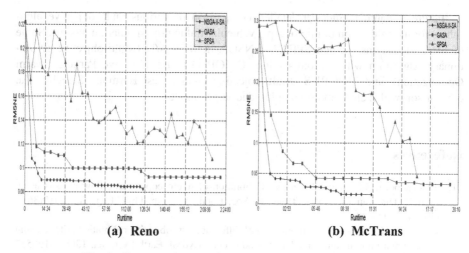

(a) **Reno**   (b) **McTrans**

Fig. 4. Convergence curve based on execution time (hh:mm:ss).

Table 2. Comparison of the NSGA-II, GASA, and SPSA algorithms.

Experiments/ criteria	Reno			McTrans		
	NSGA-II-SA	GASA	SPSA	NSGA-II-SA	GASA	SPSA
Run time	1 h 25 min	2 h 20 min	2 h 14 min	11 min	19 min	15 min
RMSNE	0.08	0.092	0.10	0.015	0.03	0.04
GEH	<5 for 100 % of cases	<5 for 100 % of cases	<5 for 93 % of cases	<5 for 100 % of cases	<5 for 100 % of cases	<5 for 100 % of cases

GASA (42.1 % less) respectively. The RMSNE were better for NSGA-II-SA in all cases. The GEH obtained with NSGA-II-SA were equal or superior.

4 Conclusions

A multi-objective memetic algorithm based on NSGA-II and simulated annealing, NSGA-II-SA, was proposed for the calibration of microscopic vehicular traffic flow simulation models. Two CORSIM vehicular traffic models were calibrated. After calibration, all parameters were within allow values (below the limit value suggested by the GEH statistic). The proposed algorithm has the ability to calibrate all parameters of the model, along with multiple performance measures and time periods, simultaneously. NSGA-II-SA was compared with two state-of-the-art algorithms, SPSA and GASA, obtaining promising results. The runtime of NSGA-II-SA and the results in terms of RMSNE were better for both experiments, with substantial improvements over SPSA and GASA. NSGA-II-SA quickly converges to the best solution for both experiments. NSGA-II-SA takes between 26.6 % and 42.1 % less time to converge than SPSA and GASA.

Future research includes a detailed comparison of various multi-objective algorithms for the calibration of microscopic vehicular traffic flow simulation models. Some of these algorithms include SPEA2, ε-NSGA-II, MOEA/D (Multi-objective Evolutionary Algorithm with Decomposition) OMOPSO (Multi-objective Particle Swarm Optimization), and MOGBHS (Multi-objective Global Best Harmony Search). The comparison will include more complex and larger models.

References

1. Hoogendoorn, S., Hoogendoorn, R.: Calibration of microscopic traffic-flow models using multiple data sources. Philos. Trans. R. Soc. Lond. A: Math. Phys. Eng. Sci. **2010**(368), 4497–4517 (1928)
2. Moussa, R., Chahinian, N.: Comparison of different multi-objective calibration criteria using a conceptual rainfall-runoff model of flood events. Hydrol. Earth Syst. Sci. **13**(4), 519–535 (2009)
3. Yu, L., et al.: Calibration of VISSIM for bus rapid transit systems in Beijing using GPS data. J. Public Transp. **9**(3), 13 (2006)
4. Garg, P.: A comparison between memetic algorithm and genetic algorithm for the cryptanalysis of simplified data encryption standard algorithm. arXiv preprint arXiv:1004. 0574 (2010)
5. Moscato, P., Cotta, C.: A modern introduction to memetic algorithms. In: Gendreau, M., Potvin, J.-Y. (eds.) Handbook of Metaheuristics, pp. 141–183. Springer, New York (2010)
6. Paz, A., et al.: Calibration of traffic flow models using a memetic algorithm. Trans. Res. Part C: Emerg. Technol. **55**, 432–443 (2015)
7. Durillo, J.J., Nebro, A.J.: jMetal: a Java framework for multi-objective optimization. Adv. Eng. Softw. **42**(10), 760–771 (2011)
8. Hadka, D., Reed, P.M., Simpson, T.W.: Diagnostic assessment of the Borg MOEA for many-objective product family design problems. In: 2012 IEEE Congress on Evolutionary Computation (CEC). IEEE (2012)
9. Deb, K., et al.: A fast and elitist multiobjective genetic algorithm: NSGA-II. IEEE Trans. Evol. Comput. **6**(2), 182–197 (2002)
10. Meneses, C.A.P., Echeverri, M.G.: Optimización multiobjetivo usando un algoritmo genético y un operador elitista basado en un ordenamiento no-dominado (NSGA-II). Scientia Et Technica **1**(35) (2007)
11. Paz, A., Molano, V., Gaviria, C.: Calibration of corsim models considering all model parameters simultaneously. In: 2012 15th International IEEE Conference on Intelligent Transportation Systems (ITSC). IEEE (2012)
12. Holm, P., Tomich, D., Sloboden, J., Lowrance, C.: Traffic Analysis Toolbox Volume IV: Guidelines for Applying CORSIM Microsimulation Modeling Software, FHWA-HOP-07-079. 348 p. January 2007. http://www.ops.fhwa.dot.gov/trafficanalysistools/tat_vol4/vol4_guidelines.pdf
13. Neri, F., Cotta, C., Moscato, P.: Handbook of Memetic Algorithms, vol. 379. Springer, Heidelberg (2012)

Fuzzy Logic: Foundations and Applications

Fuzzy Soft Set Decision Making Algorithms: Some Clarifications and Reinterpretations

José Carlos R. Alcantud[✉]

BORDA Research Unit and Multidisciplinary Institute of Enterprise (IME),
University of Salamanca, Salamanca, Spain
jcr@usal.es
http://diarium.usal.es/jcr

Abstract. We do two things in relation with fuzzy soft set decision making in this paper. Both in the score-based and fuzzy choice values approaches to decision making, the modifications that account for the model with positive and negative attributes are put forward and discussed for the most common fuzzy negation. We also provide a reinterpretation of the fuzzy choice values solution in terms of choice values associated with fuzzy opportunity costs.

Keywords: Soft set · Fuzzy soft set · Resultant fuzzy soft set · Comparison table · Decision making

1 Introduction

Since the introduction of fuzzy sets by Zadeh [1], a huge literature on their properties and applications to decision making has been produced. However in some practical problems, imprecise individual or group knowledge cannot be suitably represented by fuzzy sets (FSs): cf., Bustince et al. [2,3]. To name but a few models, Atanassov [4,5] proposes the concept of intuitionistic fuzzy set, which coincides with the notion of vague set (Bustince and Burillo [6]). Preference structures in group decision making problems under uncertainty appear in the form of the fuzzy preference relation (cf., Castro et al. [7], which provides an application to consensus-driven group recommender systems; see Alcantud et al. [8] for a different approach to consensus analysis, also Alcantud and de Andrés [9] for a fuzzy viewpoint).

Within the fuzzy framework there are also cases where the practitioner cannot proceed with a unique membership degree because she receives a set of possible input values (e.g., when several experts supply their own membership degrees). To model these situations, Torra [10] introduces hesitant fuzzy sets (HFSs) which incorporate many-valued sets of memberships (cf., Herrera et al. [11], Rodríguez et al. [12], and Xu [13]). Alcantud et al. [14] give real applications that validate the model by hesitant fuzzy sets. Alcantud and de Andrés [15] propose a segment-based approach to evaluate HFSs. Zhan and Zhu [16] give a summary of decision making methods based on (fuzzy) soft sets and rough soft sets.

O. Luaces et al. (Eds.): CAEPIA 2016, LNAI 9868, pp. 479–488, 2016.
DOI: 10.1007/978-3-319-44636-3_45

Molodtsov [17] initiates the theory of soft sets. His results are complemented e.g., by Aktaş and Çağman [18], Alcantud [19] (who proves formal relationships among soft sets, fuzzy sets, and their extensions) and Maji et al. [20].

Among the most successful extensions of the soft set model we can cite fuzzy soft sets (Maji et al. [21], also Alcantud et al. [22], Li et al. [23] and Tang [24] for applications to decision making for medical diagnosis) and incomplete soft sets (Alcantud and Santos-García [25], Han et al. [26], Zou and Xiao [27]).

Subsection 2.2 below reviews fundamental approaches to fuzzy soft set decision making. Then we analyze this problem with desirable and undesirable parameters, both in the cases of Roy and Maji [28] and Alcantud [29]. To normalize the information, the complement of the fuzzy set associated with each non-desirable attribute may be used, although the choice of the complement is not evident (cf., Klir and Yuan [30, Sect. 3.2]). In this paper we explore the decision making situation under Zadeh's fuzzy negation $c(x) = 1 - x$. Finally, we reinterpret the notion that provides the solution in Kong et al. [31].

This paper is organized as follows. Section 2 recalls some terminology and definitions. Section 3 contains our results. We conclude in Sect. 4.

2 Basic Definitions: Soft Sets, Fuzzy Soft Sets

We adopt the usual description and terminology for soft sets and fuzzy soft sets. U denotes a universe of objects and E denotes a universal set of parameters.

2.1 Soft Sets and Fuzzy Soft Sets

Definition 1 (Molodtsov [17]). A pair (F, A) is a *soft set* over U when $A \subseteq E$ and $F : A \longrightarrow \mathcal{P}(U)$, where $\mathcal{P}(U)$ denotes the power set of U.

A soft set over U is interpreted as a parameterized family of subsets of U, and A represents a set of parameters. Then for any $e \in A$, we say that $F(e)$ is the subset of U approximated by the parameter e or the set of e-approximate elements of the soft set. To put an example, if $U = \{f_1, f_2, f_3, f_4\}$ is a universe of films and A contains the parameter e that describes "3D image" and the parameter e' that describes "suitable for children aged under 7" then $F(e) = \{f_2\}$ means that the only 3D film is f_2 and $F(e') = \{f_1, f_3\}$ means that the only suitable for children aged under 7 films are f_1 and f_3. For soft set based decision making, the reader may consult Maji et al. [32], Çağman and Enginoğlu's [33] and Feng and Zhou [34].

The following notion is a natural extension of the concept of soft set:

Definition 2 (Maji et al. [21]). A pair (F, A) is a *fuzzy soft set* over U when $A \subseteq E$ and $F : A \longrightarrow \mathbf{FS}(U)$, where $\mathbf{FS}(U)$ denotes the set of all fuzzy sets on U.

Any soft set can be considered as a fuzzy soft set with the natural identification of subsets of U with FSs of U. Following with our film example above, fuzzy soft sets permit to deal with other properties like "funny" or "scary" for which partial memberships are almost compulsory.

Henceforth we assume that there are k options and n properties. In that case a soft set or fuzzy soft set can be represented both by a matrix $T = (t_{ij})_{k \times n}$ and in tabular form. Rows correspond to the k objects in U, and columns correspond to the n parameters in A (see Examples 1 and 2 below). In the case of a soft set, all cells are either 0 or 1 (this is to say, its representation is binary).

2.2 Fuzzy Soft Sets and Decision Making

The most distinctive approaches to fuzzy soft set based decision making are probably Roy and Maji [28], Kong et al. [31], Feng et al. [35] and Alcantud [29].

Roy and Maji [28] pioneered this research. Alcantud [29] is closely related to their successful proposal. This article develops and discusses a novel algorithm for fuzzy soft set based decision making from multiobserver input parameter data set. It improves the performance of Roy and Maji's algorithm at the two stages of their proposal. The following comparison between both approaches helps to introduce their structure:

Stage 1. Roy and Maji [28] propose to begin with an aggregation procedure that yields a single resultant fuzzy soft set from preliminary multi-source information. Alcantud [29] shows that their approach very often results into a large loss of information and henceforth generates uncertainty. Accordingly, [29] develops an alternative proposal that avoids such situation to a great extent.

Stage 2. In order to evaluate the alternatives from the information in the resultant fuzzy soft set, Roy and Maji [28] propose to construct a Comparison matrix that permits to compute scores for the alternatives. In [29] it is argued that a new *relative* Comparison matrix improves the performance of the algorithm of solution, because it contributes both to ensure a higher power of discrimination and to produce a well-determined solution.

As a result of these innovations the procedure in Alcantud [29] is considerably less inconclusive than existing solutions which produce ties on a regular basis (as shown in [29] both by arguments and many examples from the literature).

Remark 1. Kong et al. [31] propose a different procedure at Stage 2 without examining Stage 1. Feng et al. [35] explain that the difference between [31] and [28] is whether the criterion for making a decision should use scores (see definition in Sect. 3.1) or fuzzy choice values (that is, the sum of all membership values across attributes) attached with each option. We concur with their argument that the redesigned approach by scores in Roy and Maji [28], and afterwards in Alcantud [29], is more suitable for making decisions in an imprecise environment than fuzzy choice values. We return to the discussion about [31] in Sect. 3.2.

Concerning their own contribution, Feng et al. [35] introduce an adjustable method based on level soft sets at Stage 2. In their flexible decision mechanism the optimal choice is dependent upon the selected level soft sets.

3   Results

3.1   Comments on Score-Based Solutions

Roy and Maji [28] and Alcantud [29] share the spirit that scores are a better tool than fuzzy choice values in order to evaluate options characterized by fuzzy soft sets, and also that a resultant fuzzy soft set can be produced from more primitive data at an earlier stage.

It is worth insisting that in both cases *it is implicitly assumed that the attributes that are being examined are desirable or not negative*. The reason is that in the comparisons that produce the scores in both models, it is always better to have higher amounts. In order to fully grasp the importance of this overtone, henceforth we analyze the following situation:

Example 1. Let $U' = \{o_1, o_2\}$ be a universe of two cars, and $A = \{e_1, e_2, e_3, e_4, e_5\}$. The tabular representation of the fuzzy soft set that describes the options in terms of the parameters is given by Table 1.

Alcantud [29, Example 7] shows that both the algorithms proposed in [29] and [28] suggest that option o_2 should be selected.

However *if the parameters are some positive and some negative, this conclusion could be challenged even when the choice procedure has been fixed.*

Table 1. Tabular representation of the fuzzy soft set in Example 1.

	e_1	e_2	e_3	e_4	e_5
o_1	0.9	0.1	0.2	0.1	0.3
o_2	0.19	0.3	0.4	0.3	0.4

We proceed to discuss the latter statement with an attention to the two fundamental score-based approaches [29] and [28] (v., Sect. 3.2 below for the fuzzy choice values approach). Henceforth we suppose that in Example 1, the parameters $\{e_4, e_5\}$ are 'negative', e.g., describe attributes like "being expensive" or "pollutes above legal limits". At the same time, parameters $\{e_1, e_2, e_3\}$ are 'desirable', e.g., describe attributes like "security appliances", "efficient fuel consumption" or "fashionably designed". For simplicity this general case is labelled *mixed properties* henceforth.

In order to normalize the information in a fuzzy soft set representation, it seems only natural that *the complement of the fuzzy set associated with each non-desirable attribute should be used*. However in operational terms this is not as direct as apparent, since there is not a unique fuzzy complement or negation (cf., Klir and Yuan [30, Sect. 3.2]). In this paper we explore the case when *we fix $c(x) = 1 - x$ as the fuzzy complement*. Then one needs to subtract from 1 the membership values when the attributes are undesirable. In this fashion we produce the *normalized* matrix or tabular form of the fuzzy soft set, to which the

Table 2. Normalized tabular representation of the fuzzy soft set in Example 1. The fuzzy complement $c(x) = 1 - x$ is applied.

	e_1	e_2	e_3	e_4'	e_5'
o_1	0.9	0.1	0.2	0.9	0.7
o_2	0.19	0.3	0.4	0.7	0.6

standard versions of the algorithms can be applied. Hence in Example 1, Table 2 should replace Table 1 before implementing any solution.

Let us now discuss what adjustments the aforementioned consideration introduces in the Algorithms by [29] and [28] under mixed properties, when they are applied to the original sources of information (in our example, to Table 1).

Comments on Roy and Maji's Score-Based Solution. After normalizing the fuzzy soft set representation of Example 1 (cf., Table 2) with our selected fuzzy complement $c(x)$, Roy and Maji's standard algorithm computes a Comparison table (cf., Table 3) in a way that echoes the classical aggregation procedure due to Marquis de Condorcet. We recall that to produce cell $1, 2$ in Table 3 we count for how many characteristics option o_1 performs at least as well as o_2 (especifically, $\{e_1, e_4, e_5\}$), and in its cell $2, 1$ we count for how many characteristics option o_2 performs at least as well as o_1 (especifically, $\{e_2, e_3\}$). Also, R_i is row i's sum, and T_i is column i's sum, for each i. We are lead to conclude that o_1 is a better option because the scores associated with Table 2 are $S_1 = R_1 - T_1 = 3 - 2 = 1$ and $S_2 = R_2 - T_2 = 2 - 3 = -1$.

Table 3. Comparison table for the application of [28] in Example 1, when attributes e_4, e_5 are undesirable while the others are desirable.

	o_1	o_2	R_i
o_1	0	3	3
o_2	2	0	2
T_i	2	3	

In order to apply a Roy and Maji's inspired algorithm to the original Table 1 directly, the only caution we must make is that the Comparison table that captures their idea should be Table 3. Hence when we count for how many properties an option performs at least as well as another one and there are mixed properties as in Table 1, we must distinguish the case where the property is undesirable (and in all such cases inequalities are reversed: the smaller a membership value the better).

This is a universal feature of our framework which ensures that the conclusion by our alternative Roy-and-Maji's-type solution coincides with the solution through complements implemented above.

Comments on Alcantud's Score-Based Solution. We have identified what simple modification in Roy and Maji's [28] algorithm is needed under mixed properties in order to comply with their spirit and at the same time, coincide with the simple solution that applies [28] to normalized information. Here we replicate the analysis with solution [29]. The following algorithm is needed:

Algorithm 1 - Alcantud [29] modified for mixed properties.

Input: a general fuzzy soft set represented by a matrix $T = (t_{ij})_{k \times n}$.

Without loss of generality we reorder the n properties so that the first q properties are desirable whereas the remaining $n - q$ are not.

1. For $j = 1, \ldots, n$, let M_j be the maximum membership value of any object, i.e., $M_j = \max_{i=1,\ldots,k} t_{ij}$. For $j = q + 1, \ldots, n$, let m_j be the minimum membership value of any object, i.e., $m_j = \min_{i=1,\ldots,k} t_{ij}$.

   Now construct a $k \times k$ Comparison matrix $A' = (a'_{ij})_{k \times k}$ where for each i, j, we let a'_{ij} be the sum of the non-negative values in the finite sequence

$$\frac{t_{i1} - t_{j1}}{M_1}, \frac{t_{i2} - t_{j2}}{M_2}, \ldots, \frac{t_{iq} - t_{jq}}{M_q}, \frac{t_{jq+1} - t_{iq+1}}{1 - m_{q+1}}, \ldots, \frac{t_{jn+1} - t_{in+1}}{1 - m_{n+1}}.$$

2. Continue exactly as in [29].

Observe that in addition to changing the sign of the comparison between membership values for the non-positive properties as in the adapted Roy and Maji's algorithm, the denominator at the quotient has been changed: the relative Comparison matrix $A = (a_{ij})_{k \times k}$ in [29] is computed by summing up the non-negative values in the sequence

$$\frac{t_{i1} - t_{j1}}{M_1}, \frac{t_{i2} - t_{j2}}{M_2}, \ldots \ldots, \frac{t_{in} - t_{jn}}{M_n}$$

in order to obtain cell a_{ij}. Here is the reason for our modified algorithm:

Proposition 1. *The ranking solution in Algorithm 1 coincides with the application of the original algorithm in [29] to the normalized tabular or matrix representation of the fuzzy soft set through the fuzzy complement $c(x) = 1 - x$.*

Proof. Let $T = (t_{ij})_{k \times n}$ be the $k \times n$ matrix representation of a fuzzy soft set for which the first q properties are desirable whereas the remaining $n - q$ are not. Therefore the normalized matrix representation of the fuzzy soft set is

$$T' = \begin{pmatrix} t_{11} & \cdots & t_{1q} & 1 - t_{1q+1} & \cdots & 1 - t_{1n} \\ \vdots & & \vdots & \vdots & & \vdots \\ t_{k1} & \cdots & t_{kq} & 1 - t_{kq+1} & \cdots & 1 - t_{kn} \end{pmatrix}$$

We proceed to check that in both the procedures explained in the statement, the relative Comparison matrix is the same. In the second procedure, for each $i, j \in \{1, \ldots, k\}$, a'_{ij} is the sum of the non-negative values in

$$\frac{t_{i1} - t_{j1}}{M_1}, \ldots, \frac{t_{iq} - t_{jq}}{M_q}, \frac{t_{jq+1} - t_{iq+1}}{1 - m_{q+1}}, \ldots, \frac{t_{jn+1} - t_{in+1}}{1 - m_{n+1}}$$

This sequence coincides with

$$\frac{t_{i1} - t_{j1}}{M_1}, \ldots, \frac{t_{iq} - t_{jq}}{M_q}, \frac{(1 - t_{iq+1}) - (1 - t_{jq+1})}{M'_{q+1}}, \ldots, \frac{(1 - t_{in+1}) - (1 - t_{jn+1})}{M'_{n+1}}$$

where $M'_j = \max_{i=1,\ldots,k} t'_{ij} = \max_{i=1,\ldots,k}(1 - t_{ij}) = 1 - \min_{i=1,\ldots,k} t_{ij}$ for each $j = q + 1, \ldots, n$. Hence $a'_{ij} = a_{ij}$ where $A = (a_{ij})_{k \times k}$ is the relative Comparison matrix that arised from the application of [29] to T'. Now both procedures continue in exactly the same fashion. ∎

3.2 A Comment on Kong et al.'s Solution

In this section we provide a different interpretation of the proposal in Kong et al. [31] (which has been criticized e.g., in Feng et al. [35] or Alcantud [29]). It relies on the economic concept of "opportunity cost".

In the context of decision under uncertainty, Savage early introduced the "minimax regret" criterion that produces an associated loss table. In this table every original value is subtracted to the maximum value that any object achieves under the property that it is linked to. Operationally: for each column, we first compute the maximum value in the original decision table and then every value at that column is replaced by such maximum minus it.

By the recourse to this new opportunity cost table we are measuring for each option and attribute, how much we are losing by not choosing the option with highest membership value for the attribute. Let us give an example:

Example 2. Kong et al. [31] used the fuzzy soft set (S, P) represented by Table 4 as an example that shows the disparity of conclusions when choice values (i.e., row sums) are used instead of scores (cf., Roy and Maji [28]).

As they explain, in such example the algorithm in Roy and Maji [28] shows that option o_3 should be selected because when their scores s_i are computed, one obtains $s_3 > s_2 > s_5 > s_1 > s_6 > s_4$. However a fuzzy-choice-value-based decision produces a different ranking and optimal selection, because $c_6 > c_2 > c_3 > c_1 = c_4 = c_5$ and therefore o_6 is the suggested alternative.

If we compute the opportunity cost table associated with the fuzzy soft set (S, P) we obtain the data in Table 5. Since opportunity costs are negative, the comparisons $Op_6 < Op_2 < Op_3 < Op_1 = Op_4 = Op_5$ permit us to observe that the ranking of alternatives is identical to Kong et al.'s conclusion, i.e., $o_6 \succ o_2 \succ o_3 \succ o_1 \sim o_4 \sim o_5$. In Proposition 2 below we prove that the coincidence observed in Example 2 holds in general.

Table 4. Tabular representation of the fuzzy soft set (S, P) in Kong et al. [31, Table 1]. The input at i, j is t_{ij}, c_i is the sum of the amounts in row i (fuzzy choice value).

	p_1	p_2	p_3	p_4	p_5	Fuzzy choice value
o_1	0.1	0.5	0.3	0.4	0.3	$c_1 = 1.6$
o_2	0.3	0.5	0.2	0.3	0.6	$c_2 = 1.9$
o_3	0.1	0.7	0.4	0.5	0.1	$c_3 = 1.8$
o_4	0.7	0.2	0.2	0.2	0.3	$c_4 = 1.6$
o_5	0.2	0.6	0.3	0.2	0.3	$c_5 = 1.6$
o_6	0.9	0.2	0.1	0.1	0.8	$c_6 = 2.1$

Table 5. Opportunity cost table associated with Table 4: at each cell i, j we introduce $M_j - t_{ij}$. Op_i is the sum of the amounts in row i (opportunity cost values).

	p_1	p_2	p_3	p_4	p_5	Opportunity cost value
o_1	0.8	0.2	0.1	0.1	0.5	$Op_1 = 1.7$
o_2	0.6	0.2	0.2	0.2	0.2	$Op_2 = 1.4$
o_3	0.8	0	0	0	0.7	$Op_3 = 1.5$
o_4	0.2	0.5	0.2	0.3	0.5	$Op_4 = 1.7$
o_5	0.7	0.1	0.1	0.3	0.5	$Op_5 = 1.7$
o_6	0	0.5	0.3	0.4	0	$Op_6 = 1.2$
M_i	0.9	0.7	0.4	0.5	0.8	

Proposition 2. *The ranking solution in Kong et al. [31] does not change if we use opportunity cost tables instead of fuzzy soft set representations.*

Proof. Let $T = (t_{ij})_{k \times n}$ be the $k \times n$ matrix representation of a fuzzy soft set (F, A) over U. For each column i we define $M_i = \max\{t_{1i}, \ldots, t_{ki}\}$. Then the opportunity cost table associated with (F, A) is $T_O = (M_j - t_{ij})_{k \times n}$. Kong et al.'s fuzzy choice values are $c_i = t_{i1} + t_{i2} + \ldots + t_{in}$ for each $i = 1, \ldots, k$.

The fuzzy choice value associated with option i and the opportunity cost table is $Op(o_i) = M_1 - t_{i1} + M_2 - t_{i2} + \ldots + M_n - t_{in}$ hence if we let $M = M_1 + \ldots + M_n$ then $Op(o_i) = M - (t_{i1} + t_{i2} + \ldots + t_{in}) = M - c_i$. This justifies that a ranking of the alternatives by non-increasing fuzzy choice values coincides with a ranking of the alternatives by non-decreasing opportunity cost fuzzy values. ∎

Remark 2. Kong et al. [31] implicitly assume that the attributes are positive, because the fuzzy choice value sums up all amounts. Therefore the practitioner should exercise the same cautions as in Sect. 3.1 before applying their criterion.

4 Concluding Remarks

The attributes in a fuzzy soft set decision making analysis must be carefully examined to check if they are all positive or not. When there are both desirable and undesirable attributes, fuzzy complements or negations should be applied to one of the cases (typically, negative attributes). We discuss which modifications to the standard version of the decision algorithms in Roy and Maji [28] and Alcantud [29] permit to implement that feature when $c(x) = 1 - x$ is the fuzzy complement. A possibility for future research is the investigation when other fuzzy complements like the Sugeno class $s_\lambda(x) = \frac{1-x}{1+\lambda x}$, $\lambda \in (-1, +\infty)$, or the Yager class $c_\omega(x) = (1 - x^\omega)^{\frac{1}{\omega}}$, $\omega \in (0, +\infty)$, are preferred.

We have also provided a reinterpretation of the controversial solution by Kong et al. [31] stated in terms of choice values associated with fuzzy opportunity costs.

References

1. Zadeh, L.: Fuzzy sets. Inf. Control **8**, 338–353 (1965)
2. Bustince, H., Barrenechea, E., Pagola, M., Fernández, J., Xu, Z., Bedregal, B., Montero, J., Hagras, H., Herrera, F., De Baets, B.: A historical account of types of fuzzy sets and their relationships. IEEE Trans. Fuzzy Syst. **24**, 179–194 (2016)
3. Bustince, H., Barrenechea, E., Fernández, J., Pagola, M., Montero, J.: The origin of fuzzy extensions. In: Kacprzyk, J., Pedrycz, W. (eds.) Springer Handbook of Computational Intelligence, pp. 89–112. Springer, Berlin (2015)
4. Atanassov, K.T.: Intuitionistic fuzzy sets. Fuzzy Sets Syst. **20**, 87–96 (1986)
5. Atanassov, K.T.: More on intuitionistic fuzzy sets. Fuzzy Sets Syst. **33**(1), 37–45 (1989)
6. Bustince, H., Burillo, P.: Vague sets are intuitionistic fuzzy sets. Fuzzy Sets Syst. **79**(3), 403–405 (1996)
7. Castro, J., Quesada, F.J., Palomares, I., Martínez, L.: A consensus-driven group recommender system. Int. J. Intell. Syst. **30**(8), 887–906 (2015)
8. Alcantud, J.C.R., de Andrés Calle, R., Cascón, J.: A unifying model to measure consensus solutions in a society. Math. Comput. Model. **57**(7–8), 1876–1883 (2013)
9. Alcantud, J.C.R., de Andrés Calle, R.: A fuzzy viewpoint of consensus measures in social choice. In: Actas del XVII Congreso Español sobre Tecnologías y Lógica Fuzzy (ESTYLF 2014), pp. 87–92 (2014)
10. Torra, V.: Hesitant fuzzy sets. Int. J. Intell. Syst. **25**(6), 529–539 (2010)
11. Herrera, F., Martínez, L., Torra, V., Xu, Z.: Hesitant fuzzy sets: an emerging tool in decision making. Int. J. Intell. Syst. **29**(6), 493–944 (2014)
12. Rodríguez, R., Martínez, L., Torra, V., Xu, Z., Herrera, F.: Hesitant fuzzy sets: state of the art and future directions. Int. J. Intell. Syst. **29**, 495–524 (2014)
13. Xu, Z.: Hesitant fuzzy sets theory. Studies in Fuzziness and Soft Computing, vol. 314. Springer International Publishing, Switzerland (2014)
14. Alcantud, J.C.R., de Andrés Calle, R., Torrecillas, M.: Hesitant fuzzy worth: an innovative ranking methodology for hesitant fuzzy subsets. Appl. Soft Comput. **38**, 232–243 (2016)
15. Alcantud, J.C.R., de Andrés Calle, R.: A segment-based approach to the analysis of project evaluation problems by hesitant fuzzy sets. Int. J. Comput. Intell. Syst. **9**(2), 325–339 (2016)
16. Zhan, J., Zhu, K.: Reviews on decision making methods based on (fuzzy) soft sets and rough soft sets. J. Intell. Fuzzy Syst. **29**, 1169–1176 (2015)
17. Molodtsov, D.: Soft set theory - first results. Comput. Math. Appl. **37**, 19–31 (1999)

18. Aktaş, H., Çağman, N.: Soft sets and soft groups. Inf. Sci. **177**, 2726–2735 (2007)
19. Alcantud, J.C.R.: Some formal relationships among soft sets, fuzzy sets, and their extensions. Int. J. Approx. Reason. **68**, 45–53 (2016)
20. Maji, P., Biswas, R., Roy, A.: Soft set theory. Comput. Math. Appl. **45**, 555–562 (2003)
21. Maji, P., Biswas, R., Roy, A.: Fuzzy soft sets. J. Fuzzy Math. **9**, 589–602 (2001)
22. Alcantud, J.C.R., Santos-García, G., Hernández-Galilea, E.: Glaucoma diagnosis: a soft set based decision making procedure. In: Dorronsoro, B., Barrenechea, E., Troncoso, A., Baruque, B., Galar, M. (eds.) CAEPIA 2015. LNCS, vol. 9422, pp. 49–60. Springer, Heidelberg (2015). doi:10.1007/978-3-319-24598-0_5
23. Li, Z., Wen, G., Xie, N.: An approach to fuzzy soft sets in decision making based on grey relational analysis and Dempster-Shafer theory of evidence: an application in medical diagnosis. Artif. Intell. Med. **64**(3), 161–171 (2015)
24. Tang, H.: A novel fuzzy soft set approach in decision making based on grey relational analysis and Dempster-Shafer theory of evidence. Appl. Soft Comput. **31**, 317–325 (2015)
25. Alcantud, J.C.R., Santos-García, G.: Incomplete soft sets: new solutions for decision making problems. In: Bucciarelli, E., Silvestri, M., González, S.R. (eds.) Decision Economics, In Commemoration of the Birth Centennial of Herbert A. Simon 1916-2016 (Nobel Prize in Economics 1978). AISC, vol. 475, pp. 9–17. Springer, Heidelberg (2016). doi:10.1007/978-3-319-40111-9_2
26. Han, B.H., Li, Y., Liu, J., Geng, S., Li, H.: Elicitation criterions for restricted intersection of two incomplete soft sets. Knowl.-Based Syst. **59**, 121–131 (2014)
27. Zou, Y., Xiao, Z.: Data analysis approaches of soft sets under incomplete information. Knowl.-Based Syst. **21**(8), 941–945 (2008)
28. Roy, A., Maji, P.: A fuzzy soft set theoretic approach to decision making problems. J. Comput. Appl. Math. **203**, 412–418 (2007)
29. Alcantud, J.C.R.: A novel algorithm for fuzzy soft set based decision making from multiobserver input parameter data set. Inf. Fusion **29**, 142–148 (2016)
30. Klir, G.J., Yuan, B.: Fuzzy Sets and Fuzzy Logic: Theory and Applications. Prentice-Hall Inc., Upper Saddle River (1995)
31. Kong, Z., Gao, L., Wang, L.: Comment on "A fuzzy soft set theoretic approach to decision making problems". J. Comput. Appl. Math. **223**, 540–542 (2009)
32. Maji, P., Biswas, R., Roy, A.: An application of soft sets in a decision making problem. Comput. Math. Appl. **44**, 1077–1083 (2002)
33. Çağman, N., Enginoğlu, S.: Soft set theory and uni-int decision making. Eur. J. Oper. Res. **207**(2), 848–855 (2010)
34. Feng, Q., Zhou, Y.: Soft discernibility matrix and its applications in decision making. Appl. Soft Comput. **24**, 749–756 (2014)
35. Feng, F., Jun, Y., Liu, X., Li, L.: An adjustable approach to fuzzy soft set based decision making. J. Comput. Appl. Math. **234**, 10–20 (2010)

Some New Measures of k-Specificity

José Luis González Sánchez[✉], Ramón González del Campo,
and Luis Garmendia

Universidad Complutense de Madrid, Madrid, Spain
joselg04@ucm.es

Abstract. Measures of k-specificity are generalizations of Yager's measures of specificity to measure the tranquility when choosing k elements from the universe of discourse.

In this paper some new examples of measures of k-specificity are proposed and compared.

Keywords: Fuzzy sets · Measure of specificity · k-specificity · Defuzzification

1 Introduction

Measures of specificity play a notable role in decision making, the measurement of performance of fuzzy expert systems, and deductive reasoning systems [5].

Yager introduced the concept of specificity [3] in the earliest 1980s to measure the degree which a fuzzy subset is closed to a crisp set with one and only one element. In many applications, measures of specificity are useful to measure the amount of information contained in a fuzzy set.

Measures of k-specificity [2] extend this idea to the problem of choosing k elements, not necessarily only one; also, they can be used to defuzzificate a fuzzy set. The main idea is to decide the cardinality of the crisp set using the k that maximizes the measure of k-specificity.

2 Preliminaries

Let $X = \{e_1, ..., e_n\}$ be a finite crisp set.

Definition 1. *Fuzzy Set. A fuzzy set μ on X is a mapping such that $\mu : X \to [0, 1]$, and $\mu(e_i)$ is interpreted as the membership degree of the element e_i to the fuzzy set μ.*

Definition 2. *Singleton. Let μ be a fuzzy set on X. μ is a singleton if and only if there exists one and only one $e_i \in X$ that $\mu(e_i) = 1$ and $\mu(e_j) = 0$ $\forall e_j \in X$ with $j \neq i$.*

Definition 3. *Normal Fuzzy Set. Let μ be a fuzzy set on X. The fuzzy set μ is normal if and only if there exists $e_i \in X$ that $\mu(e_i) = 1$.*

O. Luaces et al. (Eds.): CAEPIA 2016, LNAI 9868, pp. 489–497, 2016.
DOI: 10.1007/978-3-319-44636-3_46

Definition 4. [3] *Measure of Specificity. Let* $[0,1]^X$ *be the set of fuzzy sets on* X. *Let* a_j *be the* j^{th} *greatest membership degree of a fuzzy set* μ. *A measure of specificity of a fuzzy sets is a mapping* $Sp : [0,1]^X \mapsto [0,1]$ *such that:*

(i) $Sp(\mu) = 1$ *if and only if* μ *is a singleton.*
(ii) $Sp(\emptyset) = 0$.
(iii) $Sp(\mu)$ *is strictly increasing respect* a_1.
(iv) $Sp(\mu)$ *is decreasing respect* a_j $\forall j \geq 2$.

Definition 5. [2] *Measure of k-Specificity. Let* $[0,1]^X$ *be the set of fuzzy sets on* X. *Let* a_j *be the* j^{th} *greatest membership degree of a fuzzy set* μ *and let* k *be an integer such that* $0 \leq k \leq n$. *A measure of k-specificity of fuzzy sets is mapping* $Sp_k : [0,1]^X \mapsto [0,1]$ *such that:*

(i) $Sp_k(\mu) = 1$ *if and only if* μ *is a crisp set of* k *elements.*
(ii) $Sp_k(\emptyset) = 0$ *if* $k > 0$.
(iii) $Sp_k(\mu)$ *depends on* a_j *in this way:*
   (a) $Sp_k(\mu)$ *is strictly increasing respect each* a_j *when* $1 \leq j \leq k$
   (b) $Sp_k(\mu)$ *is strictly decreasing respect each* a_j *when* $k + 1 \leq j \leq n$

Remark 1. Note that the empty set is a crisp set; thus, $Sp_k(\emptyset) = 1$ *when* $k = 0$.

Definition 6. [2] *Measure of Maximum k-Specificity. Let* $[0,1]^X$ *be the set of fuzzy sets on* X. *Let* a_j *be the* j^{th} *greatest membership degree of a fuzzy set* μ *and let* k *be an integer such that* $0 \leq k \leq n$. *Let* Sp_k *be a measure of k-specificity. A measure of maximum k-specificity of fuzzy sets is a mapping* $Sp_{max} : [0,1]^X \mapsto [0,1]$ *such that:*
$$Sp_{max}(\mu) = max_{k:0,\ldots,Card(\{a_j\})} \{Sp_k(\mu)\}.$$
The k *that maximizes the* $Sp_k(\mu)$ *is called the cardinality of* μ.

Remark 2. $Sp_{max}(\mu) = 1$ *if and only if* μ *is a crisp set.*

Definition 7. [2] *Linear measure of k-specifity. Let* $[0,1]^X$ *be the set of fuzzy sets on* X. *Let* a_j *be the* j^{th} *greatest membership degree of a fuzzy set* μ *and let* k *be an integer with* $0 \leq k \leq n$. *Let* $\boldsymbol{w}$, $\boldsymbol{w}'$ *be two sets of* k *and* $n - k$ *weights such that:* $\sum_{i=1}^{k} w_i = 1$ *and* $\sum_{j=k+1}^{n} w'_j = 1$ *and* $w_i, w'_j \in [0,1]$ *for all* i, j.
The linear measure of k-specificity of a fuzzy set μ *is defined as follows:*

$$Sp_{k,\boldsymbol{w},\boldsymbol{w}'}(\mu) = \begin{cases} \sum_{j=1}^{k} a_j w_j - \sum_{j=k+1}^{n} a_j w'_j & \text{if } k > 0 \\ 1 - \sum_{j=1}^{n} a_j w_j & \text{if } k = 0 \end{cases}$$

Definition 8. [2] *Uniform Linear measure of k-specifity. Let* $w_i = \frac{1}{k}$ *for* $1 \leq i \leq k$ *and* $w'_i = \frac{1}{(n-k)}$ *for* $k + 1 \leq j \leq n$. *The Uniform Linear measure of k-specificity is defined as follows:*

$$Sp_k(\mu) = \begin{cases} \sum_{j=1}^{k} a_j \frac{1}{k} - \sum_{j=k+1}^{n} a_j \frac{1}{(n-k)} & \text{if } k > 0 \\ 1 - \sum_{j=1}^{n} a_j \frac{1}{n} & \text{if } k = 0 \end{cases}$$

Remark 3. [2] Let Sp_k be the Uniform Linear measure of k-specificity. Let N be the negation operator $N(x) = 1 - x$, then $Sp_k(\mu) = Sp_{n-k}(N(\mu))$ for all $k : 0, ..., n$.

Definition 9. [6] *Fractional Measure of specificity. Le μ be a fuzzy set on X, and let a_j be the jth greatest membership degree of μ.*

The Fractional measure of specificity of μ is $Sp(\mu) = \dfrac{a_1^2}{\sum\limits_{j=1}^{n} a_j}$

Definition 10. [4] *The Product measure of specificity. Le μ be a fuzzy set on X, and let a_j be the jth greatest membership degree of μ. The Product measure of specificity is* $Sp(\mu) = a_1 \prod\limits_{j=2}^{n} (qa_j + (1 - a_j))$ *where q is in* $[0, 1]$.

3   Some New Measures of k-Specificity

The Fractional and Product measures of specificity are extended to define respectively the Fractional and Product measures of k-specificity.

Let $X = \{e_1, ..., e_n\}$ be a finite crisp set with n elements and let $[0, 1]^X$ be the set of fuzzy sets on the universe X. Let μ be a fuzzy set on X and let a_j be the jth greatest membership degree. Let k be an integer such that $0 \leq k \leq n$.

Proposition 1. *Let $\mathcal{F} = \{Sp_{k,m,p}\}$ be a family of mappings $[0, 1]^X \mapsto [0, 1]$ with $m, p \in \mathbb{N}$, $m \geq 2$ and $1 \leq p < m$ such that*

$$Sp_{k,m,p}(\mu) = \begin{cases} \dfrac{\left(\sum\limits_{j=1}^{k} a_j\right)^m}{k^{m-p}\left(\sum\limits_{j=1}^{n} a_j\right)^p} & \text{when } 1 \leq k \leq n, \mu \neq \emptyset \\ 0 & \text{when } 1 \leq k \leq n, \mu = \emptyset \\ 1 - a_1^m & \text{when } k = 0 \end{cases}$$

Let $Sp_k \in \mathcal{F}$, then Sp_k is a k-specificity measure on $[0, 1]^X$.

Proof. (i) $Sp_k(\mu) = 1$ if and only if μ is a crisp set with k elements.

   (a) If μ is a crisp set with k elements on X, then $a_j = 1 \ \forall j : 1 \leq j \leq k$ and $a_j = 0 \ \forall j : k+1 \leq n$, so $\sum\limits_{j=1}^{n} a_j = \sum\limits_{j=1}^{k} a_j + \sum\limits_{j=k+1}^{n} a_j = \sum\limits_{j=1}^{k} 1 = k$. That is, numerator and denominator are equal, $k^m = k^{m-p}k^p$, and the specificity value is 1.

   (b) If $Sp(\mu) = 1$, then in the fraction the numerator is equal to the denominator, so we can write the equality as $(\sum\limits_{j=1}^{k} a_j)^{m-p}(\sum\limits_{j=1}^{k} a_j)^p = k^{m-p}(\sum\limits_{j=1}^{k} a_j + \sum\limits_{j=k+1}^{n} a_j)^p$. In this equality, both factor on the right are respectively higher than the two factors on the left. $\sum\limits_{j=1}^{k} a_j = k$ and $\sum\limits_{j=k+1}^{n} a_j = 0$; thus, $a_j = 1$

when $1 \leq j \leq k$ and $a_j = 0$ when $k + 1 \leq j \leq n$, so μ is a crisp set with k elements.

(ii) $Sp_0(\emptyset) = 0$ when $k \geq 1$ by definition.

(iii) $Sp_k(\mu)$ is strictly increasing respect each a_j when $1 \leq j \leq k$ and it is strictly decreasing respect each a_j.

Since μ is not the empty set, at least is $a_1 > 0$, and the first partial derivative $\frac{\partial Sp_k(\mu)}{\partial a_j}$ exists for every $a_j, 1 \leq k \leq n$.

(a) When $1 \leq j \leq k$,

$$\frac{\partial Sp_k(\mu)}{\partial a_j} = \frac{m\left(\sum_{j=1}^{k} a_j\right)^{m-1} k^{m-p}\left(\sum_{j=1}^{n} a_j\right)^{p} - pk^{m-p}\left(\sum_{j=1}^{n} a_j\right)^{p-1}\left(\sum_{j=1}^{k} a_j\right)^{m}}{\left(k^{m-p}\left(\sum_{j=1}^{n} a_j\right)^{p}\right)^2} \quad \text{In this}$$

fraction, the denominator is a strictly positive number, so its sign is given by the numerator, and it is:

$$k^{m-p}\left(\sum_{j=1}^{k} a_j\right)^{m-1}\left(\sum_{j=1}^{n} a_j\right)^{p-1}\left(m\sum_{j=1}^{n} a_j - p\sum_{j=1}^{k} a_j\right) > 0.$$

Note that inside the third parenthesis is $m > p$ and $\sum_{j=1}^{n} a_j \geq \sum_{j=1}^{k} a_j$.

That is, $Sp_k(\mu)$ is strictly increasing respect each a_j when $1 \leq j \leq k$.

(b) When $k + 1 \leq j \leq n, \mu \neq \emptyset$

$$\frac{\partial Sp_k(\mu)}{\partial a_j} = \frac{-pk^{m-p}\left(\sum_{j=1}^{n} a_j\right)^{p-1}\left(\sum_{j=1}^{k} a_j\right)^{m}}{\left(k^{m-p}\left(\sum_{j=1}^{n} a_j\right)^{p}\right)^2} < 0.$$

So, $Sp_k(\mu)$, is strictly decreasing respect each $a_j, k + 1 \leq j \leq n$

Definition 11. *The Fractional measure is a mapping $Sp_k^F : [0,1]^X \mapsto [0,1]$ such that:*

$$Sp_k^F(\mu) = \begin{cases} \dfrac{\left(\sum_{j=1}^{k} a_j\right)^2}{k\sum_{j=1}^{n} a_j} & \text{when } 1 \leq k \leq n, \mu \neq \emptyset \\ 0 & \text{when } 1 \leq k \leq n, \mu = \emptyset \\ 1 - a_1^2 & \text{when } k = 0 \end{cases}$$

Proposition 2. *The Fractional measure Sp_k^F is a measure of k-specificity on $[0,1]^X$.*

Proof. The Fractional measure Sp_k^F is a member of the family $\mathcal{F}$ defined in Proposition 1; namely, with $m = 2$ and $p = 1$, so Sp_k^F is a measure of specificity on $[0,1]^X$.

Remark 4. The Fractional measure of k-specificity is an extension of the Fractional measure of specificity that has been defined in [1].

Example 1. Le be $X = \{e_1, e_2, e_3, e_4, e_5\}$ be a crisp set with $n = 5$ elements.
Consider the fuzzy set μ on X defined by $\mu(e_i) = \{0.2, 0.7, 0, 0.9, 0.5\}$

Reordering μ we obtain $\{0.9|e_4, 0.7|e_2, 0.5|e_5, 0.2|e_1, 0|e_3\}$, thus is $\{a_i\} = \{0.9, 0.7, 0.5, 0.2, 0\}$. We calculate the Fractional measure of k-specificity $Sp_k^F(\mu)$ for $0 \le k \le n = 5$.

For $k = 0$ we use the expression $Sp_0(\mu) = 1 - a_1^2 = 1 - (0.9)^2 = 0.19$

For $k = 1$, $Sp_1(\mu) = \dfrac{\left(\sum\limits_{j=1}^{1} a_j\right)^2}{1 \sum\limits_{j=1}^{5} a_j} = \dfrac{(0.9)^2}{1(0.9+0.7+0.5+0.2+0)} = 0.352$

For $k = 2$, $Sp_2(\mu) = \dfrac{\left(\sum\limits_{j=1}^{2} a_j\right)^2}{2 \sum\limits_{j=1}^{5} a_j} = \dfrac{(0.9+0.7)^2}{2(0.9+0.7+0.5+0.2+0)} = 0.556$

For $k = 3$, $Sp_3(\mu) = \dfrac{\left(\sum\limits_{j=1}^{3} a_j\right)^2}{3 \sum\limits_{j=1}^{5} a_j} = \dfrac{(0.9+0.7+0.5)^2}{3(0.9+0.7+0.5+0.2+0)} = 0.639$

For $k = 4$, $Sp_4(\mu) = \dfrac{\left(\sum\limits_{j=1}^{4} a_j\right)^2}{4 \sum\limits_{j=1}^{5} a_j} = \dfrac{(0.9+0.7+0.5+0.2)^2}{4(0.9+0.7+0.5+0.2+0)} = 0.575$

For $k = 5$, $Sp_5(\mu) = \dfrac{\left(\sum\limits_{j=1}^{5} a_j\right)^2}{5 \sum\limits_{j=1}^{5} a_j} = \dfrac{(0.9+0.7+0.5+0.2+0)^2}{5(0.9+0.7+0.5+0.2+0)} = 0.460$

The maximum k-specificity is $max_k(Sp_k(\mu)) = 0.639$ for $k = 3$, then we decide to defuzzificate μ choosing $\{e_4, e_2, e_5\}$.

Definition 12. *The Product measure is a mapping $Sp_k^P : [0,1]^X \mapsto [0,1]$ such that:*

$$Sp_k^P(\mu) = \begin{cases} \left(\prod\limits_{j=1}^{k} a_j\right)^{\frac{1}{k}} \left(\prod\limits_{j=k+1}^{n} (1 - a_j)\right)^{\frac{1}{n-k}} & when\ 1 \le k < n \\[2em] \left(\prod\limits_{j=1}^{k} a_j\right)^{\frac{1}{k}} & when\ 1 \le k = n \\[2em] \left(\prod\limits_{j=1}^{n} (1 - a_j)\right)^{\frac{1}{n}} & when\ k = 0 \end{cases}$$

Proposition 3.

Proof. (i) $Sp_k(\mu) = 1$ if and only if μ is a crisp set with k elements.
  (a) If μ is a crisp set with k elements, then $a_1 = 1$ for all $1 \le j \le k$ and $a_j = 0$ for all $k + 1 \le j \le n$; thus, every term $a_j = 1$, $(1 - a_j) = 1$, and $Sp(\mu) = 1$.
  (b) If $Sp(\mu) = 1$, then every terms must be 1,
(ii) $Sp_0(\emptyset) = 0$ when $k \ge 1$
(iii) $Sp_k(\mu)$ is strictly increasing respect each a_j when $1 \le j \le k$ and it is strictly decreasing respect each a_j when $k + 1 \le j \le n$.
  That is obvious, since $1 - a_j$ decreasing when a_j increasing.

Remark 5. The Product measure of k-specificity of μ, it is an extension of the Product measure of specificity that has been defined in Definition 10.

Proposition 4. *Let Sp_k be the Product Measure of k-specificity on X. Let N be the negation operator $N(x) = 1 - x$, then $Sp_k(\mu) = Sp_{n-k}(N(\mu))$ for all $k : 0, ..., n$.*

Proof. Let a_j be the jth greatest membership degree of the fuzzy set μ and let b_i be the ith greatest membership degree of the fuzzy set $\mu' = 1 - \mu$.

Note that is $b_1 = 1 - a_n, b_2 = 1 - a_{n-2}, ..., b_i = 1 - a_{n+1-i}, ..., b_n = 1 - a_1$.

When $n - k \geq 1$ $Sp_{n-k}(\mu') = \left(\prod_{i=1}^{n-k} b_i \right)^{\frac{1}{n-k}} \left(\prod_{i=n-k+1}^{n} (1 - b_i) \right)^{\frac{1}{n-(n-k)}} =$

$$\left(\prod_{j=k+1}^{n} (1 - a_j) \right)^{\frac{1}{n-k}} \left(\prod_{j=1}^{k} a_j \right)^{\frac{1}{k}} = Sp_k(\mu)$$

When $n - k = 0$

$$Sp_{n-k}(\mu') = \left(\prod_{i=1}^{n} (1 - b_i) \right)^{\frac{1}{n}} = \left(\prod_{j=1}^{n} a_j \right)^{\frac{1}{n}} = Sp_n(\mu)$$

Definition 13. *The Perfect Separation property. Let $N(x) = 1 - x$ be the usual negation operator. Let μ be a fuzzy set on X, and let $\mu' = N(\mu)$ be his complementary fuzzy set. Let Sp_k be a measure of k-specificity on $[0, 1]^X$, and let k_μ be the k that maximizes $Sp_k(\mu)$.*

Sp_k has the Perfect Separation property when $k_\mu = n - k_{\mu'}$ holds for every fuzzy set μ of $[0, 1]^X$.

Remark 6. A measure of k-specificity on X has the Perfect Separation property when defuzzificating any fuzzy set μ and his complementary fuzzy set μ', using the Measure of Maximum k-specificity, we obtain two complementary crisp sets on X.

Proposition 5. *The Product measure of k-specificity has the Perfect Separation property.*

Proof. It is obvious, since $Sp_k(\mu) = Sp_{n-k}(N(\mu))$ for all $k : 0, ..., n$ as we have saw in the previous proposition.

Proposition 6. *The Uniform Linear measure of k-specificity has the Perfect Separation property.*

Proof. [2] It is obvious, since $Sp_k(\mu) = Sp_{n-k}(N(\mu))$ for all $k : 0, ..., n$.

4   Comparing Measures of k-Specificity

In the next two subsections we compare the Uniform Linear, Fractional, and Product measures of k-specificity for both crisp and not crisp subsets on the universe X.

4.1   Comparing Measures of k-Specificity for the Crisp Subsets Case

Example 2. Comparing measures of k-specificity.

Le be $X = \{e_1, e_2, e_3, e_4, e_5\}$ be a crisp set with $n = 5$ elements.

Consider the fuzzy sets:

$\mu_0 = \{0|e_1, 0|e_2, 0|e_3, 0|e_4, 0|e_5\} = \{\} = \emptyset$

$\mu_1 = \{1|e_1, 0|e_2, 0|e_3, 0|e_4, 0|e_5\} = \{e_1\}$

$\mu_2 = \{1|e_1, 1|e_2, 0|e_3, 0|e_4, 0|e_5\} = \{e_1, e_2\}$

$\mu_3 = \{1|e_1, 1|e_2, 1|e_3, 0|e_4, 0|e_5\} = \{e_1, e_2, e_3\}$

$\mu_4 = \{1|e_1, 1|e_2, 1|e_3, 1|e_4, 0|e_5\} = \{e_1, e_2, e_3, e_4\}$

$\mu_5 = \{1|e_1, 1|e_2, 1|e_3, 1|e_4, 1|e_5\} = \{e_1, e_2, e_3, e_4\}$

For each one, we can calculate the Uniform Linear, Fractional, and Product measures of k-specificity (Tables 1, 2 and 3).

Table 1. Uniform linear measure of k-specificity Sp_k^L

	$Sp_k^L(\mu_0)$	$Sp_k^L(\mu_1)$	$Sp_k^L(\mu_2)$	$Sp_k^L(\mu_3)$	$Sp_k^L(\mu_4)$	$Sp_k^L(\mu_5)$
$k = 0$	1.00	0.80	0.60	0.40	0.20	0.00
$k = 1$	0.00	1.00	0.75	0.50	0.25	0.00
$k = 2$	0.00	0.50	1.00	0.67	0.33	0.00
$k = 3$	0.00	0.33	0.67	1.00	0.50	0.00
$k = 4$	0.00	0.25	0.50	0.75	1.00	0.00
$k = 5$	0.00	0.20	0.40	0.60	0.80	1.00

Table 2. Fractional measure of k-specificity Sp_k^F

	$Sp_k^F(\mu_0)$	$Sp_k^F(\mu_1)$	$Sp_k^F(\mu_2)$	$Sp_k^F(\mu_3)$	$Sp_k^F(\mu_4)$	$Sp_k^F(\mu_5)$
$k = 0$	1.00	0.00	0.00	0.00	0.00	0.00
$k = 1$	0.00	1.00	0.50	0.33	0.25	0.20
$k = 2$	0.00	0.50	1.00	0.67	0.50	0.40
$k = 3$	0.00	0.33	0.67	1.00	0.75	0.60
$k = 4$	0.00	0.25	0.50	0.75	1.00	0.80
$k = 5$	0.00	0.20	0.40	0.60	0.80	1.00

Proposition 7. *Let Sp_k be a measure of k-specificity on $[0, 1]^X$, then $Sp_k^P(\mu) \leq Sp_k(\mu)$ for every crisp subset μ of the universe X, therefore, the Product measure of k-specificity is the lowest measure of k-specificity for every crisp subset μ of the universe X.*

Note that the Uniform Linear and Fractional measures are not always comparable.

Table 3. Product measure of k-specificity Sp_k^P

	$Sp_k^P(\mu_0)$	$Sp_k^P(\mu_1)$	$Sp_k^P(\mu_2)$	$Sp_k^P(\mu_3)$	$Sp_k^P(\mu_4)$	$Sp_k^P(\mu_5)$
$k=0$	1.00	0.00	0.00	0.00	0.00	0.00
$k=1$	0.00	1.00	0.00	0.00	0.00	0.00
$k=2$	0.00	0.00	1.00	0.00	0.00	0.00
$k=3$	0.00	0.00	0.00	1.00	0.00	0.00
$k=4$	0.00	0.00	0.00	0.00	1.00	0.00
$k=5$	0.00	0.00	0.00	0.00	0.00	1.00

Proof. If μ is a crisp set with k elements, then $a_j = 1$ for every j: $1 \leq j \leq k$ and $a_j = 0$ for every j: $k+1 \leq j \leq n$. Let h be an integer such that $0 \leq h \leq n$. If $h < k$, since $(1 - a_k) = 0$, then $Sp_h^F = 0$. If $h > k$, since $a_h = 0$, then $Sp_h^F = 0$. Therefore, if Sp_k is a measure of k-specifictiy, then $Sp_k^P(\mu) \leq Sp_k(\mu)$ for every crisp subset μ on the universe X.

4.2 Comparing Measures of k-Specificity for Not Crisp Subsets

Example 3. Le be $X = \{e_1, e_2, e_3, e_4, e_5\}$ be a crisp set with $n = 5$ elements. Consider the fuzzy sets:

$\mu_6 = \{0.2|e_1, 0.7|e_2, 0|e_3, 0.9|e_4, 0.5|e_5\}$

$\mu_7 = \{0.8e_1, 0.3|e_2, 1|e_3, 0.1|e_4, 0.5|e_5\} = 1 - \mu_6 = \mu_6'$ Reordering μ_6 we obtain $\{0.9|e_4, 0.7|e_2, 0.5|e_5, 0.2|e_1, 0|e_3\}$, so $\{a_j\}_6 = \{0.9, 0.7, 0.5, 0.2, 0\}$; similarly, $\{a_j\}_7 = \{1, 0.8, 0.5, 0.3, 0.1\}$.

We can calculate the Uniform Linear Sp_k^L, the Fractional Sp_k^F, and the Product Sp_k^P measures of k-specificity of μ_6 and μ_7 (Table 4):

Table 4. Measures of k-specifcity for a fuzzy set and his complementary fuzzy set

	$Sp_k^L(\mu_6)$	$Sp_k^L(\mu_7)$	$Sp_k^F(\mu_6)$	$Sp_k^F(\mu_7)$	$Sp_k^P(\mu_6)$	$Sp_k^P(\mu_7)$
$k=0$	0.54	0.46	0.19	0.00	0.41	0.00
$k=1$	0.55	0.57	0.35	0.37	0.53	0.50
$k=2$	0.57	0.60	0.56	0.60	0.58	0.61
$k=3$	0.60	0.57	0.64	0.65	0.61	0.58
$k=4$	0.57	0.55	0.57	0.63	0.50	0.53
$k=5$	0.46	0.54	0.46	0.54	0.00	0.41

Remark 7. Note that the Uniform Linear and Product measures of k-specificity have the perfect separation property, and the Fractional measure of k-specificity does not.

Proposition 8. *The Fractional measure of k-specificity does not have the perfect separation property with the usual negation operator.*

Proof. See previous example.

Proposition 9. *The Sp_k^L, Sp_k^F, and the Sp_k^P are not totally ordered for all fuzzy sets.*

Proof. See Fig. 1.

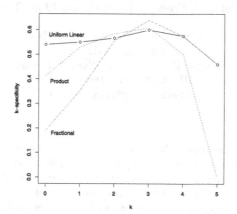

Fig. 1. Comparing three k-specifity measures of fuzzy set μ_6.

5 Conclusions

The Product and Fractional measures of k-specificity on fuzzy sets have been defined and some examples are provided. They have been compared with the known Uniform Linear measure of k-specificity. The Perfect Separation property has been defined and the lowest measure of k-specificity for crisp sets has been found.

References

1. Garmendia, L., González del Campo, R., Yager, R.R.: Recursively spreadable and reductible measures of specificity. Inf. Sci. **326**, 270–277 (2016)
2. González del Campo, R., Garmendia, L., Yager, R.R.: A measure of k-specificity of fuzzy sets and the use of maximum k-specificity. In: IV Congreso Español de informática, CEDI 2013, pp. 1134–1143 (2013)
3. Yager, R.R.: Measuring tranquility and anxiety in decision making: an application of fuzzy sets. Int. J. Gen. Syst. **8**, 139–146 (1982)
4. Yager, R.R.: Ordinal measures of specificity. Int. J. Gen. Syst. **17**, 57–72 (1990)
5. Yager, R.R.: Measures of specificity. In: Kaynak, O., Zadeh, L.A., Türkşen, B., Rudas, I.J. (eds.) Computational Intelligence: Soft Computing and Fuzzy-Neuro Integration wiht Applications. NATO ASI Series. Series F: Computer and Systems Sciences, vol. 162, pp. 94–113. Springer, Heidelberg (1998)
6. Yager, R.R.: Expansible measures of specificity. Int. J. Gen. Syst. **41**(3), 247–263 (2012)

On a Three-Valued Logic to Reason with Prototypes and Counterexamples and a Similarity-Based Generalization

Soma Dutta[1,2], Francesc Esteva[3], and Lluis Godo[3(✉)]

[1] Vistula University, Warsaw, Poland
somadutta9@gmail.com
[2] University of Warsaw, Warsaw, Poland
[3] IIIA-CSIC, Bellaterra, Spain
{esteva,godo}@iiia.csic.es

Abstract. In this paper, the meaning of a vague concept α is assumed to be rendered through two (mutually exclusive) finite sets of prototypes and counterexamples. In the remaining set of situations the concept is assumed to be applied only partially. A logical model for this setting can be fit into the three-valued Łukasiewicz's logic Ł$_3$ set up by considering, besides the usual notion of logical consequence $\models$ (based on the truth preservation), the logical consequence $\models^{\leq}$ based on the preservation of all truth-degrees as well. Moreover, we go one step further by considering a relaxed notion of consequence to some degree $a \in [0,1]$, by allowing the prototypes (counterexamples) of the premise (conclusion) be a-similar to the prototypes (counterexamples) of the conclusion (premise). We present a semantical characterization as well as an axiomatization.

1 Introduction

A vague, in the sense of gradual, property is characterized by the existence of borderline cases; that is, objects or situations for which the property only partially applies. The aim of this paper is to investigate how a logic for vague concepts can be defined starting from the most basic description of a vague property or concept α in terms of a set of prototypical situations or examples $[\alpha^+] \subseteq \Omega$, where α definitely applies, and a set of counterexamples $[\alpha^-] \subseteq \Omega$, where α does not apply for sure. In this paper we will further assume to work with *complete* descriptions of this kind: that is, for each concept α, the remaining set of situations $\Omega \setminus ([\alpha^+] \cup [\alpha^-])$ will be those where we know α only partially applies to. Of course, to be in a consistent scenario, we will require that there is no situation where α both fully applies and does not apply to, in other words, the constraint $[\alpha^+] \cap [\alpha^-] = \emptyset$ is always satisfied. In such a case, one lead to a three-valued framework, where for each situation $w \in \Omega$, the degree $app(w, \alpha)$ to which α applies at w (or, equivalently, the truth degree of the assertion "w is

© Springer International Publishing Switzerland 2016
O. Luaces et al. (Eds.): CAEPIA 2016, LNAI 9868, pp. 498–508, 2016.
DOI: 10.1007/978-3-319-44636-3_47

α") can be naturally defined as follows:

$$app(w, \alpha) = \begin{cases} 1, & \text{if } w \in [\alpha^+] \\ 0, & \text{if } w \in [\alpha^-] \\ 1/2, & \text{otherwise} \end{cases}$$

We want to emphasize that in this 3-valued model, the third value $1/2$ is not meant to represent ignorance about whether a concept applies or not to a situation, rather it is meant to represent that the concept only partially applies to a situation, or equivalently, that the situation is a borderline case for the concept (see [3] for a discussion on this topic).

The paper is structured as follows. After this short introduction, Sect. 2 is devoted to develop a logical approach to reason with vague concepts represented by examples and counterexamples based on the three-valued Łukasiewicz logic $Ł_3$. In Sect. 3 we show how by introducing a similarity relation into the picture one can define three kinds of graded notions of approximate logical consequence among vague propositions and we characterize them. Finally, in Sect. 4 we formally define a sort of graded modal logic to capture reasoning about the approximate consequences and prove completeness. We end up with some conclusions.

2 Three-Valued Logics to Reason with Examples and Counterexamples

In our framework, we assume that we have evaluations e such that for atomic concepts α, $e(\alpha) = ([\alpha^+], [\alpha^-])$, providing a disjoint pair of examples and counterexamples. A first question is how this evaluation propagates to compound concepts. We consider a language with four connectives: conjunction ($\wedge$), disjunction ($\vee$), negation ($\neg$) and implication ($\rightarrow$). Given $e(\alpha) = ([\alpha^+], [\alpha^-])$ and $e(\beta) = ([\beta^+], [\beta^-])$, the rules for $\wedge$, $\vee$ and $\neg$ seem clear as given follows:

$e(\alpha \wedge \beta) = ([\alpha^+] \cap [\beta^+], [\alpha^-] \cup [\beta^-])$
$e(\alpha \vee \beta) = ([\alpha^+] \cup [\beta^+], [\alpha^-] \cap [\beta^-])$
$e(\neg \alpha) = ([\alpha^-], [\alpha^+])$

The case for $\rightarrow$ is not that straightforward as above. Generalising the classical definition of material implication, one could take $\alpha \rightarrow \beta := \neg \alpha \vee \beta$, and hence

$e(\neg \alpha \vee \beta) = ([\alpha^-] \cup [\beta^+], [\alpha^+] \cap [\beta^-]).$

In that case, the framework turns out to be the one corresponding to the well-known Kleene's three-valued logic. However, it is also well-known that in Kleene's logic the interpretation of the intermediate value $1/2$ is usually considered as ignorance. This makes it natural to claim that if it is not known whether w is an example or counterexample of both α and β, it remains unknown whether it is an example or counterexample of $\alpha \rightarrow \beta$. However, if $1/2$ is assumed to denote a borderline case, it is perfectly natural to consider, in that case, that w is an example of $\alpha \rightarrow \beta$. This small change in the framework amounts to move from Kleene's three-valued logic to Łukasiewicz's three-valued logic. In such a case, we have

$$e(\alpha \rightarrow \beta) = ([\alpha^-] \cup [\beta^+] \cup ([\alpha^\sim] \cap [\beta^\sim]), [\alpha^+] \cap [\beta^-]),$$

where we use the notation $[\gamma^\sim] = \Omega \setminus ([\gamma^+] \cup [\gamma^-])$.

Let us formalize this framework from a three-valued logic point of view. To do so, let Var denote a (finite) set of atomic concepts, or propositional variables, from which compound concepts (or formulas) are built using the connectives $\wedge$, $\vee$, $\rightarrow$ and $\neg$. We will denote the set of formulas by $Fm_3(Var)$, in short Fm_3. Further, let Ω be the set of all possible situations, that we will identify with the set of all evaluations v of atomic concepts Var into the truth set $\{0, 1/2, 1\}$, that is $\Omega = \{0, 1/2, 1\}^{Var}$, with the following intended meaning: $v(\alpha) = 1$ means that v is an example of α (resp. v is a model of α in logical terms), $v(\alpha) = 0$ means that v is a counterexample of α (resp. v is a counter-model of α), and $v(\alpha) = 1/2$ means that v is a borderline situation for α, i.e. it is neither an example nor a counterexample. According to the previous discussion, truth-evaluations v will be extended to compound concepts according to the semantics of 3-valued Łukasiewicz logic $Ł_3$, defined by following truth-tables:

$\wedge$	0	1/2	1
0	0	0	0
1/2	0	1/2	1/2
1	0	1/2	1

$\vee$	0	1/2	1
0	0	1/2	1
1/2	1/2	1/2	1
1	1	1	1

$\rightarrow$	0	1/2	1
0	1	1	1
1/2	1/2	1	1
1	0	1/2	1

$\neg$	
0	1
1/2	1/2
1	0

These truth-tables can also be given by means of the following truth-functions: for all $x, y \in \{0, 1/2, 1\}$, $x \wedge y = \min(x, y)$, $x \vee y = \max(x, y)$, $x \rightarrow y = \min(1, 1 - x + y)$ and $\neg x = 1 - x$.

Notation. For any concept φ we will denote by $[\varphi]$ the 3-valued (fuzzy) set of models of φ, i.e. $[\varphi] : \Omega \rightarrow \{0, 1/2, 1\}$ defined as $[\varphi](w) = w(\varphi)$. We will write $[\varphi] \leq [\psi]$ when $[\varphi](w) \leq [\psi](w)$ for all $w \in \Omega$.

In $Ł_3$, a strong conjunction and a strong disjunction connectives can be defined from $\rightarrow$ and $\neg$ as follows: $\varphi \otimes \psi := \neg(\varphi \rightarrow \neg\psi)$ and $\varphi \oplus \psi := \neg\varphi \rightarrow \psi$.[1] Actually, for each concept $\varphi \in Fm_3$, the connective $\otimes$ allows one to define three related *Boolean* concepts:

$$\varphi^+ := \varphi \otimes \varphi, \quad \varphi^- := (\neg\varphi) \otimes (\neg\varphi) = (\neg\varphi)^+, \quad \varphi^\sim := \neg\varphi^+ \wedge \neg\varphi^-,$$

with the following semantics:

$$w(\varphi^+) = 1 \text{ if } w(\varphi) = 1; \quad w(\varphi^+) = 0 \text{ otherwise};$$
$$w(\varphi^\sim) = 1 \text{ if } w(\varphi) = 1/2; \, w(\varphi^\sim) = 0 \text{ otherwise};$$
$$w(\varphi^-) = 1 \text{ if } w(\varphi) = 0; \quad w(\varphi^-) = 0 \text{ otherwise};$$

and therefore $[\varphi^+], [\varphi^-], [\varphi^\sim]$ capture respectively the (classical) sets of examples, counterexamples and borderline cases of φ.

---

[1] Actually, one could take $\rightarrow$ and $\neg$ as the only primitive connectives since $\wedge$ and $\vee$ can be defined from $\rightarrow$ and $\neg$ as well: $\varphi \wedge \psi = \varphi \otimes (\varphi \rightarrow \psi)$ and $\varphi \vee \psi = (\varphi \rightarrow \psi) \rightarrow \psi$.

The usual notion of logical consequence in 3-valued Łukasiewicz logic is defined as follows: for any set of formulas $\Gamma \cup \{\varphi\}$,

$$\Gamma \models \psi \text{ if for any evaluation } v, v(\varphi) = 1 \text{ for all } \varphi \in \Gamma, \text{ then } v(\psi) = 1.$$

It is well known that this consequence relation can be axiomatized by the following axioms and rule (see e.g. [2]):

(L1) $\varphi \rightarrow (\psi \rightarrow \varphi)$,
(L2) $(\varphi \rightarrow \psi) \rightarrow ((\psi \rightarrow \chi) \rightarrow (\varphi \rightarrow \chi))$,
(L3) $(\neg\varphi \rightarrow \neg\psi) \rightarrow (\psi \rightarrow \varphi)$,
(L4) $(\varphi \vee \psi) \rightarrow (\psi \vee \varphi)$,
(L5) $\varphi \oplus \varphi \leftrightarrow \varphi \oplus \varphi \oplus \varphi$,

(MP) The rule of modus ponens: $\dfrac{\varphi, \quad \varphi \rightarrow \psi}{\psi}$.

This axiomatic system, denoted $Ł_3$, is strongly complete with respect to the above semantics; that is, for a set of formulas $\Gamma \cup \{\varphi\}$, $\Gamma \models \varphi$ iff $\Gamma \vdash \varphi$, where $\vdash$, the notion of proof for $Ł_3$, is defined from the above axioms and rule in the usual way.

Remark: In the sequel we will restrict ourselves on considerations about logical consequences from finite set of premises. In such a case, if $\Gamma = \{\varphi_1, \ldots, \varphi_n\}$ then it holds that $\Gamma \models \psi$ iff $\varphi_1 \wedge \ldots \wedge \varphi_n \models \psi$, and hence it will be enough to consider premises consisting of a single formula.

Lemma 1. *For all formulas φ, ψ, it holds that $\varphi \models \psi$ iff $[\varphi^+] \subseteq [\psi^+]$.*

This makes clear that $\models$ is indeed the consequence relation that preserves the examples of concepts. Similarly we can also consider the consequence relation that preserves counterexamples. Namely, one can contrapositively define a falsity-preserving consequence as:

$\varphi \models^C \psi$ if $\neg\psi \models \neg\varphi$, that is, if for any evaluation $v, v(\psi) = 0$ implies $v(\varphi) = 0$.

Unlike classical logic, in 3-valued Łukasiewicz logic it is not the case that $\varphi \models \psi$ iff $\neg\psi \models \neg\varphi$. As we have seen that the former amounts to require $[\varphi^+] \subseteq [\psi^+]$, while the latter, as shown next, amounts to require $[\psi^-] \subseteq [\varphi^-]$. Clearly these conditions, in general, are not equivalent, except when φ and ψ do not have borderline cases, that is, when $[\varphi^+] \cup [\varphi^-] = [\psi^+] \cup [\psi^-] = \Omega$.

Lemma 2. *For all formulas φ, ψ, it holds that $\varphi \models^C \psi$ iff $[\psi^-] \subseteq [\varphi^-]$.*

Equivalently, $\varphi \models^C \psi$ holds iff for any evaluation $v \in \Omega$, $v(\varphi) \geq 1/2$ implies $v(\psi) \geq 1/2$, or in other words, $[\varphi^+] \cup [\varphi^\sim] \subseteq [\psi^+] \cup [\psi^\sim]$. Now we define the consequence relation that preserves both examples and counterexamples in the natural way.

Definition 1. $\varphi \models^\leq \psi$ *if* $\varphi \models \psi$ *and* $\varphi \models^C \psi$, *that is, if* $[\varphi^+] \subseteq [\psi^+]$ *and* $[\psi^-] \subseteq [\varphi^-]$.

Note that, for instance, $\varphi \models \varphi^+$ holds, while $\varphi \not\models^{\leq} \varphi^+$. Indeed, while the examples of φ and φ^+ are the same, the counterexamples of φ^+ include not only the counterexamples but also those borderline cases of φ.

From the above observations, we have these equivalent characterizations of $\models^{\leq}$.

Lemma 3. *For all formulas φ, ψ, the following conditions are equivalent:*

- $\varphi \models^{\leq} \psi$,
- $\models \varphi \rightarrow \psi$,
- $[\varphi] \leq [\psi]$,
- $[\varphi \rightarrow \psi] = \Omega$.

These characterizations justify the use of the superscript $\leq$ in the symbol of consequence relation. And indeed, the consequence relation $\models^{\leq}$ is known in the literature as the *degree-preserving* companion of $\models$, as opposed to the *truth-preserving* consequence $\models$, that preserves the truth-value '1' [1].

$\models^{\leq}$ can also be axiomatized by taking as axioms those of Ł$_3$ and the following two inference rules:

$$(Adj) : \frac{\varphi, \ \psi}{\varphi \wedge \psi} \qquad (MPr) : \frac{\varphi, \ \vdash \varphi \rightarrow \psi}{\psi}$$

The resulting logic is denoted by Ł$_3^{\leq}$, and its notion of proof is denoted by $\vdash^{\leq}$. Notice that (MPr) is a weakened version of modus ponens, called restricted modus ponens, since $\varphi \rightarrow \psi$ has to be a theorem of Ł$_3$ for the rule to be applicable.

As a summary of this section, we can claim that Ł$_3^{\leq}$ (or its semantical counterpart $\models^{\leq}$) provides a more suitable logical framework to reason about concepts described by examples and counterexamples than the usual three-valued Łukasiewicz logic Ł$_3$.

3   A Similarity-Based Refined Framework

In the previous section we have discussed a logic for reasoning about vague concepts described in fact as 3-valued fuzzy sets. A more fine grained representation, moving from 3-valued to $[0, 1]$-valued fuzzy sets, can be introduced by assuming the availability of a (fuzzy) similarity relation $S : \Omega \times \Omega \rightarrow [0, 1]$ among situations. Indeed, for instance, assume that all examples of φ are examples of ψ, but some counterexamples of ψ are not counterexamples of φ. Hence, we cannot derive that ψ follows from φ according to $\models^{\leq}$. However, if these counterexamples of ψ greatly resemble to counterexamples of φ, it seems reasonable to claim that ψ follows *approximately* from φ.

Actually, starting from Ruspini's seminal work [7], a similar approach has already been investigated in the literature in order to extend the notion of entailment in classical logic in different frameworks and using formalisms, see e.g. [6]. Here we will follow this line and propose a graded generalization of the $\models^{\leq}$ in the presence of similarity relation S on the set of 3-valued Łukasiewicz interpretations Ω, that allows to draw approximate conclusions.

Since, by definition $\varphi \models^{\leq} \psi$ if both $\varphi \models \psi$ and $\varphi \models^C \psi$, that is, if $[\varphi^+] \subseteq [\psi^+]$ and $[\psi^-] \subseteq [\varphi^-]$, it seems natural to define that ψ is an approximate consequence of φ to some degree $a \in [0,1]$ when every example of φ is similar (at least to the degree a) to some example of ψ, as well as every counterexample of ψ is similar (to at least to the degree a) to some counterexample of φ. In other words, this means that to relax $\models^{\leq}$ we propose to relax both $\models$ and $\models^C$. This idea is formalized next, where we assume that a $*$-similarity relation $S : \Omega \times \Omega \to [0,1]$ be given, satisfying the properties:

- $S(w,w') = 1$ iff $w = w'$,
- $S(w,w') = S(w',w)$,
- $S(w,w') * S(w',w'') \leq S(w,w'')$,

where $*$ is a t-norm operation. Moreover, for any subset $A \subset \Omega$ and value $a \in [0,1]$ we define its a-neighborhood as

$$A^a = \{w \in \Omega \mid \text{there exists } w' \in A \text{ such that } S(w,w') \geq a\}.$$

Definition 2. *For any pair of formulas φ, ψ and for each degree $a \in [0,1]$, we define the consequence relations $\models_a, \models_a^C$ and $\models_a^{\leq}$ as follows:*

(i) $\varphi \models_a \psi$ if for every $w \in \Omega$ such that $w(\varphi) = 1$ there exists $w' \in \Omega$ with $S(w,w') \geq a$ and $w'(\psi) = 1$. In other words, $\varphi \models_a \psi$ if $[\varphi^+] \subseteq [\psi^+]^a$.

(ii) $\varphi \models_a^C \psi$ if for every $w \in \Omega$ such that $w(\psi) = 0$ there exists $w' \in \Omega$ with $S(w,w') \geq a$ and $w'(\varphi) = 0$. In other words, $\varphi \models_a^C \psi$ if $[\psi^-] \subseteq [\varphi^-]^a$.

(iii) $\varphi \models_a^{\leq} \psi$ if both $\varphi \models_a \psi$ and $\varphi \models_a^C \psi$ i.e. if both $[\varphi^+] \subseteq [\psi^+]^a$ and $[\psi^-] \subseteq [\varphi^-]^a$.

Taking into account that for any formula χ it holds $[(\neg\chi)^+] = [\chi^-]$, it is clear that $\models_a^C$ (and thus $\models_a^{\leq}$ as well) can be expressed in terms of $\models^a$.

Lemma 4. *For any formulas φ and ψ, the following conditions hold:*

- *$\varphi \models_a^C \psi$ iff $\neg\psi \models_a \neg\varphi$*
- *$\varphi \models_a^{\leq} \psi$ iff $\varphi \models_a \psi$ and $\neg\psi \models_a \neg\varphi$.*

The consequence relations $\models_a$ are very similar to the so-called approximate graded entailment relations defined in [4] and further studied in [6,9,10]. The main difference is that in [4] the authors consider classical propositions while in this paper we consider three-valued Łukasiewicz propositions. Nevertheless we can prove very similar characterizing properties for the $\models^a$'s. In the following theorem, for each evaluation $w \in \Omega$, $\overline{w}$ denotes the following proposition:

$$\overline{w} = \Big(\bigwedge_{p \in X : w(p)=1} p^+ \Big) \wedge \Big(\bigwedge_{p \in X : w(p)=1/2} p^\sim \Big) \wedge \Big(\bigwedge_{p \in X : w(p)=0} p^- \Big).$$

So, $\overline{w}$ is a (Boolean) formula which encapsulates the complete description provided by w. Moreover, for every $w' \in \Omega$, $w'(\overline{w}) = 1$ if $w' = w$ and $w'(\overline{w}) = 0$ otherwise.

Theorem 1. *The following properties hold for the family $\{\models_a\colon a \in [0,1]\}$ of graded entailment relations on $Fm_3 \times Fm_3$ induced by a $*$-similarity relation S on Ω:*

(i) *Nestedness: if $\varphi \models_a \psi$ and $b \leq a$, then $\varphi \models_b \psi$*

(ii) *$\models_1$ coincides with $\models$, while $\models \subsetneq \models_a$ if $a < 1$. Moreover, if $\psi \not\models \bot$, then $\varphi \models_0 \psi$ for any φ.*

(iii) *Positive-preservation: $\varphi \models_a \psi$ iff $\varphi^+ \models_a \psi^+$*

(iv) *$*$-Transitivity: if $\varphi \models_a \psi$ and $\psi \models_b \chi$ then $\varphi \models_{a*b} \chi$*

(v) *Left-OR: $\varphi \vee \psi \models_a \chi$ iff $\varphi \models_a \chi$ and $\psi \models_a \chi$*

(vi) *Restricted Right-OR: for all $w \in \Omega$, $\overline{w} \models_a \varphi \vee \psi$ iff $\overline{w} \models_a \varphi$ or $\overline{w} \models_a \psi$*

(vii) *Restricted symmetry: for all $w, w' \in \Omega$, $\overline{w} \models_a \overline{w'}$ iff $\overline{w'} \models_a \overline{w}$*

(viii) *Consistency preservation: if $\varphi \not\models \bot$ then $\varphi \models_a \bot$ only if $a = 0$*

(ix) *Continuity from below: If $\varphi \models_a \psi$ for all $a < b$, then $\varphi \models_b \psi$*

Conversely, for any family of graded entailment relations $\{\vdash_a\colon a \in [0,1]\}$ on $Fm_3 \times Fm_3$ satisfying the above properties, there exists a $*$-similarity relation S such that $\vdash_a = \models_a$ for each $a \in [0,1]$.

Proof (Sketch). The proof follows the same steps than the one of [4, Theorem 1] in the case of a classical propositional setting. The key points to take into account here are:

- it is easy to check that, for any formula $\varphi \in Fm_3$, φ^+ is logically equivalent in L_3 to the disjunction

$$\bigvee_{w \in \Omega \colon w(\varphi)=1} \overline{w}.$$

- $(\varphi \vee \psi)^+$ is logically equivalent to $\varphi^+ \vee \psi^+$.
- for every $w, w' \in \Omega$, $\overline{w} \models_a \overline{w'}$ iff $S(w, w') \geq a$.

For the converse direction, the latter property is used to define the corresponding similarity S for a family of consequence relations $\{\vdash_a\colon a \in [0,1]\}$ satisfying (i)–(ix) as $S(w, w') = \sup\{a \in [0,1] \mid \overline{w} \vdash_a \overline{w'}\}$.   □

Taking into account Lemma 4, a sort of dual characterization for $\models_a^C$, that we omit, can easily be derived from the above one for $\models_a$. On the other hand, the above properties also indirectly characterize $\models_a^{\leq}$ in the sense that, in our finite setting, $\models_a$ (and thus $\models_a^C$ as well) can be derived from $\models_a^{\leq}$ as well as the following lemma shows.

Lemma 5. *For any $\varphi, \psi \in Fm_3$, we have that $\varphi \models_a \psi$ iff for every $w \in \Omega$ such that $w(\varphi) = 1$ there exists $w' \in \Omega$ such that $w(\psi) = 1$ and $\overline{w} \models_a^{\leq} \overline{w'}$.*

Proof. It directly follows from properties (iv) and (v) of Theorem 1, by checking that, for every $w \in \Omega$, $\overline{w} \models_a^{\leq} \overline{w'}$ iff $\overline{w} \models_a \overline{w'}$.

However, admittedly, the resulting characterization of $\models_a^{\leq}$ we would obtain using this lemma is not very elegant.

4 A Logic to Reason About Graded Consequences $\models_a$, $\models_a^C$ and $\models_a^\leq$

In this section we will define a Boolean (meta) logic LAC3 to reason about the graded entailments $\models_a$, $\models_a^C$ and $\models_a^\leq$. The idea is to consider expressions corresponding to $\varphi \models_a \psi$, $\varphi \models_a^C \psi$ and $\varphi \models_a^\leq \psi$ as the concerned objects of our logic, and then to use Theorem 1 to devise a complete axiomatics to capture the intended meaning of such expressions.

To avoid unnecessary complications, we will make the following assumption: all $*$-similarity relations S will take values in a finite set G of $[0, 1]$, containing 0 and 1, and $*$ will be a given *finite* t-norm operation on G, that is, $(G, *)$ will be a finite totally ordered semi-group. In this way, we keep our language finitary and avoid the use of an infinitary inference rule to cope with Property (ix) of Theorem 1.

Our logic will be a two-tired logic, where at a first level we will have formulas and semantics of the 3-valued Łukasiewicz logic L3 and at the second level we will have propositional classical logic CPC.

We start by defining the syntax of LAC3, with two languages:

- Language $\mathcal{L}_0$: built from a finite set of propositional variables $Var = \{p, q, r, \ldots\}$ and using L3 connectives $\neg, \wedge, \vee, \rightarrow$. Other derived connectives are $\oplus$ and $\otimes$, defined as in Sect. 2. We will use $\top$ and $\bot$ as abbreviations for $p \rightarrow p$ and $\neg(p \rightarrow p)$ respectively, and φ^+ and φ^- as abbreviations of $\varphi \otimes \varphi$ and $(\neg \varphi)^+$ respectively.
- Language $\mathcal{L}_1$: atomic formulas of $\mathcal{L}_1$ are only of the form $\phi \succ_a^P \psi$, where ϕ, ψ are $\mathcal{L}_0$-formulas and $a \in G$, and compound $\mathcal{L}_1$-formulas are built from atomic ones with the usual Boolean connectives $\neg, \wedge, \vee, \rightarrow$.[2]
  Moreover, we will be using $\phi \succ_a^C \psi$ and $\phi \succ_a \psi$ as abbreviations of $\neg\psi \succ_a^P \neg\phi$ and $(\phi \succ_a^P \psi) \wedge (\phi \succ_a^C \psi)$ respectively.

The semantics is given by similarity Kripke models $M = (W, S, e)$ where W is a finite set of worlds, $S : W \times W \rightarrow G$ is a $*$-similarity relation, and $e : W \times Var \mapsto \{0, \frac{1}{2}, 1\}$ is a 3-valued evaluation of propositional variables in every world, which is extended to arbitrary $\mathcal{L}_0$-formulas using L3 truth-functions. For every formula $\varphi \in \mathcal{L}_0$, we define: $[\varphi]_M : W \rightarrow \{0, 1/2, 1\}$ such that $w \mapsto e(w, \varphi)$, $[\varphi^+]_M = \{w \in W \mid e(w, \varphi) = 1\}$, and $[\varphi^-]_M = \{w \in W \mid e(w, \varphi) = 0\}$.

Each similarity Kripke model $M = (W, S, e)$ induces a function $e_M : \mathcal{L}_1 \rightarrow \{0, 1\}$, which is a (Boolean) truth evaluation for $\mathcal{L}_1$-formulas defined as follows:

- for atomic $\mathcal{L}_1$-formulas:
  $e_M(\phi \succ_a^P \psi) = 1$ if $[\phi^+]_M \subseteq ([\psi^+]_M)^a$, i.e., if $\min_{w \in [\phi^+]_M} \max_{w' \in [\psi^+]_M} S(w, w') \geq a$;
  $e_M(\phi \succ_a^P \psi) = 0$ otherwise.
- for compound formulas, use the usual Boolean truth functions.

---

[2] Although we are using symbols $\wedge, \vee, \neg, \rightarrow$ for both formulas of $\mathcal{L}_0$ and $\mathcal{L}_1$, it will be clear from the context when they refer to L3 or when they refer to Boolean connectives.

Note that, by definition, $e_M(\phi \succ_a^C \psi) = 1$ iff $e_M(\neg\phi \succ_a^P \neg\psi) = 1$, and $e_M(\phi \succ_a \psi) = 1$ iff $e_M(\phi \succ_a^P \psi) = 1$ and $e_M(\phi \succ_a^C \psi) = 1$.

In the next lemma we list some useful properties of e_M.

Lemma 6. *The following conditions hold:*

- $e_M(\phi \succ_a^C \psi) = 1$ *iff* $[\psi^-]_M \subseteq ([\phi^-]_M)^a$
- $e_M(\phi \succ_a \psi) = 1$ *iff* $[\phi^+]_M \subseteq ([\psi^+]_M)^a$ *and* $[\psi^-]_M \subseteq ([\phi^-]_M)^a$
- $e_M(\phi \succ_1 \psi) = 1$ *iff* $[\phi]_M \le [\psi]_M$
- $e_M((\phi \succ_1 \psi) \wedge (\psi \succ_1 \phi)) = 1$ *iff* $[\varphi]_M = [\psi]_M$, *iff* $[\phi \leftrightarrow \psi] = W$.

Now we define the notion of logical consequence in LAC3 for $\mathcal{L}_1$-formulas.

Definition 3. *Let $T \cup \{\Phi\}$ be a set of $\mathcal{L}_1$-formulas. We say that Φ logically follows from T, written $T \models_{LAC3} \Phi$, if for every similarity Kripke model $M = (W, S, e)$, if $e_M(\Psi) = 1$ for every $\Psi \in T$, then $e_M(\Phi) = 1$ as well.*

Finally we propose the following axiomatization of LAC3.

Definition 4. *The following are the axioms for LAC3:*

(A1) Axioms of CPC for $\mathcal{L}_1$-formulas
(A2) $\phi \succ_1^P \psi$, where ϕ, ψ are such that $\phi \models \psi$
(A3) $\neg(\top \succ_1^P \to \bot)$
(A4) $(\phi \succ_a^P \psi) \to (\phi \succ_b^P \psi)$, where $a \le b$
(A5) $(\phi \succ_1^P \psi) \to (\phi^+ \wedge \neg\psi^+ \succ_1^P \bot)$
(A6) $\neg(\psi \succ_1^P \bot) \to (\phi \succ_0^P \psi)$
(A7) $(\phi \succ_a^P \bot) \to (\phi \succ_1^P \bot)$
(A8) $\neg(\overline{w} \succ_1^P \bot) \wedge (\overline{w} \succ_a^P \overline{w'}) \to (\overline{w'} \succ_a^P \overline{w})$, for $w, w' \in \Omega$
(A9) $(\phi \succ_a^P \chi) \wedge (\psi \succ_a^P \chi) \to (\phi \vee \psi \succ_a^P \chi)$
(A10) $(\overline{w} \succ_a^P \phi \vee \psi) \to (\overline{w} \succ_a^P \phi) \vee (\overline{w} \succ_c^P \psi)$
(A11) $(\phi \succ_a^P \psi) \wedge (\psi \succ_b^P \chi) \to (\phi \succ_{a*b}^P \chi)$
(A12) $(\phi \succ_a^P \psi) \leftrightarrow (\phi^+ \succ_a^P \psi^+)$

The only rule of LAC3 is modus ponens. The notion of proof defined from the above axioms and rule will be denoted $\vdash_{LAC3}$.

Finally, we have the following soundness and completeness theorem for LAC3.

Theorem 2. *For any set $T \cup \{\Phi\}$ of $\mathcal{L}_1$-formulas, it holds that $T \models_{LAC3} \Phi$ if, and only if, $T \vdash_{LAC3} \Phi$.*

Proof. One direction is soundness, and it basically follows from Theorem 1. As for the converse direction, assume $T \nvdash_{LAC3} \Phi$. The idea is to consider the graded expressions $\phi \succ_a^P \psi$ as propositional (Boolean) variables that are ruled by the axioms together with the laws of classical propositional logic CPC. Let Γ be the set of all possible instantiations of axioms (A1)–(A12). Then it implies that Φ does not follow from $T \cup \Gamma$ using CPC reasoning, i.e. $T \cup \Gamma \nvdash_{CPC} \Phi$. By completeness of CPC, there exists a Boolean interpretation v such that $v(\Psi) = 1$

for all $\Psi \in T \cup \Gamma$ and $v(\Phi) = 0$. Now we will build a $*$-similarity Kripke model M such that $e_M(\Psi) = 1$ for all $\Psi \in T$ and $e_M(\Phi) = 0$. To do that we take Ω and define $S : \Omega \times \Omega \to G$ by

$$S'(w, w') = \max\{a \in G \mid v(\overline{w} \succ_a^P \overline{w'}) = 1\}.$$

By axioms (A2), (A8) and (A11), S is a $*$-similarity. Note that, by definition and Axiom (A4), $S(w, w') \geq a$ iff $v(\overline{w} \succ_a^P \overline{w'}) = 1$. Finally we consider the model $M = (\Omega, S, e)$, where for each $w \in \Omega$ and $p \in Var$, $e(w, p) = w(p)$. What remains is to check that $e_M(\Psi) = v(\Psi)$ for every LAC3-formula Ψ. It suffices to show that, for every $\phi, \psi \in \mathcal{L}_0$ and $a \in G$, we have $e_M(\phi \succ_a^P \psi) = v(\phi \succ_a^P \psi)$, that is, to prove that

$$v(\phi \succ_a^P \psi) = 1 \quad \text{iff} \quad \min_{w \in [\phi^+]_M} \max_{w' \in [\psi^+]_M} S(w, w') \geq a.$$

First of all, recall that for every ϕ, L_3 proves the equivalence $\phi^+ \leftrightarrow \bigvee_{w \in \Omega : w(\varphi) = 1} \overline{w}$, and by axioms (A12), (A9) and (A10), we have that LAC3 proves

$$\phi \succ_a^P \psi \leftrightarrow \bigwedge_{w \in \Omega : w(\phi) = 1} \bigvee_{w' \in \Omega : w'(\psi) = 1} \overline{w} \succ_a^P \overline{w'}.$$

Therefore, $v(\phi \succ_a^P \psi) = 1$ iff for all w in Ω such that $w(\phi) = 1$, there exists w' such that $w'(\psi) = 1$ and $v(\overline{w} \succ_a^P \overline{w'}) = 1$. But, as we have previously observed, $v(\overline{w} \succ_a^P \overline{w'}) = 1$ holds iff $S(w, w') \geq a$. In other words, we actually have $v(\phi \succ_a^P \psi) = 1$ iff $\min_{w \in [\phi^+]_M} \max_{w' \in [\psi^+]_M} S(w, w') \geq a$. This concludes the proof. $\square$

5 Conclusions and Future Work

We have presented an approach towards considering graded entailments between vague concepts (or propositions) based on the similarity between both the prototypes and counterexamples of the antecedent and the consequent. This approach is a natural generalization of the Łukasiewicz's three-valued consequence ($\models^{\leq}$) that preserves truth-degrees. The provided axiomatization is for the operators $\succ_a^P$, which are based on prototypes only, while the operators $\succ_a$, based on both prototypes and counterexamples, can be naturally obtained as a derived operators in the system. To derive a complete axiomatic system directly for the operators $\succ_a$ is an issue under current investigation. Besides, we leave other interesting issues for further research. First, in this paper, we have assumed $app(\omega, \alpha)$ to be a three-valued concept, and to define $\models_a^{\leq}$ from $\models_a$ and $\models_a^C$ we have used a *conjunctive* aggregation of the two aspects of similarity, similarity among prototypes and similarity among counterexamples. Another approach could be to let $app(\omega, \alpha)$ to admit itself a finer distinction by defining $app^*(\omega, \alpha) = S(w, [\alpha]^+) \odot (1 - S(w, [\alpha^-]))$ with $S(w, [\alpha^+]) = \max_{w' \in [\alpha^+]} S(\omega, w')$ and analogously for $S(w, [\alpha^-])$. Then the extent to which α entails β can be defined based on the relationship of $app^*(\omega, \alpha)$ and $app^*(\omega, \beta)$ considering all possible situations ω. This direction seems to have lots of challenges as ⊙ might not be as simple as a conjunctive oper-ation; also different notions of consequence can be worth exploring in the line of [5,6,8].

Acknowledgments. The authors are thankful to the anonymous reviewers for their helpful comments. Esteva and Godo acknowledge partial support of the project TIN2015-71799-C2-1-P (MINECO/FEDER).

References

1. Bou, F., Esteva, F., Font, J.M., Gil, A., Godo, L., Torrens, A., Verdú, V.: Logics preserving degrees of truth from varieties of residuated lattices. J. Logic Comput. **19**(6), 1031–1069 (2009)
2. Cignoli, R., D'Ottaviano, I.M.L., Mundici, D.: Algebraic Foundations of Many-Valued Reasoning. Trends in Logic, vol. 7. Kluwer, Dordrecht (1999)
3. Ciucci, D., Dubois, D., Lawry, J.: Borderline vs. unknown: comparing three-valued representations of imperfect information. Int. J. Approx. Reason. **55**(9), 1866–1889 (2014)
4. Dubois, D., Prade, H., Esteva, F., Garcia, P., Godo, L.: A logical approach to interpolation based on similarity relations. Int. J. Approx. Reason. **17**, 1–36 (1997)
5. Dutta, S., Bedregal, B.R.C., Chakraborty, M.K.: Some instances of graded conse-quence in the context of interval-valued semantics. In: Banerjee, M., Krishna, S.N. (eds.) ICLA. LNCS, vol. 8923, pp. 74–87. Springer, Heidelberg (2015)
6. Esteva, F., Godo, L., Rodríguez, R.O., Vetterlein, T.: Logics for approximate and strong entailments. Fuzzy Sets Syst. **197**, 59–70 (2012)
7. Ruspini, E.H.: On the semantics of fuzzy logic. Int. J. Approx. Reason. **5**, 45–88 (1991)
8. Vetterlein, T.: Logic of prototypes and counterexamples: possibilities and limits. In: Alonso, J.M., et al. (eds.) Proceedings of the IFSA-EUSFLAT 2015, pp. 697–704. Atlantis Press (2015)
9. Vetterlein, T.: Logic of approximate entailment in quasimetric spaces. Int. J. Approx. Reason. **64**, 39–53 (2015)
10. Vetterlein, T., Esteva, F., Godo, L.: Logics for approximate entailment in ordered universes of discourse. Int. J. Approx. Reason. **71**, 50–63 (2016)

Author Index

Printed in the United States
By Bookmasters